Immigration and Labor

The Economic Aspects of European Immigration to the United States

AMS PRESS
NEW YORK

Immigration and Labor

The Economic Aspects of European Immigration to the United States

By

Isaac A. Hourwich, Ph.D.

Second Edition
Revised

New York
B. W. HUEBSCH, Inc.
1922

Library of Congress Cataloging in Publication Data

Hourwich, Isaac Aaronovich, 1860-1924.
Immigration and labor.

Reprint of the 1922 ed.
1. United States--Emigration and immigration.
2. United States--Economic conditions--1918-1945.
3. Labor and laboring classes--United States.
I. Title.
HD8081.A5H6 1972 331.6'2 70-170055
ISBN 0-404-03348-2

Reprinted from the edition of 1922, New York
First AMS edition published in 1972
Manufactured in the United States of America

International Standard Book Number: 0-404-03348-2

AMS PRESS INC.
NEW YORK, N. Y. 10003

PREFACE TO THE SECOND EDITION

IMMIGRATION is treated in this book solely as an economic question. In this the author followed the Immigration Commission, which was created by Congress in 1907, and presented its report in 1910. He was not unaware of the existence of a sentiment against immigration, based upon other than economic considerations. Indeed, most of the first chapter, and a part of the third, are devoted to this aspect of the question. But he concurs in the opinion of the experts of the Immigration Commission, and of the Commission on Industrial Relations, that the objections to immigration are fundamentally of an economic nature. Prior to the war, the only real power behind the agitation in favor of restriction of immigration was organized labor. Our statesmen in Washington took scant notice of the academic disquisitions in the domains of anthropology, ethnology, sociology, eugenics, and political science, which presented the old arguments of the Know-Nothings dressed up in a modern scientific garb. But they listened to union officials who proposed to reward their friends and punish their enemies on election day. Yet the opposition of labor to immigration was outweighed by the influence of capital, which regarded free trade in the labor market as indispensable for the expansion of American industry. The social revolution in Russia and its echoes in Hungary, Germany, and Italy, as well as the growth of the Socialist and Communist parties in all European countries, have aroused a fear of immigration among American capitalists. Labor and capital now united in the demand for restrictive legislation. Organized labor favored complete exclusion of immigration, capital favored a "selective" test meant to bar all immigrants infected with "Bolshevism," which is a comprehensive term for every variety of economic and political heresy. A compromise was reached by the passage of the recent immigration act, supplemented by the order of the State Department requiring the viséing of the passports of all intending immigrants by American consuls in the countries of emigration. Both are merely emergency measures, and the matter will again be before Congress at its regular session. The object of this edition is to aid in the public discussion of this question.

The first edition of this book appeared less than two years before the World War. No changes in the structure of society manifest themselves within two years under ordinary conditions. No new immigration legislation was enacted during that time. It is, therefore, reasonable to assume that the normal effects of immigration on the eve of the war were the same as at the time when this book was first published. The outbreak of the European war produced a revolutionary change. As an ardent advocate of restriction exultingly put it, "the war did to immigration what all the restrictionist agitation in the world could not have accomplished—it stopped it altogether."[1] Here was an opportunity to test the effects of the cessation of immigration upon the condition of labor in the United States. This subject is treated in the new chapter, "The Lessons of the War," dealing with labor conditions during the late war. The forecast of the probable effects of restriction of immigration, which was the concluding chapter of the first edition, has been retained, with the omission of the discussion of some of the recommendations of the Immigration Commission which are now out of date. The reader is thus enabled to verify the deductions drawn from the history of immigration prior to the war, by the experience of labor during a period without immigration. The new chapter may serve as an answer to the main criticisms of the first edition.

A reviewer in *The Quarterly Journal of Economics* scouted

[1] Prof. Henry P. Fairchild in *The New York Times* of October 12, 1919.

the "elaborate treatment . . . accorded the question, 'has emigration from Southern and Eastern Europe checked emigration from Northern and Western Europe?'" It seemed to him that "restrictionists . . . who plan and expect a revival of the older immigration, are not conspicuous." Yet this is the avowed aim of the 3 per cent quota of the immigration law which was enacted last spring.

A detailed analysis of the points raised by critics will be found in the Appendix.

ISAAC A. HOURWICH.

NEW YORK, September 15, 1921.

PREFACE TO THE FIRST EDITION

THE Immigration Commission, after three years of investigation, reached the conclusion that our immigration policy "should be based primarily upon economic or business considerations." This conclusion has determined the scope of the present book: it treats immigration solely as an economic question. For the same reason the discussion is confined to European immigration, Oriental immigration being viewed by many students primarily as a race question, which reaches out beyond the domain of economics.

The author gratefully acknowledges his indebtedness to Mr. William W. Bishop, superintendent of the Reading Room, Library of Congress, who obligingly placed at his disposal the exceptional facilities of the Library; to Mr. W. W. Husband, secretary of the Immigration Commission, who courteously gave him access to the proof sheets of the reports of the Commission, in advance of their publication; and to the young men and women who assisted him in the preparation of the material for this book.

I. A. H.

WASHINGTON, D. C., July 23, 1912.

CONTENTS

PART I.

SUMMARY REVIEW.

PART II.

TOPICAL ANALYSIS.

CHAPTER I.

STATEMENT OF THE QUESTION.

CHAPTER II.

THE REPORT OF THE IMMIGRATION COMMISSION.

CHAPTER III.

OLD AND NEW IMMIGRATION.

CHAPTER IX.

RACE SUICIDE.

CHAPTER X.

THE STANDARD OF LIVING.

CHAPTER XI.

HOME OWNERSHIP.

CHAPTER XII.

EFFECT OF IMMIGRATION ON WAGES.

CHAPTER XIII.

HOURS OF LABOR.

CHAPTER XIV.

CHILD LABOR.

CHAPTER XV.

LABOR ORGANIZATIONS.

CHAPTER XVI.

PAUPERISM AND CRIME.

CHAPTER XX.

THE IRON AND STEEL WORKERS.

CHAPTER XXI.

THE COAL MINERS.

CHAPTER XXII.

WORK ACCIDENTS.

PART IV.

CONCLUSION.

CHAPTER XXIII.

PROBABLE EFFECTS OF RESTRICTION—A FORECAST.

CHAPTER XXIV.

THE LESSONS OF THE WAR.

APPENDIX

LIST OF TABLES

APPENDIX

LIST OF DIAGRAMS

MAPS

Immigration and Labor

PART I

SUMMARY REVIEW

IT is the purpose of this review to state briefly for the benefit of the busy reader the results of our inquiry into the various phases of the immigration question. Such a summary must necessarily be dogmatic in form. Every proposition is advanced here, however, merely as a theorem, whose demonstration is presented in its proper place, in another part of the book.

It is recognized on all sides that the present movement for restriction of immigration has a purely economic object: the restriction of competition in the labor market. Organized labor demands the extension of the protectionist policy to the home market in which "hands"—the laborer's only commodity—are offered for sale. The advocates of restriction believe that every immigrant admitted to this country takes the place of some American workingman. At the inception of the restrictionist movement, in the 80's and the early 90's, they were avowedly opposed to immigration in general. The subsequent decline of immigration from the British Isles, Germany, and the Scandinavian countries and the increase of immigration from Southern and Eastern Europe have diverted the attack from immigration in general to "the new immigration" from Southern and Eastern

Europe and the Asiatic provinces of Turkey. Yet while the root of all evil is now sought in the racial makeup of the new immigration, as contrasted with the old, every objection to the immigrants from Southern and Eastern Europe is but an echo of the complaints which were made at an earlier day against the then new immigration from Ireland, Germany, and even from England. Three quarters of a century ago, as to-day, the only good immigrants were the dead immigrants.

There is no real ground for the popular opinion that the immigrants of the present generation are drawn from a poorer class than their predecessors. It is a historical fact that prior to 1820 the great majority of the immigrants were too poor to prepay their passage, which never cost as much as $50 per steerage passenger; the usual way for a poor man to secure transportation for himself and family was to contract to be sold into servitude after arrival. The next generation of immigrants was not much better off. According to contemporary testimony, the millions of Irish and Germans who came in the middle of the nineteenth century were ignorant and accustomed to a very low standard of living. Since the races of Southern and Eastern Europe have become predominant among immigrants to the United States, the steerage rates have been doubled, the increase being equivalent to a heavy head tax. The higher cost of transportation must have raised the financial standard of the new immigration, as compared with the immigrants of the 70's and the early 80's. This inference is borne out by the fact that the percentage of illiteracy is much lower among the immigrants than among their countrymen who remain at home. Illiteracy is generally the effect of poverty. The higher literacy of the immigrant may be accepted as evidence that economically the immigrant must be above the average of his mother country.

The complaint that the new immigrants do not easily "assimilate" is also as old as immigration itself. To-day the Germans are reckoned by courtesy among the "English-speaking races." But as late as the middle of the nineteenth century the growth of German colonies in all large cities caused the same apprehension in the minds of their American contemporaries as the Jewish, the Italian, and the Slav colonies of our day. Statistics show, however, that the new immigrant races number among them as large a percentage of English-speaking persons as the Germans who have lived in the United States the same length of time.

The only real difference between the old immigration and the new is that of numbers. To the workman who complains that he has been crowded out of his job by another, it would afford little comfort to feel that the man who had taken his place was of Teuton or Celtic, rather than of Latin or Slav stock. The true reason why the "old immigration" is preferred is that there is very much less of it.

As stated, the demand for restriction proceeds from the assumption that the American labor market is overstocked by immigration. Comparative statistics of industry and population in the United States show, however, that immigration merely follows opportunities for employment. In times of business expansion immigrants enter in increasing numbers; in times of business depression their numbers decline. The immigration movement is further balanced by emigration from the United States. As a rule, the causes which retard immigration also accelerate the return movement from this country. It is customary to condemn the "bird of passage," but so long as there are variations in business activity from season to season and from year to year, the American wage-earner has no cause to complain of the immigrants who choose to leave this country temporarily while there is no demand for their services, thereby reducing unemployment in its acutest stage.

It is broadly asserted by restriction advocates that the hundreds of thousands of Slav, Italian, Greek, Syrian, and other immigrant mine and mill workers have been "imported" by capitalists—in other words, that they are all contract laborers. This belief offers to the student of folk-lore a typical example of twentieth century myth-building. None of the official investigations of immigration has disclosed any evidence of importation of laborers under contract on a large scale, although prior to the enactment of the law of 1885 excluding contract laborers there was no reason to conceal the fact. It is quite conceivable that in the case of a strike a great corporation might have resorted to the importation of a large force of strikebreakers regardless of cost. As a general rule, however, with hundreds of thousands of immigrants coming to this country annually, it would be a waste of money to "induce" immigration. The few actual violations of the contract labor law that elude the vigilance of the immigration authorities cannot affect the labor market.

The real agents who regulate the immigration movement are the millions of earlier immigrants already in the United States. It is they that advance the cost of passage of a large proportion of the new immigrants. When the outlook for employment is good, they send for their relatives, or encourage their friends to come. When the demand for labor is slack, the foreign-born workman must hold his savings in reserve, to provide for possible loss of employment. At such times no wage-earner will assume the burden of providing for a relative or friend, who might for a long time be unable to secure employment. It is in this way that the business situation in the United States reacts upon the volume of immigration. The fluctuating supply of immigrant labor, like that of any other commodity, may sometimes outrun the demand and at other times lag behind it, yet, if we compare the totals for industrial cycles, comprising years of panic, of depression, and of prosperity, within the past sixty years, we find that the ratio of immigration to population has been well-nigh constant. In the long run immigration adjusts itself to the demand for labor.

This proposition seems to be inconsistent with the presence at all times of a vast number of unemployed. Apparently, there are already more men than jobs in the

United States; every new immigrant, in order to live, must take away the job from some one else who has been here before. On closer study, however, it is found that unemployment is not the effect of an absolute surplus population. It arises, notwithstanding a growing demand for labor, from the fluctuations in the distribution of the demand. The most generally recognized cause of unemployment is seasonal variation of business activity. There are trades dependent largely upon climatic conditions and partly upon social customs. In the period of maximum activity the demand for labor in such trades may often so far exceed the supply as to necessitate overtime work; yet this shortage of labor will not save a portion of the force from idleness at other times of the year. The only class of labor which is capable of shifting from one industry to another in response to variations in demand is unskilled labor. But the localization of industries sets a limit to the mobility of unskilled labor. In order to eliminate unemployment it would be necessary to dovetail the busy and the slack seasons in the various industries upon such a plan as would produce an even distribution of the work of the nation over all seasons of the year. This might be possible if all mines, mills, and transportation lines were operated by one nation-wide trust. So long, however, as production is controlled by many competing employers, each subject to his own vicissitudes of business, insecurity of employment is inevitable. The normal state of every industry is to have a larger force than can ever find employment in it at any one time. The labor reserve is as much a part of the industrial system as the regular force.

Still, the labor market being normally overstocked, it sounds plausible that the immigrant, who is accustomed to a lower standard of living at home than the American workman, will be able to underbid and displace his American competitor. If this view were correct, we should find, in the first place, a higher percentage of unemployment among the native than among the foreign-born breadwinners.

Statistics, however, show that the proportion of unemployment is the same for native and foreign-born wage-earners. The immigrant has no advantage over the native American in securing or retaining employment. In the next place, we should find more unemployment in those sections of the United States where the immigrants are most numerous. In fact, however, the ratio of unemployment in manufactures is the same in the North Atlantic States with a large immigrant population as in the South Atlantic States where the percentage of foreign-born is negligible. Coal miners are thought to have suffered most from immigration. Yet it appears that Pennsylvania, which is among the States with the highest percentages of foreign-born miners, has the second lowest percentage of unemployment. The highest ratio of unemployment, according to the latest published census data, was found in West Virginia, where the percentage of foreign-born miners was next to the lowest. A similar relation between unemployment and the proportion of immigrants is observed among cotton-mill operatives and common laborers: immigrants are not attracted to those States where opportunities for regular employment are less favorable.

Furthermore, if there existed a causal connection between immigration and unemployment, there should have been more unemployment in those years when immigration was greater, and *vice versa*. The figures show, on the contrary, that there was less unemployment during the first seven years of the present century with immigration at a high tide than during the preceding decade when immigration was at a low ebb.

Still an oversupply of labor may produce a latent form of unemployment which could be described as underemployment: all employees may be kept on the rolls, and yet be idle a part of every week. Again, however, we find that the average number of days of employment per wage-earner increases as immigration increases, and declines as immigration declines.

The relation between immigration and unemployment may thus be summed up in the following propositions: Unemployment and immigration are the effects of economic forces working in opposite directions: those which produce business expansion reduce unemployment and attract immigration; those which produce business depression increase unemployment and reduce immigration.

Yet it may be said that while immigration is not a contributory cause of unemployment, restriction of immigration might nevertheless reduce unemployment. This supposition is negatived by the experience of Australia, where emigration exceeds immigration. Australia is a new country with an area as great as that of the United States, while its population at the census of 1906 was half a million short of the population of New York City at the census of 1910. Yet Australia has as much unemployment as the State of New York, which is teeming with immigrants. It is evident that unemployment is produced by the modern organization of industry even in the absence of immigration.

There is a widespread belief that, although on the whole the United States is in need of immigrant labor, "the new immigration" has a tendency to stagnate in the overpopulated cities, while there is a keen demand for hands in agricultural sections. A retrospective view of the history of immigration shows that this tendency is not peculiar to "the new immigration." For the past ninety years public men and social theorists have sought to relieve unemployment in the cities by directing the current of immigration to the farm, but the immigrants have always preferred to seek employment in the cities. The popular mind which accounts for individual conduct by the "free will" of the individual applies the same criterion to social phenomena: the Italians and the Slavs concentrate in the cities because they have a "racial tendency" to concentrate in the cities. That most of the immigrants of those nationalities have grown up in agricultural communities and that many of them after working a few years in a great American city return home and go back to the soil, argues against the assumption of a "racial" dislike for agriculture. The real cause of the concentration of immigrants in the cities is economic. Even the "desirable" immigrant from Northern and Western Europe who lands with a capital of fifty and odd dollars lacks the funds to rent a farm. At best he can obtain employment only as a farm hand. Since the early days of Irish and German immigration, however, the growing industries of the cities have offered a better market for labor than agriculture.

The industrial development of the United States has manifested itself in a relative, and in some sections an absolute, depopulation of rural territory. There is a large migration of native Americans of native stock from country to city. This movement is the result of the revolution in American farming conditions and methods, which has tended to reduce the demand for labor on the farm. The American farm of the first half of the nineteenth century was the seat of a highly diversified industry. The members of a farm household made their own tools and part of the furniture; they were spinners and weavers; they made their own clothes, and soap and candles for their own use. With such a variety of occupations there was work for a hired man at all seasons of the year. But industrial differentiation has removed from the farm one industry after another. The time during which a hired man can be kept employed on the farm has been reduced in consequence to a few months in the year. Still until the middle of the nineteenth century the mills were quite commonly run by water power, which made for decentralization of manufactures. The small country towns accordingly offered to the farm laborer a prospect of employment when work was scarce on the farm. But the general substitution of steam for water power led to the removal of factories from small towns to great commercial centers. The opportunity to earn a full year's wages in a rural community was gone.

While in manufacturing the invention of labor-saving

machinery has resulted in the gradual displacement of the small proprietor by the wage-earner, in American agriculture, on the contrary, the machine has tended to eliminate the wage-earner. As late as the middle of the nineteenth century the agricultural methods of the American farmer differed little from those of his ancestors. Grass was mowed with a scythe. Grain was cut with a sickle and threshed with a flail. Flailing and winnowing grain was the chief farm work of the winter. Corn was planted by hand, cultivated with the hoe, and shelled by scraping the ears against the handle of a frying pan. The cultivation of a farm in this primitive way sustained a demand for steady farm help in all seasons. To-day there is some implement or machine for every kind of farm work. It is estimated that the quantity of labor saved by machinery represents the services of one and a half million men working every week day in the year.

In consequence of limited demand, agricultural labor is the least remunerative of all occupations. The hours of labor on the farm are longer than even in the steel mills of Pennsylvania. Small pay, long hours, and irregular employment is what the immigrant can expect on a farm. His preference for city work which pays better can be easily explained without delving into the mysteries of race psychology. It merely confirms the rule that immigration follows the demand for labor.

The effect of immigration upon labor in the United States has been a readjustment of the population on the scale of occupations. The majority of Americans of native parentage are engaged in farming, in business, in the professions, and in clerical pursuits. The majority of the immigrants, on the other hand, are industrial wage-earners. Only in exceptional cases has this readjustment been attended by actual displacement of the native or Americanized wage-earner. In the course of industrial evolution some trades have declined owing to the introduction of new methods of production. In such cases there was naturally a decrease of the number of native as well as of foreign-born workers. As a rule, however, the supply of immigrant labor has been absorbed by the increasing demand for labor in all industries without leaving a surplus sufficient to displace the native or older immigrant wage-earner. There were but a few occupations which showed an actual, not a relative decrease of native Americans of native stock. This decrease was due to the disinclination of the young generation to follow the pursuits of their fathers; the new accessions from native stock were insufficient to replace the older men as they were dying off, and the vacancies were gradually filled up by immigrants. But for every position given up by a native American there were many new openings filled by native American wage-earners.

The westward movement of American and Americanized wage-earners and the concentration of immigrants in a few Eastern and Central States have been interpreted as the "displacement" of the English-speaking workmen from the mills and mines of the East by the new immigration. An examination of the figures shows, however, that during the past thirty years mining and manufacturing grew much faster in the West and South than in the East and drew some of the native workers and earlier immigrants from the older manufacturing States. But the demand for labor grew in the old States as well. The places left vacant by the old employees who had gone westward had to be filled by new immigrants.

The desertion of mills and factories by native American girls has also been explained as their "displacement" by immigrants. The motive assigned is not economic, but racial: it is the social prejudice against the immigrant that has forced the American girl to quit. It seems, however, that this explanation mistakes cause for effect: the social stigma attaching to working association with immigrants is not the cause but the effect of the desertion of the mills and factories by native American women. The psychological interpretation overlooks one of the greatest economic changes that has taken place in the United States since the Civil War: the admission of women to most of the pursuits which were formerly regarded as peculiarly masculine. For every native woman of American parentage who left the mill or clothing factory there were forty women of the same nativity who found new openings. The increase of the number of native American professional women was nearly five times as great as the decrease of the number of native American factory girls. The marvelous progress of the American educational system has fitted the native American woman for other work than manual labor and has at the same time opened to her a new field in which she does not meet the competition of the immigrant.

There is absolutely no statistical proof of an oversupply of unskilled labor resulting in the displacement of native by immigrant laborers. No decrease of the number of common laborers among the native white of native or foreign parentage appears in any of the great States which serve as receptacles for immigration. The same is true of miners. In none of the States affected by the new immigration has there been a decrease in the number of native miners. Such States as Pennsylvania and Illinois showed large increases in the number of native miners, both of foreign and native parentage. The iron and steel mills are another industry from which the recent immigrants are popularly believed to have forced out the native workmen and older English-speaking immigrants.. The fact is, that in the earlier period of the industry, when immigration from Southern and Eastern Europe was negligible, the number of American employees increased very slowly; during the recent period, on the contrary, since the immigrants from Southern and Eastern Europe have been coming in large numbers, the number of American-born employees of every nativity has more than doubled. The increased employment of native Americans is recorded in the figures for every important iron- and steel-producing State, as well as for every city holding a leading place in the iron and steel industry.

The effect of immigration upon the occupational distribution of the industrial wage-earners has been the elevation of the English-speaking workmen to the status of an aristocracy of labor, while the immigrants have been employed to perform the rough work of all industries. Though the introduction of machinery has had the tendency to reduce the relative number of skilled mechanics, yet the rapid pace of industrial expansion has increased the number of skilled and supervisory positions so fast that practically all the English-speaking employees have had the opportunity to rise on the scale of occupations. This opportunity, however, was conditioned upon a corresponding increase of the total operating force. It is only because the new immigration has furnished the class of unskilled laborers that the native workmen and older immigrants have been raised to the plane of an aristocracy of labor.

Yet, while the number of native American workmen in all industries has increased, it is true that in some occupations there has been an actual decrease of the number of English, Welsh, Irish, and German workers, which has been construed as "displacement" of Americanized workers by immigrants from Southern and Eastern Europe with a lower standard of living. This interpretation overlooks the fact that native workers of native parentage, presumably with as high a standard of living as the Irish, are found in the same occupations in larger numbers than formerly. Another fact that contradicts the popular view is the increase of the number of Scotch immigrants in those very occupations which show a decline in the number of English and Irish. Judged by any standard, the Scotch are not inferior to other immigrants from the United Kingdom. The increased employment of the Scotch in the principal occupations, including even common laborers, warrants the conclusion that the decline in the numbers of English and Irish must have been due to other causes than the competition of recent immigrants with lower standards of living. A further fact that must be considered in this connection is that the

English, Welsh, and Irish farmers exhibit a greater decrease, both absolute and relative, than any other occupational group among the same nationalities. Evidently no new farmers came to fill the places of their countrymen who were carried off by death, although the aliens from Southern and Eastern Europe kept away from the farming sections and left the field open for English, Welsh, and Irish immigrants.

The real explanation of the decrease in the number of immigrants from Northern and Western Europe in the occupations which rank lowest in the social scale is that the earlier immigrants have worked their way upward. Among the breadwinners born in Northern and Western Europe, farmers, business men, professional men, and skilled mechanics outnumber those who are employed in the coarser grades of labor. The latter have been left to immigrants from Southern and Eastern Europe.

There has been a great deal of speculation to the effect that had immigration from Southern and Eastern Europe been kept out of the United States, the immigrants from Northern and Western Europe would, as of old, have supplied the demand of American industry for unskilled labor. The fallacy of this assumption is apparent from a consideration of the comparative growth of population in the United States and in the countries of Northern and Western Europe, as well as of the economic conditions in those countries. As stated before, immigration in the long run bears a constant relation to the population of the United States. Inasmuch, however, as the latter increases faster than the population of Europe, especially that of the emigration countries, the rate of emigration from those countries must increase much faster than their population in order to supply the American industries with the number of immigrants they can employ. Yet the volume of emigration from any country can not increase beyond a certain limit set by the size of its population. When that point is reached, further industrial expansion in the United States must draw upon the labor supply of other countries. In order to replace the immigrants from Southern and Eastern Europe that were absorbed by the industrial expansion of the past decade, immigration from Great Britain, Germany, and the Scandinavian countries should have risen to the Irish level, whereas Ireland ought to have been depopulated at a greater rate than in the years of the Irish famine. The recent development of those countries, however, has had a decided tendency to check emigration.

In the closing years of the nineteenth century Germany ceased to be a country of emigration, and became a country of immigration. Inasmuch as Germany draws her immigrant supply from the same sources as the United States, it is evident that the German wage-earner does not stay away from the United States in order to escape the competition of the immigrant from Southern and Eastern Europe. The transformation of Germany from an emigrant-furnishing nation to a country of immigration is the direct result of her recent economic development. Until the middle of the nineteenth century Germany was principally an agricultural country. About that time German agriculture reached the point where the growth of land values made the traditional methods of the peasant unprofitable and necessitated a transition to intensive systems of cultivation. Many a peasant who lacked the requisite capital for a change of methods was forced to dispose of his land and to seek a new home in the United States. In Prussian Poland this crisis came in the 70's and the early 80's and drove large numbers of Polish peasants to the United States. But the rapid growth of manufacturing and mining during the last twenty-five years has absorbed the whole natural increase of the rural population. At the same time, German agriculture has also made substantial progress. As a result, there is a scarcity of agricultural laborers during the busy season. The combined effect of all these causes, coupled with the disappearance of cheap lands in the United States, has been reflected in a decline of the emigration of farmers and farm laborers to the United States. The increased demand for labor has resulted in a substantial increase of the rates of wages, simultaneously with a marked reduction of the working day. These gains are in no small way due to the progress of organization among German wage-earners, which was practically prohibited prior to 1891. Since that time the membership of labor organizations has advanced by leaps and bounds, leaving behind the older British and American trade-unions. The growth of the labor movement in Germany has directly and indirectly stimulated labor legislation, which has conferred material benefits upon the German wage-earner. Whereas industrial progress in modern times has generally led to the elimination of the independent artisan who has been pushed into the ranks of wage-earners, in Germany this process has been checked by the development of co-operation. The general improvement of the economic conditions of all classes of the working people necessarily affected the rate of emigration for the past twenty years.

Yet it is worthy of note that while immigration from Germany to the United States has in recent years been much below the level of the early 80's, the average annual immigration from Germany was much higher during the past decade than during the last decade of the nineteenth century. In other words, German immigration increased with the increase of Italian and Slav immigration to the United States.

Coming next to Scandinavian immigration we find that the number of breadwinners coming to compete in the American labor market virtually reached its maximum during the past decade. The only change is that, whereas the earlier Scandinavian immigration was mostly of a family type, among the recent Scandinavian immigrants single persons vastly predominate. This change is due to the fact that the old Scandinavian immigrants came largely to settle on farms, where a family was a help, while the new Scandinavian immigrants, like the new immigration from Southern and Eastern Europe, come chiefly to seek industrial employment. That Scandinavian immigration to the United States was in no way affected by immigration from Southern and Eastern Europe is evidenced by the change in the direction of the former: whereas prior to 1890 the greater part of Scandinavian immigration was directed to the agricultural States of the Central West and Northwest, since 1890 the majority of the Scandinavian immigrants follow the current of immigration from Southern and Eastern Europe. The bulk of the Scandinavian immigrants are laborers from agricultural districts or farm workers without special mechanical skill. It is these unskilled Scandinavian laborers that have in recent years sought employment in competition with unskilled Slav and Italian laborers. The reason why the number of these Scandinavian immigrants has not grown fast enough to keep pace with the needs of American industry must be sought in the economic conditions of the Scandinavian countries. Since the opportunity eventually to secure a homestead in the United States is gone, the agricultural laborer who is dissatisfied with his condition must seek employment in industry. And here the recent industrial progress of the Scandinavian countries offers him many an opportunity at home.

The industrial development of Sweden is contemporaneous with the latest progress in engineering, which has harnessed the water power furnished in abundance by her mountains. The growth of Swedish industries has far outrun the increase of her population. As a result, Sweden has become a country of immigration. The immigration to Sweden has in recent years left a surplus over emigration.

In Denmark the last fifteen years of the nineteenth century witnessed a rise of the peasant farmer, due chiefly to the rapid spread of co-operation in all branches of farming. The progress of agriculture has attracted immigration to Denmark. During every agricultural season considerable numbers of Polish peasants come to work on the farms in Denmark.

While the wave of emigration from Great Britain and Ireland to the United States has receded from the high-water mark reached in 1880–1889, yet, eliminating that exceptional decade, we find that during the 20-year period 1890–1909, marked by the influx of immigrants from Southern and Eastern Europe, the United States received more immigrants from Great Britain and Ireland than during the 20-year period 1860–1879. Another fact that must not be lost sight of is the recent development of Canada, Australia, New Zealand, and South Africa, which has naturally drawn a part of the emigration from Great Britain and Ireland. The policy of restriction adopted in Australia, New Zealand, and South Africa has conferred a special privilege upon immigrants of British nationality. On the other hand, the governments of Canada and Australia are making systematic efforts to induce and assist immigration from the mother country. That the financial assistance offered to immigrants from the United Kingdom has diverted a part of them from the United States is but natural.

The decline of Irish immigration began as far back as 1861. It rose again in the 80's, in the turbulent years of the Irish Land League agitation, and once more during the past decade. That the "new immigration" to the United States was not the cause of the decline of Irish immigration is clear from the fact that the emigration movement from Ireland to other countries has also declined, while, on the other hand, of those Irish who did emigrate the proportion destined to the United States was higher during the period of the great influx of immigrants from Southern and Eastern Europe than in 1876–1890, when immigration from Southern and Eastern Europe was negligible. There have been forces at work to reduce the number of Irish seeking to better their condition away from home. The great Irish unrest of the 80's forced the British Parliament to enact remedial legislation, which gave to the tenant-at-will a legal title to his holding, besides reducing his rent, and converted about one third of the tenants into land proprietors. These far-reaching reforms in a country with a predominantly peasant population sufficiently account for the decline of emigration from Ireland.

It can be seen from this brief survey that immigration from Northern and Western Europe has declined, not because the condition of labor has deteriorated in the United States, but because those countries have become better homes for their citizens.

Another popular fallacy is the theory originated by General Walker, that the immigrants have displaced unborn generations of native Americans. It rests on no other foundation than a computation made in 1815 from the increase of the population of the United States between 1790 and 1810. During the century that has elapsed, the declining birth-rate has become a world-wide social phenomenon. In the Australian Commonwealth, with her vast continent as yet unsettled, with a purely Anglo-Saxon population and practically no immigration, the decline of the birth-rate has been as rapid as among Americans of native stock. Prof. Wilcox has proved by an analysis of population statistics that the decrease in the proportion of children began in the United States as early as 1810. The native birth-rate has declined with the increase of the urban population and the relative decrease of the number of farmers. The rearing of children on a farm requires less of the mother's time and attention than in the city. Moreover, the child on a farm begins to work at an earlier age than in the city. A numerous family on a farm has the advantages of a co-operative group, whereas every addition to the family of the wage-earner or of the salaried man with a fixed income tends to lower the family's standard of living. It is significant that the decline of the birth-rate is universal among those classes which are scarcely, if at all, affected by immigrant competition. Their standard of living is higher than that of the wage-earner. Yet it is precisely the desire to preserve this higher standard that accounts for the practice of race suicide. Granting, for the sake of argument, that the absence of immigration in the past would have raised the native wage-earner's standard of living to that of the middle class, it does not follow that the natural increase among the native-born would have sufficed to supply the needs of the rapidly expanding industries of the United States.

There was clearly no other source from which American industry could have drawn its labor supply than immigration from the countries of Southern and Eastern Europe. Without the immigrants from those countries the recent development of American industry would have been impossible.

An invidious distinction is drawn between the old and the new immigrants by reason of the fact that the bulk of the latter are incapable of any but unskilled work. A comparative statistical study of immigration shows that the old immigrants, like those of the present generation, were mostly unskilled laborers and farm hands. The proportion of skilled mechanics has at no time within the past fifty years been as high as one fourth of all immigrant breadwinners, for the very obvious reason that the demand in the American labor market has been mainly for unskilled laborers. Invention of machinery has had the tendency to reduce the demand for mechanical skill, and most of that demand has been supplied by native Americans. In the industrial army the commissioned and non-commissioned officers are outnumbered by the privates. It is a misconception of modern industrial organization to confuse lack of "skill," *i. e.*, ignorance of a trade, with "low efficiency." If every immigrant were a skilled mechanic, most of them would nevertheless have to accept employment as unskilled laborers. The special skill of the engineer would give him no superiority at loading coal over a common laborer, nor would the ability to read Shakespeare in the vernacular assure higher wages to a mule-driver.

The objection to the unskilled immigrant is based upon the belief that because of his lower standard of living he is satisfied with lower wages than the American or the older immigrant. It is therefore taken for granted that the effect of the great tide of immigration in recent years has been to reduce the rate of wages or to prevent it from advancing. The fallacy of this reasoning is due to the attempt to compare the wages and standard of living of the unskilled laborer with those of the skilled mechanic. In order to prove that the new immigrants have introduced a lower standard of living, the latter ought to be compared with the standard of living of unskilled laborers in the past. Housing conditions have been most dwelt upon in the discussion of the standard of living of the immigrant, because they strike the eye of the outsider. Historical studies of housing conditions show, however, that congestion was recognized as a serious evil in New York City as far back as the first half of the nineteenth century. The evil was not confined to the foreign-born population. American-born working-women lived on filthy streets in poorly ventilated houses, crowding in one or two rooms which were used both as dwelling and workshop. No better were the living conditions of the daughters of American farmers in the small mill towns of New England. They lived in company houses, half a dozen in one attic room, without tables, or chairs, or even washstands. Comparative statistics of house tenancy in Boston show that in the middle of the nineteenth century the tenement-house population was as numerous, in proportion, as in our day. The conversion of the old single-family residence into a tenement house, where a whole family was jammed in every room, was productive of filth. The inconvenience suffered by the people of New York City during the recent strike of the street cleaners was but a faint reminder of the normal conditions of the immigrant sections of New York or Boston half a century ago. These conditions are a thing of the past. The typical tenement house in the Jewish and Italian sections of New York to-day is a decided improvement upon the dwellings of the older immigrant races in the same sections a generation or two ago. On the other hand, in the South, where many of the coal mines are operated without immigrant labor, and native white Americans are employed as unskilled laborers, their homes are primitive and insanitary.

It is evident that the cause of bad housing conditions is not racial, but economic. Congestion in great cities is produced by industrial factors over which the immigrants have no control. The fundamental cause of congestion with all its attendant evils is the necessity for the wage-worker to live within an accessible distance from his place of work. In mining towns the mine company is usually the landlord, and the mine worker has no choice in the matter of housing accommodations. In so far, however, as housing conditions might affect the rates of wages of native and immigrant workmen, it is the amount of rent, not the equivalent in domestic comfort, that has to be considered. And here it is found that immigrants have to pay the same rent as, and often a higher rent than, native American wage-earners. A certain proportion among the immigrants seek to reduce their rent by taking in boarders, but the practice is not universal, and the wages of the others must therefore provide for the payment of normal rent. Moreover, the recent immigrants are mostly concentrated in great cities, where rent is high, while the native American workmen live mostly in small towns with low rents.

Nor are the food standards of the recent immigrant inferior to those of native Americans with the same income. Meat, the most expensive article of food, is consumed by the Slav in larger quantities than by native Americans. Rent and food claim by far the greater part of a workman's wages. It is thus apparent that whatever may have been the immigrant's standard of living in his home country, his expenditure in the United States is determined by the prices ruling in the United States. Contrary to common assertion, the living expenses of the native American workman in small cities and rural districts are lower than those of the recent immigrants in the great industrial centers. It is therefore not the recent immigrant that is able to underbid the native American workman, but it is, on the contrary, the latter that is in a position to accept a cheaper wage.

There is, of course, a difference between the expenses of a single and of a married workman. The necessary expenses of a single man are lower than those of one who has a family to support, and a large proportion of the recent immigrants are either single or have left their families abroad. But, while an unmarried American workman may either save or spend the difference, the recent immigrant is obliged to save a part of his earnings. He must repay the cost of his own passage; if he has left a family at home, he must save up money to pay for their passage, besides supporting them in the meantime. So when the recent immigrant is seen to deny himself every comfort in order to reduce his personal expenses to a minimum, it is a mistake to assume that he will accept a wage just sufficient to provide for his own subsistence. The Italian section hand who lives on vegetables does not save money for the railroad company. The economic interests of the American wage-earner are therefore not affected by the tendency of the recent immigrant to live as cheaply as possible and to save as much as possible. Whether he spends his wages for rent and dress, or saves his money to buy steamship tickets for his family; whether he invests his savings in a home in the United States or sends them to his parents for improving the home farm, his wants in one case are as urgent as in the other, and he must demand a wage which will enable him to satisfy them.

On the other hand, though the standard of living of the native or Americanized wage-earners be higher than that of the new immigrants, this difference is not necessarily indicative of a higher rate of wages: the higher standard is very often maintained with the earnings of the children, whereas the Southern and Eastern European immigrants are mostly young people whose children have not reached working age. The supposed difference in the standard of living can therefore have no effect upon the comparative rates of wages of English-speaking workmen and of recent immigrants.

But it is argued that the newly arrived immigrant must have work at once and is therefore glad to accept any terms. The Immigration Commission after a study of the earnings of more than half a million employees in mines and manufactures, has discovered no evidence that immigrants have been hired for less than the prevailing rates of wages.

The primary cause which has determined the movement of wages in the United States during the past thirty years has been the introduction of labor-saving machinery. The effect of the substitution of mechanical devices for human skill is the displacement of the skilled mechanic by the unskilled laborer. This tendency has been counteracted in the United States by the expansion of industry: while the ratio of skilled mechanics to the total operating force was decreasing, the increasing scale of operations prevented an actual reduction in numbers. Of course this adjustment did not proceed without friction. While, in the long run, there has been no displacement of skilled mechanics by unskilled laborers in the industrial field as a whole, yet at certain times and places individual skilled mechanics were doubtless dispensed with and had to seek new employment. The unskilled laborers who replaced them were naturally engaged at lower wages. The fact that most of these unskilled laborers were immigrants disguised the substance of the change—the substitution of unskilled for skilled labor—and made it appear as the displacement of highly-paid native by cheap immigrant labor.

To prove that immigration has virtually lowered the rates of wages, would require a comparative study of wages paid for the same class of labor in various occupations before and after the great influx of immigration. This, however, has never been attempted by the advocates of restriction. In fact, the chaotic state of our wage statistics precludes any but a fragmentary comparison for different periods. In a general way, however, all available data for the period of "the old immigration" agree in that the wages of unskilled laborers, and even of some of the skilled mechanics, did not fully provide for the support of the wage-earner and his family in accordance with their usual standards of living. The shortage had to be made up by the labor of the wife and children.

If the tendency of the new immigration were to lower the rate of wages or to retard the advance of wages, it should be expected that wages would be lower in great cities where the recent immigrants are concentrated, than in rural districts where the population is mostly of native birth. All wage statistics, concur, however, in the opposite conclusion. Since the United States has become a manufacturing country average earnings per worker have been higher in the cities than in the country. The same difference exists within the same trades between the large and the small cities. Country competition of native Americans often acts as a depressing factor upon the wages of recent immigrants. This fact has been demonstrated in the clothing industry, in the cotton mills, in the coal mines, etc.

Furthermore, if immigration tends to depress wages, this tendency must manifest itself in lower average earnings in States with a large immigrant population than in States with a predominant native population. No such tendency, however, is discernible from wage statistics. As a rule, annual earnings are higher in States with a higher percentage of foreign-born workers.

The conditions in some of the leading industries employing large numbers of recent immigrants point to the same conclusions. In the Pittsburgh steel mills the rates of wages of various grades of employees have varied directly with the proportion of recent immigrants. The wages of the aristocrats of labor, none of whom are Southern or Eastern Europeans, have been reduced in some cases as much as 40 per cent; the money wages of the skilled and semi-skilled workers, two thirds of whom are natives or old immigrants, have not advanced notwithstanding the increased cost of living, while the wages of the unskilled laborers, the bulk of whom are immigrants from Southern and Eastern Europe, have been going up.

Another typical immigrant industry is the manufacture of clothing. The clothing industry has become associated in the public mind with the sweating system, and since the employees are, with few exceptions, immigrants from Southern and Eastern Europe, the conclusion is readily reached that the root of the sweating system is in the character of the new immigration. Yet the origin of the sweating system preceded the Jewish clothing workers by more than half a century. Throughout the second quarter of the past century native American and Irish women worked in the sweat shops of New York, Boston, and Philadelphia for only board and lodging, or even for board alone, depending upon their families for other necessities, whereas the Jewish factory girls of the present day are at least self-supporting.

In the cotton mills of New England the last quarter of the nineteenth century, when the operatives were practically all of the English-speaking races, was a period of intermittent advances and reductions in wages; on the whole, wages remained stationary. The first years of the present century, up to the crisis of 1908, were marked by the advent of the Southern and Eastern Europeans into the cotton mills, and by an uninterrupted upward movement of wages. The competition of the cheap American labor of the Southern cotton mills, however, tends to keep down the wages of the Southern and Eastern European, Armenian, and Syrian immigrants employed in the New England mills.

As a general rule, the employment of large numbers of recent immigrants has gone together with substantial advances in wages. This correlation between the movements of wages and immigration is not the manifestation of some mysterious racial trait, but the plain working of the law of supply and demand. The employment of a high percentage of immigrants in any section, industry, or occupation, is an indication of an active demand for labor in excess of the native supply. Absence of immigrants is a sign of a dull labor market.

To be sure, the rise in wages is paralleled by a similar movement of prices. The employer of labor seeks to recoup the advance in wages by advancing the price of his product to the consumer. When the advance in the price of manufactured products becomes general, the wage-earner as a consumer is forced in effect to give up a part or all of his gain in the money rate of wages. The increased cost of living then stimulates further demands for advances in wages. Since combinations of capital in all fields of industry have reduced competition among employers of labor to a minimum, the wage-earners have been at a disadvantage in this continuous bargaining. In general it has been observed by economists that wages, as a rule, do not rise as fast as prices. That this rule holds true irrespective of immigration, is illustrated by the movement of wages and prices during the Civil War. With the exception of the first year, the period was one of prosperity in every branch of industry. The wage-earners were apparently in a favorable situation. The army drew hundreds of thousands of workers from industrial pursuits, while immigration declined. There were at that time no immigrants from Southern and Eastern Europe, nor was there any oversupply of unskilled labor. Yet while the depreciation of the currency caused a rapid increase in the cost of living, money wages did not keep pace with prices. In other words, real wages decreased. It must be noted that during the war a lively labor agitation was going on; strikes were usually successful. Withal, labor was unable to win increases in wages commensurate with the increased cost of living.

Among the factors tending to depress the rate of wages child labor holds a prominent place. The most significant fact to be noted concerning the relation between child labor and immigration is the large proportion of children employed in factories in States where there is practically no immigrant population, whereas the lowest per cent is found in New York, which is overrun by immigrants. The growth of manufacturing industries in the South being restricted by the natural increase of her native population, the manufacturers, in order to extend their operations, must resort to the employment of children, as did their predecessors in New England a century ago, before immigration came to supply the needs of American industry. This situation is by no means confined to the South. Absence of foreign immigration has created a demand for the labor of native American children in the canneries and shoe factories of rural and semi-rural Missouri. The principal inducement for locating new shoe factories in rural sections of Missouri appears to be the availability of the cheap labor of native American women and children, who can underbid the male immigrants employed in the shoe factories of Massachusetts. On the other hand, taking the United States as a whole, we find that during the ten-year period from 1899 to 1909, with its unprecedented immigration, the average number of children employed in factories did not increase, while their relative number decreased.

An unerring measure of the effects of immigration on labor conditions is furnished by the length of the working day. Aside from the benefits of shorter hours for the physical and mental well-being of the wage-earner, every reduction of the hours of labor, even when not accompanied by an increase of the daily or weekly wage, is equivalent to an increase of the hourly wage. Going back to the beginnings of the factory system in the United States, when the operatives were sons and daughters of American farmers, we find that the hours of labor in the factories were from sunrise to sunset, the same as on the farms to-day. The retirement of the native element and their replacement by Irish immigrants was followed by a reduction of the hours of labor in the textile mills. In recent years the mills have been run with a polyglot help made up of representatives of all the races of Southern and Eastern Europe and Asiatic Turkey. Compared with the time when the operatives were mostly

Irish, the factory workers have again won a reduction of an hour and a quarter a day. One need not take an optimistic view of labor conditions in the Massachusetts textile mills to recognize that fifty-four hours a week is a great stride in advance since the time when the regular working day was from sunrise to sunset.

The effects of the recent immigration upon the length of the working day can be best observed in the State of New York, which is affected by immigration more than any other State in the Union. The first decade of the present century has witnessed the greatest volume of immigration known in the history of the United States, and the bulk of that immigration has come from the countries of Southern and Eastern Europe. And yet the reports of the factory inspectors of the State of New York, covering an average of nearly a million factory employees annually, show for that decade a gradual reduction of the hours of labor in the State of New York. Comparing the city of New York with the remainder of the State, we find that the population of Southern and Eastern European birth in the great city increased during the same period from one sixth to about one fourth of the total population, whereas in the State outside the city of New York the immigrants from Southern and Eastern Europe constituted in 1910 only one sixteenth of the total population; yet after a decade of "undesirable immigration" more than two thirds of all factory operatives in New York City work ten hours or less on week days with a half holiday on Saturday, whereas in the remainder of the State, with a working population predominantly native, the majority still work longer hours. The lower wages of the native American wage-earners in small cities and country towns might be explained by the lower cost of living, which permits the native country worker to enjoy a greater measure of comfort than the more highly paid recent immigrant living in a large city. But the longer hours of the native American wage-earner in the country admit of no such explanation.

Among the many charges against the recent immigrants not the least important one is that their ignorant acquiescence in dangerous and unsanitary working conditions is a menace to the safety of the older employees. The Immigration Commission has accepted without criticism the employers' defense in work accidents, viz., that the majority of accidents arise from the negligence, the ignorance, and inexperience of the employees. There is, however, another side to the question. Many experts hold that most of the risks are humanly preventable, and their continuance is due to economic conditions beyond the control of the employee. Effective prevention of accidents in mines presupposes a carefully planned equipment involving considerable expense. But competition forces the mine operator to follow unsafe mining methods, which inevitably result in unnecessary sacrifice of human life. It is not the carelessness of the mine workers, but the carelessness of mine operators and their representatives that is, according to expert opinion, the cause of the high fatality rate in American mines. Similar dangerous conditions once existed in France and Belgium, but they were removed by stringent legislation and by an effective enforcement of the law. The theory which shifts the blame for accidents from the mine operator to the Slav miner tends to prevent the enactment of such legislation in the United States.

In the iron and steel mills there is the same popular disposition to shift the responsibility for accidents to "the ignorant foreigner," whereas expert opinion views the tremendous speed at which the plants are run as the real cause of danger. The greatest risk of death and personal injury is assumed by railway trainmen, who are all either Americans or natives of Northern and Western Europe. They have strong organizations and could not be replaced by non-English-speaking immigrants. Yet "acquiescence in dangerous and unsanitary working conditions" appears to be the general attitude of organized and unorganized workers alike, irrespective of nationality. Obviously, organized labor does not feel strong enough to make demands which would involve large outlays by employers for safe equipment.

Organization of labor is nowadays generally recognized in the United States as the most effective of all existing agencies for the increase of wages and improvement of working conditions. It would therefore be a cause for grave concern if it were true, as claimed, that the recent immigrants were not organizable, and that their employment threatened the existing labor organizations with disruption. The fact is, however, that the origin and growth of organized labor in the United States are contemporaneous with the period of "the new immigration," and that the immigrants from Southern and Eastern Europe are the backbone of some of the strongest labor unions. A notable example is the coal-mining industry, where the mine workers' organization has gained strength only since the Southern and Eastern Europeans have become the predominant element among them. One of the most troublesome problems which the organization of these immigrants has had to face has been the competition of the unorganized Americans of native stock.

Before 1880 all labor organizations were small in membership and their effect upon economic conditions was negligible. Like everywhere, during the infancy of organized labor, a union would spring into existence under the impulse of a strike, would flourish for a while, if successful, and would soon disintegrate. The work of organization has since been proceeding at an ever increasing pace. During the first decade of the new immigration, 1880–1890, more labor unions were organized than throughout the previous history of the United States. The majority of the trade-unionists and Knights of Labor were of foreign birth, whereas the native Americans contributed less than their quota to the membership of labor organizations. The greatest success rewarded the efforts of union organizers during the first decade of the present century, the membership of labor organizations growing faster than the number of wage-earners. Thus the greatest activity in the field of organization coincided with the unparalleled immigration of the past decade. The best field for observation of the effects of immigration upon trade-unionism is the State of New York, which receives more than its proportionate share of immigrants from Southern and Eastern Europe. A comparative study of trade-union statistics compiled by the New York Bureau of Labor and of the federal immigration statistics shows that union membership rises and falls with the rise and fall of immigration. The fluctuations of union membership depend upon the business situation, which likewise determines the fluctuations of immigration. The harmonious movement of immigration and organization among wage-earners is thus accounted for by the fact that both are stimulated by business prosperity and discouraged by business depression.

The question arises, however, whether the progress of trade-unionism would not have been greater had there been no immigration from Southern and Eastern Europe during the past decade of industrial expansion. An answer to this question is furnished by the comparative growth of trade-union membership in New York and in Kansas. The ratio of foreign-born in Kansas has been steadily decreasing since 1880. At the same time Kansas has shared in the recent industrial expansion. Statistics show that the relative number of organized workmen is much higher in New York with its large and growing Southern and Eastern European population than in Kansas, where more than nine tenths of the population are of native birth.

These comparisons prove that recent immigration has not retarded the progress of trade-unionism, except, of course, where it is the policy of the unions to exclude the recent immigrants by prohibitive initiation dues and other restrictive regulations intended to limit the number of competitors within their trades.

Language is nowadays no longer a bar to organization

among immigrants. The membership of every union includes a sufficient number of men of every nationality through whom their countrymen can be reached.

Many of the more recent immigrants from Southern and Eastern Europe had acquired a familiarity with the principles of organization in their home countries. In Italy organization has lately made rapid progress not only among industrial workers, but also among agricultural laborers. In Russia, previous to the uprising of 1905, labor organizations and strikes were treated as conspiracies, but the revolutionary year 1905 outmatched the labor-union record of any other country. The strikes of that year affected one third of all the factories employing three fifths of all factory workers. The total number of strikers, at a conservative estimate, exceeded three and a half millions. The strikers drew together wage-earners of all those nationalities which make up the bulk of our immigration from the Russian Empire: Hebrews, Poles, Lithuanians, Russians, and Ukrainians.[1] In this connection, it is worthy of note that the organizations of clothing workers in New York City, nearly all of whom are Russian and Polish Jews and Italians, comprise a higher proportion of the total number employed in the industry than the average trade-union in the United States.

If organized labor in the United States has not succeeded in welding together a majority of the wage-earners, the fault is neither with immigration in general, nor with immigration from Southern and Eastern Europe in particular. The primary cause is the substitution of machinery for human skill, which is taking the ground from the craft union. The latter, however, as a rule, does not seek to organize the unskilled laborers. Situations have arisen where the interests of the craft union have been antagonistic to organization among the unskilled. That organization among the unskilled

[1] The revolution of 1917 has made organized labor a part of the machinery of government.

is feasible, however, has been demonstrated in the coal-mining industry, in the Lawrence strike, and in the recent strikes of the steel workers.

Another obstacle to the progress of trade-unionism is that the principal industries to-day are controlled by combinations, which have reduced competition among employers of labor to a minimum. In a contest of endurance between a trust and a trade-union, the former is able to hold out longer, since it can shift the losses to the consumers. The only successful strikes against trusts have been those in which the majority of the strikers were immigrants from Southern and Eastern Europe, viz., the strikes in the anthracite coal mines of Pennsylvania and in the woolen mills of Lawrence.

One of the reasons for the greater power of resistance exhibited by the Southern and Eastern Europeans is the predominance among them of men without families.[1] The single European wage-earner who manages to save a portion of his earnings can fall back on his savings, if necessary. This relieves the pressure upon the strike fund. On the other hand, the families of recent immigrants, being inured to the most simple life in their home countries, can more easily endure the hardships of a strike than the families of native American wage-earners. The Southern and Eastern European strikers are therefore able to hold out longer in a wage contest than the native wage-earner.

The defeat of many strikes is charged against the immigrant, who, though supposedly too tractable under normal conditions, is said to be inclined to violence when aroused. Suffice it to say that strike riots are as old as strikes in the United States.

[1] The proportion of married men among the recent immigrants employed in bituminous coal mines varied from 49.4 per cent to 77.2 per cent; the proportion of married men whose families were living abroad averaged 27.9 per cent for all races, varying from 19.5 to 80.4 per cent.—*Reports of the Immigration Commission*, vol. 6, Tables 102 and 104.

On the other hand, however, the United Mine Workers of America, whose members are mostly immigrants from Southern and Eastern Europe, has put into practical operation an industrial parliament, with separate representation for employers and employees, for the regulation of the terms of employment. It can not be said then "*as a general proposition* . . . that all improvement in conditions and increases in rates of pay have been secured in spite of the presence of the recent immigrant." [1]

The results of the preceding discussion can be summed up as follows:

(1) Recent immigration has displaced none of the native American wage-earners or of the earlier immigrants, but has only covered the shortage of labor resulting from the excess of the demand over the domestic supply.

(2) Immigration varies inversely with unemployment; it has not increased the rate of unemployment.

(3) The standard of living of the recent immigrants is not lower than the standard of living of the past generations of immigrants engaged in the same occupations. Recent immigration has not lowered the standard of living of Americans and older immigrant wage-earners.

(4) Recent immigration has not reduced the rates of wages, nor has it prevented an increase in the rates of wages; it has pushed the native and older immigrant wage-earners upward on the scale of occupations.

(5) The hours of labor have been reduced contemporaneously with recent immigration.

(6) The membership of labor organizations has grown apace with recent immigration; the new immigrants have contributed their proportionate quota to the membership

[1] *Reports of the Immigration Commission*, vol. 1, p. 541.—Since the days of the Immigration Commission another experiment in industrial government, inaugurated by recent immigrants in the clothing factory of Hart, Schaffner and Marx, has attracted wide notice among labor leaders and social workers.

of every labor organization which has not discriminated against them, and they have firmly stood by their organizations in every contest.

There is consequently no specific "immigration problem." There is a general labor problem, which comprises many special problems, such as organization of labor, reduction of hours of labor, child labor, unemployment, prevention of work-accidents, etc. None of these problems being affected by immigration, their solution can not be advanced by restriction or even by complete prohibition of immigration.

The advocates of restriction are conscious of the fact that without immigration the industrial expansion of the past twenty years would have been impossible. But they believe that the pace of progress has been too fast and that the interests of labor would be furthered by a slower development of industry which would dispense with Southern and Eastern European unskilled laborers. This was the gist of the recommendations of the Immigration Commission.

The weak point in this argument is that it takes no cognizance of the cardinal principle of modern division of labor, viz., that in every industrial establishment there is a fixed proportion of skilled to unskilled laborers. Were the expansion of industry to slow down in consequence of a reduced supply of unskilled labor, the demand for skilled mechanics would eventually decline in proportion. The slow growth of industry would tend to curtail the opportunities for advancement of the wage-earners who are already here. The skilled crafts whose organizations favor the exclusion of unskilled immigrants would be the first to suffer in consequence.

On the other hand, the unemployed could gain nothing from a slow growth of industry. Seasonal and cyclical variations in the general demand for labor, as well as variations in the demands of individual employers, would continue on a reduced scale of national production. The mere exclusion of immigrants will not provide employment for sailors in the winter, or for the full winter force of a Wisconsin logging camp in the summer; nor will it revolutionize the world of fashion. In order to provide regular employment for all workers, it would be necessary to run all industries upon a common time schedule, like railway trains are run on connecting lines. No plan of such a readjustment has as yet been suggested by the advocates of immigration restriction. Certainly an adjustment of the busy and slack seasons of a quarter of a million factories will not spring up spontaneously from an act of Congress closing the gates against immigrants. The present crisis, which has followed a period with immigration reduced to insignificant proportions, demonstrates how ineffectual restriction of immigration would be as a remedy against unemployment resulting from cyclical disturbances of capitalistic industry.

As a speculative proposition, it seems quite plausible that if restriction of immigration resulted in a scarcity of labor, employers would be forced to pay scarcity rates of wages. A standing refutation of this theory is presented by the condition which actually exists in the United States throughout the agricultural sections. Few immigrants seek employment on the farms. The number of Southern and Eastern European farm laborers in the United States is negligible. Moreover, there is a constant stream of native labor from the farms to the cities, which has led to an actual decrease of the rural population in many agricultural counties. Farmers generally complain of scarcity of farm labor during the agricultural season. Nevertheless, the wages of farm laborers are lower than the wages of unskilled laborers in mines and mills where recent immigrants predominate. Scarcity of labor has not forced the farmer to pay scarcity wages, but has merely retarded the growth of farming.

The World War offered an opportunity to test the effects of restriction of immigration under the most favorable conditions. The United States became the chief producer of war supplies for the allied nations. Beginning with the spring of 1916 the supply of labor in the United States fell short of the demand. The entrance of the United States into the war withdrew more than two million workers from industry. Officers of the American Federation of Labor and avowed friends of labor were put in charge of the various war boards which were entrusted with the function of regulating wages in the leading industries. If the economic condition of the American wage-earner could be improved by suspension of immigration, its beneficial effects should have materialized during the war.

Volumes of statistics on every aspect of the economic situation during the war period have been published. They show a growth of production much in excess of the rate of the pre-war years. This unparalleled growth of industry was marked by extraordinary profits, which were far beyond anything that was necessary to stimulate initiative and enterprise.

At the same time, the growth of population lagged behind the industrial expansion. To meet the abnormal demand for common labor caused by the cessation of immigration, the Secretary of Labor, a former labor leader, was obliged to suspend the law to permit mine operators and other employers in the Southwest to import Mexican laborers under contract.

This abnormal condition brought about an unprecedented mobility of labor. Reports from every section of the country to *Bradstreet's* complained of employees "constantly being enticed from their jobs by competition between employers."[1] Employers were offering high rates of wages to union and non-union workers alike.

What, then, was the effect of this most favorable combination of economic factors upon the condition of the American wage worker?

In such war-time industries as munition plants, some of the occupations enjoyed increases in wages more than sufficient to compensate for the increase in the cost of living.

[1] *The Literary Digest*, December 1, 1917, p. 80.

On the other hand, the wages of the railroad workers, coal miners, and farm laborers, lagged behind the increase in prices. On the whole, wages did not keep pace with the increasing cost of living. The workers merely struggled to keep their old standards of living, and even in this struggle they did not always succeed.

The most telling corroboration of the decline in real wages is furnished by the investigations of medical authorities, which show a decided increase of the proportion of underfed school children during the World War.

We have thus witnessed a repetition of the labor conditions which prevailed during the Civil War. This lagging of wages behind the advancing cost of living cannot be explained by the alleged submissiveness of the immigrant wage-workers, who are said to be willing to acquiesce in the terms offered to them by the employers. The statistics of strikes during the World War show that during the three years 1916–1918 the number of strikes per year was more than twice the annual average for the period from 1881 to 1905. More than four fifths of the war-time strikes were led by unions. The annual average number of strikers rose to the unprecedented figure of 1,310,000. Moreover, during the war, the principle of collective bargaining was recognized, under the pressure of the government, by all employers engaged on government orders or in the production of essentials.

That the foreign worker can not be held responsible for the decline of real wages is further proved by the fact that the real wages of common laborers in the iron and steel industry, most of whom are foreign born, went up, whereas those of locomotive firemen, most of whom are native-born Americans, declined to a point much below the minimum budget under American standards.

Among the potent factors in the decline of real wages must be noted the movement of labor from agriculture to urban industries. As a result, agricultural production during the war remained almost stationary, while the demand for breadstuffs was increased by exports abroad. The big interests which control the produce market were thereby enabled to raise the prices of food. What the wage-earner gained in money wages he was forced to surrender in the higher prices of necessities of life.

Let us now examine what were the substitutes for immigrant labor during the war years. The movement of workers from agriculture to urban industries has already been adverted to. Public attention was attracted by the migration of Negroes from the agricultural South to the industrial North. The volume of that migration is officially estimated at nearly half a million. Agricultural regions of the Southern states began to suffer for want of the Negro worker. Another substitute for immigrant labor was found in the increased employment of women and children. The main force which was driving children into industry was the excessive cost of living. Labor commissioners and factory inspectors complained of the difficulty experienced during the war years in administering child-labor laws. The scarcity of adult labor made the employer ready to take minors into his employ.

What, then, is the outlook in the light of the experience of labor in the late war? We are passing through one of the cyclical disturbances of modern industry with their attendant acute unemployment. But this crisis will be over, and American industry will resume its usual course. If restriction of immigration is to become the settled policy of the United States, substitutes for immigrant labor will be sought.

The mines and mills of the Southern states which have failed to attract immigrants utilize the labor of farmers and their sons. The millions of tenant-farmers offer great possibilities as an industrial reserve available during the winter months. The farm being their main source of subsistence, they have been willing to offer their labor during the idle winter months more cheaply than freshly landed immigrants. The efforts of trade-union organizers among this class of English-speaking workers have met with scant success. The substitution of the cheap labor of the American farmer for the labor of the Slav or Italian immigrant, would tend to weaken the unions and to keep down wages. A stimulated movement of labor from the farm to the factory would check the growth of farming; the prices of foodstuffs would rise in consequence, which would tend to offset the advantages to the wage-earners from a possible rise of money wages.

The discontinuance of fresh supplies of immigrant labor for the mills and factories of New England would give a new impetus to the establishment of factories in the South, where there is an abundant supply of child labor.

Still, should all the substitutes for immigration prove inadequate, it does not necessarily follow that scarcity prices would rule in the American labor market. It must be borne in mind that capital is international. Billions of American capital are already invested in foreign enterprises. Heretofore these investments could not compare with the profits of American industries annually reinvested at home. If, however, a permanent scarcity of labor were created in the United States, more American capital would seek investment abroad. The increased investment of American capital in the industrial development of foreign countries, with cheap labor, must eventually react upon labor conditions in the United States. Certain of the most important American industries depend in part upon the export trade. A scarcity of labor in the United States would induce many American manufacturers to follow the example of their European competitors, who have found it more profitable to establish factories in foreign countries than to export their products to those countries. It is learned from an official report of the Commercial Secretary of the British Embassy in Berlin, that arrangements have been in progress between American capitalists and German corporations, looking toward the investment of American capital in German industry. There are other reports to the same effect. Such an emigration of American capital would materially affect the export trade of the United States and eventually cut off the avenues of employment for a number of American wage-earners.

It is evident that while restriction of immigration can limit the supply of labor, it is powerless to prevent a corresponding limitation of the demand for labor.

The true cause of the decline of real wages during the late war is to be found in the fact that advances in wages are the outcome of the slow process of collective bargaining, with occasional industrial warfare, whereas the prices of commodities are controlled by monopolistic combinations, which promptly shift every advance in wages to the consumer. Thus the rise of wages in one industry or occupation is, in effect, charged up to the working class as a whole. What is wanted in order to secure to the worker a real advance in wages is regulation of profits in the interest of the consumers, of whom the wage-earners are the most numerous element. Restriction of the supply of labor does not touch the problem of price control. Immigration laws can prevent the American capitalist from employing foreign labor in the United States. But he may find it as profitable to employ the same labor in Europe in the manufacture of goods for the world market. The reduction of the supply of labor will be neutralized by a reduction of the demand for labor in the United States.

PART II.

TOPICAL ANALYSIS

CHAPTER I

STATEMENT OF THE QUESTION

A STUDY of the immigration question involves an examination of every important phase of American economic, political, and social life. There is scarcely an ailment of our body politic that is not diagnosed—in prose and in verse—as the effect of unrestricted immigration. The immigrants are blamed for unemployment, female and child labor, the introduction of machinery, unsafe coal mines, lack of organization among wage-earners, congestion in great cities, industrial crises, inability to gain a controlling interest in stock corporations,[1] pauperism, crime, insanity, race suicide, gambling, the continental Sunday, parochial schools, atheism, political corruption, municipal misrule. The latest count in this long indictment is the McNamara conspiracy, which a noted sociologist has somehow connected with unrestricted immigration.[2] Not only has "recent immigration from Southern and Eastern Europe" lowered the American standard of living, but it threatens to lower "the average stature of the American."[3]

[1] *Reports of the Immigration Commission*, vol. 16, p. 655.

[2] Prof. E. A. Ross, in *The Survey*, December 30, 1911, p. 1425.

[3] Robert Hunter: *Poverty*, p. 269.

It is conceded that in the past immigration has been a material factor in the economic development of the United States. It is claimed, however, that the new immigrant races are of a different social type lacking the sturdy qualities of the old immigration. "In the early years of immigration, when it was difficult, if not actually dangerous, to come to the United States, there was a natural selection of the best and hardiest inhabitants of the old world, men willing to risk their all in going to a new country."[1] The pioneers of those days were eager for an opportunity to develop the untouched resources of a new land and to advance the march of civilization into the wilderness. The new immigrant, on the contrary, is attracted by the glamor of the city. To be sure, a large percentage of the new immigration comes from the farming sections of Europe; but brought up, as they are, amidst the congestion of the small agricultural towns of the old world, these new immigrants recoil at the isolation of the American farm and prefer to crowd in the congested districts of the large manufacturing cities.

The cure for the evils of immigration upon which all seem to be agreed is some method of selection which would admit all desirable immigrants and keep out the "undesirable." There is, however, no authoritative definition of a "desirable" and an "undesirable" immigrant. Mr. Prescott F. Hall, Secretary of the Immigration Restriction League, regards as "undesirable immigration" that "which is ignorant of a trade,"[2] while another writer maintains that the races having the highest percentages of unskilled laborers are the most desirable, because they do not compete with American mechanics, but men who are "skilled in tailoring, shoemaking, baking, or other trades which do not require much physical strength . . . are undesirable immigrants," because "they enter into direct competition with

[1] John Mitchell: *Organized Labor*, p. 177.

[2] Prescott F. Hall: "Selection of Immigration." *Annals of the American Academy of Social and Political Science*, July, 1904, p. 175.

the American mechanic."[1] Again Mr. Hall would treat as "undesirable immigration" that "which is averse to country life and tends to congregate in the slums of large cities," though "if our recent immigrants were able and willing to go to the West and South, these States do not want them."[2] Along with the Southeastern European immigrant who is accordingly not wanted either in the large cities, or in the agricultural West and South, the same author would class as "undesirable" all immigration "which fails to assimilate in a reasonable time."[3]

Prof. Mayo-Smith is more specific in his definition and favors the selection of immigrants with a view, among other things, to the preservation of the "social morality of the Puritans."[4]

With respect to assimilation, conditions are said to have undergone a material change. The old immigrants, scattered amidst the native American population, were quickly assimilated. Moreover, they were practically all of Teuton and Celtic stock and came from countries with a representative form of government. The recent immigrants, on the other hand, have had no training in self-government at home, and being herded together in foreign colonies, out of touch with native Americans, they are incapable of assimilation and present a growing danger to the integrity of American democratic institutions.[5]

According to some students, this country is facing a new

[1] Dr. Allan McLaughlin: "Distrust of the Immigrant." *Popular Science Monthly*, January, 1903, p. 232.

[2] Prescott F. Hall, *loc. cit.*, pp. 175, 179. [3] *Ibid.*, p. 175.

[4] Richmond Mayo-Smith: *Emigration and Immigration*, p. 5.

[5] A writer, discussing the "perils" of "un-American immigration" in 1894, gave warning that "if foreign immigration continues at the present rate and such immigration continues to come from Middle, Southern, and Northeastern Europe, in 1900 the Anglo-Saxon and Anglo-Saxon institutions will no longer be the dominant powers in moulding American life and legislation."—Rena M. Atchison, *Un-American Immigration: Its Present and Future Perils*, p. 148. (Chicago 1894.)

race problem, similar to the negro problem. In the opinion of a member of the Immigration Commission the Southern Italian is not "a white man," nor is the Syrian.[1] The presence of these races in large numbers among the working forces of our mines and mills has attached a social stigma to certain occupations; as a result of this race prejudice the native American workmen have withdrawn from those employments where they must work side by side with recent arrivals and overcrowd the less remunerative, but more respectable occupations.[2]

Still the fact is that while the root of all evil is sought in the racial make-up of the new immigration, as contrasted with the old, every complaint against the immigrants from Eastern and Southern Europe is but an echo of the complaints which were made at an earlier day against the then new immigration from Ireland, Germany, and even from England. As observed by the Industrial Commission a decade ago, "on the whole, it does not seem that the newer immigration offers any greater or more serious problems than the old, except in so far as they add to the total numbers."[3] A retrospective view of immigration will show the problems presented by a polyglot population to be by no means peculiar to our own day. If "assimilation" is taken to mean the substitution of the English language in daily intercourse for the mother tongue of the immigrant, then a century of experience proves it to be an unattainable ideal. But, if "assimilation" means an understanding of

[1] Hearings before the House Committee on Immigration and Naturalization. 61st Congress. Testimony of Hon. John L. Burnett, of Alabama, p. 407. In 1885, in reply to inquiries sent out by the Iowa Bureau of Labor Statistics, a laboring man complained that "the Bohemians . . . will get a job in preference to *a white man.*" (*VI. Biennial Report, Iowa Bureau of Labor Statistics*, p. 189.) Since that time the Bohemians have been advanced in the publications of the Immigration Restriction League to a place among the "desirable" immigrants from Northern and Western Europe.

[2] Jenks and Lauck: *The Immigration Problem*, pp. 75–76.

[3] *Reports of the Industrial Commission*, vol. xv., p. 491.

American institutions, it will readily occur to the student that one of the standard works on the constitutional history of the United States was written in German by von Holst, an alumnus of a Russian university, and another standard book on the organization of American political parties was written in French by Ostrogorsky, a Russian Jew. The politician who comes in closest personal contact with the mass of citizenship has long since adjusted himself to the conditions created by immigration and finds no difficulty in presenting the issues and the candidates of his party to a mixed constituency in a variety of languages. Moreover, a deeper insight into the social life of the immigrant will discover powerful forces making for social assimilation, in those very institutions which are popularly frowned upon as tending to perpetuate the isolation of the foreigner from American influences. The newspaper printed in a foreign language is virtually a sign of Americanization; the Lithuanian peasant at home had no newspaper in his own language; the demand for a newspaper has grown on American soil. That it apparently serves its purpose, is conceded by prominent advocates of restriction.[1] The theater where the immigrant sees a play produced in his mother tongue is likewise the outgrowth of the democratic spirit of American social life; the theater in Eastern Europe caters only to the upper classes. The numerous foreign-speaking organizations owe their existence to the political freedom of the United States. It is through all these social agencies using his native tongue as a medium of communication, that the immigrant who is not a scholar is enabled to partake of the advantages of American civilization.

It is realized by the clear-sighted advocates of restriction that "too much emphasis, in the discussion of immigration, within recent years, has been placed upon the social and political results of recent immigration. The problem at

[1] "So large a number of periodicals are published in various foreign tongues that it is by no means essential that the immigrant read English."—Jenks and Lauck, *loc. cit.*, p. 32.

present is really fundamentally an industrial one."[1] The reason the appeals for restriction to-day find a more favorable hearing than in the days of the Know-Nothing agitation, is the growth of organized labor, which demands restriction of immigration as an extension of the protective principle to the home market in which "hands"—the laborer's only commodity—are offered for sale. All doctrinaire theories of a civic character are accepted by organized labor in so far as they may be helpful in its campaign for restriction of immigration. The real attitude of organized labor, however, is candidly stated in the testimony of Mr. Roe, representing the railroad brotherhoods, before the House Committee on Immigration and Naturalization: "Every foreign workman who comes into this country takes the place of some American workingman who wants higher wages and a higher standard of living than the foreigner."[2]

All opposition to restriction of immigration is viewed with suspicion by organized labor, as emanating from the employing class or from the steamship companies, which are hiding selfish interests under a cloak of humanitarianism. This view overlooks the millions of foreign-born wage-earners who are bound by family ties with millions of workers across the sea and want them to share in the opportunities which this country holds out to the immigrant for bettering his economic and social conditions.[3] Their appeal from the present-day policy of restriction to old American traditions springs from personal affection and friendship.

It must be understood, however, that the United States no longer recognizes the Kantian "ideal demand of the new

[1] *Ibid.*, p. 197.

[2] H. R. 61st. Congress. Hearings before Committee on Immigration and Naturalization, p. 254.

[3] The claim of the pessimists, that the condition of the immigrant workman in the United States is to-day no better than in his native country (Robert Hunter: *Poverty*, p. 280), is refuted by the millions, of European workers who come to this country to stay and send for their relatives.

law of nations,"[1] that the individual may have the freedom of the world to choose his domicil, regardless of state boundaries. The enactment of the Chinese exclusion law signalized a reversion of the United States to the old doctrine of sovereignty, which invests the state with the absolute right to exclude aliens from its territory. In opposition to the cosmopolitan theory underlying the free immigration policy of the past, the policy of restriction has elaborated its own social philosophy in the following words of Mr. John Mitchell:

> To a large extent the progress of nations can best be secured by the policy of seclusion and isolation. By means of barriers which regulate, but do not prohibit, immigration, the various countries of Europe and America can individually work out their salvation, and a permanent increase in the efficiency and remuneration of the workers of the world can thus be obtained. By the maintenance of these barriers the best workingmen in each country can rise to the top, and the great mass of the workingmen can secure a larger share of the wealth produced.[2]

It goes without saying that this theory of progress can lay no claim to originality, "the policy of seclusion and isolation" having been consistently followed for many centuries by China.

Without venturing, however, into the realm of sociological speculation, and allowing that if "every foreign workman who comes into this country takes the place of some American workingman" immigration ought to be prohibited, the unprejudiced student of the immigration question will demand proof that the premises are true. When a million workers are reported to be out of employment and an equal number of immigrants are shown to have been admitted during the same year, the man in the street is apt to jump to the conclusion that the new arrivals have dis-

[1] J. C. Bluntschli: *Die Bedeutung und die Fortschritte des modernen Völkerrechts*, p. 36.

[2] John Mitchell: *Organized Labor*, p. 181. It is stated on p. viii of the book that it has been written in co-operation with Dr. Walter E. Weyl.

placed the native workmen or the older immigrants. On closer scrutiny, however, this superficial conclusion may prove wholly unwarranted. To take but one illustration, the presence of a few thousand unemployed sailors in Buffalo during the winter months is no proof of an oversupply of sailors during the navigation season or of an overstocked labor market in general. The emigration of all Slav and Italian surface laborers employed during the summer in the iron mines of the Lake Superior region would not create a single job for the unemployed sailors in the winter. On the contrary, the reduction of the working force in the mines during the season which is most favorable for their operation would have the effect of reducing the volume of iron ore carried on the lakes, in consequence of which a number of sailors could be dispensed with in the summer. It is quite obvious that the effects, if any, of immigration upon unemployment cannot be determined by deductive reasoning. The same is true of the standard of living, etc.

In order to bring to light all the facts respecting immigration, a commission was created in 1907 by an act of Congress. The results of the Commission's investigations will next be considered.

CHAPTER II

THE REPORT OF THE IMMIGRATION COMMISSION

THE most valuable contribution of the Immigration Commission to the discussion of immigration is the conclusion that it should be considered "primarily as an economic problem."[1] This statement of the question takes it out of the domain of conflicting, more or less speculative, social theories and permits of its consideration on the solid basis of measurable economic realities.

Of the forty-two volumes of the Commission's report, thirty-one contain primary facts directly or indirectly related to the economic aspects of immigration.[2]

The Commission has unanimously recommended restriction of immigration, the only dissenting opinion being confined to methods of restriction. There are few people who will go beyond the conclusions of the Commission and undertake the task of examining the evidence, presumably stored up in its voluminous report. The lay public will assume that the unanimous conclusions were reached after mature deliberation over the evidence collected by the Commission. An illuminating sidelight upon the supposed connection between its recommendations and its statistics is thrown by ex-Congressman William S. Bennet's dissenting opinion, which contains the statement that the report of the Commission was finally adopted "within a half hour of the

[1] *Reports of the Immigration Commission*, vol. 1, p. 25.

[2] Volumes 3, 4, 6–28, 34, 35, 37, and 40. The remaining portion of the report deals with ethnography, education, legislation, etc., and two of the volumes are summaries of the whole.

time" when, under the law, it had to be filed, which left "no time for the preparation of an elaborate dissent." It is legitimate to question under the circumstances whether the members of the Commission had the opportunity, amidst their manifold duties, to examine the manuscript of the forty volumes, which did not leave the printing office until more than a year after the Commission had ceased to exist. Apparently, they had before them merely the summary submitted for the Commission's approval by its experts. The unanimity of the Commission thus invests its conclusions with no other authority than the scientific weight of the statistical and descriptive reports of its experts. The most important part of the reports, viz. "Immigrants in Industries" (vols. 6–25), "was prepared under the direction of the Commission" by one expert, Prof. W. Jett Lauck (of course, with the assistance of a staff of field agents and clerks). The student is, therefore, free to judge the reports of the Commission by the same canons as other official statistical publications. The Commission finds:

That the numbers of recent immigrants "are so great and the influx is so continuous that even with the remarkable expansion of industry during the past few years there has been created an oversupply of unskilled labor, and in some of the industries this is reflected in a curtailed number of working days and a consequent yearly income among the unskilled workers which is very much less than is indicated by the daily wage rates paid."

That the standard of living of "the majority of the employees . . . is so far below that of the native American or older immigrant workman that it is impossible for the latter to successfully compete with them." That "they are content to accept wages and conditions which the native American and immigrants of the older class had come to regard as unsatisfactory . . . and as a result that class of employees was gradually replaced."

That the new immigrants have in some degree "lowered the American standard of living."

That a "characteristic of the new immigrants is the impossibility of successfully organizing them into labor unions. Several attempts at organization were made, but the constant influx of immigrants to whom prevailing conditions seemed unusually favorable contributed to the failure to organize."

That "the competition of these immigrants . . . has kept conditions in the semi-skilled and unskilled occupations from advancing."[1]

Every one of the preceding conclusions involved a comparison of the present conditions with the past. Still it is only as a rare exception that fragments of statistical information relating to the earlier period of American industrial history can be found in the numerous volumes of the reports of the Immigration Commission. No attempt has been made to utilize the vast statistical material collected by the State bureaus of labor statistics since the establishment of the Massachusetts Bureau in 1869. This is very much to be regretted. There is no other nation in the world that expends so much for the collection of statistical data and so little for their analysis as the United States. An index prepared by the United States Bureau of Labor to the publications of the State labor bureaus up to 1902 fills a volume. The data contained in these publications were collected at great cost during a period of years, but were for the most part published in an undigested form. This defect is the result of the prevailing policy of official statistical institutions to eliminate as far as practicable all interpretations of their statistics in order to escape the suspicion of partisanship. A Congressional commission, however, is free from such limitations, its very purpose being to draw conclusions and make recommendations which are of necessity open to controversy. A perusal of the single volume devoted to immigration in the report of President McKinley's Industrial Commission shows what a storehouse of original data is available at small cost in the files of official publications

[1] *Reports of the Immigration Commission*, vol. 1, pp. 38, 39.

of States and municipalities. The Immigration Commission with its vastly greater resources had the opportunity to make a contribution of inestimable value to the study of the economic and social conditions of the American people at the period of the greatest migration in the history of the world. Unfortunately the Commission expended all its efforts in search for new material, with the result, as candidly admitted by Prof. H. Parker Willis, "the editorial adviser" in the final preparation of its report, that the thirty-one volumes have added a fresh stock of ill-digested statistics to that previously accumulated.[1]

Of what value are the tables showing the rate of unemployment of a limited number of selected families when the censuses of 1890 and 1900 have collected and published such data for all bread-winners in the United States?

The fact that the wage-earners in some industries were unemployed some part of the year covered by the Commission is alone insufficient to support the conclusion that the number of working days has been "curtailed," without a comparison of the number of working days in the same industries for a series of years. "Racial displacement" prominently figures in the tables of contents of every volume and in the subheads of every chapter dealing with the condition in the manufacturing and mining industries, but an inspection of the statistical tables discloses no evidence of actual "displacement."

One example may serve as an illustration. The changes in the population of Birmingham, Alabama, have been the subject of the following commentary:

[1] "With so much actually collected in the way of detailed data, and with but scant time in which to summarize these data, lacking, moreover, a sufficient number of trained writers and statisticians to study the information acquired and to set it down with a due proportion of properly guarded inferences, it is a fact that much of the Commission's information is still undigested, and is presented in a form which affords no more than a foundation for the work of future inquirers."—H. Parker Willis in *The Survey* of January 7, 1911, p. 571.

It is even more significant, however, that with the exception of the Welsh and Norwegians there was a falling off in numbers from the countries of Great Britain and Northern Europe in 1900 as contrasted with 1890, the increase in the foreign-born population during the ten years 1890–1900 practically all arising from the arrival of races from Southern and Eastern Europe.[1]

The numbers which have given occasion to the preceding remarks were as follows:

Place of birth	*1890*	*1900.*
England...	258	233
Germany..	450	446
Ireland....	245	218
Scotland...	53	52
Sweden....	49	16

It will be observed that the total "falling off in numbers" amounted to 33 Swedes, 27 Irish, 25 English, 4 Germans, and 1 Scotch—in all, 90 persons in ten years. At the same time the native-born population increased by as many as 12,113 persons, while the total increase "from the arrival of races from Southern and Eastern Europe" was less than 214 persons. Why should the loss of the 90 natives of Great Britain and Northern Europe be interpreted as their displacement by arrivals from Southern and Eastern Europe rather than by native Americans? Moreover, the rate of mortality among those nationalities, except the Swedes, must have reduced their numbers by at least one sixth in ten years, which is more than twice their actual falling-off and suggests that there must have been some increase by immigration from the same sources. So the actual falling-off was confined to the Swedes, who—if all alive—were leaving Birmingham at the rate of three individuals per year. Was the annual loss of three Swedes "significant" enough for a city whose population increased 50 per cent from 1890 to 1900 to be noted as evidence of "racial displacement"?

"The impossibility of successfully organizing" the new immigrants "into labor unions" cannot be proved without

[1] *Reports of the Immigration Commission*, vol. 9, p. 159.

statistics of union membership. The Commission has compiled no statistical table showing the growth of labor unions in various trades during the period of recent immigration. The data collected by the Commission as a part of its study of households are too meager and fragmentary to be of any value.

The following table and commentary are a fair specimen of the Commission's trade-union statistics:[1]

TABLE 233.

AFFILIATION WITH TRADE-UNIONS OF MALES 21 YEARS OF AGE OR OVER WHO ARE WORKING FOR WAGES, BY GENERAL NATIVITY AND RACE OF INDIVIDUAL.

(*Study of households.*)

General nativity and race of individual	Number reporting complete data	Affiliated with trade-unions	
		Number	Per cent
Native-born of native father—white	47	..	0.0
Native-born of foreign father, by race of father:			
Croatian	1	..	(a)
German	3	..	(a)
Irish	1	..	(a)
Polish	2	..	(a)
Foreign-born:			
Croatian	240	2	.8
German	54	1	1.9
Irish	11	..	(a)
Polish	64	..	.0
Slovenian	1	..	(a)
Total	424	3	.7
Total native-born of foreign father	7	..	(a)
Total native-born	54	..	.0
Total foreign-born	370	3	.8

(*a*) Not computed, owing to small number involved.

The above table discloses the significant fact that an exceedingly small proportion of employees in Kansas City of foreign birth, and none of native birth, are affiliated with labor organizations.

[1] *Ibid.*, vol. 13, p. 300.

The fact that the field agents of the Commission—in a study of households, not of trade-unions—happened to come across three trade-unionists in a city of the size of Kansas City, is considered sufficient to justify the conclusion that "an exceedingly small proportion of employees in Kansas City . . . are affiliated with trade-unions"! Another table brings out the "affiliation with trade-unions" of one South Italian wage-earner among 668 householders duly "classified by nativity and race of individual."[1]

When a single trade-unionist in an unorganized mill town is enlarged into an "exhibit by general nativity and race of individual," one cannot help wondering that the economic data of the Commission have been compressed within the small compass of thirty-one volumes.

Coming to the standard of living, it is clearly insufficient to compare the sections inhabited by English-speaking skilled mechanics and their families with the settlements of the unskilled Slav laborers, with a view to showing that the former present a better appearance than the latter. The housing conditions of the new immigrants should be compared with those of the Irish and German unskilled laborers a generation ago, in order to support the conclusion that the former have "introduced a lower standard."

The statistics of earnings classified by race and nativity are spread over hundreds of tables, yet they are vitiated by the absence of a classification by occupations. The only conclusion that can be drawn from these statistics is that the weekly or annual earnings of the new immigrants are, as a rule, lower than those of the native wage-earners or the older immigrants. But when this information is collated with the fact that the new immigrants are mostly employed in unskilled occupations, while the native Americans and foreign-born employees of the older class have risen on the scale

[1] *Ibid.*, vol. 8, p. 390, Table 286. A similar table comprising two Polish trade-unionists among 441 heads of households will be found in the same volume on p. 765, Table 515, and another in vol. 11, p. 701, Table 38.

of occupations, it is readily seen that the hundreds of tables show nothing beyond the fact that supervisory positions and skilled trades are more remunerative than unskilled labor. It was hardly necessary to expend much time and labor in order to establish this fact which is a matter of common knowledge. To justify the conclusions of the Commission, proof was wanted that the rates of wages of the new immigrants in specified occupations were lower than those paid to native workmen in the same occupations and in the same localities. No such proof was produced; on the contrary, the Commission found that, as a matter of fact, the new immigrants "were not, as a rule, engaged at lower wages than had been paid to the older workmen for the same class of labor."[1] The numerous tables showing variations in weekly earnings by race are therefore meaningless.

The popular prejudice against the new immigrant races justified an unbiased comparative study of their social and economic conditions in the United States[2]. Unfortunately the experts and investigators of the Commission were themselves so completely under the sway of the popular sentiment that they perceived the effect of race differences even in small variations of the number of mine accidents, where the element of chance called for the exercise of extreme caution in drawing conclusions. The following example is typical of the generalizations which abound in the reports of the Commission. In the year 1907 there were 75 fatal and non-fatal accidents among the Lithuanians and 139 among the Poles employed by one anthracite coal company. As the Lithuanians were somewhat more numerous than the Poles, the following conclusion is drawn in the report:

The differences between the Lithuanian and Polish figures, after

---

[1] *Reports*, vol. 1, p. 38.

[2] "In studying the immigration situation in Europe the Commission was not unmindful of the fact that the widespread apprehension in the United States relative to immigration is chiefly due to this change in the character of the movement of population from Europe in recent years."—*Ibid.*, vol. 4, p. 12.

making due allowance for error in both cases, is still so great that it gives ground for the inference that ***here a real race difference is exposed.*** When it is remembered in how many other instances in this report tables have shown a ***superiority of the Lithuanians over the Poles,*** the conclusion gathers strength that the former show ***greater skill*** and carefulness in their work.[1]

In Lawrence, Massachusetts, however, "*the Lithuanians* are said to resemble the Poles in their industrial characteristics, but *are thought to be less intelligent* or at any rate more illiterate."[2] The average percentage of illiteracy among the Lithuanian immigrants admitted from 1899 to 1910 was 48.9 per cent and among the Polish immigrants admitted during the same period 35.4 per cent.[3] These averages are derived from the records of over a million individuals of both nationalities, whereas "the superiority of the Lithuanians over the Poles" is deduced from 214 accidents that occurred in one year in the mines of one company.

As far as the statistics of the Commission permit to judge of the antecedents of the Lithuanian and Polish anthracite coal workers in their native countries, it appears that none of them had worked in mines before coming to the United States; 96 per cent of the Lithuanians and 86 per cent of the Poles from whom information was received had been peasants (farmers and farm laborers) in their home countries, the proportion of farmers and farmers' sons being somewhat higher among the Poles than among the Lithuanians, viz., 70 per cent and 60 per cent, respectively, of the total number reported for each race.[4] To judge by the historical experiences of the two races, there is no warrant whatsoever for rating the mass of the Poles below the mass of the Lithuanians. For centuries they have been close neighbors. Since the organic union of Poland and Lithuania in 1386, Polish civilization was dominant in Lithuania. The ruling classes, the landed nobility and the clergy were thoroughly Polonized. Since

[1] *Reports*, vol. 16, p. 667
[2] *Ibid.*, vol. 10, p. 772.
[3] *Ibid.*, vol. 1, p. 99, Table 11.
[4] *Ibid.*, vol. 16, p. 596, Table 9.

the policy of Russianization was inaugurated in Poland and Lithuania fifty years ago, the Lithuanians have been at a disadvantage compared with the Poles; the Lithuanian language was barred from the public schools; they were denied the right to have a press in their own language, while the mass of the Lithuanian people do not understand the Russian language.

The Immigration Commission has discovered no anthropological evidence that would sustain the hypothesis of the superiority of the Lithuanian race, unless the difference of 64 accidents be accepted as such evidence. Yet it appears from the same accident statistics that the native Americans also contributed more than their share of accident victims, whereas the Irish exhibited an exceptionally low accident rate. This variation, however, must not be construed to show a superiority of the Irish over the native Americans, because "for the accident report the State mine inspector generally has to get the nationality from others, usually friends of the victim or his boss," and the information is often erroneous. "Probably the same source of error accounts for some of the Polish accident excess."[1] Still, if not all of the 64 accidents then some of them are deemed sufficient to place the Poles below the Lithuanians on the sliding scale of foreign races.

It would seem as if the investigation of the Immigration Commission proceeded upon the supposition that immigrant races represented separate zoölogical species. Thus we find the following under the head "diseases peculiar to immigrant races":

> The testimony of the physicians and hospital authorities is to the effect that *apparently* (*sic!*) there are no diseases peculiar to any one single race. The chief diseases among the aliens are the following: (a) Rheumatism; (b) heart diseases; (c) typhoid fever; (d) pneumonia—this is one of the diseases most common to the foreign population, but they seem no more subject to it than the natives.[2]

Thus it has been officially established that disease

[1] *Reports*, vol. 16, p. 667. [2] *Ibid.*, vol. 8, p. 433.

"apparently" makes no distinction of race, color, or previous condition of servitude, "the aliens" being subject, alike with native-born and naturalized citizens, to rheumatism and pneumonia. The habits of the new species are described in the language of the naturalist. We learn, *e. g.*, that among the Bulgarians beef "is usualy cooked as a stew with vegetables and eaten with bread. They also consume all forms of green vegetables in season. . . . The usual drinks are coffee and beer. Many drink hot milk in the morning."[1]

The adoption of the "race" idea as a basis for classification has inevitably led to the splitting up of all statistical data into minute groups unfit for any generalizations. The Commission has nevertheless systematically reduced all such data to percentages, which are used for comparison among races. It is an elementary rule in statistics that averages and percentages may be used for generalizations only when derived from large numbers, the reason being that where the number of observed cases is small personal characteristics or casual circumstances may affect the results. How deceptive percentages may be when derived from insufficient numbers, is illustrated by the following table compiled from the Commission's statistics, showing the "per cent of foreign-born employees (in the clothing factories investigated) who speak English, by sex, years in the United States, and race."[2]

TABLE I.

PER CENT WHO SPEAK ENGLISH, BY YEARS, IN THE UNITED STATES

	Under 5 years	5 to 9 years	10 years or over	Total
Male				
Bohemian and Moravian....	22.5	45.0	75.0	56.0
Polish....................	24.8	62.4	83.2	51.1
Female				
Bohemian and Moravian....	18.1	57.5	88.0	54.8
Polish....................	19.4	63.0	89.4	49.9

[1] *Reports*, vol. 9, p. 82.

[2] *Ibid.*, vol. 11, p. 363, Table 95.

The significance of the preceding table is in the fact that the Bohemians and Moravians are classed by the Immigration Restriction League among "desirable" immigrants, whereas the Poles belong to the "undesirable aliens from Eastern Europe." A comparison of the figures in the first three columns shows, however, that in each group classified according to length of residence in the United States the Poles show a higher percentage of males, as well as females, able to speak English, than the Bohemians. And yet when the totals are compared for both nationalities, irrespective of length of residence in the United States, it appears that the Bohemians exhibit a larger percentage of persons of either sex able to speak English, than the Poles. The reason for this arithmetical aberration is disclosed only in another part of the volume, where the number of persons in each of the preceding groups is given. It appears that about one-half of all Poles had resided in the United States less than five years and accordingly exhibited a small percentage of persons able to speak English, whereas three fourths of all males and two thirds of all females of Bohemian nationality had resided in the United States over five years and had had more time to learn English.[1]

[1] The following are the numbers relating to the two nationalities:

	Number reporting complete data	Years in the United States					
		Under 5		5 to 9		10 or over	
		Number	Number who speak English	Number	Number who speak English	Number	Number who speak English
Male							
Bohemian and Moravian..	532	129	29	111	50	292	219
Polish.......	667	302	75	181	113	184	153
Female							
Bohemian and Moravian..	347	127	23	87	50	133	117
Polish.......	431	216	42	73	46	142	127

[1] *Reports*, vol. 11, pp. 540, 541, Table 53.

The numbers reported permit of no conclusion beyond the bare fact that the Bohemians are an older immigrant race than the Poles, yet the total percentages tend to create the wholly unjustified impression that the Poles are less capable of "assimilation" than the Bohemians.[1]

The defects of the plan and statistical method of the Commission render the bulk of its report on Immigrants in Industries valueless or misleading.

[1] The reports of the Immigration Commission abound with such comparative percentages. A few samples only can be quoted in these pages. To judge by percentages, the migratory spirit reaches its extreme height—60.0 per cent—among the Greeks employed in the packing industry after they have been in the United States over ten years. On closer examination it appears, however, that there were five Greeks all told who had been in the United States more than ten years, and of their number three had visited abroad. (*Reports*, vol. 13, p. 151, Table 105.) In another place the following comment is made: "The employment of the wife or keeping boarders or lodgers is less frequent among the native-born of foreign father." This conclusion is derived from the reports on just four families whose heads are native-born of foreign father. (*Ibid.*, vol. 11, p. 311.)

CHAPTER III

OLD AND NEW IMMIGRATION

IT has come to be accepted as an unquestionable truth so often has it been repeated—that the type of the old immigrant was superior to the recent immigrants from Southern and Eastern Europe:

> Fifty, even thirty years ago, [said Gen. F. A. Walker in 1896], there was a rightful presumption regarding the average immigrant, that he was among the most enterprising, thrifty, alert, adventurous, and courageous of the community from which he came. It required no small energy, prudence, forethought, and pains to conduct the inquiries relating to his migration, to accumulate the necessary means, and to find his way across the Atlantic.[1]

The immigrants of those happy days

> did not come because they were assisted by others, they did not come because some one paid their passage to get them out of the old country, but they came because they wanted to be free. . . . They came not at the behest of the agents of the steamship lines or the agent of the large American industries, sent over to buy labor as by auction, in the market. . . . No; they came at their own behest, and did not all settle down in the centers of American life to congest it, but struck out into the prairies and forest to build homes for themselves and families.[2]

"Those were skilled artisans or progressive farmers of the thrifty, self-reliant type."[3]

[1] Francis A. Walker: *Discussions in Economics and Statistics*, p. 446.

[2] Statement of Rev. M. D. Lichliter, chaplain of the Junior Order American Mechanics before the House Committee on Immigration and Naturalization, Sixty first Congress. Hearings, p. 491.

[3] Frank Tracy Carlton: *The History and Problems of Organized Labor*, p. 328.

It is the old story of the Golden Age in a modern version. The cold facts of history, however, do not bear out this popular myth.

The great majority of immigrants to this country were so poor that they could not buy their passage, and in order to meet the obligations incurred by them for passage money and other advances, they were sold, after their arrival, into temporary servitude. . . . The prepayment of the passage was the exception, and its subsequent discharge by compulsory labor the rule.[1] The ship owners and ship merchants derived enormous profits from the sale of bodies of immigrants, as they charged very high rates for the passage, to which they added a heavy percentage —often more than a hundred per cent— for their risks. But the immigrants suffered bitterly from this traffic in human flesh. Old people, widows, and cripples would not sell well, while healthy parents with healthy children and young people of both sexes always found a ready market. If the parents were too old to work, their children had to serve so much longer to make up the difference. When one or both parents died on the voyage, their children had to serve for them. The expenses of the whole family were summed up and charged upon the survivor or survivors. Adults had to serve from three to six years; children from ten to fifteen years, till they became of age; smaller children were, without charge, surrendered to masters, who had to raise and board them. As all servants signed indentures, they were called "indentured servants." Whenever a vessel arrived at Philadelphia or New York its passengers were offered at public sale. The ship was the market-place, and the servants were struck off to the highest bidder. The country people either came themselves or sent agents or friends to procure what they wanted, be it a girl, or a "likely boy, or an old housekeeper, or a whole family. . . . Parents sold their children in order to remain free themselves. When a young man or girl had an opportunity to get married they had to pay their master five or six pounds for each year they had to serve. Yet a steerage passage never cost more than ten pounds. . . . If the master did not want to keep his servant he could sell him for the unexpired time of his term of servitude.[2]

"The newspapers of the time regularly contain advertise-

[1] Prof. Commons estimates that probably one half of all the immigrants of the colonial period landed as indentured servants. A. M. Simons: *Social Forces in American History*, p. 19.

[2] From a paper read before the American Social Science Association in New York City, in 1869, by State Commissioner of Immigration, Friedrich Kapp. *XVI. Annual Report of the New York Bureau of Labor Statistics*, pp. 964–965.

ments of the arrival of ships with 'indentured servants' to be sold. In case no buyers came to the ship the passengers were sold to agents, who chained them together and peddled them through the towns and villages."[1]

So great then was the poverty of the early immigrants that for the sum of ten pounds they were willing to sell themselves into peonage. The last sales of immigrants are reported in 1819 in Philadelphia.[2]

Nearly a century ago, the managers of the Society for the Prevention of Pauperism in the City of New York spoke of the immigrants "in the language of astonishment and apprehension":

> Through this inlet pauperism threatens us with the most overwhelming consequences. . . . The present state of Europe contributes in a thousand ways to foster unceasing immigration to the United States. . . An almost innumerable population beyond the ocean is out of employment. . . . This country is the resort of vast numbers of these needy and wretched beings. . . . They are frequently found destitute in our streets, they seek employment at our doors; they are found in our almshouses and in our hospitals; they are found at the bar of our criminal tribunals, in our bridewell, our penitentiary, and our State prison, and we lament to say that they are too often led by want, by vice, and by habit to form a phalanx of plunder and depredations, rendering our city more liable to increase of crimes and our houses of correction more crowded with convicts and felons.[3]

Eighteen years later the Mayor of New York City in a communication to the City Council complained that the streets were "filled with wandering crowds" of immigrants "clustering in our city, unacquainted with our climate, without employment, without friends, not speaking our language, and without any dependence for food, or raiment, or fireside, certain of nothing but hardship and a grave."[4]

[1] Simons, *loc. cit.*, p. 19.

[2] Kapp, *loc. cit.*, p. 965.

[3] Second Annual Report of the Managers of the Society for the Prevention of Pauperism in the City of New York, 1819. Quoted from the *Reports of the Industrial Commission*, vol. xv., p. 449.

[4] H. R., 61st Congress. Hearings before Committee on Immigration, p. 369.

This was the period when, according to Gen. F. A. Walker, the average immigrant was "enterprising, thrifty, alert, adventurous, and courageous." A contemporary writer anticipated General Walker's parallel between the old and the new immigration in almost identical language.[1]

A generation later it is again reported that "the poor and the productive classes of Europe, by hundreds of thousands, have been, and are now coming to our shores, with fixed habits and modes of life. These now constitute, mainly, the army of our unskilled laborers, are ignorant and degraded, pitifully so."[2]

Regarding the standard of living of the Irish peasantry at the beginning of the Irish exodus to America, when, according to General Walker's "rightful presumption," the average immigrant was thrifty and had accumulated the necessary means to pay his way, we have the following description from the same authority:

> The conditions under which they had been born and brought up were generally of the most squalid and degrading character. Their wretched hovels, thatched with rotting straw, scantily furnished with light, hardly ventilated at all, frequently with no floor but the clay on which they were built, were crowded beyond the bounds of comfort, health, or, as it would seem to us, of simple social decency; their beds were heaps of straw or rags; their food consisted mainly of buttermilk and potatoes, often of the worst, and commonly inadequate in amount; their clothing was scanty and shabby.[3]

---

[1] "Then our accessions of immigration were real accessions of strength from the ranks of the learned and the good, from enlightened mechanic and artisan and intelligent husbandman. Now, immigration is the accession of weakness, from the ignorant and vicious, or the priest-ridden slaves of Ireland and Germany, or the outcast tenants of the poorhouses and prisons of Europe."—From a paper entitled "Imminent Dangers to the Institutions of the United States through Foreign Immigration," etc., by S. F. B. Morse, 1835.— H. R. Sixty-first Congress. Hearings before the Committee on Immigration, p. 327.

[2] *Report of the Massachusetts Bureau of Statistics of Labor, 1869–1870*, p. 88.

[3] Walker, *loc. cit.*, p. 451. The following is quoted elsewhere by the same author from the report of Earl Devon's Commission on Irish Poverty in the 40's: "In many districts, their daily food is the potato;

Congestion was a common evil in those days, as it is to-day, and the reason for it was sought in the fact that the Irish immigrant, born in a cabin or a garret, had been used to crowding at home.[1] The *New York Weekly Tribune* of May 2, 1846, discussing a strike of Irish laborers in Brooklyn, said that their earnings were hardly sufficient to pay the rent of a decent tenement, so "they were allowed to build miserable shanties on ground allotted them by the contractors on the plot occupied by them in performing the work."[2] A quarter of a century later the dwellings of the Irish immigrants in Boston were officially characterized as "sickening kennels."[3] Says Dr. Kate H. Claghorn, comparing the old immigration with the new: "No account of filth in daily surroundings among Italians and Hebrews can outmatch the pictures drawn by observers of the habits of immigrant Irish and even Germans."[4]

The living conditions in an Irish district in 1864 were thus described by a city inspector:

> The tenants seem to wholly disregard personal cleanliness, if not the very first principles of decency, their general appearance and actions corresponding with their wretched abodes. This indifference to personal and domiciliary cleanliness is doubtless acquired from a long

---

their only beverage water; their cabins are seldom a protection against the weather; a bed or a blanket is a rare luxury; and, in nearly all, their pig and manure heap constitute their only property."—Francis A. Walker: *Political Economy*, pp. 313–314. "In the 40's, at the time of the potato famine in Ireland, many of the thousands who came to this country were in serious danger of absolute starvation if they remained at home. *Practically none of our immigrants of the present day are in such a condition*."—Jenks and Lauck: *The Immigration Problem*, p. 12.

[1] A contemporary writer had "seen in Ireland a horse, two cows, two goats, grandmother, father and mother, brother and sisters, an infant in a cradle, all in one apartment."—*Report of the Industrial Commission*, vol. xv., p. 459.

[2] *Documentary History of American Industrial Society*, vol. viii., pp. 225–226.

[3] *Report of the Massachusetts Bureau of Statistics of Labor, 1869–70*, p. 88.

[4] *Report of the Industrial Commission*, vol. xv., p. 491.

familiarity with the loathsome surroundings, wholly at variance with all moral or social improvements.[1]

A gloomy picture of the moral effects of bad housing conditions in the foreign sections of New York City in 1878, when the immigrants were only Irish and Germans, was drawn in a report of the Association for the Improvement of the Condition of the Poor:

In many quarters of the city family life and the feeling of home are almost unknown; people live in great caravansaries, which are hot and stifling in summer, disagreeable in winter, and where children associate together in the worst way. In many rooms privacy and purity are unattainable, and young girls grow up accustomed to immodesty from their earliest years. Boys herd together in gangs, and learn the practices of crime and vice before they are out of childhood. Even the laborers' families who occupy separate rooms in these buildings have no sense of home.[2]

Dr. Griscom, as early as 1842, had called attention to the "depraved effects which such modes of life exert upon the moral feelings and habits"; and the city inspector in 1851 remarks that "these over-populated houses are generally, if not always, seminaries of filthiness, indecency, and lawlessness."[3]

Dr. Claghorn concludes her review of the housing conditions of the former generations of immigrants with the following remarks:

The newer immigrants arrive here at no lower social level, to say the least, than did their predecessors. Their habits of life, their general morality and intelligence can not be called decidedly inferior. . . . The Italian ragpicker was astonishingly like his German predecessor, and the Italian laborer is of quite as high a type as the Irish laborer of a generation ago. In some cases the newer immigrants have brought about positive improvements in the quarters they have entered. Whole blocks have been transferred from nests of pauperism and vice into quiet industrial neighborhoods by the incoming of Italians and Hebrews.[4]

Throughout the nineteenth century relief against city

[1] *Report of the Industrial Commission*, p. 456.
[2] *Ibid.*, p. 459.
[3] *Loc. cit.*, p. 458.
[4] *Loc. cit.*, p. 491.

poverty was sought in directing the current of immigration to the farm. As early as 1817, "the same anxiety was felt that is felt to-day to get the immigrant out of the 'crowded' cities into the country beyond."[1] In 1819, the managers of the Society for the Prevention of Pauperism of the City of New York favored the plan of establishing "communication . . . with our great farmers and landholders in the interior" with a view to provide "ways and means . . . for the transportation of able-bodied foreigners into the interior," where labor could be provided for them "upon the soil."[2] Forty years later the Association for the Improvement of the Condition of the Poor complained of the Irish immigrants that "they had an utter distaste for felling forests and turning up the prairies for themselves. They preferred to stay where another race would furnish them with food, clothing, and labor, and hence were mostly found loitering on the lines of the public works, in villages, and in the worst portions of the large cities where they competed with negroes . . . for the most degrading employments."[3]

The old immigrants, like those of the present generation, were mostly unskilled laborers and farm hands, as will appear from an analysis of Table 2 next following.[4]

TABLE 2.

PER CENT DISTRIBUTION OF IMMIGRANTS BY OCCUPATIONS: 1861–1910.

Occupation	1861–1870	1871–1880	1881–1890	1891–1900	1901–1910
Professional	0.8	1.4	1.1	0.9	1.5
Skilled	24.0	23.1	20.4	20.1	20.2
Agricultural pursuits	17.6	18.2	14.0	11.4	24.3
Unskilled laborers	42.4	41.9	50.2	47.0	34.8
Servants	7.2	7.7	9.4	15.1	14.1
All other occupations	8.0	7.7	9.4	5.5	5.1
Total	100.0	100.0	100.0	100.0	100.0

[1] *Report of the Industrial Commission*, p. 449 [2] *Loc. cit.*, p. 462.

[3] *Report of the A. I. C. P.*, 1860, p. 50. Quoted from *Report of the Industrial Commission*, vol. xv., p. 462.

[4] For annual averages and sources of information see Appendix, Table 1.

The sharp fluctuations of the percentages of agricultural workers and common laborers indicate that the distinction between farm laborers and other laborers was probably not very accurately drawn in our immigration statistics. For the period 1901–1910 it is possible to subdivide all persons engaged in agricultural pursuits into farmers and farm laborers, the former constituting 1.6 per cent and the latter 23.0 per cent of all immigrant breadwinners.

Allowing the same percentage for the decade next preceding, with a rising tide of immigration from Eastern and Southern Europe, and estimating the maximum proportion of farmers in the "old immigration" at one half of all incoming agricultural workers,[1] we arrive at the following comparative ratios for unskilled laborers and farm help combined.

TABLE 3

RATIO OF LABORERS TO IMMIGRANT BREADWINNERS.

Period	Per cent
1861–1870	51.2
1871–1880	51.0
1881–1890	57.2
1891–1900	57.0
1901–1910	57.9

The ratio of unskilled laborers and farm hands to the total number of breadwinners exhibits but little change during the whole fifty-year period. For the half-century beginning in 1820, the proportion of unskilled laborers, exclusive of those classified under agricultural pursuits, has been computed as 46.6 per cent,[2] *i.e.*, about the same as for the later period.

[1] This is vastly more than is claimed for the "old immigration" by Professors Jenks and Lauck in their unofficial summary of the reports of the Immigration Commission, wherein they say that "the percentage of farmers as distinguished from farm laborers has always been very small, so small as not to be an appreciable factor in determining our civilization."—Jenks and Lauck, *loc. cit.*, p. 31.

[2] *Political Science Quarterly*, March, 1904; Roland P. Falkner: *Some Aspects of the Immigration Problem*, p. 49.

The percentage of skilled mechanics has varied but little for the last fifty years, and has at no time reached one quarter of all immigrant breadwinners. If this percentage is added to the estimated maximum ratio of farmers, it will be found that the aggregate of "skilled artisans and progressive farmers of the thrifty, self-reliant type" could in the good old days not have been as high as one third of the total immigration.

Still it is broadly asserted that the "new immigration" is drawn from the "poorest and least desirable" elements of the population of Italy, Austria, and Russia. "Measured either by intellectual, social, economic or material standards, the average immigrant of any particular class from these countries is far below the best of his countrymen who remain behind, and probably also below the average."[1]

No comparative study of the immigrants and their countrymen who remain at home is cited in support of this view. It still rests on the purely deductive argument, first advanced by Mayo-Smith twenty-four years ago, that, as the result of the increase of transportation facilities and the reduction of the cost of passage, "it is more and more the lower classes that are coming." In corroboration of this argument he cited the fact that the Irish and German immigrants of his day were coming from the poorer sections of their countries.[2] It is obvious, however, that the inhabitants of those sections were not all on the same economic level. Lack of opportunities in a poor country will drive people of some means to seek better luck abroad, while lack of funds will keep the poorest at home. Be that as it may, since the time of Mayo-Smith the steerage rates have been doubled. The increase in the cost of transpor-

[1] William Williams: *New Immigration*, p. 286. *Report of the Conference of Charities and Corrections*, 1906. See also Prescott F. Hall: *Selection of Immigration*, *Annals of American Academy of Political and Social Science*, July, 1904, p. 174; Robert Hunter: *Poverty*, p. 270.

[2] Richmond Mayo-Smith: "*Control of Immigration*," *Political Science Quarterly*, 1888, pp. 62, 69, 70, and 71.

tation has been tantamount to a head tax of from $18 to $27[1] and should have raised the standard of the "new immigration," as compared with the immigrants of the 70's and the early 80's.

Leaving aside, however, all speculative considerations, we have a purely objective standard of comparison, viz., the ratio of literacy. It is generally recognized that "probably the most apparent cause of illiteracy in Europe, as elsewhere, is poverty. The economic status of a people has a very decided effect upon the literacy rate. . . . Another phase of the economic factor is the need of children's service at home."[2]

While the statistics of illiteracy among immigrants to the United States are not compiled on a uniform basis with foreign statistics of illiteracy, still for a few countries and nationalities the data are fairly comparable. An examination of the figures presented in Table 4 shows that as a rule *the ratio of illiteracy among the immigrants is considerably lower than among their countrymen at home.*[3] These statistics prove that *measured by intellectual standards the average immigrant is above the average of his countrymen who remain behind.* Illiteracy being the effect of poverty (by hypothesis), one cannot escape the conclusion that, measured by economic standards, the immigrant is likewise above the average of his native country.

[1] "During the later seventies and early eighties the steerage passenger rate fluctuated from as low as $12 up as high as $25, but averaged about $17 or $18. . . . In the later eighties and early nineties . . . most of the foreign steamship companies—there were no native companies—gradually increased the steerage rates to about $38 or $39. . . . (The rates charged now) vary from about $36 to $38 and $39, depending upon the port, vessel, and so forth. Thirty-seven dollars and fifty cents is commonly quoted as the average."—Hearings before Committee on Immigration and Naturalization, H. R. 61st Congress: Statement of James H. Patten, pp. 31–32.

[2] *Reports of the Immigration Commission*, vol. 4, pp. 34–35.

[3] See Note on the Statistics of Italian Illiteracy, at end of chapter.

TABLE 4.

PER CENT OF ILLITERACY AMONG THE POPULATION OF RUSSIA, BULGARIA, SERVIA AND GREECE, AND AMONG THE IMMIGRANTS FROM THE SAME COUNTRIES.[1]

Nationality, year of enumeration, and age group	Population		Immigrants 14 years of age and over, year ended June 30 —		
			1908		1899–1910
	Male	Female	Male	Female	Both sexes.
Russia, 1897:					
Russians:					
10 to 19 years	51.3	83.6	40.1	50.8	38.4
20 years and over	62.6	89.7			
Hebrews					
10 to 19 years	41.3	58.0	21.9	40.4	26.0[2]
20 years and over	32.6	66.2			
Bulgaria, 1900:					
14 years and over	57.3	89.4	35.0	50.2	41.7
Servia, 1900:					
11 to 15 years	55.7	89.6			
16 to 20 years	58.8	90.9			
21 years and over	70.2	94.4			
Greece, 1907:					
14 years and over	42.6	82.2	26.9	57.5	

[1] *Reports of the Immigration Commission*, vol. 1, p. 99. *Report of the Commission of Immigration of the State of New York, 1909*, pp. 170 and 171. Premier Récensement Général de la Population de l'Empire de Russie, 1897. Relevé Général, Part 2, pp. 97 and 134. Bulgarie, Récensement de la population, 1900, vol. 1., p. 125. Annuaire Statistique du Royaume de Serbie pour 1900, vol. v., pp. 75–80. Grèce, Récensement de la population, 1907, vol. 1, pp. 156–157.

[2] This percentage represents the ratio of illiteracy among the Hebrews of all countries, but the bulk of Hebrew immigration comes from Russia. The population statistics of Austria classify Hebrews as Poles, Germans, etc., according to mother tongue. The ratio of illiteracy among the

The Immigration Commission on its trip to Europe sought the opinions of experts respecting the character of emigration to the United States. The conclusions reached by the Commission have none of the pessimistic sound typical of restrictionist literature. Says the Commission:

> The present movement is not recruited in the main from the lowest economic and social strata of the population. . . . Neither do the average or typical emigrants of to-day represent the lowest in the economic and social scale even among the classes from which they come, a circumstance attributable to both natural and artificial causes. In the first place, emigrating to a strange and distant country, although less of an undertaking than formerly, is still a serious and relatively difficult matter, requiring a degree of courage and resourcefulness not possessed by weaklings of any class. This natural law in the main regulated the earlier European emigration to the United States, and under its influence the present emigration, whether or not desirable as a whole, nevertheless represents the stronger and better element of the particular class from which it is drawn.[1]

Roumanian Hebrews 15 years of age and over, according to the census of 1889, was 55.6 per cent. ("Sans protection," meaning mostly Hebrews.) Résultats définitifs du dénombrement de la population de Roumanie, 1899, p. lxii.

[1] *Reports*, vol. 4 (in press). From the opinions of Americans who had long resided in Italy and of leading Italians, which are quoted in the Commission's report, a few are selected here by way of illustration.

Rev. N. W. Clark, an American, in charge of the educational work of the Methodist Church of Italy, said: "The class of emigrants who go to the United States are unquestionably the more enterprising, the better element; only those would be able to go who have the money to get tickets; many are too poor to go."

In a report to the Department of State, the American Consul at Palermo quotes the country correspondents of a Sicilian newspaper, concerning the local estimate of the character of emigration from that island. "As these accounts—says he—were in no way prepared for the foreign eye, or for any official or political purpose, but only by way of a routine chronicle of the happenings of life in the minor communities, they are spontaneous and unbiased and have an authority that can hardly be impeached." One of the correspondents says of the emigrants that they are not "driven out by dire want and necessity; they are lured rather by the desire to better themselves in the world and make a possible fortune. . . . Many are of a class

The social prejudice against the immigrant which it is sought to justify by his alleged inferiority, antedates the influx of the "undesirable aliens from Eastern and Southern Europe." Suffice it to recall the agitation of the Know-Nothing days, with its rioting and outbreaks of mob violence against the Irish, the desecration of their churches, the petty persecution of Irish children in the public schools, the denunciation of the Germans, the mobbing of German newspapers and Turner halls.[1]

> Probably the most important element in this antipathy was the pure contempt which men usually feel for those whose standards of life seem inferior. This feeling was felt towards all immigrants of the poorer class, irrespective of their race. To the mind of the average American the typical immigrant was a being uncleanly in habits, uncouth in speech, lax in the moralities, ignorant in mind, and unskilled in labor. . . . The immigrant bore a stamp of social inequality.[2]

The manifestations of this social prejudice in the industrial field seventy years ago were much the same as to-day.

> About the year 1836 to 1840, very material changes took place among . . . the general laboring help in all departments of industry. The profuse immigrations from Ireland. . . crowded into all the fields of labor, and crowded out the former occupants. Under the prejudice of nationality . . . the American element, the daughters of independent farmers, educated in our common schools . . . retired from mill and factory, and all the older establishments, and can no longer be found therein. Their places were taken up in the old, and all the new were filled by the new immigrants.[3]

---

possessing some little property." Another correspondent speaks of the emigrants as "*the enterprising and robust youth . . . confiding in their strength.*" According to him, "this emigration . . . *comprises even people of fairly easy circumstances.*"

[1] H. J. Desmond: *The Know-Nothing Party*, pp. 7–105. Louis Dow Scisco: *Political Nativism in New York State*, pp. 19, 248–249. Herrmann Von Holst: *Constitutional History of the United States*, vol. v., pp. 188–190. James Schouler: *History of the United States*, vol. v., pp. 305–306.

[2] Scisco, *loc. cit.*, p. 19.

[3] *First Report of the Massachusetts Bureau of Statistics of Labor*, 1870, p. 91.

By a strange inconsistency those who object to the coming of the immigrant as strongly object to his going. Why the "bird of passage" should have been the subject of popular censure is from an economic point of view inconceivable. So long as there are variations in business activity from year to year and from season to season, which result in unemployment, the American wage-earners should be the last to object if a class of wage-earners choose to leave the country temporarily while there is no demand for their services, thereby relieving competition for jobs in its acutest shape. From the point of view of the present immigration policy as well, the departure of the "bird of passage" ought to be approved as the best assurance that he would not "become a public charge." Still if an immigrant who comes to this country when there is work to be done and leaves when he is not wanted is to be regarded as an "undesirable alien," it is of interest to know how the "new immigration" compares in this respect with the "old immigration." "The one conclusion to be drawn from the record of departures from the United States," says the Immigration Commission, "is that as a whole the races or peoples composing the old immigration are essentially permanent settlers, and that a large proportion of the newer immigrants are simply transients."[1]

"The one conclusion" is, however, not the only one, for in another volume the Commission takes a more hopeful view, to wit:

> It is inaccurate to speak of the immigrant population as being only temporarily in this country. It is true, no doubt, that most of the recent immigrants hope at first to return some day to their native land, but the whole history of immigration goes to show that with the passing years and the growth of the inevitable ties, whether domestic, financial, or political, binding the immigrant to his new abode, these hopes decline and finally disappear.[2]

Inasmuch as the conclusions of the Commission contradict

[1] *Reports of the Immigration Commission*, vol. 4, p. 40.

[2] *Ibid.*, vol. 8, p. 657.

each other, we must go back to the facts from which they are drawn. The Immigration Commission in its investigation paid considerable attention to this question. The foreign-born workmen in iron and steel mills are classed by popular belief among the most "undesirable" elements of the "new immigration." The comparative frequency among them of the objectionable character addicted to the habit of visiting his old home and parents, may accordingly be accepted as typical of the races of the "new immigration." The Commission's data, presented in Table 5, show that the English-speaking races harbor among them a higher proportion of these offenders than all Eastern and Southern European races, except the North Italians and the Slovaks. The former, however, do not differ in this respect from the Scotch, while the Slovaks exceed the Swedes by a fraction of 1 per cent.

TABLE 5.

VISITS ABROAD MADE BY FOREIGN-BORN EMPLOYEES IN IRON AND STEEL MILLS, BY RACES.[1]

Northern and Western European Races.		Southern and Eastern European Races.	
Nationality.	*Per cent.*	*Nationality.*	*Per cent.*
Canadian	46.1	Italian, North	27.6
Scotch	27.6	Slovak	21.4
Welsh	24.7	Italian, South	20.7
English	24.0	Magyar	20.3
Swedish	21.0	Roumanian	15.1
		Croatian	14.3
		Slovenian	13.9
		Servian	12.2
		Russian	10.2
		Greek	8.8
		Bohemian and Moravian	8.5
		Polish	6.6
		Lithuanian	6.2

Even the vexed problem of "assimilation" appears to be as old as immigration itself. Benjamin Franklin, in a

[1] *Reports of the Immigration Commission*, vol. 8, p. 152, Table 110.

personal letter dated Philadelphia, May 9, 1753, characterized the Germans of Pennsylvania in the following terms:

> Those who come hither are generally the most stupid of their own nation, and as ignorance is often attended with great credulity, when knavery would mislead it . . . it is almost impossible to remove any prejudice they may entertain. . . . Not being used to liberty they know not how to make modest use of it. . . . I remember when they modestly declined intermeddling with our elections; but now they come in droves and carry all before them, except in one or two counties.
>
> Few of their children know English. They import only books from Germany, and of the six printing houses in the Province, two are entirely German, two half German, half English, and but two are entirely English. They have one German newspaper and one half German. Advertisements intended to be general are now printed in Dutch and English. The signs in our streets (Philadelphia) have inscriptions in both languages, and some places only in German. They begin, of late, to make all their bonds and other legal instruments in their own language, which (though I think it ought not to be) are allowed in our courts, where the German business so increases, that there is continued need of interpreters, and I suppose in a few years they will also be necessary in the Assembly, to tell one half of our legislators what the other half says. In short, unless the stream of importation could be turned from this to other colonies, as you very judiciously propose, they will soon outnumber us, that all the advantages we will have will in my opinion, be not able to preserve our language, and even our government will become precarious.[1]

Franklin's apprehensions concerning the Legislature of Pennsylvania were all but justified at the convention of the State of Pennsylvania held at Philadelphia from July 15 to September 28, 1776, whose minutes were ordered published weekly in English and German.[2] This practice was still continued as late as 1790.[3]

The conditions in Pennsylvania were by no means exceptional. Says Prof. McMaster of the same period:

[1] Frank Ried Diffenderffer: *The German Immigration into Pennsylvània, 1700 to 1775*, Part II, pp. 110–113.

[2] *Pennsylvania House Journal*, vol. i, p. 57, Friday, July 26, 1776, P.M.

[3] *Journal of the Senate of the Commonwealth of Pennsylvania*, vol i, 1790–1791, p. 22, Thursday, December 16, 1790.

> Diverse as the inhabitants of the States . . . were in occupations, they were not less diverse in opinions, in customs, and habits. . . . Differences of race, differences of nationality, of religious opinions, of manners, of tastes, even of speech, were still distinctly marked. . . . In New York the Dutch element prevailed and the language of Holland was very generally spoken.[1]

With the great influx of Irish and German immigrants in the middle of the nineteenth century, distinct colonies of those nationalities grew up in the larger cities.

> So large are the aggregations of different foreign nationalities [says a report of that day] that they no longer conform to our habits, opinions, and manners, but, on the contrary, create for themselves distinct communities, almost as impervious to American sentiments and influences as are the inhabitants of Dublin or Hamburg. . . . They have their own theaters, recreations, amusements, military and national organizations; to a great extent their own schools, churches, and trade unions; their own newspapers and periodical literature.[2]

The Irish were accused of "clannishness,"[3] like the "immigrants from Eastern and Southern Europe" in our day, although "to a large extent this going apart of the Irish was but natural in view of the contemptuous manner in which the 'nativist' Americans treated them."[4] It took three generations to raise "the Celts and the Teutons" to a place among the "more desirable immigrants from Northern and Western Europe."

Have the new immigrants given evidence of an assimilability inferior to that exhibited by the Germans? Some evidence on this subject, collected by the Immigration Commission, is given in Table 6 next below, relating to the families of employees in the slaughtering and packing houses of Kansas City:

[1] John Bach McMaster: *History of the People of the United States*, vol. i., pp. 10–11.

[2] *Report of the Industrial Commission*, vol. xv., p. 455.

[3] Scisco, *loc. cit.*, p. 19.

[4] Desmond, *loc. cit.*, p. 9.

TABLE 6.

PER CENT OF POLISH AND GERMAN EMPLOYEES OF PACKING HOUSES IN KANSAS CITY AND THEIR FOREIGN-BORN CHILDREN SIX YEARS OF AGE OR OVER WHO SPEAK ENGLISH, BY YEARS IN THE UNITED STATES.[1]

Years in the United States	Polish	German
Under 5	26.1	20.0
5 to 9	73.2	70.0
10 or over	100.0	95.8

It can be seen from this table that the Polish workmen and their children born abroad number among them a larger percentage of English-speaking persons than the Germans who have lived in the United States the same length of time. This example need not be the general rule, but it shows that the general classification of the Germans as "English-speaking" and of the Poles as non-English-speaking is purely a matter of prejudice.

It is obviously not the character of the new immigration that is the real cause of the popular feeling. The opposition of organized labor, the main social force behind the present agitation for restriction, originated at a time when the numbers of immigrants from Eastern and Southern Europe were too small to attract attention. Resolutions in opposition to immigration were adopted by the National Labor Union as early as 1868.[2] The report of the president to the convention of the Cigarmakers' Union held in 1879 discussed immigration among "the evils which affect the trade."[3]

The report of the New York Bureau of Labor Statistics for 1885, in a summary of the testimony taken on the sub-

[1] *Reports of the Immigration Commission*, vol. 13, Table 256, p. 329.

[2] *Documentary History of American Industrial Society*, vol. ix., pp. 221–222.

[3] *Cigarmakers' Official Journal*, vol. v., No. 1, September 15, 1879, p. 2. Editorial articles against immigration appeared in the official organ of the Cigarmakers' Union before that, in the issues of June 10, 1878, and January 10, 1879.

ject of immigration, records a growing feeling of opposition to foreign labor. Every reason which is urged to-day against the admission of immigrants from Southern and Eastern Europe is recited in that testimony, although five sixths of the immigration in the fiscal year 1885, and still more during the prior years, came from Canada and Northern and Western Europe.[1] Thirteen years later an inquiry addressed by the New York Bureau of Labor to officers of labor organizations elicited the following reply from the Brotherhood of Carpenters and Joiners No. 382, of New York: "Immigrants from Northern Europe—Danes and Swedes—interfere very much with the keeping up of the wages in the trade. That is the principal thing we find fault with."[2]

The only apparent difference between the old immigration and the new is that of numbers. The reason why the "old immigration" is to-day viewed with greater favor than the new is that there is much less of it. It is so stated in the testimony of the representative of the railway brotherhoods before the House Committee on Immigration and Naturalization:

> A good many people are apt to consider themselves better than some other nationality. It is a matter of opinion, and, for my part, I am not discussing this subject with any such narrow view of the situation. I am not prepared to say that the Italian or the Slav or the Hungarian or the Mexican has not the natural attributes that go to make up good citizenship. . . . It is not a question of whether or not they possess those qualities. . . . The question is whether or not . . . a foreigner brought into this country is replacing or ruinously competing with some one who is already here.[3]

This is the question to which the attention of the unpreju-

[1] *Reports of the Immigration Commission*, vol. 1, pp. 63 and 87.

[2] *XVI Annual Report of New York Bureau of Labor Statistics*, 1898, p. 1047.

[3] Hearings before Committee on Immigration and Naturalization. H. R. 61st Congress, pp. 251–252.

diced student of the immigration problem should address itself.

NOTE: THE STATISTICS OF ITALIAN ILLITERACY

The Immigration Commission concedes that "it is impossible," from a comparison of Italian statistics of illiteracy with our own statistics of illiteracy among Italian immigrants, "to determine whether the proportion of illiterates among Italian immigrants to the United States is greater or less than among corresponding classes in Italy."[1] It immediately seeks to weaken this conclusion by selecting for comparison the statistics of illiteracy among persons contracting marriage, on the assumption that "in the matter of age the marriage group would probably correspond rather closely to the immigrant group." As a result of this selection it appears "that in 1905 36.9 per cent of the total population contracting marriage and 48.8 per cent of the immigrants were illiterate." A comparison of the tables in question (28 and 32) shows that the ratio of illiteracy among persons contracting marriage in 1901 was 32.7 per cent for males and 46.1 per cent for females, whereas among the population at large 21 years of age and over the ratio of illiteracy was 43.9 per cent and 60.4 per cent respectively. This difference is readily accounted for by the fact that the marriage group is younger than the adult population as a whole, and the younger generations have had the benefit of the progress of education in Italy; the ratio of illiteracy among the adult population of both sexes in 1901 was 52.3 per cent, as compared with 63.4 per cent in 1882.[2]

On the other hand, while the immigrants contain a large percentage of young men of marriageable age, yet there are among them quite a number of men who have been married several years. Moreover, "the marriage group . . . is drawn from all sections of the country and from all classes of the population, while immigrants are largely from the peasant class of the more southern compartimenti." It is evident that a comparison of the marriage group with the immigrant group must be unfavorable to the latter. If the immigrants are compared with the total population 21 years of age and over, the results are quite different. The percentage of illiteracy in Northern Italy, according to the census of 1901, fluctuated between 16.8 and 46.8 per cent for males and between 28.8 and 59.6 per cent for females 21 years of age and over, whereas among North Italian immigrants of both sexes 14 years of age and over, for the fiscal year 1901, the ratio of illiteracy was only 15.3 per cent.[3] In Southern Italy the percentage of illiteracy among adults widely differs from one district to another; in some the

---

[1] *Reports of the Immigration Commission*, vol. 4, p. 192.

[2] *Ibid.*, Table 27.

[3] *Ibid.*, Tables 28 and 33.

ratio of illiteracy is lower, in some higher than among South Italian immigrants.

Even if the marriage group furnished a proper standard for comparison the variations of the illiteracy rate by administrative divisions would make the results uncertain. In two districts the ratio of illiteracy would be below and in two others above the percentage of illiteracy among the North Italian immigrants. In Southern Italy two districts show a higher percentage of illiteracy among males than the average among South Italian immigrants of both sexes, and the percentage of illiterates among women is in all but three districts higher than among the immigrants of both sexes. The Commission would have been on safer ground, had it adhered to its original conclusion, instead of speculating on the basis of such incommensurable figures.

CHAPTER IV

IMMIGRATION AND THE LABOR MARKET

THE main question in all present discussion of immigration is: Does immigration injure the economic interests of the American wage-earner? The demand for restriction of immigration proceeds from the assumption that immigration overcrowds the American labor market, hordes of willing workers being driven by fear of starvation to compete for one job. To remedy this evil foreign immigration must be restricted: keep the "undesirable" immigrants out, and the American workingmen will be kept busy. The more consistent advocates of this view, as previously stated, regard all immigrants as undesirable. It is an echo of the Malthusian theory, that population increases faster than the means of subsistence, with this modification, however, that the cause of the disproportion is found, not in the natural propagation of the human species, but in immigration, which is believed to outrun the opportunities of employment. In order to test the accuracy of this assumption, let us first take an inventory of the industrial progress of the United States compared with the growth of population for the last twenty years.

The population of the continental United States increased between 1890 and 1910 from 63,000,000 to 92,000,000, *i. e.*, 46 per cent. During the same period, the production of coal in the United States more than trebled, the increase being from 140,000,000 to 448,000,000 long tons.[1] As the exports of coal from the United States are insig-

[1] *Statistical Abstract of the United States*, 1911, Table 335.

nificant,[1] these figures indicate that to-day three times as much coal is consumed in this country as twenty years ago. Coal is the foundation of modern industry. The increased consumption of coal indicates that the consumption of steam has increased threefold, *i. e.*, that the whole American industry has grown in proportion. The production of steel, another basic article of modern industry, increased during the twenty-year period 1889–1909 seven-fold, from 3,400,000 to 24,000,000 long tons. The production of copper more than quadrupled, viz., from 101,000 to 488,000 tons. The number of ton-miles of freight carried over American railways nearly trebled from 1890 to 1909, the increase being from seventy-seven billions to two hundred and nineteen billions. The total amount of bank clearings in the United States likewise nearly trebled in the twenty-year period between 1890 and 1910, having grown from $58,000,000,000 to $169,000,000,000.[2] The increase in the amount of bank clearings may be accepted as a fair index of the aggregate industrial expansion.[3] Thus, while the economic activities of the people of the United States have trebled during the last twenty years, population has increased by less than one half.

The introduction of labor-saving machinery has lessened the potential demand for new laborers, yet the pace of industrial development has been faster than the progress of invention. The growing demand for bituminous coal necessitated an increase of the working force from 192,000 in 1890 to 556,000 in 1910.[4] The number of railway employees increased from 749,301 in 1890 to 1,502,823 in 1909,

[1] The exports of bituminous coal from the United States in 1891–1910 fluctuated between 1.5 and 3.1 per cent of the annual production. —*Statistical Abstract of the United States*, 1910, p. 541.

[2] *Statistical Abstract of the United States*, 1910, Table No. 335.

[3] Professor Irving Fisher estimates that the total trade of the United States increased from $191,000,000,000 to $387,000,000,000 in the thirteen years 1896–1909.—*The Purchasing Power of Money*, p. 304.

[4] *Mineral Resources of the United States*, 1908, pp. 25, 41. United States Geological Survey. *The Production of Coal in 1910*, p. 41.

i. e., exactly 100 per cent.[1] The average number of wage-earners employed in manufactures increased between 1889 and 1909 from 4,200,000 to 6,600,000,[2] *i. e.*, 57 per cent.

The unbiased testimony of figures shows that the demand for labor within the last twenty years has outrun the growth of population, both through natural increase and through immigration. The investigators of the Immigration Commission sought to ascertain from employers of labor the "reason for employing immigrants," and were told that "they found it necessary either to employ immigrant labor or delay industrial advancement."[3] A number of specific instances are quoted in the Commission's reports. In the Birmingham iron and steel district, Alabama, where the number of immigrants is insignificant, "the largest employers of labor . . . state that under normal conditions, at the present stage of the industrial development of the district, the ordinary labor supply which may be relied upon continuously affords about 50 per cent of the total necessary to operate all plants and mines at their full capacity."[4] In the centers of immigration, on the other hand, the clothing manufacturers likewise claim "that the industry has developed faster than the number of clothing workers has increased." With the revival of business after the depression of 1908 they found it "almost impossible to keep their pay-rolls full."[5]

According to an investigation made by the United States Bureau of Labor,

> the demand for laborers of all kinds in all lines of industry greatly exceeded the supply during the year 1906. One of the great lines of railroad reported an increase in its construction and track gangs of 41 per cent in 1906 over 1905. . . . The men employed were all

---

[1] *Interstate Commerce Commission, Twelfth Annual Report on the Statistics of Railways*, p. 40, and *Twenty-second Annual Report*, p. 34.

[2] *Bureau of the Census, Manufactures*, 1905, Part I., p. xxxvi. Census Bureau's Preliminary Summary for 1909. Advance Statement to the Press of October 18, 1911.

[3] Jenks and Lauck, *loc. cit.*, p. 140.

[4] *Reports of the Immigration Commission*, vol. 9, p. 151.

[5] *Ibid.*, vol. 11, p. 411.

Italian immigrants. . . . Another large railway system reported an increase of 44 per cent in this class of workers in 1906 over 1905. The increase of one company was 24 per cent in this class of common labor. An iron and steel company with a total of 147,343 employees in 1904 increased it to 180,158 employees in 1905 and to 217,109 in 1906.

Conditions are perhaps best summed up in this extract from a letter received from the President of one of the largest railroads:

> Our work was delayed in both years—1905 and 1906—by the inability to get workmen. This is true not only of railroads but of the industries along our lines. Our patrons were constantly giving as the excuse for not promptly unloading cars that they are unable to get the laborers to do the work. There was not only a scarcity of common laborers in the country, but we found it impossible, under existing conditions, to get an adequate number of workmen for our shops.[1]

Statements of employers of labor, however, are discounted; what is meant by "a scant labor supply" is simply, it is thought, "the inability of the manufacturers and mine operators to secure labor at the same wages in the face of the growing labor needs of the country."[2] Aside from the admission implied in this interpretation, that the demand for labor is growing faster than the supply, there is unimpeachable evidence to the same effect in the report of the Bureau of Labor, to which reference has been made above. The Bureau's investigator examined the books of a number of employment agencies for 1906 and found that they had been unable to supply more than a fraction of their orders for help.[3]

[1] Frank J. Sheridan: "Italian, Slavic, and Hungarian Unskilled Immigrant Laborers in the United States." *Bulletin of the Bureau of Labor*, No. 72, pp. 424–425.

[2] Jenks and Lauck, *loc. cit.*, pp. 17, 140.

[3] "A personal examination of the books of record of another agency, covering a period of eight months, from April 1 to November 30, 1906, showed that 165 employers in the States of New York, New Jersey, Connecticut, Pennsylvania, and Virginia made application for 8668 Italian laborers from this one agency. The agency supplied fewer than 1500. Another agency, where no fees were charged, had applications

Doubtless, demand and supply in the labor market are fluctuating. During the twenty-year period under consideration, this country has gone through two industrial crises, when great numbers of wage-earners were suddenly thrown out of employment. The question is, what, if any, is the interdependence between the vicissitudes of the labor market and immigration?

The Industrial Commission, in 1901, from a comparative study of the number of immigrants and price index numbers for a period of sixty years, arrived at the conclusion that "immigration follows business conditions in obedience to the opportunities for employment: In times of business expansion, when capital is seeking investment and the resources of the country are being eagerly developed . . . immigrants enter in increasing numbers to take a share of the increasing wages and employment, but in times of business depression their numbers decline."[1]

The report of the Industrial Commission appeared after a decade of declining immigration. Has the unprecedented immigration of recent years changed its relation to business conditions in this country?

A comparative view of the fluctuations of business and immigration for the past thirty years, since the tide has set in from Eastern and Southern Europe, can be gained from a glance at Diagram I.[2] It will be observed that the curves representing the production of coal, the volume of railway freight, bank clearings, and immigration run in

---

in seven months for 37,058, and could supply but 3705 newly arrived Italian immigrants. One effect of the scarcity is reported by an Italian agency as follows:

"'Since about July, 1906, on account of the great scarcity, employers pay from $3.00 to $5.00 per man for common laborers. Not for twenty-two years have there been such high fees offered. Since the demand set in the laborer pays no fees.'" (*Bulletin of the Bureau of Labor*, No. 72, pp. 424–425.)

[1] *Reports of the Industrial Commission*, vol. xv., pp. 308, 309. See also chart opposite p. 305.

[2] Based upon the figures of the *Statistical Abstract of the United States*.

DIAGRAM I.

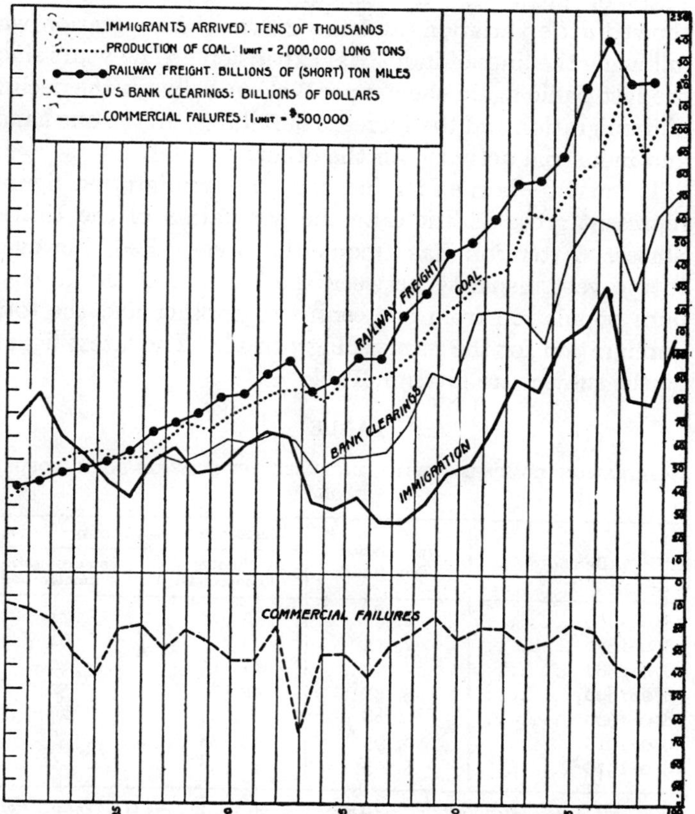

I. Immigration and business conditions, 1880–1910.

harmony. On the other hand, the decrease of immigration from 1880 to 1899 runs almost parallel with the increase of commercial failures, and *vice versa*. During the following years of prosperity the amount of commercial failures showed little variation, and the curve of immigration was following the lines of industrial expansion. The years since the last panic again show a parallelism between the decline of immigration and the increase of failures, on the one hand, and industrial activity, on the other.

It must be borne in mind that the immigration figures represent gross additions to the population of the United States. Attention has frequently been called, however, to the vast disparity between the increase of the foreign-born population from one census to another and the total immigration for the intervening period. The latest figures on the subject are given in Table 7.

TABLE 7.

IMMIGRATION COMPARED WITH INCREASE OF FOREIGN-BORN POPULATION.[1]

Decade	Immigration (Thousands)	Increase in foreign-born population	
		Number (Thousands)	Per cent ratio to immigration
1850–1860..........	2,598	1,928	74
1860–1870..........	2,315	1,428	62
1870–1880..........	2,812	1,113	40
1880–1890..........	5,247	2,570	50
1890–1900..........	3,688	1,092	29
1900–1910..........	8,795	3,175	36
1910–1920[2].........	5,565	358	6

[1] *Reports of the Immigration Commission*, vol. I., pp. 64, 135.—*XIII. Census. Population*, vol. i., p. 781.

[2] The comparative figures for the last decade do not include Orientals, the preliminary returns of the XIV. Census made public by the Bureau of the Census being confined to foreign-born white. The total number of white immigrants for the period from July 1, 1910, to June 30, 1920, has been computed from the *Report of the Commissioner-General of Immigration* for 1920, Table XV., pp. 181–182.

The difference between gross immigration and the net increase of the foreign-born population is the combined result of mortality and emigration. As the foreign-born population increases, an ever larger number of new arrivals

DIAGRAM II.

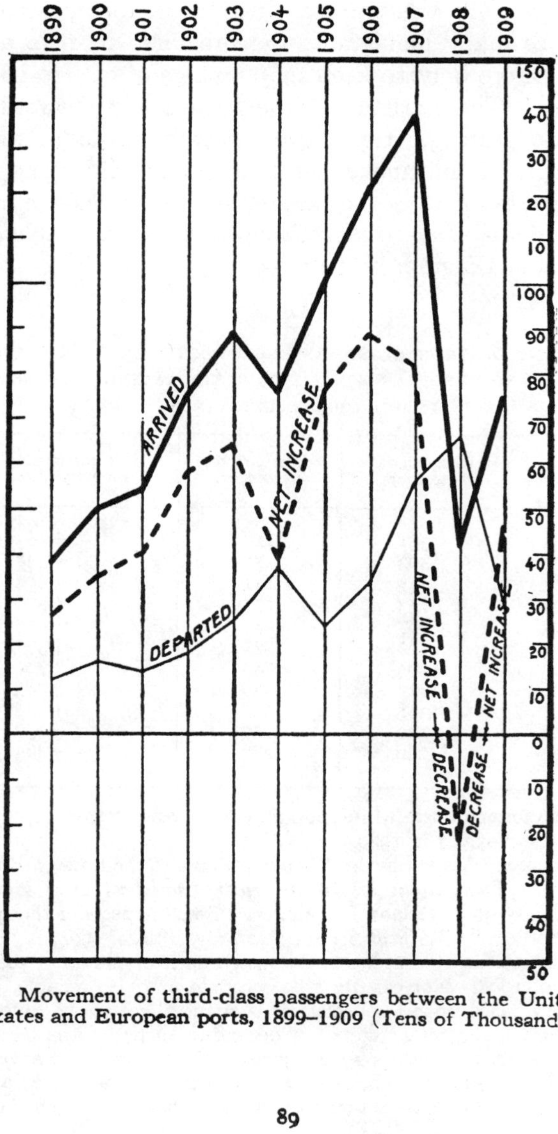

II. Movement of third-class passengers between the United States and European ports, 1899–1909 (Tens of Thousands)

merely fill up the places of their predecessors claimed by death. The foreign-born white population of the United States in 1920 was twice as great as in 1880[1]; accordingly twice as many immigrants were required in 1920 as forty years before only to keep the numbers of foreign-born stationary. The statistics of the inward and outward transatlantic passenger traffic are generally taken to represent the immigration and emigration movement.[2] The respective figures for 1899–1909 are reproduced in Table 8 from the *Reports of the Immigration Commission*, vol. 4, Table 26, and plotted in Diagram II. on p. 89.

TABLE 8.

MOVEMENT OF THIRD CLASS PASSENGERS BETWEEN THE UNITED STATES AND EUROPEAN PORTS DURING THE CALENDAR YEARS 1899 TO 1909. (THOUSANDS.)

Year	West-bound passengers	East-bound passengers	Net immigration (+) or emigration (−)
1899	381	118	+263
1900	503	156	+347
1901	545	141	+404
1902	753	177	+576
1903	887	252	+635
1904	762	371	+391
1905	1004	244	+760
1906	1223	338	+885
1907	1378	555	+823
1908	420	657	−237
1909	750	287	+463

[1] The foreign-born white population increased from 6,559,679 in 1880 to 13,703,987 in 1920.

[2] Richmond-Mayo-Smith: "Immigration and the Foreign-Born Population." *Publications of the American Statistical Association*, vol. iii., pp. 305–306. Roland P. Falkner: "Some Aspects of the Immigration Problem." *Political Science Quarterly*, March, 1904, p. 38.

Our statistics of emigration do not go back of the fiscal year ended June 30, 1908. Nor can they be accepted as quite reliable, being of necessity based upon the declarations of the aliens at the time of their departure. The total number of departing aliens for the period from July 1, 1907, to June 30, 1920, exceeded the number of avowed "emigrants" by 2,513,000, whereas the total number of admitted aliens exceeded the number of immigrants only by 1,867,000, which shows that

DIAGRAM III.

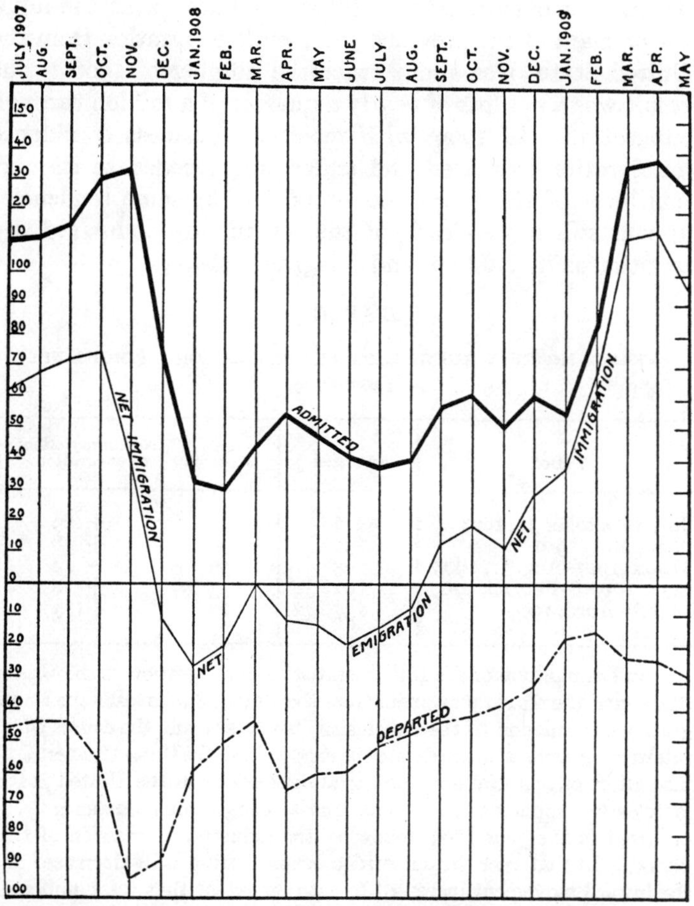

III. Monthly immigration and emigration, from July, 1907, to May, 1909 (thousands).

646,000 persons classified as "non-emigrant aliens," *i. e.*, 26 per cent, of that class, did not return to the United States. See Appendix, Table XXX.

It will be observed that the tide of immigration was rising until 1907, with a slight set-back during the Presidential year 1904. During the industrial crisis of 1908 immigration dropped at once nearly a million, compared with the high-water mark of the previous year, while emigration from the United States was about twice the number of 1906. The result was a net loss of nearly a quarter of a million through emigration. In 1909, with returning business confidence immigration increased and emigration receded to its normal level of the years 1903–1906.[1] The same tendencies appear still more clearly if the returns are compared by months, as in Table 9, and Diagram III. on p. 91.[2]

TABLE 9.

AVERAGE MONTHLY IMMIGRATION AND EMIGRATION. (THOUSANDS), 1907–1909.

Period	Admitted	Departed	Net immigration (+) or emigration (−)
July 1–October 31, 1907	116	47	+ 69
November, 1907	132	94	+ 38
Dec. 1, 1907–Aug. 31, 1908	45	59	− 14
Sept. 1, 1908–Feb. 28, 1909	61	33	+ 28
March–April, 1909	137	24	+113

[1] An examination of the Italian statistics of emigration to the United States and the return movement from the United States leads the Immigration Commission to the conclusion "that as a rule the causes which retard emigration also accelerate the exodus from the United States. . . . The effect of financial and industrial depressions in the United States is clearly apparent. . . . The most conspicuous instance . . . occurred in the year 1894, following the industrial depression of that period. In that year the outward movement from Italy decreased and the inward movement increased to such an extent that the number returning was 848 to every 1000 emigrating. The same tendency was shown again in 1904, immediately following the financial depression of the preceding year."—*Reports of the Immigration Commission*, vol. 4, p. 229.

[2] *Annual Reports of the Commissioner-General of Immigration*, 1908, p. 228, and 1910, p. 14. The monthly figures are for immigrant and emigrant aliens, as defined in the statistics of the Bureau of Immigration. These two classes are not identical with third-class passengers arriving

From July 1, to October 31, 1907, immigration and emigration went on normally. The latter part of October witnessed the outbreak of the crisis, and the next month emigration doubled. Immigration still remained normal, inasmuch as those who arrived here in November had left their homes before the crisis. But from December immigration dropped to one third of the number of arrivals in November. During the next nine months emigration exceeded immigration by 14,000 persons monthly. From September 1, 1908, the situation began to improve, and the number of immigrants went up again, while departures went down. In the spring of the next year immigration and emigration resumed their normal relation. It is evident that the immigration movement promptly responds to the business situation in the United States.

The question arises: How does immigration adjust itself to business conditions in America? The method by which this adjustment is effected is thus described by the Immigration Commission:

> It is entirely safe to assert that letters from persons who have emigrated to friends at home have be n the immediate cause of by far the greater part of the remarkable movement from Southern and Eastern Europe to the United States during the past twenty-five years. There is hardly a village or community in Southern Italy and Sicily that has not contributed a portion of its population to swell the tide of emigration to the United States, and the same is true of large areas of Austria, Hungary, Greece, Turkey, and the Balkan States. . . . It was frequently stated to members of the Commission that letters from persons who had emigrated to America were passed from hand to hand until most of the emigrants' friends and neighbors were acquainted with the contents. In periods of industrial activity, as a rule, the letters so circulated contain optimistic references to wages and opportunities for employment in the United States. . . . The reverse is true during seasons of industrial depression in the United States. At such times intending emigrants are quickly informed by their friends in the United

---

and departing. Those aliens who go to Europe with the expectation of returning may never come again, yet they are not included among "emigrant aliens." As a result, the net emigration is lower in this than in the preceding table.

States relative to conditions of employment, and a great falling off in the tide of emigration is the immediate result. . . . Emigrants as a rule are practically assured that employment awaits them in America before they leave their homes for ports of embarkation. . . . In fact it may be said that immigrants, or at least newly-arrived immigrants, are substantially the agencies which keep the American labor market supplied with unskilled laborers from Europe. . . . As a rule, each immigrant simply informs his nearest friends that employment can be had and advises them to come. It is these personal appeals which, more than all other agencies, promote and regulate the tide of European emigration to America.[1]

These conclusions of the Immigration Commission are corroborated by Table 10.

TABLE 10.

IMMIGRANTS' CONNECTIONS IN THE UNITED STATES.[2]

Immigrant aliens admitted	Numbers (Thousands)			Percentages		
	1908	1909	1910	1908	1909	1910
Total	783	752	1042	100	100	100
Going to join:						
Relative........	596	583	857	76	77	82
Friend.........	128	122	133	16	17	13
Neither........	59	47	52	8	6	5

It appears that most of the immigrants come to join relatives, and that only a small proportion of those who land here have neither relatives nor friends to meet them on arrival. This percentage is much smaller for the new immigration than for the old, viz., 3 per cent for the former as against 10.6 per cent for the latter.[3]

There is a remarkable coincidence of the percentage ratios for the fiscal years ending June 30, 1908 and 1909.

[1] *Reports of the Immigration Commission*, vol. 1, pp. 187–189.

[2] *Annual Reports of the Commissioner-General of Immigration*, 1908, p. 15; 1909, p. 23; 1910, p. 21.

[3] *Reports of the Immigration Commission*, vol. 4, Table 38. The figures are for 1908 and 1909.

Both were partly affected by the crisis. On the other hand, the year 1910 shows an addition of 274,000, *i. e.* 47 per cent, to the number of immigrants coming to join their relatives, while the number of persons who came in 1908–1910 to join friends, and the number of those who seemingly had neither relatives nor friends in the United States, exhibit only slight fluctuations from year to year. This means that, as soon as conditions improved, the first thought of the older immigrants was of their kin whom they had left behind; friends came next.

The correctness of this interpretation is supported by Table 11, which shows the fluctuations in the number of immigrants whose passage was paid by their American relatives, compared with the number of dependents admitted—in official terminology, "no occupation (including women and children)"— and also the fluctuations in the number of persons whose passage was paid by persons "other than self or relative," *i. e.* by friends.[1] The fiscal year ending June 30, 1908, included four prosperous months from July to October, 1907. Moreover, many of those who reached the United States later in the year had been provided with steamship tickets before the crisis. Their American relatives and friends must have been saving the money with which their passage was paid, for some months previous to their landing. Steamship tickets are quite commonly sold on small weekly payments. The full effect of the crisis therefore manifested itself during the next fiscal year (beginning July 1, 1908), when the number of immigrants who arrived on tickets prepaid by their American relatives dropped twenty per cent. In 1910 their number again came up to the level of 1908. In 1908 the number of such immigrants exceeded by 32,000 the number of dependents coming to join their relatives who had preceded them. Evidently some of the resident aliens had raised the means to send for their brothers, sisters, and

[1] *Report of the Commissioner-General of Immigration*, 1908, pp. 15, 35; 1909, pp. 23, 46; 1910, pp. 21, 57.

other self-supporting relatives, in addition to the members of their immediate households. In 1909 the number of immigrants assisted by their American relatives was barely equal to the total number of dependents who came to join their husbands and fathers. Apparently while employment was scarce the foreign-born workman could spare no money to send for his more distant relatives. In 1910 improved business conditions again brought to this country quite a number of breadwinners (14,000) whose passage was paid by their American relatives. The number of immigrants assisted by their American friends showed similar fluctuations.

TABLE 11.

ASSISTED IMMIGRATION

Year Ending June 30	1908	1909	1910
Assisted immigrants (thousands):			
Passage paid by relative	275	220	274
Dependents	243	221	260
Difference	+32	− 1	+14
Passage paid by friend	10	8	12

Another potent agency which regulates immigration is the great number of returning immigrants. As a rule, says the Immigration Commission, they are those who have succeeded. "The money they can show makes a vivid impression. They are dispensers of information and inspiration, and are often willing to follow up the inspiration by loans to prospective emigrants."[1] During the ten-year period 1900–1909, three million people returned to Europe from the United States. (See Table 8 above.)

Compared with this army of promoters of immigration,

[1] *Reports of the Immigration Commission*, vol. 4, p. 58.

the much blamed steamship agent fades into insignificance. A simple calculation will show that the number of steamship agents is grossly exaggerated by popular imagination. In order to make something by "stimulating immigration," an agent must sell at least one ticket a week; his commission on $37, which is the average cost of passage from Europe, could not be too great at that. A good many tickets are prepaid on this side; yet if every steamship ticket were sold through an agent, the annual emigration of a million persons could barely support twenty thousand agents. This scarcely equals one per cent of the volunteer force of immigration promoters who have returned from America within the past ten years,—with every allowance made for duplications. It is clearly against all sense of proportion to magnify the "propaganda" of a few thousand ticket agents into a contributing cause of this modern *Völkerwanderung.*[1] The facts brought to light by the investigation of the Immigration Commission in Europe will tend to dissipate this popular delusion. The Commission found that in Greece, which "according to its population furnishes more immigrants to the United States than any other country . . . solicitation by steamship companies probably plays relatively a small part even as a contributory cause of the movement." In Austria "government officials and others interested in the emigration situation expressed the belief that the solicitations of agents had little effect on the emigration movement, which was influenced almost entirely by economic conditions." Unquestionably, steamship agents in all parts of Europe solicit business in competition with one another, but they do it, as Mr. T. V. Powderly has found, "much as insurance agents do. . . . One method adopted is to translate editorials and articles from American newspapers relative to the prosperity of the United States, which articles are distributed among pros-

[1] There are some people who similarly believe that the trade-union movement of our days is "stimulated" by the "labor agitators," walking delegates, and business agents of the unions.

pective emigrants." The Immigration Commission learned in Hungary that steamship agents addressed "personal letters to prospective emigrants advising how to leave Hungary without the consent of the government. Letters of this nature were presented to the Commission. Some of them are accompanied by crudely drawn maps indicating the location of all the Hungarian control stations on the Austrian border, and the routes of travel by which such stations can be avoided."[1] It is clear that such letters can appeal only to those who have already made up their minds to emigrate. The immigrant is not as simple-minded and credulous as he is popularly represented to be. "Several American States have attempted to attract immigrants by the distribution in Europe of literature advertising the attractions of such States. A few States have sent commissioners to various countries for the purpose of inducing immigration, but although some measure of success has attended such efforts, the propaganda has had little effect on the immigration movement as a whole."[2] There appears to be no sound reason why the "editorials and articles from American newspapers relative to the prosperity of the United States," circulated by a steamship agent, should have a greater effect with the European peasant than the literature distributed by an official representative of an American State. The conclusion reached by the Immigration Commission is that "immigration from Europe proceeds according to well-defined individual plans rather than in a haphazard way."[3] The Commission qualifies this conclusion by the statement that since "selling steerage tickets to America is the sole or chief occupation of large numbers of persons in Southern and Eastern Europe," and since "these local agents, as a rule, solicit business," they "consequently encourage emigration."[4] This argument might be made broader by substituting the principal for the agent: it is the steamship companies that encourage emigration by

[1] *Reports of the Immigration Commission*, vol. 4, p. 63.
[2] *Ibid.*, vol. 1, p. 192. [3] *Ibid.*, p. 188. [4] *Ibid.*, vol. 4, p. 62.

making it their business to sell steerage tickets to America, for it is a self-evident truth that should the steamship companies discontinue the sale of steerage tickets, emigration would be discouraged. Inasmuch, however, as the Immigration Commission recognizes the difficulty for the ordinary laborer in Southern and Eastern Europe to raise the price of a steerage ticket, "no matter how strong the desire to emigrate may be," the question is, by what means the local agents encourage the emigration of impecunious laborers who have no relatives or friends in America willing to advance them the price of a ticket. The popular answer is that the "new immigration" is largely "stimulated" by employers of labor masquerading as "friends" of the immigrants. It is believed that "the ends of the earth have been ransacked in the search for the low standards of living combined with patient industriousness."[1]

Representatives of labor speak indiscriminately of all Slav and Italian immigration as "imported," in other words as contract labor. The truth is that the frequency of the practice in recent times has been greatly exaggerated by popular imagination. The investigations of the Immigration Commission, both in the United States and in Europe, failed to disclose any evidence of systematic importation of contract laborers.[2] In the Connellsville coke region of Pennsylvania, old inhabitants remember that as far back as 1882 "some companies had agents in Europe soliciting and encouraging the immigration of Slovaks, Poles, and Bohemians . . . and *some immigrants may have been imported as contract laborers.*"[3] Of what little consequence these importations could have been, is clear from the fact that eight years later, at the census of 1890, there were

[1] John R. Commons: *Races and Immigrants in America*, p. 152.

[2] The inquiries made by the Commission in Europe "did not disclose that actual contracts involving promises of employment between employers in the United States and laborers in Europe were responsible for any considerable part of the present emigration movement." *Reports*, vol. 4 p. 60. No figures or specific cases are cited. See also, further, Chapter XIX.

[3] *Ibid.*, vol. 6, p. 257.

enumerated in Fayette and Westmoreland counties (the Connellsville region) 4788 natives of Hungary, Bohemia, and Poland, of both sexes, all ages, and all occupations.[1] It is quite conceivable that in the case of a strike a great corporation might have resorted to the importation of a force of strikebreakers regardless of cost. There is a "legend" in the Pennsylvania anthracite field that during a strike in 1870 a breaker belonging to Eckley B. Coxe was burned down, whereupon he secured through his superintendent "two shiploads of his Hungarian countrymen to man the new structure. *There is no evidence of any further importations of immigrants by the mine owners, since there has been no necessity for such an effort.*"[2] With immigration running into hundreds of thousands annually, there is no economic advantage in importing a few thousand a year, as they could have no effect upon labor conditions in general.[3] On the other hand, their importation would involve an outlay of money for their passage without any guarantee of repayment, as the contract of employment could not be enforced in law in case the laborer chose to break it. It is not usual for an employer of labor in this country to advance a sum equal to a month's wages without any security to a laborer in his employ. That the personal credit of the laborer should be enhanced by his absence from the United States hardly accords with common experience. Apart from economic considerations, the Immigration Commission finds that "owing to the rigidity of the law and the fact that special provision is made for its enforcement there are probably at the present time relatively few actual contract laborers admitted."[4] This conclusion

[1] *Population of the United States, XI. Census*, vol. i., p. 654 (computed).

[2] *Reports of the Immigration Commission*, vol. 16, p. 661.

[3] A sound view of the question is taken by Prof. Adams and Dr. Sumner in their book on *Labor Problems*, where they say that under the influence of the increase of immigration it is no longer profitable to "induce" immigration (pp. 90–91).

[4] *Reports*, vol. 1, p. 29.

ought to be accepted as final. It would be impossible for any corporation or labor agent to operate on a large scale in violation of the law without being detected. Human experience has no record of a secret guarded by a multitude. The few violations of the contract labor law that elude the vigilance of the immigration officials cannot affect the labor market.

The supply of immigrant labor is regulated by free competition, like that of any other commodity. It may sometimes exceed the demand and at other times fall short of it; in the long run, however, supply adjusts itself to demand.

If we compare the totals for industrial cycles, including years of panic, of depression, and of prosperity, we find a remarkable regularity in the ratio of immigration to population. In Table 12 the addition to population through immigration during the twenty-year period 1891–1910 is collated with the corresponding figures for the preceding two periods of equal length.

TABLE 12.

POPULATION AND IMMIGRATION

Census Population		Immigration for twenty years following		
Year	Thousands	Thousands	Percentage ratio to population at preceding census	Period
1850.....	23,192	5,019	21.2	1851–1870
1870......	38,558	8,059	20.9	1871–1890
1890.....	62,622	12,483	19.9	1891–1910

These figures show that during the past sixty years, notwithstanding the fluctuations from year to year, in the long run the ratio of immigration to population has been well-nigh constant, with a slightly declining tendency as population has grown. Although the total number of immigrants for the period 1891–1910 was 50 per cent in excess of the total for the preceding period, yet the addition to population was relatively smaller during the later period.

It has also been shown (see Table 2) that the per cent distribution of immigrants by occupations has undergone little change during the past half-century, notwithstanding the rise and fall in numbers from decade to decade. The ratio of skilled mechanics has during the last thirty years remained at 20 per cent, while unskilled laborers have made up 57 per cent of all immigrants. This regularity indicates that the demand for labor determines the character, as well as the volume of immigration.

CHAPTER V

THE DEMAND FOR LABOR IN AGRICULTURE

THE preference of the "new" immigrants for city employments over agricultural pursuits is viewed with apprehension by philanthropists and sociologists. It is evident, however, that even the "desirable" immigrant from Northern and Western Europe who brings with him on an average $55[1] lacks the necessary means to rent a farm, let alone to buy one.[2] At best he can only obtain employment as a farm hand, which depends primarily upon the demand for farm labor. And here he is confronted with the fact that the American farmer cannot keep his own sons on the farm.

The industrial development of the United States has manifested itself in a relative decrease, and in some sections in a numerical decrease of the rural population. In New England and New York an actual depopulation of the rural districts was recorded by the census of 1890. The next census showed a loss of rural population in New Jersey, Delaware, Ohio, and Kansas. Maryland and Illinois sustained similar losses from 1880 to 1890, but recovered them within the next ten years.[3] The published bulletins of the last census show a numerical decrease of the rural population in the following States of the Central West:

[1] *Reports of the Immigration Commission*, vol. 4 (in press).

[2] The average value per farm, exclusive of real estate, in 1900, amounted to $1173. H. W. Quaintance: *The Influence of Farm Machinery on Production and Labor*, p. 58.

[3] *Supplementary Analysis, XII. Census*, p. 78, Table XXXIX.

TABLE 13.

DECREASE OF THE POPULATION OF RURAL TERRITORY, 1900–1910

State	Number	Per cent
Illinois............	111,963	7.0
Indiana...........	132,266	9.5
Iowa..............	152,673	12.1
Kansas............	4,919	0.5
Michigan..........	9,946	0.8
Missouri..........	133,489	8.0
Ohio..............	93,055	5.3
Wisconsin.........	8,201	0.7

Even where the total rural population of a State has increased since 1900, the maps given in the census bulletins show a few agricultural counties with a declining population.

This depopulation of rural territory is due to emigration of native Americans of native stock. The figures for 1910 are as yet not available; the census of 1900 recorded in Kansas a loss of 2.8 per cent of the native population of native parentage in settlements of less than 2500 inhabitants, and in Nebraska a loss of 1.3 per cent of the same element. In New England, New York, and New Jersey the loss was still greater; the maximum was reached in Connecticut, viz., 16.7 per cent.[1]

The popular way to account for a social phenomenon is to seek an explanation in the personal tastes and dislikes of individuals or racial groups. "Much has been said of a mad rush to cities," said Prof. Charles H. Cooley before the Michigan Political Science Association, in July, 1902, "and the movement has often been spoken of as if it were altogether a kind of dissipation, like going to the saloon. But if there were no solider ground for the migration than this we should find the migrants plunged into pauperism and vice after they get to the cities, instead of pursuing useful remunerative labor as is ordinarily the case. The real causes of the decrease of rural population are chiefly economic." These causes affect the native and the foreign

[1] *Supplementary Analysis, XII. Census*, pp. 620–627, Tables 10 and 11.

DIAGRAM IV.

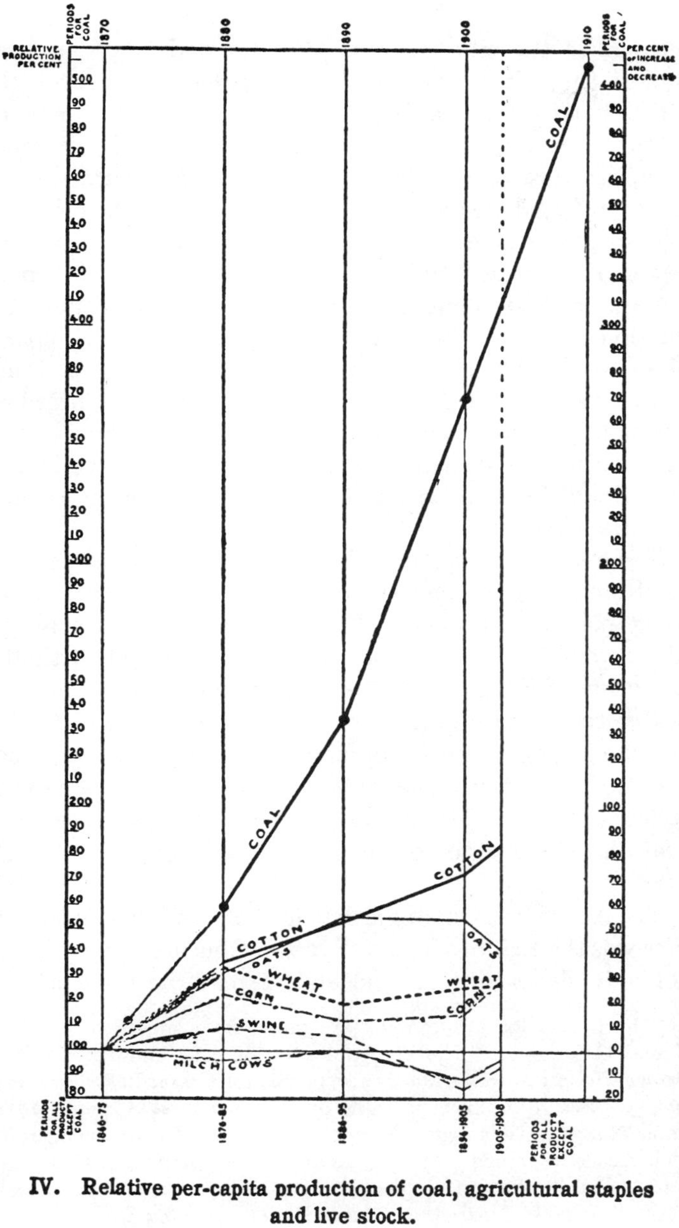

IV. Relative per-capita production of coal, agricultural staples and live stock.

current to the cities alike. Since the early days of Irish and German immigration the growing industries of the cities have offered a better market for labor than agriculture. A comparative view of the demand for labor in agriculture and in industry since 1870 is furnished in Diagram IV, where the per capita production of the principal agricultural staples and live stock is compared with the per capita production of coal, the latter being chosen as the measure of industrial expansion.[1] Whereas the production of coal has quadrupled, the increase of the output of cotton is only about 90 per cent, the increase of other farm products less than 50 per cent, and stock breeding has not kept pace with the increase of population. It is patent that the demand for farm hands must have lagged far behind the demand for labor in manufacturing, mining and transportation.

The relative number of persons engaged in agriculture fell from 21.79 per cent of the total population in 1840 to 15.43 per cent in 1870. This decrease was not confined to any one State or section, but was universal, with the exception of Florida. In New York and all New England States there was during the same period an absolute decrease of the agricultural population from 869,000 to 697,000, *i. e.*, 20 per cent.[2] The revolution wrought in American farming by the industrial development of the past seventy years has tended to reduce the demand for labor on the farm.

The American farm of the first half of the nineteenth century was the seat of a highly diversified business, comprising not only the raising of food and of material for clothing,

[1] The figures for Diagram IV are taken from an article by Prof. Homer C. Price on "The Reorganization of American Farming" in *Popular Science Monthly*, May, 1910, p. 464; the *Census Report on Mines and Quarries*, 1902, p. 669, Table 6; and *Statistical Abstract*, 1911, Table No. 335. The figures for agricultural products are averages for each decade beginning 1866–1875 and for the quadrennial period 1905–1908. Coal production per capita is for each census year since 1870.

[2] *Bulletin of the Department of Labor*, No. 11, pp. 400, 402.

but also the preparation and manufacture of these products.[1] Wakefield, in 1833, gave the following description of the American farmer:

> Free Americans, who cultivate the soil, follow many other occupations. Some portion of the furniture and tools which they use is commonly made by themselves. They frequently build their own houses, and carry to market, at whatever distance, the produce of their own industry. They are spinners and weavers, they make soap and candles, as well as, in many cases, shoes and clothes for their own use.[2]

With such a variety of occupations there was work for a hired man at all seasons of the year. But the development of manufactures has differentiated from the farming business one industry after another and removed them from the farm.[3] The time during which a hired man can be kept employed on the farm has been reduced in consequence to a few months in the year.

Still until the middle of the nineteenth century the mills were quite commonly run by water power, the supply of which determined their location. The small country towns were alive with little industries, which offered to the farm laborer a prospect of employment during the winter when work was scarce on the farm.[4] But the general substitution of steam for water power and the consequent concentration of industry removed the factories from the small towns to

[1] L. H. Bailey: *The State and the Farmer*, pp. 6, 7.

[2] E. G. Wakefield: *England and America*, vol. i., pp. 21, 22.

[3] "At the present time, throughout probably the greater part of the country . . . butter-making is ordinarily done away from the farm," but in 1870, "butter was made . . . on the farms and as part of farm work. The development of the agricultural implement industry is another instance. The manufacture of the implements and machines from being a feature of farm work has become a distinct branch of manufactures, employing, according to the returns of the XII census, during the census year reported on, an 'average number' of 46,582 persons besides 10,046 salaried officials, clerks, etc."—M. W. Quaintance, *loc. cit.*, pp. 44–45, 74.

[4] *Report of the Industrial Commission*, vol. x., pp. cl. and 889. *Report on Condition of Woman and Child Wage-Earners in the United States*, vol. ix., p. 48.

the great manufacturing cities. The opportunity to earn a full year's wages in a rural community was gone, and the farm laborer followed the factory to the city.[1]

Along with the progress of division of labor between farm and factory, the invention of labor-saving machinery tended to displace the wage-earner from agriculture. Down to the middle of the nineteenth century the agricultural methods of the American farmer were as primitive as those of the Russian peasant of the present. The first patent for a cast-iron plow was granted as early as 1797, but it took many years before it had overcome the prejudice of the farmers who believed that the use of cast-iron "poisoned the land." About 1850, cast-iron plows had come into general use, but grass was still mowed with the scythe, grain was cut with the sickle and threshed with the flail. Flailing and winnowing grain was the chief farm work of the winter. As late as the year 1870, the editor of the *New American Farm Book* questioned the advisability of using the large threshing machines and advised for the "moderate farmer" the use of a hand thresher as the more economical, permitting the work to be done "in winter, when there is more leisure to do it." Corn was planted by hand, cultivated with the hoe, and shelled by scraping the ears against the handle of a frying pan or the blade of a shovel. The cultivation of a farm in this crude way required a great deal of labor and sustained a steady demand for farm help in all seasons. To-day "there is hardly a phase of farm work that has not been essentially changed by the introduction of some new implement or machine." For planting corn

> the farmer now uses a check-row planter drawn by horses and depositing the seed at regular intervals so that the rows may be cultivated with equal facility either in the direction of the planting or across. As a means of cultivating the corn . . . the farmer quite commonly uses a riding plow. Steam power corn-huskers and corn-shellers are found. Instead of the old hand-method of shelling corn . . . by which . . .

[1] *Report of the Industrial Commission*, vol. x., p. cxlix.

hardly six bushels could be shelled in a day, the farmer may now have his corn shelled at the rate of a bushel a minute and the machine which does the work will also "carry off the cobs to a pile or into a wagon, and deliver the corn into sacks." Mowing machines, horse hay-rakes, tedders, and stackers have revolutionized the work of making hay. It formerly required eleven hours of man-labor to cut and cure a ton of hay. Now the same work may be done in one hour and thirty minutes.

"The increased effectiveness of man-labor power when aided by the use of machinery . . . varies from 150 per cent in the case of rye to 2244 per cent in the case of barley." On the whole, the quantity of labor now requisite for the production of the principal crop averages "a little over one fifth of the quantity which would be requisite under the former hand methods of cultivation." Confining the comparison to the period of the "new immigration," "we shall find that the effectiveness of the average (agricultural) worker in the United States was greater, by nearly 60 per cent, in 1900 than in 1880."

The quantity of labor saved by machinery in producing the average crop of the last decade of the past century, as compared with hand methods in use in the middle of the century, is estimated by Professor Quaintance at 450,000,000 days.[1] The saving represents the labor of one and a half million men working three hundred days in the year. This figure suggests the reason why the new immigration does not go to the farming sections of the United States. As the per capita production of agricultural staples did not increase as fast as the efficiency of agricultural implements and machinery, there was an actual as well as a relative displacement of labor. The same writer estimates the average quantity of labor spent in producing the annual crops of the principal cereals during the period from 1840 to 1870, at 173,000,000 work days, and the average number of work days used for producing the annual crops of the period 1893–1896, at 120,000,000. There was accordingly an actual displace-

[1] Quaintance, *loc. cit.*, pp. 7, 8, 10, 18, 23, 30, 73.

ment of 42 per cent of farm labor.[1] Since the number of farmers had meantime increased, there must have been an actual decrease in the number of hired farm hands. In North Dakota a farmer who owns two quarter-sections of land generally takes care of the farm himself, with his family, until spring, and employs very little help during his busy season.[2] As a rule, agricultural laborers are in demand only during the harvesting season.

In consequence of limited demand, "agricultural labor is . . . the least paid of all the great groups of occupations, even allowing for the laborer's garden and other privileges."[3] Aside from the consensus of expert opinion, this fact is established by statistical evidence for Kansas and California. The former is predominantly agricultural, the latter industrial, but the XIII. Census shows an increase of 71.2 per cent in the value of implements and machinery since 1900, an increase of 89.2 per cent in the value of live stock, and an increase of 34.5 per cent in the rural population of California. Judged by the increase in the value of buildings and machinery since 1900 both States are representative of the average for the United States.[4] Their wage statistics may therefore be accepted as typical (see Tables 14 and 15).

The hours of labor on the farms are longer than even in the steel mills of Pennsylvania. In the Northwest and in the South the general custom is to work from sunrise until sunset; in Maryland the hours of labor in the dairying business are generally from 4 or 5 o'clock in the morning to 7 or 8 o'clock at night, and about the same in other agricultural pursuits.[5] It is true that the hours are so long

[1] Quaintance, *loc. cit.*, pp. 32–33.

[2] *Report of the Industrial Commission*, vol. x., p. 846. More than one half of the farms of North Dakota at the XII. Census were of a smaller size.—*XII. Census, Agriculture*, Part I., Table 4, pp. 30 *et seq.*

[3] *Report of the Industrial Commission*, vol. x., pp. xx. See also *Bulletin of the Bureau of Labor*, No. 72 (September, 1907), p. 406.

[4] *XIII. Census*, vol. i, *Population*, p. 62, Table 39; vol. v., *Agriculture*, p. 79, Table 29.

[5] *Report of the Industrial Commission*, vol. x., pp. xx., cxix., cxx., cxxi. The witness from Maryland testified that he "once heard a public

TABLE 14.

AVERAGE ANNUAL EARNINGS OF FARM LABORERS IN KANSAS, COMPARED WITH EARNINGS IN SIMILAR NON-AGRICULTURAL OCCUPATIONS IN THE SAME STATE, 1900.[1]

Occupation	Number reported	Average annual earnings	Average number of days unemployed	Average number of hours per day
Laborers:				
On farms.........	35	$296[2]	51	11.6
In building trades.	19	323	93	9.3
On railroads......	637	335	..	..
Coal miners......	24	357	113	8.4

TABLE 15.

DISTRIBUTION OF WHITE MALE LABORERS, EMPLOYED IN AGRICULTURE AND OTHER PURSUITS IN CALIFORNIA, BY RATES OF WAGES PER WEEK (WITHOUT BOARD), 1906.[3]

Character of employment	Number reported			Per cent		
	$12.00 or less	Over $12.00	Total	$12.00 or less	Over $12.00	Total
Agriculture.................	689	15	704	97.9	2.1	100
Stores and factories.........	2156	1964	4120	52.3	47.7	100
Lumber woods and saw mills	1610	3492	5102	31.6	68.4	100
Railway construction in and around San Francisco...	556	1746	2302	24.2	75.8	100

speaker say that the farmers settled the eight-hour question by having eight hours before dinner and eight after."

[1] *XVI. Annual Report of the Kansas Bureau of Labor*, pp. 128–131, 153.

[2] Including the cost of board for ten months estimated at $90, given in Table 2, p. 122.

[3] Compiled from *XII. Biennial Report of the Bureau of Labor Statistics of the State of California (1905–1906)*, pp. 76–77, 80–161, 165.

only in harvest and threshing time. After the rush is over the working day averages about ten hours. But at that time very few laborers are retained on the farms.

Long hours, small pay, and irregular employment are what the immigrant can expect on a farm. His preference for other employment seems to call for no explanation by special racial characteristics; it is merely another illustration of the rule that immigration follows the demand for labor. "In the settlement of agricultural districts a point is reached beyond which any considerable growth of agricultural population is possible only if there is a change to more intensive forms of agriculture. . . . If there is no such change, the further growth of population must consist in the development of urban or non-agricultural communities."[1]

This point has been reached in the United States. The public domain has practically all passed into private occupation. Land values during the last decade have climbed to unheard-of heights.[2] At the same time Western Canada offers to settlers vast areas of public land practically free.

[1] *XII. Census, Supplementary Analysis*, p. 303.

[2] The highest average value per acre in 1900 was found for Illinois, viz., $46. At the XIII. Census the following States exceeded that maximum:

State	*Value per acre*
California	$47.00
New Jersey	48.00
Ohio	53.00
Indiana	62.00
Iowa	82.00
Illinois	95.00

The lowest average value in 1900 was in Wyoming, viz., $2.88; in 1910 the average value in that State reached $10.00 per acre. The lowest average in 1910 was $8.77, computed for New Mexico. The average value per acre for the United States doubled from 1900 to 1910, but the maximum increase was as high as 475 per cent, viz., from $6.00 to $34.00 in Arizona. *XIII. Census*, vol. v., *Agriculture*, p. 80, Table 30.

It seems that for some time to come the Canadian Northwest will furnish the same opportunities for extensive agriculture as the Western States did a generation ago. Western farmers find it profitable to dispose of their land in the United States and to take up public land in Western Canada.[1] The emigration of American farmers to Canada has reached considerable proportions.[2] In the United States a market for agricultural labor may grow up in the future with the eventual spread of intensive agriculture. But this is a problem for the American farmer to solve. The immigrant should not be burdened with the mission to reform the methods of American agriculture.

[1] The average value of land and buildings per farm in Iowa increased from the XII. to the XIII. Census by more than $8000. Practically all of this represented increased land value. "Canadian officials estimate that in the fiscal year 1909 the United States emigrants brought to Canada, in stock, cash, and effects, upwards of $60,000,000." (*Reports of the Immigration Commission*, vol. 2, p. 616.) This is equivalent to an average of $1000 per individual immigrant, or to $4000 per family.

[2] In 1910 the number of emigrants from the United States to Canada reached 103,984.—*Ibid.*

CHAPTER VI

UNEMPLOYMENT

A. The Causes of Unemployment

AS far back as 1901 Prof. John R. Commons, in his report on immigration prepared for the Industrial Commission, reached the conclusion that immigrants come to this country "in obedience to the opportunities for employment."[1] Still the force of statistics must apparently yield to the living proof, furnished by the ever-present "army of the unemployed," that there are already more men than jobs in the United States. There seems to be no escape from the conclusion that every new immigrant, in order to live, must take away the job from some one else who has been here before.[2] A study of the sources of unemployment shows the fallacy of the premises upon which the popular argument is based.

Unemployment in its present form is a problem peculiar to our industrial system, but alternations of work and involuntary idleness were incidents of the life on the old New England farm as well. The disappearance of slavery in New England was in no small degree due to the long winters during which the time of the negro slave could not be fully

[1] *Report of the Industrial Commission*, vol. xv., p. 309.

[2] "The popular conception is of industry as rigidly limited—a sphere of cast iron in which men struggle for living room; in which the greater the room taken by any one man the less must there be for others; in which the greater the number of men the worst must be the case of all."—W. H. Beveridge: *Unemployment, a Problem of Industry*, p. 11.

employed. The introduction of the factory system in New England at the close of the eighteenth century was advocated on the ground that it would "give employment to a great number of persons, especially females who now eat the bread of idleness."[1]

On the old farm, however, work and leisure were shared by all members of the household and all were supported by the work of the busy months. The differentiation of lumbering, dairying, slaughtering, tool making, canning, spinning, weaving, dressmaking, etc., from farming has destroyed the former co-ordination of those occupations. Nowadays, whenever work in any of them grows scarce, some of the workers are cut off from the pay-roll and become "unemployed."

The most generally recognized cause of unemployment is seasonal variation of business activity. According to the census of 1900, among masons and plasterers more than one half were out of work a portion of the year. Next follow brick- and tile-makers, of whom nearly one half were at times unemployed. Among paper-hangers, the proportion was 44 per cent; among carpenters and painters, over 40 per cent; among fishermen, about one half; among sailors, one third. All these occupations are dependent upon the weather. Other trades are dependent upon and decline with these. Then there are trades dependent partly upon the weather and partly upon social customs; more than one fourth (27 per cent) of all tailors were out of work at some period during the year 1900.[2] In the busiest season the supply of labor in such trades may oftentimes be short of the demand, necessitating overtime work;

[1] Helen L. Sumner: "History of Women in Industry in the United States," *Report on Condition of Woman and Child Wage-Earners in United States*, vol. ix., p. 43. See also pp. 38, 39. In the early years of the nineteenth century the mills employed many farm girls who were "not constantly at work, but as they had leisure from other household employment."—*Ibid.*, p. 47. See also Simons: *Social Forces in American History*, p. 172 *et seq.*

[2] *Occupations at the XII. Census*, Tables LXXXVII., and XC.

yet even this shortage of labor will not save a portion of the force engaged in such trades from idleness at other times of the year. A reduction of the number of competitors for positions in such trades would obviously not relieve the situation. Masonry may serve as an example. Out of every 1000 masons 555 were unemployed some time during the census year 1900 and there was steady work all year around for only 445.[1] Could the number of masons in the United States have been reduced to the 445 who had steady work in 1900, unemployment would thereby not have been eliminated. On the contrary, many of the 445 who were employed all year around when there were 555 more masons in busy times would have lost part of their working time with the exclusion of their competitors. The explanation of this apparent paradox is that there is steady work on a building for about one half of the total number employed at the busiest time—probably inside work which does not depend upon the weather. But a building cannot be constructed all inside. If the number of masons were reduced from 1000 to 500, the building operations at the busiest season would necessarily have to be reduced one half, with the result that during the slack season there would be only enough inside work for 250 and the other 195 of the 445 who had steady work in 1900 would now go idle. The same condition exists to a greater or lesser degree in many other industries.

In order to eliminate unemployment it would be necessary to dovetail the busy and the slack seasons in the various industries upon such a plan as would produce an even distribution of the work of the nation over all seasons of the year. This might be possible if all mines, mills, and transportation lines were operated by one nation-wide combine. Such an adjustment of half a million independent business establishments, however, is not feasible for more than one season. In the first place, the periods of the highest and lowest demand for labor are largly contemporaneous, in

[1] *Occupations at the XII. Census*, p. ccxxxii., Table CX.

all industries (see Diagram V).[1] The highest number employed in manufactures, in the United States as a whole as well as in every one of the principal States, is found in the spring and in the fall, the lowest in winter. The workman who is laid off in January has, as a rule, no opportunity to secure other work.

In the second place, even when the slack period in one industry coincides with the busiest period in another, the mobility of labor is quite limited. The skilled trades admit of no shifting from one occupation to another. May was the busiest month of the year 1899 (see Diagram V). In 51 industries an additional force of 400,000 men was at work in excess of the permanent force employed at all times of the year, including the slack season. On the other hand, there were four industries for which May was the dullest month, but the aggregate number laid off in those industries was less than 7000. And yet with all that demand for labor some of them must have remained out of work. There were, *e.g.*, 1924 idle jewelry workers. Help was wanted in brick yards, 74,000 men; carpenter shops, 71,000; custom tailoring shops, 16,000; carriage and wagon shops, 14,000; planing mills, 13,000; cigar factories, 6000; cheese factories, 5000, etc. There was not a single industry, however, among the 51, which could furnish employment to the 1924 idle jewelry workers.[2] Had every one of the extra 400,000 men been deported to Europe, the 1924 idle jewelers would nevertheless have remained unemployed. Even if all the laborers in the brickyards were of unadulterated Puritan stock, a jewelry worker would consider it beneath his social status to do rough work in a brickyard while waiting for the resumption of work at Tiffany's. The natural tendency is for the fact of seasonal fluctuation to be recognized as a normal incident of the industry and to be allowed for in the standard of wages.

The only class of labor which is capable of shifting from

[1] Based upon figures of *XII. Census Report on Manufactures*, vol. 1, Table 3, p. 62.

[2] See Appendix, Table II.

DIAGRAM V.

Scale for States: 1 unit = 10,000. For the United States: 1 unit = 100,000.

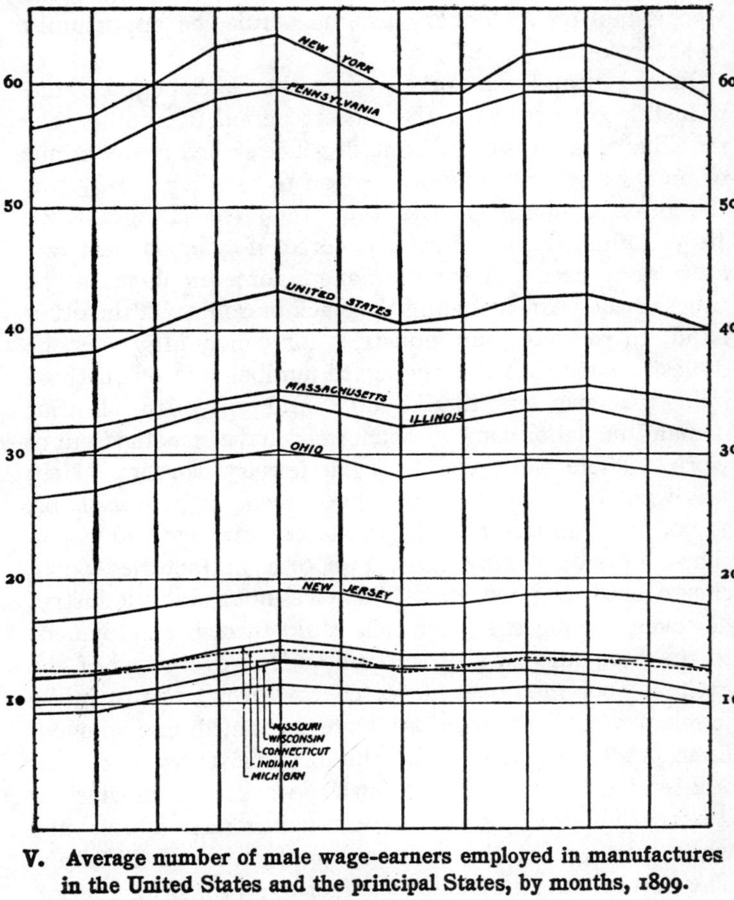

V. Average number of male wage-earners employed in manufactures in the United States and the principal States, by months, 1899.

one industry to another is unskilled labor. Yet the localization of industries sets also a limit to the mobility of unskilled labor. By way of illustration let us compare the iron and steel and the lumber industry. Both employ large numbers of unskilled laborers. The variation between the greatest and the least number of men employed is over 200,000 in the latter and only 80,000 in the former. Assuming that busy and dull times dovetail in the two industries, we shall nevertheless find interchange of unskilled labor between them restricted by geographical location. Nearly one half of the iron and steel workers are employed in Pennsylvania; there were 38,000 of them unemployed at one time or another in 1899, whereas the highest number of extra men hired during the same year in the lumber industry of the same State was about 9000; more than three fourths of the idle iron and steel workers of Pennsylvania could find no employment in the lumber industry within their own State. The same was true of Ohio, where there were at one time or another 13,000 unemployed iron and steel workers, while only 6300 temporary men found employment in the lumber industry within the same State. Men were wanted in the lumber camps of Michigan, Wisconsin, and Minnesota,[1] but the laborer who is employed on and off in a steel mill around Pittsburgh will not take the risk in the intervals to hunt for a temporary job in the lumber camps of Minnesota.

The local and seasonal divergencies between the supply of and the demand for labor have called into existence the labor agent or the "padrone," whose business is that of a broker in the labor market. To declaim against him is as futile as to condemn the broker in the Produce Exchange. The casual or "discontinuous" laborer in New York City has no means to learn that men are wanted by a railway company in the West or South. The labor agent, who is in communication with railway companies, building contractors, and other great employers of labor, renders a service

[1] *XII. Census, Manufactures*, Part I, Table 4, pp. 254–255, 286–291.

both to the employer and to the laborer. Being in business for profit, he charges a commission for his services. That a broker of this class is apt to take advantage of his client does not mark him as an exception to the general run of mankind in kindred occupations. It is a common error to think that the labor agent is the specific product of Italian or Greek immigration. We learn from the recent report of Dr. Helen L. Sumner on the *History of Women in Industry in the United States* that during the early years of the factory system, before the era of immigration, the New England factories "put forth systematic efforts to attract the farmers' daughters of the surrounding country." A common

> method of securing girls for the factories was to send out agents to the country districts who were paid a stipulated sum per head for hiring girls. As early as 1831 the Dedham (Mass.) *Patriot* announced that "a valuable cargo, consisting of 50 females, was recently imported into this State from 'Down East' by one of the Boston packets. . . ." The Cabotville *Chronicle* spoke in 1864 of a "long, low, black, wagon" which makes regular trips to the North of the State, cruising around in Vermont and New Hampshire with a "commander" whose heart must be as black as his craft, who is paid a dollar a head for all he brings to the market, and more in proportion to the distance, if they bring them from such a distance that they cannot easily get back. This is done by "hoisting false colors," and representing to the girls that they can tend more machinery than is possible and that the work is so very neat, and the wages such that they can dress in silks and spend half their time in reading.[1]

The abuses of unscrupulous labor agents must not blind us, however, to the fact that they perform a necessary social function, viz., that of distributing the labor supply where it is wanted. The main shortcoming of this system of distribution of labor is its inadequacy. The total number of laborers shipped by all employment agencies out of New York City to twenty-six States in more than two years (May 1, 1904, to July 31, 1906) was only 40,737,[2] *i.e.*, about

[1] *Report on Condition of Woman and Child Wage-Earners in the United States*, vol. ix., pp. 80–81

[2] Frank J. Sheridan: "Italian, Slavic, and Hungarian Unskilled Im-

17,000 a year. The total number of laborers who were unemployed at any time during the census year 1900 (the latest for which data are available) was 40,108[1] and the rate of unemployment in 1904–1906, as far as can be judged, was about the same as in 1900.[2] It is safe to say that the labor agencies were able to place outside of New York City less than one half of all unemployed laborers. The majority stayed in New York waiting for work "to pick up."

We come next to the cyclical fluctuations of business which result in variations of the number employed from year to year. A temporary decline in business means unemployment for a number of wage-earners who were employed the year before. Such fluctuations of business occur in countries with a net emigration, like Great Britain, or in France whose population is practically stationary, as well as in the United States. The effect of these fluctuations of business activity "is the requirement in each trade of reserves of labor to meet the fluctuations of work incidental to years of prosperity."[3] An illustration of the range of these cyclical fluctuations is given in Diagram VI. on p. 125.[4]

The most important cause of unemployment in point of numbers affected, however, is to be found in the fact that "the actual demand is that of each of many separate employers in many different places."[5] The effect of this "dissipation of the demand for labor in each trade"[6] upon

---

migrant Laborers in United States," *Bulletin of the Bureau of Labor*, No. 72, p. 417.

[1] *Occupations at the XII. Census*, Table XLIII., p. 634.

[2] According to the statistics of the New York Bureau of Labor, the ratio of unemployed in 1900 was 21.0 per cent; in 1904, 30.5 per cent; in 1905, 14.6 per cent and in 1906, 8.6 per cent, averaging for 1904–1906, 17.9 per cent. (*Report of the New York Bureau of Labor Statistics*, 1908, p. xviii., Table 10.) While these figures relate to members of labor unions only, they may serve as a standard of comparison of general business conditions in various years.

[3] Beveridge, *loc. cit.*, p. 13.

[4] Based on *Report of the New York Bureau of Labor Statistics*, 1910, p. viii.

[5] Beveridge, *loc. cit.*, p. 10.

[6] *Ibid.*, p. 13.

the mass of wage-earners can be measured by the difference between the aggregate number of hands required by all establishments at their busiest seasons and the aggregate minimum number employed when business is at its lowest ebb. To be sure, this difference does not represent the amount of unemployment at any given date, since the seasonal variations are not simultaneous in all industries and a considerable portion of the unskilled laborers readily shift from one industry to another. But every change of position involves some period of unemployment, as it requires some time to find a new job. This is clearly demonstrated by the census statistics of manufactures. The difference between the greatest and the least average number employed during any month in the year is far short of the difference between the aggregate greatest and the aggregate least number employed in all establishments during the same year, as shown in Table 16 next below:

TABLE 16.

RANGE OF FLUCTUATIONS OF EMPLOYMENT, 1899 AND 1904[1]

Number employed (thousands)	1899		1904	
	Simultaneously, monthly average	Aggregate in all establishments at any time during the year	Simultaneously, monthly average	Aggregate in all establishments at any time during the year
Maximum......	5567	7069	5677	7017
Minimum......	4938	4527	5262	4599
Difference....	629	2545	415	2418
Percentage to aggregate minimum.	14	56	9	53

[1] Compiled from *XII. Census Report on Manufactures*, Part I, p. 59, Table 3; *Census Report on Manufactures*, 1905, Part I, p. lxxix., Table XXVII.

In order to ascertain the total number of wage-earners who had steady employment during the year, the number employed by each individual manufacturer on the slackest day in his own business must be added to similar numbers for all others, though the days may not have coincided. It appears that this number was less than the lowest monthly average, which means that even in the worst month of the year more people are wanted on an average than can be given permanent employment. On the other hand, while during the best month of the year 1899 only fourteen additional wage-earners were needed over and above every one hundred who had permanent employment, actually four times as many persons were hired for temporary jobs during the same year. In 1904, the proportion was still more striking, the number of persons hired temporarily was nearly six times greater than the actual temporary force needed at the busiest time during the year. In either year there were over one half as many temporary jobs as permanent positions. Of course, these figures comprise many duplications; there may have been few wage-earners over the greatest number that could actually have been employed at the same time; in that case each of the temporary employees had about four different jobs during the year 1899 and six during the year 1904. The unemployment intervening between one temporary job and another clearly did not depend upon the number of applicants for jobs, but was determined by the vicissitudes of business.

The whole problem of unemployment is admirably elucidated in Mr. Beveridge's exhaustive treatise on the subject, from which the following is condensed:

A general and normal excess of the supply of labor over the demand appears to be explicable only by an excessively rapid increase of population. But such an explanatior does not square with the facts showing irreducible minimum of unemployment precisely in those industries which have grown with exceptional rapidity in recent years.

The general formula for the supply of labor in an industry appears to be this: for work requiring, if concentrated at one spot, at most ninety-eight men, there will actually be eighty in regular employment; there will be a hundred in all, so that at all times two at least are out of work. The twenty, however, are as much part of the industrial system as are the eighty; the reserve is as indispensable as the regulars. The idleness, now of some, now of others, of the reserve is mainly responsible for the irreducible minimum of unemployment. The figures here given have only an illustrative value; the proportion of regular and reserve and irreducible minimum vary from trade to trade. The principle is of the greatest generality. The rule for each trade is to have more men than are called for together even at the busiest moment.

The normal state of every industry is to be overcrowded with labor, in the sense of having drawn into it more men than can ever find employment in it at any one time. This is the direct consequence of the work of each industry being distributed between many separate employees each subject to fluctuations of fortune. *It depends upon the nature of the demand for labor, not upon the volume of the whole supply.*

To speak of the reserve of labor in a trade may become, in fact, only another way of speaking of the whole volume of unemployment in it. The change, however, is not one of words alone. It implies a revolution of mental attitude. It involves perception of unemployment, not as a thing standing by itself—an inexplicable excrescence on the industrial system—but as a thing directly related to that system and as necessary to it as are capital and labor themselves.

Unemployment is not to be identified as a problem of general over-population. Unemployment arises because, while the supply of labor grows steadily, the demand for labor, in growing, varies incessantly in volume, distribution, and character. This variation in several of its forms at least flows directly from the control of production by many competing employers. It is obvious that, so long as the industrial world is split up into separate groups of producers—each group with a life of its own, and growing or decaying in ceaseless attrition upon its neighbors—there must be insecurity of employment. Unemployment, in other words, is to some extent at least part of the price of industrial competition—part of the waste without which there could be no competition at all.[1]

B. Unemployment and Immigration

It has been shown that unemployment does not depend upon the volume of the supply of labor, but is determined by the nature of the demand for labor, which produces a "relative surplus-population." Is it not possible, however

[1] Beveridge, *loc. cit.*, pp. 70, 76, 99, 100, 103, 235.—"A surplus laboring population is . . . a condition of existence of the capitalist mode of

DIAGRAM VI.

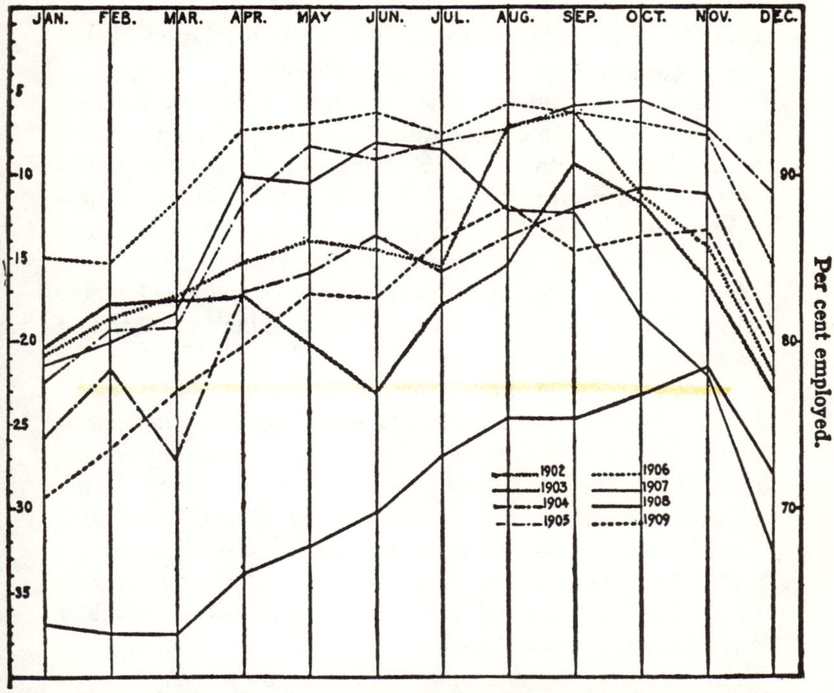

VI. Per cent. of employed and unemployed members of trade unions in the State of New York, by months, 1902–1909.

production. . . . With accumulation, and the development of productiveness of labor that accompanies it, the power of sudden expansion of capital grows also. . . . There must be the possibility of throwing great masses of men suddenly on the decisive points without injury to the scale of production in other spheres. . . . The whole form of the movement of modern industry depends, therefore, upon the constant transformation of a part of the laboring population into unemployed or half-employed hands. . . . Taking them as a whole, the general movements of wages are exclusively regulated by the expansion and contraction of the industrial reserve army. . . . They are, therefore, not determined by the variations of the absolute number of the working population, but by the varying proportions in which the working class is divided into active and reserve army, by the increase or diminution in the relative amount of the surplus population."—Karl Marx, *Capital*, part I., ch. xxv., sec. 3.

that the effects of "the normal glutting of the labor market"[1] may be aggravated by immigration?

It is asserted, indeed, on the strength of the investigation of the Immigration Commission "that the point of complete saturation has already been reached in the employment of recent immigrants in mining and manufacturing establishments."[2] The Commission holds "that even with the remarkable expansion of industry during the past few years there has been created an oversupply of unskilled labor, which "is reflected in a curtailed number of working days."[3]

It is further argued that the oversupply of unskilled labor indirectly affects the skilled trades; more workers who might otherwise find employment as unskilled laborers are pushed up the scale to compete for skilled positions. This is especially felt in slack seasons when skilled mechanics would welcome any kind of work, even unskilled, which would tide them over the hard times. But the oversupply of unskilled labor restricts their opportunities in this field and intensifies competition in the skilled trades. When two competitors apply for one job in an overstocked labor market, the cheaper man will outbid the other. It is accordingly inevitable that the immigrant with a lower standard of living must displace the American workman.

If this theory is correct, we must find a higher percentage of unemployment among the native than among the foreign-born breadwinners. In fact, however, we find the following percentages of unemployment ascertained by the census for

[1] Beveridge, *loc. cit.*, p. 13.

[2] Jenks and Lauck, *loc. cit.*, p. 197.

[3] *Reports of the Immigration Commission*, vol. 1, p. 39. The Commission does not consistently adhere to this view. Elsewhere, in discussing the causes of the outward movement of immigrants leaving the United States permanently, the Commission says: "That it is not due to lack of opportunity for employment, except in a period of depression, is evident from the fact that there is a steady influx of European laborers who have little or no difficulty in finding employment here."—*Ibid.*, vol. 4 (in press).

1900: native white males, 21.2 per cent; foreign white males 21.0 per cent.[1]

The difference between the two classes is negligible. The figures do not sustain the theory that the immigrants have an advantage over the native American workmen in the matter of securing employment. Has the "cheap" immigrant a better chance to hold his job, once secured, than the native American workman? An answer to this question is found in the following table reproduced from the *Reports of the Immigration Commission*, vol. 8, p. 87.

TABLE 17.

PER CENT DISTRIBUTION OF NATIVE AND FOREIGN-BORN MALE IRON AND STEEL WORKERS 16 YEARS OF AGE AND OVER BY NUMBER OF MONTHS OF EMPLOYMENT

Number of months employed	Native born		Foreign born
	Of native father	Of foreign father	
9 and over	60.2	50.2	41.4
6 and under 9	23.4	28.3	32.3
3 and under 6	13.5	17.1	20.1
Less than 3	2.9	4.4	6.2
Total	100.0	100.0	100.0

[1] *Occupations at the XII. Census*, p. ccxxvi. The census averages for unemployment among female breadwinners are not reliable. The highest ratios of unemployment were found among school teachers, 61.2 per cent, and in agricultural pursuits, 44.3 per cent, (p. ccxxxi), whereas the ratio for manufactures was 22.4 per cent, for domestic and personal service, 17.1 per cent, and for trade and transportation, 11.1 per cent (p. ccxxviii). The teachers' vacation was included by the compilers of the census data under unemployment. Similarly, we find that in most of the census tables on occupations female members of farmers' families who were helping on the farm were lumped together with hired help under the common designation of "agricultural laborers." These "farm laborers (members of family)" numbered two thirds of all "agricultural laborers" (*ibid.*, p. 7). The part of the year when there was no work for them on the farm was also counted as "unemployment."

The statistics of the Immigration Commission do not show that the immigrant holds his position longer than the American-born workman. On the contrary, in the iron and steel industry, which is among those most affected by immigration, the native workman is given more steady employment than the immigrant.

If there exists a causal connection between immigration and unemployment, we must expect to find more unemployment in those sections of the United States where the immigrants are mostly concentrated. This assumption is disproved by Table 18 next following:

TABLE 18.

COMPARATIVE PERCENTAGES OF UNEMPLOYED AND OF FOREIGN-BORN BREADWINNERS BY GEOGRAPHICAL DIVISIONS, 1900[1]

Geographical divisions	Ratio of foreign white to total number of breadwinners	Ratio of breadwinners unemployed during a portion of the year to total number in each class and division	
		Manufacturing and mechanical pursuits	Domestic and personal service (including laborers)
Continental United States	*19.7*	*27.2*	*28.1*
South Atlantic	2.9	25.2	28.1
South Central	3.7	28.6	31.0
North Central	23.5	29.5	30.7
Western	27.7	28.1	28.6
North Atlantic	31.5	25.7	24.3

As a result of this method of classification, the number of "unemployed" female agricultural laborers (293,707) exceeded by nearly one third the total number of hired female farm help (222,597). These two classes of occupations furnished two fifths of all unemployed females (494,202 out of a total of 1,241,492), while the ratio of foreign-born was only 5.3 per cent for teachers and 0.8 per cent for agricultural laborers (*ibid.*, pp. 10–11, Table 2). In consequence the average percentage of "unemployment" for native white women in all occupations appears to be higher than for foreign-born. It is evident that the census data on unemploy ent among women are misleading, which is conceded in the census report.

[1] *Occupations at the XII. Census*, Table XCIII., pp. lxxxi., ccxxxv., and ccxxxvi., Tables XVII. and XCIII.

A glance at the table shows that the percentage of unemployment is not affected by the percentage of foreign-born engaged in the main classes of occupations. The variation of the ratio of unemployment from section to section is confined within narrow limits. The ratio of unemployment in manufactures is the same for the South Atlantic and the North Atlantic States, though there are very few foreign-born in the South Atlantic States, while in the North Atlantic States they constitute nearly one third of all operatives. In all other sections of the country the ratio of unemployment is slightly higher than in the North Atlantic States, while the percentage of foreign-born breadwinners engaged in manufactures is less, and in the South Central States much less than in the North Atlantic States. The same is true of the miscellaneous collection of occupations lumped together in census statistics under the head of "domestic and personal service," which includes unskilled laborers. We find the lowest ratio of unemployment in the North Atlantic States, with 31.5 per cent of foreign-born breadwinners and the highest in the South Central States, with but 3.7 per cent of foreign-born breadwinners.

Comparative statistics showing the ratio of unemployment and the percentage of foreign-born breadwinners by sex and by States are available for the manufacturing industries at the XII. Census. The measure of unemployment, for the purposes of this comparison, is the difference between the total greatest and the total least monthly average number employed, expressed as a percentage of the greatest monthly average. The data for manufactures relate to the calendar year 1899 and the distribution of breadwinners by nativity is for the summer of 1900. The dates are sufficiently close to make the figures comparable.[1]

There is considerable variation of the ratio of unemployment, as well as of that of foreign-born, by States. There are some States with a high percentage of foreign-born and

[1] See Appendix, Table III.

low ratio of unemployment and *vice versa*; there are others with high percentages both of foreign-born and of unemployment and *vice versa*. The ratio of unemployment seems sometimes to rise and sometimes to fall with the percentages of foreign-born. But a significant correlation between the two ratios is disclosed if all States are combined into two areas according to the ratio of foreign-born engaged in manufactures and mechanical pursuits:

I. Those States where the ratio of foreign-born in manufactures is below the average for the United States;

II. Those States where that ratio is above the average for the United States.

The statistics relating to each area are summarized separately for male and female wage-earners in Tables 19 and 20.

TABLE 19.

GREATEST AND LEAST NUMBER OF MALE WAGE-EARNERS EMPLOYED IN MANUFACTURES DURING ANY ONE MONTH OF THE YEAR 1899, GREATEST NUMBER OF UNEMPLOYED, AND PERCENTAGE OF FOREIGN-BORN MALES ENGAGED IN MANUFACTURES AND MECHANICAL PURSUITS IN 1900, BY GROUPS OF STATES.

States with percentage of foreign-born in manufactures and mechanical pursuits	Employed in manufactures (thousands)		Unemployed sometime		Per cent ratio of foreign-born to all males in manufactures and mechanical pursuits.	
	Least number	Greatest number	Thousands	Percent of greatest number employed	Least	Greatest
Below the average..	1224	1501	277	18.5	1.0	31.9
Above the average..	2524	2907	383	13.2	33.2	53.8
Total........	3748	4408	660	15.0	Average 32.7	

TABLE 20.

GREATEST AND LEAST NUMBER OF FEMALE WAGE-EARNERS EMPLOYED IN MANUFACTURES DURING ANY ONE MONTH OF THE YEAR 1899, GREATEST NUMBER OF UNEMPLOYED, AND PERCENTAGE OF FOREIGN-BORN FEMALES ENGAGED IN MANUFACTURES AND MECHANICAL PURSUITS, IN 1900, BY GROUPS OF STATES.

States with percentage of foreign-born in manufactures and mechanical pursuits	Employed in manufactures (thousands)		Unemployed sometime		Per cent ratio of foreign-born to all females in manufactures and mechanical pursuits	
	Least number	Greatest number	Thousands	Per cent of greatest number employed	Least	Greatest
Below the average..	352	442	90	20.4	0.2	20.3
Above the average..	573	668	95	14.2	22.7	46.2
Total.........	925	1110	185	16.4	Average 21.4	

Combining all the States where the immigrants furnish from one third to more than one half of all males engaged in manufactures and mechanical pursuits, we find that the ratio of unemployment in that area as a whole is lower than in the other area, where the immigrants are few in numbers, rising in no State to one third of all males employed in manufacturing industries and falling as low as 1 per cent. The same rule holds true with regard to female wage-earners employed in manufactures. On the whole, *unemployment is in inverse ratio to the relative number of foreign-born.*

The underlying cause of this relation will be apparent, if we remember that the number of foreign-born wage-earners is regulated by immigration and emigration and that both movements promptly respond to changes in the business situation. (See Chapter IV.)

Still the variation of the ratio of unemployment by States may be affected by the localization of industries; certain industries concentrated in a State with a small foreign-born population may through climatic or other causes be more subject to ebb and flow than other industries located in a

State with a large immigrant population. The ratio of unemployment must therefore be compared for different occupations with a varying percentage of foreign-born breadwinners.

Diagram VII furnishes the data for a comparative study of fifty leading occupations which gave employment, in 1900, to seven and a half million male breadwinners.[1]

If it be true that unemployment is intensified by immigration, the aggregations of solid black bars representing unemployment and striped bars representing the percentage of foreign-born male breadwinners in each occupation should be expected to display some similarity in outline. No such tendency is suggested by the diagram; the variation of the ratio of unemployment for different occupations shows no effects of immigration.

Although the number of occupations selected for comparison, as well as the number of persons engaged in them, is very large and well distributed over all sections of the country, yet, in order to eliminate the possible effect of localization of industries, we shall next compare the variations of the ratios of unemployment and of the percentage of foreign-born within the same occupations by States. Space forbids an exhaustive treatment of all the leading occupations shown in Diagram VII. Our study will be confined to three occupation groups: bituminous coal-miners, common laborers, and cotton-mill operatives. The first two have been selected in view of the popular belief, accepted by the Immigration Commission, that they are suffering from an oversupply of unskilled immigrant labor. The cotton-mill operatives, on the other hand, afford the opportunity to contrast the New England mills, where the majority of the workers are of foreign birth, with the Southern mills dependent almost exclusively upon native labor.

Diagram VIII presents in graphic form the ratio of un-

[1] The comparative figures for these occupations, as well as for the leading occupations of female breadwinners are given in the Appendix, Table IV.

DIAGRAM VII

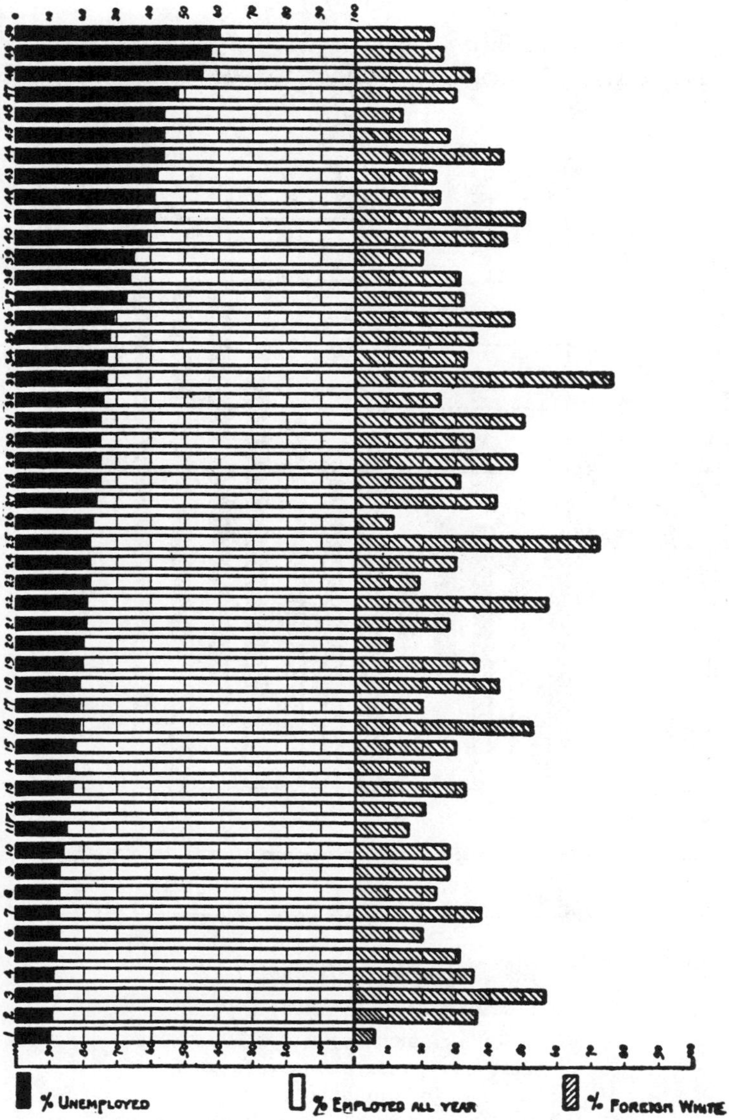

VII. Per cent unemployed at any time during the year and per cent of foreign-born in fifty leading occupations, 1900.

employment in bituminous coal-mining collated with the percentage of foreign-born miners. The former ratio has

Diagram VIII

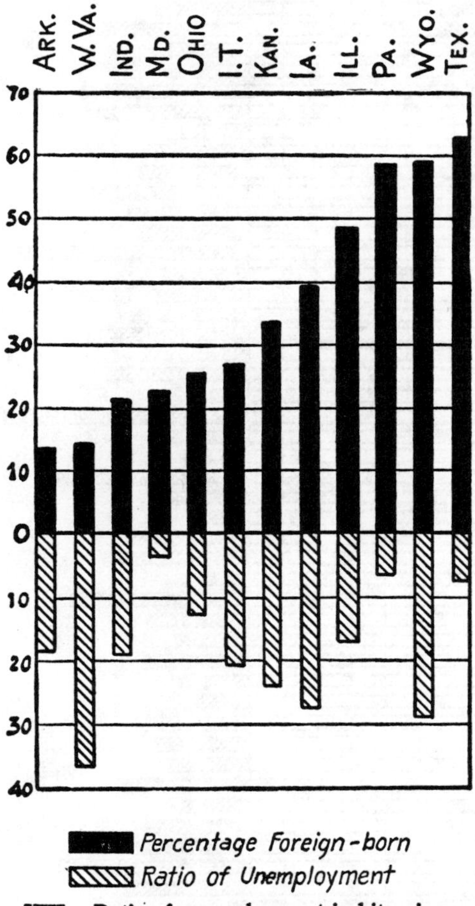

VIII. Ratio of unemployment in bituminous coal mines, 1902, and percentage of foreign-born miners, 1900.

been computed by the method applied above to manufactures. The greatest and the least number of wage-earners are taken from the census report on *Mines and*

Quarries for 1902, while the percentage of foreign-born is that for 1900, but the dates are sufficiently near for comparative purposes.[1] As the statistics of occupations by States do not distinguish coal miners from other miners and quarrymen, the comparison is confined to those States where coal mining was practically the only mining industry.[2] The diagram includes, however, all principal coal-mining States in 1902 which produced 83 per cent of the total coal output of the United States.[3] No connection between unemployment and immigration is disclosed by the diagram. Pennsylvania, which holds the third highest place according to the percentage of foreign-born miners, stands next to the State with the lowest ratio of unemployment. The highest ratio of unemployment is found in West Virginia, where the percentage of foreign-born miners is next to the lowest

Similar variations by States appear in the statistics relating to the other two occupations selected for comparison. To further trace the interdependence, if any, between immigration and unemployment in these occupations, we shall again combine all States into two areas, first, according to the percentage of foreign-born; and next, in the same manner, according to the ratio of unemployment. The results of these combinations are summarized in Tables 21 and 22.[4]

An examination of Table 21 shows that the percentage of unemployment is slightly less in the area where the immigrants furnish 44 per cent of all common labor, than in the rest of the United States where the foreign-born laborers constitute one tenth of the total number. The

[1] See Appendix, Table V.

[2] In Pennsylvania a large number of coal miners were employed in the anthracite mines; the latter, however, were affected by the strike of 1902 and could for this reason not be included in a comparison between the greatest and the least number employed. But the employment of immigrants is general in both classes of mines.

[3] *Mines and Quarries*, p. 680.

[4] Detailed statistical data for each State will be found in the Appendix Tables VI. and VII.

TABLE 21.

LABORERS (MALE), FOREIGN-BORN AND UNEMPLOYED, 1900.

Areas	Total	Foreign-born		Unemployed	
		Number	Per cent	Number	Per cent
With percentage of foreign-born:					
Above the average...	1,317,218	580,682	44.1	570,401	43.3
Below the average...	1,188,029	122,853	10.3	539,324	45.4
With percentage of unemployed:					
Above the average...	1,031,548	252,453	24.4	498,881	48.4
Below the average...	1,473,699	451,082	30.6	610,844	41.5
Total..........	2,505,247	703,535	28.1	1,109,725	44.3

TABLE 22.

COTTON-MILL OPERATIVES (MALE), FOREIGN-BORN AND UNEMPLOYED, 1900.

Areas	Total	Foreign-born		Unemployed	
		Number	Per cent	Number	Per cent
With percentage of foreign-born:					
Above the average...	65,984	46,009	69.7	7,725	11.7
Below the average...	59,031	1,982	3.4	8,551	14.5
Total..........	125,015	47,991	38.4	16,276	13.0
With percentage of unemployed:[1]					
Above the average...	52,882	10,479	19.8	8,380	15.6
Below the average...	71,719	37,499	52.3	7,842	9.1
Total..........	124,601	47,978	38.5	16,222	13.0

[1] Exclusive of Kentucky where the percentage of unemployed is equal to the average.

difference is negligible. Evidently conditions of employment of unskilled laborers are everywhere such that well-nigh one half of them, whether native or foreign-born, have no steady work and lose a part of their time during the year in changing from one situation to another. If the arrangement of the States is reversed and they are grouped into two areas according to whether the percentage of unemployment is above or below the average for the United States as a whole, it appears that in the area with the higher ratio of unemployment the percentage of foreign-born laborers is lower.

The same relation is disclosed by Table 22 with regard to male cotton-mill operatives. In the area with 70 per cent of foreign-born operatives the percentage of unemployed is slightly less than in the area where 96 per cent of all operatives are of native birth. Reversing the arrangement we find again that in the area with the higher ratio of unemployment only one fifth of all operative are foreign-born, whereas, in the area with the lower ratio of unemployment over one half of the operative force are immigrants. In other words, immigrants, as a rule, are not attracted to the cotton mills of those States where opportunities for steady employment are less favorable.

The preceding analysis justifies the conclusion that there is no causal connection between unemployment and immigration, the ratio of unemployment within the same occupation being substantially the same in areas with a large immigrant population and with practically none at all.

The preceding conclusions have been derived from an inquiry into the conditions of employment for one census year. We shall next examine whether there is any connection between immigration and unemployment compared for a series of years. The Massachusetts Bureau of Labor Statistics has collected annual statistics of the greatest and the least number of wage-earners employed in factories since the middle of the 80's. Table 23 shows the variation of the ratio of unemployment for twenty years from 1888 to 1908. The standard of comparison is the same as before, viz., the difference between the greatest and the least number employed.[1]

TABLE 23.

RATIO OF UNEMPLOYMENT IN MASSACHUSETTS, 1888–1908[2]

Year	Per cent	Year	Per cent	Year	Per cent
1888	23	1895	26	1902	23
1889	23	1896	33	1903	25
1890	22	1897	28	1904	26
1891	22	1898	30	1905	23
1892	23	1899	26	1906	29
1893	36	1900	27	1907	25
1894	33	1901	25	1908	33

The years 1893, 1894, and 1908 show the effects of industrial crises, and the year 1896 those of the unsettled business situation produced by the free silver agitation. With those exceptions the variation of the ratio of unemployment from year to year is small. The ratio is lower for the seven years of the present century characterized by heavy immigration than for the preceding decade when immigration was small. The relation between unemployment and immigration is shown graphically in Diagram IX.[3] It is clearly seen that with increasing immigration unemploy-

[1] The returns are not complete, especially for the earlier years; a comparison of the numbers employed would therefore be misleading. Nevertheless, the numbers reported are so large that the percentage of unemployment could not be materially varied by the addition of the missing figures. The inquiries of the Bureau call for the number employed during the current and the preceding year. As a result the figures for the previous year published in every annual report are more complete than those published the year before. A comparison of the percentage of unemployment for each year computed from the numbers published in two consecutive reports shows that the variations do not exceed a fraction of 1 per cent. In Table 23 fractions of 1 per cent have been omitted.

[2] See Appendix, Table VIII.

[3] See Appendix, Table IX.

ment decreases, and with declining immigration unemployment increases. The tendency disclosed by this diagram

DIAGRAM IX

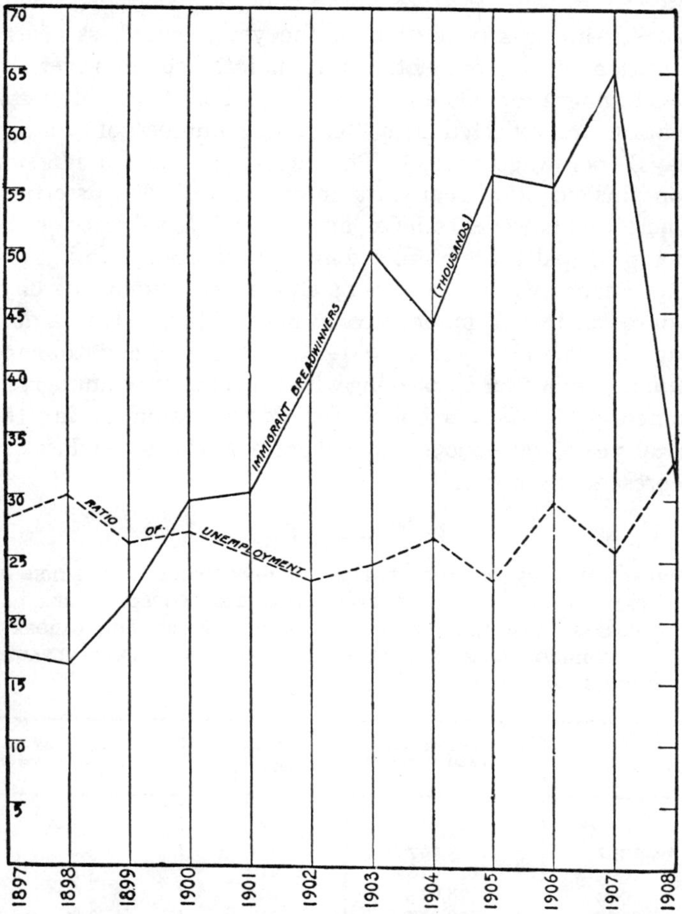

IX. Ratio of unemployment of factory workers in Massachusetts and number of immigrant breadwinners destined for Massachusetts, 1897–1908.

is but a corroboration of the rule that immigration follows the demand for labor. The condition in Massachusetts, which is a manufacturing State with a large immigrant population, may be accepted as typical.

Heretofore we have dealt with unemployment as expressed in the relative number of wage-earners unemployed during any portion of the year, regardless of the duration of employment. It is maintained, however, by the Immigration Commission, that the effects of immigration are reflected in a "curtailed number of working days" per wage-earner. The report of the Commission contains no statistical data in support of this assertion. There are, however, official figures on this subject for the two principal States affected by immigration, New York and Pennsylvania. Table 24 shows the number of days worked in the bituminous coal mines of Pennsylvania during the calendar years 1901–1909, the average tonnage mined per day per man, along with the number of immigrant miners and laborers bound for Pennsylvania during the fiscal years 1901–1909. In Diagram X the same data are represented graphically.

TABLE 24.

AVERAGE NUMBER OF DAYS WORKED IN BITUMINOUS COAL MINES OF PENNSYLVANIA, AVERAGE PRODUCTION PER EMPLOYEE PER DAY WORKED, AND NUMBER OF IMMIGRANT MINERS AND LABORERS (INCLUDING FARM LABORERS) DESTINED FOR PENNSYLVANIA, 1901–1909.[1]

Year	Immigrants (fiscal years)	Days (calendar years)	Tons per day (calendar years)
1901	63,713	216	3.5
1902	95,967	221	3.6
1903	114,018	216	3.4
1904	78,625	190	3.6
1905	127,417	216	3.6
1906	116,923	239	3.4
1907	141,830	238	3.7
1908	54,813	184	3.6
1909	69,291	210	3.7

[1] *Reports of the Commissioner of Immigration*, 1901, Table VII.; 1902–

Diagram X.

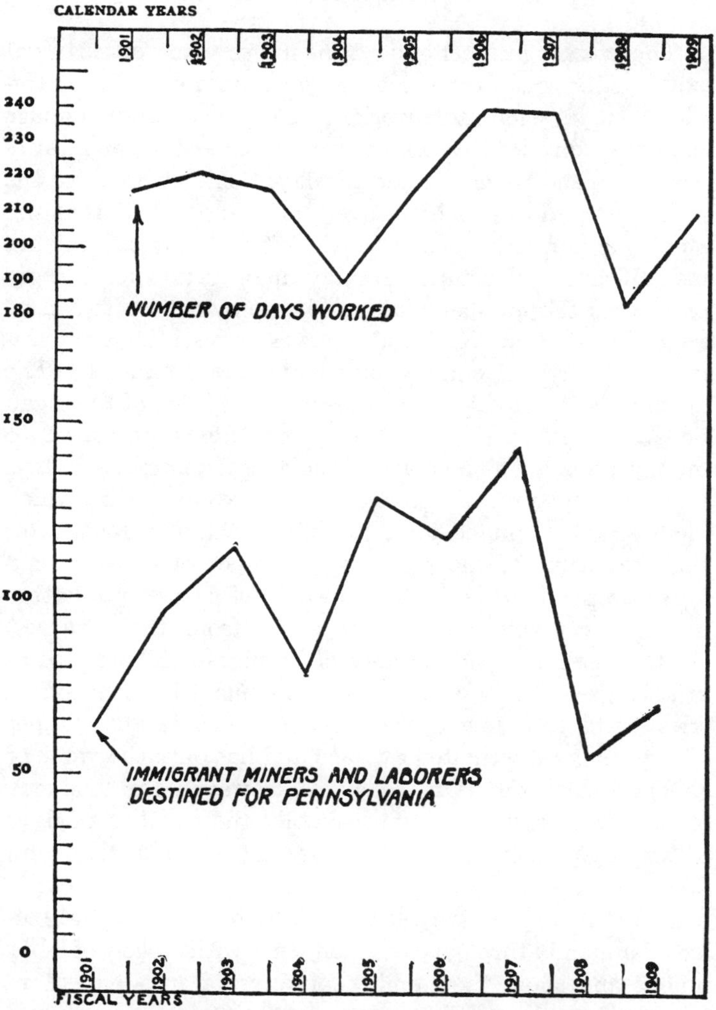

Average number of days worked in the bituminous coal mines of Pennsylvania and number of immigrant miners and laborers destined for Pennsylvania, 1901–1909

Scale for immigrants: 1 unit = 1000

The average number of days the mines were worked might not be identical with the average number of days of employment for each mine worker. But the average tonnage mined per day worked serves as a measure of the amount of work furnished every miner per day. The average for the nine-year period is a little over three and a half tons per employee per day, the fluctuations from year to year are insignificant. The number of days in operation accordingly represents the number of days of employment. It can be seen from Diagram X. that the curves representing immigration and days of employment run almost parallel. The deviations from that course are slight, and one of them can be accounted for by temporary conditions unrelated to immigration. The increase of the average number of days worked in 1902 was due to the anthracite coal strike, which increased the demand for bituminous coal. In 1903, after the settlement of the strike, the number of days worked again dropped to the level of 1901. Of course, no mathematical accuracy must be expected from these curves. On the one hand, the number of immigrant laborers comprises a great many who found employment in other industries than bituminous coal mines; on the other, the number of days is not a weighted average and has only the value of an approximation. On the whole, however, the tendency of the two curves is unmistakable; the number of days of employment rises and falls as immigration rises and falls.

The statistics of the New York Labor Bureau are collected annually through correspondence with officers of labor unions and show the number of days of employment in organized trades. While these statistics relate primarily to the skilled crafts only, yet indirectly they reflect the conditions in the industrial field as a whole. Nowadays there are few skilled crafts that do not enter as a part into a larger industrial system. Unemployment of the engineer

---

1908, Table IX; 1909, p. 57. *Reports of the Department of Mines of Pennsylvania*, Part II., for the years 1901 to 1909.

or fireman means unemployment for a number of factory hands.

In Diagram XI. days of employment are plotted along with the number of immigrants, exclusive of dependents,[1] who gave New York as their destination on landing.[2] The two upper curves represent the average number of days of employment during the first and the third quarter of every year from 1897 to 1909,[3] the lowest heavy line represents immigration of breadwinners. Contrary to the general assumption, the rise of the immigration curve is not followed by a decline of the curves representing duration of employment. On the whole, the three curves move in a uniform direction; the number of days of work increases as immigration increases, and declines as immigration declines. In the fall of 1900 (a presidential year), there was less work on an average than in the fall of 1899, but the middle curve shows that conditions improved in the spring of 1901. These fluctuations were reflected in the total immigration for the fiscal year ended June 30, 1901, which remained almost stationary. A divergence between the employment and immigration curves strikes the eye in 1907. The spring of that year was marked by a decline of employment compared with the preceding year, and the opportunities in the fall showed no progress compared with the previous fall, whereas the immigration curve was still rising. The effects of the curtailment of the days of employment were reflected in the immigration curve next year. On the other hand immigration continued to decline when the condition of the labor market began to improve. The conclusion that can be drawn from this divergence is that it takes some time before the conditions of the labor market are reflected in the immigration movement. As stated in a preceding

[1] "No occupation (mostly women and children)," in Immigration Bureau terminology.

[2] For detailed figures see Appendix, Table XXIII.

[3] *Annual Report of the New York Bureau of Labor Statistics*, 1909, vol. ii, p. xvii., Table 5.

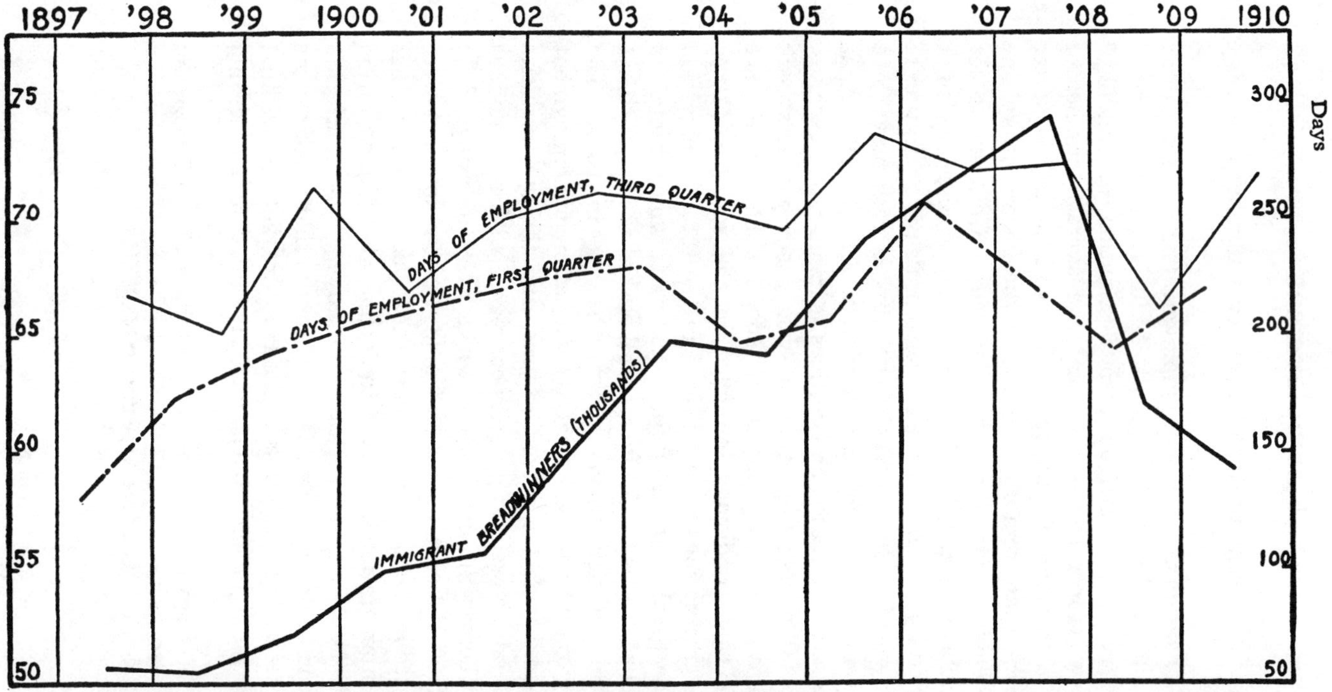

XI. Days of employment in organized trades in the State of New York and number of immigrant breadwinners destined for New York, 1897–1909

chapter, the arrivals of immigrants in the United States at any given time are the result of preparations made some months before their embarkation on the other side. Viewed as a whole, however, the diagram strongly contradicts the assumption that immigration results in the curtailment of the days of employment. During the ten normal years 1897–1906, which preceded the crisis of 1907, the number of working days increased with the increase of immigration. It could not have been a fortuitous coincidence. No one claims that the arrival of the immigrants was the cause of the increase of the per capita share of work. By the method of exclusion there is room for no other inference than that immigration has merely responded to the increased demand for labor.

The preceding analysis may be summed up in the following proposition:

Unemployment and immigration are the effects of economic forces working in opposite directions; that which produces business expansion reduces unemployment and attracts immigration; that which produces business depression increases unemployment and reduces immigration.

Yet it may be said that while immigration is not a contributory cause of unemployment, restriction of immigration would nevertheless reduce unemployment. An answer to this argument is furnished by the example of Australia, where immigration does not keep up with emigration, and yet unemployment is an ever-present problem, precisely as in the United States. Australia is a new country with abundant natural resources. Its area is as great as that of the continental United States (exclusive of Alaska), while its population at the census of 1906 was a million short of the United States figure for 1800. The Australian statistics of unemployment essentially differ from ours. The XII. Census counted all breadwinners who were idle at any time during the twelve months preceding the date of enumeration. The statistics of the New York Bureau of Labor comprise all wage-earners who were unemployed during the first or the third quarter of the year. The Australian statistics, on the other hand, give the number unemployed on the date of enumeration. A comparison of the Australian ratio of unemployment with the New York ratio must therefore be favorable to Australia and unfavorable to New York. Still the comparison is highly instructive. The Australian ratio in 1901 varied from 3.96 per cent for South Australia to 6.73 per cent for New South Wales.[1] In the State of New York the total amount of unemployment for the three summer months, July, August, and September, fluctuated during the years 1897–1907 between 1.9 per cent and 6.5 per cent.[2] It thus appears that Australia with an excess of emigration over immigration is suffering from unemployment at least as much as the State of New York, which is teeming with immigrants. It is evident that unemployment is created by the modern organization of industry even in the absence of all immigration.

Unemployment not being the result of overpopulation, it necessarily follows that limitation of the number of wage-earners can promise no relief against unemployment. To be effective, any proposed remedy must attack the problem of unemployment, not collaterally, through restriction of immigration, but directly.

A radical remedy for the evils of unemployment is offered by the Code of Labor Laws of the Russian Soviet Government. The law assures to every able-bodied citizen "the right to employment" at his trade or vocation at the standard wage fixed for such class of work. The Government, through its employment service, undertakes to find a job for every unemployed worker. Every person who is out of work may register at the local office of the Division of Distribution of Labor Power. All establishments in need of workers may

[1] Victor S. Clark: "Labor Conditions in Australia," *Bulletin of the Bureau of Labor*, No. 56 p. 180.

[2] *Annual Report of the New York Bureau of Labor Statistics*, 1909, vol. ii., p. xvii., Table 5.

likewise register with the local government employment office their demand for labor, stating the qualifications of workers and the kind of work required, as well as the terms of employment. The local office assigns the applicants in the order of their registration. In case the local supply of workers is insufficient to meet the demand for a certain class of workers, the local employment office communicates with other offices within the same region. If the supply of labor of a certain class is in excess of the demand, the applicant for work may be temporarily offered a job outside of his trade. An applicant for whom no employment can be found is entitled to draw a benefit, equal to his standard wages, out of an unemployment insurance fund levied on all employers of labor, including government institutions. Whenever a worker is directed to a position below his grade of work, he is entitled to draw upon the unemployment insurance fund for the difference between his standard rate of wages and that actually offered to him.[1]

[1] *Code of Labor Laws.* Compilation of the Statutes and Orders of the Labor and Farmer Government, December 10, 1918, Sections 10, 20–23, 26, 28–30, and Supp. to Sec. 79, §§6, 7, 14, 15. A summary of that Code appears in the *Monthly Labor Review* of the U. S. Dept. of Labor, April, 1920, pp. 210–214.

CHAPTER VII

RACIAL STRATIFICATION

INDUSTRIAL evolution has broken down the stable organization of ancient and mediæval societies, in which every individual had a fixed place and the son followed the occupation of the father. Modern industrial society tends to revert to the nomadic type. People come and go, and others settle in their places. There were, in 1900, thirteen and a half million persons born in the United States who were living outside of their native States. There is no record of migration within State limits. Assuming that the number of native citizens migrating within their State of birth is equal to the number migrating to contiguous States, six millions more may be added to the migratory population, making in all about 30 per cent of the total native population.[1] Yet when it is learned that of the 2,653,000 native Missourians who were living in the United States, 618,000 resided outside of their native State, while 855,000 natives of other States settled in Missouri,[2] no one takes it that the Missourians were "displaced" by the "invasion" of a host nearly a million strong from Southern and Eastern States. It is only when the new-comers are of foreign birth that the impression of "racial displacement" is created.

There was one great racial displacement in America: the Indian was displaced from his land by the European invasion. The invasion and the displacement in that instance

[1] *XII. Census, Supplementary Analysis*, p. 281.

[2] *Ibid.*, Table 61, pp. 850 *et seq.*

were physical acts, not metaphors. When the term "racial displacement" is applied to immigration, it suggests the idea of a virtual crowding out of the native American by the alien invader.[1] No doubt, in the shifting of population from East to West, from country to city, the racial composition of many settlements has changed. Within the memory of the present generation the Irish and German colonies of New York City gradually moved out of the sections they had occupied in the 80's and early 90's of the past century and in their places Jewish and Italian colonies grew up. Still the old Irish or German settler of ten or twenty years ago can be located in another section of the great city, and the public is conscious of the fact that he has simply moved from one neighborhood to another which seemed to him more attractive. The population of New York City, however, is large enough to fill several States. Were the same population spread over a hundred cities of about forty thousand inhabitants each and had the German residents of one city gradually moved out of it to others within a radius of twenty-five miles, their places being filled by a new race, the change would be keenly felt by many. The grocer, the butcher, the hotelkeeper, the physician, the lawyer, would be losing patronage. In their minds the change would be reflected as the "displacement" of the old

[1] The definition of the word "displacement" given by the Oxford English Dictionary is as follows:

Displacement: The act of displacing or fact of being displaced. Removal of a thing by substitution of something else in its place.—1880, *Library Universal Knowledge*: "The displacement of human labor through machinery."

Hydrostatics: The displacing of a liquid by a body immersed in or floating on it.

Displace:

1. To remove or shift from its place; to put out of the usual place.
2. To remove from a position, dignity, or office.
3. To oust (something) from its place and occupy it instead. . . . (*b*) to take the place of, supplant, replace.—A. R. Wallace, "*Darwinism*"; "This weed . . . absolutely displaced every other plant on the ground."

settlers by the new-comers. And yet the element of crowding out, even in a metaphorical sense, might be wholly absent. The abandonment of the New England farms may serve as an illustration. No one "displaced" the New England farmer; the population of many a town fell off, but few new settlers, native or foreign-born, came to take the places of those who had gone. The old homesteads were left to decay and their proprietors went West, where they found better opportunities. And now we witness the same movement in Iowa, whose population has decreased since 1900, the farmers being attracted by cheaper lands in Western Canada.

Is it not possible that a similar process has been going on in manufacturing, in mining, in railroading? Where there was a wilderness thirty years ago, several new States with a substantial population have grown up. The railroads of the West needed employees, who had to come from the East. From 1879 to 1909, the manufactures of New England and the Middle Atlantic States added one and a half million wage-earners to their personnel, whereas the industrial development of the rest of the country created opportunities for two and one third million new hands, as shown in Table 25 next below. The manufactures in the West and South grew much faster than in the East and drew some of the native workers and earlier immigrants from the older manufacturing States. Still the demand for labor in those States also grew. The places left vacant by the old employees who had gone westward had to be filled by new immigrants. The term "displacement" would be misapplied to such a migration of wage-earners, as much as in the case of the migration of the New England farmer.

Let us see what light can be thrown upon this question by the statistics of occupations. According to the figures of the XII. Census, covering the whole area of the United States, the economic stratification within the principal elements of the white population in 1900 exhibited very characteristic differences, as appears from Table 26.

TABLE 25.

AVERAGE NUMBER OF WAGE-EARNERS EMPLOYED IN MANUFACTURES (THOUSANDS), 1879–1909.[1]

Geographic divisions	1879	1909	Increase	
			Number	Per cent
New England and Middle Atlantic States	1790	3309	1519	85
All other States	940	3306	2366	252
Total, United States	2730	6615	3885	142

TABLE 26.

PER CENT DISTRIBUTION OF MALE BREADWINNERS 21 YEARS OF AGE AND OVER, BY NATIVITY AND CLASS OF OCCUPATIONS, 1900.[2]

Occupation groups.	Native white		Foreign white
	Native parents	Foreign parents	
Industrial wage-earners	27.6	40.8	52.8
Business[3] and professional pursuits, commercial and clerical employment	57.7	43.9	35.5
All others	14.7	15.3	11.7

The majority of Americans of native parentage, in 1900, were engaged in farming, in business, in the professions, and in all sorts of commercial and clerical pursuits. The majority of the immigrants, on the other hand, were industrial wage-earners.[4]

The question is, was this adjustment of native and foreign elements on the scale of occupations attended by actual "racial displacement"? Comparing the numbers

[1] *XII. Census*, vol. vii., pp. clxxii–clxxiii.—*XIII. Census, Manufactures*, vol. viii., p. 542.

[2] Isaac A. Hourwich, "The Social-Economic Classes of the Population of the United States." *The Journal of Political Economy*, April, 1911, p. 327.

[3] Including farming.

[4] Speaking of the immigrants in a "representative" coal-mining community (Shenandoah, Pa.), the Immigration Commission states

of persons engaged in each occupation at the censuses of 1900 and 1890, we find a decrease of native breadwinners in the following occupations:

TABLE 27.

OCCUPATIONS IN WHICH THE NUMBER OF NATIVE-BORN DECREASED, 1890–1900.[1]

Native-born of native parentage.	Decrease (Thousands)
Male:	
Carpenters and joiners	25
Boot- and shoe-makers and repairers	12
Woodworkers, including cabinet makers and coopers	7
Masons	6
Boatmen, canalmen, pilots, and sailors	3
Dairymen	2
Brick and tile makers	1
Tailors	1
All others	19
Total	76
Female:	
Seamstresses	9
Tailoresses	1
Textile mill operatives	2
Dairywomen	1
Total	13
Both sexes	89
Native-born of foreign parentage.	
Male:	
Brick and tile makers	1
Dairymen	1
All others	1
Total	3
Female:	
Cotton mill operatives	1
Tailoresses	1
Total	2
Both sexes	5
GRAND TOTAL	94

that they "have done practically nothing in the way of initiating new industries. . . . A few small candy and cigar factories and blacksmith shops have been established by foreigners, but these are insignificant in number and size." (*Reports*, vol. 16, p. 655.) All schools of political economy agree that "initiating new industries" is the function of capital. But the majority of the foreigners are wage-earners.

[1] See Appendix, Table X.

In all, from 1890 to 1900, 94,000 native breadwinners dropped out of the occupations enumerated in the preceding table. If we were to assume that this figure represents actual displacement (which it does not, as will presently be shown), it would amount to only 2.5 per cent of the total immigration for the decade 1890–1900. At the same time the increase of native white of native parentage in all occupations, exclusive of farming, exceeded two and a half millions. It means that there were twenty-five other opportunities for every position given up by the native breadwinners of the above enumerated classes.

The figure 94,000 must not be mistaken, however, for the number of individuals discharged from their former positions. In the first place, an allowance must be made for decrease by death. Taking those occupations which are specified in the statistics of mortality at the XII. Census, we obtain the following comparative ratios:

TABLE 28.

DECREASE FROM ALL CAUSES, COMPARED WITH LOSS BY DEATH AMONG NATIVE WHITE MALES OF NATIVE PARENTAGE, IN SELECTED OCCUPATIONS, 1890–1900.[1]

Occupations	Number engaged (Thousands)		Per cent of total for each occupation		
	1890	1900	Decrease	Loss by death	Net accessions (+) or defections (−)
Masons	65	59	− 9.2	−19.9	+10.7
Boatmen, canalmen, pilots, and sailors	37	34	− 8.1	−18.8	+10.7
Carpenters and joiners	354	329	− 7.1	−17.2	+10.1
Tailors	15	14	− 6.7	−11.8	+ 5.1
Boot- and shoemakers and repairers	71	59	−16.9	− 9.4	− 7.5

[1] *XII. Census, Vital Statistics*, vol. i., p. ccix. *Occupations at the XII. Census*, Table 2. *Compendium of the XI. Census*, Part III: Population, Table 78.

The decrease of the number of native white males of native parentage in all but the last occupation included in the preceding table is accordingly accounted for by the fact that the new accessions from that class were insufficient to fill the places of those who died.

On the other hand, an actual decrease of the number of American workmen of native stock was found among shoemakers and repairers. On closer scrutiny, however, it appears that this decrease was merely a part of a general decline of the trade, which manifested itself in a decrease of the number of foreign-born shoemakers as well. Among other occupations of the same class were brick and tile makers, whose total number was reduced by 10,000, and dairymen whose number was reduced by 8000; more than one half of those reductions affected foreign-born workers (7000 in the former and 4000 in the latter occupation). The same is true of the other occupations specified in Table 27. As far as can be judged from census figures, there was consequently no "displacement" of native by foreign workmen.

Coming to female wage-earners, we find that while there was a decrease of 13,000 American women of native stock and of 2000 native of immigrant parentage employed as seamstresses, tailoresses, textile mill operatives, and dairywomen, the number of servants and waitresses showed a decrease of 41,000 foreign-born, contemporaneous with an increase of 16,000 white American girls of native stock and 47,000 native daughters of immigrants. It may be inferred from these figures that the women of the "new immigration" showed a tendency to prefer factory work to domestic service, while the tendency among native American girls was in the opposite direction.[1]

[1] Most of the female factory workers being young, the decrease by mortality may be disregarded. On the other hand, however, "women enter industry only temporarily. The census shows that the great majority of them who are at work are between 16 and 30 years of age—that is, they are in industry until they get married." (Nearing: *Wages*

On the whole, the number of native women of native parentage in gainful occupations increased by more than half a million, as against a possible displacement of 13,000; in other words, for every native woman of native parentage who left the mill or clothing factory there were forty women of the same nativity who found new openings. The increase of the number of professional women of that class was 63,000, *i. e.*, nearly five times as great as the decrease of the number of native American factory girls. The loss of the 2000 positions by native women of foreign parentage was compensated by an increase of 348,000 in the number of the same nativity employed in all occupations.

It is evident from these figures that the "displacement," if there was any, was negligible, and moreover that it did not manifest itself in those occupations which are believed to be affected by immigration. The three occupations mostly spoken of in connection with "racial displacement" viz., laborers, miners, and iron and steel workers, show increasing numbers of native workmen of native parentage.

Unskilled laborers appear in census statistics under two designations: "agricultural laborers," and "laborers not specified." At the census of 1890, many farm laborers in agricultural districts were reported simply as "laborers," while at the census of 1900 the distinction between these two classes was more strictly drawn. In consequence, the increase of the number of non-agricultural laborers, appearing from the census returns for 1900, is below the actual figure. The increase of the number of non-agricultural laborers identified as such and classified by race and nativity is given in Table 29 next below:

---

in the United States, pp. 173–174.) Within a period of ten years the number of women of every nativity engaged in a given occupation would accordingly be greatly reduced by marriage, unless there were others of the same class to fill their places.

TABLE 29.

INCREASE OF THE NUMBER OF LABORERS IN THE UNITED STATES, CLASSIFIED BY RACE AND NATIVITY, 1890–1900.[1]

Race and Nativity	(Thousands).
Native white	458
Native father	333
Foreign father	125
Foreign-born	41
Colored	158
Total	657

It appears from Table 29 that only 6 per cent of the additional demand for unskilled labor was supplied by immigrants. Since the percentage of foreign-born among agricultural laborers is much smaller than among other unskilled laborers,[2] the underestimate of the numerical increase of the foreign-born in the latter class is smaller than for the occupation in general; the percentage of increase of foreign-born laborers must accordingly be rather overestimated than underestimated. In other words, immigration during the decade 1890–1900 was barely sufficient to make up for the natural decrease of unskilled laborers by death.

Yet the totals for the country at large might conceal local displacements of considerable magnitude. Turning to the State figures for 1890 and 1900 we find a decrease of the number of native white laborers of native parentage in the following States: Colorado, 1000 men; Delaware, 100 men; Utah, 100 men; and Rhode Island, 300 men.[3] But in the first three States the number of foreign-born laborers likewise decreased. The total "displacement" of native white laborers of native parentage by immigrants

[1] *Occupations at the XII. Census*, Table 2, pp. 10 and 11. *XI. Census, Population*, Part II., Table 82, p. 354; Table 78, p. 304.

[2] The ratio of foreign-born in 1900 was 5.8 per cent among agricultural laborers and 27.1 per cent among "laborers not specified." —*Occupations at the XII. Census*, Table 2, pp. 10 and 11.

[3] *Ibid.*, Table 41, pp. 220–423. *XI. Census, Population*, Part II., Table 116, pp. 530–627.

was thus represented by a decrease of 300 men in the State of Rhode Island, or by thirty men annually. It is within the range of possibility that those thirty men may have crossed the State line to Massachusetts or Connecticut, the first of which, shows an increase of 2100 and the second an increase of 1400 native white laborers of native parentage. No decrease of the number of common laborers among the native white of native parentage appears in any of the great States which serve as centres of attraction for immigration. The native white of foreign parentage show an increase during the same period in every State and territory.

What has been said of laborers is equally applicable to miners, as can be seen from Table 30, two thirds of the increased demand for miners having been supplied by native-born workmen and only one third by immigrants.

TABLE 30.

INCREASE OF THE NUMBER OF MINERS IN THE UNITED STATES, CLASSIFIED BY NATIVITY (THOUSANDS), 1890–1900.[1]

Native white	108
Native parents	73
Foreign parents	35
Colored	13
Foreign-born	61
Total	182

Comparing the number of miners by States in 1890 and 1900, we find a decrease in the employment of native white miners only in the following States[2]:

[1] *XI. Census, Population*, Part II., p. 304, Table 78, and pp. 354 and 355, Table 82. *Occupations at the XII. Census*, Table 2, pp. 12 and 13.

[2] XI. *Census, Population*, Part II., Table 116, pp. 540, 564, 582, 584, 594, 608, and 616. *Occupations at the XII. Census*, Table 41, pp. 242, 294, 332, 334, 358, 386 and 400.

TABLE 31.

DECREASE OF THE NUMBER OF NATIVE WHITE MINERS, 1890–1900, BY STATES.

State	Decrease
Maine	200
New Hampshire	100
Vermont	200
Connecticut	200
North and South Dakota	100
Nevada	500
Total	1300

The total loss of 1300 positions by native miners would have been amply compensated by the employment of 70,000 American miners of native stock in excess of the number employed at the preceding census. In fact, however, not all of this decrease represents "racial displacement." In Connecticut, Maine, and Nevada, it was due to a general decline of the mining and quarrying industry, which affected all employees, native as well as foreign-born. The actual "displacement" was confined to 400 men in New Hampshire, Vermont, and the Dakotas, without any allowance for decrease by death. None of these States was affected by the "new immigration." Such States as Pennsylvania and Illinois, on the other hand, showed large increases in the number of native miners, both of foreign and of native parentage.

The statistics of iron and steel workers classified by race and nativity appear in Table 32. The fundamental fact brought out by the table is the difference in the rate of industrial expansion between the two last decades of the past century; while in 1880–1890 the increase in the number of employees was equal to about one fourth, during the period 1890–1900 the demand for labor doubled. The effect of this difference is seen in the fact that during the first period, when the number of immigrants from Southern and Eastern Europe was negligible, only 12,000 additional American workmen found employment in the iron and steel industry, or one man to every six who had been employed in 1880; during the period 1890–1900, on the other hand, when immigrants from Southern and Eastern Europe began to come in, the number of native employees of every nativity more than doubled. For every one additional American workman engaged in 1880–1890, eight new American workmen were added to the labor forces in 1890–1900, and there was still room for immigrants.

TABLE 32.

NUMBER OF IRON AND STEEL WORKERS IN THE UNITED STATES, BY RACE AND NATIVITY (THOUSANDS), 1880, 1890, AND 1900.[1]

Race and Nativity	1880	1890	1900	Increase	
				1880–1890	1890–1900
Native-born, total	73	85	184	12	99
White, total	(*)	79	172	..	93
Native parents	(*)	45	94	12	49
Foreign parents	(*)	34	78	..	44
Colored	(*)	6	12	..	.6
Foreign-born, total	42	58	103	16	45
Eastern and Southern Europe	..	3	24	3	21
All other countries	42	55	79	13	24
Grand total	115	143	287	28	144

(*) Not reported.

As stated above, an increase of the total number of native workmen in the United States does not preclude the possibility of local displacements of native workmen by immigrants. As an actual fact, however, no evidence of such displacements can be discovered by a comparison of the distribution of iron and steel workers by States in 1890 and 1900. In two States only the census returns for 1900 showed a decrease of native white iron and steel workers since 1890, viz., in Montana 100 men, and Nebraska 300 men; total, 400 men. Neither of these States holds an important place in the iron and steel industry. Both

[1] Compiled from the *Reports of the Immigration Commission*, vol. 8, pp. 21–22, Tables 14 and 15, and vol. 1, pp. 784, 785, Table 4.

States show a general decline of the number of iron and steel workers from 1890 to 1900, viz., Montana from 600 to 300 and Nebraska from 1000 to 500. This decline affected foreign-born as well as native workers. Alabama alone shows a displacement of the majority of colored iron and steel workers (1300 out of a total of 1700) by immigrants. But while the aggregate decrease of the number of native white and colored workers through racial displacement and other causes did not exceed 1700 men in three States, the total increase of the number of native-born iron and steel workers in the United States was as high as 99,000, distributed over all important iron- and steel-producing States.[1]

We may go one step further, following the lead of the Immigration Commission into four of the principal centers of the iron and steel industry, but we shall look in vain for evidence of "racial displacement." The results of the comparison are presented in Table 33.

TABLE 33.

INCREASE OF THE NUMBER OF IRON AND STEEL WORKERS IN THE PRINCIPAL CITIES OF THE MIDDLE WEST BY RACE AND NATIVITY, 1890–1900.[2]

City	Native-born				Foreign white	Grand total
	White		Colored	Total		
	Native parents	Foreign parents				
Chicago, Illinois	404	1522	21	1947	1166	6113
Milwaukee, Wisconsin	110	1002	1	1113	1324	2437
Cleveland, Ohio	222	1031	39	1292	2377	3669
Toledo, Ohio	83	152	1	236	249	485
Total for the 4 cities	819	3707	62	4588	8116	12,704

[1] *XII. Census, Occupations*, Table 41, pp. 220–423; *XI. Census, Population*, Part II., pp. 530–627.

[2] Computed from *Reports of the Immigration Commission*, vol. 9, p. 9, Tables 559 and 560.

In every one of the four cities chosen for comparison by the Commission we find an actual increase in the number of native workers of native and foreign parentage, white and colored. Of course, this fact does not mean that every individual worker of old American stock who had been employed in the iron and steel mills of Chicago or Cleveland in 1890 was holding his old place in 1900. Some surely have left the mills and gone to other occupations, while their particular places may have been filled by immigrants, which gives occasion to old-timers to speak in a reminiscent mood of "racial displacement." But the scientific investigator must look beyond individual life stories to the movements of population as reflected in great numbers. The effect of immigration upon the distribution of the native- and foreign-born labor forces is shown in Table 34 next following, compiled from material collected by the Immigration Commission.

"In this table skilled laborers are arbitrarily considered to be those who are receiving more than $1.45 per day (14½ cents per hour), and unskilled laborers those receiving $1.45 or less per day. The classification is made upon the basis of the wage-scale of the steel company, which provides for a maximum payment of $1.45 for a day of ten hours to unskilled or common laborers."

The effect of immigration upon the distribution of the labor forces in the iron and steel industry is apparent from the following table; all but one tenth of the native and Northern and Western European workmen have been shifted to skilled occupations, while nine tenths of all unskilled positions have been filled by new immigrants from Southern and Eastern Europe. "The change is sometimes described as a forcing out of the American and Americanized foreign employees. That is hardly accurate, however," says the Immigration Commission, "for the

TABLE 34.

NUMBER AND PER CENT OF SKILLED AND UNSKILLED LABORERS IN ONE IRON AND STEEL CONCERN, 1907.[1]

Nationality	Number			Per cent of total for each national group	
	Total	Skilled	Unskilled	Skilled	Unskilled
Native white:	5257	4678	579	89.0	11.0
Foreign-born:					
From Northern and Western Europe.........					
Scotch.......	27	27	0	100.0	0.0
French.......	31	30	1	96.8	3.2
Swedish......	59	55	4	93.2	6.8
German......	1687	1530	157	90.7	9.3
Welsh.......	440	395	45	89.8	10.2
English......	386	346	40	89.6	10.4
Irish.........	841	743	98	88.3	11.7
From Southern and Eastern Europe:					
Bohemian....	38	7	31	18.4	81.6
Magyar......	731	96	635	13.1	86.9
Slovak.......	2434	280	2154	11.5	88.5
Polish.......	1371	126	1245	9.2	90.8
Croatian.....	1391	84	1307	6.0	94.0
Italian.......	964	5	959	.5	95.5
Recapitulation:					
From Northern and Western Europe.........	3471	3126	345	90.1	9.9
From Southern and Eastern Europe........	6929	598	6331	8.6	91.4
Total white...	15,657	8402	7253	53.8	46.2

[1] Compiled from the *Reports of the Immigration Commission*, vol. 8, p. 350, Table 252.

immigrant does not appear to underbid the American, or at the present time to be even competing with him in any serious way for the better-paid positions."[1] In reality, the "racial displacement" has manifested itself in that

> a part of the earlier employees who remained in the industries in which they were employed before the advent of the Southern and Eastern European, have been able, because of the demand growing out of the general industrial expansion, to rise to more skilled and responsible executive and technical positions which required employees of training and experience . . .
>
> The same tendency asserts itself in the distribution of employees according to race in bituminous coal mines, where all occupations of a higher grade are filled by native Americans or older immigrants and their children, while the Southern and Eastern Europeans are confined to pick mining and unskilled and common labor. The same situation exists in other branches of manufacturing enterprise.[2]

This racial distribution of the operating forces has developed a deep social tendency which constitutes the main distinction between American and European labor conditions. It is pretty generally accepted by European economists, nowadays, that concentration of industry has reduced the ratio of proprietors to wage-earners and thereby diminished the probability of a wage-earner working his way up to the status of a proprietor; at the same time the introduction of machinery has reduced the relative number of skilled mechanics to a minority of the operating force, leaving to the mass of unskilled laborers few opportunities for advancement on the scale of occupations. As a result, the average European laborer has come to regard his place in the industrial system as fixed. Such has not been the attitude of the American wage-earner. Though the introduction of machinery has had the tendency in the United States, as in Europe, to reduce the relative number of skilled mechanics, yet the rapid pace of industrial expansion has increased the number of skilled and supervisory positions

[1] *Reports of the Immigration Commission*, vol. 8, p. 583.

[2] Jenks and Lauck, *loc. cit.*, pp. 195, 196.

so fast that all but "the thriftless, unprogressive elements of the original operating forces"[1] have had the opportunity to advance on the scale of occupations. The few examples of "captains of industry" who have risen from the ranks of labor will inspire only the most optimistic. But the presence of great numbers of commonplace American workmen who started at the bottom and have advanced to better paid positions in the mills has kept up in the average American wage-earner the ambition to rise individually.

A good illustration of these tendencies is furnished by the statistics of the iron and steel industry. Of the 15,657 white iron and steel workers employed in all plants of Industrial Concern No. 1 in 1907, about one half were American and Americanized skilled men. (See Table 34 above.) Looking back to the time before the advent of the immigrants from Southern and Eastern Europe, we shall find that the opportunity for all of the original operating forces to advance to skilled positions was conditioned upon the concern doubling its force within the period of working efficiency of one generation. It has been shown that the total number employed in the iron and steel industry of the United States doubled from 1890 to 1900. It is easy to calculate what the opportunities of the "English-speaking"[2] wage-earners

[1] Jenks and Lauck, *loc. cit.*, p. 194.

[2] The Immigration Commission has adopted the race classification popularly used in mill towns and mining camps. This classification is thus explained by Mr. Fitch: "By the Eastern European immigration the labor force has been cleft horizontally into two great divisions. The upper stratum includes what is known in mill parlance as the 'English-speaking men'; the lower contains the 'Hunkies' or 'Ginnies.' Or, if you prefer, the former are the 'white men,' the latter the 'foreigners.' An 'English-speaking' man may be neither native American, nor English, nor Irish. He may be one of these, or he may be German, Scandinavian, or Dutch. It is sufficient if the land of his birth be somewhere west of the Russian Empire or north of Austria-Hungary. A 'Hunky' is not necessarily a Hungarian. He may belong to any of the Slavic races. 'Ginny' seems to include all the 'Hunkies' with the Italians thrown in."—*The Pittsburgh Survey: The Steel Workers*, pp. 147–148.

would have been, had the rate of expansion during that decade been as slow as in 1880–1890. Of the total number employed by Concern No. 1, 8728 were Americans or older immigrants; the others belonged to the new immigrant races. Had the concern progressed at the 1880–1890 rate, the force would have been increased by one fourth, approximately to 11,000. Only one half of this number, *i. e.*, 5500, could have been given skilled employment, while the other 2304 of the 7804 English-speaking workmen who were so employed in 1907 would have had to content themselves with unskilled work. In other words, a slower expansion of the industry recommended by the Immigration Commission[1] would have deprived more than thirty per cent of the "English-speaking" workmen of opportunities for advancement. Their standard of living would necessarily have remained that of unskilled laborers. It is only because the new immigration has furnished the class of unskilled laborers that the native workmen and older immigrants have been raised to the plane of an aristocracy of labor. This evolution must not be lost sight of in the discussion of "racial displacement."

That the statistics of iron and steel workers show an increase of 49,000 native-born of native parentage from 1890 to 1900, does not mean that the same individuals were employed in 1900 as ten years before. Some surely have advanced on the scale of occupations and others succeeded them in the mills, still the figures do not disclose the change of individuals. But when English-speaking workers of foreign birth are classified separately, the shifting of a number of Englishmen, Welshmen, and Irishmen to other, more remunerative pursuits, will manifest itself in a corresponding reduction of their numbers employed in the iron and steel industry, unless there have been new immigrants of the same nationalities to take their places. This may be observed in many industries. It has been shown that actual displacement of native- by foreign-born wage-earners

[1] *Reports of the Immigration Commission*, vol. 1, p. 45.

is exceptional and negligible. But there has been a decrease of the number of English, Welsh, and Irish workers in certain occupations, simultaneously with an increase of the number of recent immigrants and native American workers in the same occupations. Upon a superficial glance this coincidence might be interpreted as the forcing out of Americanized workers by immigrants from Southern and Eastern Europe with a lower standard of living. Such an interpretation would not harmonize with the fact that new native workers of native parentage, presumably with as high a standard of living as the Irish, have entered the industry in large numbers. A comparative study of the distribution of the foreign-born workers by country of birth and occupation will bring out the real tendencies of the industrial readjustment produced by immigration.

We find in the first place, that the total number of English, Welsh, Irish, and German male breadwinners in the United States decreased from 1890 to 1900 as follows:

TABLE 35.

NUMBER OF ENGLISH, WELSH, IRISH, AND GERMAN MALE BREADWINNERS (THOUSANDS), 1890 and 1900.[1]

Nationality	Number		Decrease 1890–1900	
	1890	1900	Number	Per cent
English and Welsh	487	439	48	9.9
Irish	805	714	91	11.3
German	1338	1276	62	4.6

It must be borne in mind that the number of foreign-born can increase only by immigration, since their children born in this country are classified as native. Had there been no immigration, the four nationalities named should have lost

[1] See Appendix, Table XI.

by death from 1890 to 1900 about 20 per cent of their numbers.[1] The actual per cent of decrease indicates that the net immigration of the English and Welsh, Irish, and Germans must have been equal respectively to about 10 per cent, 9 per cent, and 15 per cent of their numbers in 1890. In other words, there was no "displacement" of those nationalities by the races of the new immigration.

In the next place, the reduction in numbers affected only certain occupations, while others showed an increase. Among the English and Welsh, the latter class comprised the following occupations: manufacturers, with an increase of 5000; agents and salesmen, with an increase of 3900; and professional men, with an increase of 2500. All other occupations showed a decrease; the greatest numerical decrease was found among the farmers, viz. 14,500 men, or 20 per cent, which was somewhat in excess of the death roll for the ten-year period.[2] Apparently, no new farmers came from England and Wales to fill the places of their countrymen who were carried off by death. This fact, obviously, had nothing to do with the "new immigration," since the "undesirable aliens from Southern and Eastern Europe" kept away from the farming sections and left the field open for English and Welsh immigrants.

The tendency characterizing the readjustment which took place in the occupational field is brought out in the following comparative statement of selected occupations which exhibited a marked divergence, one way or the other, between the percentage of decrease of the number employed and the occupational death-rate:

[1] The annual death-rate among the foreign-born, according to the census of 1900, varied from 19 to 20.6 per 1000.—*XII. Census, Vital Statistics*, Part I., p. xc.

[2] The annual death-rate for farmers and farm laborers according to the XII. Census was 17.6 per 1000.—*XII. Census, Vital Statistics*, Part I., p. 209.

TABLE 36.

SHIFTING OF ENGLISH AND WELSH MALE BREADWINNERS IN SELECTED OCCUPATIONS, 1890–1900.[1]

Selected occupations.	Per cent ratio to total engaged in each occupation.		
	Aggregate decrease	Loss by death	Net accretion (+) or defection (−)
Bookkeepers, accountants, and clerks	−0.6	−13.6	+13.0
Retail merchants	−8.3	−16.4	+8.1
Machinists and blacksmiths	−2.8	−10.5[2]	+7.7
Textile mill operatives	−17.6	−8.8	−8.8
Miners and quarrymen	−20.8	−9.6	−11.2
Tailors	−39.5	−11.8	−27.7

The preceding table indicates that while the English and Welsh were leaving the mines, the textile mills, and the tailor shops, their numbers were increasing in some of the better paid skilled trades and in mercantile pursuits.

The tendency among the Irish was substantially the same as among the English and Welsh. There were 5000 more manufacturers in 1900 than in 1890; 4700 more agents and salesmen, and 500 more professional men. All other specified occupations showed a decrease. The greatest decrease, both numerical and relative, appeared among farmers, viz., 26,000, or 28 per cent, which was much in excess of the loss by death. It is evident not only that the soil had no attraction for the recent Irish immigrants, but that it could not hold the older Irish farmers who must have given up farming for other pursuits. The direction in which the Irish shifted within non-agricultural pursuits is indicated in Table 37 next below:

[1] See Appendix, Table XI.

[2] The death-rate for 1900 among machinists was 10.5 and among blacksmiths 18.3 per 1000. (*Vital Statistics, loc. cit.*) In order to make the estimates in this table more conservative, the lower rate has been selected.

TABLE 37.

SHIFTING OF IRISH MALE BREADWINNERS IN SELECTED OCCUPATIONS, 1890–1900.[1]

Selected occupations	Per cent ratio to total engaged in each occupation		
	Aggregate decrease	Loss by death	Net accretion (+) or defection (−)
Bookkeepers, accountants, and clerks	0.0	−13.6	+13.6
Machinists and blacksmiths	−2.3	−10.5[1]	+8.2
Building trades	−10.3	−17.0[2]	+6.7
Steam railroad employees	−14.5	−10.8	−3.7
Miners and quarrymen	−18.0	−9.6	−8.4
Textile mill operatives	−25.5	−8.8	−15.7
Tailors	−34.5	−11.8	−22.7

Simultaneously with the movement of the Irish from the mines, the textile mills, the tailor shops and, presumably, from the lower grades of the railroad service, their number increased in the skilled trades and in clerical pursuits.

The occupational changes among the Germans display the same tendencies as have been traced among the English-speaking races, with some variation of detail. The census returns for 1900 record an increase since 1890 in the following occupations: manufacturers, 7000; agents and salesmen, 11,000; professional men, 2000; machinists and blacksmiths, 3000. City laborers, farm laborers, and all other specified occupations show a numerical decrease. In some of the latter, however, the loss by death was partly offset by accretions from the same nationality, while in others actual defections added to the natural decrease by death. The comparative statistics for both classes of occupations are presented in the following table:

[1] See footnotes to Table 36.

[2] The death-rate for masons in 1900 was 19.9 per 1000; for carpenters and joiners 17.2; for plasterers and whitewashers 17.0. (*Vital Statistics, loc. cit.*)

TABLE 38.

SHIFTING OF GERMAN MALE BREADWINNERS IN SELECTED OCCUPATIONS 1890–1900.[1]

Selected occupations	Per cent ratio to total engaged in each occupation		
	Aggregate decrease	Loss by death	Net accretion (+) or defection (−)
Farmers	−6.7	−17.6	+10.9
Retail merchants	−4.5	−16.4	+11.9
Building trades	−12.5	−17.0	+4.5
Miners and quarrymen	−1.0	−9.6	+8.6
Tailors	−22.0	−11.0	−10.2
Textile mill operatives	−22.6	− 8.8	−13.8

Unlike the English, Welsh, and Irish, the Germans, during the last decade of the nineteenth century, show accretions among the farmers, on the one hand, and among the miners and quarrymen, on the other. Defections from textile mills and tailor shops are paralleled by increases among retail merchants and in the building trades.

The ultimate effect of immigration from Southern and Eastern Europe upon the readjustment of the various races of foreign-born breadwinners on the scale of occupations appears from the table on page 171.

The earlier immigrants have worked their way upward, leaving the coarse grades of labor to later immigrants from Southern and Eastern Europe. It will be observed that the natives of Austria-Hungary furnish a strikingly high proportion of mine, mill, and factory workers compared with the Germans and Irish. The Poles and Italians furnish a proportion of common laborers higher than the Irish and much higher than the Germans and the British. On the other hand, one fifth of the Germans and Swedes are farmers, whereas the percentage of farmers among the natives of Poland and Austria is very small, and among the Hungarians and Italians it is negligible. The races of the "old

[1] See footnotes to Table 36.

immigration" likewise show higher percentages of skilled mechanics and of persons engaged in business and the professions.

TABLE 39.

PRINCIPAL NATIONALITIES OF MALE BREADWINNERS CLASSIFIED BY OCCUPATION GROUPS (PER CENT), 1900.[1]

Nationality	Farmers, planters, and overseers	Business, professional and clerical pursuits[2]	Skilled trades[3]	Mine, mill, and factory workers[4]	Laborers (not on farms)	All others	Total
Scotch	12.7	18.7	16.5	13.4	5.7	33.0	100
English and Welsh	13.1	17.7	13.2	18.0	6.4	31.6	100
Irish	9.4	12.1	9.3	8.7	22.3	38.2	100
Germans	20.7	15.3	11.1	6.9	10.2	35.8	100
Swedes	20.9	7.7	13.5	10.9	12.8	34.2	100
Poles	5.7	8.7	5.1	23.2	29.1	28.2	100
Italians	1.6	10.2	4.7	14.5	33.2	35.8	100
Austrians	5.2	10.8	4.6	31.7	18.8	28.9	100
Hungarians	1.6	8.4	3.0	40.7	22.3	24.0	100

To throw the social gradation among the various nationalities more into relief, all specified occupations of the preceding table are combined in Table 40 under two heads: (1) higher grade, comprising skilled mechanics, business and professional men and farmers, and (2) lower grade, comprising mine, mill, and factory workers and unskilled laborers in general. Nearly one half of all the British, German, and Swedish immigrants are farmers, skilled mechanics, professional and business men; less than one fourth are employed in the coarser grades of labor. Among the races of the old immigration the proportion is reversed.

[1] *Reports of the Immigration Commission*, vol. 1, Table A, pp. 821–829.

[2] Include: Saloonkeepers and bartenders; agents; bookkeepers and accountants; clerks and copyists; merchants and dealers (not wholesale); salesmen; manufacturers and officials, etc.; and professional service.

[3] Include: Building trades; blacksmiths; machinists; printers, lithographers, and pressmen, and tobacco and cigar factory operatives.

[4] Include: Iron and steel workers; miners and quarrymen; saw- and planing-mill employees; tailors; and textile mill operatives.

TABLE 40.

PER CENT DISTRIBUTION OF FOREIGN-BORN MALE BREAD-WINNERS ACCORDING TO NATIONALITY AND GRADE OF OCCUPATION, 1900

Nationality (as determined by country of birth)	Higher-grade	Lower-grade
Scotch	47.9	19.1
German	47.1	17.1
English and Welsh	44.0	24.4
Swedes	42.1	23.7
Irish	30.8	31.1
Austrian	20.6	50.5
Polish	19.5	52.3
Italian	16.5	47.7
Hungarian	13.0	62.3

A comparison of the Scotch with other English-speaking immigrants throws a new light upon the subject of "racial displacement." Judged by occupational standards, the Scotch stand higher than other immigrants from the British Isles. And yet, while the English, Welsh, and Irish in the United States decreased in number from 1890 to 1900, the Scotch showed an increase of 10 per cent, which was equivalent to a net immigration of about 30 per cent. Increased numbers in the principal occupations are the rule among the Scotch during that decade, decreases the exception. Even common laborers show an increase.[1] But

[1] See Appendix, Table XI.

In the census returns for 1890 the distinction between agricultural laborers and other laborers in agricultural districts was not strictly drawn. For this reason comparisons for each class taken separately are not reliable when the differences are close. The combined number of city laborers and farm laborers among the Scotch was 14,300 in 1890 and 14,500 in 1900. The only two occupations which show a numerical decrease in excess of the probable loss by death are miners and textile mill operatives. The miners showed an aggregate decrease of 2100 men, which was equivalent to 17.8 per cent, as against a death-rate of 9.6 per cent; among the textile mill operatives the corresponding percentages were respectively 23.4 per cent and 8.8 per cent. The number of tailors decreased from 1100 to 1000, which approximately corresponds to the death-rate among tailors.

these decreases were amply compensated by increases in other occupations. These facts command attention. The Scotchman's "progress toward assimilation" is not questioned. It is not claimed that his standard of living is lower than the Irish, or the English; nor has "ready acceptance of a low wage," or "willingness to accept indefinitely without protest certain conditions of employment," been discovered among his "general characteristics."[1] The increase of the Scotch in this country, contemporaneous with a decrease of the English and Irish, warrants the supposition that the decline of emigration from England and Ireland may be the effect of changed conditions in those countries rather than in the United States. This subject will be more fully treated in a subsequent chapter.

As the latest available figures for the whole country date back to 1900, the question arises whether the relations disclosed by them have not been materially modified by the heavy immigration of the first decade of the present century. A partial view of its effects, restricted to the first half of that period and to one industrial State with a large foreign-born population, can be gained from a comparison of the results of the Massachusetts census of 1905 with those of the United States census of 1900. According to the changes which took place in the interval, all classes of manual labor and clerical occupations fall into five groups:

I. Occupations in which the increased demand for labor manifested itself in a general increase of native, as well as foreign-born breadwinners.

II. Specified occupations in which the demand for labor decreased, reducing both the native and the foreign-born force.

III. Laborers, not specified.

IV. Occupations in which native workers were displaced by immigrants.

V. Occupations in which foreign-born workers were displaced by native-born.

[1] Jenks and Lauck, *loc. cit.*, pp. 195–196.

Laborers have been segregated into a separate group for the reason that an increase or decrease among them is likely to be affected by a difference in the method of classification as much as by real economic changes. The comparative importance of these five groups appears from Table 41. The Massachusetts census draws no distinction between native-born of native and of foreign parentage. On the whole, native breadwinners show a greater increase than foreign-born.

TABLE 41.

INCREASE (+) AND DECREASE (−) OF THE NUMBER OF BREADWINNERS IN MASSACHUSETTS CLASSIFIED BY SEX, NATIVITY, AND OCCUPATION GROUPS (THOUSANDS), 1900–1905.[1]

Nativity and Sex	Occupation groups					
	I	II	III	IV	V	Total
Both Sexes:						
Native	+79.9	−17.3	−7.7	−2.8	+1.0	+53.1
Foreign-born	+57.3	−5.8	−11.1	+3.9	−0.4	+43.9
Total	+137.2	−23.1	−18.8	+1.1	+0.6	+97.0
Male:						
Native	+48.9	−12.8	−7.7	−2.7	+0.5	+26.2
Foreign-born	+41.5	−3.1	−11.1	+3.8	−0.4	+30.7
Total	+90.4	−15.9	−18.8	+1.1	+0.1	+56.9
Female:						
Native	+31.0	−4.5	......	−0.1	+0.5	+26.9
Foreign-born	+15.8	−2.7	......	+0.1	−0.0	+13.2
Total	+46.8	−7.2	......	+0.0	+0.5	+40.1

The increase of the native-born is greatest where the increase of the foreign-born is greatest. On the contrary a substantial decrease of native-born breadwinners is found in the second group of occupations where the number of

[1] *Occupations at the XII. Census*, Table 34, pp. 154 *ff*., and Table 41, pp. 300–305. *Census of the Commonwealth of Massachusetts*, 1905, vol. ii., Occupations, Table I., pp. 9–117.

foreign-born likewise shows a large decrease. The gains of the foreign-born at the expense of the native and *vice-versa* are insignificant. The decrease of native breadwinners in all occupations aggregated 27,800 persons, but it was offset by a net increase of 80,900 in all other classes of manual labor and clerical occupations, that is to say the loss of one position was compensated by the gain of three. No account is taken here of the increase of native-born breadwinners in business and professional service.

As stated above, it is uncertain whether the decrease of the number of laborers was due to industrial changes or to the whims of statistical classification. The details for all other occupations showing a decrease of the number of native breadwinners are given in Table 42.

TABLE 42.

SPECIFIED OCCUPATIONS IN MASSACHUSETTS WITH A DECREASING NUMBER OF NATIVE BREADWINNERS, CLASSIFIED BY SEX AND NATIVITY, 1900–1905.[1]

Occupations	Decrease (Thousands)		Occupations	Decrease (Thousands)
GROUP II	Native	Foreign-born	GROUP IV	NATIVE
Males:			*Males.*	
Agricultural laborers...	2.5	.3	Hucksters and peddlers	.6
Butchers............	1.3	.1	Boatmen and sailors...	.4
Carpenters and joiners.	2.8	.4	Engineers and firemen..	.3
Gold and silver workers	2.2	1.0	Porters and helpers.....	.3
Packers and shippers..	1.0	.2	Tin plate and tinware workers............	.2
All others[2]...........	3.0	1.1	Barbers and hairdressers	.2
Total...........	12.8	3.1	Miners and quarrymen.	.1
			All others[3]...........	.6
Females:			Total...........	2.7
Housekeepers and stewardesses......	1.8	1.5		
Servants and waitresses	1.5	.9	*Females:*	
Dressmakers........	1.2	.2		
Total...........	4.5	2.6	Agricultural laborers, hucksters, and peddlers	1
Both sexes........	17.3	5.7	Both sexes.........	2.8

[1] See footnote to Table 41.

[2] Includes bakers, blacksmiths, brick and tile makers, confectioners, coopers, gunsmiths, locksmiths and bell hangers, harness and saddle

As appears from the preceding table, the only possible "displacement" of native- by foreign-born did not exceed 2800 breadwinners in five years, which was less than 3 per cent of the increase of native-born in all occupations exclusive of business and professional service. The total number of immigrant breadwinners who gave Massachusetts as their destination in 1901–1905 reached 220,000 persons of both sexes.[1] Assuming that 2800 native hucksters and peddlers, boatmen, and sailors, etc., were virtually displaced by the immigrants, we find that the measure of "displacement" was equal to one native for every seventy-eight immigrants.

These results disclose no material change in the racial make-up of the industrial forces during the first five years of the present century; what was true in 1900 remained so as late as 1905. The immigrants did not "crowd" the native wage-earners, but were absorbed in those occupations where native workers found employment in increasing numbers. Actual "displacement" was a negligible quantity.

---

makers and repairers, hostlers, marble and stone cutters, masons (brick and stone), meat and fruit canners, packers, etc., millers, shirt, collar and cuff makers, stewards, and wheelwrights.

[3] Includes brassworkers, cabinet makers, candle, soap, and tallow makers, copper workers, engravers, paper hangers, rope and cordage factory operatives, sail, awning, and tent makers, tobacco and cigar operatives, and upholsterers.

[1] *Annual Reports of the Commissioner-General of Immigration*: 1901, p. 17, Table VIII.; 1902, p. 29, Table IX.; 1903, p. 32, Table IX.; 1904, p. 30, Table IX.; 1905, p. 34, Table IX.

CHAPTER VIII

EMIGRATION FROM NORTHERN AND WESTERN EUROPE

A. Introductory

THE great influx of Italian, Slav; and Jewish immigrants since 1890 coincides with a decrease of immigration from Northern and Western Europe. This coincidence has been generally accepted as proof that immigration from Southern and Eastern Europe has checked the current of "more desirable" immigration from Northern and Western Europe. This assertion has been clothed in the scientific garb of "the Gresham law of immigration"; bad immigration, it is said, tends to drive out good immigration. The *cum hoc, ergo propter hoc* method of reasoning has scarcely ever appeared so undisguised as in this newly discovered "law." No attempt has been made to inquire into the conditions of the countries from which the "old immigration" was drawn, with a view to ascertaining, if possible, whether there were any causes tending to check emigration from those countries.

It has been shown in Chapter IV. that in the long run immigration bears an almost constant relation to the population of the United States. Inasmuch, however, as the latter increases faster than the population of Europe, especially that of the emigration countries, the rate of emigration from those countries must increase much faster than their population in order to supply the industries of the United States with the number of immigrants they can employ. Yet the sources of emigration are not unlimited,

We may speak, metaphorically, of a Slav "invasion," but such figures of speech merely obscure the real nature of present-day phenomena. The Norman invaders of a thousand years ago financed their expeditions by robbing the peaceable population on their way. All they needed was the spirit of adventure. To-day that spirit alone will not carry their descendants across the ocean. The funds for emigration must be raised by the emigrants themselves, or by their relatives and friends. The volume of emigration from a given country can, therefore, not increase beyond a certain limit set by the size of its population. When that point is reached, further industrial expansion in the United States must draw upon the labor supply of other countries.

During the ten-year period 1881–1890 the countries of Northern and Western Europe furnished 72 per cent of the total immigration to the United States.[1] This period included the years of the maximum immigration from Germany and the Scandinavian countries and of the greatest immigration from the United Kingdom since the Irish famine of the '40's of the past century. To maintain the same ratio to the total immigration of the past decade, 1901–1910, the countries of Northern and Western Europe should have furnished six and one third million immigrants, *i. e.*, two thirds more than in 1881–1890. In order to replace the immigrants from Southern and Eastern Europe that were absorbed by the industrial expansion of the past decade, immigration from Northern and Western Europe should have risen 117 per cent above the highest water-mark reached in 1881–1890.

During the same period the population of Ireland decreased 14 per cent, and the population of the other countries of Northern and Western Europe increased from 12.5 to 25.2 per cent.[2] Unless we allow ourselves to be

[1] *Reports of the Immigration Commission*, vol. 1, Table 6, pp. 61–63.

[2] The rates of increase for each of the principal countries were as follows:

carried away by imagination, does past experience warrant the assumption that the volume of immigration from those countries could have so far outrun the increase of their population?

The total immigration from Ireland to the United States for 1891–1900 was equal to 655,000 persons.[1] An increase of 117 per cent would have brought up this figure to 1,400,000 (in round numbers), *i. e.*, to 31 per cent of the population of Ireland at the census of 1901.[2] Such a rate of depopulation was not reached even in the years of the Irish famine.[3]

It is needless to repeat this calculation for Great Britain and the Scandinavian countries. It could be shown by a simple computation that, in order to replace the "new immigration" emigration from those countries should have risen to the Irish level. Their recent economic development, on the contrary, as will next be shown, has had a decided tendency to check emigration.

		Per cent
England and Wales	1881–1901	25.2
Scotland	1881–1901	19.7
Germany	1880–1900	24.6
Denmark	1881–1900	24.4
Norway	1875–1900	23.1
Sweden	1880–1900	12.5

(Computed from *Statesman's Year Book*, 1910, pp. 13, 17; and *British Statistical Abstract of the Principal and Other Foreign Countries*, No. 16, p. 8; No. 35, pp. 8, 10.)

[1] *Reports of the Immigration Commission*, vol. 1, Table 9, pp. 89–92.

[2] *Statistical Abstract for the United Kingdom*, Table 114, p. 361.

[3] The lowest numerical and relative decrease was in 1871–1881, viz., 237,541 persons, equivalent to 4.4 per cent. The total emigration during the same period was 618,650. The natural increase of population through the excess of births over deaths was accordingly 381,109 persons, *i. e.*, 7 per cent of the population at the census of 1878. Allowing the same rate for the natural increase of the population of Ireland in 1901–1910, we obtain 24 per cent as the rate of decrease in our hypothetical case, as against 19.8 per cent for the decade 1841–1851 comprising the years of the great Irish famine. (The figures are taken from the *Statistical Abstract for the United Kingdom*, No. 56, p. 361, Table 114.)

B. Germany

In the closing years of the nineteenth century Germany ceased to be a country of emigration, and became a country of immigration. This transformation is seen from the following table:

TABLE 43.

FOREIGN-BORN POPULATION OF GERMANY, NET EMIGRATION AND NET IMMIGRATION (THOUSANDS).[1]

Year	Foreign-born population			Net emigration (−) or net immigration (+)
	Number	Increase		
		Total	Annual average	
1880	419	...	...	...
1885	433	14	3	−980
1890	513	80	16	−331
1895	...	...	...	−449
1900	830	317	32	+ 94
1905	...	...	...	+ 52

The increase of the foreign-born population of Germany during the years 1900–1907 averaged 79,000 annually.[2] The annual increase of the foreign-born population of the United States in 1870–1880 averaged 107,000, and in 1890–1900, 109,000. It can be readily seen by comparison that immigration to Germany is growing to respectable proportions. Two thirds of the foreign-born male breadwinners are engaged in industrial pursuits. This fact alone would furnish a sufficient explanation of the decline of German immigration to the United States; when there is a call for large masses of immigrant labor, native wage-earners will find a good market at home.[3]

It is worthy of note, on the other hand, that Germany

[1] *Die Statistik in Deutschland nach ihrem heutigen Stand*, I Band (1911), Dr. Herrmann Losch, "Wanderungsstatistik," p. 485. Dr. Friedrich Zahn, "Deutschlands wirtschaftliche Entwickelung," *Annalen des Deutschen Reichs*, 1910, p. 405.

[2] *Ibid.*

[3] See Appendix, Table XII.

draws her immigrant supply from the same sources as the United States. During the twenty years from 1880 to 1900, three fourths of all immigrants to Germany came from Austria-Hungary, Russia, and Italy.[1] Moreover, the Polish or Italian immigrant to the United States comes from a higher social layer than his countryman who goes to Germany, the cost of passage from any of these countries to Germany being purely nominal in comparison with the cost of a transatlantic trip. It is evident that the German wage-earner cannot avoid coming in contact with the immigrant from Southern and Eastern Europe by staying away from the United States.

In addition to her permanent foreign-born population Germany has a large floating immigrant labor supply, the so-called "birds of passage," mostly Poles and other Slavs from Russia and Galicia. The latest official data relating to migration from Galicia to Germany place the total number at 26,283 for the year 1899. The movement has considerably grown since that time. Austrian statisticians variously estimate the number for the year 1905 at from 60,000 to 100,000.[2]

The migration of working men and women from Russian Poland to Germany for temporary employment has grown in the following proportion:

TABLE 44.

MIGRATION OF WORKERS FROM RUSSIAN POLAND TO GERMANY FOR TEMPORARY EMPLOYMENT, 1890–1904.[3]

Year	Thousands
1890	17
1900	119
1901	140
1902	136
1903	142
1904	138

[1] See Appendix, Table XIII.

[2] *Münchener Volkswirtschaftliche Studien*, J. von Trzcinski, "Russisch-Polnische und galizische Wanderarbeiter im Grossherzogtum Posen," p. 44.

[3] *Reports of the Warsaw Statistical Committee. Bulletin XXII.*, p. 2,

About 95 per cent of the temporary immigrants from Russian Poland find employment as agricultural laborers.[1] But the demand for them is the direct result of the movement of Polish peasants from the rural districts of Prussian Poland to the great industrial cities of Germany and particularly to the coal mining districts.

In 1898 there were 57,000 foreign-speaking mine workers in Western Germany out of a total of 198,000, *i. e.*, 28.7 per cent, nearly all of whom were Poles from Prussian Poland.[2] According to the latest statistics for the Ruhr district, which produces one half of Germany's coal output, the number of Polish miners has grown to 100,000 out of a total of 350,000.[3] Evidently, there must have been some other cause than reluctance to compete with Polish immigrants that has "operated to prevent the further coming" of German miners to the bituminous regions of Pennsylvania,[4] since they have no alternative but to work with Polish immigrants on either side of the Atlantic.

The transformation of Germany from an emigrant-furnishing nation to a country of immigration is the direct result of her recent industrial expansion. Its extent can be gauged by the comparative growth of production of coal and pig iron in Germany and the two other leading industrial countries, the United States and Great Britain, as represented graphically in Diagrams XII[5] and XIII.[6] In coal mining Germany has, in recent years, outrun Great

---

Warsaw, 1906. (In Russian.) *General Analysis of the Statistics of Migration of Workers for Temporary Employment*, etc. By K. G. Vobly.

[1] *Ibid.*, p. 21.

[2] J. Karski, *Die Polnischen Wanderarbeiter*, "Die Neue Zeit," 1900–1901, pp. 722, 723.

[3] V. Maisky: "The Tragedy of the German Coal Miners," (in Russian) *Russkoye Bogatstvo*, April, 1912, pp. 35, 47.

[4] *Reports of the Immigration Commission*, vol. 6, p. 427.

[5] Based upon the Report of the United States Geological Survey, *Production of Coal in 1909*, p. 60.

[6] Figures are taken from *The Mineral Industry*, 1893, p. 351; 1896. p. 334; 1900, p. 395; 1910, p. 381.

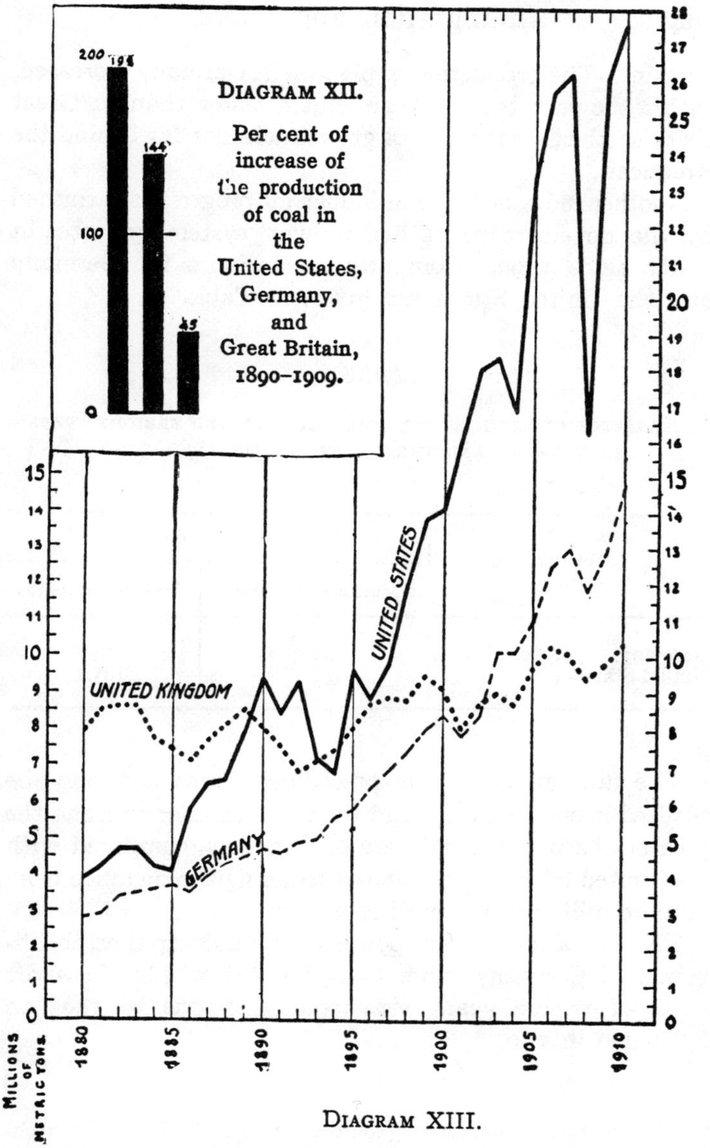

DIAGRAM XII.

Per cent of increase of the production of coal in the United States, Germany, and Great Britain, 1890–1909.

DIAGRAM XIII.

Production of pig iron in Germany, the United States, and the United Kingdom, 1880–1910.

Britain. The production of pig iron in Germany increased, within the past twenty years, much faster than in Great Britain; the German rate of growth was not far behind the American.

Another index of German industrial progress is furnished by the development of her railway system and freight traffic since 1890. Comparative statistics for Germany and the United States are given in Table 45.

TABLE 45.

COMPARATIVE GROWTH OF RAILROAD MILEAGE AND FREIGHT TRAFFIC IN GERMANY AND THE UNITED STATES, 1890–1900.[1]

Country	Per cent increase	
	Mileage in operation	Ton-miles of freight
Germany	41.3	135.7
United States	46.7	183.4

The full import of the preceding figures can only be realized if one bears in mind the much smaller area and the greater density of population of Germany, compared with the United States, both factors reducing the distance from mine to mill and from mill to market.

The use of mechanical power in the industrial establishments of Germany more than doubled within the short space of twelve years, viz., from 3,400,000 in 1895 to 8,800,000 in 1907.[2]

[1] Computed from the following sources: Dr. Friedrich Zahn, "Deutschlands wirtschaftliche Entwickelung," *Annalen des Deutschen Reichs*, 1911, No. 3–4, p. 189; *Statistical Abstract of the United States*, 1910, p. 715.

[2] Zahn, *loc. cit.*, p. 175.

The effect of the industrial progress of Germany upon the labor market is shown in the comparative increase of the number of breadwinners engaged in trade and manufactures and of the population at large, as shown in Table 46 next following:

TABLE 46.

PER CENT INCREASE OF THE POPULATION OF GERMANY AND OF THE NUMBER OF BREADWINNERS IN TRADE AND MANUFACTURES, 1882–1907.[1]

Period	Population	Breadwinners
1882–1895	14.5	39.9
1895–1907	19.2	39.7

The increased demand for labor in the industrial establishments of Germany resulted in a substantial increase of the rate of wages.

"The rate of wages has risen during the recent past . . . more than the price of the necessities of life, showing that the German workingman has shared in the prosperity of the country."[2] It is admitted by the German trade-unions that the condition of labor has materially improved.[3]

[1] Zahn, *loc. cit.*, p. 164.

[2] Earl Dean Howard: *The Cause and Extent of the Recent Industrial Progress of Germany*, p. 118.

[3] Zahn, *loc. cit.*, p. 227. If an opinion coming from official sources is preferred, the following quotation from a recent speech by Mr. von Berlepsch, former Prussian Minister of Commerce, will be of interest: "Slowly and by little steps rises the well-being of the general body of the people; and no small number of those classes of the population which thirty years ago obtained a bare subsistence have now made their way into a middle class and enjoy a fairly adequate income."—Howard, *loc. cit.*, p. 181.

The average annual earnings upon which membership dues to the trade-union insurance fund were figured increased from 638 marks in 1890 to 953 marks in 1909, *i. e.*, 50 per cent. The upward tendency of wages is not confined to the skilled trades, but has affected all classes of labor. Unbiased evidence of this fact is furnished by the statistics compiled by local authorities under the provisions of the sick-insurance law, and showing the prevailing rates of wages of day laborers in the large cities.[1]

The rate of increase of the average annual earnings of coal miners appears from the following table:

TABLE 47.

AVERAGE ANNUAL EARNINGS IN PRUSSIAN COAL MINES, 1890–1910.[2]

District	Number of wage-earners (thousands) 1910	Annual earnings, marks		
		1890	1910	Per cent of increase
Upper Silesia..........	116	671	964	43.6
Lower Silesia..........	28	735	974	32.5
Dortmund............	335	1,067	1,382	24.8
Aix-la-Chapelle.........	22	878	1,375	56.6
Halle.................	40	730	1,089	49.1

At the same time there has been a marked reduction in the number of hours of work per day.[3] Furthermore "there is also less changing of employment and less non-employment in Germany," than in the United States, since, "in most cases the law requires at least a two weeks' notice before the employee can be discharged."[4]

All these improvements are in no small degree due to the progress of organization among German wage-earners, which became possible only after the repeal of the anti-Socialist law on October 1, 1890. Under the operation of

[1] Howard, *loc. cit.*, pp. 114–115. Statistical tables on the subject of wages are given on pp. 112–113.

[2] Zahn, *loc. cit.*, p. 228.

[3] Howard, *loc. cit.*, p. 117.

[4] *Ibid.*, pp. 126–127.

that law, only local trade-unions, without national affiliations, had been tolerated, and those, only so long as they confined themselves to mutual benefit and educational objects; by executive order of April 11, 1886, strikes of any character were declared to be "revolutionary manifestations." The first national labor convention was held in 1892. It was not until January 1, 1900, however, that all laws restricting the right of federating independent local unions were unequivocally repealed.[1] Since that time the membership of labor organizations has progressed by leaps and bounds, leaving behind the older British and American trade-unions, as appears from the following table:

TABLE 48.

MEMBERSHIP OF TRADE-UNIONS IN GERMANY, 1890–1900.[2]

Year	(Thousands)
1890	301
National unions:	
1900	932
1901	935
1902	1017
1903	1191
1904	1371
1905	1727
1906	2129
1907	2330
1908	2203
1909	2212
1910	2435
Total, including unaffiliated local unions, 1910:	
Germany	2688
United States and Canada (estimated)	2625
Great Britain and Ireland	2427

The ratio of organized workers to the total number of wage-earners enumerated in 1907 was estimated at 28 per cent.[3]

[1] *Handwörterbuch der Staatswissenschaften*, vol. iv., pp. 1147–1149.

[2] *Statistische Beilage des Correspondenz-Blatt der General-Commission der Gewerkschaften Deutschlands*, 1911, No. 6, pp. 161–163; *New York Labor Bulletin*, No. 48 (September, 1911), p. 418. The membership for the United States and Canada seems overestimated.

[3] *Handwörterbuch der Staatswissenschaften*, vol. iv., p. 1175.

A noteworthy development of the German labor movement is the progress of organization among female wage-earners, who are, as a rule, unorganized in this country. The efforts of German unions among the women were stimulated, above all altruistic considerations, by recognition of the depressing effect of the competition of unorganized female labor upon the wages of men. The extent to which the women have responded to the efforts of the unions can be measured by the following figures:

TABLE 49.

PROGRESS OF ORGANIZATION AMONG FEMALE WAGE-EARNERS, IN GERMANY, 1895–1910.[1]

Year	Number of organized women (thousands)	Per cent of total union membership
1895	7	2.7
1900	23	3.3
1905	74	5.7
1906	119	7.1
1907	137	7.3
1908	138	7.6
1909	134	7.3
1910	162	8.0

The assistance rendered by German unions to their members can be measured by the expenditures of the Social-democratic *Gewerkschaften*, *i. e.*, the national unions affiliated with the largest and most influential of the German federations of labor. The figures are given in Table 50.

The progress of the labor movement in Germany has directly and indirectly stimulated labor legislation, which has resulted in a material improvement of the condition of labor:

As a rule [says Dr. Howard], the factories are kept in a much better condition, and have more arrangements for the comfort of the men,

[1] *Statistische Beilage des Correspondenz-Blatt der General-Commission der Gewerkschaften Deutschlands*, 1911, No. 6, pp. 163, 168.

than in the United States. This is the general opinion of writers who compare the conditions prevailing in the two countries, and it seems to be confirmed by direct observation. The factories usually have good light and air, are clean and orderly. The sanitary arrangements and the facilities for washing and changing clothes are splendid. Most of the factories are provided with lockers for the men, so that they need not leave the place in their working clothes.[1]

TABLE 50.

COMPARATIVE SUMMARY OF THE PRINCIPAL EXPENSES OF THE NATIONAL ORGANIZATIONS AFFILIATED WITH THE "GENERAL COMMISSION OF THE TRADE-UNIONS OF GERMANY," 1895–1910.[2]

Object	Millions of marks		
	1895	1900	1910
Strikes	0.3	2.7	20.4
Unemployed benefits	0.2	0.5	6.1
Sick and death benefits and sundry benevolent expenses	0.5	1.0	11.2

Germany was the first nation to introduce a system of workingmen's insurance under the control of the government. "The introduction of insurance laws protecting the workingman against sickness and accidents, and promising him a pension in his old age, has had a tendency to decrease the chances of misfortune in life."[3]

In 1909 there were insured under the provisions of that law over 13,000,000 persons against sickness, over 15,000,000 against old age and invalidity, and nearly 24,000,000 persons against accident, in a total population of 64,000,000 of whom there were less than 19,000,000 wage-earners.[4]

The expansion of industry and the resulting improvement of the condition of industrial wage-earners have drawn to the cities and mining sections the whole natural increase of the rural population.[5]

[1] Howard, *loc. cit.*, pp. 127–128.

[2] *Ibid.*, p. 189.

[3] *Ibid.*, pp. 124, 131.

[4] Zahn, *loc. cit.*, *Annalen des Deutschen Reichs*, 1911, p. 232.

[5] At the foundation of the German Empire in 1871, its rural popula-

At the same time, German agriculture, stimulated by the increase of the country's population and fostered by a protective tariff, also showed substantial progress, as can be seen from Table 51 below. As a result, there is a scarcity of agricultural laborers during the busy season, which is only partially relieved by the immigration of Polish and Russian temporary laborers. Although organization among agricultural laborers is seriously restricted by law, yet, as an effect of economic causes alone, the wages of agricultural laborers have continually advanced.[1]

TABLE 51.

AGRICULTURAL PROGRESS IN GERMANY, 1895–1909.[2]

Crop	Total yield Millions of tons		Yield per hectar tons	
	1895	1909	1895	1909
Rye	7.7	11.4	1.3	1.9
Wheat	3.2	3.8	1.6	2.1
Spring barley	2.8	3.5	1.7	2.1
Potatoes	37.8	46.7	12.4	14.1
Oats	6.2	9.1	1.6	2.1

The combined effect of all these causes was reflected in the rate of emigration from rural districts. Towards the middle of the past century the growth of land values had made the primitive methods of farming unprofitable, and necessitated the introduction of more intensive systems of cultivation. In Prussian Poland the change was somewhat retarded by its general economic backwardness, but in the '70's and in the early '80's it drove large numbers of Polish peasants to the United States. These Poles constituted a large element of the German immigration to the United States and were counted in our immigration statistics as

tion constituted 64 per cent in a total of 41,000,000; at the census of 1900 the total population numbered 56,000,000, but the proportion of rural population had declined to 46 per cent.—Howard, *loc. cit.*, p. 31.

[1] Howard, *loc. cit.*, p. 68.

[2] Zahn, *loc. cit.*, *Annalen des Deutschen Reichs*, 1910, p. 578.

"Germans."[1] But the rapid development of German industry within the last twenty-five years opened for these peasants new opportunities at home. This fact, coupled with the disappearance of cheap lands in the United States, has resulted in a falling off in the emigration of farmers and farm laborers to the United States.

As a general rule, industrial progress in modern times has tended to eliminate the independent artisan, the small trader, and the small-scale farmer and to push them into the ranks of wage-earners. In Germany, however, this process has been checked by the development of co-operation.[2] Its recent progress can be seen from the following table:

TABLE 52.

CO-OPERATIVE ASSOCIATIONS IN GERMANY, 1903–1908.[3]

Year	Number of Associations (thousands)	Membership (millions)	Per cent ratio to population
1903	21	3.1	5.4
1904	22	3.4	5.8
1905	24	3.6	6.2
1906	25	3.8	6.3
1907	26	4.0	6.7
1908	27	4.3	7.2

The general improvement of the living conditions of the broad masses, which characterizes the recent economic development of Germany, must necessarily have affected the rate of emigration during the past twenty years. On the other hand, the tide of German emigration in the early '80's was swelled by political oppression. Under the "minor state of siege," proclaimed by virtue of the anti-Socialist law of 1878, all labor unions were "put under the ban alike with the political organizations of the Social-Democracy. Of the 25 existing unions 16 were dissolved by the govern-

[1] Trzcinski, *loc. cit.*, pp. 3 and 128.

[2] Zahn: *Annalen des Deutschen Reichs*, 1911, No. 3–4, p. 226.

[3] *Ibid.*, p. 227.

ment, the others disbanded voluntarily."[1] The membership of the organizations directly affected was estimated at 50,000. The widespread discontent created by these repressive measures led many workingmen to seek liberty in the United States. The repeal of the "exceptional laws" in 1890 removed the political stimulus to emigration.

The cumulative effect of all these causes upon emigration from Germany can be learned from the following table.

TABLE 53.

ANNUAL AVERAGE IMMIGRATION FROM GERMANY (THOUSANDS), 1875–1910.[2]

Occupation	1875–1878	1879–1890	1891–1898	1899–1910
Skilled mechanics	4.8	15.1	6.3	11.5
Farmers and farm laborers	3.7	12.2	4.4	8.0[3]
Laborers	3.4	20.1	8.1	7.5
Servants	.6	2.6	2.9	7.3
All other miscellaneous	3.3	4.3	2.2	3.9
Total	15.8	54.3	23.9	38.2

In 1879–1890, contemporaneously with the operation of the exceptional laws of 1878, the average annual immigration from Germany to the United States rose 244 per cent above the average level of the preceding four-year period. On the other hand, the average for the twelve-year period 1899–1910 dropped only one third below the level of the preceding period of equal length, 1879–1890. The immigration of skilled mechanics decreased by 3600 annually,

[1] *Handwörterbuch der Staatswissenschaften*, vol. iv., p. 1146.

[2] *Monthly Summary of Commerce and Finance, June, 1903*, pp. 4408–4411. *Reports of the Immigration Commission*, vol. 1, p. 100. *Annual Reports of the Commissioner-General of Immigration:* 1899–1900, Table VII.; 1901–1904, Table IX.; 1905–1908, Table VIII.; 1909–1910, Table X.

[3] Of this number 1110 were farmers and the rest farm laborers.

i. e., by about one fourth. The immigration of farmers and farm laborers dropped 4200 annually, *i. e.*, more than one third, from the high level reached in 1879–1890. The decrease of the immigration of agricultural workers doubtless bears some relation to the decline in the demand for agricultural labor and the increase of land values in the United States.

In order to determine the effect, if any, of immigration from Southern and Eastern Europe upon immigration from Germany, the annual average immigration of unskilled laborers must be considered. The line of demarkation between farm laborers and "laborers not specified" was not clearly drawn in our earlier immigration statistics. Moreover, many agricultural laborers come to the United States to seek industrial employment. If both classes of laborers are merged into one, and an allowance is made for the number of farmers combined with farm laborers prior to 1899,[1] the immigration of unskilled laborers may be estimated for 1891–1898 at 11,400 persons annually. In 1899–1910 this average rose to 14,400. At the same time the rate of immigration from Southern and Eastern Europe rose from 48 per cent of the total immigration for the first period, to 72 per cent for the last.[2] It is evident that the competition of the Italian and Slav unskilled laborer did not deter the German unskilled laborer from coming to the United States. On the whole, the average annual immigration from Germany during the period 1899–1910 increased by 14,300, *i. e.*, 60 per cent over the average for 1891–1898.

[1] The average number of farmers for the period 1891–1898 was estimated at 1100 annually, the same as recorded by immigration statistics for 1899–1910, although the combined number of farmers and farm laborers during the former period was only about one half of the total for the latter. In this manner every precaution was taken against overrating the increase of immigration of unskilled laborers during the last period.

[2] Computed from *Reports of the Immigration Commission*, vol. 1, Table 6, pp. 61–64.

The United States has always been the chief destination of the bulk of German emigrants. Complete data regarding the destination of German emigrants are available only since 1890. The figures will be found in Table 54 next following, with the rate of immigration from Southern and Eastern Europe to the United States in a parallel column. The results are presented graphically in Diagram XIV.

TABLE 54.

EMIGRATION FROM GERMANY TO ALL COUNTRIES OUTSIDE THE UNITED STATES, 1890–1904.[1]

Year	Number of emigrants from Germany to countries outside of United States	Immigration from Southern and Eastern Europe to the United States, per cent of total
1890	7338	35.3
1891	7043	41.2
1892	4533	46.6
1893	9428	44.3
1894	5062	44.9
1895	4995	42.1
1896	4817	57.0
1897	4285,	56.8
1898	3658	62.4
1899	4518	68.0
1900	2606	72.4
1901	2161	73.6
1902	2887	75.1
1903	2661	72.1
1904	1899	68.4

The preceding table and Diagram XIV clearly show the absence of any connection between emigration from Germany and immigration from Southern and Eastern Europe to the United States. Emigration from Germany to other countries was highest in 1890, 1891, and 1893, when immigration from Southern and Eastern Europe to the United States varied from 35.3 to 44.3 per cent of the total immigration to the United States. Since 1893 emigration from

[1] *Vierteljahrshefte zur Statistik des Deutschen Reichs, 1905. Die überseeische Auswanderung im Jahre 1904,* Part I., p. 120, Table 1. *Reports of the Immigration Commission,* vol. 1, Table 6, p. 61.

Diagram XIV.

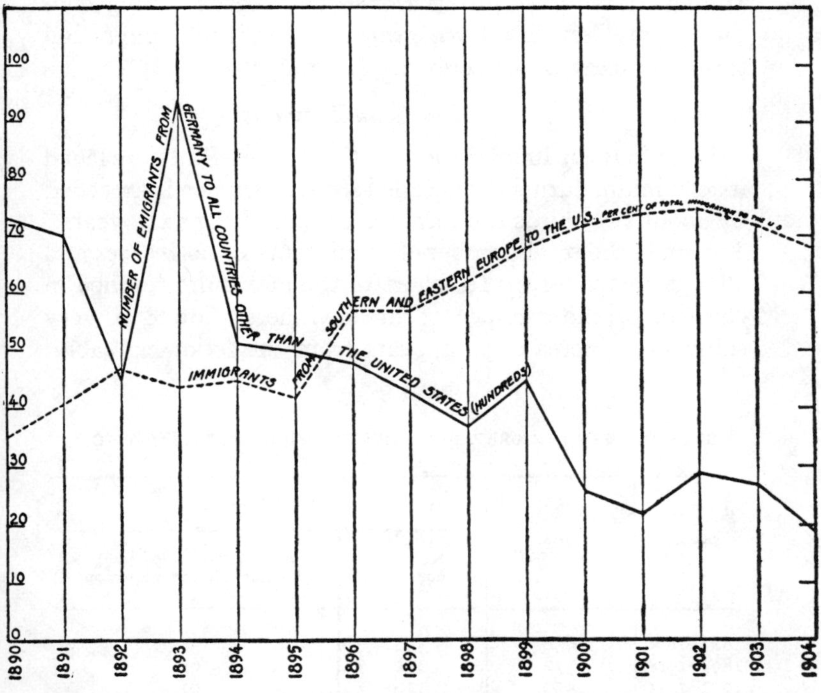

XIV. Emigration from Germany to all countries outside of the United States and per cent of Southern and Eastern European immigration to the total immigration to the United States, 1890–1904.

Germany to other countries than the United States steadily declined, while immigration from Southern and Eastern Europe to the United States advanced from 44.3 to 75.1 per cent of the total.

It is, evidently, not because living conditions in the United States have grown worse, but because living conditions in Germany have grown better, that emigration from Germany to all countries has fallen off.

C. The Scandinavians

Scandinavian immigration to the United States reached its maximum during the decade 1881–1890, when it exceeded by about two thirds the total for the preceding sixty years.[1] Yet while the total number of immigrants of both sexes and all ages in 1901–1910 fell short of the maximum reached in 1881–1890, the number of breadwinners showed a very substantial increase, as appears from the following table:

TABLE 55.

SCANDINAVIAN IMMIGRATION TO THE UNITED STATES, 1881–1910.[2]

Period	Total (thousands)	Breadwinners[3]	
		Number (thousands)	Per cent ratio to total Scandinavian immigration
1881–1890	656	356	54
1891–1900	372	241	65
1901–1910	530	429	81

[1] The total number admitted up to 1880 was 397,011, the total for 1881–1890 was 656,494. Computed from *Reports of the Immigration Commission*, vol. 1, Table 9, pp. 66–96.

[2] *Monthly Summary of Commerce and Finance, June, 1903*, pp. 4408–4411; *Report of the Immigration Commission*, vol. 1, Tables 12–13. *Annual Reports of the Commissioner-General of Immigration:* 1899–1900, Table VIII.; 1901–1904, Table IX.; 1905–1908, Table VIII.; 1909–1910, Table X.

[3] All immigrants exclusive of dependents, described in immigration statistics as "without occupation (mostly women and children)."

As shown by the figures, the number of Scandinavians coming to compete in the American labor market actually increased: the total for 1901–1910 exceeded by 20 per cent that for 1881–1890. The population of the Scandinavian countries increased at the same time approximately 22 per cent.[1] Emigration kept pace with population.

The only observable change is that, whereas the earlier Scandinavian immigration was mostly of a family type, among the recent Scandinavian immigrants single persons vastly predominate; in 1881–1890 there were 46 dependents to every 54 immigrant breadwinners, in 1901–1910 only 19 to 81. In this respect the Scandinavian immigrants of the present day are very much like the immigrants from Southern and Eastern Europe. The cause of this change in the matter of the family relations of the Scandinavian immigrants is evidently not racial, but economic. The old Scandinavian immigration came largely to settle on farms,[2] where a family was a help, while the new Scandinavian immigration, like the new immigration from Southern and Eastern Europe, comes chiefly to seek industrial employment. A single person, without family responsibilities, can more easily hazard the uncertainties of emigration to a strange land; a married wage-earner will as a rule leave his family behind, until he feels certain of his ability to provide for them in the new country.

That Scandinavian immigration to the United States was in no way affected by immigration from Southern and Eastern Europe is evidenced by the change in the direction

[1] Computed from *Statistical Abstract of the Principal and other Foreign Countries (British)*, No. XVI., p. 8; No. XXXV., pp. 8, 10.

[2] At the census of 1900, 49.8 per cent of all Norwegians, 42.3 per cent of all Danes, and 30.2 per cent of all Swedes in the United States were reported as engaged in agricultural pursuits. It is probable that some of those who were described by the enumerators in agricultural districts as laborers were agricultural laborers. Both groups combined numbered 59.3 per cent of all Norwegians, 52.3 per cent of all Danes, and 43 per cent of all Swedes.—*Reports of the Immigration Commission*, vol. 28, Table 1A, pp. 216 *et seq.*

of the former; whereas prior to 1890 the greater part of Scandinavian immigration was directed to the agricultural States of the Central West and the Northwest, since 1890 the majority of the Scandinavian immigrants follow the current of immigration from Southern and Eastern Europe. The figures are presented in Table 56. The increase of the number of foreign-born from Scandinavian countries and from Southern and Eastern Europe in 1880–1910 represents the net results of immigration from those countries, as reduced by emigration and death. In Diagram XV a graphic representation of the same figures is furnished, each number being expressed in the area of the corresponding semicircle or quadrant. The black quadrants represent Scandinavians, the shaded semicircles and quadrants natives of Southern and Eastern Europe. The left side represents the eleven Western States indicated on the map, the right side, all other States and Territories.

TABLE 56.

INCREASE OF FOREIGN-BORN FROM THE SCANDINAVIAN COUNTRIES AND FROM EASTERN AND SOUTHERN EUROPE, 1880–1910, BY GEOGRAPHIC DIVISIONS (THOUSANDS).[1]

Period	Scandinavians		Natives of Southern and Eastern Europe	
	Eleven Western States	All other States and Territories	Eleven Western States	All other States and Territories
1880–1890......	251	242	45	474
1890–1900......	39	92	39	976
1900–1910......	89	99	189	2850

If it were true that the Scandinavians stayed away from the United States because they were reluctant to compete with immigrants from Southern and Eastern Europe, we should expect to find that the recent Scandinavian immigrants, like their predecessors, were headed for the West

[1] See Appendix, Table XIV.

DIAGRAM XV.

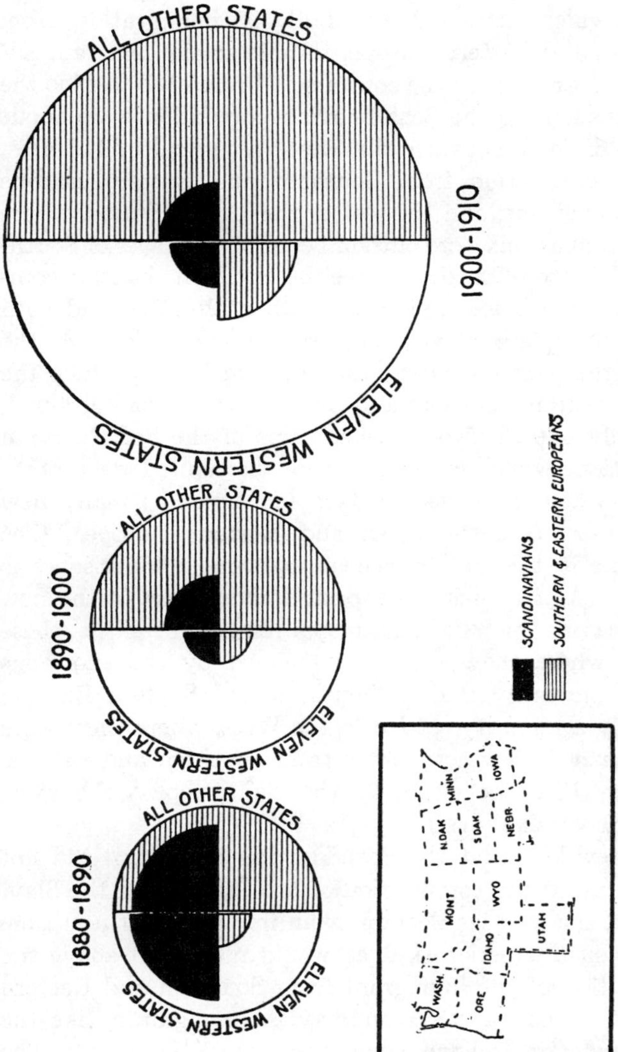

XV. Increase of Scandinavians and of Southern and Eastern Europeans in a group of eleven Western States and in the remainder of the United States, 1880–1910.

where the field was comparatively clear, and avoided those States which attracted the bulk of immigration from Southern and Eastern Europe. Table 56 and Diagram XV furnish clear proof to the contrary. From 1880 to 1890 the net accessions to the Scandinavian population were about evenly divided between the western agricultural States, where immigration from Southern and Eastern Europe was insignificant, and the rest of the United States, where the Scandinavians were outnumbered by the races of Southern and Eastern Europe. (See the circle on the left; compare the two black quadrants with each other and with the shaded quadrant and semicircle on each side.) At the end of the next ten years, the Western States, where the accretions from Southern and Eastern Europe had declined, held only one third of the net gains of the Scandinavian population, while two thirds were distributed over other States, where they had to face ten times as many new competitors from Southern and Eastern Europe. (See the circle in the middle; repeat the same comparisons, as above.) Again during the past decade most of the new Scandinavian population sought employment in these States, where they were overwhelmed by the enormous tide of immigration from Southern and Eastern Europe, and only a minority settled in the West, where there were comparatively few newcomers from Southern and Eastern Europe. (See the circle on the right; repeat the same comparisons as above.)

It is evident that the Scandinavian immigrant did not seek to avoid the competition of the Italian and the Slav. Nor did the average Scandinavian immigrant at any time display such superior skill as would place him above the competition of the immigrant from Southern and Eastern Europe. Most of the Scandinavian immigrants, like the Slavs and the Italians, come from rural districts.[1] The

[1] According to Swedish official statistics, the ratio of emigrants from rural districts to the total emigration was 76 per cent in 1891–1900 and 77 per cent in 1901–1908. (Computed from Gustav Sundbärg's

distribution of Scandinavian immigrants by occupation has undergone no material change since 1881, as witnessed by the following table:

TABLE 57.

DISTRIBUTION OF SCANDINAVIAN IMMIGRANT BREADWINNERS BY MAIN CLASSES OF OCCUPATIONS (THOUSANDS), 1881–1910.[1]

Occupations	1881–1890	1891–1900	1901–1910
Skilled mechanics	46	35	91
Agricultural workers, laborers, and servants[2]	305	202	325
All others	5	4	13
Total	356	241	429

While there were twice as many skilled mechanics among the Scandinavian immigrants in 1901–1910 as in 1881–1890, yet the bulk of them have always been laborers or farm workers without special mechanical skill. The number of unskilled laborers in 1901–1910 was greater than in 1881–1890, and it was these unskilled Scandinavian laborers that sought employment in competition with unskilled Slav and Italian laborers. If the increase of immigration from the Scandinavian countries was not fast enough to satisfy the preference of certain social theorists for the races of Northern Europe, the explanation of this comparatively slow growth must be sought in the economic conditions of those countries, not in the immigration from Southern and Eastern Europe to the United States.

Ekonomisk-Statistisk Beskrifning öfver Sveriges Olika Landsdelar, p. 20, Table 22.)

[1] See footnotes to Table 55.

[2] From a comparison of the distribution of the Scandinavian immigrants by occupation in our immigration statistics with the Swedish statistics of occupations of emigrants, it appears that the distinction between agricultural workers, laborers, and servants in our official statistics is not reliable. (Compare American sources cited in footnote to Table 55 and Gustav Sundbärg, *op. cit.*, p. 20, Table 22.)

D. Norway

The merging of all Scandinavians into one racial group in United States statistics has obscured the fact that while the total immigration from Sweden and Denmark (including dependents) has declined since 1881–1890, immigration from Norway reached its maximum during the decade 1901–1910, as shown in the table next below:

TABLE 58.

IMMIGRATION FROM NORWAY TO THE UNITED STATES.[1]

Period	Number
Up to 1880	148,341
1881–1890	176,586
1891–1900	95,014
1901–1910	190,505
Total	610,446

The number of Norwegian immigrants of both sexes and all ages in 1901–1910 was double the total for the preceding ten-year period and 8 per cent above the high watermark reached in 1881–1890. All that can be said is that the rate of increase of the population of Norway from 1875 to 1900 was 23.1 per cent, *i. e.*, approximately 18 per cent in twenty years, so that, taking the emigration of 1881–1890 as a standard, it will be found that emigration from Norway has not increased as fast as her population.

It will be remembered that the majority of the Scandinavian emigrants came from agricultural districts. One half of the Norwegians who came to the United States before 1900 were engaged in agricultural pursuits. Since the opportunity eventually to secure a homestead in the United States is gone, the Norwegian agricultural laborer who is dissatisfied with his condition must seek employment in industry. And here the development of the Norwegian industry offers him many an opportunity at home. The recent industrial progress of Norway can be gauged by the

[1] *Reports of the Immigration Commission*, vol. 1, Table 9, pp. 66–96.

fact that from 1897 to 1908 the quantity of horsepower used increased 146.5 per cent. The average number of wage-earners reduced to the basis of 300 working days per year, increased during the same period 45 per cent, while the total population increased during the same period only 9 per cent.[1] The rapid development of home industry absorbed a portion of the agricultural surplus population which under former conditions might have found an outlet in emigration.

E. Denmark

The total immigration from Denmark to the United States up to and including 1910 numbered only a quarter of a million, distributed as follows:

TABLE 59.

IMMIGRATION FROM DENMARK TO THE UNITED STATES, 1820–1910.[2]

Period	Number
Up to 1880	53,774
1881–1890	88,132
1891–1900	50,231
1901–1910	65,285
Total	257,422

While immigration was greater during the last ten-year period than during the preceding, yet it did not reach the high level of 1881–1890. Since nearly one half of all Danes in the United States in 1900 were engaged in agricultural pursuits, the decrease of Danish immigration to the United States might have some relation to the decline in the demand for farm help in the United States.

On the other hand, the last fifteen years of the nineteenth century "witnessed a great improvement in the condition of life all round of the Danish peasant farmer."[3] Among

[1] *Statistique Industrielle pour l'année 1908, éditée par l'office des Assurances de l'État*, pp. 18*, 230*, Kristiania, 1911.

[2] *Reports of the Immigration Commission*, vol. 1, pp. 66–96, 176–204.

[3] Erik Givskov, "Peasant Farming in Denmark," *The Economic Journal*, vol. viii (1903), p. 646.

the causes of that improvement, the most important one is the rapid spread of co-operation in all branches of farming. The first co-operative creamery was established in 1882. According to a special census taken in 1906, there were 1068 such creameries whose membership embraced 82.3 per cent of all dairy farms. The co-operative creameries controlled 93 per cent of the total milk production of the country. The first co-operative association of exporters of eggs was established in 1890. In 1906 there were 790 such associations with a membership of over 50,000 farmers, who owned in the aggregate over 1,900,000 hens. There were in 1905, thirty-two co-operative slaughter houses with a membership of 63,000 farmers who owned one half of all the swine of the country.[1] As a result, the export of agricultural products from Denmark increased sixfold in twenty years, viz., from an annual average of 49,000,000 crowns[2] in 1881–1885 to 313,000,000 crowns in 1901–1905.[3]

The progress of agriculture has turned Denmark into a country of immigration. Considerable numbers of Polish peasants come during every agricultural season to work on the farms in Denmark; in 1907, their number was 6251,[4] which was equal to three fourths of the average annual emigration of the period 1881–1890.

The manufacturing industries of the country have also made progress. The total horsepower used in manufactures increased 156 per cent from 1897 to 1906. The number of wage-earners increased 15.4 per cent, while the population increased only 3.5 per cent from 1901 to 1906, *i. e.*, about 11 per cent in nine years.[5] The industrial progress of Den-

[1] *Danmarks Statistik. Landbrugets Andelsvirk somhed.* Udgivet at Statens Statistiske Bureau, 1906, pp. 8, 20, 24, 41, 43, 51, 67, 69.

[2] 1 crown = 26.8 cents.

[3] Danemark, *Précis de Statistique*, 1907, pp. 14–15.

[4] Statistique de Danemark, *Annuaire Statistique*, 1908, p. 129, Table 98.

[5] Danemark, *Précis de Statistique*, 1907, p. 13. British *Statistical Abstract for the Principal and other Foreign Countries*, No. XXXV., pp. 8, 10.

mark encouraged organization among wage-earners. In 1908, 60 per cent of all industrial workers in Denmark were organized.[1]

The improvement of the condition of the Danish people within the last twenty-five years is sufficient to account for the decrease of emigration from that country, irrespective of the immigration from Southern and Eastern Europe to the United States.

F. Sweden

The emigration movement from Sweden for the past half-century is classified by country of destination in the following table:

TABLE 60.

ANNUAL AVERAGE EMIGRATION FROM SWEDEN BY DESTINATION, (THOUSANDS), 1861–1908.[2]

Period	To non-European countries	To European countries
1861–1870	8.9	3.4
1871–1880	10.1	4.9
1881–1890	32.4	5.2
1891–1900	20.4	4.2
1901–1908	22.6	3.4

Emigration from Sweden, after reaching its highest point in 1881–1890, began to decline. The fact to be noted is that this declining tendency affected alike emigration over-sea as well as to European countries. The probable causes of the decline of each movement must be examined separately.

A study of the sources of Swedish emigration shows that the greater part of it came from rural districts, but the

[1] *Handwörterbuch der Staatswissenschaften*, vol. iv., p. 1210.

[2] Compiled from Gustav Sundbärg's *Ekonomisk-Statistisk Beskrifning öfver Sveriges Olika Landsdelar*, 1910, p. 95, Table 45.

general decline of the movement did not affect the urban and the rural districts in the same degree. The difference appears from the following figures:

TABLE 61.

AVERAGE ANNUAL EMIGRATION FROM CITIES AND RURAL DISTRICTS OF SWEDEN (THOUSANDS), 1881–1907.[1]

Period	From rural districts	From cities	Total
1881–1890	30.4	7.2	37.6
1891–1900	18.7	6.0	24.7
1901–1907	21.3	6.4	27.7

We find that the decline of the total emigration is due to the decline of emigration from the rural districts. A comparison of the last two tables further shows that the decrease of the average rural emigration from 1881–1890 to 1901–1907 is approximately equal to the decrease of the average emigration to non-European countries during the same period. If it is remembered that 30.2 per cent of the Swedes who had settled in the United States in the past century were engaged in agriculture and that during the last twenty years the direction of Scandinavian immigration to the United States turned from the West to the East, the reason of the decline of emigration from the rural districts of Sweden will be apparent: the United States no longer holds out to the Swedish peasant the hope of becoming a farmer. The Swedish peasant who is dissatisfied with his surroundings must look for industrial employment. And he finds that there are ample opportunities in Sweden which attract immigrants from foreign countries.

A comparison of the emigration from Sweden to other European countries with the immigration to Sweden from those countries brings out the fact that during the past decade the balance for the first time turned in favor of Sweden:

[1] Sundbärg, *loc. cit.*, p. 13, Table 17 (computed).

TABLE 62.

ANNUAL AVERAGE EMIGRATION FROM SWEDEN TO OTHER EUROPEAN COUNTRIES AND IMMIGRATION TO SWEDEN FROM OTHER EUROPEAN COUNTRIES (THOUSANDS), 1881–1908.[1]

Annual average	Emigration	Immigration	Net immigration (+) or emigration (−)
1881–1890	5.2	2.9	−2.3
1891–1900	4.2	3.1	−1.1
1901–1908	3.4	4.1	+ .7

It appears from Table 62 that while emigration from Sweden to other European countries has been decreasing from decade to decade, immigration to Sweden from those countries has been on the increase. The net result of these movements during the last period was a slight surplus of immigration over emigration. Evidently economic opportunities in Sweden must have sufficiently improved to attract more foreigners while fewer Swedish people left the country.

The industrial progress of Sweden is contemporaneous with the recent development of hydraulic and hydro-electric engineering, which has harnessed the water power furnished in abundance by her mountains. More than one half of her motive power used in 1907 was derived from water power, either directly or in the form of electric current generated by water power. The increase in the use of water power since 1896 amounted to 134 per cent.[2] As an index of Sweden's industrial advance since the time when her emigration was at its highest level, may be used the production of iron ore, which increased from an annual average of 900,000 tons in 1881–1890 to an average of more than 3,500,000 in 1901–1905, *i. e.*, nearly fourfold.[3]

[1] Sundbärg, *loc. cit.*, pp. 95–96, Tables 45–46.

[2] Out of a total of 607,000 horse-power used for driving machinery or generating electric power, 330,000 was water power.—*Sveriges Officiella Statistik. Fabriker och Handtverk*, 1907, pp. xxix. and 118.

[3] Eli F. Heckscher, *Till Belysning af Järnvägarnas Betydelse för Sveriges Ekonomiska Utveckling*, p. 91.

The number of wage-earners in Swedish factories increased from 202,000 in 1896 to 303,000 in 1907, *i. e.*, at the rate of 50 per cent in eleven years.[1] The growth of Swedish industries far outran the increase of her population. The factories offered employment to an average of 9000 new hands annually, which was approximately equal to the decrease in the annual average emigration from 1881–1890 to 1901–1908.

To what extent the wage-earners of Sweden have improved the opportunities of the industrial situation, is shown by the rapid progress of organization of labor and the spread of collective bargaining. The total membership of labor organizations increased from 50,000 in 1900 to 260,000 in 1908. The proportion of organized workers to the total number of industrial wage-earners was estimated at 45 per cent.[2] A highly instructive account of the progress of collective bargaining is given in a Swedish government report, from which the following is condensed.[3]

About one half of the total number of wage-earners were employed in establishments which had adopted the system of collective bargaining. In the coal mines, sugar factories, and potteries collective bargaining was practically the general rule. In trade and transportation nearly all the employees of private telephone companies, about 90 per cent of all employees of electric street railways, and 66 per cent of the employees on private steam railways were working under collective trade agreements. In the building trades about three fourths of the total number and in the factories and hand trades about one half were employed under the same system. The principal industries where collective bargaining has been adopted and the percentage of the total number of wage-earners affected in each of them are given in the following table:

[1] *Sveriges Officiella Statistik. Fabriker och Handtverk*, 1907, p. xxviii. There are no comparable figures prior to 1896.

[2] *Handwörterbuch der Staatswissenschaften*, vol. iv, p. 1211.

[3] *Kollektivaftal Angående Arbets-och—Löneförhållenden i Sverige* (Stockholm, 1910), pp. 246–249.

TABLE 63.

PER CENT OF WAGE-EARNERS EMPLOYED UNDER THE SYSTEM OF COLLECTIVE BARGAINING IN THE PRINCIPAL INDUSTRIES OF SWEDEN.

Industry	Per cent
Printing	93
Fertilizers	82
Rubber	82
Matches	79
Tobacco manufactures	75
Collieries	71
Machinery	68
Jewelry	63
Cabinet making	47
Glass	47
Iron and steel	44
Leather	42
Textiles	35

In all of these industries [says the official report] it is chiefly the large-scale establishments that have adopted collective bargaining, whereas those establishments, where it is absent, generally belong to the small-scale industry. Whenever a trust or a combine is organized in an industry, collective labor agreements generally comprise a greater number of factories within, than without the combination.

A noteworthy feature of these trade agreements is the provision for compensation in cases of work accidents which are not within the law of 1901. Provisions of this character are found in 1313 agreements affecting 67 per cent of the total number of wage-earners coming under the operation of this system.

It will not be disputed that the Slav and Italian immigrants to the United States are not responsible for the utilization of the water power supply of the Scandinavian mountain range, with the resulting industrial upheaval which created a lively demand for labor in Sweden. That nevertheless the immigration of unskilled laborers from Sweden to the United States continues and grows, is the best evidence that many of them consider the opportunities in the United States superior to those which are open to them at home.

G. *The United Kingdom*

Emigrants from the British Isles enjoy a great advantage

over those of all other nations in that the main fields of modern immigration are controlled by English-speaking peoples. An Englishman or an Irishman is equally at home in the United States, in Canada, Australia, New Zealand, and South Africa. The recent development of those countries has naturally attracted a part of the emigration from Great Britain and Ireland. Furthermore, the policy of restriction adopted in Australia, New Zealand, and South Africa has conferred a special privilege upon immigrants of British nationality.

On the other hand, the governments of Canada and Australia are making systematic efforts to induce immigration from the mother country.[1] Contract laborers may be freely imported into Canada, as well as into Australia. Salaried agents of the Dominion government are stationed in the large cities of Great Britain to promote emigration to Canada. A bonus of £1 is paid to the booking agent on each ticket to Canada sold to a British subject who is engaged in the occupation of farmer, farm laborer, gardener, stableman, carter, railway surface man, navvy, or miner, and who signifies his intention to follow farming or railway construction work in Canada.[2] Not content with the work of regular immigration agents, Canada has been sending agricultural delegates to Great Britain. The Salvation Army is also utilized as an agency to promote emigration to Canada, and grants of money are made to the Army for that purpose. Canada annually receives a considerable number of English immigrants, who have been sent by private or state aid from the mother country.[3] Canada also encourages the immigration of poor and homeless British children to her borders. This immigration is chiefly recruited from the orphan or industrial homes of the British Isles.[4]

[1] *Reports of the Immigration Commission*, vol. 2, pp. 607–631.

[2] *Ibid.*, pp. 607–608.

[3] In 1907, 12,336 persons were sent to Canada by London charitable societies alone.

[4] It is officially estimated that during the last 50 years nearly 60,000

The Australian government furnishes land to settlers at a nominal price payable in small installments. Moreover, in all the states except Tasmania, allowances are made to settlers for improving their holdings. By way of further inducements, the states pay the passage, wholly or in part, of immigrants from the United Kingdom whose purpose it is to settle on the land or to engage in farming or other work of a similar nature. Assistance is also offered to domestic servants and other persons who can satisfy the Australian agent in London that they would make desirable settlers in Australia. The policy of assisting immigration has been pursued by the several states of Australia for a greater part of the time since their settlement. According to official information 653,698 state-aided immigrants have been admitted to the Australian states.[1]

That all these efforts should have diverted from the United States a part of the British emigration was inevitable, irrespective of any causes originating in the United States. As shown in a preceding chapter, the rise of land values in the United States and the agricultural opportunities of the Canadian Northwest have, during the past decade, resulted in an emigration of American farmers to Canada. Withal, it is a noteworthy fact that the movement to the United States has been affected less than is generally imagined.

Compared with the annual average for the period 1880–1889, emigration from Great Britain and Ireland to the United States has considerably declined. But as appears from Table 64 the decade 1880–1889 cannot be taken as a standard for comparison. The only period approaching it was the decade 1850–1859, when over a million people emigrated from Ireland.[2] Eliminating the two exceptional

---

juvenile immigrants have been transported from the British Isles to Canada. From 1901 to 1909, inclusive, 19,034 of this class were sent to Canada.

[1] *Ibid.*, pp. 631–635.

[2] *Census of Ireland, 1901*, p. 168, Table 41.

decades, we find that during the twenty-year period 1890–1909, 2,425,000 immigrants came from Great Britain and Ireland to the United States as against 2,254,000 in 1860–1879.[1]

TABLE 64.

NUMBER OF EMIGRANTS FROM THE UNITED KINGDOM, BY DESTINATION (THOUSANDS), 1840–1909.

Period	Destination				
	United States	North American Colonies	Australia, New Zealand, and South Africa	Other countries	Total
1840–1849	912	428	127	27	1 495
1850–1859	1 631	259	499	52	2 440
1860–1869	1 179	145	286	60	1 670
1870–1879	1 074	184	296	100	1 554
1880–1889	1 728	300	376	164	2 568
1890–1899	1 196	191	234	171	1 792
1900–1909	1 230	706	477	300	2 612

The number of English and Irish immigrants since 1890 who found the conditions in the United States attractive was 8500 in excess of the annual average for the period 1860–1879 preceding the "new immigration."

To be sure, the figures of gross immigration alone are not conclusive, as they conceal many unsuccessful ventures ending in a return movement to the home country. In Table 65 are therefore presented the figures of net emigration from the British Isles by countries of destination since 1895, when immigration from Southern and Eastern Europe to the United States for the first time outran the "old immigration."

[1] The Civil War reduced emigration from the United Kingdom to the United States only in 1861 and 1862. During the next three years the number of emigrants bound for the United States rose to a higher level than that of 1855–1860 or 1874–1879. See Appendix, Table XV.

[2] See Appendix, Table XV.

TABLE 65.

NET EMIGRATION OF BRITISH SUBJECTS FROM THE UNITED KINGDOM BY COUNTRIES OF DESTINATION (THOUSANDS), 1895–1909.

Year ended March 31	Destination								
	British Possessions					Foreign Countries			Grand Total
	British North America	Australia and New Zealand	Cape of Good Hope and Natal	Other British Possessions	Total[2]	United States	Other Foreign Countries	Total	
1895	6	1	12	1	20	56		56	76
1896	6	1	10	2	19	40	1	41	60
1897	6	4	6	3	19	31	1	32	51
1898	8	4	6	2	20	29		29	49
1899	8	4	−6	1	7	39		39	46
1900	8	6	7	2	23	48		48	71
1901	7	6	9	3	25	46	1	47	72
1902	15	4	28	3	50	52		52	102
1903	46	4	28	3	81	65	1	66	147
1904	51	5	−1	4	59	67	1	68	127
1905	63	7	3	4	77	61	1	62	139
1906	91	10	−3	7	105	86	4	90	195
1907	117	14	−5	5	131	100	4	104	235
1908	42	21	−5	1	59	31	1	32	91
1909	52	25	3	2	82	56	2	58	140

As appears from Diagram XVI, where the same figures are shown graphically, the curves representing net emigration to the United States and to British possessions exhibit a tendency to rise and fall together. From 1898 to 1907 the net immigration to the United States was steadily rising with slight deviations in the years ended March 31, 1901, and 1905, *i. e.*, in the two presidential years. Since the latter year, the immigration countries of the British Empire have drawn and held more immigrants than the United

[1] Computed from *Statistical Abstract of the United Kingdom*, No. 57, pp. 363–364, Tables 117, 118, 119.

[2] Includes 22,719 passengers from 1895 to 1907 whose nationality is not specified.

States, but the net immigration to the United States also increased. The drop in 1908 affected the net immigration to Canada as much as that to the United States. In 1909 the net immigration to the United States exhibited a greater increase, both absolute and relative, than the net immigra-

DIAGRAM XVI.

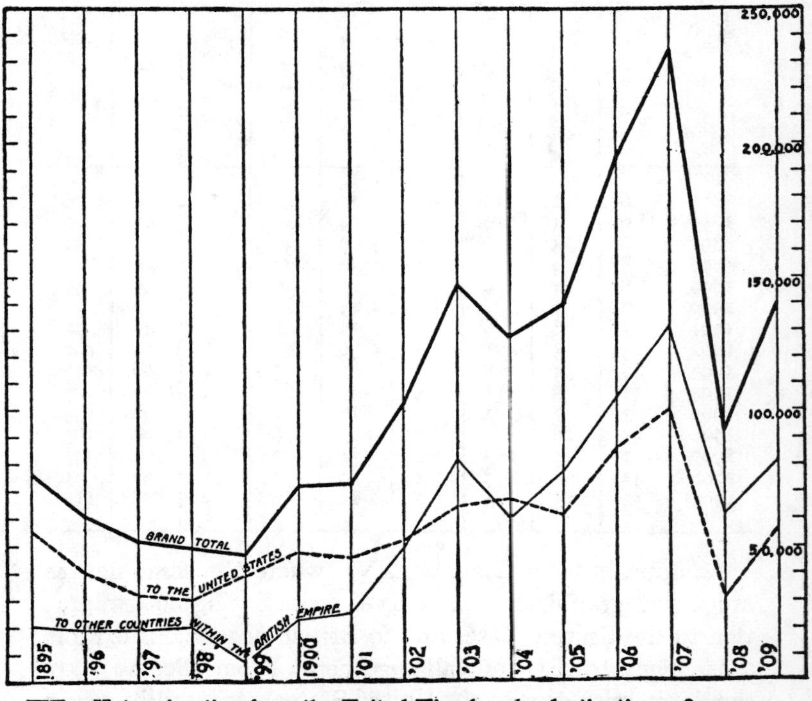

XVI. Net emigration from the United Kingdom by destination, 1895–1909.

tion to all British possessions. Obviously, conditions in the United States, notwithstanding immigration from Southern and Eastern Europe, compared favorably with those in other immigration countries.

Another factor determining the volume of emigration, that must not be lost sight of, is the improvement of living conditions in Great Britain. In the first place, there has been a decrease in the cost of living. Measuring the cost of living by wholesale prices and taking the Board of Trade index number for 1900 as 100, official estimates put the cost of living in 1878–1887 at 119.5 and in 1898–1907 at 97.8. At the same time the rates of wages have increased.[1] An estimate of the course of average real wages in the second half of the nineteenth century is reproduced in the following table:

TABLE 66.

AVERAGE REAL WAGES IN GREAT BRITAIN, 1850–1900.

Year	Per Cent
1850	50
1860	55
1870	60
1880	70
1890	84
1895	93
1900	100

During the decade 1850–1859, when immigration from the British Isles to the United States reached its maximum, relative to population, and the decade 1880–1889, when it reached its numerical maximum, the real wages averaged from 50 to 55 per cent and from 70 to 84 per cent, respectively, of the wages of 1900. The improvement is sufficient to account for the reduction in the rate of emigration from the United Kingdom.

H. Ireland

Emigration from Ireland to all countries reached its maximum during the decade ended March 31, 1861, and has since declined. The tide rose again during the '80's, in the turbulent years of the Irish Land League agitation, and once more during the past decade, but not as high as the water-mark reached in 1852–1861. The figures are given in Table 67 below.

[1] Beveridge, *loc. cit.*, p. 9.

[2] *Ibid.*, quoting: A. L. Bowley, *National Progress in Wealth and Trade*, p. 33.

TABLE 67.

ANNUAL AVERAGE EMIGRATION FROM IRELAND, MAY 1, 1851, TO MARCH 31, 1908.[1]

Years ended March 31	(Thousands)
1852–1861	115
1862–1871	77
1872–1881	62
1882–1891	77
1892–1901	43
1902–1908	50

There are no accurate statistics showing the distribution of Irish emigrants by destination previous to 1876. The subsequent years 1876–1908 for which such statistics are available may be divided with respect to the racial composition of the immigration to the United States into two periods of nearly equal length; previous to 1891 the races of Northern and Western Europe furnished the bulk of the immigrants, whereas during the more recent period the races of Southern and Eastern Europe became the predominant element among them. The figures are presented in Table 67 on page 216.

Two facts are worthy of note in the following comparative table: first, that the decline of emigration from Ireland has affected the movement to other countries, as well as to the United States, and second, that the proportion of Irish emigrants destined to the United States during the period of the great influx of immigrants from Southern and Eastern Europe was higher than in 1876–1890, when immigration from Southern and Eastern Europe was negligible.

That the "new immigration" to the United States was not the cause of the decline of Irish emigration is clear from the fact that the decline had set in as early as 1861–1870, at least twenty years before the immigrants from Southern and Eastern Europe became sufficiently numerous to attract

[1] The enumeration of emigrants from Irish ports did not commence until May 1, 1851.

Census of Ireland, 1901, Part II., p. 168, Table 41. *Statistical Abstract of the United Kingdom*, No. 56, p. 365.

notice. The conclusion suggested by the statistics of Irish emigration is that there must have been forces at work to reduce the number of Irish seeking a better home than their native country.

TABLE 68.

ANNUAL AVERAGE EMIGRATION FROM IRELAND, BY DESTINATION, 1876–1908.[1]

Period	To the United States			To other countries (thousands)
	Total (thousands)	(Thousands)	Per cent of total	
1876–1890[2]	69	50	72	19
1891–1908[3]	46	38	83	8

The change in the economic condition of the Irish people since the '80's may be summed up in the following words of Mr. Dillon:

> The wretched land system was responsible for most of the misery which the poor suffered. Successive land purchases are gradually restoring the worse than homeless tenants to the land, and each family so restored becomes decently prosperous, because for the first time there is offered a chance to make a living. . . . The helpless, hopeless tenants and the evicted families are being made independent. . . . The thousands who have been put in the way of making decent farms and homes have become hopeful and self-reliant instead of despairing. . . . Those families who were struggling against starvation on the rocky hillsides are now cultivating fertile fields.[4]

That this is not mere rhetoric a few figures will show.

[1] Computed from the following sources: *Census of Ireland, 1881*, Part II., p. 74; 1891, Part II., p. 74; 1901, Part II., p. 74; 1901, Part II., Table 41, p. 168; *Statistical Abstract of the United Kingdom*, No. 48, p. 255; No. 56, p. 365; *Reports of the Immigration Commission*, vol. 1, Table 9, pp. 76–92.

[2] Calendar years.

[3] Total emigration from Ireland for 17¼ years, from January 1, 1891, to March 31, 1908; immigration to the United States for 17 years from January 1, 1891, to December 31, 1908.

[4] Hugh Sutherland: *Ireland Yesterday and To-day* (1909), p. 108.

Under the operation of the several purchase acts passed since 1885, more than 214,000 tenants have been enabled to buy their land with the assistance of the government.[1] This number is equal to one third of all families enumerated in rural areas at the census of 1901.[2] Under the provisions of the Wyndham Act of 1903, the government is authorized to expend $800,000,000 in loans to tenants at 3¼ per cent for the purchase of land, which is to be paid for in 68½ years.[3] Furthermore, the rent of the tenants has been substantially reduced by law, to which must be added the creation of a legal interest of a marketable character, together with a chance of further abatements in the future.[4]

Other legislation has been enacted for the benefit of agricultural laborers. "County authorities are able to borrow government funds for the erection of decent sanitary dwellings, which rent for 1 shilling a week. Nearly 50,000 of these neat cottages have been erected."[5]

Another factor which has materially contributed to the improvement of the condition of the Irish farmers has been the co-operative movement which dates from 1889. In 1903 there were more than 800 co-operative societies with an aggregate membership of 80,000 farmers.[6] Perhaps, the most important among these societies are the co-operative agricultural banks, which—in the language of Sir Horace Plunkett—"perform the apparent miracle of giving solvency to a community composed almost entirely of insolvent individuals."[7] There are more than 200 of these banks which lend money to farmers at 5 or 6 per cent per annum for agricultural improvements.[8]

The improvement of the condition of the tenants has

[1] *Ibid.*, p. 114.

[2] *The Census of Ireland,—General Report*, Table 49, p. 173.

[3] Sutherland, *loc. cit.*, p. 114.

[4] C. F. Bastable: "Some Features of the Economic Movement in Ireland, 1880–1900," *Economic Journal*, 1901, No. xi., pp. 33, 39.

[5] Sutherland, *loc. cit.*, p. 183.

[6] Horace Plunkett: *Ireland in the New Century*, p. 192.

[7] *Ibid.*, p. 195.

[8] *Ibid.*, pp. 192, 197.

affected the labor market; there has been a substantial gain in the real wages of farm laborers.[1]

The improvement of the living conditions of the Irish people is reflected in the statistics of housing accommodations. The census of Ireland divides all houses into four classes: "In the lowest of the four classes are comprised houses built of mud or perishable material, having only one room and window; in the third a better description of house, varying from one to four rooms and windows; in the second what might be considered a good farmhouse, having from five to nine rooms and windows; and in the first class all houses of a better description than the preceding."[2]

TABLE 69.

FAMILIES OCCUPYING EACH CLASS OF INHABITED HOUSES IN RURAL AREAS OF IRELAND, 1861–1901.[3]

Census period	Number (thousands)				Per cent				Total
	I class	II class	III class	IV class	I class	II class	III class	IV class	
1861	29	291	471	90	3.3	33.0	53.5	10.2	100
1881	36	309	356	39	4.9	41.7	48.1	5.3	100
1891	40	332	288	20	5.8	48.9	42.4	2.9	100
1901	41	353	230	9	6.4	55.8	36.4	1.4	100

While housing conditions in Ireland to-day are still far from ideal, yet they show evidence of very real improvement, compared with the days when emigration from Ireland was at its maximum. The number of one-room huts with one window, built of mud or other material of the same class, decreased since 1861 from 90,000 to 9,000. In 1861, there were but one in three houses that might be considered good farm houses; forty years later about the same proportion fell below that definition.

[1] Bastable, *loc. cit.*, p. 38.

[2] *Census of Ireland, General Report for 1901*, p. 11.

[3] Computed from the *Census of Ireland, General Report*, Table 49, p. 173

The results of the census of 1911 have as yet not been published. In Mr. Dillon's opinion, "Ireland has made more progress in the last ten years than during the previous two hundred years."[1] Is it reasonable to assume that the same rate of emigration from Ireland could be maintained to-day as half a century ago?

I. Conclusion

To sum up the preceding review of economic conditions in the countries of Northern and Western Europe, it is not because the "new immigration" has had an unfavorable effect upon labor conditions in the United States, but because those countries have become better homes for their citizens, that fewer of them are nowadays coming to the United States. If this country is to have immigration, it will have to come from other sources. To be sure, it may be argued that this country has no further need of immigration in general and can therefore dispense with immigrants from Southern and Eastern Europe. Be it as it may, it is a fallacy to assume that they could be replaced by potential immigration from Northern and Western Europe.

[1] Sutherland, *loc. cit.*, p. 108.

CHAPTER IX

RACE SUICIDE

IT cannot be seriously disputed that the great immigration of recent years has come in response to a demand for labor in the United States. Industrial progress and improvement of the condition of the wage-earners and farmers in the countries of Northern and Western Europe rendered the supply of immigrant labor from those sources inadequate. Without the immigrants from Southern and Eastern Europe, the rapid industrial expansion of the past decade would have been impossible. But it seems to the Immigration Commission, that "there is ground for argument or speculation" that "less immigration of a character tending to keep down wages and working conditions might have been attended by a larger natural increase among the native-born portion of the population."[1]

This theory, originated by Gen. Francis A. Walker, until lately held unchallenged the field of economic and sociological discussion. General Walker believed that immigration had caused a decline in the birth-rate of the native American population:

> The American shrank from the industrial competition thus thrust upon him. He was unwilling himself to engage in the lowest kind of day-labor with these new elements of the population; he was even more unwilling to bring sons and daughters into the world to enter into that competition. Foreign immigration into this country has . . . amounted not to a re-enforcement of our population, but to a replacement of native by foreign stock. . . . If the foreigners had not come, the native element would long have filled the places the foreigners usurped.[2]

---

[1] *Reports of the Immigration Commission*, vol. 1, p. 494.

[2] Francis A. Walker: *Discussions in Economics and Statistics*, pp. 422–425.

In proof of his theory, General Walker maintained that the decline of the birth-rate

> among Americans began at the very time when foreign immigration first assumed considerable proportions; it showed itself first and in the highest degree in those regions, in those States, and in the very counties into which the foreigners most largely entered. It proceeded for a long time in such a way as absolutely to offset the foreign arrivals, so that in 1850, in spite of the incoming of two and a half millions of foreigners during thirty years, our population differed by less than ten thousand from the population which would have existed, according to the previous rate of increase, without re-enforcement from abroad. These three facts . . . constitute a statistical demonstration such as is rarely attained in regard to the operation of any social or economic force.[1]

General Walker's statistical demonstration consisted in a comparison of the census figures from 1820 to 1890 with a calculation made by Elkanah Watson in 1815 on the basis of the increase of population from 1790 to 1810. The census figures for 1820–1850 closely coincided with Watson's estimates.[2] Yet, whereas prior to 1820 immigration was insignificant, from 1820 to 1850, 2,500,000 foreigners were added to the population of the United States without increasing it to any appreciable degree. The inference seemed to be incontrovertible that the development of the natural resources of the United States made provision for a fixed population at every census, so that the two-and-a-half million foreigners merely usurped the places of as many unborn Americans. At every subsequent census Watson's calculations proved to be overestimated, viz.: in 1860 by over 300,000, in 1870 by 3,770,000, in 1880 by more than

[1] Walker, *loc. cit.*, p. 441.

[2] *Ibid.*, pp. 120–122:

Year	Watson's estimates	The census	Difference
1820	9,625,734	9,633,822	+ 8,088
1830	12,833,645	12,866,020	+32,375
1840	17,116,526	17,069,453	−47,073
1850	23,185,368	23,191,876	+ 6,508

six millions, and in 1890 by over fourteen millions. Chief among the social and economic causes of this shortage compared with Watson's calculation was, according to General Walker, "the access of vast hordes of foreign immigrants bringing with them a standard of living at which our own people revolted."[1] The revolt assumed the form of a strike of American parents against child-bearing.

This conclusion illustrates in a striking manner the effect of a preconceived idea upon the reasoning ability of a scientific writer. Twenty years before promulgating his theory, General Walker had made light of Watson's predictions. Writing in 1873 on the results of the IX. Census (1870), he dwelt upon the social change which

> began when the people of the United States began to leave agricultural for manufacturing pursuits; to turn from the country to the town; to live in up-and-down houses. . . . A close observer must discern causes now working within the nation, which render it little less than absurd longer to apply the former rates of growth to the computation of our population at 1880, 1890, or 1900. . . . It would be merely an attempt at imposture to assume that numerical data exist for determining, within eight or ten or twelve millions, the population of the country thirty years from the date of the last census. As long as one simple force was operating expansively upon a homogeneous people, within a territory affording fertile lands beyond the ability of the existing population to occupy, so long it was no miracle to predict with accuracy the results of the census. But in the eddy and swirl of social and industrial currents through which the nation is now passing, it is wholly impossible to estimate the rate of its progress.[2]

Still General Walker's later theory stands and falls with Watson's predictions.

A reaction against that theory was led by Prof. Walter F. Willcox, in the *Supplementary Analysis of the Results of the XII. Census*. Later, in a paper read at the annual meeting of the American Statistical Association in St. Louis in 1910,[3] Professor Willcox proved by an analysis

[1] Walker, *loc. cit.*, p. 426. [2] *Ibid.*, p. 43.

[3] "The Change in the Proportion of Children in the United States" etc., by W. F. Willcox: *Quarterly Publications of the American Statistical Association*, March, 1911.

of population statistics "that the decrease in the proportion of children began in the United States as early as 1810."[1] The number of children under five years of age to one hundred women of the child-bearing age decreased in 1810–1830 by 9.9, and in 1880–1900 by 9.4. Thus the twenty-year period of the recent immigration did not substantially differ in this respect from the time when, according to General Walker himself, immigration had not affected the birth-rate among native Americans.

Moreover, the declining birth-rate is a world-wide social phenomenon of the present day. In the Australian Commonwealth, with her vast continent as yet unsettled and practically no immigration, as well as in New Zealand, "the decline of the birth-rate has probably been as rapid," says Professor Willcox, "as among native American stock." [2]

The greater decline of the native birth-rate in those sections and counties into which the foreigners most largely enter, goes together with the growth of the urban population. The percentage ratio of native white children of native parentage under five years of age, to native women of child-bearing age averaged in 1900 for cities with 25,000 inhabitants or over—29.6, and for smaller cities and rural territory—52.2. The latter ratio, of course, is subject to great variation, the limits being 76.7 in Louisiana and 29.1 in Massachusetts.[3] As indicated by these two extremes

[1] Walker, *loc. cit,*, pp. 495–496.

[2] *Supplementary Analysis. XII. Census*, p. 410. Carlton, *loc. cit.*, p. 347.

"So alarming has this phenomenon of the falling birth-rate become in the Australian colonies, that in New South Wales a special governmental commission has voluminously reported upon the subject. It is estimated that there has been a decline of about one third in the fruitfulness of the people in fifteen years. New Zealand even complains of the lack of children to fill her schools."—"Race Progress and Immigration," by William Z. Ripley, *Annals of the American Academy of Political and Social Science*, vol. xxxiv., pp. 132–133.

[3] *Supplementary Analysis*, *XII. Census*, Table XXII., p. 434.

Per cent ratio of native white children under 5 years of age, born of native mothers, to native white females 15 to 44 years of age in cities of less than 25,000 inhabitants and rural territory, 1900.

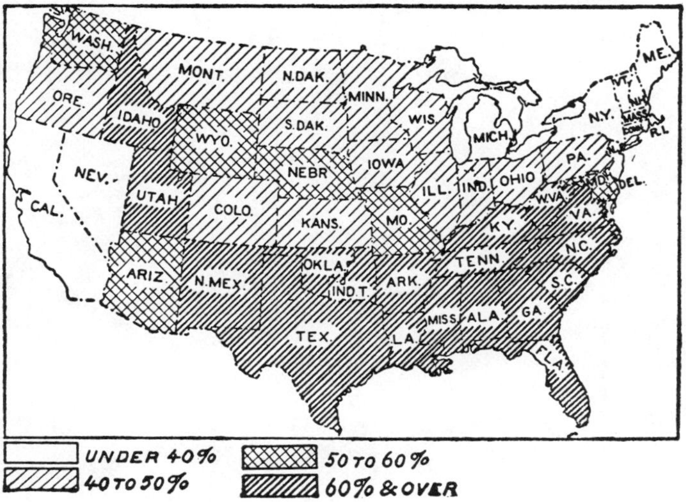

the variation of the statistical average is to a great extent purely arithmetical, being due to the heterogeneous character of the settlements combined in this class; on the one hand, there are the manufacturing towns of Massachusetts, on the other, the purely agricultural settlements of Louisiana. The connection between the agricultural character of the population of this class of settlements and the ratio of native-born children to native women of child-bearing age can be seen from Table 70 in which all States are divided into four areas, according to the ratio of native-born children under five, and the percentage of "farmers, planters, and overseers" to the total number of breadwinners for each group is given in a parallel column.

TABLE 70.

PER CENT RATIO OF NATIVE WHITE CHILDREN UNDER 5 YEARS OF AGE, BORN OF NATIVE MOTHERS, TO NATIVE WHITE FEMALES, 15 TO 44 YEARS OF AGE, IN CITIES OF LESS THAN 25,000 INHABITANTS AND RURAL TERRITORY, AND PER CENT RATIO OF NATIVE WHITE MALE FARMERS, PLANTERS, AND OVERSEERS TO THE TOTAL NUMBER OF WHITE MALE BREADWINNERS, 1900, BY AREAS COMPRISING STATES AND TERRITORIES GROUPED ACCORDING TO RATIO OF CHILDREN, 1900. (THE STATES ARE SHOWN ON THE MAP FACING THE TABLE.)

	Areas	Children[1]	Farmers, etc.[2]
I	Over 60 per cent	67.2	38.4
II	50 to 60 per cent	54.2	26.4
III	40 to 50 per cent	47.5	21.6
IV	Under 40 per cent	35.3	13.3
	Continental United States	52.2	24.7

The preceding table clearly shows that the native birthrate declines with the percentage of farmers among the

[1] *Supplementary Analysis, XII. Census*, Table XXII, p. 434.
[2] *Occupations at the XII. Census*, Table 41, pp. 220 *et seq.* (computed).

native population. The rearing of children on a farm requires less of the mother's time and attention than in the city. Moreover, the child on a farm begins to work at an earlier age than in the city. A numerous family on a farm has the advantages of a co-operative group, whereas every addition to the family of the wage-earner, or of the salaried employee with a fixed income, tends to lower the family's standard of living.

On the other hand, the decline of the birth-rate is universal among those classes which are scarcely, if at all, affected by immigrant competition. This observation, advanced by students in America and in England,[1] was substantiated by the Report of the National Birth Rate Commission on the declining birth-rate in the United Kingdom. The results of its studies are summarized in the following proposition:

> Such statistical evidence as is available for establishing a comparison of the birth-rate among the different social and pecuniary grades of our population indicates that the better-to-do classes restrict more closely the size of their families, and that even among certain of the wage-earning classes the birth-rate varies inversely with the income.[2]

Analyzing the interrelation between the declining birth-rate and "the condition of the working-class," the Commission concludes:

---

[1] A. Lapthorn Smith: "Higher Education of Women and Race Suicide," *Popular Science Monthly*, March, 1905, pp. 468, 470. Arthur Newsholme: *The Declining Birth-Rate*, pp. 32, 33, 42–43.

[2] *The Declining Birth-Rate, Its Causes and Effects*, p. 44. By way of illustration, the statistics of births in 1911, provided by the Registrar-General for England and Wales are quoted in the table next following (*Ibid.*, p. 9). The returns were classified according to the occupation of the father and summarized "in descending order of social grade." The figures represent the ratio of births per 1,000 married males under the age of 55.

Social Class	*Births per 1,000*
1. Upper and middle class	119
2. Intermediate	132
3. Skilled workmen	153
4. Intermediate class	158
5. Unskilled workmen	213

that every rise in the condition of the artisan tends at present to lower the birth-rate in his class. Wherever political and social conditions bring a man or a class into a position in which he hopes to rise or fears to fall, the family will be restricted. That class of motives, which we may blame as love of comfort, snobbishness, vulgar ambition, timorousness, or praise as proper pride, desire for self-improvement, and prudence, is the most potent cause of family restriction.[1]

In relation to the United States, similar views were expressed by the late Dr. Billings as far back as 1893. It is the desire of "the lower middle classes" to maintain "social position," along with "the great increase in the use of things which were formerly considered as luxuries, but which now have become almost necessities" that accounts in part for "the deliberate and voluntary avoidance or prevention of child-bearing."[2] Still "the lower middle classes" are scarcely affected by immigration. Their standard of living is, as a rule, higher than that of the wage-earner. Yet it is precisely this higher standard that is productive of a "desire to have fewer children." All speculation to the effect that an increase in the rate of wages "might have been attended" in the past, or is likely to be attended in the future, "by a larger natural increase among the native-born portion of the population," has accordingly no foundation of fact.

---

[1] *Ibid.*, pp. 41–42.

[2] *Supplementary Analysis, XII. Census*, p. 410.

CHAPTER X

THE STANDARD OF LIVING.

A. Introductory

IN so far as immigration is an economic movement, it is obvious that the immigrant's standard of living in his home country must have been below the American standard. This is as true of the old as of the new immigration. Those immigrants only are an exception to this rule who seek to escape from political or religious oppression. Its victims are not confined to the poorer classes, but include people of means and of standing in the community, whose standard of living is often superior to that of the native American mechanic. Since 1890, however, of all the races which have come to this country, the Jews, the Poles, the Lithuanians, the Russians, the Finns, and the Armenians, have furnished the only immigrants of this class. As to all others, it was just the higher standard of living of the American wage-earner that induced them, like most races that preceded them, to emigrate to the United States. If the lower standard of living to which the immigrant has been accustomed at home tends to reduce the American standard of living, then these effects of immigration must have manifested themselves in the days of the Irish and German immigration as much as to-day. At most there may be only a difference of degree. That the standard of living of the recent immigrant employed as an unskilled laborer is lower than that of the native American mechanic or of the older immigrant engaged in skilled work, is no new discovery. To prove, however, that the new immigrants have introduced a lower standard of living, it is necessary to show that the standard of living of the recent immigrants employed as unskilled laborers is lower than that of the Irish and German immigrants of past generations who were doing the same grade of work, or of the native American unskilled workers of the time before the Irish and German immigration. The experts of the Immigration Commission, however, have simply taken for granted that the standard of living of the present-day American or Americanized skilled mechanic is identical with that of the unskilled laborer of the same racial stocks in the days before the new immigration. This assumption is not borne out by American economic history.

The housing conditions of the foreign-born population have been most dwelt upon in the discussion of the standard of living of the immigrant, because they strike the eye of the outsider. On this subject there are ample comparative data. New York has always had more than its proportionate share of newly arrived immigrants; its housing problem, as affected by immigration, therefore, calls for separate treatment.

B. Congestion in New York City

Overcrowding was recognized as a serious evil in New York City as far back as 1834. A city inspector for that year attributed the high rate of mortality to "the crowded and filthy state" in which the population of New York lived.[1] As the city was growing, the well-to-do residents were moving northward and their old dwellings were let to the poor. The traditional American one-family house was adapted to the requirements of a population of independent artisans and small shopkeepers, many of whom were home-owners. With the growth of great cities and the rise of land values, and with the development of a

[1] *Report of the Industrial Commission*, vol. xv., p. 452.

wage-earning class, the one-family house became the cause of congestion in its worst form. The rental of such a house was beyond the reach of the wage-earner. Each room was let out to a separate family. Naturally, such improvised dwellings lacked the most necessary accommodations. The basement of the one-family house of the old type, formerly used as a dining-room and kitchen, developed into a separate cellar apartment.

Towards the middle of the '40's there had grown up in New York a great "cellar population." A pen picture of the condition of the cellars is given in a report on the *Sanitary Condition of the Laboring Population*, which was published in 1845:

> The most offensive of all places of residence are the cellars. It is almost impossible, when contemplating the circumstances and conditions of the poor beings who inhabit these holes, to maintain the proper degree of calmness requisite for a thorough inspection of their miseries and sound judgment respecting them. You must descend to them; you must feel the blast of foul air, as it meets your face on opening the door; you must grope in the dark or hesitate until your eye becomes accustomed to the gloomy place, to enable you to find your way through the entry over the broken floor, the boards of which are protected from your tread by a half inch of hard dirt; you must inhale the suffocating vapor of the heated rooms; and in the dark, dim recesses endeavor to find the inmates by the sound of their voices, or chance to see their figures moving between you and the flickering light of a window, coated with dirt and festooned with cobwebs—or, if in search of an invalid, take care that you do not fall full length upon the bed with her, by stumbling against the rags and straw dignified by that name, lying upon the floor, under the window, if window there is.[1]

The occupants of these tenements were "principally Irish and German" whose habits were described in 1837 as "more or less filthy." An account of one of these houses, in the rear of No. 49 Elizabeth Street, is given in an official report of a city physician:

> The front building, a small two-story frame house, was partly occu-

[1] *Report of the Industrial Commission*, vol. xv., p. 453.

pied by the proprietor or lessee of the building as a liquor store and partly sublet to several Irish families. A covered alleyway led to the rear of the building. This was a double frame house of three stories in height. It stood in the center of the yard, ranged next the fence, where a number of pigsties and stables had surrounded the yard on three sides. From the quantity of filth, liquid and otherwise, thus caused, the ground, I suppose, had been rendered almost impassable, and to remedy this, the yard had been completely boarded over so that the earth could nowhere be seen. These boards were partially decayed, and by a little pressure, even in dry weather, a thick, greenish, fluid could be forced up through the crevices.[1]

These evils were not confined, however, to the foreign-born population. The living conditions of the sewing women, a large majority of whom were American-born, were thus described by the *New York Tribune*, in the same year 1845:

> These women generally "keep house"—that is, they rent a single room, or perhaps two small rooms, in the upper story of some poor, ill-constructed, unventilated house in a filthy street, constantly kept so by the absence of back yards and the neglect of the street inspector—where a sickening and deadly miasma pervades the atmosphere and in summer renders it totally unfit to be inhaled by human lungs depositing the seeds of debility and disease with every inspiration In these rooms all the processes of cooking, eating, sleeping, washing, working, and living are indiscriminately performed.[2]

Bad as these conditions were, they were not the worst. The wages of Irish laborers in Brooklyn were so low that they could not afford to pay any rent at all, so "they were allowed to build miserable shanties on ground allotted them by the contractors on the plot occupied by them in performing the work."[3]

In the '60's there was a "shanty population" of about 20,000 on the upper west side of Manhattan Island. It was composed of Germans and Irish. They were largely

[1] *Report of the Industrial Commission*, vol. xv., pp. 452–453.

[2] Helen L. Sumner: *Report of Woman and Child Wage-Earners in the United States*, vol. ix., p. 135.

[3] *Documentary History of American Industrial Society*, vol. viii., pp. 225–226; quoting from *New York Weekly Tribune*, May 2, 1846, p. 3, col. 3.

day laborers, employed by contractors in grading, paving, and sewering the streets, and in the removal of rock, or in excavating for public purposes. In a typical shanty, according to an inspector of the council of hygiene, "domiciliary and personal cleanliness is almost impossible. In one room are found the family, chairs, usually dirty and broken, cooking utensils, stove, often a bed, a dog or cat, and sometimes more or less poultry. On the outside, by the door in many cases, are pigs and goats and additional poultry. There is no sink or drainage, and the slops are thrown upon the ground."[1]

Gloomy pictures of the housing conditions which prevailed in the '60's are drawn in contemporary reports of medical inspectors. They speak in general terms of "the contracted alleys; the underground, murky, and pestilential cellars; the tenement house, with its hundreds of occupants where each cooks, eats, and sleeps in a single room without light or ventilation, surrounded with filth, in an atmosphere foul, fetid, and deadly."[2]

> The Thirteenth Ward was densely crowded with working classes, the majority of whom were Irish; Germans ranked next, and Americans last. . . . The ward showed a high rate of sickness and mortality, owing to the over-crowded and ill-ventilated dwellings and to the ignorant and careless habits of the people themselves. . . . From Fortieth to Fiftieth Street the foreign population was mainly Irish or of Irish descent, packed in filthy tenements and of the most unclean and degraded personal habits. . . . The tenement houses in which most of the foreign population found their homes were certainly little calculated to develop high social and moral types, and indeed brought to bear influences working directly the other way.[3]

The following description of the tenements in Sheriff Street, which was then settled by Germans, is quoted from contemporary sources:

> The attic rooms are used to deposit the filthy rags and bones as they are taken from the gutters and slaughterhouses. The yards are filled with dirty rags hung up to dry, sending forth their stench to all the

[1] *Report of the Industrial Commission*, vol. xv., p. 457.

[2] *Ibid.*, p. 454.

[3] *Ibid.*, p. 458.

neighborhood. . . . The tenants are all Germans. . . . They are exceedingly filthy in person and their bedclothes are as dirty as the floors they walk on. Their food is of the poorest quality, and their feet and hands, doubtless their whole bodies are suffering from what they call rheumatism, but which in reality is a prostrate nervous system, the result of foul air and inadequate supply of nutritious food. . . . The yards are all small and the sinks running over with filth. . . . Not one decent sleeping apartment can be found on the entire premises and not one stove properly arranged. The carbonic-acid gas, in conjunction with the other emanations from bones, rags, and human filth, defies description. The rooms are 6 by 10 feet; bedrooms 5 by 6 feet. The inhabitants lead a miserable existence, and their children wilt and die in their infancy.[1]

When at length the tenement dwellers crowded the old one-family residences to the utmost limit of their capacity, the further growth of population led to the utilization of the back yards, for building purposes. A special type of rear tenement came into existence. The terrible conditions that arose from lack of ventilation and sanitary conveniences are vividly depicted in a report of a city inspector concerning a square of front and rear tenements which were occupied mostly by Irish:

In a majority of rear tenements . . . the apartments are dirty, dark, and often reeking with filth, the walls wholly innocent of whitewash, and the atmosphere impregnated with the disagreeable odor so peculiar to tenant houses. In some the sun never shines, and the apartments are so dark that unless seated near the window it is impossible to read ordinary type; and yet the inspector often hears the hackneyed expression, "We have no sickness, thank God," uttered by those whose sunken eyes, pale cheeks, and colorless lips speak more eloquently than words of the anæmic condition inevitably resulting from the absence of pure, fresh air, and the general light of the sun. . . . The tenants seem to wholly disregard personal cleanliness, if not the very first principles of decency, their general appearance and actions corresponding with their wretched abodes. This indifference to personal and domiciliary cleanliness is doubtless acquired from a long familiarity with the loathsome surroundings, wholly at variance with all moral or social improvements, as well as the first principles of hygienic science.[2]

The fundamental cause of congestion with all its attend-

[1] *Report of the Industrial Commission*, vol. xv., p. 461. [2] *Ibid.*, p. 456.

ant evils is the fact that wage-workers must live within an accessible distance from their places of work. This necessity puts the owners of real estate in the factory district in a position of advantage over the tenants.

The landlord took the utmost advantage of the situation by charging the highest possible prices for the poorest possible accommodations, and disregarding every law of health and decency in erecting big barracks meant for occupation by the poor.

An inspector for the council of hygiene in 1864 thus reports the landlords' methods with regard to repairs:

Every expenditure of money which the law does not enforce to make is refused; and blinds half swung and ready to fall and crash with the first strong wind; doors long off their hinges, which open and shut by being taken up bodily and put out of or in the way; chimneys as apt to conduct the smoke into the room as out of it; stagnant, seething, overflowing privies, left uncleansed through the hot months of summer, though pestilence itself should breed from them; hydrants out of repair and flooding sink and entry; stairs which shake and quiver with every step as you ascend them; and all this day after day, month after month, year in and year out.[1]

Such were the housing conditions to which the "old immigrants" of Teuton and Celtic stock submitted for more than a quarter of a century, at a time when the population of New York was but a fraction of its present size, and there was still an abundance of unimproved land in the upper part of Manhattan Island. These conditions are a thing of the past. The typical tenement house in the Jewish and Italian sections of New York to-day is a decided improvement upon the dwellings of the Irish and the Germans in the same sections a generation or two ago. "The visitor of 1900 could go about dry-shod, at least, in tenement yards and courts where thirty-five years before the accumulation of what should have gone off in sewers and drains made access almost impossible."[2]

The causes of the present congestion in New York City

[1] *Report of the Industrial Commission*, vol. xv., p. 459.
[2] *Ibid.*, p. 488.

have been the subject of an exhaustive investigation by Professor Pratt, of the New York School of Philanthropy. Although believing that restriction of immigration would have "salutary results in different directions," he found from the mass of statistical evidence collected by him, that congestion is produced by industrial factors which are not related to immigration and over which the immigrants have no control. We must abstain, for want of space, from quoting his statistics. His conclusions are reproduced in condensed form, yet, as nearly as possible verbatim, in the following abstract[1]:

"New York City is the great mart of the American continent. Every company or corporation of any size or importance has offices, usually its principal offices, in New York City. The New York market, therefore, is an exceedingly important factor in the concentration of manufacturers in that city. The fact that New York City is large and commercially great, makes it a desirable place in which to locate a manufacturing enterprise. A very large and increasing importance should be attached to this element as a factor in the congestion of manufactures in New York City. During the last half century New York has been changing from a purely commercial city to a manufacturing center as well. The value of manufactured products has increased nearly tenfold. The great bulk of the manufacturing in greater New York is carried on in Manhattan below Fourteenth Street, on that small but immensely valuable one-hundredth of the city's total land area. Of the whole number of workers engaged in manufactures in Manhattan, 321,488, or 66.8 per cent, work in factories below Fourteenth Street, while only 160,368 or 33.2 per cent work in the much larger area above Fourteenth Street. The problem of congestion of population, then, seems to be closely linked with that of congestion of industries.

"Population must live within an accessible distance of its place of work. Hence, it is scarcely necessary to point out how important a cause of congestion of population the concentration of industry, trade, and commerce becomes.

[1] Edward Ewing Pratt: *Industrial Causes of Congestion of Population in New York City*, pp. 14, 15, 17, 20, 21, 39, 42, 94, 97, 138, 145, 146, 155, 166, 167, 182, 183, 185, 186, 187, 188, 204.

The conditions of labor exercise a preponderating influence upon the lives of the workers. Long hours and low pay have compelling force and necessitate the residence of the overworked and underpaid in the over-crowded and congested districts of New York City. Even the efficient workman counts the carfare to distant points a drain on his income, and locates near the industrial districts. The conclusion indicated is irresistible, that the factory and the workshop are the predominant factor in the lives of these workers, and that the factories in the crowded sections of Manhattan are largely responsible for the problem of congestion of population which confronts the city in these districts. The latter being limited in size, buildings must be erected which will house many families. Some students of the problem have discovered the fact that in the most congested districts there are to be found the largest proportions of aliens. The conclusion is then drawn that congestion is due to immigration. The best that can be said of this generalization is that it is indeed a hasty one. The tendency for people to group themselves together in a strange land is most natural. The newly arrived immigrant seeks his friends or relatives,—if he has none, he seeks companionship where he can understand and where he can be understood. From this little nationality group, he makes his start in the struggle of the New World. These steady accessions of newly arrived immigrants no doubt augment the crowded districts, but they are scarcely an important cause. Similar tendencies of congregation among immigrants are found in sparsely settled Minnesota and in the Dakotas, but we do not find congestion. The logical explanation is, that there are other and perhaps more fundamental causes at work.

"One of the most powerful lodestones of the city is the city itself, and within the city, the center is the magnet. These advantages of the city and the center of the city are not purely pleasurable, but are social in the best sense of the word. It is at the center of a great city like New York that educational and cultural facilities are found most highly developed. As a shrewd employer of men once said, 'A man can get more for nothing in New York City than he can buy with his whole wage in a small town.' He can get more pleasure, more excitement, more education, than he can anywhere else. The city contributes to every side of a man, no matter how varied his nature. This is true, in general, of the city; it is pre-eminently true of the center of the city's population, where congestion has occurred, or is likely to occur.

"Congestion is often attributed to the inordinate desire of certain races or nationalities to congregate. The Jews and the Italians have each been accused of causing congestion. These recent arrivals have no doubt largely inhabited congested districts, but it seems unjust and unscientific to assert that congestion is caused by these groups of people. In fact the entire reasoning underlying this theory of congestion is based on *a priori logic and is open to serious* objections. The returns of workers employed in Lower Manhattan, in the uptown factories, in Brooklyn, near Brooklyn Bridge, in Williamsburg, in Queens Borough, near the 34th Street Ferry, and in suburban factories located on the outskirts of Greater New York, display certain uniform tendencies which may be formulated as follows:

"A working population tends to live in the immediate vicinity of its place of employment.

"The distribution of a working population is greatly influenced by such industrial factors as hours of work and wages. The degree of distribution may be termed residence-mobility.

"The residence-mobility of a working population varies inversely with the length of the working day or week. The longer the working day the intenser the congestion.

"The residence-mobility of a working population varies directly with the wages or labor. The workers earning the lowest wages are the most congested.

"The nationality or race of the workers has no appreciable effect upon the residence-mobility of a working population.

"In the most congested districts a large proportion of the workers find it impossible to secure adequate or comfortable living quarters. Hence we find that the workers employed in Lower Manhattan take, on the average, a longer time in getting to and from work than the workers in any other group. Nor do the workers employed near Manhattan show any tendency whatever, that could be interpreted as indicating a preference for the congested districts. The workers prefer to live near their places of employment. This is the tendency despite nationality, which may be urging them to live among their countrymen. These facts indicate that the recently-arrived Italian or Russian

Jew does not prefer to live in the congested districts. They are found to reside near their places of work, and when the two alternatives are open to them, the larger proportion embraces the opportunity to live among decent surroundings. The most important finding in the investigation of the group of workers employed in Brooklyn near the Brooklyn Bridge is the relatively small proportion who live in Manhattan, in spite of its accessibility. With the crowded down-town colony of Little Italy easily accessible, only 37.8 per cent of these Italians live in Lower Manhattan. Of the group working in Brooklyn, there are more than fifty per cent less Italians, and almost fifty per cent less Russians and Jews living in Manhattan, than of the groups that are employed in Manhattan. This fact shows the effect of concentrating industries in Manhattan and demonstrates what a difference exists when the factories are located only just outside. Manufacturers in suburban sites within accessible distance of Manhattan remove their workmen from the congested districts. The workmen, when given the chance, prefer to live in the less crowded sections. This is true even of the much-maligned Italian and Jew.

"When the influence of immigration and the distribution of the various nationalities are carefully considered, the tendency of our immigrant people to live in congested districts near the work places cannot occasion very great surprise, in view of the fact that our foreign population is the most unskilled, and therefore, the lowest paid, and that it is employed in industries working the longest hours. This tendency—and the fact that aliens form the largest part of our most congested population is admitted—has been frequently seized upon as the explanation of congestion, and hence these theorists have demanded restriction of immigration as a remedy for congestion. However, if congestion were due to the desire or willingness of our alien population to live in congested districts, we should expect those employed within a reasonable distance of Manhattan to make every effort to live there. But this is exactly contrary to the facts as brought out in the preceding study. The Italians, Jews, and Slavic peoples, who have oftenest been indicted for congestion, have proved themselves innocent and their positive unwillingness to live in Manhattan, when escape is offered, is evidenced by every group of workers in the factories outside of Lower Manhattan.

If, therefore, this mass of evidence has any weight, the oftrepeated theory of congestion—that it is the result of the preference of the people, the gregarious instinct—is disproved.

"The basic cause of congestion in all great cities is to be found in the failure on the part of the community to provide necessary safeguards. The first of these negative causes is the lack of proper planning of the city. Had our cities been laid out on broad, comprehensive plans, had our streets been laid out on wide, intelligent lines, and adequate parks provided, had our industrial and commercial districts been segregated, and our residence districts reserved, some of the very tap-roots of congestion would have been removed.

"The lack of adequate building laws is closely linked to that of city planning. The limitation of the area of the lot which can be built upon, the height of the house, the size of the rooms, are all factors which would definitely and certainly confine and limit congestion. But even those laws we have, have not been adequately enforced. Had our laws been enforced in the best possible manner, we would have gained a little in preventing congestion. Of the local conditions peculiar to New York, which with thought and foresight might have been prevented, the first and foremost is the lack of adequate rapid transit. Whenever it has been advantageous to do business in Lower Manhattan, it has been convenient, because of lack of transit facilities, both to have a permanent place of business there and to live there. Transit not only converged on Lower Manhattan, but what there was of it simply conveyed people into the crowded districts and 'dumped' them. Had transit facilities to neighboring localities been convenient and adequate, the population might have availed itself of the advantages of the central city, and business might have flourished in other than down-town Manhattan districts. Important factors in the campaign for the relief of congestion of population in Manhattan are: first, the removal of factories from Manhattan, and their distribution according to some comprehensive plan throughout the outlying suburbs; second, the enactment of laws to prevent the reproduction of bad living and housing conditions in the other neighborhoods. This is city planning."

It is evident from Professor Pratt's analysis that congestion in New York City is not wrought by the habits or standards of living of the immigrants from Eastern and Southern Europe, but is forced upon them by conditions not of their own making.

As regards the effects of this congestion upon the rate of wages, on the other hand, the determining factor is not the discomfort suffered by the immigrant, but the amount he must expend for rent. And it is a well-known fact that house rent in New York is higher than in the rest of the United States. The average rent in New York City for a normal workingman's family, according to latest pre-war statistics, was $13.50 to $14.00 a month, whereas in the rest of the United States, it ranged from $8.25 to $11.00 per month.[1] The Jewish or Italian immigrant in New York City was compelled to expend for rent about $1.00 a week more than the wage-earners in small towns where the native American workmen predominate. The American workman may be better housed, yet when the manufacturer employing immigrant labor in New York must meet in the nation's market his competitor employing native American labor in a small country town, it is the native American workman, rather than the immigrant recently arrived in New York from Southern or Eastern Europe, that can be induced or coerced to accept a lower wage.

C. *Housing Conditions in the Country at Large*

In a retrospective view of the New England textile manufacturing towns of the period when the operatives in

[1] Amos G. Warner; *American Charities*, p. 180. "Not only is the cost of housing less in cities outside of New York, but the accommodations enjoyed are better. Detached houses are the rule, with no question of access to light and air. The number of rooms is 3, in only 1 case of the 53 (Rochester); only 6 report 4 rooms, and 7 and 8 rooms are of frequent occurrence. . . . For $8.00 a month in the smaller towns of the State, and $10.00 or $11.00 in the cities like Syracuse, better accommoations can be secured than for $15.00 in Manhattan."—Chapin: *The Standard of Living in New York City*, p. 303.

the mills were recruited among the farm girls of the neighborhood, the Immigration Commission has discovered a description of their living conditions "which affords a pleasing contrast with the Lowell of the present." "The life in the boarding houses was very agreeable. These houses belonged to the corporation,"[1] *i. e.*, they were "company houses," in modern parlance. Dr. Sumner, however, in her *History of Women in Industry in the United States*, written for the U. S. Bureau of Labor, quotes other contemporary testimony less bucolic in character. From the same town of Lowell, complaints were made in 1845 that a dozen or more of the "daughters of New England" were crowded into "the same hot, ill-ventilated attic." The boarding houses of the Tremont mills in 1847 were described in the following extract from a letter:

> 'T is quite common for us to write on the cover of a bandbox, and sit upon a trunk, as tables or chairs in our sleeping rooms are all out of the question, because there is no room for such articles, as 4 to 6 occupy every room, and of course trunks and bandboxes constitute furniture for the rooms we occupy. A thing called a light-stand, a little more than a foot square, is our table for the use of 6. Wash-stands are uncommon articles—it has never been my lot to enjoy their use, except at my own expense.[2]

Comparative statistics of house tenancy in Boston in 1855 and 1900 show that in the middle of the nineteenth century the tenement house population was as numerous, in proportion, as in our day. This can be seen from Table 71 on page 242.

Overcrowded and filthy tenement houses were as prevalent forty years ago in Boston, as in New York. There also the conversion of the single family house into a tenement house, where a whole family was jammed in every room, was productive "of filth and grime." An early report of the Massachusetts Labor Bureau, describing the

[1] *Reports of the Immigration Commission*, vol. 1, pp. 508–509.

[2] Helen L. Sumner: *Report of Woman and Child Wage-Earners in the United States*, vol. ix., pp. 87–88.

tenement houses of Boston and their surroundings, speaks of "hovels rotting with damp and mould," of "puddles reeking with stenchy garbage," of "putrid cesspools and uncleansed drains, befouled with unspeakable nastiness."[1]

TABLE 71.

PER CENT DISTRIBUTION OF THE FAMILIES OF BOSTON ACCORDING TO NUMBER OF FAMILIES PER HOUSE, 1855 AND 1900.[2]

Living in	Per cent of families 1855	1900
1 family houses	31.8	32.2
2 family houses	23.5	26.5
Tenements with 3 or more families	44.7	41.3
Total	100.0	100.0

The degree of congestion at the close of the '60's is exemplified by the description of a block of tenements consisting of fifty-six rooms which were occupied by fifty-four families, mostly Irish. There were also a few English and colored families among them. The stairways were rotten and dangerous. The ventilation of the rooms was very poor. Washing, ironing, and drying were all done in the only room which was both a living room and a sleeping room.[3]

The two-room tenements on Meander Street consisted of a living and a sleeping room, both dark and damp and dirty. Other tenements visited were old, rickety frame houses with plastering broken down and full of holes through which rain and sun freely entered. In the summer the houses swarmed with vermin. These houses were occupied by American and Irish tenants.

Another tenement house in Kingston Court was a wooden building consisting of six apartments, some with three rooms and some with only one to each. The living rooms

[1] *Massachusetts Bureau of Statistics of Labor. 3d Annual Report* (1871–1872), pp. 437–438.

[2] *Census of Boston*, 1855, p. 11 (percentages computed); *XII. Census of United States. Population*, Part II., p. 186, Table XCVIII.

[3] *Reports of the Massachusetts Bureau of Labor Statistics*, 1870, pp. 164–180.

were 10 by 14; the sleeping rooms 7 by 9. The sun never penetrated the sleeping rooms. Water was obtained from a hydrant in the yard upon which twenty-six families depended. Broken windows patched up with boards and rags, rickety and broken-down stairs were not unusual. We quote the concluding sentence of the report:

> We could describe other tenement-house abominations of the same foulness and beastly defilement, but it would be but a repetition of nastiness and negligence, and for which neither memory or dictionary could supply words not yet used, or language adequate to the filthy picturing.[1]

In the smaller Massachusetts towns, the working people were as badly housed as in Boston. The following is reproduced from contemporary testimony given by a canvasser who went through many of the tenements of Danvers:

> Take them as a whole, they are horrid; those belonging to the factory especially. There are tenement houses there that ought not to be occupied. Four families have complained to me, that if they go to bed at night and there comes a shower, they have to rise up and put dishes in different places to catch the water, and that they can't sleep in their beds; and to prove it I went and examined and saw it was actually worse than they had said; one house, especially, where a person came to me, and I saw he did n't look right, and I said, "Are you going to work?" "No," he says, "had no sleep last night." It had been raining and his mother had been baking and preparing things for the house, and, in the morning almost everything had swum off and gone away—in all directions. . . . Another house, I was almost afraid to go into. I could see right through into the cellar; the plastering was entirely off the ceiling and they told me it leaked in just about the same way. There is another house, where there is a yard square without a shingle on it; and then another has an addition to it, and you can put your whole arm right in betwixt the two. It is more like a pig-pen than a decent house . . . when people are in the water-closet, the people on the road can see them. There is not a good tenement in the village.[2]

[1] *Reports of the Massachusetts Bureau of Labor Statistics*, 1871, pp. 517–531.

[2] *Ibid.*, pp. 442–443.

The same conditions were reported from Salem. The houses were seldom repaired, the plumbing was very poor, and the pump water was often made unfit for drinking purposes by the washings of the yard. The odor in the houses was bad. The following description of a house at No. 18 Lemon Street, is quoted as an extreme case, which nevertheless indicates what conditions were tolerated in those days:

> In connection with the kitchen, and only separated by a door was the pantry, quite reluctantly shown us by the mistress. She said that it being very much out of repair, and not fit to be used as such, they concluded it was best to turn it into a cowshed. Here were two cows, and all the accompaniments usually found in a stable, in direct connection with the kitchen, filling the house with its unmitigated stench. In this place pigs and hens were once kept, besides the cow, the former on all occasions making the freest use of the domestic apartments.[1]

About the same time (1872) shanty dwellers were found among the laborers of Massachusetts. The paymaster of tunnel laborers employed at North Adams in 1872 testified that many of them lived in shanties on the works and even kept boarders. "The miners, rockmen, etc., who have no families, board at the shanties. They are filthy, dirty places. . . ."[2]

The congestion and squalor of the past were no better than the worst housing conditions that were found by the investigators of the Immigration Commission among the immigrants from Southern and Eastern Europe. Yet the tenement-house dwellers of forty years ago were all of Teuton and Celtic stock. As stated in a previous chapter, contemporary observers sought to explain the bad housing conditions of the Irish immigrants by the low standard of living of the people of Ireland.[3] Although living conditions

[1] *Reports of the Massachusetts Bureau of Labor Statistics*, 1870, pp. 372 and 380.

[2] *Massachusetts Bureau of Statistics of Labor. Third Annual Report* (1871–1872), pp. 440–441.

[3] *Report of the Industrial Commission*, vol. xv., p. 459.

in Ireland have greatly improved since those days, yet they still remain far below the average of the most overcrowded sections of the great American cities.

The investigation of the Immigration Commission was confined to "the overcrowded, poor quarters of the city"; in the households investigated, the average number of persons per room was 1.34.[1] In the city of Dublin, according to the census of 1901, four fifths of all tenements consisted of four rooms or less with an average of 2.20 persons per room. More than one third of all tenements had three persons or more per room. Three fifths of all tenements consisted of one or two rooms only.[2] In the whole of Ireland, one third of all families lived in two rooms or less.[3] There were 38,086 families of three or more persons living in one room each. These extremes of congestion comprised 4.2 per cent of all Irish families. The details are given in Table 72.

TABLE 72.

NUMBER OF TENEMENTS OF ONE ROOM OCCUPIED BY THREE OR MORE PERSONS, 1901.[4]

Occupied by	Number of tenements
3 persons	12,867
4 persons	8,932
5 persons	6,250
6 persons	4,400
7 persons	2,701
8 persons	1,530
9 persons	786
10 persons	364
11 persons	138
12 persons or more	68
Total	38,036

If it is maintained that the immigrant tends to transplant to the American soil the standard of living of his native country, it must follow from the latest statistics of housing conditions in Ireland that even the present-day Irish immi-

[1] Jenks and Lauck, *loc. cit.*, pp. 117, 119.

[2] See Appendix, Table XVI.

[3] *Census of Ireland*, 1901. *General Report*, p. 112, Table 9; p. 173, Table 49.

[4] *Ibid.*, Table 10.

grants are open to the same objection as the immigrants from Southern and Eastern Europe. The fact that the investigation of the Immigration Commission discovered among the Irish no overcrowding approaching that of their mother country must be taken to mean one of two things: either its investigators overlooked the recent Irish immigrants and selected only old Irish settlers who had in the course of time advanced on the social scale, or else the standard of living of the recent Irish immigrants in the United States was not determined by their living conditions in Ireland, but depended upon their earning ability in this country. In either case the race theory of economics fathered by the Commission fails.

That bad housing conditions are not the exclusive characteristic of the immigrant, but are found under like economic conditions among the native wage-earners as well, has been shown by the investigation of the Immigration Commission in Alabama, where there are practically no foreigners whose competition might be supposed to have forced down the American standard of living. In the outlying towns, beyond the territory immediately adjacent to Birmingham, many of the bituminous coal mines are operated exclusively by native labor and native white Americans are employed as unskilled laborers. "In these environments the home of the native white laborer is frequently devoid of the more modern equipment and sanitation."[1] Mr. Streightoff, in his study of the standard of living, uses stronger language. According to him, "in the Southern mill towns conditions are about at their worst." The number of foreign-born wage-earners in the Southern mills is negligible and cannot affect the housing situation. The mill workers are country people of old American stock. And yet the company houses in which they live "are neither sheathed, plastered, nor papered, and the tenants suffer intensely from the occasional cold weather."[2]

[1] *Reports of the Immigration Commission*, vol. 9, p. 229.

[2] Streightoff: *The Standard of Living*, pp. 76–77 and 92.

The preceding comparison between the present and the past, on the one hand, and between native and foreign-born mill and mine workers, on the other, irresistibly leads to the conclusion that the cause of bad housing conditions is not racial, but economic. That the difference among wage-earners in this respect "depends, of course . . . upon the income," is admitted, "to a considerable extent," by the experts of the Immigration Commission with the qualification, however, that the difference depends "apparently also upon the insistence" of the tenants themselves upon having proper accommodations.[1] If the South Italian or Irish laborers, or the Southern white mill hands, are not so well housed as their Welsh foreman, or English engineer, it is because, apart from their inability to raise the rent of a substantial dwelling, they do not "insist" upon having it for the money they are able to pay. That the English or German laborers and factory hands of past generations lived in filthy tenements, must have been due, by the same method of reasoning, to lack of "insistence" on their part upon better accommodations. This view implies a belief that the law of supply and demand will assure to the wage-workers such homes as they will "insist" upon. The economic distinction between land and other forms of property is lost sight of.

The inadequacy of the law of supply and demand in the matter of housing was conclusively demonstrated by all investigations of the New York housing system, which "agreed in showing the landlord, rather than the helpless tenant, as the primitive cause of tenement evils."[2]

In the mill towns and mining camps of to-day, as in the

[1] "There seems to be a decided difference . . . among the various races—the South Italians and the Syrians among the recent immigrants, the Irish among the older immigrants, not being so well provided with sanitary equipment as are the other races. This depends, of course, to a considerable extent, upon the income, but apparently also upon the insistence of the persons themselves upon having proper water supply and toilet accommodations."—Jenks and Lauck, *loc. cit.*, p. 126.

[2] *Report of the Industrial Commission*, vol. xv., p. 459.

mill towns of Massachusetts in the days of the "old immigration," the helplessness of the tenant is aggravated by the combination of the landlord and mill owner in the same individual or corporation, whose income is derived from house rents, as well as from manufacturing or mining. "In many industrial localities," say Professors Jenks and Lauck, "especially in those connected with the mining industry, the so-called 'company-house' system prevails under which the industrial worker . . . must live in a house owned by the operating company and rented to him."[1] This system is as common in the Anglo-Saxon towns of the South, as in the Slav settlements of Pennsylvania.[2] If the mill or mine worker were to "insist" upon a better dwelling, he could not hold his position.

The Immigration Commission made no systematic inquiries to ascertain the landlords' share of responsibility for the overcrowding and unsanitary conditions of the houses occupied by the new immigrants in industrial communities. The outspoken tendency of its investigation was to lay the whole blame upon the habits of the immigrants. There are scattered in its reports, however, occasional items of information which tell the other side of the story. The following description of a "company house" is illuminating:

> The type of company house most frequently seen in the locality adjacent to Birmingham is a one-story frame building containing from two to four rooms, the four-room houses being frequently divided into two apartments. . . . They are usually devoid of any modern conveniences, such as bath or flush toilet.

But these houses are "built in close proximity to the steel, iron, or coke yard in which the laborers are employed,"[3] and they have no other choice but to take such houses as the company provides for them, or to travel a distance to and from work.

[1] Jenks and Lauck, *loc. cit.*, p. 279

[2] Streightoff, *loc. cit.*, pp. 76–77.

[3] *Reports of the Immigration Commission*, vol. 9, p. 232.

From an account relating to another locality we learn that the rent paid by the recent immigrants "is excessive, and yields an unusually large rate of return to his landlord."[1] It may be surmised from this illustration that the income from company houses also very likely "pays more than the ordinary return on the cost of the building."

The effect of the emphasis, however, laid by the Commission upon the "tendency . . . characteristic of the South Italian and Slav races" to "settle in that section of the town where . . . the house rent is reduced to a minimum"[2] is to divert public attention from the responsibility of the mine and mill operators for the insanitary condition of the tenements provided by them for their employees.[3] The police power of the State is ample to protect the health of the community from the ill effects of insanitary housing conditions. Considered on its own merits, as a problem in public hygiene, the housing of the mine and mill operatives, whether native or foreign-born, has therefore no relevancy to the subject of immigration.

In reality, however, the housing problem is drawn into

[1] *Reports of the Immigration Commission*, vol. 9, pp. 93–94.

[2] *Ibid.*, p. 229.

[3] The following is quoted from a "description of a typical mining and coke village" in Pennsylvania:

"The typical company village is exceedingly insanitary. . . . The water supply of the coal and coke town is very impure and a source of disease. The companies usually 'clean up' the towns once a year; sometimes twice, but often not at all. There is little to stimulate cleanliness on the part of the tenants under such circumstances. *The mine operators say that the existing conditions result from the fact that the foreigner is too dirty for the town to be other than what it is*, but whether this is true or not, it seems that very little effort is made to improve the living conditions." (*Ibid.*, vol. 6, p. 323.)

The defense is very typical, indeed. Because "the foreigner is dirty," the mining company which owns the village provides him with impure water which is a source of disease, and cleans up the village only twice a year. It is evident that the tenants cannot build water-works, nor can they install a system of sewerage. It would not avail them to "insist" upon these improvements, as there is no place to which they could move in case of refusal, these conditions being "typical."

the discussion of immigration only collaterally, as an argument in support of a theory. The Immigration Commission has filled its volumes with statistical tables, some of which show that the English-speaking wage-workers are better housed than the immigrants from Southern and Eastern Europe, and others that the earnings of the former are higher. The impression conveyed by the race classification[1] is that the wages of the immigrants from Southern and Eastern Europe are low because they are willing to live in crowded quarters, whereas the wages of the English-speaking workmen are higher, because they "insist" upon the American standard of living. The Immigration Commission's own statistics, however, contain a refutation of this theory.

In the first place, it appears that there is the widest variation among wage-earners of each race with respect to housing, which shows that there is no common standard of living for all wage-earners of the same race, but that it varies for the individuals of the same race. Neither do the low rents paid by some of them force down the earnings of others of the same race, as demonstrated by the wide variations in earnings among individuals of the same race.

In the second place, it is found that "the household of immigrants, as compared with the native born wage-earners pays, generally speaking, the same if not higher rent per room."[2] In some districts the average monthly rent per apartment is also higher for recent immigrants than for American wage-earners of native parentage. In Ensley,

[1] Some of the "race" distinctions are unique. Thus we are informed that the Macedonians paid $5.53 per apartment, whereas the Greeks paid $5.94 and the Bulgarians only $4.28. (*Ibid.*, vol. 9, p. 234, Table 687.) It can be found in the Commission's own *Dictionary of Races* that Macedonia is merely a political division with a mixed population consisting chiefly of Bulgarians and Greeks. Professors Jenks and Lauck also comment upon the per capita monthly rent payments of the Bulgarians who paid only $0.97, and the Macedonians who paid $0.78. (Jenks and Lauck, *loc. cit.*, pp. 131–132.)

[2] Jenks and Lauck, *loc. cit.*, p. 122.

Ala., *e. g.*, the latter paid on an average $5.40 per apartment, the Greeks, $5.94, and the Poles, $5.98. The lowest average rent per room was paid by the native white of native parentage, viz., $1.38; the new immigrants ranged in the following order: Slovaks, $1.73; Bulgarians, $1.82; Poles, $1.91; South Italians, $2.09; Greeks, $2.93.[1]

It is believed, however, that the difference in rent is reduced by overcrowding, which is "most frequently shown by the keeping of boarders or lodgers."[2] Great stress is laid upon the fact that the Southern and Eastern Europeans "break the independence of family life by taking boarders or lodgers into the home," whereas "the native American and older immigrant employees maintain an independent form of family life," though they send their wives and children to the factory.[3] It is worthy of note, as a historical parallel, that in 1873 General Walker spoke of "the *detestable American vice* of 'boarding' . . . uprooting the ancient and honored institutions of the family."[4] The Commission has laboriously figured out for each race the percentage of families taking lodgers or boarders. Aside from the merits of this criterion which will be considered later, it is open to question, whether the figures of the Commission may be accepted as typical. A similar investigation recently made by the United States Bureau of Labor led to widely divergent results. Out of 1139 American households studied by the Immigration Commission only 10 per cent had boarders or lodgers; out of 15,161 American households, however, studied by the Bureau of Labor 22.23 per cent kept boarders or lodgers. The variation of the percentage by race in the statistics of the Immigration Commission was from 0 to 79.3 per cent, whereas in the statistics of the United States Bureau of Labor the range of variation was from 16.50 to 30.77 per

[1] *Reports of the Immigration Commission*, vol. 9., p. 234, Table 687.

[2] Jenks and Lauck, *loc. cit.*, p. 122.

[3] Jenks and Lauck, *loc. cit.*, pp. 158, 161.

[4] Walker: *Discussions in Economics and Statistics*, p. 43.

cent. The discrepancies between the two series of figures relating to the old immigration are shown in Table 73.

TABLE 73.

PER CENT OF FAMILIES KEEPING BOARDERS OR LODGERS AMONG THE RACES OF THE OLD IMMIGRATION.[1]

Nativity	Source of information	
	Immigration Commission	United States Bureau of Labor
Norwegian	.0	20.13
Welsh	2.2	26.89
Scotch	4.1	23.51
Canadian French	6.3	26.78
Irish	6.4	30.71
English	7.1	25.92
German	9.6	23.79

That two official investigations separated by a brief interval of six or seven years have brought such widely divergent results, can probably be accounted for by the fact that the investigations of the Immigration Commission were concentrated upon selected industrial communities, where the English-speaking immigrants were mostly high-priced skilled mechanics, whereas the new immigrants were nearly all unskilled laborers; it has been shown, however, in Chapter VII. that each race is represented in every occupation. The investigation of the United States Bureau of Labor, on the other hand, was made in the leading industrial centers of thirty-three States and is believed to be "representative of the industrial portion of the country as a whole."[2]

Apart, however, from the doubtful value of the statistics collected by the Immigration Commission on the subject of boarders and lodgers, the fatal defect of its race per-

[1] Jenks and Lauck, *loc. cit.*, p. 160. *Eighteenth Annual Report of the Commissioner of Labor*, p. 261.

[2] *Eighteenth Annual Report of the Commissioner of Labor*, p. 39.

centages is that they assume by implication a communistic system of housekeeping among the foreign-born. In reality, however, the 52 per cent of the Croatians who keep boarders or lodgers do not help to pay the rent of the other 48 per cent who keep none. The latter must themselves pay the rent in full, which is at least as high as that paid by the natives. It is evident that the wages of those who have no lodgers must be sufficient to enable them to pay the same rent as the native Americans, which goes to show that those of them who do keep lodgers do not force down the earnings of their countrymen.

That overcrowding is not a racial characteristic, but an economic phenomenon, appears from the following table showing the comparative frequency of the practice of keeping boarders or lodgers in families of foreign-born garment workers and woolen mill operatives classified by annual earnings.

TABLE 74.

PER CENT OF FOREIGN-BORN FAMILIES IN WHICH WIFE HAS EMPLOYMENT OR KEEPS BOARDERS OR LODGERS, BY YEARLY EARNINGS OF HUSBAND.[1]

Husband's earnings.	Per cent of wives keeping boarders or lodgers	
	Garment workers	Woolen mill operatives
Under $400	28.2	61.4
$400 and under $600	30.6	45.3
$600 and over	19.9	7.1

The nationalities comprised in the preceding table are Scotch, Irish, Germans, Norwegians, French, Bohemians, Hebrews, Lithuanians, Poles, South Italians, and Syrians. As shown by the figures, the percentage of families with boarders and lodgers[2] decreases with the increase of earnings.

[1] *Reports of the Immigration Commission*, vol. 10, Table 38, p. 685; vol. 11, Table 45, p. 310.

[2] The comparative value of the figures could not be affected by the

The same effect is produced by differences in rent. Among iron and steel workers "both the native and foreign households exhibit the smallest proportion having boarders or lodgers in the South." The reason is that rents are considerably lower in the South than in other sections of the country.[1] Of the South Italian iron workers in the Pittsburgh district 70.6 per cent keep boarders and lodgers, whereas in the Birmingham district there are only 3 per cent with boarders and lodgers. Among the Slovaks the percentages are respectively 43.9 and 15.0.[2]

The United States Bureau of Labor has made a comparison of the expenditures for rent per person in 3908 foreign and 7248 native "normal" families, which have no children of working age, nor any boarders or lodgers. The results for the North Atlantic and North Central States compare as follows:

TABLE 75.

AVERAGE ANNUAL RENT PER FAMILY AND PER INDIVIDUAL IN NORMAL FAMILIES, BY NATIVITY, IN NORTHERN STATES.[3]

Nativity	North Atlantic		North Central	
	Per family	Per individual	Per family	Per individual
Native..........	$125.54	$33.25	$97.58	$24.45
Foreign.........	118.21	29.09	91.94	22.02
Difference	$7.33	$ 4.16	$ 5.64	$ 2.43

small proportion of married women working for wages who were found in only 5 per cent of all foreign-born households studied by the Immigration Commission.

[1] Cottages very similar to, but not so good as those for which the southern mill operatives pay a rent of $3.00 to $3.50 per month, rent in Southwestern Illinois at from $14.00 to $16.00 per month. (*Ibid.*, vol. 9, p. 93.)

[2] *Ibid.*, vol. 8, p. 105.

[3] *Eighteenth Annual Report of the Commissioner of Labor*, Table V., H. and O., pp. 578, 589, 590. Other sections are omitted from this com-

The difference in the amount of rent paid by native and foreign-born wage-earners amounts to fourteen cents a week per family or eight cents a week per person in the North Atlantic States and to eleven cents a week per family or five cents a week per person in the North Central States. This is the extent to which the scrimping on rent enables the average immigrant to underbid the native wage-earner in the labor market. In Table 75 all foreign-born are combined in one group. In Table 76 the foreign-born are distinguished by nationality for the country as a whole.

TABLE 76.

ANNUAL RENT PER FAMILY AND PER INDIVIDUAL IN NORMAL FAMILIES, BY NATIVITY OF HEAD OF FAMILY.[1]

Nativity of head of family	Per family	Per individual
Native white:	$112	$29
Foreign-born	111	27
Old immigration:		
Canada	109	27
England	125	31
Ireland	117	28
Sweden	119	30
Germany	109	26
New immigration:		
Austria-Hungary	90	22
Russia	101	23
Italy	97	25

Another fundamental fact which has been noted by all students of the housing problem is that the wage-earner must expend more for rent in proportion to his income in a large city than in a small town. "Whereas the average outlay for rent in the income group $400–$500 in the city is $120 or $125, that in the country as a whole is $86.54."[2] The significance of this difference lies in the fact

parison because the averages for natives in the South may be reduced by the inclusion of negroes.

[1] *Eighteenth Annual Report of the Commissioner of Labor*, Table V., J. and P., pp. 581 and 591 respectively.

[2] Streightoff: *The Standard of Living*, p. 12.

that the recent immigrants are mostly concentrated in great cities, where rent is high, while the native American workmen predominate in small towns with low rents. So when the article produced by immigrant labor in a large city must compete in the market with the article produced by native American labor in a small country town, it is not the recent immigrant that is able to underbid the native American workman, but on the contrary the latter is in a position to accept a cheaper wage.[1]

D. Food

The Immigration Commission has expressed the opinion that "while it [the new immigration] may not have lowered in a marked degree the American standard of living it has introduced a lower standard which has become prevalent in the unskilled industry at large."[2] This conclusion rests solely on the meagre statistics which were collected by the Commission on the subject of housing. The inconclusiveness of these statistics has been shown in the preceding section. The food expenditure which absorbs about two fifths of the workman's income,[3] was not included by the Commission in the regular program of its statistical investigation. Its reports contain but a few budgets picked up here and there in a casual way. It notes, however, "that, generally speaking, the expenditures for meat are considerably higher in the case of the more recent immigrants than in the case of the older immigrant races and the whites native-born of native father."[4] By way of illustration

[1] The Industrial Commission found that the average rent paid by a family of a garment worker in the city was $8.95 per month for three rooms, whereas the country garment workers who did not own their houses paid on an average $4.59 for a whole house. (*Report of the Industrial Commission*, vol. xv., p. 730.) The difference in rent amounted to $4.37 per month, *i. e.*, to $1.00 per week.

[2] *Reports of the Immigration Commission*, vol. 1, p. 39.

[3] *Eighteenth Annual Report of the Commissioner of Labor*, p. 96.

[4] *Reports of the Immigration Commission*, vol. 6, p. 356.

the following items are quoted from some of the published budgets.

The Magyar is a great consumer of meat. A butcher states that a group of eight Magyar men on an average eat 4 pounds of beef, 5 pounds of pork, 3 pounds of Polish sausage, and 4 pounds of veal, and often in addition, bacon and ham and other cured meats, each day. (Thus on an average, each man eats 2 pounds of meat each day.)

The Bulgarians. Among them bread is the staple article of diet. Each man will consume a three-pound loaf of bread per day. They also use a small quantity of meat each day, usually about a pound per man. (The experts of the Commission consider one pound a day per man "a small quantity." Few boarding houses patronized by university professors serve meat in greater quantities.)

The kind of food consumed daily by a Bulgarian couple was about as follows[1]:

Breakfast: Tea, cream, cheese, bread.

Dinner: Bread, some kind of meat or stew.

Supper: Bread, meat stew, or eggs.

Presumably these budgets were published by the Immigration Commission, because they were regarded as representative.

How do these food standards compare with the standard of the native American workingman? We may accept as the official definition of the American food standard the ration fixed by act of Congress for enlisted men on the warships of the American navy. A specimen bill of fare prepared in accordance with the Navy ration prescribed by Congress, is as follows[2]:

Breakfast: Baked beans, tomato catsup, bread, butter, coffee.

[1] *Reports of the Immigration Commission*, vol. 9, pp. 82–96.

[2] Frank J. Sheridan: "Italian, Slavic, and Hungarian Unskilled Immigrant Laborers in the United States." *Bulletin of the Bureau of Labor*, No. 72, p. 466.

Dinner: Roast beef, brown gravy, string beans, sweet potatoes, cottage pudding, vanilla sauce, bread, coffee.

Supper: Cold boiled ham, canned peaches, bread, butter, tea.

Judged by this official standard, the Hungarian and Bulgarian workmen, with their daily fare of one or two pounds of meat per man, do not appear to have "introduced a lower standard."

Concerning the Italians, material for a comparison of their food expenditure with that of native white Americans is furnished in the *Report of the Immigration Commission* on iron and steel manufacturing in the South. The Italians whose budgets were reported were all unskilled, earning from $7.50 to $12.50 per week, with the exception of one foreman of unskilled laborers, who was earning $15.00 and had an 18-year-old boy who contributed $7.00 a week to the family income. The Americans were all skilled mechanics with a weekly income of from $18.00 to $25.00, except one carpenter whose wages were $12.00 a week. In Table 77 the food expenditures of these families have been reduced to nutrition units per man per day according to the scale adopted by the United States Department of Agriculture.[1]

Although the budgets secured by the investigation of

TABLE 77.

AVERAGE EXPENDITURE PER MAN PER DAY OF SELECTED FAMILIES OF SOUTH ITALIAN AND NATIVE WHITE WORKERS IN THE IRON AND STEEL DISTRICT OF THE SOUTH.[2]

South Italian	Cents	Native White	Cents
No. 3	41	No. 13	62
No. 7	37	No. 10	36
No. 6	36	No. 11	36
No. 2	30	No. 9	32
No. 4	28	No. 12	29

[1] For an explanation of the method used, see Robert Coit Chapin: *The Standard of Living among Workingmen's Families in New York City*, pp. 125–126.

[2] For details see Appendix, Table XVII.

the Immigration Commission included none for unskilled American workmen and only one for an Italian employed in a supervisory capacity, all the rest relating to unskilled Italian laborers, yet the preceding table shows that the food expenditure of the South Italian laborer is the same as that of the Southern white skilled mechanic.[1]

A special investigation of the expenditures of single laborers in construction camps was made by the Bureau of Labor in 1906. Fresh and salt meats were found to be essential parts of the bills of fare of "Hungarian" and "Slav"[2] laborers. The same information was obtained concerning Hungarian laborers in an iron and steel plant in Ohio: "They used beef as a rule three times a day." At Hansford, Pa., the bill of fare of Hungarians and Slavs on week days was as follows:

"Breakfast: Bread and coffee. Lunch: Four or five sandwiches (beef). Dinner in the evening: Soup, boiled or roast beef, one half to three fourths of a pound a head. Vegetables and coffee."

According to Dr. Roberts, who has made a study of the conditions of labor in the anthracite coal mines, "the Slavs have good bread made of the best wheat or rye; they consume daily about a pound of beef for boiling or of fat pork or bologna sausage, a quantity of potatoes, cabbage, milk, coffee, and beer, butter and cheese, sugar, eggs, and fish."

An earlier investigation made by the Bureau of Labor among the Slav and Hungarian workmen in the iron mines of Pennsylvania showed that, in 1890, their bill of fare included "two pounds of meat per man per day, one for dinner and one for supper."[3]

[1] The one exceptionally high average, 62 cents per man per day, was obtained from a native machinist, who was employed in the railroad shops at $23.00 per week and had only his wife and a small child dependent upon him.

[2] The term "Hungarian" often comprises all immigrants from Hungary, most of whom belong to various Slav races. Bulgarians are also "Slavs."

[3] *Bulletin of the Bureau of Labor*, No. 72, p. 475.

With respect to Italians, a distinction must be drawn between families and single men, or married men whose families have remained in Italy. It is learned from the investigation of the Bureau of Labor, that men who are employed in construction camps live principally on vegetables and reduce their expenditures to a minimum, in an effort to save as much as possible of their wages. Italian families, however, do not differ in the matter of food expenditures from families of other nationalities with the same income. Beside the budgets of the Immigration Commission which have been analyzed above, this fact is brought out in Professor Chapin's monograph on the standard of living among New York workingmen, based upon a canvass of 391 families in the summer of 1907.

The following table, giving the classification of food expenditures by income and nationality, is compiled from Professor Chapin's budget statistics, the nationalities being arranged in the descending order of their average expenditure per man per day:

TABLE 78.

AVERAGE FOOD EXPENDITURES PER MAN PER DAY, BY INCOME AND NATIONALITY[1]

Income group and nationality	Expenditure Cents
$600 to $699:	
Italian	31.1
Bohemian	25.5
Teutonic	25.3
Austrian, Hungarian, and other S. E. European	24.0
Native white	23.9
Colored	23.5
Russian	23.1
Irish	20.8
$700 to $799:	
Italian	31.2
Irish	30.0
Teutonic	26.4
Native white	26.0
Colored	25.7
Austrian, Hungarian, and other S. E. European	25.1
Bohemian	24.3

[1] Robert Chapin, *loc. cit.*, p. 141.

Income group and nationality	Expenditure Cents
$800 to $899:	
Italian	33.9
Native white	32.4
Bohemian	30.2
Teutonic	29.5
Irish	26.5
$900 to $999:	
Native white	33.8
Teutonic	31.6
Italian	31.5
Irish	31.4
Austrian, Hungarian, and other Southeastern European	31.1
Bohemian	28.5
$1000 to $1099:	
Native white	38.1
Italian	34.3
Irish	32.0
Teutonic	31.9

The Italians in every income group expended more for food than the Hungarians and Slavs. In every income group below $900 per year, they expended more for food than any other nationality, including native Americans.[1] Among the families with an income from $900 to $1000, the Italians expended as much as the Teutons and the Irish, and more than the Bohemians who are regarded as "desirable" immigrants. In the highest group the Italian expended more than the Celts and the Teutons. According to Professor Underhill, of Yale University, who has made a study of the nutritive value of various foods, 22 cents per man per day must be regarded as the minimum upon which physical existence can be maintained.[2] It appears from the preceding table, that the Irish were the only race which denied themselves that minimum when their earnings were low. To sum up, Professor Chapin's analysis gives no indication of a sliding scale of racial standards of living.

[1] All the native Americans but one were sons of native fathers, or of immigrants from Northern and Western Europe. The one exception was the son of a Bohemian father, but Bohemians are not among the "undesirable."—Chapin, *loc. cit.*, p. 39.

[2] Chapin, *loc. cit.*, p. 126.

The most extensive investigation of its kind, comprising more than 25,000 family budgets, was made by the United States Bureau of Labor ten years ago. Table 79, compiled from its report, is a comparative statement of food expenditures of "normal" families classified by annual income and country of birth. A "normal" family, it will be remembered, is one supported solely by the earnings of husband and father. All families with abnormally low incomes (under $400 annually) have been excluded from this comparison. No nationality with less than ten families in each income group is shown separately, but all foreign-born are included in the total.

TABLE 79.

EXPENDITURES FOR FOOD IN NORMAL FAMILIES WITH AN INCOME FROM $400 TO $700, CLASSIFIED BY NATIVITY AND INCOME.[1]

Nativity of head of family	Income		
	$400–$499	$500–$599	$600–$699
Native white	$212	$245	$260
Foreign-born	229	255	276
Old Immigration:			
Canada	228	250	267
England	235	257	270
Ireland	231	261	278
Sweden	237	248	273
Germany	224	254	277
New Immigration:			
Austria-Hungary	252	267	289
Russia	235	273	291
Italy	214	235	263

The lowest expenditures for food within the same income group were found among native white workmen with incomes under $500 and above $600; in the middle group the lowest place was held by the Italians, the next to the lowest by native white Americans. The highest expendi-

[1] *Eighteenth Annual Report of the Commissioner of Labor*, Table V D. pp. 560–563.

tures were reported by the Russians in the two groups with incomes of $500 and over. In the lowest income group the highest expenditure for food was found among natives of Austria-Hungary, while the Russians were on a par with the English and above the Irish, the Canadians and the Germans. In the other two groups, the natives of Austria-Hungary expended more than the native Americans and more than any of the "old immigrants." The Italians expended more than the native Americans in the two extreme groups, and only $10.00 less per year, *i. e.*, three cents a day less per family in the middle group. It is possible that the higher expenditure for food among the "undesirable" races is accounted for by the size of the family, but the earnings of the head of the family must cover the expense of supporting all its members. It is therefore, the total expense rather than the average per individual that may, by supposition, affect the rate of wages.

Still, if we turn to the comparative table of the same report in which the expenditure for food of native and foreign families is reduced to a uniform basis of units of consumption,[1] we observe the same tendency as shown by the comparison of total expenditures. We learn from that table:

(1) That among the families having no children the natives of Russia expended $145.24 per one hundred units of consumption, while the natives of the United States expended only $119.85;

(2) That among the families with two children, the Russians expended $107.35 as against $95.24 expended by Americans;

(3) That among families with three children, the average expense of the Russians was $108.11, whereas the Americans expended only $85.06;

(4) That an Italian family with one child expended on an average $124.73, while an American family of the

[1] *Eighteenth Annual Report of the Commission of Labor*, Table V D., p. 102.

same size was contented with $109.94, an English family with $107.19, and a Norwegian with $87.53;

(5) That an Austro-Hungarian family without children or with one child expended more for food than a Scotch family of the same size;

(6) That an Austro-Hungarian family with two children needed $117.22, while a native American family of the same size could exist on $95.24, and an English family on $105.86;

(7) That an Austro-Hungarian family with three children, expended $98.65 per one hundred units of consumption as compared with $85.00 expended by an average American family of the same size, and with $85.20 expended by an average English family;

(8) That an Austro-Hungarian family with four or five children, expended more than a Scotch family;

(9) That the Scotch were in every group inferior to the Russians;

(10) That English families with less than five children had a lower expenditure for food than Russian families of equal size.[1]

These budgets have been quoted here as the best evidence that has been collected on the comparative standards of living of native and foreign-born wage-earners. Still, large as the number of individual families included in the canvass of the Bureau of Labor may look at a superficial glance, it affords too narrow a foundation for nice distinctions. Food expenditures vary with the size and the income of the family, and with geographical location affecting the prices of food-stuffs. If the food expenditures are to be compared by nationality, under uniform conditions as to location, size of family, and income, some of the groups must be so minute as to preclude the possibility of any reliable generalizations. The last table commented upon may serve as an illustration; among the foreign nationalities, there is no group of more than seventeen

[1] *Eighteenth Annual Report of the Commission of Labor*, p. 631, Table VI E.

families, while most of the groups contain less than ten families, and twenty-one consist of only one family. Variations in individual cases, however, are very wide. The only conclusion that is warranted by such statistics as are available is a negative one, viz., that the existence of a race standard of living determining the rate of wages for every race is not proven.[1] "The actual standard that prevails is set primarily by the wages paid and the prices charged."[2]

E. Clothing

In no other respect is the assimilation of the immigrant accomplished so rapidly as in the matter of dress. The mandates of Herbert Spencer's "ceremonial government" cannot be disobeyed. "Many of the recent immigrants," says the Immigration Commission, "still have some articles of clothing which they brought with them from Europe. Most of their clothing, however, practically all, is made in this country and purchased by them here."[3] The prices which the alien workman must pay in an American department store for shoes and clothes are fixed, not by his im-

[1] In a later work, published in 1917, the chief expert of the Immigration Commission seems to have come to recognize that the standard of living of the new immigrants is not lower than, but different from, that of the native wage-earners. Whereas the immigrant seeks primarily physical comfort, with the sophisticated American worker the conventional plays a conspicuous part in his family budget. To put it in Professor Lauck's words:

"It is significant to note that *all newer immigrants spend a greater proportion of their total expenditures for food than do the native wage-earners.* This seems to be due to the fact that their standard of living is less subject to demands created by desires other than for food. In a sense, their standard is more elemental. They are more free to satisfy their natural physical wants, and less restricted than native wage-earners, by the pressure of other wants upon their income. *In the selection of their diet it seems to be the consensus of observations that the newer immigrant has the advantage over the native wage-earners.*" W. Jett Lauck and Edgar Sydenstricker: *The Condition of Labor in American Industries*, p. 288.

[2] Chapin, *loc. cit.*, pp. 249–250.

[3] *Reports of the Immigration Commission*, vol. 9, p. 81.

ported individual or racial psychology, but by the American manufacturer, the American railway manager, and the American department store proprietor, every one of them eager to make an American profit, in order to maintain an American standard of living for himself.

The Immigration Commission secured the transcripts of store accounts, which showed that the prices paid for wearing apparel by immigrants from Southern and Eastern Europe were the same as those advertised in Washington, D. C., by the department stores and tailor shops catering to the trade of government clerks.[1]

The United States Bureau of Labor has published comparative statistics showing for each nationality the average annual expenditure for clothing. It can be seen at a glance that the expenditure for clothing among the native, as well as among the foreign-born, increases with the increase of their earnings.[2] Whether, or not, the wage-earner's standard of living determines his wages, *i. e.*, whether, or not, he is paid higher wages because he wears better clothes, it is self-evident that his ability to buy clothes is limited by his earnings. A comparison of race standards in the matter of clothing must therefore be made for workmen of the same earning capacity. Table 80 on page 267 follows the arrangement of Table 79.

It can be seen from Table 80 that in each of the income groups the variations of expenditure by race are confined within very narrow limits, the margin between the highest and lowest expenditure not exceeding $10.00 a year. It is evident that such a margin is too small to produce an appreciable effect upon the rate of wages.[3]

[1] *Reports of the Immigration Commission*, vol. 9, pp. 81, 84.

[2] *Eighteenth Annual Report of the Commissioner of Labor*, Table V,D.

[3] It must be borne in mind, that the numbers of families in each group being small, the variations may be due to differences in the size of the families, in geographical location, etc. Even the earnings may vary within each income group as much as $99.00 per year. Some allowance must be made for the inaccuracy of the figures, inasmuch as they are all mere estimates.

TABLE 80.

EXPENDITURE FOR CLOTHING IN NORMAL FAMILIES OF UNSKILLED LABORERS, CLASSIFIED BY INCOME AND NATIVITY.[1]

Country of birth	Income		
	$400–$499	$500–$599	$600–$699
Native	$53	$66	$79
Foreign-born, generally	53	63	78
Old Immigration:			
Canada	57	61	82
England	58	67	75
Ireland	51	61	73
Sweden	48	64	78
Germany	52	63	80
New Immigration:			
Austria-Hungary	57	61	82
Russia	52	64	74
Italy	52	57	73

F. Savings

The expenses of a normal family for housing, food, and clothing amount in the aggregate to about three fourths of the total expenditure for all objects.[2] The preceding analysis has shown that the variations of these principal items of a workingman's budget are not affected by race. Table 81 on page 268 points in the same direction. It can be seen from the comparative figures that the average wage-earner's family of every nationality lives practically up to its income. A very small margin is left for savings. But while the native workman may save or spend at pleasure, the newly-arrived immigrant must save money.

"Before the immigrant can realize any return from his labor in the form of American wages, he must incur the following expense or indebtedness, for even if one or all costs are prepaid for him by relative, friend, or other person, he eventually pays them all by deductions from his wages or otherwise:

[1] *Eighteenth Annual Report of the Commissioner of Labor*, pp. 560–563.

[2] *Ibid.*, p. 581, Table 5K.

TABLE 81.

SURPLUS OF INCOME OVER EXPENDITURE OF NORMAL FAMILIES; CLASSIFIED BY COUNTRY OF BIRTH.[1]

Country of birth	Amount	Per cent of income
Native	$ 37	5.6
Foreign-born generally	26	4.1
Old immigration:		
Canada	41	6 1
England	40	5.8
Sweden	38	4.2
Germany	23	3.6
Ireland	15	2.6
New Immigration:		
Italy	25	4.6
Austria-Hungary	14	2.5
Russia	4	0.6

1. Cost of preparation at his home in Europe for the journey.
2. Cost of transportation from his home to the European seaport.
3. Cost of emigrant head tax to his Government.
4. Cost of immigrant head tax to the United States Government.
5. Cost of steamship transportation, European port to the United States.
6. Cost of labor agency for securing employment at port of entry, if used.
7. Cost of transportation, United States port of entry to place of employment.
8. Cost of living from port of entry to place of destination."[2]

The cost of items 3–5 and 7 is further on estimated at $40.00 for a single Italian, Slav, or Hungarian immigrant. If the immigrant has left wife and children in his native country, he must save money to pay their passage. In order to meet these demands the immigrant must curtail his expenses for the necessities of life. This is accomplished

[1] *Eighteenth Annual Report of the Commissioner of Labor*, p. 581, Tables V, J and K.

[2] *Bulletin of the Bureau of Labor*, No. 72, pp. 411–412.

in various ways. Living in crowded tenements is one of them. Co-operative boarding, which has been given the odious name of "the boarding boss system," enables the Slav laborer to reduce his board bill much below the price the individualistic Anglo-Saxon has to pay in a boarding house, though, as has been shown, the fare under the co-operative system is at least as wholesome and abundant as in an average boarding house.

The fact, however, that the immigrant who has no family in the United States is at first content to deny himself many comforts does not warrant the apprehension that he will be satisfied with a wage just sufficient to provide the bare necessities of life. The Italian railroad laborer who subsists on vegetables does not work for the mere price of his vegetables, but saves about 80 per cent of his wages. "Ninety-five per cent of the Italian laborers save from $25.00 to $30.00 of their wages per month. For eight months' work this would amount to over $200 per man."[1] It is a matter of general knowledge that large sums of money are annually sent home by the immigrants. A member of the Immigration Commission who visited a Greek mountain village from which two hundred immigrants had gone to the United States was told that each of the men sent back about $200 annually.[2] It was learned from the records of a post-office in a township of Russian Poland that thirty-seven workmen who had immigrated from that township to the United States sent home in 1903 the sum of 47,862 roubles, *i. e.*, an average of $665 per emigrant.[3] That these are not isolated cases is indicated by the number of international money orders sent from the United States to Europe, which averaged, in 1907–1909, about three millions a year.[4] Moreover, hundreds of

[1] *Bulletin of the Bureau of Labor*, No. 72, pp. 469–470, 477, 481.

[2] *Reports of the Immigration Commission*, vol. 4 (in press).

[3] *Reports of the Warsaw Statistical Committee*, *Bulletin* XXII. K. B. Vobly: *General Analysis of the Statistics of Migration of Workers for Temporary Employment and of the Statistics of Emigration*, p. 29.

[4] *Reports of the Immigration Commission*, vol. 37, p. 280.

thousands of immigrants annually return home, and their passage must be paid out of their savings. The total amount sent abroad by immigrants in the year 1907 is estimated by the Immigration Commission at $275,000,000. This estimate "does not take into account the large sums carried abroad by returning immigrants."[1]

A better idea of the average amount an immigrant manages to save from his wages can be gained from the economic effects produced by the flow of American money into the rural districts of Southern and Eastern Europe. In Greece

> much of the money sent home by emigrants is for the payment of old debts and cancellation of mortgages, a considerable part . . . for deposits, loans, the purchases of real estate or the improvement of property already owned. . . . Many houses were . . . built by money sent back by emigrants. . . . Usury is receding, fleeing from the glitter of abundant gold which has inundated towns and villages. . . . Nor is it surprising that the rate of interest should have fallen from 20, 15, and 10 per cent to 6 and 5 per cent.[2]

In Southern Italy, those who return from America purchase a house with a small estate. In Austria-Hungary, the enormous influx of money goes partly to pay old debts and to bring over families, but most of it to support relatives at home, to invest in land, to build homes, to make improvements, and to buy agricultural machinery. "The desire of the returning emigrant to invest in land has led to a considerable increase in its value, particularly in Croatia, Galicia, and the Slovak district of Hungary. . . . In Galicia the buying of large estates by associations of emigrants has become a common practice. Very often from 50,000 to 90,000 acres a year are thus bought up and subdivided among the peasant purchasers. The money is either contributed from the savings of the associated peasants or borrowed from friends who are still in America." Reports from all emigration countries concur in the statement that the standard of living of the peasants who have

[1] *Reports of the Immigration Commission*, vol. 37, p. 277.
[2] *Ibid.*, vol. 4, p. 413.

returned from the United States is above that of their neighbors. The roomy cottages built by them with money earned in the United States are in striking contrast with the surrounding poverty and dirt. In short, according to the Immigration Commission, the savings of the immigrants "are an important factor in promoting the general economic welfare of several European countries." It is evident that the wages of the immigrants must needs be sufficient to enable them to invest hundreds of millions of dollars in the uplifting of the economic conditions of their native countries, after paying American prices for all necessities of life. Viewed solely with an eye to the economic interests of the American wage-earner, the efforts of the average immigrant from Southern and Eastern Europe "to live upon the basis of minimum cheapness, and to save as much as possible," at the sacrifice of comfort,[1] is a matter of no concern to his competitors in the labor market. Whether he spends his wages on rent, food, and clothing, or saves his money to buy steamship tickets for his family, whether he deposits his savings in a local bank, or sends them to his parents for improving the home farm, his wants in one case are as great and as imperative as in the other, and he must demand a wage which will enable him to satisfy them. Furthermore, contrary to learned opinion, a wage-earner who is able to save four fifths of his earnings need not accept "employment on the terms offered or suffer from actual want," for he can live four months on the savings of one, and is therefore "in a position to take exception to wages or working conditions"[2] a great deal more readily than the native wage-earner who lives to the limit of his income. This fact has been proved more than once in recent years by the long drawn out strikes of Southern and Eastern European mine and factory operatives.

There is a tendency to view with disapproval "the sending back to the old country of the savings of the immigrant," upon the old Mercantilist theory that every dollar invested

[1] Jenks and Lauck, *loc. cit.*, pp. 183–184. [2] *Ibid.*

by him in his home country is a loss to the United States: "America should have the productive influence of not only the labor but also of the capital made from the savings."[1] The same objection certainly applies with far greater force to the investment of American capital in foreign industrial enterprises. One important fact is overlooked in this objection, viz., that the money which is invested in the home farm provides for the relatives of the immigrant who stay in the old country. Were that money invested in the United States they would have to be brought over to the United States. While the capital invested in the United States would be increased, the supply of labor would likewise be increased. Money being dearer in Europe than in the United States, the savings that are ample to provide employment for the immigrants' relatives at home, would be insufficient, if invested in American industries, to keep an equal number of persons employed in the United States. Their immigration would accordingly tend to increase the supply of labor out of proportion to the demand.

The only economic interests affected in a real, not in an imaginary way, by the thrifty habits ("the low standard of living") of the recent immigrant, is the mercantile business which seeks the trade of the wage-earner as a consumer. With many manufacturing and mining concerns the commissary is an important part of the industry.

In fact, [says the Immigration Commission] according to the statements of some of the small operators, commissaries as a rule return not only a 20 per cent net profit in normal times to the company, but the system goes so far as to largely determine the race of employees. In certain cases it was stated that negroes were preferred because their improvident habits prevented them from being able to live on a cash income, paid monthly, and thus forced them to draw their wages weekly, and even daily, in the form of commissary checks or store credits. Currency payments were made monthly partly for this purpose. As a result, the negroes are always a little in debt to the commissaries. . . . Their wants are confined to the supply of goods furnished by the commissaries, with the exception of whiskey, and they have no funds for

[1] Jenks and Lauck, *loc. cit.*, p. 16.

any other purpose than that of bare subsistence . . . . For the same reason these employers do not encourage immigrant laborers, and in some cases refuse to employ them altogether. The immigrant exhibits a strong tendency to get his wages in cash and to live on the lowest level possible to maintain subsistence. . . . He seeks the cheapest places. . . . A careful and detailed inquiry into a comparison of prices in the commissaries and in the city markets and groceries revealed a slight increase in the general run of prices in the former over the latter.[1]

The Croatians are good livers in comparison with the other foreign races, and they do not stint themselves in food or drink [say Professors Jenks and Lauck]. Although extravagant, they do not, however, spend as much as the negroes, who loiter about the commissaries looking for something for which to spend their money. The Croatians know what they want and buy it freely, but if there is a surplus of their wages it is saved. The Italians, living as they do, very cheaply, buy little from the commissaries. In a general way the laborers are required to patronize the commissaries[2]. . . .

From the point of view of the proprietor of the commissary store, an immigrant with a "low standard of living," who buys in the cheapest store, or saves his money instead of leaving it in the commissary, is, naturally enough, "undesirable."

[1] *Reports of the Immigration Commission*, vol. 9, p. 190.

[2] Jenks and Lauck, *loc. cit.*, p. 176.

CHAPTER XI

HOME OWNERSHIP

OWNERSHIP of homes by wage-earners has been advocated as a proposition of practical social reform, ever since the condition of labor has been recognized as a distinct social problem. The Immigration Commission has given a prominent place in its investigation to home ownership among immigrant races on the ground that "the proportion of the families in a given group of workmen who live in homes owned by themselves may fairly be regarded as an indication, at least, of the social and industrial progress of the group."[1]

The Commission fully realizes "that the wage-earner is living and working in a large urban or industrial center where the acquisition of real estate is beyond his resources," while in small mining towns "the industrial worker is practically not permitted to buy a home, but must live in a house owned by the operating company."[2] The mining companies find it "a better policy to retain the houses because of large profits arising from rent payments and for the additional reason that mine workers may be evicted in the event of a strike."[3] Moreover, the ownership of a home, even when within the reach of the wage-earner, often does not pay as an investment:

> If an employee should invest in a home near his work and for any reason he should be thrown out of work, the property would not be valuable, because there are no other industries near in which he could

[1] *Reports of the Immigration Commission*, vol. 7, p. 267.

[2] *Ibid.*, vol. 1, p. 467.

[3] *Ibid.*, vol. 6, p. 452.

find employment. The coal mines often have periods when work is irregular, or suspend operations for months at a time, which facts tend to make coal-mining labor migratory.[1]

These conditions are not peculiar to coal mining alone, but exist generally.[2] Nevertheless, after all that is said, the Commission regards "the number and percentage of families owning their homes," as indications of "racial inclinations toward the acquisition of property."[3] It is noted that "the recent immigrant has no property or other restraining interests which attach him to a community," and the fact is officially recorded among the "salient characteristics of the *recent* immigrant labor supply."[4] This is an error. As far back as 1878, a noted New York philanthropist spoke in almost the same terms of the immigrants of his day, who were mostly Irish and Germans:

> They do not own the house nor any part of it, nor have any interest in it. . . . The general effect of the system is the existence of a proletaire class, who have no interest in the permanent well-being of the community, who have no sense of home, and who live without any deep root in the soil.[5]

It is obvious that the subject of home ownership is viewed in these opinions from the standpoint of a middle-class resident of a rural community, not from that of a wage-earner.[6] A farmer, a shopkeeper, or a professional man, is

[1] *Reports of the Immigration Commission*, vol. 7, p. 206.

[2] An English writer who would encourage "the acquirement by workingmen of their homes," recognizes that "a difficulty exists in the fact that a large portion of the working classes are migrating, owing to the changes and irregularities of their means of livelihood."—T. L. Worthington: *Dwellings of the People*, (2d edition, 1901), p. 60.

[3] *Reports of the Immigration Commission*, vol. 1, p. 467. This view is expressed with all due "qualifications," "reservations," and "limitations."

[4] *Ibid.*, pp. 498, 500—"This characteristic has both a good and a bad influence . . . . Probably, the bad effect of this characteristic is greater than the good, all things considered." Jenks and Lauck, *loc. cit*, p. 185.

[5] *Report of the Industrial Commission*, vol. xv., p. 459.

[6] "The idea that the working man must buy his dwelling rests upon the reactionary conception that the condition created by modern large scale industry is a pathological degeneration, and that society must be forcibly steered against the stream which has been running for over

by the nature of his occupation attached to a certain community. With him the ownership of a home is a profitable investment. Considered, however, from the point of view of the wage-earner who lives "in a town dominated by a single industry, home ownership would seriously hinder his defense of his rights in a disagreement with his employers." [1] In a small town, where many of the workmen own their homes

> trade-unionism means but little [to them]. If, however, trade-unionism becomes a factor and organization follows, with accompanying demands for shorter hours and more pay, these men would think long and well of their little homes . . . before engaging upon a strike, the outcome of which may possibly mean the loss of many things they greatly prize. It seems that the employers have the upper hand.[2]

A wage-earner, on the contrary, who has no property interests attaching him to a certain community, is "free to follow the best industrial inducements." [3]

Inasmuch, however, as the ownership of a home is regarded "as a mark of thrift" [4] it is instructive to compare the extent of home ownership at present and in the past, before "the Slav invasion," and still earlier, before immigration became a social factor in the United States.

As early as 1790, when Boston had a population of 18,320, the average number of families to each house in the town was 1.46, which means that at least one third of all Boston families lived in rented houses, even on the assumption that all one-family houses were occupied by their owners and that in the two-family houses one dwelling was occupied by the owner. Half a century later, at the city census of 1845, the proportion of home owners in Boston was found to be only 17.5 per cent.[4] The population of Boston was then only 114,000, and the percentage of foreign-born and

---

a century, into a condition . . . which is generally nothing but an idealized restoration of the moribund small handicraft."—Friedrich Engels: *Zur Wohnungsfrage.*

[1] Streightoff, *loc. cit.*, p. 84. [2] Pratt, *loc. cit.*, p. 99.

[3] *Reports of the Immigration Commission*, vol. 1, p. 500.

[4] *Ibid.*, vol. 6, p. 451. [5] *Census of Boston*, 1845, p. 55.

their children born in Boston was 32.61.[1] In other words, there were 67.39 per cent of native Americans of native parentage, of whom at most only one fourth owned their homes, even if there was not a single home owner among the foreign-born. The percentage of home owners has since slightly increased, as shown in the following table:

TABLE 82.

PER CENT OF HOME OWNERS IN THE POPULATION OF BOSTON, 1845–1900.[2]

Year	Per cent
1845	17.5
1890	18.4[3]
1900	18.9

The most thorough-going statistical study of home ownership in the United States was made at the census of 1890. The data for that year reflect the standard of living of native Americans at a time when it could not have been affected by immigration from Southern and Eastern Europe. It will be seen from Table 83 on page 278 that of all American householders of native stock who were living in cities with a population of from 50,000 to 250,000 in 1890, only a little over one fourth owned their homes; in larger cities the percentage was still smaller. And it must be borne in mind that these percentages relate to people in all walks of life, not to wage-earners alone. The prevailing "American standard" in cities is accordingly the standard of a tenant, not that of a home owner.

[1] *Census of Boston*, pp. 26 and 37. The percentage of persons born of foreign parents in the United States outside of Boston could not have affected the situation, as appears from the fact that of the native children of foreign parents there were 10,105 under the age of 20 and only 80 over the age of 20. Evidently, immigration was new and the native children of foreign parents were still very young.

[2] *Report on Farms and Homes in the United States at the XI. Census*, p. 32. *XII. Census, Population*, Part II., Table CVI., p. ccv.

[3] The population of Suffolk County representing the economic, though not the municipal, Boston, included 19.36 per cent home-owners.

TABLE 83.

PERCENTAGE OF NATIVE WHITE HOME OWNERS TO ALL OCCUPANTS, CLASSIFIED BY PARENT NATIVITY, IN CITIES WITH A POPULATION OF 50,000 AND OVER.[1]

Population	Per cent of home owners	
	Native parentage	Foreign parentage
50,000 to 250,000..	27.6	26.4
250,000 and over...	21.5	17.7

This fact is not due, however, to a racial disinclination of the American of native stock toward the acquisition of property, but to the fact that the value of a house is beyond the reach of the majority of householders. The proof will be found in Table 84:

TABLE 84.

PERCENTAGES OF HOME OWNERS CLASSIFIED BY VALUE OF HOMES, 1890.[2]

Value	United States	Cities classified by population	
		8,000 to 100,000	100,000 and over
Under $500...............	0.63	0.21	0.04
$500 and under $1000.......	3.56	2.46	0.61
$1000 and under $2500......	17.41	17.94	9.24
$2500 and under $5000......	22.35	25.93	17.95
$5000 and over.............	56.05	53.46	72.16

More than one half of all homes in the United States were valued in 1890 at $5000 and over; in cities with a population of 100,000 and over the proportion of homes of the same value was nearly three fourths.

The relative number of home owners decreased with the growth of the density of population and the resulting

[1] *Farms and Homes, XI. Census,* Table 73, p. 204.

[2] *Ibid.*, Table 39, p. 87

increase of the value of real estate, as shown in Table 85, where all States and Territories are divided into two areas:

I. With ratio of home owners to total families above the average for the United States;

II. With ratio of home owners to total families below the average for the United States.

TABLE 85.

HOME OWNERSHIP AND VALUE OF REAL ESTATE IN AREAS WITH RATIO OF HOME OWNERS TO TOTAL FAMILIES ABOVE (I) AND BELOW (II) THE AVERAGE, 1890.[1]

Areas	Per cent of home owners	Population per square mile	Average value per home (including incumbrances)
I	46.34	12	$ 2656
II	30.53	53	3828

To be sure, some of the homes were incumbered (three eighths of all homes in cities with a population of 100,000 and over, and less in smaller cities and towns[2]), but the average incumbrance in the United States covered only 37.7 per cent of the value.[3] The average equity of the owner ranged from $3200 in cities with a population of 100,000 and over, down to $1400 in settlements of less than 8000 inhabitants.[4]

Age is an important factor in home ownership; under the age of forty-five the majority were tenants (see Diagram XVII).[5] This was the rule in every section of the country, in those where the percentage of foreign-born was high, as well as in those where it was low. The percentage of home-owners increases with advancing years, and it is only in old age that a majority become home-owners. It takes a lifetime of savings to acquire a home. Now it must be remembered that most of the immigrants are under the

[1] *Farms and Homes, XI. Census*, Table 16, p. 42.

[2] *Ibid.*, Table 14, p.34.

[3] *Ibid.*, Tables 104–106, pp. 421–428. [4] *Ibid.*, Table 38, pp. 83–86.

[5] *Ibid.*, p. 224, Diagram 32.

DIAGRAM XVII. PER CENT RATIO OF HOME OWNERS AND TENANTS TO

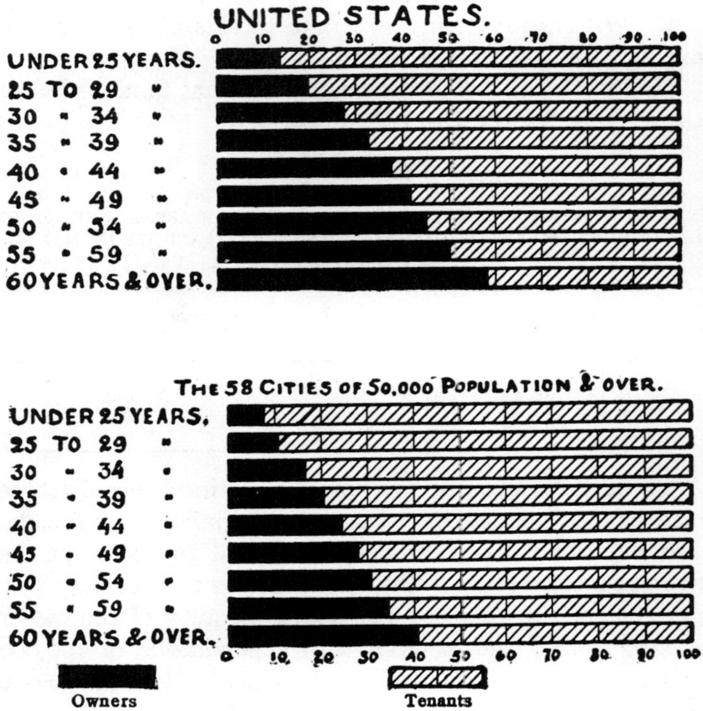

age of forty-five on arrival. It was found in 1890, when immigration from Southern and Eastern Europe was insignificant, that "by far the principal portion of the foreign-born owners of farms and homes have been in this country fifteen years and over."[1] Of all industrial workers from Southern and Eastern Europe, however, who were covered by the investigation of the Immigration Commission, only from 0.9 per cent (Roumanians) to 18.2 per cent (Russian Jews) had been in the United States fifteen years or over.[2] According to the standard set by the immigrants from North-

[1] *Farms and Homes, XI. Census*, p. 163.

[2] Jenks and Lauck, *loc. cit.*, p. 477.

ALL HOME FAMILIES, CLASSIFIED BY AGE PERIODS AND BY GEOGRAPHICAL DIVISIONS, 1890.

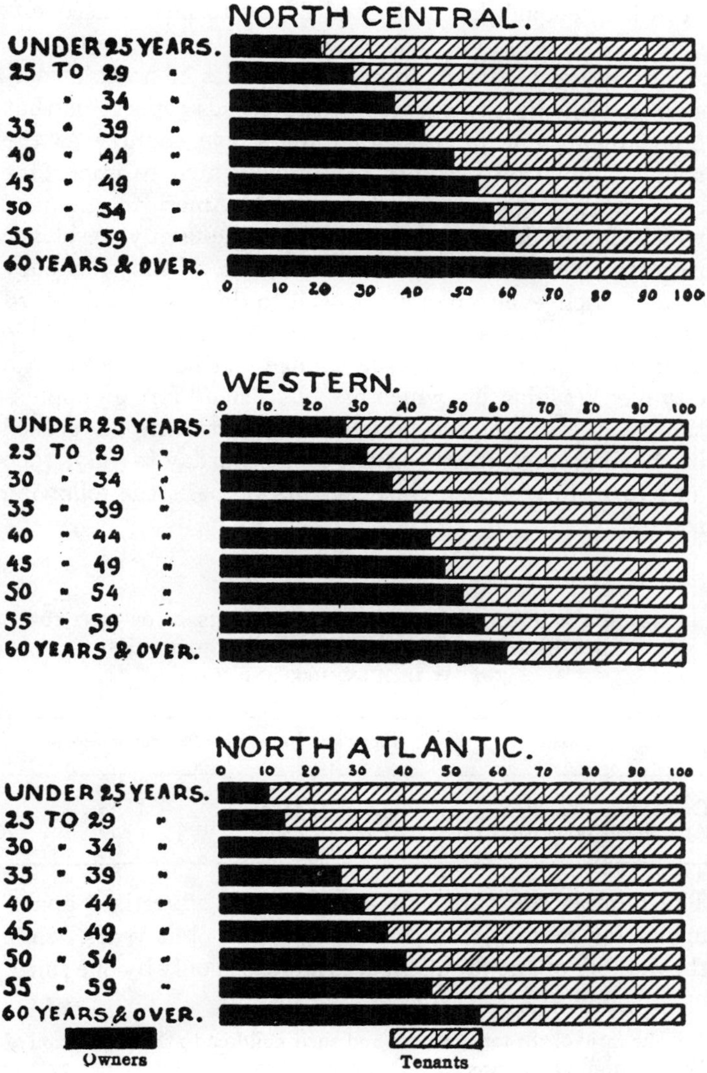

ern and Western Europe, the overwhelming majority of the immigrants from Southern and Eastern Europe had not been long enough in the United States to have raised sufficient funds for buying real estate.

The inference drawn from the statistics of home ownership in 1890 by the authors of the census report "is that home tenancy is increasing in the whole country as the urban population becomes numerically a more important element of the population."[1] The old American standard which found its expression in the one-family residence retreats before the apartment house. This tendency asserts itself even among the well-to-do who could afford to buy a home for the rental they pay for a fashionable apartment. The rate of the change can be observed in a city like Washington, which has but a small foreign population.[2] A count of the houses and apartments advertised in the *Washington Star* on the last Saturday in July, 1900 and 1910, for rent to white tenants brought the following results:

TABLE 86.

NUMBER OF HOUSES AND APARTMENTS ADVERTISED FOR RENT TO WHITE TENANTS IN WASHINGTON, D. C., ON THE LAST SATURDAY IN JULY, 1900 AND 1910.

For rent	1900	1910	Per cent of increase
One-family houses........	882	1169	33
Apartment houses.........	64	580	806

The number of apartment houses which advertised apartments for rent increased ninefold within ten years, while the number of one-family houses increased only by one third.

[1] *Farms and Homes, XI. Census*, p. 54.

[2] The ratio of the foreign-born and their children to the population of Washington, D. C., was only 20.6 per cent in 1900 and 21 per cent in 1910. *XIII. Census*, vol. 1, p. 150.

It is clear from this example that the tendency toward the apartment house or tenement house has no connection with immigration. It is in line with the general tendency toward concentration characteristic of modern times.[1]

[1] This has come to be recognized by industrial experts. In the opinion of Mr. Henry Wright, an architect who during the war was town planner of Emergency Fleet Corporation towns and has since made a study of housing conditions for the community planning committee of the American Institute of Architects, the time has come for "a scientific revolution of our methods of building houses." Speaking of the present housing situation to a writer for the *Globe* of New York, he was quoted (in the issue of June 1, 1920) to have said:

"'Own Your Own Home' campaigns to-day are essentially buncombe. They cannot provide houses for the laboring classes; under present conditions no one belonging to the laboring classes can afford to 'own his own home.' . . . We must do away with the old sales system and its single lot, single family house, and surplus street, and come to group and multi-family house building with its savings of billions for the country in street maintenance, constructional costs, and proportion of land to houses."

CHAPTER XII

EFFECT OF IMMIGRATION ON WAGES

THAT wages in many occupations are barely sufficient to provide for the necessities of life, has been established by all investigations of the cost of living. That unskilled labor receives a lower wage than skilled labor, is a truism. That the standard of living of unskilled laborers must be lower than that of skilled mechanics, is the necessary consequence of the difference in the rates of their compensation. Inasmuch, however, as the skilled mechanics are mostly native Americans and older immigrants, whereas the unskilled laborers are mostly new immigrants, the average man with a prejudice against the foreigner overlooks the difference in the grade of the service rendered, and jumps to the conclusion that the American mechanic commands higher wages because he insists upon maintaining an American standard of living, whereas the foreign unskilled laborer is willing to accept lower wages, because he is satisfied with a lower standard of living.

It has been shown, however, that the standard of living of the new immigrants is not lower than that of their predecessors in the same grades of employment, or than that of the present generation of native Americans engaged in unskilled labor in the South, where there is practically no competition of immigrant labor. Granting that the standard of living determines the rate of wages, there is no escape from the conclusion that the wages of the new immigrants can not be lower than those of the past generation of immigrants who in their day were engaged in unskilled labor. In other words the logical deduction from the premises is, that the new immigration could not have depressed the rate of wages.

On the other hand, though the standard of living of the native or Americanized foreign-born wage-earners be higher than that of the new immigrants, this difference is not necessarily indicative of a higher rate of wages: the higher standard may be maintained on the earnings of several members of the family.

> As a matter of fact, present-day industrial families in the United States find it necessary to add to the earnings of the husband through the employment of wives and children outside the home and the keeping of boarders and lodgers within the home. The native American and older immigrant employees maintain an independent form of family life, but the earnings of the heads are supplemented by the wages of the wives and children. On the other hand, the Southern and Eastern European families have recourse to the keeping of boarders and lodgers as a supplementary source of family income. . . . That contributions of children are less general in the latter class of families is probably due to the fact that children of these households have not in any considerable proportions reached working age.[1]

It is argued that the newly-arrived immigrant must have work at once and is therefore eager to accept any terms:

> Another salient fact in connection with the recent immigrant labor supply has been the necessitous condition of the newcomers upon their arrival in America's industrial communities. Immigrants from the South and East of Europe have usually had but a few dollars in their possession when their final destination in this country has been reached. . . . Consequently, finding it absolutely imperative to engage in work at once, they have not been in a position to take exception to wages or working conditions, but must obtain employment on the terms offered or suffer from actual want.[2]

Still, the investigations of the United States Bureau of Labor have shown that only one half of the families of native American wage-earners (51.25 per cent) are able to save, whereas one third (32.2 per cent) are barely able to

[1] Jenks and Lauck, *loc. cit.*, pp. 157–158, 161.
[2] *Ibid.*, pp. 183–184.

make both ends meet, and about one in every seven (15.55 per cent) have a deficit.[1] Only after the annual income of the native American wage-earner with a normal family has reached $700 is there a surplus left over average expenses.[2] Making allowance for unemployment, an annual income of $700 may be taken as equivalent to about $2.50 a day, which is approximately the dividing line between skilled and unskilled labor. It thus appears that one half of the native American wage-earners, or roughly speaking all unskilled laborers, have no savings and are therefore in the same "necessitous condition" as "the newcomers upon their arrival": they "must obtain employment on the terms offered or suffer from actual want." The terms of competition are therefore not changed by the arrival of the immigrant.

It is further argued that the immigrant is at a particular disadvantage, being a stranger in a strange land:

> The immigrant unfamiliar with American conditions, often not even understanding the language in which he must make his contract, and ignorant of the working methods which are new to him, while naturally preferring the best that he can get, is often willing to work under conditions and at wages which would not appeal to American workingmen, but which to him seem ample and satisfactory, because they are so much better than he has ever known before. Moreover, when the wage-earner is one unfamiliar, as are most immigrants, with American conditions, he is likely to be eager, perhaps too eager, to secure work at almost any wage above that affording a mere subsistence. Usually he is not in touch with the American workingman or with trade unions, and does not know what he could do by proper effort. He is not a member of their trade organization, and cannot bargain through officials who know the conditions. Moreover, if he is one who is expecting as soon as possible to return to his home country with his savings, what he dreads most of all is lack of work, and he is willing to take low wages and bad working conditions, rather than be idle even for a short time and see any of his savings disappear. In the large majority of cases, doubtless, the immediate inducement to the emigrants to leave home and sail for America comes in the form of a personal letter from friends or members of their own families already in the United States. It is thus

[1] *Sixteenth Annual Report of the Commissioner of Labor*, p. 68.

[2] *Ibid.*, p. 592.

that they learn of the much higher wages and the better living conditions; and usually they are practically sure of a job almost as soon as they arrive, at wages which seem to them more than satisfactory.[1]

This statement contains its own refutation. If the immigrants "usually are practically sure of a job almost as soon as they arrive," then there is no occasion for them "to be eager to secure work at almost any wage, etc." Since "in the large majority of cases" the immigrants come in response to "a personal letter from friends or members of their own families already in the United States," it is erroneous to say that they are "not in touch with the American workingman," unless the term "American" be used in the narrow sense of native American. But the immigrant loses nothing in a pecuniary way by not being in touch with the native workman, since the latter usually works at a skilled trade, whereas the former in most cases seeks employment as a common laborer. On the other hand, in all establishments employing immigrant labor the new applicant, as a rule, finds some one through whom he makes his contract in his native language. It has been shown in the discussion of the standard of living that the new immigrant has obligations which do not permit him "to work at any wage above that affording a mere subsistence." As for affiliation with trade unions, it must be borne in mind that they comprise only a small minority of all wage-earners, native as well as foreign-born, and are mostly confined to skilled trades, whereas most of the immigrants are unskilled. Lastly, it is recognized by the Immigration Commission that "it is inaccurate to speak of the immigrant population as being only temporary in this country": most of the recent immigrants come to stay.[2]

The object for which the Immigration Commission was created was to supply statistical facts which should take

[1] Jenks and Lauck, *loc. cit.*, pp. 18–19.

[2] See *supra*, p. 74.—*Reports of the Immigration Commission*, vol. 8, p. 657.

the place of speculation. After a study of the racial composition of the operating forces in the principal industries, based upon information received for more than half a million wage-earners in mines and manufactures, the Commission discovered no evidence "that it was usual for employers to engage recent immigrants at wages actually lower than those prevailing at the time of their employment in the industry where they were employed."[1]

> One of the most striking facts indicated by a comparison of the earnings of the races in the different industries [say Professors Jenks and Lauck] is that *earning ability is more the outcome of industrial opportunity or conditions of employment than of racial efficiency and progress.* This fact becomes evident when the average weekly earnings of the members of a race, or several races, in the cotton or woolen and worsted goods industry, are considered in connection with the earnings of the same race or races in other industries. The Lithuanians, for example, earn an average of $12.24 weekly in the manufacture of agricultural implements and vehicles, $11.60 in clothing, $13.60 in copper mining and smelting, $9.87 in furniture, $12.89 in iron and steel, $11.98 in iron-ore mining, $9.50 in leather, $12.85 in oil refining, $10.87 in shoes, $10.67 in sugar refining, but only $7.86 in cotton and $7.97 in woolen and worsted manufacturing. The same condition of affairs is shown by other races in different industries.[2]

That the economists who directed the investigations of the Immigration Commission regard it as a "striking" fact that earning ability is the outcome of economic conditions rather than of racial characteristics, indicates that they expected to find the opposite, viz., that earning ability was determined by racial factors. Yet, notwithstanding the "evident fact" brought to light by the investigations of the Commission, that individuals of the same race, with presumably the same "racial standards," are paid varying rates of wages in different industries, the Commission persists in the view that the rate of wages is determined by the standard of living of the wage-earners. The statistics of the Commission show that the earnings of the immigrants

[1] *Reports of the Immigration Commission*, vol. I, pp. 494, 541.
[2] Jenks and Lauck, *loc. cit.*, pp. 145–146.

increase with the length of residence in the United States; there is a ready explanation that "the immigrants of long residence have acquired a higher standard of living and, consequently, demand a higher wage."[1] It would seem as though wages were regulated in accordance with the communistic ideal, "to everybody according to his wants." The question arises, however, why should the employer grant the demand of the immigrant of long residence for a higher wage when there is said to be an "oversupply" of recent immigrants willing to accept "almost any wage above that affording a mere subsistence"? The statistics of the Commission give no answer to this question, because the basis of its classification is race, not character of employment, each race being treated as a homogeneous unit. The real explanation of the variation in wages among individuals of the same race is that the immigrant of long residence has advanced on the scale of occupations and is paid a higher wage for a higher grade of labor. Since he receives a higher wage, he has "consequently" acquired a higher standard of living.

The primary cause which has determined the movement of wages in the United States during the past thirty years has been the introduction of labor-saving machinery. The effect of the substitution of mechanical devices for human skill is the displacement of the skilled mechanic by the unskilled laborer. This tendency has been counteracted in the United States by the expansion of industry: while the ratio of skilled mechanics to the total operating force was decreasing, the increasing scale of operations prevented an actual reduction in numbers. The growing demand for unskilled labor was supplied by immigration.[2] Of course,

[1] *Reports of the Immigration Commission*, vol. 2, p. 370.

[2] Prof. Commons, in the *Reports of the Industrial Commission*, vol. xv., p. 305, says: "In manufactures, mining, and transportation there has been a rapid advance in machinery and a better organization and division of labor, whereby the resources of the country are made more productive. This advance in machinery and division of labor often appears in itself to be a means of displacing labor and so of

this readjustment did not proceed without friction. While, in the long run, there may have been no displacement of skilled mechanics by unskilled laborers in the industrial field as a whole, at certain times and places individual skilled mechanics were doubtless dispensed with and had to seek new employment. As the unskilled laborers who replaced them were naturally engaged at lower wages, and as most of them were immigrants, the change reflected itself in the minds of the displaced American mechanics as substitution of cheap immigrant labor for highly paid American labor.

The English, Scotch, Welsh, and Irish miners, *e. g.*, for some time successfully resisted the introduction of machinery. Their resistance was overcome by the employment of Slavs and Italians.[1] The impression was thus created that the introduction of machinery was the effect of Slav and Italian immigration. According to Professors Jenks and Lauck, "the lack of skill and industrial training of the recent immigrants in the United States has stimulated the invention of mechanical methods and processes which might be conducted by unskilled industrial workers as a substitute for the skilled operatives formerly required."[2] This idea had been anticipated by Mr. Leiserson, who expressed the belief that one of the effects "of the influx of Slavs is that lack of intelligence makes improved machinery and a perfected organization of the mining processes absolutely essential. There is a direct connection between the increasing number of unintelligent mining laborers and the use of mining machinery during the last ten or fifteen years." The author is ready to accept at face value the contention of the coal operators "that the scarcity of intelligent labor compelled them to adopt machinery wherever possible."[3] Presumably, but for the immigration

---

depressing wages, and *such would be the case if industry as a whole were not continually expanding.*"

[1] *Report of the Industrial Commission*, vol. xv., pp. xxiii., xxxiv.

[2] Jenks and Lauck, *loc. cit.*, pp. 186–187.

[3] William M. Leiserson: "Labor Conditions in the Mines of the Pitts-

of the "unintelligent" Slavs, American industry might have gone on forever without improved machinery, and instead of perfecting the organization of the mining processes the mine operators would have encouraged the "arts and crafts" movement in bituminous coal mining.

This theory ignores the elementary proposition of political economy, that the main object of labor-saving machinery is to dispense precisely with "intelligent," *i. e.*, high-priced labor, and that, on the contrary, an abundant supply of cheap labor would retard the introduction of improved machinery.[1]

The conditions in the coal mines of West Virginia may serve as an example: "The low level of wages in West Virginia may be inferred from the low rate of introduction of machinery," says Prof. John R. Commons. This fact, according to him, is of special significance because

burgh District." *Annals of the American Academy of Political and Social Science*, March, 1909, pp. 318–319.

[1] "If labor is cheap . . . somewhat more labor will be employed and somewhat less machinery installed. . . . If wages are high . . . more machinery will be introduced and somewhat less labor employed." C. J. Bullock, Assistant Professor of Political Economy in Harvard University, *The Elements of Economics*, pp.79–80.—"Higher wages for labor will induce entrepreneurs to economize in the use of labor. . . . In the printing industry, for example, a rise in wages would make it profitable for employing printers to use more labor-saving machinery." *Outlines of Economics*, by Richard T. Ely, Professor of Political Economy in the University of Wisconsin, revised and enlarged by the author and Thomas S. Adams; Max O. Lorenz, Ph.D., Assistant Professor of Political Science in the University of Wisconsin; Allyn A. Young, Ph.D., Professor of Economics in Leland Stanford Junior University (New York, 1909), p. 369.—"Every rise of wages will have a tendency to determine the saved capital in a greater proportion than before to the employment of machinery. Machinery and labor are in constant competition, and the former can frequently not be employed until labor rises." David Ricardo: *Principles of Political Economy and Taxation* (London, 1891), p. 386.—"Where abundance of cheap labor . . . can be obtained, . . . the development of machinery has been generally slower." John A. Hobson: *The Evolution of Modern Capitalism*, p. 69; also p. 81. *Cf.* also Karl Marx: *Capital*, Book I., Chapter XV: Machinery and Modern Industry, Sec. 2.

"the miners of West Virginia are mainly native Americans, who have only recently turned from home industry to mining."[1]

It is patent that the movement of labor from agriculture to mining and manufactures would, even in the absence of all immigration, have overcome the resistance of the English-speaking miners to the introduction of machinery. The number of mines is not fixed. New mines are continually being opened. The operator of a new machine-equipped mine need not face the resistance of old pick-miners; he can engage an entirely new force of operatives, free from any traditions. His competition will ultimately force the owners of old mines to introduce machinery or go out of business. The resistance of English-speaking miners might have some time been strong enough to prevent the introduction of machinery, but at no time could it have forced a mine operator to run his mine at a loss. The shutting down of the unprofitable mines would have put an end to the resistance of the pick-miners. Absence of immigration might have retarded the growth of American industry, but it could not have checked the introduction of machinery.

Machinery has so radically changed the technique of all industries that a comparison between past and present wages is beset with extreme difficulties. Many old occupations are gone, and even though the name may have remained the same, the substance has changed: a steel-worker to-day is not the same as a steel-worker thirty years ago.[2] A comparison of average wages or earnings for two different periods may therefore be quite misleading. It is possible for the average to show a decrease, though in reality the wages may have increased. This will be clear from the following example in which all figures are purely

[1] *Reports of the Industrial Commission*, vol. xv., p. 410.

[2] For a discussion of this subject see R. Mayo-Smith: *Statistics and Economics*, pp. 91–102. (*Publications of the American Economic Association*, vol. iii., Nos. 4, 5.)

arbitrary. Suppose, the working force of a mill in 1882 consisted of 1000 men, of whom 750 were skilled mechanics whose wages averaged $3.50 a day, and 250 were unskilled laborers hired at $1.25 a day. The average wage for all mill workers was, accordingly, $3.00 per day. Suppose, further, that in the thirty years that have elapsed since, the business of the mill has grown and two new departments have been added, with 1000 mcn in each. But owing to the installation of new machinery the same 750 skilled mechanics have been distributed over the three plants, and the additional force of 2000 men consists solely of unskilledlaborers. Suppose, the wages of the skilled mechanics have been raised from $3.50 to an average of $5.00 per day, and the wages of unskilled laborers from $1.25 to an average of $2.00 per day. The average for the three plants, however, would be $2.75 per day, *i. e.*, twenty-five cents less than thirty years ago, notwithstanding the substantial gain in the wages of all employees. The same defect is inherent in the latest refinements of the average, the "median," the "quartile," the "decile," etc.

Moreover, our wage statistics present a huge mass of fragmentary and heterogeneous data, which in their present undigested form "are well-nigh inaccessible."[1] The use

[1] Nearing: *Wages in the United States*, p. 7. The defects of our wage statistics are well stated by Professor Nearing in the following paragraphs:

"At every turn the need arose for an accurate, concise statement of the wages being paid in the various parts of the United States, yet to date no study has been made which supplies the need. Ryan's Estimate is old, and at best incomplete; Mrs. Moore's statement, like the statement in the 1903 Report of the Commissioner of Labor, is of standards of living primarily, and only incidentally of wages. In neither case is the ground covered sufficiently to warrant valuable wage deductions. The Wage Study accompanying the Census of 1900 is old, and rather inadequate, as the compilers themselves point out. . . . The available data on the subject of wages exist chiefly in the reports of State bureaus of labor, and are unfortunately of such a nature as to render comparison with data of a decade since (in the few cases where such data exist) most unsatisfactory. . . . New York wage statistics

of wage statistics, such as they are, for an analysis of the effects of immigration on wages is restricted by lack of comparable statistics of occupations by nativity.[1]

On the other hand, a rise or a fall in money wages is no indication of an increase or decrease of the resources of the wage-earners, unless coupled with comparative statistics of the cost of living. The various index numbers of prices, however, admit of a wide margin of error. An illustration is furnished by the curve plotted by Mr. Streightoff from the figures of the United States Bureau of Labor on "real wages."[2] It appears that during the period from 1890 to 1907, the purchasing power of full-time weekly wages was at its maximum in 1896, when, according to the statistics of the Massachusetts Bureau, the ratio of unemployment was as high as during the crisis year 1908;[3] the country had

relate to members of labor unions only; the average wage statistics of Pennsylvania are incomplete—even those cited are wretchedly compiled and presented; Illinois has published no recent statement of wages except in department stores; Missouri, Michigan, and Indiana publish little or no wage data. The statistics for Ohio are excellent, but very diffuse and unconcentrated. . . . Therefore, of the ten leading industrial States, three present worthy wage data; the statistics of two are far from satisfactory; while five of the ten States furnish no current wage material of value to this study. Deplorable as is the lack of statistics in these great industrial States, the conditions in the country at large are infinitely worse. Of the forty-seven States of the Union, not more than five publish up-to-date wage statistics. Of the remaining States, a score publish statistics of average wages only, which, in some cases, are so unrepresentative as to be valueless." (Pp. 9–15.)

"The last Bulletin of the Federal Bureau of Labor relating to wages was published in 1908. . . . The material as a whole permits of practically no deduction, save that wages are considerably higher in the West than in any other section of the country, and that the wages in some trades are very much higher than in others." (Pp. 138–139.)

[1] For example, though the average wages of coal miners can be computed from census statistics for every State, it is impossible to ascertain for many States the percentage of Slavs among coal miners, because coal miners are combined in census statistics with metalliferous miners and quarrymen.

[2] Streightoff, *loc. cit.*, Chart XI.

[3] See Ch. VI., Table 23 and Diagram IX.

not recovered from the effects of the crisis of 1893–1894, and the industrial situation was again disturbed by the uncertainty of a Presidential campaign fought on one of the most vital economic issues, the money question. No trust can be placed in statistics which lead to conclusions so glaringly at variance with facts still fresh in people's memory.

Overlooking, however, the inadequacy of our wage statistics, let us examine the material, such as it is, bearing upon the relation between immigration and wages.

We have seen that in the 40's the wages of Irish street laborers in Brooklyn were insufficient to provide for rent, and they were compelled to live in shanties.[1] Bad as the housing accommodations of the Italian street laborers may be to-day, they nevertheless earn enough to pay rent, which is indisputable proof of an increase in "real wages."

A generation later, a statistical inquiry into the earnings of 75,000 wage-earners in the State of Massachusetts led the Bureau of Labor Statistics to the conclusion that "the average earnings of a majority of the skilled laborers in this State do not reach the average cost of the necessities of life," with the result that "the children of the poor are taken away early from school, and brought into the labor market; the son to the factory, store, or shop, and the daughter to the life and wages of a factory or cash girl, or of a serving woman."[2] Evidently the skilled mechanics forty years ago did not fare better than the wage-earners of our own day.

In the same report there is a comparison of earnings and expenses in Massachusetts for 1800, 1830, and 1860. It is estimated that in 1800 the master mason alone of all craftsmen earned more than his expenses, whereas master carpenters and master painters could not pay their expenses; journeymen carpenters, masons, and painters were in the same category. In 1830 a journeyman mason earned barely

[1] *New York Weekly Tribune*, May 2, 1846. Quoted in *Documentary History of American Industrial Society*, vol. viii., pp. 225–226.

[2] *Third Annual Report of the Massachusetts Bureau of Statistics of Labor* (1871–1872), pp. 531–532.

enough to support a family of four, but the earnings of a journeyman carpenter were still insufficient to provide for a family of the same size. The wages of a laborer were estimated at $226 a year, which was equivalent to a little over one half of the estimated expenses of an average family of four persons. In 1860 neither a master carpenter, nor a master painter earned enough to support a family; no journeyman in the building trades was able to support a family solely on his own earnings. The earnings of a common laborer remained, as thirty years before, at a little over one half of the estimated cost of supporting a family.[1]

The Bureau of Statistics of New Jersey in its early days published a number of workmen's budgets. A compilation of the data for 1885 will be found in the Appendix, Tables XIX. and XX. The workmen were either native, or immigrants from Northern and Western Europe. Immigration from Southern and Eastern Europe was still too insignificant to affect the labor situation. It appears that of all wage-earners in specified occupations only glass-workers and blacksmiths earned enough to support on their wages an average family of about five persons. Other skilled mechanics, such as machinists and carpenters, needed the assistance of members of their households to support a family of the same size, while workers in textile mills could not meet expenses even with the assistance of members of their families. Among unskilled laborers there were some whose earnings were sufficient to support their families, but their expenses averaged only $1 a day. Those families whose expenses averaged about $1.50 a day or more were barely able to keep above water with the aid of the children's earnings. None of the Irish laborers could make both ends meet, although their expenses were somewhat below those of the other English-speaking laborers.

There are similar budget data in the report of the Ohio Bureau of Labor Statistics for 1885. In a few trades, the

[1] *Third Annual Report of the Massachusetts Bureau of Statistics of Labor*, (1871–1872), pp. 514–517. See Appendix, Table XVIII.

average earnings were insufficient to provide for the support of the wage-earner and his family. The average deficit per family for each occupation is shown in Table 87:

TABLE 87.

AVERAGE ANNUAL DEFICIT PER WORKING FAMILY IN OHIO, BY OCCUPATIONS, 1885.[1]

Occupation	Persons in family	Annual deficit
Stone-cutters	5.0	$ 2
Machinists	4.2	15
Cabinet-makers	4.5	56
Iron-workers	5.7	66
Wood-carvers	5.6	113
Cigar-makers	4.8	114
Miners	5.8	119

Among the skilled mechanics the stone-cutters and the machinists were on the border line between surplus and deficit; the cabinet-makers, wood-carvers and cigar-makers depended upon outside sources, in addition to their wages; likewise the iron-workers and the miners. The proportion of immigrants from Southern and Eastern Europe in those occupations five years later varied in Ohio between 2.1 and 5.3 per cent.

One fact may be taken as firmly established by the preceding statistics, fragmentary and insufficient as they are for other purposes, viz., that in the days of "the old immigration" the wages of unskilled laborers, and even of some of the skilled mechanics, did not fully provide for the support of the wage-earner and his family in accordance with their usual standards of living. The shortage had to be made up by the wife and children.

If the tendency of the new immigration be to lower the rate of wages or to retard the advance of wages, it should be expected that wages would be lower in great cities where the recent immigrants are concentrated, than in rural districts where the population is mostly of native birth. All

[1] See Appendix, Table XXI.

wage statistics concur, however, in the opposite conclusion. Though the census reports have since 1900 repeatedly warned against the use of census returns for the computation of average earnings, yet the defects of the census statistics of wages do not preclude a fair comparison between the earnings of urban and rural factory operatives. The average number of wage-earners in either case has been computed on a uniform basis of 300 working days per wage-earner. While individual returns may be mere estimates of questionable accuracy, yet these defects are insufficient to obscure a pronounced tendency, such as shown in Table 88.

TABLE 88.

AVERAGE EARNINGS OF FACTORY WORKERS, FOR A YEAR OF 300 WORKING DAYS, 1904.[1]

Location	Men	Women	Children
Urban	$566	$307	$186
Rural	479	264	158

An examination of previous census reports on manufactures as far back as 1870 proves that since the United States has become a manufacturing country average earnings per worker have been higher in the cities than in the country.[2] The effect of this difference is "that the country competition of native Americans where the cost of living is low often acts as a depressing effect on wages in the same occupation in cities."[3] Prof. Commons gives the following explanation

[1] Computed from the *Report of the Census of Manufactures*, 1905, Part I., United States by Industries, Table I., p. xxxv.

[2] See *XII. Census Reports. Manufactures*, Part I., pp. ccxx., ccxxi., Tables IV.–VI.; p. cclix., Tables XXVII. and XXVIII. This difference might be accounted for in part by the employment of relatively greater numbers of women and children in smaller cities and rural settlements. The effect upon the wage situation, however, is the same, whether the better paid workman of the city is underbid by a man, woman, or child employed in a country town.

[3] *Reports of the Industrial Commission*, vol. xv., p. xxiv.

of "the pressure to reduce wages" which "proceeds from the cheaper labor of country districts employed in the same line of production":

> Wages are necessarily higher in cities than in the country for the corresponding standard of living. In the city there are such additional demands as car fare, the food costs more and must be paid for in cash, because the laborer does not have his patch of ground from which, by the help of wife and children and by his own extra work mornings and evenings and idle days, he can secure a large share of his necessary food supplies.[1]

In other words, the American wage-earner in a country district gives more of his time to making a living than the city worker.

The same difference exists within the same trades between the large cities and the smaller cities. The Industrial Commission, in its volume on immigration, quotes the following from the reports of the New York Bureau of Labor:

> Wages at the present time (in 1898) are good throughout the large cities, where it must be borne in mind the men employed in the building trades have themselves been immigrants. In the smaller cities, where the wages are much less than in the larger cities, it is the older American labor which controls the field.[2]

Another way to trace the connection, if any, between immigration and wages, is to compare the average earnings by States with reference to the percentage of foreign-born; if immigration tends to depress wages, this tendency will manifest itself in lower average earnings for States with a large immigrant population, and *vice versa*. No such tendency is disclosed by wage statistics. In Tables 89 and 90 the average earnings of male and female wage-workers above the age of sixteen in the principal manufacturing States are collated with the percentages of all foreign-born and of Southern and Eastern Europeans of the same sex engaged in manufactures and mechanical pursuits. Southern States

[1] *Reports of the Industrial Commission*, vol. xv., p. 316.

[2] *Ibid.*, p. 426.

where the negroes constitute more than 10 per cent of all persons of both sexes engaged in manufactures have been excluded from this table, in order to eliminate the influence of negro competition upon the average earnings.[1]

TABLE 89.

AVERAGE ANNUAL EARNINGS OF MALE EMPLOYEES IN MANUFACTURES, COLLATED WITH THE PERCENTAGES OF FOREIGN-BORN, IN THE PRINCIPAL STATES, 1900.

State	Average annual earnings	Per cent of all males in manufactures and mechanical pursuits	
		Foreign-born	Southern and Eastern Europeans
Colorado	$ 639	38.3	10.0
California	589	34.4	4.5
Washington	578	34.9	3.3
New York	558	44.9	15.4
New Mexico	531	27.9	6.8
Connecticut	530	41.6	8.6
Illinois	530	44.7	8.7
Massachusetts	527	46.3	4.8
New Jersey	519	38.5	9.4
Oregon	518	28.8	2.1
Pennsylvania	511	33.2	13.4
Nebraska	510	30.7	3.0
Kansas	495	19.3	3.0
Rhode Island	485	47.0	5.1
Delaware	471	17.7	4.4
Texas	445	18.9	2.2

No definite relation between wages and immigration can be deduced from the preceding tables. States with widely differing percentages of foreign-born male operatives have the same average earnings, *e. g.*, Illinois, Connecticut, and New Mexico, while States with the same percentages of foreign-born male wage-earners widely differ with respect to rates of wages, *e. g.*, Colorado and New Jersey. Higher

[1] *XII. Census. Manufactures*, Part I., p. cxv., Table XXXIX.; *Population*, Part I., pp. cii.–civ., Table XLVI.; p. cvi., Table XLVIII., also p. cxiv., Table LIII.

percentages of foreign-born go together with higher average earnings, *e. g.*, Rhode Island has more than twice as many foreign-born in proportion as Texas, and the rate of wages in Rhode Island is higher than in Texas. And, on the contrary, lower percentages of foreign-born go together with higher average wages, *e. g.*, Kansas and Rhode Island. Neither does immigration from Southern and Eastern Europe appear to affect the average earnings. New York with the highest percentage of immigrants from Southern and Eastern Europe has a higher average than Oregon with the lowest percentage of immigrants from Southern and Eastern Europe. The average earnings of women likewise bear no definite relation to the per cent of foreign-born breadwinners. In Massachusetts, which has the maximum per cent (40.6) of foreign-born breadwinners in

TABLE 90.

AVERAGE ANNUAL EARNINGS OF FEMALE EMPLOYEES IN MANUFACTURES, COLLATED WITH THE PERCENTAGES OF FOREIGN-BORN, IN THE PRINCIPAL STATES, 1900.

State	Average annual earnings	Percentage of all foreign-born females in manufactures and mechanical pursuits
Colorado	$ 355	14.9
Massachusetts	319	40.6
Washington	316	19.0
Rhode Island	304	39.5
Connecticut	302	27.9
New York	298	29.6
Illinois	288	26.1
California	279	17.0
New Jersey	276	25.3
Pennsylvania	262	13.0
Nebraska	258	15.8
New Mexico	255	3.9
Texas	253	10.4
Oregon	249	12.3
Kansas	235	6.6
Delaware	211	6.7

manufacturing and mechanical pursuits, the average earnings are $319, whereas in New Mexico, which has the minimum per cent of foreign-born breadwinners (3.9), the average earnings are $255. The lowest average earnings, $211 annually, are found in Delaware, with 6.7 per cent of foreign-born women employed in manufactures, while in Massachusetts, with six times as many foreign-born, the average annual earnings were 52 per cent above the Delaware average. The preponderance of evidence, to use a legal term, supports the conclusion that, as a rule, the annual earnings are higher in States with a higher percentage of foreign-born factory workers. But making allowance for the few exceptions to this rule, the least that can be said is that there is no proof of a tendency of immigration, old or new, to depress the rate of wages.

The preceding conclusions based upon an examination of census statistics of average earnings are corroborated by the results of Prof. Nearing's study of wage statistics published by State labor bureaus. He finds "that average wages are rather constant for a given industry from State to State, and from city to city within a State."[1] As the percentage of immigrants among the wage-earners employed in each industry greatly varies from State to State and from city to city, it is evident that immigration does not affect the rate of wages.

"The opportunities for the new hands depend upon the expansion of industry and the resources of the country," says Professor Commons. "Provided this expansion occurs, there is no overcrowding of the labor market. The new resources and new investments demand new labor; and, if the expansion is strong enough, the new labor as well as the existing labor may secure advances in wages."[2]

It is broadly asserted by Professors Jenks and Lauck that the large supply of Southern and Eastern European labor "has seriously retarded the advance of wages in those occu-

[1] Nearing, *loc. cit.*, pp. 145–146.

[2] *Report of the Industrial Commission*, vol. xv., p. 305.

pations where such labor could be used to advantage." The case of section hands on the railroads is cited as a specific example: their wages are said to have "varied little during the last fifteen years, although the wages in other lines of industry have advanced materially."[1] This conclusion is at variance with the statistics of the Interstate Commerce Commission, which furnish an accurate record of the yearly fluctuations of average daily wages for the main classes of railway employees.[2] In order to bring out the effect of the supply of Southern and Eastern European labor upon the wages of section hands on the railways, the variations in their wages must be compared with the variations in the wages of other railway employees. It should not be lost sight of that the rates of wages are governed by demand, as well as by supply, not by supply alone. That wages in other lines of industry have advanced more rapidly, may have been due to a greater demand for labor in those lines. It is only when the comparison is confined to railway employees that the changes in the rates of wages can be observed under uniform conditions. The data for such a comparison are presented in graphic form in Diagram XVIII. Of the eight classes shown on the diagram all but the lowest two consist of English-speaking employees, while the two lowest grades are filled very largely by immigrants from Southern and Eastern Europe. The engineers, conductors, and firemen have strong organizations, while the laborers and trackmen are unorganized. The raises secured by the latter have come solely through the operation of the law of supply and demand. The wage curves for all classes but general office clerks show a rising tendency; the variations from year to year are almost parallel. The office clerks are the only class whose wages have remained practically sta-

[1] Jenks and Lauck, *loc. cit.*, pp. 206–207. In a preceding paragraph this specific example is qualified by the statement that "in certain cases they [immigrants hired for railroad section work] have been paid even more than the laborers previously employed, the latter being insufficient in number to meet the increasing demand." (p. 206).

[2] *Statistical Abstract of the United States*, 1910, Table 169, p. 266.

tionary; considering the increased cost of living, their real wages have in fact declined. The clerical force is, with few exceptions, either of native or of Northern and Western European birth. Thus while the wages of Southern and Eastern European section hands have been raised to meet

DIAGRAM XVIII.

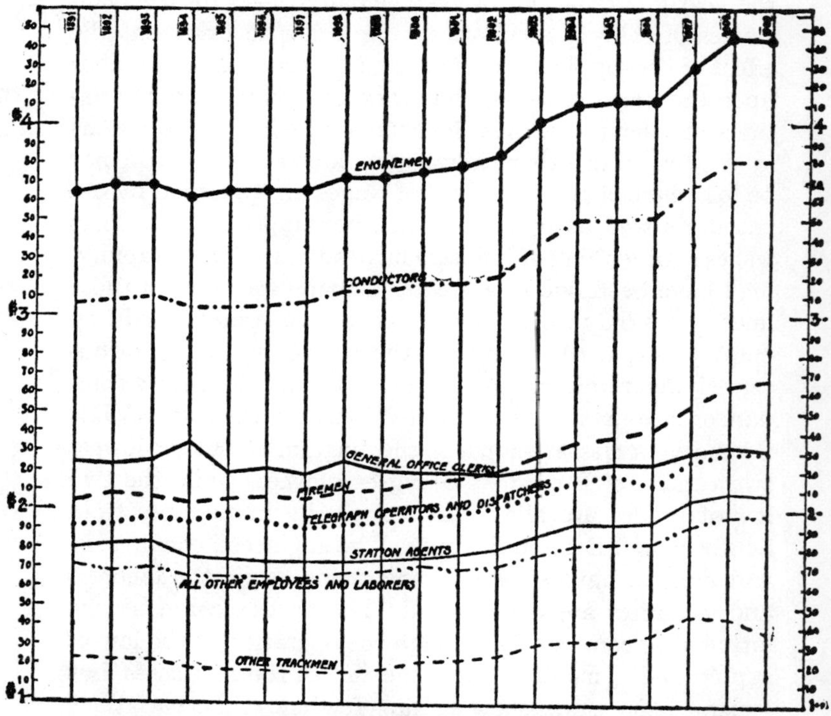

XVIII. Average daily wages of railroad employees, 1891–1909.

the increased cost of living, the salary of the American office clerk has not been advanced.

The Immigration Commission seeks to hold immigration from Southern and Eastern Europe responsible even for the low pay of clerical help:

"There is the general feeling that in so far as the recent

immigrants are entering occupations in which Americans are engaged, they are rendering those occupations undesirable. The American laborer does not care in many cases to work with the 'Hunkie,' and he resents the latter's presence and in many cases transfers his own labor to an occupation such as a clerkship at lower wages."[1]

Thus because the American street laborer deems it beneath his station in life to work side by side with a "Hunkie," he is said to be willing to accept at a sacrifice a more respectable position at a desk in a railway or mining office. The Commission has produced no statistics to show the percentage of clerical employees with a previous experience as section hands and mine laborers. On the other hand, preference for clerical work among the children of American mechanics antedates the advent of the "Hunkie." A discussion of the subject is found in a report of the Illinois Bureau of Labor as far back as 1886. First among the reasons "why the American-bred youth seek clerkships" is noted "the distaste of the American youth for the trades."[2] Obviously, the Slav and Italian laborers ought not to be burdened with responsibility for the oversupply of native American labor in clerical pursuits.

No evidence of the alleged tendency of Southern and Eastern European labor to retard the advance of wages can be found in the two basic industries which are generally regarded as representative of the conditions produced by recent immigration—the coal and the iron and steel industry. In the latter, the Immigration Commission finds, "the extensive employment of recent immigrants has been attended by an increase in rates of wages due to the general scarcity of labor in the face of the remarkable industrial expansion of recent years."[3] This statement should be

[1] *Reports of the Immigration Commission*, vol. 9, p. 583.

[2] *Fourth Annual Report of the Bureau of Statistics of Labor of the State of Illinois*, p. 227.

[3] *Reports of the Immigration Commission*, vol. 9, p. 440.

supplemented by the fact, brought to light by the Pittsburgh Survey, that while the wages of the Southern and Eastern European laborers in the steel mills have increased, the wages of the semi-skilled and skilled men—mostly Americans or old immigrants of the English-speaking races—have remained stationary, which is in effect equivalent to a lowering of the standard of wages; and the money wages of the labor aristocracy, none of whom are Southern and Eastern Europeans, have been actually reduced.[1] The same tendency is observed in the unionized coal mines of the Pittsburgh district: the wages of the unskilled men are much higher than those paid for the same grade of labor in the steel mills, whereas the wages of the skilled men are the same in the mills and mines for work of the same class. In the coal mines, as in the steel mills, unskilled work is done almost exclusively by Southern and Eastern Europeans, while the skilled men are mostly of the "English-speaking" races.[2]

To be sure, there is a continuous readjustment of wages to prices. The employer of labor seeks to recoup the advance in wages, by advancing the price of his product to the consumer. When the advance in the price of manufactured products becomes general, the wage-earner, as a consumer, is forced in effect to give up a part or all of his gain in the money rate of wages. The increased cost of living then stimulates further demands for advances in wages. Since combinations of capital in all fields of industry have reduced competition among employers of labor to a minimum, the wage-earners have been at a disadvantage in this continuous bargaining. The Immigration Commission holds that the bargaining power of labor has been impaired by "the availability of the large supply of recent immigrant labor," which "has undoubtedly had the effect of preventing an increase of wages to the extent which would have

[1] This subject is specially treated further, in Chapter XX., on the Steel-Workers.

[2] See Chapter XXI., on the Coal Miners.

been necessary had the expansion in the local industries occurred without the availability of the Southern and Eastern Europeans."[1]

Instead of conjecturing what "would have resulted . . . from the increased demand for labor,"[2] under imaginary conditions, it is safer to inquire what were the actual effects of business prosperity on wages in past American history "without the availability of the Southern and Eastern Europeans." A fair basis for comparison is offered by the Civil War period. "With the exception of the first year, the Civil War period was one of prosperity in manufactures, transportation, mining, and agriculture. Profits were large . . . New woolen factories were opened; many were operated day and night. Dividends of ten to twenty per cent were common; and larger returns were not unknown."[3] On the other hand, the cost of living rose as rapidly as in recent years; though the causes were different, the effect upon the wage-earner's budget was the same. The wage-earners were apparently in a favorable situation: "The war caused an unprecedented drain of workers from the productive industries into the army,"[4] whereas immigration dropped during the first two years.[5] The effect of that situation on wages is shown graphically in Diagram XIX., reproduced in part from Chart XII. of

[1] *Reports*, vol. 8, p. 440. The sentence is self-contradictory in form, presuming to state "the effect" which a hypothetical condition "has undoubtedly had", although, as a matter of fact, the combination of causes which "would have" made the effect "necessary" never occurred. This idea is not original with the Immigration Commission. It is referred to in the following terms by Prof. Commons in his report on immigration: "It is possible, of course, that the presence of immigrants in large numbers may prevent wages from reaching as high a level in time of prosperity as they otherwise would reach, but *this cannot, in the nature of the case, be demonstrated.*"—*Reports of the Industrial Commission*, vol. xv., p. 309.

[2] *Reports of the Immigration Commission*, vol. 1, pp. 540–541.

[3] Frank Tracy Carlton: *The History and Problems of Organized Labor*, pp. 52–53.

[4] *Ibid.*, p. 51.

[5] *Reports of the Immigration Commission*, vol. 1, pp. 79–80.

DIAGRAM XIX.

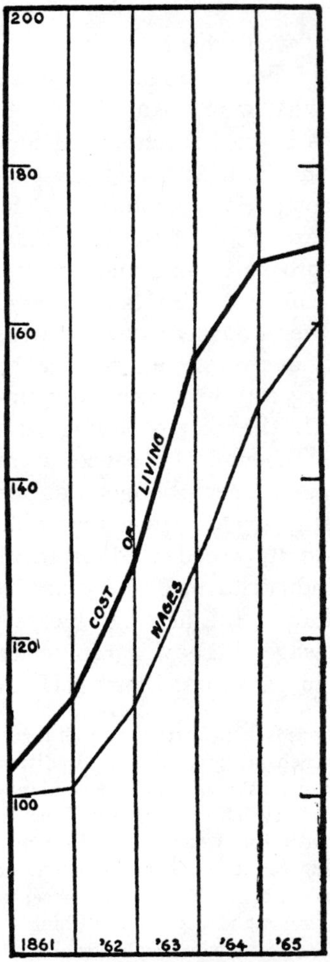

XIX. Medians of relative cost of living and average of biennial medians of relative wages, 1861–1865.

Prof. Wesley C. Mitchell's painstaking study of "Gold, Prices, and Wages under the Greenback Standard." The cost of living rose more rapidly than money wages. In other words, "without the availability of Southern and Eastern Europeans," real wages decreased.[1]

It must be noted that "after 1862 labor agitation became considerable. . . . Until near the end of the war strikes were usually successful; but they were not sufficiently successful to cause the increase in wages to keep pace with rising prices."[2] This comparison shows that the hypothesis of the Immigration Commission concerning the extent of the increase of wages "which would have been necessary had the expansion of American industries occurred without the availability of the

[1] The decrease in real wages during the period of the Civil War, according to the Aldrich Report, was as follows (Carlton, *loc, cit.*, p. 55):

Year	Per cent
1861	100
1862	87
1863	74
1864	66
1865	66

[2] *Ibid.*, pp. 57–58.

Southern and Eastern Europeans," does not fit the facts of American economic history.

The facts brought to light by the investigations of the Immigration Commission furnish ground for the assumption—paradoxical as it may seem at a superficial glance—that the availability of the large supply of recent immigrant labor has prevented a reduction of the wages of the older employees.

The prime force which has made industrial expansion so rapid in recent times has been the general introduction of labor-saving machinery. The immediate effect of the introduction of every new machine has been the displacement of the trained mechanic by the unskilled laborer. To be sure, the cheapness of machine-made products stimulates consumption of manufactured goods and creates an increased demand for labor, which in the long run offsets the loss of employment caused by the introduction of machinery. But this is true only on the assumption of a considerable industrial expansion. To use bituminous coal mining as an example: in the mines of West Virginia a team of two skilled pick-miners can produce 10 tons of coal a day; but, where machine mining has been introduced, one machine runner with one helper and eight loaders can turn out 50 tons a day.[1] Accordingly, if a force of 100 skilled pick-miners produced 500 tons of coal per day, the same output would be produced with the aid of machinery by a force of 20 skilled machine men and 80 laborers. It may be assumed that the requisite number of common laborers would be found in the home market. In order to provide skilled work for the 80 pick-miners displaced by the machine, the daily output of coal must be increased to 2500 tons, which would require an additional supply of 320 unskilled laborers. Suppose, through restriction of immigration, the additional supply of unskilled labor were cut down one half. The total available supply of labor would then consist of the 20 pick-

[1] *Annual Report of the Department of Mines, West Virginia* (1909), pp. xi., 73, 152, 153.

miners who might find employment as machine runners and helpers, the 80 laborers who would displace an equal number of pick-miners, the 80 pick-miners displaced by the machine, and an additional supply of 160 unskilled immigrant laborers, in all 340 men. The force of operatives could then be increased only to 34 teams, consisting of 68 skilled miners and 272 laborers; there would be only 48 vacancies of a higher grade for the 80 skilled miners displaced by machinery; and the remaining 32 would have to accept employment at loading coal—of course at the usual wages paid for common labor. The fact noted by the Immigration Commission, that only "a small part" of the old employees, consisting of the inefficient element, are in competition with the recent immigrants, is of course the "result of the expansion of the industry," which has opened to "the larger proportion" opportunities for "advancement to the more skilled and responsible positions."[1] These opportunities, however, were conditional upon the availability of a proportionate supply of immigrant labor for unskilled and subordinate positions.

[1] *Reports of the Immigration Commission*, vol. 1, p. 236.

CHAPTER XIII

HOURS OF LABOR

EVERY reduction of the hours of labor, even when not accompanied by an increase of the daily or weekly wage, is equivalent to an increase of the hourly wage. Moreover, a reduction in the day's work, all other things being equal, provides more days of work for every employee, which brings a direct increase of earnings. The length of the working day accordingly offers a fair measure of the effects of immigration on labor conditions. It is not complicated by the variations of the purchasing power of money, nor is it affected by the uncertainties of the index numbers. A reduction of hours is an unerring arithmetical fact. And, fortunately, the publications of the Federal and State labor bureaus furnish ample material for a comparative study of the hours of labor from the beginnings of the factory system in the United States.

There is unconscious humor in the first report of the Massachusetts Bureau of Labor Statistics on early factory conditions:

> The earliest operatives in our mills were of the home population—an active, intelligent, industrious, thrifty, well-educated, orderly, and cleanly body of young men and women, . . . daughters of independent farmers, educated in our common schools, (for years they supplied a periodical with articles written wholly by themselves,) who could think and act for themselves, who knew right from wrong, fair treatment from oppression, and who would be grateful for the one, and would not submit to the other.[1]

[1] *Report of the Massachusetts Bureau of Statistics of Labor*, 1869–1870, pp. 91–92.

Interpolated amid this eulogy of "the American element" is the following matter-of-fact statement: "The system of long hours was first adopted. . . . The general length of time per day was 14 or 15 hours." Further on it is related that "the customary time" was "from sunrise to sunset, which, in one half of the year, would give from sixteen to twelve hours, and in the other half, from nine hours to twelve."

The subject is treated more thoroughly in the recent report of the United States Bureau of Labor on "Woman and Child Wage-Earners."

> The hours of labor in textile factories in the early part of the nineteenth century were much longer than within recent years. In Massachusetts in 1825 the "time of employment" in incorporated manufacturing companies was "generally 12 or 13 hours each day, excepting the Sabbath." Of the places which reported the number of hours in that year, at only two, Ludlow and Newbury, were the hours as low as 11 a day. . . . At Duxboro the hours were from sunrise to sunset, and at Troy (Fall River) and Wellington the employees worked "all day." In 1826, 15 or 16 hours constituted . . . the working day at Ware, Mass. . . .
>
> By the thirties the hours appear to have been, if anything, longer. At Fall River, about 1830, the hours were from 5 a.m., or as soon as light, to 7:30 p. m., or till dark in summer, with one half hour for breakfast and the same time for dinner at noon, making a day of 13½ hours. In general the hours of labor in textile factories in New Hampshire, Rhode Island, and Massachusetts in 1832 were said to be 13 a day. But at the Eagle Mill, Griswold, Conn., it was said that 15 hours and 10 minutes actual labor in the mill were required.
>
> At Paterson, N. J., in 1835, the women and children were obliged to be at work at 4:30 in the morning. They were allowed half an hour for breakfast and three-quarters of an hour for dinner, and then worked as long as they could see. . . . At Manayunk, Philadelphia, in 1833, the hours of work were said to be 13 a day. And a little later the hours at the Schuylkill factory, Philadelphia, were "from sunrise to sunset, from the 21st of March to the 20th September, inclusively, and from sunrise until 8 o'clock p. m. during the remainder of the year." One hour was allowed for dinner and half an hour for breakfast during the first-mentioned six months, and one hour for dinner during the other half year. On Saturdays the mill was stopped "one hour before sunset for the purpose of cleaning the machinery."

Overtime, too, was frequent. Many of the corporations at Lowell . . . ran "a certain quantity of their machinery, certain portions of the year, until 9, and half past 9 o'clock at night, with the same set of hands.". . . Even the operatives were often against a reduction of hours, believing that it would result in a reduction of wages. Harriet Farley, editor of the *Lowell Offering* . . . thought it would work hardship to widows who were toiling for their children, to children who were toiling for their parents, and to many others.[1]

Toward the close of the '30's Irish immigration began to pour into the mills of Massachusetts. "Under the prejudice of nationality . . . the American element . . . retired from mill and factory."[2] The retirement of the "daughters of independent farmers" and their replacement by Irish immigrants was followed by a reduction of the hours of labor in the textile mills. In 1872 the working day averaged 11 hours.[3] A generation before, in 1835, it was only after a strike that the native American mill hands at Paterson, N. J., won a reduction of the working day to an average of 11½ hours.[4]

Later immigration from Southern and Eastern Europe brought new racial elements to the mills and factories of Massachusetts. The effect of the "new immigration" upon hours of labor is shown in Table 91.

TABLE 91.

WEEKLY HOURS OF LABOR IN MASSACHUSETTS, 1872 AND 1903.[5]

Industry	1872	1903	Reduction
Boots and shoes	59	53	6
Cotton goods	66	58	8
Woolen goods	66	58	8

[1] *Report of Woman and Child Wage-Earners in United States*, vol. ix., pp. 62–63, 66.

[2] *Report of the Massachusetts Bureau of Statistics of Labor*, 1869–1870, pp. 91–92.

[3] See Table 91.

[4] *Report of Woman and Child Wage-Earners*, vol. ix., p. 63.

[5] Figures computed from *Report of the Massachusetts Bureau of Labor Statistics*, 1872, pp. 119–217; *Nineteenth Annual Report of the Commissioner of Labor*, Table V.

The factory workers of Massachusetts gained during the period of the new immigration an average reduction of 7.3 hours a week, or about an hour and a quarter per day. In the woolen mills the gain in time was even slightly above the average, although forty years ago the mill operatives were mostly Irish immigrants, whereas lately the mills have been run with a polyglot help made up of all the races of Southern and Eastern Europe and Asiatic Turkey (as has been brought to public attention by the recent strike at Lawrence). The conditions in the textile mills of Massachusetts are certainly far from ideal; nevertheless fifty-eight hours a week are a great stride in advance since the period when the customary time was from sunrise to sunset, "as long as they could see." And it cannot be "said that all improvements in conditions" of the textile workers "have been secured in spite of the presence of the recent immigrant,"[1] because there was no one else to secure those improvements for them.

Taking the United States as a whole, we find that since the beginning of the "new immigration" the hours of labor have been gradually reduced; "the decrease in the hours of labor in 1907, as compared with 1890, was 5.7 per cent."[2] This fact shows at least that the recent immigrant has not hindered the movement toward better conditions of employment. It would require some proof to sustain the contention of the Immigration Commission that "his availability and his general characteristics and attitude have constituted a passive opposition which has been most effective."[3]

The Commission has made no investigation on the subject of hours of labor, except in a casual way. There is a table giving the hours of work in one unnamed steel concern. It appears that in the blast furnace department all hands, skilled and unskilled alike, work twelve hours. In all other departments the unskilled laborers work ten hours, whereas

[1] *Reports of the Immigration Commission*, vol. 1, p. 541

[2] *Bulletin of the Bureau of Labor*, No. 77, p. 4.

[3] *Reports of the Immigration Commission*, vol. 1, p. 541.

the hours of the skilled and semi-skilled employees vary as follows: in 7 occupations, 8 hours; in 143 occupations, 10 hours; in 269 occupations, 12 hours. In the coal mines operated by the same concern, the laborers work 10 hours, whereas the skilled and semi-skilled employees in 34 out of 42 occupations work 12 hours, and only in 8 occupations 10 hours.[1] The unskilled laborers in the mines and mills are mostly recent immigrants from Southern and Eastern Europe, whereas the skilled and semi-skilled positions are filled almost exclusively by native Americans and old English-speaking immigrants. The Immigration Commission itself says that "the immigrant does not appear . . . at the present time to be even competing with him [the American] in any serious way for the better-paid positions."[2] It is evident that the longer hours of the English-speaking employees are not the result of recent immigration, since the recent immigrants themselves work shorter hours.

The report on the cotton industry shows that in 1845 the working day in the cotton mills averaged 12 hours and 10 minutes; the shortest days were in December and January, averaging 11 hours and 24 minutes, and the longest in April were as high as 13 hours and 31 minutes. At the time the report was written, the working hours were 56 per week, *i. e.*, 10 hours per day with a half holiday on Saturday.[3] Thus sixty years of immigration have been attended by a reduction of 2 hours and 50 minutes in the length of the working day in the cotton mills.

The most complete statistics of hours of labor are contained in the reports of the factory inspectors of the State of New York, covering an average of nearly a million factory employees annually, for 1901–1910. New York is affected by immigration more than any other State in the Union. The period under consideration has witnessed the greatest volume of immigration known in the history of the United

[1] *Reports of the Immigration Commission*, vol. 8, Table 281, pp. 377–381.
[2] *Ibid.*, vol. 8, p. 583.
[3] *Ibid.*, vol. 11, pp. 273 and 290.

States, and the bulk of that immigration has been from the countries of Southern and Eastern Europe. The reports on factory inspection in the State of New York, therefore, offer the results of observation, under conditions best calculated to bring out the effects of immigration. Moreover, the figures for the city of New York can be compared with those for the rest of the State. In the city of New York the foreign-born population furnished in 1900, 50.7 per cent of all persons engaged in manufactures and mechanical pursuits, while in the State outside of New York the ratio was only 22.9 per cent. The natives of Southern and Eastern Europe constituted in the same year 16.1 per cent of the total population of New York City, and 2.1 per cent of the total population of the State outside of New York City. By 1910 their proportion in New York City increased to 24.1 per cent and in the remainder of the State to 6.6 per cent.[1]

The per cent distribution of factory operatives by the number of hours of work in and outside of New York City is given in Table 92 on the next page. The figures show:

(1) That the decade of the heaviest immigration from Southern and Eastern Europe was marked by a gradual reduction of the hours of labor in the State of New York;

(2) That the percentage of factory operatives working ten hours or less on week days with a half-holiday on Saturday was much greater in New York City with its large colonies of alien workers than in the remainder of the State with a working population predominantly native;

(3) That after a decade of "undesirable immigration" more than two thirds of all factory workers in New York City work ten hours or less on week days with a half holiday on Saturday, whereas in the remainder of the State the majority still work longer hours.

The preconceived notions about the "general character-

[1] *XIII. Census. Population*, vol. i, pp. 79, 148, 825–827, 832 (computed).

istics" of the recent immigrant do not stand the scrutiny of incontrovertible statistical figures.

TABLE 92.

PER CENT DISTRIBUTION OF FACTORY OPERATIVES BY WEEKLY HOURS OF LABOR IN NEW YORK CITY AND IN NEW YORK STATE OUTSIDE OF NEW YORK CITY, 1901–1909.[1]

Year	New York City		New York State outside of New York City	
	57 hours or less	58 hours and over	57 hours or less	58 hours and over
1901	53.7	46.3	17.8	82.2
1902	54.8	45.2	22.2	77.8
1903	65.8	34.2	25.2	74.8
1904	67.4	32.6	31.8	68.2
1905	68.8	31.2	34.5	65.5
1906	69.0	31.0	35.0	65.0
1907	71.2	28.8	38.5	61.5
1908	70.9	29.1	40.9	59.1
1909	71.5	28.5	39.5	60.5
1910	75.5	24.5	40.4	59.6

[1] *Annual Report of the New York Bureau of Labor*, vol. ii., 1910, Table 31, p. xlvi.

CHAPTER XIV

CHILD LABOR

CHILD labor has a depressing effect upon the rate of wages. Thousands of children of immigrants are employed in the mills of New England and the Middle Atlantic States. The inference which readily suggests itself to the popular mind is that child labor is the product of immigration. It is a historical fact, however, that child labor originated in the United States with the introduction of the factory system during the first quarter of the nineteenth century. Early writers on economic subjects favored the employment of children in factories, because it would save adult male labor for agriculture, fishing, shipping, and the skilled trades. Child labor was advocated on religious and philanthropic grounds. The various immigrant races which succeeded one another in the nineteenth century found child labor as an integral part of the factory system in the United States.[1]

During the ten-year period from 1899 to 1909, with its unprecedented immigration, the average number of children employed in factories remained stationary, viz., in 1899–161,276, in 1909–162,493, while the relative number decreased from 3.4 per cent to 2.4 per cent of all wage-earners.[2]

[1] Carlton, *loc. cit.*, pp. 380–385.

[2] *XIII. Census*, vol. viii. *Manufactures*, p. 253. It is probable that the number of children at work has decreased as well. The number of wage-earners for 1899, owing to the method of computation followed at the XII. Census, was considerably underestimated: The average number was computed "by using 12, the number of calendar months, as a divisor into the total of the average numbers reported for each month." The effect of this method is shown in the case of twelve

The most significant fact to be noted concerning the relation between child labor and immigration is the large proportion of children employed in factories in States where there is practically no immigrant population. Children of native-born American parents are drawn into the mills as a substitute for immigrant labor. This conclusion is derived from Table 93, showing the dependence of factories upon child labor in six leading manufacturing States, according to the recent census.

TABLE 93.

PER CENT OF CHILDREN UNDER 16 EMPLOYED IN FACTORIES, IN THE UNITED STATES AND IN SIX LEADING MANUFACTURING STATES, 1909, AND PER CENT OF FOREIGN-BORN, 1910.[1]

State	Per cent of children to all wage-earners	Per cent of foreign-born to total population
United States	2.4	14.7
South Carolina	12.9	0.4
North Carolina	11.3	0.3
Massachusetts	3.5	31.5
Pennsylvania	3.3	18.8
Illinois	1.5	21.4
New York	0.8	30.2

In the four leading manufacturing States of the North with a large immigrant population, child labor holds a subordinate place in the industrial organization, while in North and South Carolina one in every eight or nine factory operatives is under the age of 16. The lowest per cent of child workers is in New York, which is overrun by immigrants, old and new.

selected industries, where the average number computed "as an abstract unit (like the foot-pound)" was 475,473, whereas the total "computed on the basis of time in operation would have exceeded 650,000," the variation being as high as 36 per cent.—*XII. Census. Manufactures*, Part I., pp. cvi., cx., and cxi.

[1] *XIII. Census*, vol. viii.: *Manufactures*, pp. 270–271; vol. i: *Population*, pp. 161–162.

The latest available statistics of the distribution of children employed in manufactures by nativity relate to the year 1900. The figures are given in Table 94.

TABLE 94.

DISTRIBUTION, BY PARENT NATIVITY AND COLOR, OF THE NUMBER OF CHILDREN OF BOTH SEXES, 10 TO 15 YEARS OF AGE, ENGAGED IN MANUFACTURES AND MECHANICAL PURSUITS, BY GEOGRAPHICAL DIVISIONS, 1900.[1]

Race and Nativity	Continental United States	North Atlantic Division	North Central Division	Western Division	South Atlantic Division	South Central Division
Number:						
White:						
Native parents	114,881	46,534	19,155	1,696	35,292	12,204
Foreign parents	159,679	104,574	44,796	3,199	4,172	3,038
Colored........	9,309	493	679	288	4,784	3,065
Total.......	283,869	151,601	64,630	5,083	44,248	18,307
Per cent:						
White:						
Native parents	40.5	30.7	29.6	31.4	79.8	66.7
Foreign parents	56.3	69.0	69.3	62.9	9.4	16.6
Colored........	3.2	0.3	1.1	5.7	10.8	16.7
Total........	100.0	100.0	100.0	100.0	100.0	100.0

In the country at large, the percentage ratio of children of each nativity employed in manufactures corresponded to the percentage of all breadwinners of the same nativity, engaged in manufacturing and mechanical pursuits.[2] In other words, on the whole the foreign-born sent to the factories no more than their quota of children. There is a marked difference, however, in the ratio of children of native parents for each section of the country: in the South the

[1] *Occupations, XII. Census*, Table LVIII., p. clix.

[2] The per cent distribution, by parent nativity and color, of persons of all ages engaged in manufactures in the United States was as follows: white of native parentage, 39.8 per cent; white of foreign parentage, 56.0 per cent; colored, 4.2 per cent.—*Ibid.*, Table XXXVI., p. cxiii.

overwhelming majority of factory workers under 16 years of age are children of native parents.

Another important fact is the age distribution of children employed in factories. The Immigration Commission in its study of households of cotton-mill operatives in the North Atlantic States found but *one child under 14 years of age* at work in a total of 795 children between 6 and 13 years, and that a French-Canadian.[1] There are as yet no comparable data more recent than the census figures for 1900. The latter are presented in Table 95.

TABLE 95.

COTTON-MILL OPERATIVES UNDER 14 YEARS OF AGE IN THE PRINCIPAL MANUFACTURING STATES, 1900.[2]

State	Number
New England:	
Maine	602
New Hampshire	527
Massachusetts	199
Connecticut	50
Rhode Island	615
Middle Atlantic:	
New York	51
New Jersey	116
Pennsylvania	311
Southern:	
North Carolina	5515
South Carolina	103
Georgia	2637
Alabama	1608

While, as has been shown above, the absolute number of children employed in factories is greater in the North than in the South, the children under 14 in the cotton mills of the South far outnumber those of the same age in the great manufacturing States of the North. This is, no doubt, due to the child-labor laws of the Northern States.

No one in the Northern States to-day defends the employment of children under 14 in factories. In the Southern States, however, the economic needs of the growing manufacturing industries have produced eloquent advocates of

[1] *Reports of the Immigration Commission*, vol. 10, Table 46, p. 419.

[2] *Occupations at the XII. Census*, Table LXV., pp. clxix.–clxxxv.

child labor in positions of influence.[1] Foreign-born wage-earners are a negligible factor in the Southern labor market. The growth of manufacturing industries in the South is restricted by the natural increase of the native population. In order to extend their operations, the manufacturers of the South must resort to the employment of children, as did their predecessors in New England a century ago before immigration came to supply the needs of American industry.

This situation is by no means confined to the South. Absence of foreign immigration has created a demand for the labor of native American children in the canneries and shoe factories of rural and semi-urban Missouri.

The rural districts of Missouri lost, from 1900 to 1910, 3.5 per cent of their population. The total population of the State increased only 6 per cent. The foreign-born in 1910, as well as in 1900, constituted 7 per cent of the total population of the State at large, and only 3.3 per cent of the State outside of St. Louis and Kansas City. The additions to the foreign-born population through immigration since the census of 1900 averaged only 1310 persons annually, but the increase was concentrated in St. Louis and Kansas City, whereas the remainder of the State lost in ten years 8380 of its foreign-born population.[2] The statistics of the State Labor Bureau show an increase of the number of working children in the smaller cities, the towns and rural sections, "which can be traced to the large number of shoe factories and canneries which sprang up, outside of St. Louis, Kansas City, and St. Joseph, during 1908." The foreign-born labor supply in those sections is negligible. The Commissioner of Labor offers the following explanation for the increase in the employment of children:

[1] "The cotton mills are set forth . . . as the savior of the people, religiously, educationally, and, according to Dr. Stiles, physically." —*Annals of the American Academy of Political and Social Science*, Supplement, March, 1910. A. J. McKelway: The Mill or the Farm, p. 54.

[2] *XIII. Census. Population*, vol. i., pp. 27, 61, 135, 149, 178 (computed).

The increase in working women and children in 1908 over 1907, shown by these statistics, does not mean that conditions are such that those who ought to remain at home and take care of domestic affairs must go out into the world and toil, but in reality is due to an increase in the number of establishments in which the light, delicate touch of a gentle hand is needed, instead of strength, endurance, and mechanical labor. . . . It is necessary to state here that while the canning industry of Missouri is still in its infancy, the year 1908 was probably the best the State has ever had in this line, and that is why more employees were needed. . . . The increase in child labor was not due to the stringency, the increased cost of living, or to the poorer condition of the masses, but, instead, to an increased demand for these workers from the new canneries and shoe factories. Both these lines have a class of very light work, suitable only for boys and girls, which does not pay enough weekly for older persons. This assertion is not made in defence of child labor, but merely to explain why it exists in canneries and shoe factories.[1]

The explanation sounds very similar to that offered in the Southern States.[2] It accounts, as far as it goes, for the employment of children in canneries: an agricultural community is the natural location for the canning industry, outside labor is scarce in rural districts and the canning season is short. No local advantage for the shoe factories, however, exists in rural Missouri. The centre of the shoe manufacturing industry is Massachusetts, which in 1905 contributed 45 per cent of the total output of the United States.[3] The seat of the shoe-manufacturing industry of Missouri is St. Louis, whose output increased from 74 per cent of the total for the State in 1899 to 81 per cent in 1904.[4]

[1] *Reports of the Missouri Bureau of Labor Statistics*, 1909, pp. 320–321.

[2] "The cotton mills were the most powerful opponents [of theLouisiana child-labor law], ably seconded by the canning industries. To hear the representatives of both these industries, one, not knowing any better, would have been convinced that the most healthful, remunerative, educational place in the entire world in which to develop children was in a cotton mill or an oyster cannery. One fairly tingled to spend the rest of life shucking oysters or peeling shrimp." Supplement, *Annals of the Am. Acad. of Political and Social Science*, March, 1909. Jean M. Gordon: *The Forward Step in Louisiana*, p. 163.

[3] *Census Report, Manufactures*. 1905, Part I., p. ccxxx.

[4] *Ibid.*, pp. ccxxx. and ccxxxi. (computed).

The principal inducement for locating new shoe factories in rural sections of Missouri appears to be the availability of cheap labor of native American women and children, who can underbid the male immigrants employed in the shoe factories of Massachusetts.

CHAPTER XV

LABOR ORGANIZATIONS

THE Immigration Commission has made the statement that "the recent immigrant has not, as a rule, affiliated himself with labor unions, unless compelled to do so as a preliminary step toward acquiring work. . . . Where he has united with the labor organizations he has usually refused to maintain his membership for any extended period of time, thus rendering difficult the unionizing of the occupation or industry in which he has been engaged." This assertion could be proved only by a statistical study of the membership of labor organizations. It is a characteristic fact that with a Federal Bureau of Labor and a number of State labor bureaus we have no compilation of the total number of organized workers in the United States for a series of years.[1] A great deal of information on the subject is scattered in the published reports of labor conventions. The inevitable gaps could be supplied from the records of labor organizations. The Immigration Commission, however, made no effort to secure statistics of union membership in a systematic way from official sources, but confined its inquiries in the main to the heads of the households covered by its investigation. The report of the Commission contains data concerning 3325 trade unionists, whereas the total membership of labor organizations in the United States was estimated for 1910 at 2,625,000.[2] The reports of the Commission contain a few fragmentary data on the membership of labor organizations, apparently obtained from their

[1] *Reports of the Industrial Commission*, vol. xvii., p. xviii.

[2] *New York Labor Bulletin*, September, 1911, p. 418.

officials, but these data flatly contradict the conclusions of the Commission.

We learn that "practically 36 per cent of the total number of clothing workers in New York are organized; while 80 per cent of the cutters are members of the cutters' union. Of the organized workers, about 60 per cent are Russian and Polish Hebrews, 30 per cent Italians, and 10 per cent persons of other races including foreign and native-born."[1] To understand the meaning of these percentages, we must compare them with the percentage of organized workers in all industries. The total number of male industrial wage-earners in the United States at the census of 1900 can be estimated at 8,600,000[2]; since very few women are affiliated with labor organizations the number of males alone need be taken into consideration in computing the percentage of organized workers. The increase of the population of the United States from 1900 to 1910 was 21 per cent. The number of male industrial wage-earners in 1910 can accordingly be estimated at 10,400,000, and the proportion of organized workingmen in all industries at 25 per cent. Thus while, on an average, only 25 per cent of all male wage-earners in the United States were affiliated with labor organizations, among the clothing workers in New York City 36 per cent were organized, all but one tenth of the organized workers being Russian and Polish Hebrews and Italians. Of the most skilled among them, the cutters, 80 per cent were members of their union, *i.e.*, relatively thrice as many as in all industries of the country at large.

Of course, the question is whether the condition in the clothing industry of New York may be accepted as typical. The reports of the Immigration Commission furnish no comparable data for the industries of the country at large. The results of the study of households comprise less than two trade-unionists in every 1000. Still, this being the only

[1] *Reports of the Immigration Commission*, vol. 11, p. 388.

[2] I. A. Hourwich, "Social-Economic Classes of the Population of the United States," *Journal of Political Economy*, March, 1911, p. 205.

statistical evidence which the Immigration Commission has produced in support of its conclusions regarding the attitude of recent immigrants toward trade unions, it is worthy of note that upon the Commission's own showing trade-unionism is as strong among the immigrants as among the native American workmen. The ratio of organized workers to all male wage-earners in each population group is shown in Table 96.

TABLE 96.

ORGANIZATION OF NATIVE AND IMMIGRANT LABOR.[1]

Nativity of wage-earners	Percentage organized
Native-born of native father:	
White	13.9
Negro	17.9
Native-born of foreign father	14.1
Foreign-born	13.4

While on the whole trade-unionism is very weak in the field covered by the investigation of the Commission, it is manifest from the practical uniformity of the percentages for each group that distinctions of birth, race, and color do not explain this weakness.

Neither could a line be drawn in respect of unionism between the "desirable" immigrants from Northern and Western Europe and the "undesirable aliens from Southern and Eastern Europe." This fact is brought to light by the comparison in Table 97 of the principal immigrant races that are represented by at least 500 persons each[2] in the statistics of the Immigration Commission. On the whole, the average percentage of union men among the "undesirable aliens" is higher than among the immigrants of the preferred races.

[1] *Reports of the Immigration Commission*, vol. 1, p. 417.

[2] Smaller groups have been omitted because, where the numbers are small, the ratios are liable to be influenced by exceptional circumstances and local conditions; for example, the highest percentage of organized workmen, 100 per cent, was found among the Mexicans, because the investigators of the Commission chanced to come across 56 Mexican miners in a unionized mine.—*Ibid.*, pp. 418–419.

TABLE 97.

ORGANIZATION OF IMMIGRANT LABOR[1]

"Desirable" races	Total number	Organized	
		Number	Per cent
French Canadian	573	133	23.2
English	524	87	16.6
Irish	724	107	14.8
Swedish	515	48	9.3
Bohemian and Moravian	537	26	4.8
German	1,101	51	4.6
Total	3,974	452	11.4
"Undesirable" races			
North Italian	881	351	39.8
Lithuanian	1,408	497	35.3
Hebrew	761	163	21.4
Ruthenian	684	144	21.1
Slovak	1,706	234	13.7
South Italian	2,428	258	10.5
Magyar	1,501	146	9.7
Polish	3,280	313	9.5
Total	12,649	2,106	16.6

The percentage of trade-unionists among North Italians is nearly three times as high as among native Americans of native parentage; the Lithuanians furnish twice as many as the more desirable Englishmen; the Hebrews twice as many as the Swedes; the Ruthenians are far ahead of the Americans of native stock; even the South Italians can boast a percentage twice as high as the Germans; the Magyars and the Slovaks march in front of the Swedes; and the Poles, who are at the tail end of the procession of undesirables from Eastern Europe, still outnumber two to one their more

[1] *Reports of the Immigration Commission*, vol. 1, p. 418.

favored kinsmen, the Bohemians and Moravians. Considering that the native Americans and the members of the races which contributed most largely to the earlier immigration are, as a rule, engaged in higher occupations, where they are for the most part segregated from the recent immigrants, it is clear that the latter could not be an obstacle in the way of organization among the skilled men; and that they have not been an obstacle is shown by the fact that the recent immigrants themselves furnish a higher percentage of organized workmen.

As usual, when the facts do not fit its theory, the Commission seeks to qualify the plain language of the figures:

> These figures must not, however, be taken as representative of racial tendencies except in a few cases, for the reason that the information shown for one race may be for but one or two industries in which the race is employed and which are so controlled by labor organizations that membership in the labor unions is necessary to secure employment. On the other hand, a race or several races may be employed in an industry or industries in which no labor unions exist. . . . The fact that certain races are most extensively employed in highly unionized localities and industries is indicative of comparatively greater assimilation and progressiveness on the part of the members of such races.[1]

The Commission thus assumes that affiliation of immigrants with labor organizations is a sign of their "assimilation," which implies that organization of labor is a native growth, and that the foreigner merely imitates the ways of the native. This view has no foundation in the history of organized labor in the United States. The fact is that the membership of most of the labor organizations has from their inception been very largely foreign-born.

Historians have traced the embryo of labor organization in America to the colonial period. Labor organizations sprang up here and there during the first quarter of the nineteenth century. Between 1825 and 1850 a number of labor conventions were held. But all labor organizations

[1] *Reports of the Immigration Commission*, vol. 1, p. 419.

before the Civil War were ephemeral and soon disintegrated. Their effect upon economic conditions was negligible.[1]

The depreciation of the currency and the consequent rise of the cost of living during the Civil War stimulated organization among workmen. Still the figures made accessible by the research of Dr. Fite "plainly caution the present generation against exaggerating the importance of the war-time unions; they were numerous and bold in leadership, but they were small in membership and embraced only a small part of the labor world."[2]

The plan of the X. Census comprised an inquiry into the subject of trade unions in the United States. The statistical data collected were fragmentary. The development of labor organizations up to 1880 is summed up as follows:

"But very few of the unions reported upon, so far as their age could be learned, have had a long existence. The history of unionism in most cases is that an organization is effected under the stress of some difficulty, flourishes for a while, and then dies out, to be brought to life again in case of urgent need."[3]

Five years later, Col. Richard J. Hinton, a strong labor sympathizer, contrasting the British with the American labor organizations, noted with regret that "in the United States the whole movement has hardly reached the stage of toleration."[4]

Official inquiries made about the same time in Illinois (1886) and New Jersey (1887) established the fact that the majority of the trade-unionists and Knights of Labor were

[1] *Mass. Report on Statistics of Labor*, 1906, "The Incorporation of Trade Unions," Part. III., pp. 131–134. Frank Tracy Carlton. *The History and Problems of Organized Labor*, p. 41.

[2] Emerson David Fite: *Social and Industrial Conditions during the Civil War*, pp. 204–205.

[3] *X. Census*, vol. xx. *Report on Trade Societies in the United States*, p. 3.

[4] Richard J. Hinton, "American Labor Organizations," *The North American Review*, January, 1885, p. 49. An official report for the same year states that "trade unions in America are in their infancy yet." *Ninth Annual Report of the Ohio Bureau of Labor Statistics* (1885, p. 20).

of foreign birth, whereas the native Americans contributed less than their quota to the membership of labor organizations.[1] This fact had been generally known before from common observation. In the report of the New Jersey Bureau of Statistics of Labor for 1884, immigration was held directly responsible for the organization of labor unions. The writer of an article on "Immigration and the Labor Problem," after stating that native Americans are displaced by laborers "coming from countries in which wages are lower than our standard" and where the standard of living is therefore lower, goes on to say that

> to the American laborer of twenty-five or thirty years since, such an occurrence would have been an inconvenience but not altogether a disaster. Failing to obtain the work he wanted at one place or in one trade, he would turn to another and yet another, until he had found something by which he could live. But the foreign-born operative has but little of this cat-like facility of falling upon his feet. He knows but a single trade; often, in the subdivision of mechanical employments, which is almost uniformily prevalent and becoming still more so, only a small fraction of that. Thrown out of his place, he must find another almost precisely similar, or acquire a new training by a slow and painful process, during which he earns little or nothing, and he has in far the greater number of cases nothing laid up. That men should grow desperate and wicked under such circumstances is not surprising. That they should combine in leagues of various kinds; limit the hours of labor, or the amount of work to be done in a given time; refuse to work with apprentices, or men outside of their own associations; strike, and agree not only to remain idle themselves, but to prevent others from working; . . . is the most natural thing in the world.[2]

Thus, as late as 1884, the organization of labor unions was decried in a State report as un-American, the work of foreigners grown "desperate and wicked." Ten years later the Minnesota Bureau of Labor undertook an investigation to disprove that view. It is instructive to contrast the state of public opinion in the early 90's as reflected in the report

[1] The results of those inquiries are given in the Appendix, Table XXII.

[2] *Seventh Annual Report of the New Jersey Bureau of Statistics of Labor and Industries* (1884), pp. 289–290.

of the Minnesota Labor Bureau,[1] with the sentiment of our own day, when a Congressional commission regards unionism as a manifestation of Americanism:

> It has been repeatedly charged by a certain class of writers that American trade unions are conspiracies to prevent American boys from acquiring skilled crafts. This charge has been most clearly stated by the *Century Magazine*, May, 1893. It says: "Under the present conditions of trade instruction and employment in this country the American boy has no rights which organized labor is bound to respect. He is denied instruction as an apprentice, and if he be taught his trade in a trade school he is refused admission to nearly all trade unions and is boycotted if he attempts to work as a non-union man. The questions of his character and skill enter into the matter only to discriminate against him. All the trade unions of the country are controlled by foreigners, who comprise the great body of their members; while they refuse admission to the trained American boy, they admit all foreign applicants with little or no regard to their training or skill. In fact the doors of organized labor in America, which are closed and barred against American boys, swing open wide and free to all foreign-comers. Labor in free America is free to all save sons of Americans." The same magazine, in its issue of July, 1893, says: "They (the trade unions) are afraid of America's independent ideas in their unions, knowing, as they do, that American workmen are not so servile and not so easily led as the more ignorant foreign workmen."[2]

The report of the Minnesota Bureau of Labor then proceeds to disprove, by figures relative to Minnesota labor unions, the statements made in the *Century* articles. It shows that in the three large cities of the State 62 per cent of males of voting age at the census of 1890 were foreign-born, whereas of the total number of trade unionists who replied to the inquiries of the Bureau, 58.54 per cent were

[1] *Fourth Biennial Report of the Minnesota Bureau of Labor* (1893-94), p. 175.

[2] The author of a doctor's dissertation, submitted to the University of Chicago at the same time, strongly advocated restriction of immigration, to ward off a "peril" which threatened American labor in "the fact that our trade unions are almost exclusively controlled by foreigners . . . incapable by long oppression in the industrial slavery of Europe to understand or appreciate the true dignity or interests of American labor."—Rena M. Atchison: *Un-American Immigration*, p. 105.

born in the United States and 41.46 per cent were foreign-born. But a table in the report shows 11 of the unions with more than 62 per cent of foreign-born members. Those trades were the granite cutters with 70.09, bricklayers with 72.10, tailors with 100, bakers with 100, carpenters with 75.75, stonecutters with 72.75, blacksmiths with 100 per cent of foreign-born members.

The change of public sentiment from 1894, when the "ignorant foreign workmen" were accused of organizing labor unions, to 1910, when the ignorant foreigners were accused of keeping away from labor unions, is symptomatic of the progress of organized labor during the intervening period. In 1894, when the "ignorant foreigners" comprised mainly the races of "the old immigration," trade unionism was still weak; after eighteen years of "undesirable immigration from Southern and Eastern Europe," organized labor has gained in numbers and won public recognition.

An idea of the comparative strength of labor organizations in the days of the old and the new immigration can be gained from the distribution of the number of existing unions by the period of their organizations, as shown in Table 98.

Very few of the existing unions were organized prior to 1880. The work of organization has since been proceeding at an increasing rate of speed. During the first decade of the new immigration, 1880–1890, more unions were organized and survived than throughout the whole previous history of the United States. In the next decade, 1890–1900, when immigration from Southern and Eastern Europe first outran "the old immigration," the number of new unions organized in five of the six States (all but Illinois) exceeded the total number of unions which had survived from previous times. But the greatest success rewarded the efforts of union organizers during the first decade of the present century. In Massachusetts, Connecticut, and Minnesota more new unions were organized since 1900 than during the whole ninteenth century. It must be borne in mind that

Massachusetts and Connecticut have received large accessions to their population from Southern and Eastern Europe. Thus the greatest activity in the field of organization coincided with the unparalleled new immigration of the past decade.

TABLE 98.

NUMBER AND DATE OF ORGANIZATION OF ACTIVE LABOR UNIONS IN SIX INDUSTRIAL STATES.[1]

Period	Massachusetts	Connecticut	Ohio	Illinois	Missouri[2]	Minnesota
Total number:						
Prior to 1880...	32	24	40	65	40	11
1880–1889......	116	61	126	254	75	62
1890–1899......	197	108	710	278	241	107
Since 1900......	658[3]	285[4]	......	......	243	197[5]
Annual average:						
1880–1889......	12	6	13	25	8	6
1890–1899......	20	11	71	28	24	11
Since 1900......	73	28	......	91[6]	30	22

The aggregate membership of labor organizations in the United States and Canada was estimated by the Industrial Commission at 1,300,000 for July 1, 1901.[7] The aggregate

[1] Compiled from *Report on Statistics of Labor, Massachusetts*, 1908, pp. 185–186. *Ohio Bureau of Labor Statistics, 24th Annual Report*, 1900, p. 297. *Minnesota Labor Report*, 1905-6, p. 365; *ibid.*, 1907-8, p. 83. *Report of the Bureau of Labor Statistics of Illinois*, 1886, p. 198; *ibid.*, 1901, p. 298. *Report of the Connecticut Bureau of Labor Statistics*, 1909–1910, p. 217. *32d Annual Report of the Missouri Bureau of Labor.* [2] Periods: Up to 1880; 1881–1890; 1891–1900; 1901–1908.

[3] 1900–1908. [4] 1900–1909. [5] 1900–1908. [6] In 1900–1901—183.

[7] The total membership of enumerated unions was estimated at 1,208,000, to which was added an arbitrary allowance of 191,100 for the Knights of Labor "and unenumerated organizations." The former were at the time in a moribund condition, and the Industrial Commission believed that its estimate was subject to a probable error of 100,000.—*Reports of the Industrial Commission*, vol. xvii., p. xix.

membership of all unions in 1910 was estimated by the New York Bureau of Labor at 2,625,000 for the United States and Canada.[1] Thus in nine years from 1901 to 1910, with their unprecedented immigration, the membership of labor organizations doubled, whereas the average number of wage-earners employed in manufactures increased from 1899 to 1909 only about 40 per cent,[2] the number of railway employees from 1900 to 1910, 67 per cent,[3] etc.

The reports of the New York Bureau of Labor Statistics since 1897 furnish a record of the annual increase or decrease of union membership, which permits of a comparative study of the relation between trade-unionism and immigration. New York State is the receptacle of more than its proportionate share of "the new immigration." New York City is a temporary stopping-place for many a stranded immigrant lacking the funds for continuing his journey to final destination. The evil effects of immigration, if such they be, must appear in aggravated form in the State of New York. The relation between union membership and immigration is shown graphically in Diagram XX.[4] The curves representing trade-union membership and the immigration of breadwinners[5] run almost parallel, showing that union

[1] *New York Labor Bulletin*, Sept., 1911, p. 418.

[2] *XIII. Census*, volume viii. *Manufactures*, p. 240. The real increase of the average number of wage-earners is smaller, because the number for 1910 is the average of 12 monthly pay-rolls, whereas in 1900 the average number was computed "by using 12, the number of calendar months, as a divisor into the total of the average numbers reported for each month." The effect of this change of method is shown in the case of twelve selected industries, where the average number computed "as an abstract unit (like the foot-pound)" was 475,473, whereas the total "computed on the basis of time in operation would have exceeded 650,000," the variation being as high as 36 per cent.—*XII. Census. Manufactures*, Part I., pp. cvi., cx., cxi.

[3] Interstate Commerce Commission. *Twenty-third Annual Report of the Statistics of Railways*, pp. 33–34.

[4] The figures from which the latter is plotted will be found in the Appendix, Table XXIII.

[5] All immigrants save those that have "no occupation (including women and children)," in official terminology.

membership rises and falls as immigration rises and falls. The New York statistics thus disprove the conclusion of the

DIAGRAM XX.

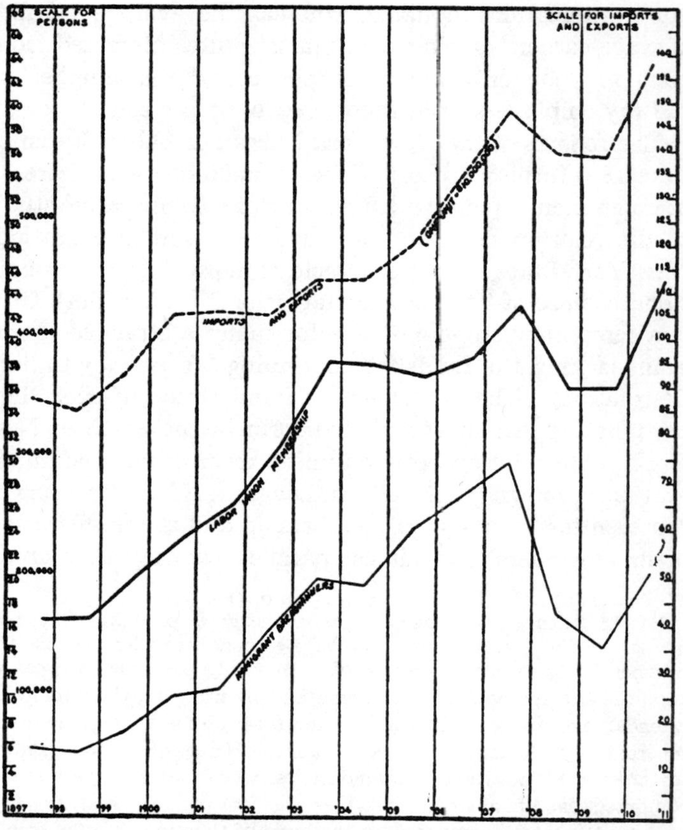

XX. Labor union membership in the State of New York, number of immigrant bread-winners destined for the State of New York and combined imports and exports through the port of New York. 1897–1910.

Immigration Commission that "his (the recent immigrant's) availability and his general characteristics and attitude have constituted a passive opposition which has been most effective."[1] The third curve represents the aggregate exports and imports through the port of New York. The import and export trade of New York gives employment, directly and indirectly, to a large portion of the population of the city. It feeds the traffic of all railways in the State with terminals in New York. The fluctuations of the export trade may therefore be taken as an index of the business situation in the State of New York. It will be observed that the curve of union membership follows very closely the curve of foreign trade. The fluctuations of union membership accordingly depend upon the business situation. The latter likewise determines the fluctuations of immigration. The harmonious movement of immigration and organization among workers is thus accounted for by the fact that both are stimulated by business prosperity and discouraged by business depression.

The question may be raised, however: given the industrial expansion of the past decade, would not the progress of trade-unionism have been greater "without the availability of the recent immigrant labor supply"? An answer to this question is furnished by the comparative statistics of union membership in the States of New York and Kansas for 1900–1909. While New York has received great numbers of immigrants during this period, the ratio of foreign-born in Kansas has been steadily decreasing since 1880: in the latter year the ratio was 11 per cent, in 1910 only 8 per cent. The proportion of foreign-born from Southern and Eastern Europe to the population of Kansas was only 2 per cent.[2] At the same time Kansas has shared in the industrial expansion of the period, as witnessed by the amounts paid out in wages to factory operatives in 1899 and 1909, shown in Table 99. While the increase in the United States at large amounted to 71 per cent and in New York City to

[1] *Reports of the Immigration Commission*, vol. i., p. 541.

[2] *Statistical Abstract*, 1910, Table 25, p. 53. *XIII. Census. Population*, vol. i., p. 817; vol. ii., p. 669.

65 per cent, in Kansas it reached 100 per cent. The comparative growth of trade-unionism in New York and Kansas in 1900–1909 must accordingly reveal the effects of

TABLE 99.

TOTAL WAGES PAID TO FACTORY OPERATIVES IN THE UNITED STATES AND IN THE STATES OF NEW YORK AND KANSAS (MILLIONS OF DOLLARS), 1899 AND 1909.[1]

	1899	1909	Per cent of increase
United States.......	2008	3427	71
New York..........	337	557	65
Kansas.............	13	26	100

industrial expansion upon the progress of organization among the wage-earners, with and without the availability of the recent immigrant.

Table 100 shows the ratio of organized workers in each of the two States to its total urban population.[2] The relative number of organized workmen is higher in New York with a large and growing immigrant population drawn from Southern and Eastern Europe than in Kansas with a small and decreasing foreign-born population. Prior to the recent crisis the percentage of organized workmen in New York was more than twice as high as in Kansas. The industrial depression of 1909 reduced the percentage of organized workmen in New York, while in Kansas the year 1908 was a record year for labor organizations. Yet even then the proportion of organized workmen in New York remained higher than in Kansas.

[1] *XIII. Census*, vol. viii. *Manufactures*, Table III, pp. 542, 543.

[2] Urban population is defined by the census as "that residing in cities and other incorporated places of 2500 inhabitants or more." (*XIII. Census*, vol. i. *Population*, p. 53.) The population for 1900 is that enumerated by the census. The urban population for each subsequent year is estimated in accordance with the method followed by the United

TABLE 100.

PER CENT RATIO OF TRADE-UNION MEMBERSHIP TO URBAN POPULATION IN NEW YORK AND KANSAS, 1900–1909.[1]

Year	New York	Kansas
1900	4.6	1.9
1901	5.0	2.3
1902	5.8	2.1
1903	6.7	2.6
1904	6.4	3.0
1905	6.1	3.0
1906	6.2	2.8
1907	6.6	2.9
1908	5.5	5.2
1909	5.3	4.4

The preceding ratios may be affected by the character of the urban population in the two States: if the proportion of wage-earners to the whole population in New York was higher than in Kansas, the difference might in a measure account for the higher percentage of organized workmen. These doubts are resolved by Diagram XXI., which shows for each State the ratio of union membership to the number of industrial wage-earners at the XII. Census.[2] The curve for New York runs throughout the whole period above that for Kansas.

These differences are by no means accidental. In the early period of trade-unionism in the United States, when it was generally regarded as a "foreign" plant and denounced as "un-American," contemporary observers sought to explain the aloofness of the native American wage-earners from labor organizations by their "indisposition to identify themselves permanently with any class."

> The foreign workman has the tradition of many generations and the walls of caste to restrain him within certain limits as to his occupation;

States Bureau of Statistics, by adding to the population of the preceding year one tenth of the increase from 1900 to 1910.

[1] See Appendix, Table XXIV. [2] *Ibid.*

DIAGRAM XXI.

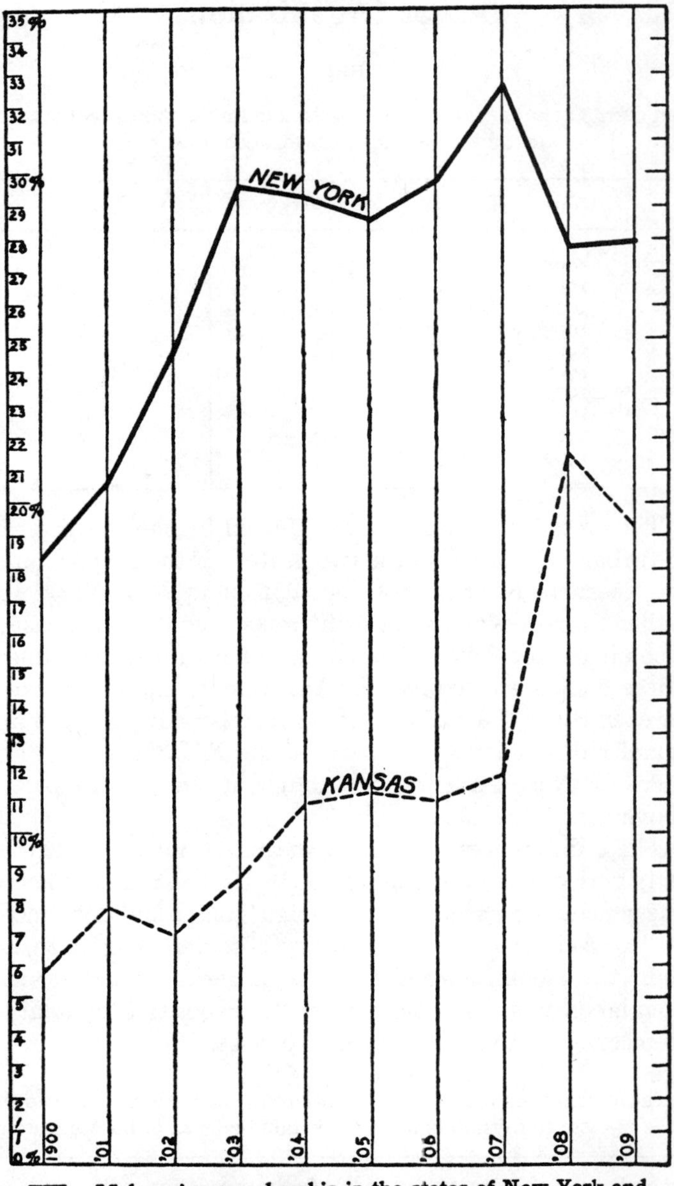

XXI. Male union membership in the states of New York and Kansas, 1900-1909; Per cent. ratio to the number of industrial wage-earners in 1900.

he has no possibilities beyond a given sphere, and is trained and developed within it. Thus environed, his career and ambitions lie in the paths his fathers have trod, and his associations with his fellow craftsmen make the trade union his natural and necessary place. Transported to this country he brings his feelings for the union and his class associations with him as a habit. But the American mechanic's boy is born to no conditions in life from which he may not rise, or hope to rise, or which at least he may not abandon for better or worse. All the precepts of the schools and teachings of observation suggest other ways of making a living, or at least other avenues in life, than those of his father.[1]

In a later publication of the Massachusetts Labor Bureau the unstable character of trade unions in New England up to 1880 is explained by the fact "that early New England workmen seldom regarded their condition as journeymen as likely to be permanent. They nearly all looked forward with some degree of hope to a time when they would become employers."[2]

This condition still exists in smaller communities where many of the native American wage-earners are home-owners,[3] and in country districts where the factory workers are drawn from the farms of the neighborhood. As a result, we find labor better organized in New York City with a high percentage of recent immigrants than in the remainder of the State of New York, with a predominantly native population.

In Table 101, the distribution of male trade-union membership between the city of New York and the remainder of the State is presented in parallel columns with the distribution of male breadwinners in non-agricultural pursuits.

In New York City one half of all breadwinners in 1900 were foreign-born, whereas in the remainder of the State three fourths were of native birth. At the same time New York City had more than its proportionate share of trade-

[1] *Fourth Annual Report of the Illinois Bureau of Statistics of Labor* (1886), p. 228.

[2] *Massachusetts Labor Bulletin*, No. 10, April, 1899, p. 55.

[3] Pratt, *loc. cit.*, p. 99.

TABLE 101.

COMPARATIVE UNION MEMBERSHIP IN THE STATE OF NEW YORK AND IN THE CITY OF NEW YORK, 1900.[1]

Geographical division	Union membership (male)		Male breadwinners in non-agricultural pursuits—per cent	
	Thousands	Per cent	All Nativities	Foreign-born Ratio to total
State	234	100	100	....
New York City	146	62	56	51
Outside of New York City	88	38	44	26

union membership. The margin in favor of New York City would be still greater if instead of all breadwinners industrial wage-earners alone were considered, the proportion of the latter being larger outside of the great cities than in cities with a population of over 300,000.[2]

The figures are for the year 1900. The conditions have not changed since, as appears from Table 102 on p. 343.

The membership of the trade unions in New York City more than doubled from 1900 to 1910, whereas in the remainder of the State it increased by less than three fifths. This difference was not due to a proportionate increase of the population of New York City compared with the urban population of the remainder of the State: while the population of New York City increased somewhat faster than the urban population outside of New York City, the relative number of organized workers in New York City increased still faster. The figures furnish unmistakable evidence of greater progress of trade unions at the gate of the United States, parallel with the growth of the foreign-born popu-

[1] *Report of the New York Bureau of Labor Statistics*, 1910, vol. ii., pp. xlix., l., 15. *Occupations, XII. Census*, Tables 41 and 43.

[2] Hourwich, *loc. cit.*. *Journal of Political Economy*, April, 1911, p. 324.

TABLE 102.

COMPARATIVE UNION MEMBERSHIP IN THE STATE OF NEW YORK AND IN THE CITY OF NEW YORK, 1900–1910.[1]

Both sexes	Year	State	New York City	Outside of New York City
Union membership:		Thousands	Thousands	Thousands
Absolute number	1900	245	154	91
" "	1910	482	338	144
		Per cent	Per cent	Per cent
Increase		....	119	58
Relative number:	1900	100	63	37
" "	1910	100	70	30
Urban population:	1900	100	64	36
" "	1910	100	66	34
Foreign-born white: Ratio to urban population.	1900	....	37	23
	1910	....	40	23

lation, than in the remainder of the State where eight ninths of the population are American-born.

Still, the strength of organized labor is measured above mere numbers by its ability to marshal its forces in contests ver terms of employment. The strike statistics which have been collected by the United States Bureau of Labor do not extend to the period prior to 1881, but there are official figures for Massachusetts going as far back as 1830, and for Pennsylvania as far as 1835. The data are presented in Table 103 on the next page:

[1] *Report of the New York Bureau of Labor Statistics*, 1910, vol. ii., pp. xlix., l., 15. *XIII. Census. Population*, vol. i., pp. 179, 191 (computed).

TABLE 103.

NUMBER OF STRIKES IN MASSACHUSETTS, 1830–1905, AND PENNSYLVANIA, 1835–1905.[1]

	Massachusetts	Pennsylvania
Period:		
Prior to 1880	159	152
1881–1905:		
Total	2774	4156
Annual average	111	166

Making every allowance for the incompleteness of the reports of early strikes, we see once more from the figures for two of the leading industrial States that in the days of "the old immigration" the labor movement was negligible: the average number of strikes in Pennsylvania during one year since 1881 exceeds the total for the preceding half-century.

In order to trace the effect, if any, of the new immigration upon the strike movement, the period 1896–1905, when immigration from Southern and Eastern Europe became predominant, is next compared with the ten-year period next preceding.

Table 104 shows an increase of the number of strikers in general, and of organized strikers in particular. Taking the number of industrial wage-earners in 1890 as the average for 1886–1895 and the number in 1900 as the average for 1896–1905, we find an increase of 34 per cent[2]; the annual average number of strikers increased at the same time 29 per cent, and the annual average of organized strikers 38 per cent. In other words the strike movement kept

[1] *Eleventh Annual Report of the Bureau of Labor Statistics of Massachusetts*, 1880, p. 65. *Report of the Secretary of the Internal Affairs of Pennsylvania*, Part III., *Industrial Statistics*, 1880–1881, p. 388. *Twenty-first Annual Report of the Commissioner of Labor*, 1906, pp. 492–495.

[2] Hourwich, loc. cit. *Journal of Political Economy*, March, 1911, p. 213.

TABLE 104.

STRIKES AND IMMIGRATION OF BREADWINNERS BY DECENNIAL PERIODS, 1886–1905.[1]

Period	Annual average number (thousands)				Per cent of establishments in which strikes failed	
	Immigrant bread winners	Strikers				
		Total	Organized	Unorganized	Organized	Unorganized
1886–1895......	241	267	208	59	41.8	55.2
1896–1905......	389	344	287	57	29.6	58.4

pace with the growing number of industrial wage-earners. The percentage of unsuccessful organized strikes decreased. The movement was apparently not affected either by the increase of immigration, or by the change in its racial make-up.

Immigrants from Southern and Eastern Europe have at times acted as strike breakers, but so have native Americans.[2] In 1904, during the strike of the miners of the Alabama district, "the operators brought in Magyars, Slovaks, Greeks, Servians, Italians, and Finns, *as well as native whites*, as strike breakers."[3] It is a matter of common

[1] *XXI. Annual Report of the Commissioner of Labor*, Table IV, pp. 478–479, and Table V, pp. 490–491. *Reports of the Commissioner-General of Immigration*, 1903–1905. *Summary of Commerce and Finance*, June 1903, pp. 4422–4423. *Statistical Abstract of the United States*, 1910, p. 246, Table 150.

[2] In the big strike of 1877 "many American girls, it was said, acted as strike breakers, replacing Bohemian women." In the cigar industry, in general, "when immigrant women went on strike they were replaced with comparative ease by American girls."—*Report of Woman and Child Wage-Earners in the United States*, vol. ix., p. 199–201.

[3] *Reports of the Immigration Commission*, vol. 9, p. 197. In 1908, "during the strike [of the miners of Birmingham], considerable numbers of immigrants were brought in as strike breakers, but in not so great a proportion as native whites from other coal-mining sections." —*Ibid.*, p. 200.

knowledge, however, that in many strikes of national dimensions, most of the participants were immigrants from Southern and Eastern Europe.

The Immigration Commission has given expression to the popular condemnation of the Southern and Eastern European immigrants for their alleged "tractability" and their "willingness *seemingly* to accept indefinitely without protest certain wages and conditions of employment."[1] It is worthy of note that the same criticism was directed against English immigrants when they were among the "new immigration." The following, from a labor paper published in 1845, has a familiar sound:

> Capital is striving to fill the country with foreign workmen. *English workmen, whose abject condition in their own country has made them tame, submissive* and "peaceable orderly citizens"; that is, work 14 and 16 hours per day, for what capital sees fit to give them, and if it is not enough to provide them a comfortable house to shelter their wives and children and furnish them with decent food and clothes, why they must live in cellars, go hungry and ragged.[2]

To-day the complaint against the immigrants from Southern and Eastern Europe who are "mainly, unskilled laborers," is that "on the whole" they "have not shown the same readiness to join trade-unions . . . as have those coming from the older immigration from the north and west of Europe."[3] In general, as shown, the supposed connection between trade-unionism and the points of the compass is not sustained by the statistics of the Immigration Commission. In regard to unskilled laborers, in particular, it must be borne in mind that "on the whole" they are not eligible "to join trade-unions," the latter being confined mainly to skilled crafts.

There is a tendency among certain theorists to idealize

[1] *Reports of the Immigration Commission*, vol. 1, pp. 531, 541. Jenks and Lauck, *loc. cit.*, pp. 191, 206–207.

[2] *Documentary History of American Industrial Society*, vol. viii., 1840–1860. *Voice of History*, Fitchburg, Massachusetts, Oct. 9, 1845.

[3] Jenks and Lauck, *loc. cit.*, p. 207.

the trade-union in the abstract as the economic organization of "the working class." The craft union, as it exists in real life, not in theory, partakes of the nature of the mediæval guild: its object is to assure work to its members. To accomplish this purpose, it seeks to limit the number of competitors.[1]

To criticise individual union leaders for this attitude is to betray a misconception of the essence of the craft union: its exclusiveness is not an "abuse," it is a policy. To organize "the working class" is not the aim of the trade union.[2] It strives only to organize as many fellow-crafts-

[1] The policy of the flint-glass workers' union is thus described in the *Reports of the Industrial Commission*, vol. xv., p. 325: "Being a highly skilled trade, it is not troubled by the immigration of unskilled laborers. Those who come to this country are mainly from Norway, Sweden, and Alsace-Lorraine, where they have learned their trade. There are two considerations which restrict the entrance of immigrants. First, the initiation fee imposed by the union. This fee was formerly $100 for foreigners, and $3 for Americans. The fee has been reduced to $50 for foreigners, the American fee remaining at $3. There is an opinion in the union that this extreme discrimination against foreigners is not advantageous, as it compels them to enter non-union shops instead of joining the union. This is known to have been the fact in at least one large non-union establishment manned mainly by foreigners." In this case discrimination was practised against highly skilled immigrants from Northern and Western Europe, usually classified as "desirable."

[2] The philosophy of trade-unionism is expressed without equivocation in the following quotation from the testimony of Mr. A. A. Roe, representing the railway brotherhoods, before the committee on Immigration and Naturalization:

"*Mr. Roe.* I take this position, without any hesitancy at all, that as I see it, the influx displaces the workman of this country, the wage-earner, and causes a competition for his position, increases the number of applicants for work. This brought into existence the organizations, drove men together. They had to get into the organizations to give them power to maintain their position, to save the comforts of their homes, and if you say that is a good thing, well and good.

"*Mr. Sabath.* It is a good condition: organization is a good condition, and if they are responsible for any improvements in the condition of the workingmen, then they are entitled to thanks.

"*Mr. Roe.* *A better condition would be one that would not require the*

men as are necessary to control the trade. There is no place for the unskilled laborer in the trade-union of the prevailing type. There are situations where the interests of the craft union may be antagonistic to organization among the unskilled, as has been exemplified in the recent Lawrence strike.

The United Textile Workers' Union of America, of which Mr. John Golden is president, for many years previous to the strike, had at Lawrence an organization confined to the skilled men in the mills. It was easy for the mill owners to satisfy the demands of the few skilled men, who were but a very small fraction of the whole labor force. They were willing to remain at work. The demands of the thousands of unskilled workers, however, could not be satisfied without a greater financial sacrifice than the mill owners were prepared to make. The suspension of work caused by the strike of the immigrants from Southern and Eastern Europe and Asia Minor was an injury to the members of the United Textile Workers' Union, who had nothing to gain from the success of the strike. Viewing the controversy not from an altruistic, but from a business point of view, they naturally sided with the mill owners against the strikers, "comforted that the whirligig of time was bringing them around as bulwarks of conservatism even in the eyes of the employers."[1] This diversity of economic interests of the aristocracy of skilled labor and of the masses of unskilled men, women, and children accounts for the fact that "the English-speaking labor men have not been urged by such a missionary zeal toward the recent immigrants as should have been theirs on human grounds no more than on the basis of sound association among the whole labor force."[2]

---

organization; would not make the organization necessary. *A better condition would be one where* hours, conditions of employment, and wages were such that *organization of labor for these purposes was unnecessary.*" —Hearings before the Commission on Immigration and Naturalization, House of Representatives, Sixty-first Congress, p. 256.

[1] Robert A. Woods: "The Clod Stirs," *The Survey*, March 16, 1912, pp. 1930–1931.

[2] *Ibid.*

Discussing the possibilities of organization among the unskilled, a student of organized labor says:

> The immigrant is usually accustomed to some form of social organization. He is not as individualistic as is the typical American. He can be organized with others into labor unions; and when the unskilled immigrants from a variety of birthplaces are thus associated, the resulting union is usually strong, coherent, and easily directed by capable and enthusiastic leaders. The McKees Rocks strike furnishes an excellent illustration of the solidarity of the unskilled when organized.[1]

On the home training of Italian immigrants in organization the report of the Immigration Commission contains interesting material, which unfortunately has been disregarded in its conclusions.

> In recent years the labor-union movement has grown rapidly and to large proportions among the industrial as well as the agricultural workers of Italy, and it is said that the activities of the unions have helped to advance wages in both fields. In 1907, according to *Annuario Statistico* for 1905–1907, there were 2950 industrial unions in the Kingdom, with a total of 362,533 members. From 1901 to 1904, inclusive, there were 3032 industrial strikes, involving 621,737 workers, and in the various years from 63 to 80 per cent of the strikes were reported as "successful" or "partly successful."[2]

The most noteworthy feature of this movement is the progress of organization among farm hands, which has no counterpart in the United States. The statistics presented in Table 105 show that even the despised South Italian farm laborer is capable of organization and concerted action.

On the labor movement in Russia, a compilation of statistics from Russian official sources has been published by the United States Bureau of Labor.

Previous to the revolution of 1905, labor organizations and strikes were treated as conspiracies in Russia. During the revolution the severity of the law was relaxed for a short time, but with the suppression of the revolution the old repressive policy was resumed. Thus the only oppor-

[1] Carlton: *loc. cit.*, pp. 346–347.

[2] *Reports of the Immigration Commission*, vol. 4 (in press).

TABLE 105.

AGRICULTURAL LABOR UNIONS AND STRIKES AMONG AGRICULTURAL LABORERS IN ITALY.[1]

Geographical division	Local unions, 1901		Strikes, 1901 to 1904 inclusive	
	Number	Membership	Number	Participants
Northern Italy....	289	49,884	701	171,911
The rest of the Kingdom.......	1014	229,629	404	315,229
Total........	1303	278,513	1105[2]	487,140

tunity the wage-warners of the Russian Empire had to show their capacity for organization and concerted action was in 1905. According to the statistics published by the Russian government, the total number of strikers in factories and mines during the year 1905 was 2,915,000. This figure does not include the railways and the postal-telegraph service, which were completely paralyzed by the strikes of 1905.[3] According to the census of 1897, the total number of railroad employees, exclusive of administrative officials, was 682,000 and the total number of employees in the postal-telegraph service, exclusive of higher officials, was 75,000.[4] The total number of strikers for the year 1905 may therefore be conservatively estimated at 3,672,000. The highest number of strikers recorded in the United States for any one year between 1881 and 1905 was 533,000, in 1902.[5] The strikes in the factories of the Russian Empire in 1905 affected 32.6 per cent of all establishments under

[1] *Reports of the Immigration Commission*, vol. 4, Table 17 (condensed).

[2] Of the 1105 strikes among agricultural laborers a large majority were reported as successful or partly successful.

[3] *Bulletin of the Bureau of Labor*, No. 86: I. M. Rubinow, *Foreign Statistical Publications*, Russia, p. 284.

[4] *Prémier Récensement Général de la Population de l'Empire de Russie*, 1897, vol. ii., pp. 11, 250–251.

[5] *Statistical Abstract of the United States*, 1909, p. 240.

factory inspection, comprising 60 per cent of all wage-earners.[1]

The strikes in the Russian Empire drew together wage-earners of all those nationalities which make up the bulk of our immigration from Russia: Hebrews, Poles, Lithuanians, Russians, and Ruthenians (South Russians).

It is evident that a good many of the immigrants from Russia, Poland, and Italy bring with them an understanding of the aims of organized labor. These immigrants serve as a nucleus of organization among their countrymen.[2] This fact has been brought to the attention of the American public in the recent strikes of the garment workers and textile mill operatives.

From all available data it is clear that if organized labor in the United States has not succeeded in welding together a majority of the wage-earners and in securing for them a greater share of the prosperity of the country, the fault is not with immigration in general, nor with immigration from Southern and Eastern Europe in particular. Race prejudice, which the coming of the immigrant has increased among the English-speaking workers is considered by some writers among the contributory causes which have retarded the development of unionism in this country.[3] The primary cause, however, is the substitution of machinery for human skill, which is taking the ground from the craft union. Since the unskilled labor which has superseded the labor of the skilled mechanic is performed by recent immigrants, the breakdown of the old organization is conceived by the trade-unionist as the effect of recent immigration. This view is given expression in the following statement:

In the occupations and industries in which the pressure of the competition of the recent immigrant has been directly felt, either because

[1] *Bulletin of the Bureau of Labor*, No. 86, pp. 271–272.

[2] Since these lines were written (in 1912) the revolution in Russia and the great strikes of 1920 in Italy have made labor a dominant force in the economic and political life of those countries.

[3] Carlton, *loc. cit.*, p. 63.

the nature of the work was such as to permit of the immediate employment of the immigrant or through the invention of improved machinery his employment was made possible in occupations which formerly required training and apprenticeship, the labor organizations have been, in a great many cases, completely overwhelmed and disrupted.[1]

Where the invention of improved machinery has dispensed with the necessity of training and apprenticeship, it is plain that labor organizations which were built upon special training and apprenticeship were doomed to die a natural death for want of supporters. Could a union of blacksmiths be maintained in a modern foundry where steam hammers are used? With the occupation of the blacksmith gone, his union must inevitably have been "disrupted" even in a purely American community without a single immigrant from Southern and Eastern Europe.

Another obstacle to the progress of trade-unionism is that the principal industries to-day are controlled by combinations, which have reduced competition among employers of labor to a minimum. A trust can afford to hold out in a strike as long as it chooses, since it can shift its losses to the consumers. The workmen, on the contrary, cannot strike without end. As a result, "the unions have practically disappeared from the trusts, and are disappearing from the large corporations."[2]

[1] Jenks and Lauck, *loc. cit.*, p. 192.

[2] Prof. Commons in the *American Journal of Sociology*, vol. xiii., (1908), p. 759.

CHAPTER XVI

PAUPERISM AND CRIME

A. Introductory

THE preceding review of comparative statistics and descriptive history of labor conditions in the past and present has disclosed no evidence in support of the view that the economic interests of the wage-earner have suffered in consequence of immigration. But it is claimed that the evil effects of immigration show themselves in an alarming increase of pauperism and crime. The statistics of dependency and delinquency, however, give no occasion for alarm. According to an investigation made by the Bureau of Immigration, the total number of inmates of penal institutions, insane asylums, and almshouses in 1908 was 610,477,[1] which included native and naturalized citizens and aliens. The enumeration of the same classes by the Bureau of the Census in 1904 gave their number as 634,877.[2] A comparison of these figures clearly shows that the large immigration of the five-year period 1903–1908 was accompanied by an actual decrease of pauperism and crime.

Whether or not the number of paupers in charitable institutions can "serve as a general index of prevailing distress,"[3] is beside the question: the contention is that pauperism is

[1] *Report of the Commissioner-General of Immigration*, 1908, p. 96.

[2] *Benevolent Institutions*, p. 12. *Paupers in Almshouses*, p. 6. *Insane and Feeble-minded in Hospitals and Institutions*, pp. 6, 107. *Prisoners and Juvenile Delinquents*, pp. 14, 228.

[3] *Paupers in Almhouses*, p. 8.

on the increase, whereas the latest statistics show that the millions of recent immigrants imposed no new burdens upon the charitable and penal institutions of the country.

B. Pauperism

The Immigration Commission, in its conclusions, notes a decrease of pauperism among immigrants of the present day, compared with the past.

> The number of those admitted who receive assistance from organized charity in cities is relatively small. In the Commission's investigation which covered the activities of the associated charities in 43 cities, including practically all the larger immigrant centers except New York, it was found that a small percentage of the cases represented immigrants who had been in the United States three years or under, while nearly half of all the foreign-born cases were those who had been in the United States twenty years or more. This investigation was conducted during the winter of 1908–09 before industrial activities had been fully resumed following the financial depression of 1907–8, and this inquiry showed that the recent immigrants, even in cities in times of relative industrial inactivity, did not seek charitable assistance in any considerable numbers.[1]

The records of the charitable institutions of New York City also show that the recent immigrant races furnish a much smaller relative number of applicants for charity than the old immigrant races. Table 106 gives the nativity of lodgers who were sheltered in the Municipal Lodging House in New York City during the first quarter of the year 1908, when the crisis was in its acutest stage.

The immigrants from Southern and Eastern Europe furnished less than their proportion of homeless men even in a period of industrial depression. The population tables of the XIII. Census for New York City are not as detailed as those of the XII. Census. It may be inferred, however, from the published figures that the ratio of pauperism relative to population must have been still more favorable to the races of Southern and Eastern Europe than shown in Table 106.

[1] *Reports of the Immigration Commission*, vol. 1, p. 36.

TABLE 106.

PER CENT DISTRIBUTION, BY NATIVITY, OF LODGERS AT MUNICIPAL LODGING HOUSE IN NEW YORK CITY DURING JANUARY, FEBRUARY, AND MARCH, 1908, AND OF THE MALE POPULATION 21 YEARS OF AGE AND OVER AT THE XII. CENSUS.[1]

Nativity	Lodgers 1908	Males of full age, 1900
Total	100.0	100.0
English-speaking:		
United States	46.2	45.7
Ireland	21.1	10.9
England, Scotland, and Wales	6.9	4.1
Germany	9.5	15.3
Scandinavian	1.7	2.0
France	0.5	0.6
Russia	4.0	5.8
Austria	2.3	2.8
Italy	1.4	6.3
Miscellaneous	6.4	6.3
English-speaking	74.2	60.7
All others	25.8	39.3
Native	46.2	45.7
Foreign-born	53.8	54.3
Northern and Western Europe	39.7	32.9
Eastern and Southern Europe	7.7	14.9
Other countries	6.4	6.3

The increase of the Russian population of New York City in 1900–1910 was 168 per cent, which raised it to 10.3 per cent of the total population of the city; the proportion of adult males in a national group comprising many recent immigrants must necessarily have increased at a greater rate. The increase of the Italians amounted to 134 per cent, and that of the Austrians to 110 per cent.[2]

It might be argued that the higher ratio of dependency

[1] *Report of the Commission of Immigration of the State of New York*, p. 201. *XII. Census. Population*, Part I., Table 83, pp. 938–945; Table 80, pp. 930–931.

[2] *XIII. Census. Population*, vol. i., pp. 178, 826–827.

among the Irish is the result of their "displacement by the Southern and Eastern Europeans." It was shown, however, by the Industrial Commission that in pauperism the Irish had always been in the lead. The demonstration of this fact is given in Table 107, which shows that in 1885–1895, when the Italians and Hebrews from Russia and Austria were but a small fraction of the population of New York City, and even as far back as 1854–1860, when there were practically none at all, the preponderance of the Irish among the recipients of charity was as great as in more recent years.

TABLE 107.

PER CENT DISTRIBUTION, BY NATIVITY, OF FOREIGN-BORN RECIPIENTS OF CHARITY, 1854–1860, AND 1885–1895, AND OF THE POPULATION OF NEW YORK CITY, 1855 AND 1890.[1]

Country of birth	Population 1855	Relief granted 1854–1860	Population 1890	Almshouse paupers 1885–1895
Total for all nativities	100.0	100.0	100.0	100.0
Ireland	27.9	69.0	12.6	60.4
England, Scotland, and Wales	5.1	4.5	3.1	6.6
Germany	15.2	10.8	14.0	14.0
Italy	.....	....	2.6	0.7
Russia and Austria-Hungary (Hebrews)	.....	....	3.0	0.0

The proportion of English and Irish paupers in Boston in the '30's and '40's was about the same as in New York City half a century later:

TABLE 108.

COMPARATIVE PERCENTAGE OF ENGLISH AND IRISH PAUPERS IN BOSTON, 1837–1845, AND IN NEW YORK CITY, 1885–1895.[2]

In Boston	1837–1840	61.7
	1841–1845	59.2
In New York City	1885–1895	64.8

[1] *Report of the Industrial Commission*, vol. xv., pp. 460, 480.

[2] *Census of Boston*, 1845, pp. 110–111. *Report of the Industrial Commission*, vol. xv., p. 480.

It is evident from the preceding figures that recent immigration is not responsible for the high percentage of pauperism among the old English-speaking immigrants. Dr. Kate H. Claghorn, after an exhaustive statistical study of immigration in its relation to pauperism, comes to the conclusion that pauperism "is the result of a considerable period of life and experiences here." It is not the able-bodied workmen and their families, but the industrial invalids that make up the lists of applicants for charity.[1]

Unemployment is responsible for but a minority of the cases of pauperism, as appears from Table 109, based upon a classification of 7225 Charity Organization Society cases in New York City:

TABLE 109.

PER CENT DISTRIBUTION OF CHARITY CASES IN NEW YORK CITY, BY NATIVITY AND CAUSES OF NEED (YEAR).[2]

Nativity	Per cent of total for each nationality		
	Unemployment	Other misfortune	All other causes
American	24.57	44.27	31.16
English	24.68	43.47	31.85
Irish	18.87	47.39	33.74
German	28.62	50.66	20.72
Italian	30.85	47.66	21.49
Russian and Polish	23.87	61.26	14.87

[1] "The census of 1890 showed that 92 per cent of the foreign-born male almshouse paupers had been in this country ten years or more. . . Overwork, poor food, and life in the airless, sunless, and crowded tenements of the city, or in the equally crowded and even more unsanitary dwellings of the mill or the mining town—the conditions accompanying the early stages of the immigrant's progress—tend strongly to break down the physical health of the sturdy Italian or Austrian peasants, or even of the Jews, more accustomed to the unsanitary conditions of city life." —Kate H. Claghorn: *Immigration in its Relation to Pauperism. Annals of the American Academy of Political and Social Science*, July, 1904, pp. 187–200.

[2] *Ibid.*, p. 199.

C. Crime

One of the favorite arguments against immigration since the days of the Know-Nothings has been the assertion that "the foreigner in proportion to his numbers furnishes by far the greater part of crime."[1] In the middle of the nineteenth century the Irish immigrant was the object of popular odium as $\frac{1}{154}$ of a potential criminal.[2] Fifty years later the suspicion turned upon "the undesirable immigrants from Southern and Eastern Europe." Although the latest statistics of prisoners, published by the Bureau of the Census simultaneously with the creation of the Immigration Commission, showed "that the popular belief that the foreign-born are filling the prisons has little foundation in fact,"[3] yet the Immigration Commission approached the subject under the influence of the popular prejudice. In its report on *Emigration Conditions in Europe* the Commission lends its support to "the not unfounded belief that certain kinds of criminality are inherent in the Italian race." Accompanying this inherent criminal tendency, in the opinion of the Commission, "is also a seemingly inherent ability to avoid arrest and conviction." The evidence in support of this indictment of the whole Italian race is merely circumstantial. There has been a "remarkable decrease in the number of murders and homicides in Italy," and, it is alleged, there has been a "startling growth of Italian criminality of the same nature in the United States." Although it "obviously cannot be mathematically determined" . . . "to what extent emigration is responsible for the decrease of crime in

[1] Sydney G. Fisher: "Immigration and Crime," *Popular Science Monthly*, September, 1896, p. 625.

[2] "The newspapers and pamphlets of that time published statistics which showed that, although the foreign population was only an eighth of the whole, yet it furnished . . . 1000 more criminals than all the remaining seven eighths of the people. . . .—Every one-hundred and fifty-four of them produced a criminal."—*Ibid.* These early statistics were discredited by later criticism. *Cf.* Roland P. Falkner: *Statistics of Crime in United States.*

[3] *Prisoners*, 1904, p. 41.

Italy," yet "in view of the fact that the decrease has been coincident with the emigration movement, and also with the" supposed "growth of Italian criminality in the United States, it is impossible to avoid the conclusion that these . . . results . . . had been due in large part to the emigration to this country of criminals and the criminally inclined." The Commission concedes that "there are of course other elements which should be taken into consideration, such as the advance of civilization and the better enforcement of law in parts of Italy," but these considerations are of little weight. To be sure, according to Italian statistics of crime, "Sicily, which has a large emigration, and Liguria, which has much the smallest emigration in proportion to population, show nearly the same per cent of decrease," in murders and homicides. But these facts are of no consequence. The homicidal tendency of the Italian immigrant is proved, on the one hand, by the fact that in certain provinces which "furnish the greatest number of transoceanic emigrants according to the population, there has been an exceptionally large decrease in the number of murders and homicides committed," and, on the other hand, by the fact, "that the prevalence of murder and homicide is as a rule much greater in Compartimenti which furnish the largest number of transoceanic emigrants, and consequently are the source of the greater part of the Italian movement to the United States."[1]

This criminological theory is significant in so far only as it betrays the bias of the Commission against the immigrant. Yet, notwithstanding its strong prejudice, which no evidence could overcome, the results of its investigation prove to the satisfaction of its own interpreters, that, "undue significance has been attached" to the supposed effects of immigration upon criminality.

"The number of . . . criminals arriving . . . taken as a percentage of the whole coming is so small that little heed need be paid to it."

"Although available statistical material is too small to

[1] *Reports of the Immigration Commission*, vol. 4, pp. 204, 205, 209.

draw positive conclusions, such material as is available would indicate that immigrants are no more inclined toward criminality on the whole than are native Americans."

"It is impossible to produce satisfactory evidence that immigration has resulted in an increase of crime out of proportion to the increase in the adult population."[1]

The State of New York, which is more affected by immigration than any other State in the Union, has compiled annual statistics of crime commencing with the year 1830. The results of an analysis of these statistics, by the writer, are briefly summed up in the following paragraphs.[2]

Surveying the general trend for the seventy-five year period 1830–1905, we find that the increase of crime has merely kept pace with the growth of population. The relative rate of criminality in 1890 was the same as in 1840, notwithstanding the change in the racial composition of the population of the State. In the year 1900 there was just one more conviction for every 100,000 of the population than in 1890, and in 1905 four convictions per 100,000 people in excess of 1900. The fluctuations of the movement of population and of the rate of criminality indicate that the causes which are favorable to the growth of population tend to reduce crime, and *vice versa*, the causes which retard the growth of population are productive of an increase of crime.

The effects of immigration upon criminality can be traced from 1850 when the census inquiries for the first time took notice of nativity. The statistics for the half-century following show that an increase of the percentage of the foreign-born population is accompanied by a decrease of criminality, and vice versa. During the latest ten-year period, 1900–1909, the wave of criminality rose when immigration was at its lowest ebb, while the high-tide of immigration was contemporaneous with a decrease of crime.

[1] Jenks and Lauck, *loc. cit.*, pp. 51, 52, 65.

[2] For a detailed statistical analysis of the data upon which these conclusions are based, the reader is referred to an article by the present writer on "Immigration and Crime," in *The American Journal of Sociology*, January, 1912.

Thus it is found that in the social profit-and-loss account, crime and immigration figure on the opposite sides of the ledger. Immigration does not impair the worker's opportunities to earn a living; on the contrary increase of immigration goes parallel with increase of business prosperity and decrease of crime.

PART III.

IMMIGRANTS IN THE LEADING INDUSTRIES

[The Immigration Commission has devoted several volumes of its report to a description of labor conditions in special industries which are generally believed to typify the evils of recent immigration. Of these, five will be considered in this part.]

CHAPTER XVII

THE GARMENT WORKERS

THE manufacture of clothing in the United States is an immigrant industry. Immigrants have furnished the labor and in most instances the capital.[1] The labor conditions in this industry have attracted wide public attention by frequent strikes, ever since the Russian Jews have become the predominant element among the operatives. The clothing industry has become associated in the public mind with the sweating system, and since the employees are, with few exceptions, immigrants from Southern and Eastern Europe, the conclusion is readily reached that the root of the sweating system is in the character of the new immigration. This view draws support from the attitude of the United Garment Workers of America, an organization of Jewish garment workers, which, at its annual convention in 1905, adopted a resolution demanding restriction of further immigration for the protection of the foreign-born workers already here.[2] And yet a dispassionate study of

[1] *Reports of the Immigration Committee*, vol. 11, p. 417.

[2] John R. Commons, *Races and Immigrants in America*, p. 115.

the clothing industry shows that labor conditions have very substantially improved with the coming of the "new immigration."

The sweating system did not originate with the Jewish clothing workers: it preceded them by more than half a century. In the *Report of Woman and Child Wage-Earners in the United States*, recently published by the United States Bureau of Labor, we find a vast amount of information on the employment of women in the clothing industry in the first third of the nineteenth century, at the time when the wage-earners were nearly all American-born.

> The history of this period, like that of the better-known period of the machine, is a tale of long hours, low wages, and exploitation. The "sweating system," indeed, in the broad sense of that term, was established in this country at the very beginning of the ready-made garment business and has developed simultaneously with that business. The contract system established stages and degrees of sweating, but a study of the sweating system would have to extend back at least as far as the beginning, in 1828, of Matthew Carey's agitation in the interests of . . . the working women, of whom he estimated that there were in Philadelphia, New York, Boston, and Baltimore between 18,000 and 20,000. . . . The disclosures made by Matthew Carey during the course of his investigation and agitation in behalf of the sewing women seem, though quaintly worded, very modern in their substance. It was set forth, for example, in the resolutions passed at a meeting in Philadelphia on February 21, 1829, that "it requires great expertness, unceasing industry from sunrise till 10 or 11 o'clock at night, constant employment (which very few of them have) without any interruption whatever from sickness, or attention to their families, to earn a dollar and a half a week, and, in many cases, a half or a third of their time is expended in attending their children, and no small portion in traveling eight, ten or fourteen squares for work, and as many to take it back when finished." . . . The committee appointed at this meeting reported: "That . . . the wages paid to seamstresses who work in their own apartments—to spoolers, to spinners, to folders of printed books—and in many cases to those who take in washing, are utterly inadequate to their support, even if fully employed . . . whereas the work is so precarious that they are often unemployed—sometimes for a whole week together, and very frequently one or two days in each week."[1]

---

[1] Helen L. Sumner: "History of Women in Industries of the United

In Boston (in 1830) the average weekly wages of a woman garment worker, when fully employed, were given by a contemporary writer as but a dollar or a dollar and a quarter, while the common rent of a room was a dollar a week.[1]

In other words, the weekly wages of a Boston working woman were barely sufficient to provide for rent. While fully employed, she was not self-supporting, but had to depend upon her family for the necessities of life.

In Baltimore, too, in 1833, the wages of sewing women were declared not sufficient for the genteel support of the single individual who performs the work, although she may use every effort of industry which her constitution is capable of sustaining.[2]

Instances of the sweating system are again recorded in 1844, still before the first inrush of Irish immigration. It was reported

that a man and two women working together from twelve to sixteen hours a day earned a dollar amongst them, and that the women, if they did not belong to the family, received each about $1.25 a week for their work, the man paying out of the remaining $3.50 about $1.00 a week for rent of his garret.[3]

From 1850, the Irish workers became predominant in the clothing industry. At that period the clothing industry in New York City was in its infancy. There were no factories, and the workers occupied small rooms or sweatshops.[4]

In 1853 the investigation of the clothing trade made by the New York *Tribune* disclosed the existence of a "middle system." For example, near one of the streets running from the Bowery to the East River an old Irish woman was found who had four girls at work for her, their compensation consisting solely of food for six days of the week. In another case a woman had hired four "learners," two of whom received only board and lodging, and the other two $1.00 a week each without food.[5]

States." *Report of Woman and Child Wage-Earners in the United States*, vol. ix., pp. 123–124. [1] *Ibid.*, p. 125. [2] *Ibid.*, p. 126.

[3] *Ibid.*, p. 141.

[4] *Reports of the Immigration Commission*, vol. 11, p. 369.

[5] Sumner, *loc. cit.*, pp. 141–142.

According to the Immigration Commission, the "displacement of the old races by the new, or recent, immigrants" has been "one resulting through the willingness of the 'raw' immigrants to accept lower wages than those who have been in this country for a longer period of time."[1] Yet when the earnings of the "raw" immigrant women of the present day are compared with those of the "old races," it is found that the native American and the Irish working women of past generations were "willing" to work only for board and lodging, or even for board alone, depending upon their families for other necessities, whereas the Jewish factory girls are at least self-supporting. The question is not whether wages to-day are all that could be desired, but whether they have been reduced by recent immigration, and Dr. Sumner's historical research proves the contrary.

One of the chief factors which kept down the wages of working women in the early history of the clothing industry was country competition.

"We know instances," said the New York *Morning News*, in 1845, "where shirtwaist makers put their work out in the country in the winter at 11 cents each. The work is done by those who do not make it a means of living, but use it merely as an auxiliary to dress." The *Voice of Industry* too, stated in 1845 that "a gentleman told us, the other day, that he saw the daughter of a respectable farmer making shirts at 11 cents apiece, for one of the dealers. He asked her whether she thought it a sufficient price. 'No,' said she, 'if I were obliged to support myself, I could not do it by this work; but I merely employ my time which otherwise I should not use.'"

In the same year the chairwoman of a meeting of working women in New York said that she knew several employers who paid only from 10 to 18 cents per day, and that one employer, who offered girls 20 cents per day, told them that if they did not take it "he would obtain girls from Connecticut who would work for less even than what he offered."

By 1850, the cheap labor of the farmhouse is said to have been employed "in the getting up of clothing, skirts, stocks, hosiery, suspenders, carriage trappings, buttons, and a hundred other light things."[2]

---

[1] *Reports of the Immigration Commission*, vol. 11., p. 369.

[2] Sumner, *loc. cit.*, pp. 140–141.

These conditions have changed as the direct result of immigration. The rapid growth of the wage-working population created a market for ready-made clothing.

> These new branches of work, whereby a product, which when formerly made by the custom tailor, the dressmaker, or the housewife cost higher prices than most of the people could afford, is now made in the latest styles, enable all classes of people to be better dressed and to spend much more money every year for clothing. Herein the immigrant has created his own employment.[1]

The expansion of the clothing industry was made possible by the introduction of the factory system with its greater efficiency than home work. The operation of a factory requires a regular force of employees whose livelihood must be provided for by their wages. This is the reason why the immigrant girl from Southern or Eastern Europe cannot accept the low wages which the daughters of native American farmers regarded as satisfactory. A development peculiar to the factory method of clothing manufacturing was the substitution of male for female labor, with a consequent increase of the rate of wages.

The view that the new immigrants tend to lower the wages of the older immigrants apparently finds support in the statistics of the Immigration Commission, which show for each race at present employed in the clothing industry "a general increase in weekly earnings with the increased period of residence."[2] In other words, the earnings of the recent immigrants are lower than those of the older immigrants, because, it is explained, "the immigrants of long residence have acquired a higher standard of living and consequently demand a higher wage."[3] Quite naturally then, "the older employees are unable to meet the competition of the recent immigrants, whose demands are not great."[4]

The reasoning sounds plausible, still it will not stand close

[1] *Report of the Industrial Commission*, vol. xv., p. xxvii.

[2] *Reports of the Immigration Commission*, vol. 11, p. 380.

[3] *Ibid.*, p. 370.

[4] *Ibid.*

scrutiny. Indeed, if the fact that the older immigrants "demand a higher wage" be sufficient to secure to them an actual increase in weekly earnings, then there is nothing to prevent them from demanding and securing a higher wage, notwithstanding the competition of the recent immigrants. If, on the contrary, the older employees are unable to meet the competition of the recent immigrants, then the increased period of residence could not help them to a "general increase in weekly earnings." The fallacy of the Commission's reasoning is due to the fact that it mistakes cause for effect: higher earnings are not the effect, but the cause, of a higher standard of living. Wages in the labor market are not determined by the amount the worker desires to spend, but by the services he is able to render. It is plain that competition would not permit the clothing manufacturer to pay higher wages to an older employee merely as a reward for long residence, if recent immigrants could be hired to do the same work more cheaply. If the older employees are able to command, not merely to "demand," a higher wage, it is evidently because their services are worth more than the "inexperienced labor" of the newcomers. And it is equally evident that the immigrants who "must have work on landing in New York, and . . . find their way to the clothing manufactories,"[1] do not compete with the older employees for the higher positions requiring experience.

But it is said that the new immigrants "annually crowd the shops of the city (of New York) in thousands, forcing workers who have preceded them to move up in the scale of occupation or to enter other employment. . . . Some of the displaced workers have opened tailoring or repair shops of their own, others have gone into the shops of custom tailors, and many have entered other lines of work."[2] In every-day language, the opening of a shop by a former wage-worker is not called "displacement," but advance-

[1] *Reports of the Immigration Commission*, vol. 11, p. 370.
[2] *Ibid.*

ment. Custom tailoring requires a higher grade of skill than the manufacturing of ready-made clothing. If a clothing worker vacates his place in the factory to accept a better position with a custom tailor and the vacancy is filled by a new immigrant, no one in the trade will conceive the change as "displacement" of the older employee by a new hand. There remain only the undefined "other lines of work," into which the incoming thousands are said to have crowded those of their predecessors whom they could not "force" to move up. A sidelight upon this residue is thrown by the narrative of the history of the clothing industry in Baltimore. The first people employed in the clothing shops of that city were

> the Germans, who entered the country in large numbers immediately after the Civil War. Since that time the Russian Hebrews, Lithuanians, Poles, Italians, and Bohemians have settled in the city and found employment in the clothing shops, *displacing* the Germans in the unskilled occupations, and *forcing them up into higher work.* It is also noticed that, as the Russian Hebrews and Poles work up into the skilled occupations, the Germans leave the industry and enter new fields. This *displacement seems to be self-displacement*, as there is work for all—more work than there are laborers—but the Germans are progressive, and *as the new races have engaged in the clothing industry they have risen in the scale of occupations*, and in many instances have left the industry and found employment in other skilled trades.[1]

Thus we learn that, at least in Baltimore, those who have left the industry have "found employment in other skilled trades," and that the "displacement" is therefore "self-displacement"; in other words, no displacement at all. Expressed in more exact language, the report of the Commission shows that the clothing industry of Baltimore has grown more rapidly than the supply of labor. The expansion of the industry created new positions for skilled workers; these positions were filled first by Germans, next by Russian Hebrews and Poles. This expansion not being confined to the manufacturing of clothing, other indus-

[1] *Reports of the Immigration Commission*, vol. 11, p. 411.

tries offered opportunities of which the Germans availed themselves.

It is reasonable to assume that if there is "more work than there are laborers" in Baltimore, the clothing manufacturers of that city would have sufficient enterprise to import some of the thousands who "crowd the shops" of New York City. The fact is that the expansion of the clothing industry in New York has been a great deal faster than in Baltimore, as appears from Table 110 below. It is therefore quite probable that the relation between the demand for, and supply of, labor in the shops of New York is the same as in Baltimore.

TABLE 110.

COMPARATIVE GROWTH OF THE VALUE OF THE PRODUCTS OF THE CLOTHING INDUSTRY IN NEW YORK AND BALTIMORE, 1890–1905.[1]

City	Millions of dollars			Per cent of increase		
	1890	1900	1905	1890–1900	1900–1905	1890–1905
New York....	119	206	306	73	49	157
Baltimore.....	16	20	23	25	15	44

The statistics of the Immigration Commission do not disclose any tendency on the part of the new immigrant races to accept lower wages than the immigrants of older races. (See Table 111 on page 370.) The percentage of recent German immigrants earning $15 a week or over is much less than the percentage of Hebrews and Russians and about the same as the percentage of Italians with the same average earnings. On the opposite end, the percentage of Germans earning less than $10 a week within the first five years of their residence in the United States is somewhat greater than that of Hebrews, Russians, Poles, and

[1] *Census Reports, Manufactures*, 1905, Part I, Table CLXVIII., p. ccxxxiii.

Bohemians. These figures show that the "new immigration" does not underbid the immigrants of the older races. On the other hand, the variation in the earnings of representatives of each race indicates that the rate of wages is not determined by racial factors, but depends upon the personal qualifications and opportunities of individual workers.

TABLE III.

PER CENT DISTRIBUTION OF FOREIGN-BORN ADULT MALE CLOTHING WORKERS, 18 YEARS OF AGE AND OVER, RESIDING IN THE UNITED STATES LESS THAN FIVE YEARS, BY RACE AND WEEKLY EARNINGS.[1]

Race	Under $10	$10 to $15	$15 and over
Hebrew (not Russian)	33.9	42.2	23.9
Hebrew (Russian)	39.1	39.9	21.0
Russian	35.3	46.8	17.9
Lithuanian	40.2	49.8	10.0
Italian, North	45.3	45.3	9.4
German	40.0	51.4	8.6
Italian, South	57.6	33.9	8.5
Polish	37.4	54.1	8.5
Bohemian and Moravian	35.5	57.0	7.5

The Immigration Commission speaks in general terms of the "availability of cheap woman and child labor of the immigrant households" for locating "men's and women's clothing manufacturing establishments" in certain districts "developed in connection with some of the principal industries of the country."[2] But the statistics of the Commission show that the earnings of recent immigrant women and children in the clothing industry are higher than those of native Americans. Thus, adult Russian Hebrew women averaged $8.09 per week, Polish women, $8.07, North Italian women, $7.54, whereas native women of native American parentage earned only $7.41 per week. The majority of Polish women (55.4 per cent) earned more than $7.50 per

[1] *Reports of the Immigration Commission*, vol. II, p. 301, Table 35.
[2] *Ibid.*, vol. I, p. 541.

week, while the majority of American women of native parentage (57.2 per cent) earned less than that amount.[1] The same is true of girls between the ages of 14 and 18. Russian Hebrew girls earned on an average $6.13 per week, other Hebrew girls $6.24, South Italian girls $5.56, Polish girls $5.25, whereas native American girls of native parentage made only $5.02 per week. Nearly one half (45.9 per cent) of the latter earned less than $5 while only a little over one fourth (27.4 per cent) of the Russian Hebrew girls earned less than that amount.[2]

Confronted with these facts, Professors Jenks and Lauck seek to explain them by the assumption that "the lower earnings of the American women" are due "to their inability and disinclination to work such long hours as the foreign-born females in the case of certain piece-rate occupations, as, for example, the clothing industry."[3] This explanation, however, is purely a matter of conjecture, since the Immigration Commission has made no inquiries regarding hours of labor in the clothing industry. As shown above, the hours were long in the factories and sweatshops when the women workers were all Americans, and were reduced with the coming of immigrants. The inquiry of the Industrial Commission concerning the hours of labor in the clothing industry in Pennsylvania brought out the fact that the working hours averaged ten per day alike in the city shops where the employees were Jews and Italians, and in country shops, where none but Americans were employed.[4]

The investigations of the Industrial Commission also disclosed the fact that in the beginning of the twentieth century, as half a century before, the American country workers were willing to work for lower wages than the immigrants in the cities.

In the country districts of Pennsylvania the garment workers are Americans, some of whom can be further distinguished as "Pennsyl-

---

[1] *Reports of the Immigration Commission.* vol. 11, p. 293, Table 26.

[2] *Ibid.*, p. 298, Table 32.

[3] Jenks and Lauck, *loc. cit.*, p. 143.

[4] *Report of the Industrial Commission*, vol. xv., p. 725.

vania Dutch." In New Jersey they are Americans and German-Americans . . . but there is no evidence of a lower standard of living than among their American neighbors. In spite of this, *it is these people and their American co-workers who are accepting a lower rate of wages than the Jews in the city.*[1]

The most striking difference between the country and town shops is that the operators in the town shops are invariably men and in the country shops they are women. . . . The women coat operators in the country who get the highest wages paid women receive $5.34, and the city women basters on vests are receiving $6.59. Here we find women in the city engaged in a lower class of work and receiving higher pay than the women in the country who are doing the highest grade of work.[2]

The same difference existed between the wages of men in city and country shops: Jewish pressers in the city averaged $11.38 per week, whereas American pressers in the country earned only $7.62 per week.[3]

Because the native American country workers were willing to accept lower wages than the recent immigrants in the cities, the contractors found it profitable to give more steady employment to country than to city workers. While the latter averaged but twenty-eight working weeks in the year, the former were given forty-four weeks, with the result that their annual earnings at lower rates of wages exceeded the earnings of city workers at higher rates.[4]

What enables the American country workers of Pennsylvania to underbid the Jewish garment workers of Philadelphia is the fact that

the country home workers are usually simply supplementing other earnings. They are farmers' wives and daughters and those of farm laborers. They make clothing in the intervals of housework and farm work, for most of them help in the haying and harvesting. . . . Where the shop replaces the farming-out system, the employees are drawn from these same farmers' families, and a low standard of wages, influenced by the home earnings, prevails throughout.[5]

Another—no less important—cause of the "low standard of wages" of native American country workers is their

[1] *Report of the Industrial Commission*, vol. xv., p. 730.

[2] *Ibid.*, pp. 727–729.

[3] *Ibid.*, p. 726.

[4] *Ibid.*, p. 725.

[5] *Ibid.*, pp. 727–728.

isolation, in consequence of which "they must accept his [the contractor's] rate of payment offered through the driver who delivers the goods."[1] The Southern and Eastern European clothing workers in the cities, on the contrary, are comparatively well organized. As shown in Chapter XV the percentage of organized workers among them is above the average for the country. Their capacity for concerted action finds full expression only in strikes which rally around the unions many workers not regularly affiliated with them. *The highest per cent of employees joining in strikes in 1887–1905 was found among clothing workers,* as shown in Table 112:

TABLE 112.

PER CENT OF STRIKING EMPLOYEES IN THE CLOTHING INDUSTRY AND IN ALL INDUSTRIES IN THE UNITED STATES, 1887–1905.[2]

Industry	Male	Female
Women's clothing	86.94	62.11
Men's clothing	81.84	43.06
All industries	44.91	28.15

The strikes were, as a rule, led by organizations. Of the 20,559 establishments involved in strikes during the twenty-five year period from 1881 to 1905, in only 355 were the strikes not ordered by labor organizations, the annual averages being 835 and 13 establishments, respectively. The proportion of unorganized strikes among workers on men's clothing was 10 per cent; among workers on women's clothing 16 per cent, whereas the average for all industries was 31 per cent.[3]

The percentage of thoroughly successful strikes of clothing workers for the period 1881–1905 was much above the average, viz.: the percentage in establishments manufacturing men's

[1] *Report of the Industrial Commission*, vol. xv., p. 728.

[2] *Twenty-first Annual Report of the Commissioner of Labor*, pp. 90–91.

[3] *Ibid.*, pp. 35–36.

clothing, 75.51, and in establishments manufacturing women's clothing 66.37, whereas the average for all industries in the United States was only 47.94.[1] These figures will enable the student to appraise at its true value the conclusion of the Immigration Commission that "*as a general proposition* it may be said that *all* improvement in conditions and increases in rates of pay have been secured in spite of the presence of the recent immigrant."[2]

The strike statistics published by the United States Bureau of Labor permit of a comparison between the recent period beginning with the fiscal year 1895, when the immigrants from Southern and Eastern Europe for the first time outnumbered all others, and the earlier period from January 1, 1881, to June 30, 1894. During the 80's the principal nationalities employed in the clothing shops were the Germans and the Irish:[3] since 1895 the Jews and the Italians have become the predominating element among the workers. It appears that during the thirteen and a half years previous to the fiscal year 1895 the average annual number of strikers in the clothing industry was 9,094, and during the eleven and a half years following it rose to 38,683.[4]

This is the unbiased testimony of figures in answer to the sweeping generalizations of the Immigration Commission about the reluctance of the Southern and Eastern Europeans "to enter labor disputes involving loss of time," their "ready acceptance of a low wage and existing working conditions" and "willingness seemingly to accept indefinitely without protest certain wages and conditions of employment."[5]

[1] *Twenty-first Annual Report of the Commissioner of Labor*, pp. 81–82.

[2] *Reports of the Immigration Commission*, vol. 1, p. 540.

[3] *Ibid.*, vol. 1, pp. 516–517.

[4] Computed from *Annual Reports of the Commissioner of Labor:* X., p. 1567; XVI., pp. 15, 34, 355; XXI., p. 16.

[5] *Reports of the Immigration Commission*, vol. 1, pp. 530–540.

CHAPTER XVIII

THE COTTON MILLS

THE cotton mills furnish a good field for the study of the effects of immigration upon the condition of labor in the United States. According to the investigation of the Immigration Commission, 68.7 per cent of the operatives in the New England States were of foreign birth. The races of the "old immigration" were represented by 37.8 per cent, and those of the "new immigration" by 30.9 per cent.[1] The latter are mostly recent arrivals. In 1900 the proportion of immigrants from Southern and Eastern Europe and their American-born children varied from 3.1 per cent in New Hampshire to 13.2 per cent in Massachusetts.[2]

The Immigration Commission has obtained from one of the largest and oldest mill corporations figures showing the movement of wages since 1875.[3] The movement may be divided into two periods: (1) from 1875 to 1898 and (2) from 1899 to 1908. The first period, when the cotton-mill operatives were practically all English-speaking, was one of intermittent advances and reductions; on the whole wages remained stationary. The second period, which is marked by the advent of the Southern and Eastern Europeans into the cotton mills, is conspicuous by an uninterrupted upward movement of wages, which was checked only by the crisis of 1908. Still, even after the reduction

[1] *Reports of the Immigration Commission*, vol. 10, Table 7, pp. 14–15.
[2] *Ibid.*, Table 19, p. 36.
[3] *Ibid.*, p. 291.

made on March 30, 1908, wages remained 15 per cent above the level of 1898. To be sure, the first period was one of falling prices, which enabled the cotton-mill operatives to maintain their usual standard of living notwithstanding the reductions in wages, whereas, on the other hand, the second period was one of rapidly rising prices which offset the increase in wages. It is therefore possible that the operatives were not better off during the later period of rising wages than during the earlier period. Still, assuming that every cut in wages merely restored the previous relation between earnings and the cost of living, it is plain that these reductions must have caused dissatisfaction among the wage-earners. However, the operatives of the New England cotton mills, all of them of Teutonic and Celtic stock, acquiesced in these reductions. On the other hand, though the advances in 1899–1907 may have been nullified by the rising cost of living, each increase in wages was nevertheless the outcome of successful bargaining by the operatives for better terms of employment.

Still the question is whether the industrial expansion of the period from 1899 to 1907 might not have enabled the operatives to win more substantial advances had there been no immigration from Southern and Eastern Europe. The only method by which such results could have been accomplished was organization.

> The more recent immigrant employees from Southern and Eastern Europe and Asia, however, [says the Immigration Commission in its summary volume], have been a constant menace to the labor organizations, and have been directly and indirectly instrumental in weakening the unions and threatening their disruption. The divergence in language and the high degree of illiteracy and ignorance among the recent operatives have made their work of organization among them very difficult and expensive.[1]

This conclusion is at variance with the facts recited in the special report of the Commission on "Cotton goods manufacturing in the North Atlantic States":

[1] *Reports of the Immigration Commission*, vol. 1, p. 537.

"Fall River, Mass., is the only distinctly trade-union locality in New England," yet there, as elsewhere, the unions are confined to the skilled occupations, whereas the recent immigrants upon entering the cotton mills "take up unskilled work. . . . Many of them never advance beyond the unskilled work. These occupations are not organized, and *the coming of the foreigner there does not concern the textile unions*."[1] In Cohoes, N. Y., likewise, "*the unions manifest little interest in the immigrant employees until they have advanced to the occupations controlled by the labor organizations*."[2] It is evident that "their work of organization" among the unskilled immigrants could have been neither "difficult" nor "expensive."

With regard to skilled occupations the Immigration Commission has reached two diametrically opposite conclusions. In the abstract of the reports on immigrants in manufacturing and mining it maintains that

> the advancement *in large numbers* of the Southern and Eastern Europeans to weaving, spinning, beaming, and similar occupations *has tended to bring them into more direct competition with the Americans and older immigrant employees*, and to destroy the advantage which the latter class, *who control and direct the unions*, formerly possessed.[3]

In the special report on cotton goods manufacturing the Commission says, on the contrary, that

> *at no time has there been a sharp competition between unionized laborers* on the one hand, and *unorganized immigrant laborers in large numbers* on the other.[4]

The latter conclusion is supported by the following statements:

> The textile occupations themselves, which are unionized, are protected, by the long time required to attain proficiency, from any sudden or immediate competition of unorganized foreigners. . . . Automatic or improved machinery might change this situation, and the coming of

[1] *Reports of the Immigration Commission*, vol. 10, pp. 123, 124.
[2] *Ibid.*, p. 123. [3] *Ibid.*, vol. 1, p. 538. [4] *Ibid.*, vol. 10, p. 124.

the immigrant might then be a more serious matter for the unions and might subject them to a disastrous competition from unorganized workers accustomed to a lower standard of living, . . . *but that is not the condition at present*. . . . As regards the attitude of the immigrants toward the unions, when they advance to the skilled, organized occupations, *even if they do not join the unions, they do not oppose the organization or cut under the unions' wages*. . . . At the time of strikes the recent immigrants come into the unions in large numbers. . . . In times of strikes these foreigners have stood by the unions, even though previously they may not have been members.[1]

The recent immigrants have not been used as strike-breakers.[2]

The only specific strike described in the report of the Commission took place in Lowell, Mass.,[3] in 1903. It is characterized as "the only serious controversy between the cotton manufacturers and the operatives" of that city. The history of that controversy is briefly as follows. The mill owners having refused an increase in wages, the unions declared a strike. The mill owners on the same day responded by a lockout. While the mills remained closed, pro-union meetings were held among the Greeks, the Poles, and the Portuguese, and organizations were formed among them. "At the commencement of the agitation for a ten per cent increase in wages, the membership of the unions constituted but a small fraction of the employees in the mills; gradually, however, this membership increased as the strike sentiment grew." The unions were defeated, however, by an unexpected turn in the cotton market.

The price of raw cotton began to rise to such an extent that the manufacturers who had provided themselves with the necessary supply in advance were able to sell at a considerable profit. One mill actually declared a 4 per cent dividend, on the basis of raw cotton sold at a good advance, due to the high prices during the strike. In this way it would have been possible for them to minimize, or even neutralize entirely

[1] *Reports of the Immigration Commission*, vol. 10, pp. 124, 125.

[2] *Ibid.*, vol. 1, p. 538.

[3] For some unknown reasons, the name of the city is hidden under the designation of "Community A." The disguise is betrayed, however, in Table 125 on p. 232, which is a reproduction of Table 24 on p. 45, where Lowell, Mass., is named.

the loss occasioned by the idleness of their plants caused by the strike. It thus became a matter of indifference to them whether work was resumed or not. When this situation generally became known the strike was doomed.[1]

After a suspension of work lasting nine weeks the manufacturers reopened the mills. From one third to two thirds of the locked-out operatives returned to the mills on the first day. The ranks of the strikers began to weaken, and after staying out for three weeks the unions unanimously voted to call the strike off.[2]

To form a fair judgment of the endurance shown by the Lowell strikers, the length of time they stayed out must be compared with the average duration of strikes in the cotton mills of Massachusetts. The races of Southern and Eastern Europe in 1909 supplied 34 per cent of the total number of operatives in the Lowell cotton mills.[3] In the State at large the proportion of immigrants from Southern and Eastern Europe and Asia among the mill operatives of the State varied as follows:

TABLE 113.

PERCENTAGE OF IMMIGRANTS FROM SOUTHERN AND EASTERN EUROPE AMONG THE TEXTILE MILL OPERATIVES OF MASSACHUSETTS, 1880–1900.[4]

Mills	Year	Per cent
Cotton (immigrants and their children)....	1900	13.2
Textile (immigrants only)...............	1890	2.3
" " "	1880	0.5

The average duration of strikes in the cotton mills of Massachusetts for the twenty-year period from 1881 to 1900 was only thirty-six days.[5] Thus the length of time

[1] *Reports of the Immigration Commission*, vol. 1, pp. 292, 293.
[2] *Ibid.*
[3] *Ibid.*, Table 130, p. 237.
[4] *Ibid.*, Tables 14, 17, and 19.
[5] *Sixteenth Annual Report of the Commissioner of Labor*, Table 3, p. 216.

the Lowell strikers stayed out in 1903 was three quarters in excess of the average for the period when nearly all the operatives were of the English-speaking races. Going over the annals of the strikes in the cotton mills of Massachusetts from 1881–1890, when there were scarcely any immigrants from Southern and Eastern Europe and Asia among the operatives, we find only one strike that can compare in extent with the Lowell strike of 1903; it was in 1889, when 9000 weavers in thirty-four mills at Fall River struck for a 10 per cent increase in wages. After staying out only seventeen days they returned to work on the old terms.[1]

Thus when the Greek, Portuguese, and Polish strikers in 1903 surrendered after nine weeks of idleness, during which they received no aid from the unions, they gave an exhibition in endurance and adherence to a common purpose, that was far above the average for any race of cotton-mill operatives. Moreover, since the proportion of the strikers who returned to the mills on the first day varied from one third to two thirds, whereas the proportion of Southern and Eastern Europeans among the operatives was less than one third,[2] it is evident that a good many of the English-speaking operatives must have surrendered simultaneously with the Southern and Eastern Europeans.

The history of this strike is prefaced by the Commission with the following remark:

> *It is not thought that the presence of immigrants in such large numbers* in Community A *has exerted a decisive influence upon the success of trade-unionism in the community.* The weakness of the unions in Community A is to be traced to less general causes of a local character.[3]

The reader is at a loss to reconcile this conclusion, and the facts leading up to it, with the general statement,

[1] *Tenth Annual Report of the Commissioner of Labor*, vol. I, Table 1, pp. 364–414.

[2] In 1909 the proportion was 34 per cent, but in 1900 only 13.2 per cent; the proportion in 1903 must have been somewhere between these two figures.

[3] *Reports of the Immigration Commission*, vol. 10, p. 291.

quoted above from the abstract of the reports on immigrants in manufacturing and mining, to the effect that "the more recent immigrant employees from Southern and Eastern Europe and Asia . . . have been a constant menace to the labor organizations, and have been directly and indirectly instrumental in weakening the unions and threatening their disruption."[1]

Considering:

(1) That the unskilled operatives have at no time been organized;

(2) That the recent immigrants seldom advance to the skilled crafts;

(3) That when they do advance to skilled occupations they either join the unions of their crafts or stand by the unions though not affiliated with them;

(4) That with the machinery heretofore in use there has been no room for competition between organized skilled operatives and unorganized immigrant unskilled laborers;

(5) That in past strikes the recent immigrants have stood by the strikers and have never acted as strike-breakers:—

It is evident that the presence of recent immigrants has been no hindrance to union activity. The failure of the unions to secure better terms from the mill corporations than they did must therefore be due to other causes than immigration.

The real cause of low wages in the cotton mills of New England is the competition of the Southern cotton mills. The subject is only hinted at in the report of the Immigration Commission. No immigrants being employed in the Southern mills, the latter were apparently considered beyond the scope of the Commission's investigation. A

[1] *Reports of the Immigration Commission*, vol. i., p. 537. Unfortunately, the full report on cotton manufacturing has been printed only as a Senate document and is accessible to a very limited number of readers, whereas the misleading conclusions of the abstract on immigration in manufacturing and mining have received wide circulation through the free mailing list of the Commission.

thorough discussion of the subject is found in the report of the Massachusetts Bureau of Labor Statistics for 1906.

Comparing labor conditions in New England and Southern mills, the Massachusetts report says, by inference, that when the sons and daughters of the farmers of the surrounding country were replaced in the Northern mills by foreigners, strikes and lockouts followed, and the doors were opened to the trade unions, with the result that hours of labor were reduced, wages were increased, and child labor was restricted.[1] The development of the cotton manufacturing industry in the South, with its natural advantages and "cheap labor," has made successful competition impossible for Massachusetts mills, unless Massachusetts will "retrograde and increase its hours of labor, reduce its wages, and employ its children to meet the South in a battle on its own ground."[2]

The "cheap labor" of the Southern cotton mills is the labor of the native white of native stock, who constitute 99 per cent of all cotton-mill operatives in North Carolina, 97 per cent in Georgia and Alabama.[3] The average yearly earnings of the Southern operatives compared as follows with those of the New England operatives, many of whom were Southern and Eastern European, Armenian, and Syrian immigrants:

[1] "When the native stock is all employed, the South must look to the immigrant, and then will come the test of her ability to withstand the enactment of just labor laws. She will be compelled to readjust her hours of labor, increase her wages, discharge her child labor, and open her doors to the trade union. She will go through the same experience as the North. The North's first operatives were the sons and daughters of the native farmers round about, but the grandchildren would not follow in their parents' footsteps, preferring to go into other business. This the South is finding to be the case with the children they are attempting to educate, and foreigners must soon be taken to replace them. Then will come a repetition of the experience of the Northern mills. Strikes and lockouts will follow." *Thirty-Sixth Annual Report Massachusetts Bureau of Statistics of Labor* (1906), Part II: Cotton Manufactures in Massachusetts and the Southern States, p. 102.

[2] *Ibid.*, p. 106.

[3] *Occupations at the XII. Census*, Table 41 (computed).

TABLE 114.

AVERAGE YEARLY EARNINGS OF COTTON-MILL OPERATIVES, BY SEX AND AGE IN THE PRINCIPAL STATES, 1904.[1]

State	Men	Women	Children under 16 years
New Hampshire	$418	$337	$188
Massachusetts	410	340	233
Rhode Island	409	334	222
Connecticut	392	325	219
New York	394	310	188
Pennsylvania	524	314	193
North Carolina	256	194	130
South Carolina	244	199	138
Georgia	283	199	126
Alabama	272	205	130

As can be seen from the preceding table the average earnings of adult men in South Carolina are only slightly above the average earnings of children in Massachusetts; the highest average earnings of adult men in the Southern mills are much below the average earnings of women employed in the Northern mills. This is a reversal of the usual relation between men's and women's wages. It is this competition of the cheap American labor of the Southern mills that keeps down the wages of the Southern and Eastern European, Armenian, and Syrian immigrants employed in the cotton mills of the North.

[1] *Census of Manufactures*, 1905, vol. i., Table 5, p. 188.

CHAPTER XIX

THE WOOLEN MILLS

THE recent strike in the woolen mills of Lawrence has forcibly drawn public attention to the condition of labor in the woolen industry. It developed in the hearings held before the Committee of the House of Representatives, and through investigations made by leading magazine writers and social workers, that in this industry, protected from foreign competition by the tariff and from domestic competition by a high degree of centralization, the wages of married men were insufficient for the support of their families. The fact that the strikers were mostly recent immigrants diverted the discussion from the issues of the strike to the subject of immigration. It was readily believed that they had been "imported" because of their low standard of living, for the express purpose of reducing the wages of native American and other English-speaking operatives. Professor Lauck, author of the report of the Immigration Commission on "Immigrants in Industries," writing in the *North American Review* on the Lawrence strike, claimed that

> the American mill hand . . . because of his inability to work under the same conditions and at the same wages as the recent immigrant, has been forced to leave the woolen-goods manufacturing industry.[1]

It has been taken as a self-evident truth that the wages of the recent immigrants were low *because* they lived in con-

[1] W. Jett Lauck: "The Lesson from Lawrence," *North American Review*, May, 1912, p. 664.

gested quarters, and *because* they were underfed and poorly clad. There has accordingly been little disposition among people usually friendly to labor to waste sympathy upon men and women who were "willing" to deny themselves the barest necessities of life for the mere privilege of working in the mills. "The lesson from Lawrence" is to these good people that the solution of the labor problem is in keeping out the foreign laborer. As usual in all arguments inspired by this theory, no regard is paid to historical perspective.

The American operative was not "forced to leave the woolen-goods manufacturing industry" by the coming of the recent immigrants, because he had left it long before. According to the census of 1880, there were among the 10,395 operatives of the cotton and woolen mills of Lawrence only 4111 native Americans, *i. e.*, only 40 per cent, including persons of native and of foreign parentage. The majority were immigrants from Ireland, Great Britain, and Canada, with a sprinkling of Germans (4 per cent).[1] The immigrants from all other countries numbered 1 per cent of all operatives. Thus, if the prevalence of immigrants among the operatives be the result of the "forcing out" of native Americans, it is clear that they were forced out by English-speaking immigrants.

Even as recently as 1900 the immigrants from Italy, Russia, Poland, and Austria-Hungary and their American-born children, employed in the woolen and worsted mills of Lawrence, numbered only 721 persons of both sexes, *i. e.*, 10 per cent of all operatives, whereas the total number of native Americans of native parentage did not exceed 374, *i. é.*, 5.2 per cent of the total force.[2] If it be true that all but this little remnant of American operatives had been "forced out" of the mills, is there any reason to attribute their ousting to the pressure of the 10 per cent made up of "recent immigrants" rather than to that of the 85 per cent

[1] *Population, X. Census*, Table XXXVI., p. 882.

[2] *Occupations at the XII. Census* Table 43.

representing the English-speaking immigrants and their native-born children? Suppose the 10 per cent contingent of recent immigrants forced out as many Americans, there were still 90 per cent of the places in the mills to be filled, and the contest for these places was between native Americans of native parentage and English-speaking immigrants and their children. Detailed figures are given in Table 115.

TABLE 115.

DISTRIBUTION OF THE OPERATIVES OF BOTH SEXES IN THE WOOLEN AND WORSTED MILLS OF LAWRENCE, MASSACHUSETTS, BY PARENT NATIVITY, 1900.[1]

Nativity	Number	Per cent
Total	7180	100.0
Native parentage	374	5.2
Foreign parentage	6806	94.8
Native born	2005	27.9
Foreign born	4801	66.9
Country of birth of parents:		
Canada (English)	182	2.6
Canada (French)	673	9.4
Great Britain	1361	18.9
Ireland	2078	28.9
Germany	872	12.2
Scandinavian	7	.0
Austria-Hungary	45	.6
Italy	402	5.6
Poland	130	1.9
Russia	144	2.0
Other countries and mixed parentage	911	12.7

It is only since the federal census of 1900 that the immigrants from Southern and Eastern Europe and Syria have become a conspicuous element among the woolen-mill operatives of Lawrence. The report of the Immigration Commission contains figures which "are practically a census of the local establishments" for 1909. According to those figures, 35.5 per cent of the operatives were immigrants

[1] *Occupations at the XII. Census*, Table 43.

from Southern and Eastern Europe and Turkey. But the proportion of native Americans of native parentage was 6.9 per cent, as against 5.2 per cent in 1900. *Since the advent of the "new immigrants" the number of native Americans of native parentage employed in the woolen and worsted mills of Lawrence has more than doubled.* The proof of this fact is given in Table 116 next following:

TABLE 116.

NUMBER OF NATIVE AMERICANS OF NATIVE PARENTAGE EMPLOYED IN THE WOOLEN AND WORSTED MILLS OF LAWRENCE, 1900 AND 1909.[1]

Sex	1900				1909	Per cent increase 1900–1909
	Woolen mill operatives	Worsted mill operatives	Textile mill operatives not otherwise specified.[2]	Total		
Male.....	142	33	45	220	690	213
Female...	147	52	63	262	545	108
Total.	289	85	108	482	1235	156

The only inference justified by the figures of the Immigration Commission is that the same economic conditions which have brought the recent immigrants to the Lawrence woolen mills have also induced increasing numbers of native Americans of native stock to accept employment in the same mills. In 1909, the average number of wage-earners in the woolen mills was 20,203, as against an average number of 12,216 employed in 1904.[3] These figures are

[1] *Occupations at the XII. Census*, Table 43. *Report of the Immigration Commission*, vol. 10, Table 81, p. 742. The same figures are duplicated in Table 85, p. 752.

[2] As some of these operatives may have been employed in woolen and worsted mills, their total number is included in this comparative table. The percentage of increase is thereby reduced below the actual figure.

[3] *XIII. Census*, vol. ix: *Manufacturers*, p. 527.

indicative of a great expansion of the industry in recent years, which has created new places both for native Americans and for new immigrants.

What has been the effect of this expansion upon the rates of wages? Professor Lauck, speaking for the Immigration Commission, holds that "the rate of wages in the presence of a large supply of immigrant laborers tends to decline."[1] This *obiter dictum*, however, is unsupported by figures. The statistics of wages quoted further in the report decidedly contradict the opinion of their compiler. In the thirteen occupations selected by him for comparison, "these figures indicate an apparent increase of 19.65 per cent in the rate of weekly wages . . . during the past twenty years." In another mill the average earnings of weavers show "an increase of 75 per cent."[2] If there be such a tendency as that enunciated by Professor Lauck, its operation has apparently been suspended at Lawrence during the past twenty years.

The statistics of the Immigration Commission furnish material for a comparison of the variation in the rates of wages in the presence and in the absence of the recent immigrant labor supply, viz., from 1889 to 1899 and from 1899 to 1909. In 1890 the population of Lawrence numbered in all 159 immigrants from Austria, Portugal, Italy, Russia, and Turkey.[3] By 1900, as stated, their number in the woolen mills reached only 8.6 per cent of all operatives. Their presence in the mills was certainly a negligible factor in determining the rates of wages. In the ten years following, however, their numbers increased to 35.5 per cent of the total force. As elsewhere, they have taken over "the simpler, cruder processes," while the English-speaking operatives have been assigned to the higher grades of work.[4] It is therefore, possible to observe the effect of recent immigration upon the rates of wages for unskilled labor, as well as the effect of the absence of the competition of recent

[1] *Reports of the Immigration Commission*, vol. 10, p. 773.
[2] *Ibid.*, pp. 773, 774. [3] *Ibid.*, p. 750. [4] *Ibid.*, p. 772.

immigrants upon the rates of wages in those occupations to which they are not admitted. The comparative rates of increase in the wage scales are presented in Table 117.

TABLE 117.

PER CENT INCREASE IN THE RATES OF WAGES PAID BY ONE OF THE TWO LARGEST WORSTED MILLS IN LAWRENCE TO SKILLED AND UNSKILLED OPERATIVES, IN 1889–1899, AND 1899–1909.[1]

Occupation	Per week		Per hour	
	1889–1899	1899–1909	1889–1899	1899–1909
Skilled:				
Loom fixers	0.0	16.4	0.0	20.5
Wool sorters	4.7	23.3	0.0	0.0
Warp dressers	0.0	5.9	0.0	9.5
Unskilled:				
Doffers	16.7	31.2	16.7	35.7
Spinners	5.3	{8.3, 18.0, 34.3}	5.3	{25.0, 35.0, 40.0}
Comb minders	0.0	12.1	0.0	16.0
Drawing girls:				
Highest grade	0.0	5.5	0.0	10.0
Lowest grade	0.0	28.9	0.0	33.4
Dyehouse hands	0.0	16.8	0.0	20.8

The preceding table demonstrates:

(1) That from 1889 to 1899, the rates of wages of the skilled operatives remained stationary, and that they increased from 1899 to 1909, *i. e.*, during the period of the great influx of immigrants from Southern and Eastern Europe and Turkey;

(2) That in three of the unskilled occupations the rates of wages remained stationary in 1889–1899, in the absence of "the new immigration," and increased in 1899–1909, in the presence of that immigration; that the wages of spinners were raised during the earlier period 5.3 per cent and during

[1] The percentages have been computed from the rates per week and per hour quoted in the *Reports of the Immigration Commission*, vol. 10, p. 774. Occupations for which two or more rates were given in 1899 and only one in 1889 and 1909 have been omitted.

the recent period from 8.3 to 34.3 per cent; that the wages of doffers increased during the first period 16.7 per cent and during the second 31.2 per cent;

(3) That since the immigrants from Southern and Eastern Europe and Asiatic Turkey have begun to enter the unskilled occupations in large numbers, the percentage of increase in the wages of unskilled operatives has been greater than the percentage of increase in the rates of skilled workers, who are practically all of the English-speaking races.

If the rates of wages are affected by the racial characteristics of the immigrants, then the preceding figures admit of no other conclusion than that the immigrants from Southern and Eastern Europe and Asiatic Turkey have a racial "tendency" to push the wages upward, whereas the English-speaking workmen are willing to acquiesce for a long time (10 years) in such wages as the recent immigrants would consider unsatisfactory. This palpably unsound conclusion is the logical consequence of the false assumption underlying the report of the Immigration Commission on immigrants in manufacturing. The only other possible interpretation of the preceding table of variations in the rates of wages is that the wages remained stationary in 1889–1899 because the growth of the woolen industry was slow during those years and that the wages increased in 1899–1909 owing to the rapid expansion of the woolen industry, which created an active demand for labor. The rapid increase of the number of recent immigrant employees was the effect of the increased demand for labor at higher wages.

The growth of a Western city, like Los Angeles, from a city of 102,000 inhabitants in 1900 to one of 319,000 in 1910 through migration of native citizens, is accepted by the American public as a matter of course. But the average American, being out of touch with the strange peoples whom he sees filling the mills of his growing city, does not realize the simple fact that "the channel of communication between the economic opportunity or labor demand in the

United States and the labor supply abroad is ordinarily the oral or written accounts of immigrants who have worked in the worsted and cotton mills." The native resident of Lawrence, who may never have been as far away from home as New York, cannot imagine how these thousands of strangers could have found their way to his town without "some organized effort." "Everywhere one goes in the city tales are told of the efforts made by one woolen company to procure laborers in Europe."[1] The Commission has made an effort to investigate these tales with the following results:

> One informant had a cousin in Glasgow who had written concerning pictures of the new mill which he had seen, and concerning an agent of the woolen company. Nothing more definite could be learned. Another informant who was much exercised over reports of this sort had written to the Secretary of the Wool Sorters' Union of Bradford, England, a district said to have been well covered with advertising matter, asking for information. The English trade-union official had, however, seen no advertisements of this sort. A clergyman in close touch with the industrial situation expressed himself as "convinced that agents are sent to Europe to get labor." The priest of the Italian congregation, one of the largest of the foreign churches—the greater part of whose membership has come from abroad within the past few years—states that *accounts of the mills and assertions that "wages of $10 a week" are paid have appeared in Italian and other European newspapers.*[2]

It is evident that in this age of the daily press news of the American labor market travels fast all over the globe. It is not at all impossible that the Table on page 774 of the *Report of the Immigration Commission on Cotton Goods Manufacturing*, showing that some classes of the operatives in the Lawrence mills earned as much as $14, $15, and even $16 a week, may yet be republished in some Old World newspaper and have the effect of stimulating the immigration of a fresh supply of Italian or Syrian laborers for the Lawrence woolen mills.

In view of the general conclusion of the Immigration

[1] *Reports of the Immigration Commission*, vol. 10., p. 770.

[2] *Ibid.*

Commission that the recent immigrants are willing to work "indefinitely without protest" for low wages,[1] it is interesting to note the characterization of the recent immigrants by a number of superintendents and foremen of the two largest Lawrence mills. "While opinions differ somewhat, there appears to be a considerable uniformity of judgment as to their characteristics." The Italians are quick to leave their positions if they see any apparent advantage elsewhere. One mill superintendent stated that "they no sooner get a job than they want something better; they work in droves; discharge one and they all go."[2]

That such characteristics are favorable to concerted action for economic improvement, has been demonstrated by the recent strike of the polyglot working force at the Lawrence mills. An observer whose sympathies were with old-line trade-unionism, noted with surprise that "the capacity of this great host of recent immigrants, representing a number of supposedly alienated nationalities, for continuous, effective solidarity is one of the revelations of the present strike."[3]

The measure of success achieved by these alien strikers can be realized by comparison with the statistics of strikes for the twenty-year period 1881–1900, when the operatives in the woolen and worsted mills of Massachusetts were practically all of the English-speaking races. During that period there were in all 81 strikes, of which only 9 were declared by labor organizations, while 72 were unorganized movements, like the recent strike at Lawrence. The aggregate number of strikers in the State of Massachusetts for the twenty years was only 5618, *i. e.*, about one third of the number engaged in the one recent strike at Lawrence. The aggregate number thrown out of employment by the strikes was 10,144 for the whole period, but 16,117 opera-

[1] *Reports of the Immigration Commission*, vol. 1, p. 541.

[2] *Ibid.*, vol. 10, p. 771.

[3] *The Survey*, March 16, 1912, p. 1930: "The Clod Stirs." By Robert A. Woods, head worker of South End House of Boston.

tives remained at work while the strikes were on. Of the 83 mills involved only 31 were forced to close while 52 were able to run with the majority that remained at work.[1]

Thus with all odds against them, the recent immigrants speaking in sixteen different languages, have given proof of far greater cohesion than the English-speaking operatives of former years.

[1] *Sixteenth Annual Report of the Commissioner of Labor*, Table iv., pp. 332–355.

CHAPTER XX

THE IRON AND STEEL WORKERS

THE twelve-hour day, the twenty-four-hour shift, and Sunday labor, not as an emergency, but as an integral part of the system, have of late caused wide discussion of the iron and steel industry. The public conscience demanded to know who was responsible for those labor conditions. The offenders were easily discovered. Inasmuch as three fourths of the unskilled men working those long hours were found to be Southern and Eastern Europeans, it became evident that it was they who were to blame for accepting such intolerable working conditions. A representative of a labor constituency, speaking on the floor of Congress, declared that "in the steel mills of Pittsburgh, Chicago, and Milwaukee, where thirty years ago the so-called princes of labor used to get from $10 to $15 a day, the modern white coolies get $1.75 for twelve hours a day, seven days in the week," the change being due to the "Slavonians, Italians, Greeks, Russians, and Armenians," who "have been *brought into this country by the million*" and "simply because they have a lower standard of living . . . have *crowded out* the Americans, Germans, Englishmen, and Irishmen," from the mills.[1]

Such generalizations as these represent the popular conception of the causes of long hours and low wages in the iron and steel industry. The principal fallacy underlying

[1] Speech of Hon. Victor L. Berger, of Wisconsin, in the House of Representatives, Wednesday, June 14, 1911. *Congressional Record*, pp. 2026–2030.

this interpretation has been shown in Chapter VII.: there has been no "crowding out" of American, English, Irish, or German steel workers by immigrants "brought" from Southern and Eastern Europe. The development of the iron and steel industry has been so rapid that all but a small percentage of the English-speaking workmen have been advanced to higher positions and their places have been filled with Southern and Eastern Europeans. The new immigrants do not compete with the native and older immigrant workmen, and can therefore not affect their wages.

The parallel between the "princes of labor" and the "white coolies" is equally without an historical foundation. Princes have at all times been few. "The old reputation of the steel industry as one of exceptionally high wages is false so far as the rank and file are concerned," says Mr. Fitch of the Pittsburgh Survey staff, who has made a study of the steel workers, "neither, on the other hand, should it be singled out as an unusual type, as an industry in which the majority of the men are paid at the lowest rates."[1] The rollers, heaters, and other skilled men, whose earnings in the early days often exceeded the salary of the superintendent, were only a small fraction of the total force.

The high earnings of the few skilled men often represented profit rather than wages. In the early '80's the contract system was the prevailing method of hiring labor in the mills:

> A man would contract with the company to run a single mill, from the furnaces to the piling beds of the shears, and like any other contractor he derived his profit from the margin between what the company paid him for the tonnage turned out and what he paid the men for it. The contractor, while usually known as the roller, frequently did no work at all, having two practical rollers employed on the mill. At the same time he secured a considerable income for himself by paying the men as low wages as possible, and *steel workers got a reputation for being very highly paid workmen on account of the large earnings of these contractors.* A statement from the proprietor of one of the "largest rolling mills in

[1] John A. Fitch, "The Steel Workers." *The Pittsburgh Survey*, p. 150.

the District," regarding wages paid in his mill in 1881–1882, was to the effect that under the contract system one steel worker had made $25,000 in a year. A sheet shearer made $12.00 per day and paid his helper $2.00. A hammerman in charge of both turns made $17.00 per day and paid his helper $2.50.[1]

The proportion of employees who were paid each rate of wages in the rolling mills of Ohio in 1884, when the number of Southern and Eastern Europeans among them was negligible, appears from Table 118. The number of

TABLE 118.

CLASSIFICATION OF EMPLOYEES IN SELECTED ROLLING MILLS OF OHIO BY RATES OF WEEKLY WAGES, 1884.[2]

Rates of weekly wages	Skilled[3]	Semi-skilled	Laborers	Total	
				Number	Per cent
Under $10	—	—	699	699	32.3
$10 to $12	—	—	360	360	16.9
$12 to $15	—	199	—	199	9.6
$15 to $18	—	95	—	95	4.5
$18 to $25	415	4	—	419	19.6
$25 to $30	147	—	—	147	6.9
$30 to $60	158	—	—	158	7.5
$60 and over	57	—	—	57	2.7
Total	777	298	1059	2134	100.0

"princes of labor" did not exceed 57 in a total force of 2134, *i. e.*, 2.7 per cent. On the other hand, the number of "white coolies" who were paid less than $10 a week, *i. e.*, less than $1.75 per day, was then as high as one third of the total force, and those who were paid less than $12 a week numbered nearly one half of all employees. There is no reason to assume that the wages in Ohio materially

[1] Fitch, *loc. cit.*, p. 99.

[2] *Report of the Ohio Bureau of Labor Statistics*, 1885, Table 51, pp. 185–186. The statistics comprise only those mills for which complete data were available.

[3] Includes: Rollers, nailers, heaters, and puddlers.

differed from those paid at the time in other centers of the iron and steel industry.

The Immigration Commission made a comparative statistical study of the rates of wages paid by one steel company at different periods, going as far back as 1880, and reached the following conclusion:

> An inspection of the wage scale paid by the steel company during the past eighteen years—the period marked by the coming of the immigrants in greatest numbers—reveals the fact that wages have risen and fallen in good and bad times equally for skilled labor, largely free from direct immigration competition, and for unskilled labor, now largely performed by immigrants.[1]

The wage scale appearing in the report includes no rolling mills where exceptionally high rates were earned by a few men of special skill. The highest rate appearing in the scale for 1880 is $3 per day paid to engineers; the highest in 1885 is $3.42 for brick masons. Neither of these two classes were iron and steel workers in a proper sense. The highest paid among iron and steel workers proper in 1880 were boiler-makers, whose maximum rate was $2.75. But the wages of laborers in 1880 were as low as $1.10, and in 1885 as low as $1. There was a general drop in the rates of wages at the blast furnaces and in the Bessemer department between 1880 and 1885, when immigration from Southern and Eastern Europe was insignificant. There was also a drop in the rates for several occupations from 1890 to 1895, which was obviously due to the effects of the crisis of 1893. Since 1895 wages at the blast furnaces and in the Bessemer department have been on the increase, while in the mechanical department, the wages of skilled mechanics have been subject to sharp fluctuations. On the other hand, the wages of unskilled laborers, most of whom are from Southern and Eastern Europe, have steadily

[1] *Reports of the Immigration Commission*, vol. 8, p. 601.

risen, while the pay of the engineers, who are mostly "English-speaking," has not come up to the 1880 level. A summary of the figures is given in Table 119 next below.[1]

TABLE 119.

DAILY WAGES OF EMPLOYEES IN STEEL COMPANY NO. 1, 1880–1908.

Year	Laborers		Other unskilled or semi-skilled		All others	
	Lowest	Highest	Lowest	Highest	Lowest	Highest
1880	$1.10	$1.23	$1.05	$1.55	$1.60	$3.00
1885	1.00	1.04	.68	1.48	1.54	3.42
1890	1.00	1.10	.75	1.25	1.26	2.70
1895	1.00	1.10	1.00	1.35	1.45	3.00
1900	1.00	1.20	1.15	1.50	1.55	3.65
1903	1.30	1.30	1.10	2.10	2.25	3.24
1908	1.38	1.45	1.20	2.20	2.25	3.60

As stated, the wage statistics of the Immigration Commission do not include rolling mills. From data published by the Ohio Bureau of Labor Statistics it appears that the average wages of laborers in rolling mills increased, from 1884 to 1902, 50 per cent, as shown in Table 120:

TABLE 120.

COMPARATIVE WAGES OF LABORERS IN ROLLING MILLS, OHIO, 1884–1902.[2]

Year	Number reported	Average daily wages
1884	4,134	$1.05
1902	11,560	1.58

An intelligent comparison of the wages of iron and steel workers at present and in the period preceding the immigra-

[1] For details of the scale, see Appendix, Table XXV.

[2] *Reports of the Ohio Bureau of Labor Statistics*, 1885, p. 187; 1903, p. 429.

tion of Southern and Eastern Europeans must take into consideration the revolution in technical methods which has occurred in the iron and steel industry during the intervening years. Prior to 1890, less than one half of all pig iron produced was made into steel; in 1909 all but 7 per cent of the pig iron reached the market as steel. Until 1890 the manufacture of iron other than steel exhibited a rapid growth; from 1880 to 1890 its output doubled. Since the latter year, however, it began to decline; from 5,000,000 tons in 1890 it dropped to about 1,800,000 tons in 1909. The majority of the men who had acquired skill in the iron mills found their occupations gone. Judged by the tonnage of pig iron, the change must have affected as many iron workers as there had been employed in all the mills in 1887. At the same time the production of steel has increased sixfold since 1890.[1] This marvelous growth was made possible only by the adoption of new methods of steel-making. All these changes necessitated a thorough readjustment of the laboring forces. The transformation is well described in the following excerpts from Mr. Fitch's study of *The Steel Workers:*

> Through the revolutionary changes in method, machinery has displaced men to a remarkable extent. The proportion of skilled steel workers needed for the operation of a plant has decreased. At the same time, the large companies have so increased their capacity that they are employing more men than ever before, until to-day 60 per cent of the men employed in the steel industry are unskilled, and that 60 per cent is greater in numbers than the total working force twenty years ago. In no part of the steel manufacture have inventions and improvements had such an effect upon working conditions as in the rolling mills. Twenty years ago these mills were alive with men. To-day you will find large numbers of men in the guide and merchant mills, but at the blooming mills, the plate mills, and the structural and rail mills, you have to look sharply not to miss them entirely. These mills have become largely automatic. The two improvements that have contributed most to the cutting-down of the laboring force are the electric crane and the movable roll tables. . . . The electric crane

[1] Computed from *Statistical Abstract of the United States*, 1911, p. 710.

operates over the whole length of the mill. Heavy material, that formerly a dozen moved with difficulty, is now picked up and moved easily by two men, working with a crane. Roll changing has become an easier and swifter process through the aid of the crane, and practically all the heavy lifting and carrying within the mill is thus accomplished by electric power. . . . As in the case of blast furnace improvements, the effect has been to reduce the number of men employed. . . .

This tendency to make processes automatic has resulted not only in a lessened cost with an increased tonnage, but it has also reinforced the control of the employers over their men. When the roll tables were introduced, they threw many roughers and catchers out of employment; beyond that, they lessened the importance to the employers of the men remaining. Men can learn to pull levers more easily than they can reach the skilled mastery of a position where the greatest dependence is on the man and the least on the machine. Accordingly this development has lessened the value to the employer of all the men in a plant, and at the same time has made the job of every man, skilled and unskilled, to a greater or less degree insecure. . . . The aim to-day seems to be to make the whole process as mechanical as possible. Fifteen or twenty years ago a large proportion of the employees in any steel plant were skilled men. The percentage of the highly skilled has steadily grown less, and the percentage of the unskilled has as steadily increased. The plants of the Carnegie Steel Company in Allegheny County employ in seasons of prosperity an aggregate of over 23,000 men. Of these about 17 per cent are skilled, 21 per cent semi-skilled, and 62 per cent unskilled, according to the classification employed by the company.[1]

Taking the classification of Table 118 as a standard of comparison, we find that in 1884 more than one third of all men employed in rolling mills were skilled, whereas by 1907 their proportion had shrunk to 17 per cent. Had there been no expansion in the steel industry, more than one half of the skilled men employed in 1884 would have been reduced to the semi-skilled grade. But as the growth of production outran the progress of labor-saving methods and machinery, the skilled and semi-skilled men who were displaced from one department were absorbed in others, and still there were openings in the higher grades which were filled by promotion from the ranks of the older unskilled men. Of course the whole trend of the technical progress

[1] Fitch, *loc. cit.*, pp. 3–4, 55–56, 139–141.

in the steel industry being toward elimination of human skill, the advancement of the minority to skilled and semi-skilled positions depended upon the employment of ever-increasing numbers of unskilled laborers. For reasons explained in Chapter VIII.,

> English, Irish, and German immigration began to fall off at just about the time that the steel industry began to expand so rapidly and at the same time to introduce the automatic processes. This created a tremendous market for unskilled labor just as the field of immigration was shifting from Northwestern to Southeastern Europe. Slavs coming to America to perform the unskilled manual labor, and finding it in the steel industry, sent for their relatives and neighbors. These automatic accretions, through letters and friends returning to the old country and spreading the tidings of where work is to be had, are at once the most natural and most widespread factors in mobilizing an immigrant labor force.[1]

Mr. Fitch is careful to note that "*the newer immigrants are not working for less pay for a day's rough work than the races they replaced. The money wages paid for common labor in the Pittsburgh steel mills have been going up* during the period referred to."[2] It is clear that the recent immigrants were not "brought" to this country to undercut the wages of the older employees.

> The Irish were not driven out of the blast furnaces by a fresh immigration with lower standards of living [says Mr. Fitch further]; rather the conditions in the industry—the twelve-hour day, the days and the weeks without a day of rest, the twenty-four-hour shift—made the life intolerable. They could make as good a living working fewer hours a day, and only six days in the week, in other positions and in other industries. So the Irish worker went out and the Slav came in.[3]

The effect of these readjustments on the distribution of the working force by race and occupation in the Pittsburgh district can be seen from Table 121.

The average proportion of Southern and Eastern Europeans among the iron and steel workers, according to the investigations of the Immigration Commission, was 44.5

[1] Fitch, *loc. cit.*, p. 143.
[2] *Ibid.*, pp. 142–143.
[3] *Ibid.*, p. 146.

TABLE 121.

EMPLOYEES OF CARNEGIE STEEL COMPANY PLANTS IN ALLEGHENY COUNTY, PENNSYLVANIA, CLASSIFIED BY SKILL AND RACIAL GROUP, MARCH, 1907.[1]

Race and nativity	Number				Per cent distribution							
					By race and nativity				By skill within each racial group			
	All grades	Skilled	Semi-skilled	Unskilled	All grades	Skilled	Semi-skilled	Unskilled	All grades	Skilled	Semi-skilled	Unskilled
Total	23,337	3,988	4,989	14,360	100.0	100.0	100.0	100.0	100.0	17.1	21.4	61.5
Native:												
White	5,705	2,316	1,879	1,510	24.5	58.0	37.7	10.5	100.0	40.6	22.9	26.5
Colored	331	66	76	189	1.4	1.7	1.5	1.3	100.0	20.0	32.9	57.1
Foreign-born:												
Teuton	1,820	714	585	521	7.8	17.9	11.7	3.6	100.0	39.2	32.1	28.7
Celt	1,401	474	407	520	6.0	11.9	8.2	3.6	100.0	33.8	29.1	37.1
Slav	13,003	359	1,946	10,698	55.7	9.0	39.0	74.6	100.0	2.8	15.0	82.2
All others	1,077	59	96	922	4.6	1.5	1.9	6.4	100.0	5.4	9.0	85.6
Recapitulation:												
English-speaking white	8,926	3,504	2,871	2,551	38.3	87.8	57.6	17.7	100.0	39.2	32.2	28.6
Southern and Eastern Europeans	14,080	418	2,042	11,620	60.3	10.5	40.9	81.0	100.0	3.0	14.5	82.5

[1] *The Pittsburgh Survey,* "The Steel Workers," Table A, p. 349; Table B, p. 350.

per cent in the East and 49.4 per cent in the Middle West.[1] The proportion of Slavs among the employees of the Carnegie Steel Company was accordingly above the average, which ought to emphasize the effects of immigration upon labor conditions in the iron and steel industry.

The classification of employees by the Carnegie Steel Company is different from that followed in Table 34.[2] The Immigration Commission draws the dividing line between skilled and unskilled occupations at $1.45 a day, whereas the Carnegie Steel Company includes among the unskilled some occupations with a higher average wage. Moreover, the Immigration Commission has disregarded the semi-skilled class. According to the classification of the company, a little over one sixth of the "unskilled" employees in 1907 were English-speaking; of the semi-skilled two fifths were immigrants from Southern and Eastern Europe; among the skilled only one tenth were of the new immigrant races.

The wages of each of these classes have been variously affected by the changes in machinery and methods. The wages of unskilled laborers, five sixths of whom are immigrants from Southern and Eastern Europe, "have increased in the last few years. In 1892 they received 14 cents an hour at Homestead. In 1907–08 their pay was 16½ cents an hour in the mills of the United States Steel Corporation—an advance of 18 per cent over the hourly pay of 1892. This increase fell short by 4 per cent in keeping pace with the increased cost of necessities as indicated by the *Bureau of Labor Bulletin*. . . . In May, 1910, announcement was made of a general increase in wages for all employees of the United States Steel Corporation. It was described as approximating 6 per cent over existing rates. Common laborers' pay was increased in the mills of the Corporation in the Pittsburg district from 16½ cents an hour to 17½ cents. This is an increase of 25 per cent over the 14-cent rate paid in 1892."

[1] Compiled from the *Reports of the Immigration Commission*, vol. 8, Table 23, pp. 34–35.

[2] See Chapter VII.

At the opposite extreme are placed, by Mr. Fitch, "the men of highest skill, headed by the rollers and heaters, who have gangs working under them and are practically foremen. These men represent not over 5 per cent of all employees." They are only a minority among the men classed by the company as skilled. Of the latter class, as stated, only one tenth are Southern and Eastern Europeans; it is reasonably certain, however, that none of them are among "the men at the top."[1] These "aristocrats of labor" have had their earnings reduced since 1892. The cuts vary, according to position, from 5.39 per cent to 41.20 per cent.

The intermediate 35 per cent are "the real steel workers. . . . They are men skilled in steel manufacture. . . . These men are individually essential to the industry." Their wages have remained in a "stationary condition, and if compared with the increased cost of living," exhibit a "downward tendency." The proportion of Slavs among them can be estimated at 31 per cent.[2] This class holds in every respect an intermediate place; they have not fared as well relatively as the immigrants from Southern and Eastern Europe who form the bulk of the unskilled force; still with one third among them drawn from the new immigration they have done better than the "aristocrats of labor" who do not come in contact with the new immigrants.

The question arises, has not the competition of the Slav prevented the wages of the skilled men below the grade of foreman from rising apace with the cost of living? An

[1] "I was unable to learn of any Slavs who had worked up to positions as rollers or heaters in the Pittsburgh mills," says Miss Byington in her study of Homestead. "This is due without doubt to the poorer industrial equipment of the immigrants, as well as to the unwillingness of the foremen to give the better positions to them."—*The Pittsburgh Survey*, "Homestead," p. 148.

[2] This ratio is obtained by computation from Table 121, allowing 5 per cent of all employees for the "men at the top" and placing all skilled and semi-skilled Southern and Eastern Europeans in the intermediate class.

answer to this question may be found if the wages of the Pittsburgh skilled men are compared with those of the skilled men employed in the Southern mills where there is very little competition from new immigration.

The boundary line drawn by the Immigration Commission between skilled and unskilled workers—$1.45 per day—obviously does not fit the conditions in the Pittsburgh district, where common laborers were paid 16.5 cents per hour previous to the recent raise. The recent report of the United States Bureau of Labor on labor conditions in the iron and steel industry divides all employees into three classes: (1) The lowest class, of the same grade as common laborers, whose earnings are less than 18 cents per hour; (2) the highest class, whose earnings are 25 cents and over per hour; and (3) the intermediate class, from 18 to 25 cents. The proportions of these classes in the total number of employees are: 49.7 per cent for the unskilled, 23.6 per cent for the skilled, and 26.7 per cent for the intermediate.[1] The latter class differs too widely from the intermediate class of the Pittsburgh Survey to be comparable with it. A fairly uniform basis, however, can be selected from the three classifications, as follows:

(1) From the Pittsburgh Survey: all employees earning over $2.50 per day.[2]

(2) From the report of the Bureau of Labor: all employees earning 25 cents and over, per hour.

(3) From the report of the Immigration Commission: all male employees 18 years of age and over who earn $17.50 and over per week.

The close similarity of the three groups appears from the comparative table on page 406.

The proportion of Southern and Eastern Europeans in this grade was 16.1 per cent in the East, while in the South the aggregate of Southern and Eastern Europeans and

[1] *Summary of Wages and Hours of Labor from the Report on Conditions of Employment in the Iron and Steel Industry in the United States*, p. 26.

[2] Fitch, *loc. cit.*, Table 8, p. 163.

negroes in the same grade was only 2.2 per cent. Thus in the East there were relatively about twice as many English-speaking employees receiving the highest rates as in the South, notwithstanding the much higher percentage of Southern and Eastern Europeans competing for the same positions in the East.

TABLE 122.

PER CENT OF SKILLED IRON AND STEEL WORKERS, BY LOCATION.

Location	Source	Earnings		
		25c. and over per hour	$2.50 and over per day	$17.50 and over per week
Allegheny County	Pittsburgh Survey	....	28.17	....
Pittsburgh District	U. S. Bureau of Labor	24.96	....	....
East...........	Immigration Commission	....	....	24.0
South..........	Immigration Commission; U. S. Bureau of Labor	13.26	....	13.6

In order to assemble into one group all Southern mill-workers who perform the same grade of labor as the men employed in Eastern mills at $17.50 per week and upwards, we must descend one step and admit all Southern iron and steel workers earning $15 per week.

As can be seen from Table 123 on page 407, two fifths (42 per cent) of the skilled iron and steel workers in the Southern mills earn only from $15 to $17.50 per week, whereas all employees of the same grade in the Eastern mills are paid not less than $17.50 per week. The difference cannot be explained by the competition of Southern and Eastern Europeans or negroes, because the aggregate of those two racial groups among Southern iron and steel workers earning $15 and over does not exceed 1.8 per cent, whereas in the Eastern mills the Southern and Eastern Europeans constitute 16.1 per cent of all mill men earning $17.50 and upwards.

TABLE 123.

PER CENT OF SKILLED IRON AND STEEL WORKERS WITH SPECIFIED EARNINGS IN EASTERN AND SOUTHERN MILLS.[1]

District	Earnings per week	Per cent of all employees	Per cent within the grade
South.....	$15 to $17.50	9.8	42
	$17.50 and over	13.6	58
	$15 and over	23.4	100
East......	$17.50 and over	24.0	100

There is considerable variation in the proportion of skilled and unskilled labor employed in various departments of iron and steel mills. This variation may affect geographical comparisons which take no account of industrial specialization. In order to eliminate this source of error the proportions of employees earning 25 cents per hour and over in productive occupations[2] are compared in Table 124 by departments. The figures show that, in all departments but one, a larger proportion of all employees are paid those rates in the Pittsburgh district than in the South. It may be assumed that the substitution of machinery for human skill in the Pittsburgh district is as far advanced as in the Southern mills; the proportion of skilled

[1] *Reports of the Immigration Commission*, vol. 9, pp. 134, 355.

[2] The following table is confined to "productive occupations" in order to exclude from the comparison, as far as possible, others than iron and steel workers. "The wages of workmen in mechanical trades are much more nearly standardized in the different districts than of the employees in the productive occupations, who are dependent almost entirely on the iron and steel industry for employment." *Summary of Wages and Hours of Labor in the Iron and Steel Industry*, p. 33.

men in each department of the Pittsburgh mills may, therefore, be accepted as the standard. It follows, accordingly, that in the Southern mills a fraction varying from one sixth to two thirds of all skilled men are paid less than 25 cents per hour, whereas in the Pittsburgh district all men of the same class are paid 25 cents and over.

TABLE 124.

PER CENT OF EMPLOYEES IN EACH DEPARTMENT EARNING 25 CENTS AND OVER PER HOUR, IN THE PITTSBURGH AND THE SOUTHERN DISTRICT.[1]

Department	Pittsburgh	South	Difference	
			Per cent of all employees	Per cent of Pittsburgh ratio
Puddling mills..........	70	58	−12	−17
Blooming mills.........	47	31	−16	−34
Bar mills...............	38	22	−16	−42
Bessemer converters....	36	20	−16	−44
Miscellaneous mills.....	35	65	+30	....
Open-hearth furnaces...	28	22	−6	−22
Blast furnaces.........	6	2	−4	−67

The exception noted above applies to eleven miscellaneous rod mills in the United States employing a total of 333 men at 25 cents and over per hour,[2] *i. e.*, about ⅓ per cent of the total in productive occupations. The number is too small to affect the labor situation.[3]

The preceding comparisons lead to the conclusion that *the rates of wages of iron and steel workers vary inversely as the ratio of recent immigrants:* The wages of the unskilled, the bulk of whom are Slavs, have kept pace with the cost of living; the wages of the "aristocrats of labor," none of whom are Slavs, have been reduced; the money wages of

[1] *Summary of Wages and Hours of Labor in the Iron and Steel Industry*, p. 32.

[2] *Ibid.*, pp. 16 and 25.

[3] At the present writing the full report of the Bureau of Labor is still in press, while the published summary does not go into details of a local character.

other skilled men, two thirds of whom are English-speaking, have remained stationary—the wages of this class of employees are lower in the South, where they meet no immigrant competition, than in the Pittsburgh District.

This correlation between the percentage of recent immigrants and the variation of the rate of wages is not the manifestation of some innate racial predisposition to higher wages, but the working of the law of supply and demand in the labor market. The employment of a high percentage of immigrants in any section, industry, or occupation is an indication of an active demand for labor in excess of the native supply. Absence of immigrants is a sign of a dull market for labor. The wages of the unskilled Slav laborers have been raised because of the increasing demand for unskilled labor, not in the steel industry alone, but in other industries as well. The unskilled Slavs "can dig ditches or heave coal any day just as well as they can throw chains around piles of steel billets or shovel scrap into furnaces." On the contrary, the skilled English-speaking steel workers, though "individually essential to the industry . . . could not enter any other industry without a reduction in earning power, because they are skilled only as steel workers."[1] Hence their acquiescence in a lowered rate of wages, whereas the unskilled Slav with his supposedly "lower standard of living" has been able to command as high a wage (measured by purchasing power) as his English-speaking predecessor.

Long hours and Sunday work have not come with the new immigration. "Sunday work has been general in blast furnaces in this country from the beginning."[2] In rolling mills the practice has varied. There were some mills which ran on Sundays, as far back as the 80's, before "the Slav invasion." The Amalgamated Association of Iron and Steel Workers in the days of its power raised no objection to labor on Sunday. Its main concern was solely with wages, and it is a historical fact, worthy of notice,

[1] Fitch, *loc. cit.*, p. 154. [2] *Ibid.*, p. 168.

that the twelve-hour day was staunchly defended by the organized iron and steel workers when the steel manufacturers, prompted by technical considerations, attempted to reduce the day to eight hours.

The twelve-hour day was the outgrowth of metallurgical conditions in the old iron mills. In puddling one charge has to be melted, worked, and taken out before the next can go in. From the beginning of the industry in the Pittsburgh District, five charges or "heats" have been a day's work for a puddler. In the mills rolling sheet iron, too, the working day was determined by the number of heats. In the early days of the iron industry five heats took about twelve hours. This was the basis of the twelve-hour day with the two-shift system. With the progress of improvements in furnace construction and methods, it became possible to finish a turn of five heats in a shorter time and the actual working day gradually shrank to one of ten hours and even less. As a result of the shortened time, there came to be periods of idleness between shifts. In a sheet mill this interim between shifts was especially objectionable, for sheet iron is rolled so thin that good results can be obtained only when the rolls are expanded by the heat. The rolls are so shaped that when cold they cannot turn out a sheet of uniform thickness; consequently after a period of idleness hot scrap is sent through them until they reach the correct expansion. To avoid these periods of idleness, the manufacturers, in the 80's, sought to introduce an eight-hour day. This was for a long time resisted by the union, which stood firmly for the twelve-hour shift. The reason for this unusual attitude was that the skilled men who belonged to the union were paid at piece rates and apprehended a loss of a part of their earnings in case they might not be able to turn out five heats in eight hours. The question was discussed at several national conventions. Some of the officers took the ground that a reduction of hours was desirable even if it originally involved a loss of earnings to individuals. The introduction of a three-shift system would create a demand for half as many more skilled men as were employed at the time and would eventually enable the members of the union to win an increase in piece rates. But the rank and file of the membership could not see so far ahead and forced the officers to insist upon the twelve-hour day. Some lodges which had accepted the eight-hour shift were suspended. One of the presidents of the union who supported the manufacturers in their effort to introduce the eight-hour day was denounced by the membership as a traitor to the cause of labor. The controversy lasted several years in the 80's, when the iron and steel workers were all of the English-speaking races. Later the union relaxed its rule against the eight-hour system, but the manufacturers had meanwhile readjusted themselves to the old twelve-hour shift.[1] This episode characterizes the spirit of the Amalgamated Association.

The Association was originally organized as a union of skilled iron workers and was very strong in the iron industry. But with the decline of the latter the power of the organization began to wane. It never gained strength in the steel mills. Out of 3800 men at Homestead when the strike began in 1892, only 752 were members in good standing of the Amalgamated Association. "The Association has always been an organization of skilled workers and has centered its efforts on securing better conditions for that class of labor alone," says Mr. Fitch. "It was only in 1889 that the constitution permitted the admission of all men, *except, however, common laborers.*"[2]

Nevertheless, when the Amalgamated Association struck in 1892, the common laborers, the despised Hungarians and Slavs, stood by it.[3] The defeat of the Homestead strike broke the organization. It had been rapidly increas-

[1] See Fitch, *loc. cit.*, pp. 90–97. [2] *Ibid.* pp. 97, 98.

[3] "A great cause was in the balance, and in their humble way the army of the poor Hungarians and Slavs understood it," says a trade-union historian of the Homestead strike.—Myron R. Stowell: *Fort Frick, or the Siege of Homestead*, p. 86.

ing its membership since 1885, when it had numbered only 5700, to the year preceding the great strike, when it reported to the national convention a membership of 24,000, organized in 290 lodges. During the year following the strike, it lost about one half of that number. There were slight increases at times in later years; since 1903, however, it has been gradually declining, until it had, in 1910, only 103 lodges with a little over 8000 members.[1] This is less than 5 per cent of the total number of iron and steel workers in the United States.[2]

The strength of the organization of the iron and steel workers in the 80's lay in their special skill. Though a minority of the force, they were indispensable to the industry, because they could not be replaced. It is for this very reason that they barred common laborers from their organization: they did not want to become involved in controversies over the wages of day laborers who could easily be replaced by others. But when improved machinery displaced the skill of the mechanic the organization of the skilled iron and steel workers lost its foothold. To-day, says Mr. Fitch—

> every man is in training for the next position above. If all of the rollers in the Homestead plant were to strike to-morrow the work would go on, and only temporary inconvenience, if any, would be suffered. There would simply be a step up along the line: the tableman would take the rolls, the hooker would manipulate the tables, perhaps one of the shearmen's helpers would take the hooker's position, and somewhere, away down the line, an unskilled yard laborer would be taken to fill the vacancy in the lowest position involving skill. The course would vary in the different styles of mills, as the positions vary in number and character, but the operating principle is everywhere the same. In the open hearth department the line of promotion runs through common labor, metal wheelers, stock handlers, cinder-pit man, second helper, and first helper to melter foreman. In this way the companies develop and train their own men. . . . Thus the working

---

[1] Fitch, *loc. cit.*, p. 297.

[2] In May, 1910, there were 172,706 workers employed in the steel mills of the United States.—*Summary of Wages and Hours of Labor in the Iron and Steel Industry*, p. 17.

force is pyramided and is held together by the ambition of the men lower down; even a serious break in the ranks adjusts itself all but automatically.[1]

In 1909, an attempt was made by "the men lower down" to unite all mill workers in a common demand for better terms of employment. In the McKees Rocks strike the leaders and the rank and file were mostly recent immigrants. Of this strike Mr. Fitch has the following to say:

> In the summer of 1909 there was a demonstration of the spirit of immigrant workmen that opened the eyes of the public to qualities heretofore unknown. For many weeks at McKees Rocks they persisted in their strike against the Pressed Steel Car Company. It had been thought that the Slavs were too sluggish to resist their employers, and unable to organize along industrial lines. It was proved in this conflict that neither theory was correct.[2]

---

[1] Fitch, *loc. cit.*, pp. 141, 142.

[2] *Ibid.*, pp. 237, 238.

CHAPTER XXI

THE COAL MINERS

THE Immigration Commission considered the coal-mining industry as typical of the conditions created by immigration, and gave it accordingly the most prominent place in its report. Two volumes are devoted to bituminous coal, and a portion of a third to anthracite. The findings of the Commission may be briefly summed up as follows: the English-speaking mine workers do not desire to associate with the immigrants from Southern and Eastern Europe, consequently those immigrants are undesirable. There are in the reports some valuable data on the economic side of the question, but they have had no part in shaping the conclusions of the Commission. It views the conditions in the coal-mining industry with the eyes of the English-speaking trade-union officials, who apprehend in the multitudes of Slav and Italian mine workers a growing menace to their influence in the organization.

To follow the Commission's summary historical review of the coal-mining industry, the conflict between the English-speaking and non-English-speaking races began in the 80's, when a series of unsuccessful strikes forced "a greater or less number of natives, English, Irish, Scotch, and Germans," to leave "Pennsylvania in search of better working conditions in the Middle West or the localities in the Southwest or West to which the recent immigrants had not penetrated in important numbers." The same situation was repeated in the 90's in West Virginia. The "constantly growing number of Southern and Eastern Europeans . . . completely inundated the older employees," with the result that many of them "moved westward in search of better working conditions," and "the immigrants from Southern and Eastern Europe were left in undisputed control of the situation." In their new retreat the English-speaking miners remained undisturbed until the first decade of the present century, when the advancing columns of the Southern and Eastern Europeans reached them there. "As the pressure, resulting from the increase in numbers of the recent immigrants has become stronger . . . the older immigrants and natives," who were unable to change their occupation, moved "from localities and mines where the competition of the Southern and Eastern European has been most strongly felt to other localities in the Middle West or Southwest." But soon the first detachments of the Southern and Eastern Europeans made their appearance in the Southwestern fields and forced the "Americans and individual members of the English, Irish, Scotch, and Welsh races" to retreat to New Mexico and Colorado. The narrative concludes with the following statement, which sounds the keynote, as it were, of the whole report:

> *From the standpoint of the natives and the older immigrant employees,* it therefore seems clearly apparent that the competition of recent immigrants has caused a gradual displacement, commencing in Pennsylvania and extending westward, until at the present time the representatives of the pioneer employees in the bituminous mining industry are making their last stand in the Southwest, and especially in Kansas, where they are gradually being weakened and are withdrawing to the newly opened fields of the West, to which the recent immigrant has not come in important numbers. Along with this displacement of the older employees in the different coal-producing areas has proceeded the elimination of a correspondingly large proportion from the industry and the development of such working and living conditions that the sons of natives and the second generation of immigrant races have only to a very small extent consented to enter the industry.[1]

The story of the pioneers "making their last stand" against the invaders has a pathetic sound uncommon in

[1] *Reports of the Immigration Commission,* vol. 1, p. 536.

PRODUCTION OF COAL IN STATES WITH AN ANNUAL

1880

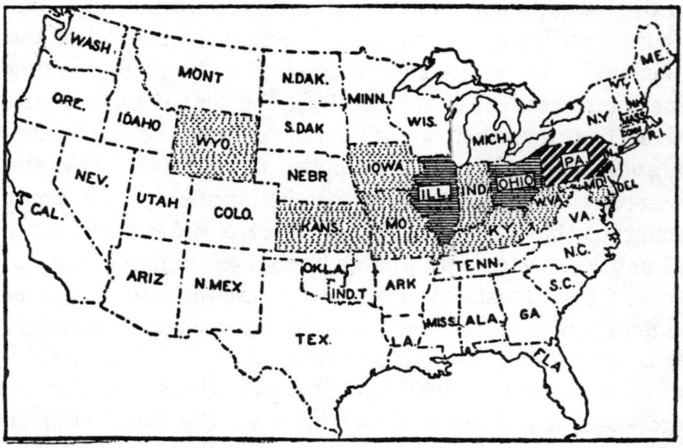

1890

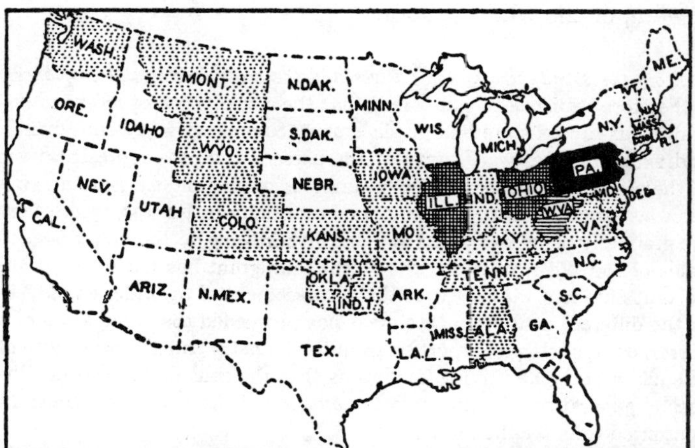

1 TO 4 | 5 TO 9 | 10 TO 19
20 TO 39 | 40 TO 79 | 80 & OVER

(1 unit = 1,000,000 tons)

OUTPUT OF NOT LESS THAN 1,000,000 TONS.

1900

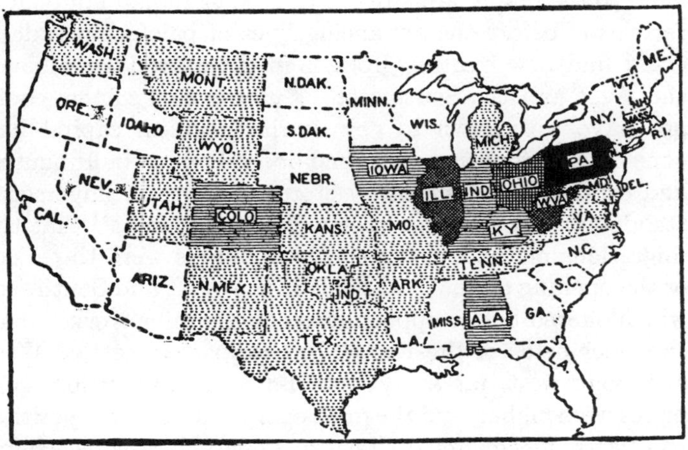

1910

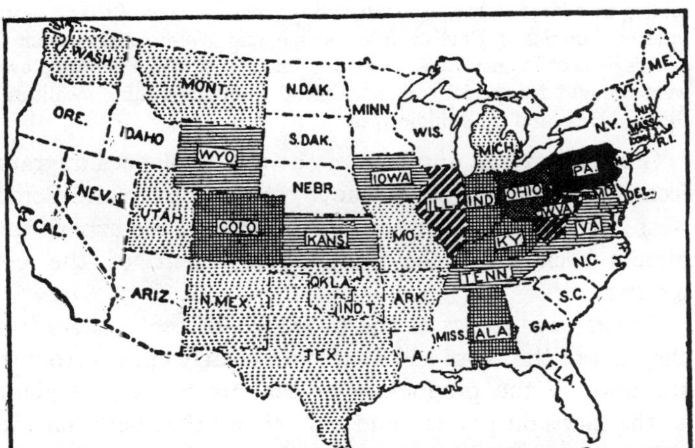

1 TO 4 | 5 TO 9 | 10 TO 19

20 TO 39 | 40 TO 79 | 80 & OVER

(1 unit = 1,000,000 tons)

official statistical publications. It does not belong, however, to the realm of history. A tribe of Indian huntsmen, retreating before the advancing lines of paleface invaders, could find new hunting-grounds in the untrodden wilds of the West and the Southwest. But the coal miners could not have withdrawn to new territory unless capital had gone there before them, and had opened mines, built houses, and established commissary stores. From an impersonal standpoint "it therefore seems clearly apparent" that the migrations of the English-speaking miners were the effect of the opening of new coal-fields in the West and Southwest which offered better opportunities to the mine worker than the older fields of the East. In the sparsely settled West and Southwest, far away from Eastern competition, coal prices were higher, and the mine operators were in a position to offer inducements to Eastern miners who were willing to go westward. Turning from the summary to the materials of the Immigration Commission we learn that

> both Kansas and Oklahoma were sparsely settled about 1880, when mining on a large scale was begun, and the management of the properties induced Americans, English, Irish, Scotch, and Welsh to come from the coal regions of Pennsylvania to work in the mines. The first employees were brought by special car or trainload from the mining localities of Pennsylvania and the Middle West.[1]

Gradually large numbers of the old employees migrated from the Middle West to the West, the South and Southwest "where there was an active demand for experienced miners because of the rapid development of the coal industry."[2]

The motive forces of the migration of coal miners from the East to the West and Southwest clearly appear from the statistics of the production of coal by States. A glance at the maps on pp. 416 and 417[3] shows that between 1880

[1] *Reports of the Immigration Commission*, vol. 6, p. 22; vol. 7, pp. 9, 11, 15.

[2] *Ibid.*, vol. 6, pp. 666, 667.

[3] The figures for these maps are taken from the *Report of the United States Geological Survey on Coal*, 1910, p. 14. States producing less than 1,000,000 tons are not included.

and 1890 coal mining developed in Virginia, Tennessee, and Alabama in the South; in Oklahoma and Indian Territory in the Southwest; and in Colorado, Montana, and Washington in the West; that between 1890 and 1900 new fields were opened in Michigan, Arkansas, Texas, New Mexico, and Utah; and that while this development was going on in the West and Southwest, production in the old States was also fast increasing. It is plain that the men to work in the new mines had to come from somewhere. The increase of the population of the United States, both by births and immigration, did not keep pace with the growth of coal production, as can be seen from Table 125 next below. The progress of machine mining has been slow: in 1910 less than one half (41.74 per cent) of the total output of bituminous coal was machine-mined.[1] Certainly the native population alone was insufficient to supply the increasing demand for labor.[2] The extent of the demand can be seen from Diagram XXII.[3]

TABLE 125.

GROWTH OF POPULATION AND OF THE PRODUCTION OF COAL, 1880–1910.[4]

Year	Per capita production, tons.	Per cent of increase for decade	
		Population	Coal production
1880	1.5	....	....
1890	2.5	25.5	85.4
1900	3.5	20.7	91.0
1910	5.5	21.0	86.0

[1] *United States Geological Survey: The Production of Coal in the United States*, 1910, p. 51.

[2] This is the unanimous testimony coming from all sections of the country. See *Reports of the Immigration Commission*, vol. 6, p. 23; vol. 7. pp. 145, 146, 156, 217, 220.

[3] The figures for the diagram are taken from the compilation in the *Reports of the Immigration Commission*, vol. 6, p. 5, Table 5.

[4] *Mines and Quarries*, 1902, p. 669, Table 6. *United States Geological*

The development of coal mining outside of Pennsylvania from 1880 to 1889 was sufficient to have absorbed every old employee who had been working in the bituminous coal

DIAGRAM XXII.

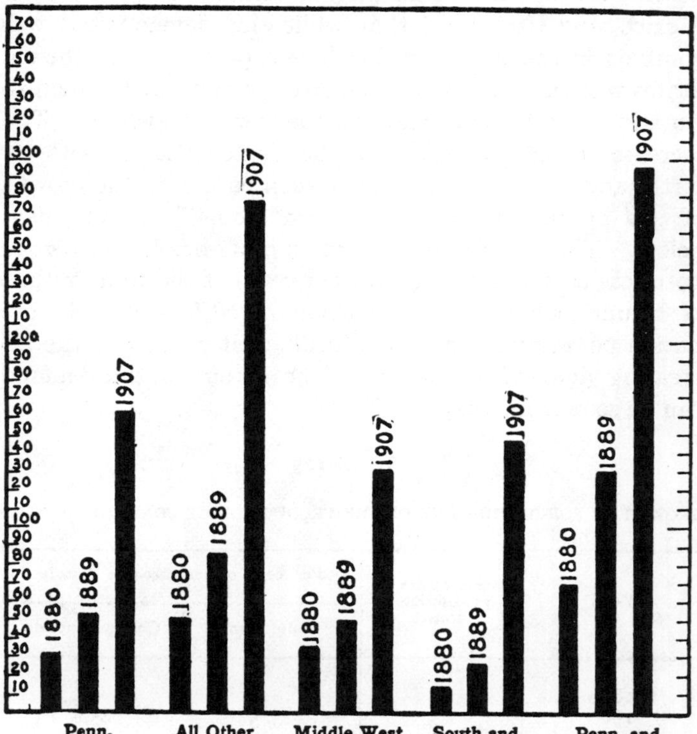

XXII. Number of persons employed in bituminous coal mines, 1880, 1889, and 1907 (thousands)

mines of Pennsylvania in 1880. The development of mining in the South and Southwest since 1889 has been sufficient to have furnished employment to every wage-earner who had been at work in the bituminous coal mines

Survey: Production of Coal, 1910, p. 21. *XIII. Census. Population*, vol. i., p. 24.

of Pennsylvania and the Middle West in 1889. At the same time the additions since 1889 to the force employed in the bituminous coal mines of Pennsylvania alone have equaled the increase in the operating forces of the Southern and Southwestern mines, while the additions to the number of employees in the Middle West since 1889 have exceeded the total number of the mine workers of Pennsylvania for that year. This growth of the industry stimulated a great deal of shifting of labor from one place to another.

The main inducement for experienced miners to migrate westward was the greater opportunity for advancement in the rapidly developing coal mines of the new fields. The proportion of supervisory or better-paid positions in an old coal mine, like in any other establishment, is limited. The opening of every new mine, however, creates new positions for skilled and experienced miners. While the expansion of mining operations in the older States offered many opportunities for advancement to old employees, still in no single concern could all the employees be raised to higher positions at one time. The more ambitious, to whom the road to promotion at their old places appeared too long, sought better opportunities in new fields. Their places had to be filled by new immigrants. There was no "displacement"[1] of the old by the new employees; the Southern and Eastern Europeans did not "inundate" the older employees, but merely filled the vacuum produced by the continuous pumping out of the older employees. The ultimate result of these migrations within the coal-mining industry has been that "the largest portion of those remaining, including the most efficient and progressive element, have, as a result of the expansion of the industry, secured advancement to the more skilled and responsible positions."[2]

The openings for the English-speaking mine workers were not confined to mining.

[1] The misuse of the word "displacement" in the *Reports of the Immigration Commission* has been adverted to, in Chapter VII.

[2] *Reports of the Immigration Commission*, vol. 1, p. 537.

> The period of development in coal mining and coke manufacturing was also a period of great expansion in manufacturing industries . . . so that for the intelligent and ambitious American, German, English, Irish, or Scotch employee there were abundant opportunities to secure . . . more pleasant or better paid work in shops and factories near home.[1]

Moreover, the growth of mining communities has created business opportunities for alert Americans and English-speaking immigrants. An illustration is furnished by the Borough of South Fork, Cambria County, Pennsylvania, alias "Representative Community B,"[2] where "the English-speaking races seem to leave the mines as soon as they accumulate earnings and to enter mercantile pursuits or seek more remunerative or more pleasant work of other kinds. The greater number of the business and professional men in the town were formerly mine workers."[3]

The Immigration Commission believes that this advancement is "probably without direct connection with recent immigration."[4] This is, however, a mistaken view. "Bituminous coal is practically the only product of the locality."[5] It is owing only to "the opening of the new mines and the extension of the old ones"[6] that the population of the "representative community" has grown from 1295 in 1890 to 2635 in 1900 and to 4592 in 1910. Two thirds of this increase were due to immigration, not counting the native-born children of immigrants.[7] And it is ob-

[1] *Reports of the Immigration Commission*, p. 335. The quotation relates to Pennsylvania, but the same is true of the United States in general.

[2] The description of that community contains nothing of a confidential nature that would warrant the withholding of its name from the public in an official report. Moreover, the disguise is too thin to be effective: there is only one incorporated place in the State of Pennsylvania that had a population of 2635 in 1900 (*XIII. Census: Population*, vol. iii., p. 558).

[3] *Reports of the Immigration Commission*, vol. 6, p. 563. See also p. 426.

[4] *Ibid.*, p. 563.

[5] *Ibid.*, p. 532.

[6] *Ibid.*, p. 563.

[7] In 1900 the total number of foreign-born in the borough was 587; in 1908 it was estimated at 1900.—*Ibid.*, p. 533.

viously the increase of the population of the borough that has made room for more professional and business men.

Speaking generally, the "employees displaced as miners" could not "have gone into manufacturing plants and shops . . . into street railways and trolley service, or into business for themselves,"[1] had not the recent immigrants furnished the labor to do the disagreeable and dangerous work in the manufacturing plants and mines and the passengers to ride on the trolley cars.

"The displaced employees did not better their economic condition," however, in the Middle West—says the Immigration Commission. The "subsequent history of the old employees" in that section is recited as follows:

> No extensive data are available as to the subsequent history of the pioneer miners in the Middle West who were displaced by the recent immigrant. It is well known, and has already been pointed out, that many of them advanced in the industrial scale, becoming foremen and attaining other responsible positions. It has also been mentioned that a large number abandoned the occupation of miner for positions as day or shift men. Many also migrated and located in other sections of the Middle West where hand mining continued to be followed, and many also moved to other coal-fields, principally to Kansas and Oklahoma, in the Southwest. The reports from several communities also show that many of the former miners who left the industry entirely . . . entered mercantile, clerical, mechanical, and other lines of work. The reports further unite in the statement, however, that the displaced employees did not better their economic condition.[2]

There are irreconcilable contradictions in this "history." It seems inconceivable that those of the "displaced" pick miners who "advanced in the industrial scale, becoming foremen and attaining other responsible positions" (there are alleged to have been "many of them"), "did not better their economic condition." It is contrary to common experience that the "*displaced*" miners "who *left* the industry" to enter mercantile or mechanical lines of work should not be earning more as business men or mechanics

[1] *Reports of the Immigration Commission*, vol. 6, p. 426.
[2] *Ibid.*, p. 668.

than they had been earning with pick and shovel inside of a coal mine. The "data . . . as to the subsequent history of the pioneer miners" are admittedly scarce. The loose "statement" of the anonymous "reports" is clearly sheer hearsay, which deserves no place in an official report.

The Immigration Commission attaches undue importance to the social prejudice against "a Hunkey's job," which it considers "one of the strongest forces toward the displacement of the older employees either from the industry or from certain occupations within the industry."[1] The Commission mistakes here cause for effect. The contempt for "a Hunkey's job" did not exist so long as the bulk of the English-speaking operatives were employed on that grade of work. Yet, then as now, the "tendency" on the part of the native American "to abandon the occupation of coal digging and to enter the better class of positions about the mines" must have been "decidedly marked,"[2] whenever an opportunity presented itself. We further learn that "the exodus of former operatives from the industry" was stimulated by "the fact that there were opportunities to secure work which paid as well or better than mining, that this work was often more agreeable and less dangerous."[3] It was only after their elevation (or "displacement," as the Commission would have it) from the ranks of coal diggers to the more exalted station of mine bosses and street car conductors that they began to look down upon those who had succeeded them. This caste feeling is far too general in all climes and conditions of life to be classed among the effects of "recent immigration."

Still more strained is the argument that the recent immigration "is preventing them [the English-speaking miners] from allowing their children to enter the industry. The prosperous miner educates his children for softer-handed work and they have to move away from Community

[1] *Reports of the Immigration Commission*, vol. 6, p. 426.
[2] *Ibid.*, vol. 7, p. 221. [3] *Ibid.*, vol. 6, p. 335

A [Shenandoah, Pa.] to find it. The well-to-do storekeeper and the professional man moves away to find a more suitable environment for his growing children."[1] This statement implies that but for the recent immigrant, a prosperous American father, who has the means to educate his son for "softer-handed work," would allow him to do the disagreeable and dangerous work of a coal miner. Could a "well-to-do storekeeper" or a professional man find better opportunities for his son in a coal-mining town like Shenandoah with a population of 25,000, were all the coal miners men of pure Anglo-Saxon blood?

The increasing consumption of coal by the expanding American industries which has drawn to our coal mines the great masses of Southern and Eastern European immigrants, has also stimulated the introduction of mining machinery. The tendency of machinery is to replace the skilled miner by the unskilled laborer. The old American, English, Welsh, and Irish miners were pick miners. The introduction of mining machines, though gradual, must have displaced many of them and forced them to seek employment elsewhere. To be sure, the expansion of the coal-mining industry has been so rapid that the displaced pick miners soon found more remunerative employment as machine runners or in supervisory capacities. But this industrial transformation did not proceed without social waste and friction. When a new labor-saving machine is introduced, no provision is made for the men whose labor is to be dispensed with. The time, however short, spent in search of other employment may cause them hardship and anxiety. Meanwhile, they see their places taken by aliens speaking a foreign tongue. The impression is created that it is these unskilled foreigners who have displaced the English-speaking miners. The pick miners, like labor in general, opposed

[1] *Reports of the Immigration Commission*, vol. 16, p. 661. Community A is situated in Schuylkill County, Pa., and can be identified by the number of its inhabitants given on p. 663 (*XIII. Census: Population*, vol. iii., p. 558).

the introduction of machinery.[1] It naturally appeared to them that without the recent immigrants who were willing to work at the machines the introduction of mining machinery would have been impossible. These views of the English-speaking miners have found their way into the reports of the Industrial Commission[2] and of the Immigration Commission.[3] Mine operators who certainly know the economic advantage of the use of machinery have assumed an apologetic attitude by throwing the blame upon the immigrant, whose lack of "skill" makes the use of machinery imperative.[4] The truth is that a team of inexperienced, unskilled Slavs working under one machine runner are more efficient than an equal number of skilled and experienced English-speaking pick miners.

The comparative efficiency of pick and machine mining appears from the following calculation based on the report of the Ohio Chief Inspector of Mines for 1909. To every

[1] *Reports of the Immigration Commission*, vol. 6, p. 662.

[2] *Reports of the Industrial Commission*, vol. xv., p. xxxiv.

[3] "To some extent, the employment of the recent immigrant may have stimulated the use of mining machinery, inasmuch as this machinery renders it possible to employ in large numbers inexperienced and untrained men."—*Reports of the Immigration Commission*, vol. 6, pp. 423, 424. Elsewhere, under the significant caption "Deterioration of working conditions and methods caused by employment of recent immigrants," the Commission quotes the opinions of "the miners and union officials," who criticize the operators, "who, to fill abnormal demands for coal, employed inexperienced immigrants in such large numbers that it was impossible to teach them to mine by approved methods. . . . The statement is then made by the old employee that this state of affairs . . . leads to the introduction of machines."—*Ibid.*, p. 670.

[4] "The operators claim that, owing to the large percentage of immigrants at work in the mines who are unskilled, they are forced to use machines in order to maintain a good quality of coal, because where no machines are used the recent immigrants 'shoot the coal off the solid' instead of properly undercutting it, and, with excessive charges of powder, they thus produce a much larger percentage of slack coal than is produced when undercutting is done with the machine or by hand." —*Ibid.*, p. 650.

five pick miners there was employed one inside day hand. An average day's work per pick miner was 2.2 tons of lump coal, or 3.3 tons "run of mine." The average daily production per inside man was accordingly 1.8 tons of lump coal or 2.7 tons "run of mine." In machine mining there were on an average eight loaders, drillers, and shooters to each runner, and two other inside day hands to one runner. The average quantity cut by each machine runner per day was twenty-nine tons of lump coal or forty-three tons "run of mine." The average daily production per inside hand was 2.6 tons of lump coal or 3.9 tons "run of mine."[1] The margin in favor of machine mining was 0.8 tons of lump, or 1.2 tons "run of mine" per inside man, which was equivalent to a saving of 30 per cent. Moreover, with pick mining, ten out of every twelve inside men were skilled miners, whereas with machine mining only one in every eleven was a skilled man and the other ten were semi-skilled day men or unskilled coal loaders. The average price per ton paid to contract-miners is accordingly lower for machine mining than for pick mining. In Illinois the margin varied in 1901–1911 from 11.3 to 16.9 cents per ton.[2] The saving resulting from machine mining is estimated by an authority as follows:

At a mine producing 1000 tons per day and having a 15 cent margin in favor of machine mining, the gross saving would be about $150 a day, or $30,000 per year of 200 days. . . . The $30,000 saving will pay for the machine plant, installation, and cost of maintenance, as well as interest and depreciation, in about one year's time. The advantages of coal cutting are: (1) an increased percentage of large coal; (2) the coal is mined in a firmer and better condition; (3) a more regular line of face is obtained, leading to more systematic timbering; (4) increased safety conditions for the miner; (5) thin seams can be profitably mined; (6) increased output; and (7) fewer explosives are required for getting down the coal.[3]

---

[1] *Thirty-Fifth Annual Report of the Chief Inspector of Mines, Ohio*, pp. 90, 93, 94, 99, 100.

[2] *Illinois Coal Report*, 1911, p. 121.

[3] *Coal and Coke*, by Floyd W. Parsons, "The Mineral Industry," 1909, pp. 143, 144.

To imagine that the opposition of the English-speaking miners could have forced the mine operators to waive these savings, is to assume that without Slav and Italian immigration the laws of modern industrial evolution would have been suspended in the United States.

Statistics show that machine mining has made great progress in States with a small percentage of Southern and Eastern European coal miners and has been lagging behind in States with a large percentage of Southern and Eastern European coal miners. This fact stands out conspicuously in Diagram XXIII.[1] In 1900, the greatest progress of machine mining was reported from Ohio, while West Virginia was the most backward State, though the proportion of Southern and Eastern European miners in both States was the same. More than four fifths of the machine product of Ohio must have been mined by English-speaking men. The second rank in the order of the percentages of machine-mined coal was held by Kentucky, where the proportion of Southern and Eastern European miners was negligible. In Indiana likewise more than four fifths of all machine-mined coal was produced by English-speaking mine workers. On the other hand, Pennsylvania had four times as many Slavs, Italians, etc., working in coal mines as Ohio, yet machine mining was less advanced in Pennsylvania than in Ohio. In Pennsylvania and Illinois the percentage of machine-mined coal was greater than the percentage of Southern and Eastern European miners. Bearing in mind the greater average production per man where mining is done by machines, it can be clearly seen that a great deal of pick mining in those two States must have been done by Southern and Eastern Europeans. The occupation statistics of the census of 1910 have as yet not

[1] See Appendix, Table XXVI. The production of bituminous coal in the States shown in the diagram amounted in 1910 to 80 per cent of the total for the United States, and their aggregate production of machine-mined coal for the ten-year period 1900–1909 to 90 per cent of the total output of machine-mined coal in the United States.

DIAGRAM XXIII.

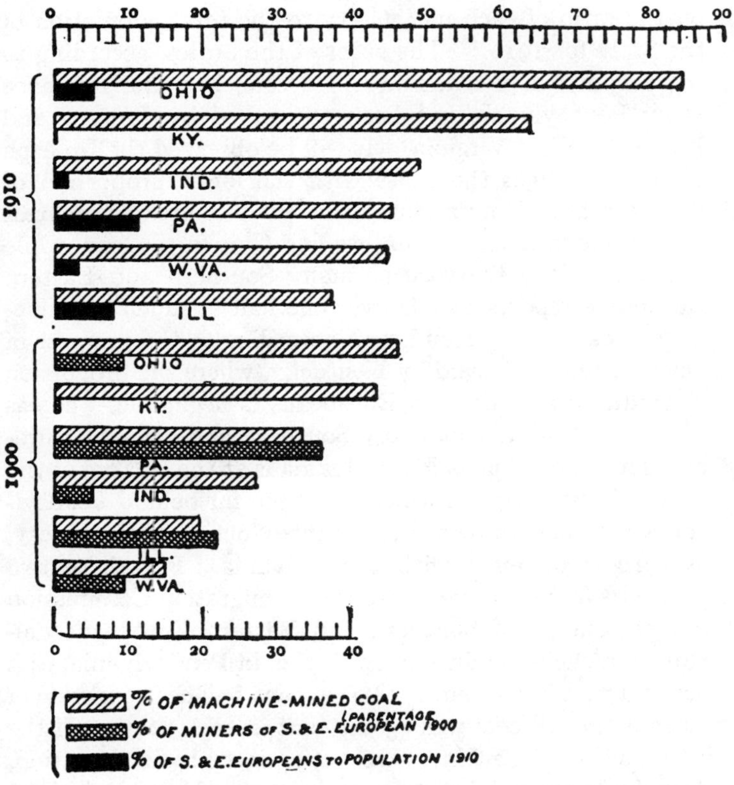

XXIII. Per cent of bituminous coal mined by machine, 1900 and 1910, compared with per cent ratio of Southern and Eastern European miners to all miners, 1900; and with per cent ratio of Southern and Eastern Europeans to the total population, 1910, for the principal States.

been published. Still for the purposes of the present comparison a fairly accurate index of the employment of Southern and Eastern Europeans in the mines is furnished by the ratio of each nationality to the total population of the State for 1910.[1] The order of the States, according to the proportion of machine-mined coal, has changed since 1900: Pennsylvania has been outranked by Indiana and Illinois by West Virginia. It will be observed that in each of these changes the State with the lower proportion of Southern and Eastern Europeans exhibits greater progress of machine mining. Again, we find Ohio in the lead, while Pennsylvania with twice as many Southern and Eastern Europeans reports a little over one half as much machine-mined coal. The second rank according to the progress of machine mining is held by Kentucky, where the proportion of Southern and Eastern Europeans is negligible, whereas Illinois with almost as many Southern and Eastern Europeans in proportion as Pennsylvania is at the bottom of the scale. West Virginia, which had been far behind Pennsylvania in 1900 with regard to the introduction of machinery, in 1910 stood even with Pennsylvania. For these two States we find in the report of the Immigration Commission the percentage of Southern and Eastern Europeans employed in the coal mines in 1908, viz., in Pennsylvania, 64.3 per cent; in West Virginia, 28.9 per cent.[2] The proportion of machine-mined coal was 45 per cent in each State. If the introduction of machinery were stimulated by immigration, it might be expected that the percentage of machine-mined coal in Pennsylvania would be twice as high as in West Virginia. Assuming that in West Virginia all unskilled labor connected with machine mining was done by recent immigrants and negroes, it can be seen at a glance that in the mines of Pennsylvania where the Southern and Eastern

[1] This can be clearly seen from a comparison of the three series of percentages of Southern and Eastern Europeans in Table XXVI of the Appendix.

[2] *Reports of the Immigration Commission*, vol. 6, Tables 140 and 143.

Europeans predominate, a large proportion of them must have been employed at pick mining.[1]

There are many factors of a local character, such as railway freights, market conditions, the nature of the coal deposit, etc., which may produce variations in the percentage of machine-mined coal for individual States. A definite tendency, however, becomes apparent if the six States are combined into two groups: (1) Ohio, Kentucky, and Indiana, and (2) Pennsylvania, West Virginia, and Illinois. In the first group the percentage of machine-mined coal for 1910 was higher than in the second group. In 1900, Ohio was in advance of Pennsylvania, while Kentucky and Indiana were in advance of Illinois and West Virginia; taken as a whole, the first group had a larger percentage of machine-mined coal than the second. At the same time the proportion of Southern and Eastern Europeans was larger in the second group, taken as a whole, than in the first. In 1900, as well as in 1910, Pennsylvania had a higher percentage than Ohio, West Virginia, and Illinois.

On the whole, then, it seems, the percentage of machine-mined coal is higher in that group which has the lower percentage of recent immigrants. This conclusion is in accord with economic conditions: where the supply of labor grows slowly, resort must be had to machinery to satisfy the rapidly growing demand for coal.

[1] The proportion of Southern and Eastern European miners employed at machine and pick mining can be calculated as follows: An allowance of 30 per cent must be made for the saving of labor by machinery. Of a team of nine working at a mining machine, one, the runner, is an English-speaking miner. Exclusive of the runners, the mining of 45 per cent of the output required the services of $(\frac{8}{9})$ 45 (0.70) = 28 per cent of all mine workers. The proportion of Southern and Eastern Europeans being 65 per cent of the total employed, there was a surplus of 37 per cent equal to 37 ÷ 65 = 57 per cent of all Southern and Eastern Europeans, for whom there was no place at machine mining. In this calculation no account is taken of the English-speaking semi-skilled men employed at machine mining. If an allowance be made for them, the percentage of Southern and Eastern Europeans who could not have been utilized at machine mining would be still larger.

The Immigration Commission states that in every section of the country a period in the development of the coal-mining industry was reached when the supply of labor, first, of native Americans, and later of English-speaking immigrants, became inadequate "to satisfy the demand and recourse was necessarily had by the mining operators to immigrants from Southern and Eastern Europe. Without the employment of mine workers drawn from this class of immigrants, the growth in the bituminous mining industry would have been impossible."[1] At the same time the Immigration Commission believes that one of the effects of recent immigration, "which seems to be well established, is the decrease of the average number of working days annually available to the older employee."[2] The inconsistency of the two statements has apparently escaped the attention of the Commission. The evidence by which the last-quoted statement is "established" is not given in the report of the Commission, beyond the bare "allegation" of "the older miners" of Illinois that "even under normal industrial conditions there are two miners for every place that offers steady work for one miner."‡

The fact is, as noted by the Commission, that coal mining is a seasonal trade.[3] The demand is greatest in the fall and winter, and declines with warm weather. The mine operators run their mines in accordance with market conditions, as can be seen from Diagram XXIV.[4] In this

[1] *Reports of the Immigration Commission*, vol. 6, p. 423. See also pp. 23, 24, 260, 661; vol. 7. pp. 216–217; in the South "the demand for labor has outgrown the supply"; vol. 16, pp. 592, 655.

[2] *Ibid.*, vol. 6, p. 668. [3] *Ibid.*, vol. 6, pp. 97, 668.

[4] Based on *Thirteenth Annual Coal Report, Illinois*, 1911, pp. 54–55.

‡ The Commission quotes, in the same connection (vol vi., p. 669), "the conviction on the part of natives that a preference is shown for the immigrants in the distribution of work." If the statistics of the Immigration Commission may be trusted, they disprove this conviction on the part of the natives. The figures which are given in Table 343 (p. 649) of the same volume, relate to the Middle West, where that "conviction" is said to prevail. The native and Southern and Eastern

DIAGRAM XXIV.

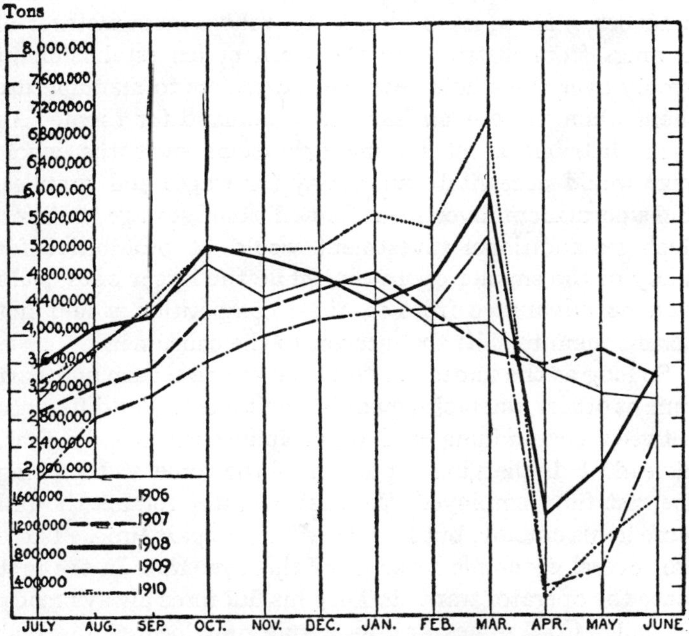

XXIV. Coal production by months in Illinois, 1906–1910.

European miners were distributed by the number of months worked in 1907 as follows:

Months	Per cent working	
	Native-born	Italians, Lithuanians, and Poles
12	18.2	1.3
9 and over	68.2	49.7
6 and over	100.0	96.7

It must be understood, however, that these statistics are of as little value as the opinions of the few "old miners" quoted by the Immigration Commission. The total number of native miners included in its "study of households" was only 371 for all bituminous mines in the United States and 79 for all anthracite mines. (*Ibid.*, vol. 6, p. 97; vol. 16, p. 619.) The number is too small to serve as a basis for any

respect the mine operators do not differ from other entrepreneurs. There is nothing to prevent a manufacturer of awnings from distributing the work of his establishment evenly over the whole year; yet he prefers to manufacture them when there is an immediate demand for them. An even distribution of mining operations over the whole year would necessitate an outlay for wages and supplies, and a permanent investment for additional storage facilities. Such an additional investment would be prohibitive for many of the smaller operators, while the larger ones could gain no advantage from it, since competition would not permit them to shift the interest to the consumer.

So long as the mines run full time at one season and part time at others, unemployment is inevitable. The difference between coal mining and other industries is only that, instead of discharging a portion of the force and keeping the rest fully employed, the coal operator retains the full force in his employ, but keeps them all on part time. There are several economic reasons for this system. In the first place the operator wants to keep his full force always ready on call. Coal mines are, as a rule, not located in great urban centres where there is at all times an available supply of men seeking employment. Chief among the contributory causes is the real estate interest of the mining company. Every operator who opens a new mine in an unsettled locality must provide houses for his employees. After having invested in workmen's dwellings, the mine operator is interested in keeping them occupied. To lay off a part of his employees during the summer months would involve a loss of rent, as they would leave in order to seek employment elsewhere. Where the mining company is also running a general store for its employees, it wants to retain

conclusions. The greatest variation between the native and foreign-born appears in the percentage of bituminous coal miners employed six months and over, viz., 82.2 for the native and 88.8 for the foreign-born (*ibid.*, vol. 6, p. 97). The difference of 6.6 per cent represents only twenty-three native workers scattered all over the United States.

them as customers. While the mine operators are guided in their policy by business considerations, rather than by philanthropy, the mine workers as a class have no ground for complaint against this policy, so long as coal mining remains a seasonal trade. The other alternative would be full employment for some and complete idleness and want for the others.

Inasmuch as the demand for coal fluctuates from year to year, it is inevitable that when the demand suffers a temporary decline, there should not be enough work to give full time employment to all the men who were needed during the previous season of maximum activity. An illustration of these fluctuations can be seen in Diagram XXIV. This is the basis of the complaint of the miners that too rapid a pace of development eventually leads to under-employment.[1] These cyclical variations, however, are not peculiar to coal mining alone, but are incidents of the modern industrial development in all lines of production. In fact the fluctuations in the demand for coal are merely the reflections of the fluctuations in the industrial field as a whole. That they are not the product of immigration, but, on the contrary, they run parallel with the fluctuations of immigration, has been shown in Chapter VI. (See Diagram X.)

The fluctuating character of the coal-mining industry produces a migratory type of mine worker. To the old employee, however, who is permanently working at one mine, these migratory applicants for work naturally appear as one of the causes of fluctuation in the opportunities for employment. The Immigration Commission is voicing the complaint of "the older employee to the effect that the recent immigrants being largely unmarried and at the same time, migratory in their habits, move readily from one locality to another, always seeking the community where there is a demand for labor and thus cause, in numerous instances, an oversupply of labor, which reacts to the injury

[1] *Reports of the Immigration Commission*, vol. 6, p. 669.

of the employees permanently working and living in the locality affected."[1] The recent immigrants accordingly cause an oversupply of labor by seeking a place "where there is a demand for labor," whereas if they stayed where there is no demand for their labor there would supposedly be no oversupply of labor. But what of "the older employees" who are permanently living in the communities where there is no demand for the labor of the migratory immigrants? Might they not regard it as an "injury" to themselves if the immigrants resolved to abandon their migratory habits and stay where there is no demand for them? The oldest inhabitants of a mining town are naturally inclined to view every question from the angle of their local interests. But their criterion need not be generally accepted as representative of the interests of labor at large.

Complaints have often been made that, apart from the fluctuations in the demand for coal, under-employment in the anthracite mines is the result of a deliberate policy on the part of the operators to employ a larger force than might be required when the mines run at full capacity.[2] There was a good foundation for this complaint in the past. In the '70's, after the breakdown of the union of anthracite coal miners, the coal companies engaged a larger force which resulted in the curtailment of the average production per man. This was, however, in the days of British, Irish, and German immigration. During the last ten years, *i. e.*, since the beginning of the new immigration, the average annual production per man has been fast increasing.

The following table shows an increase of the average annual number employed from 44,000 in 1870–1874 to 68,000 in 1875–1879, while the average annual output increased only 10 per cent. The expansion of the business obviously did not call for an increase of 55 per cent

[1] *Reports of the Immigration Commission*, vol. 6, p. 669.

[2] *Reports of the Industrial Commission*, vol. xv., p. 405. Peter Roberts, *The Anthracite Coal Industry*, pp. 126–127.

in the number of employees. As a result the average tonnage per employee declined 28 per cent. It rose again during the first half of the '80's still remaining 20 per cent

TABLE 126.

NUMBER OF WAGE-EARNERS EMPLOYED IN ANTHRACITE COAL MINES, AND PRODUCTION OF COAL BY FIVE-YEAR PERIODS, 1870–1909.

Period	Average annual number employed[1] (thousands)	Average annual production[2] (long tons)	
		Total millions	Per employee
1870–1874	44	20	448
1875–1879	68	22	322
1880–1884	85	31	361
1885–1889	110	38	342
1890–1894	130	46	350
1895–1899	145	50	343
1900–1904	151	56	372
1905–1909	171	71	417

below the average of 1870–1874. It declined again during the second half of the '80's and remained stationary until 1900. Since that time a marked improvement is noticeable. The annual average per employee in 1900–1904 was higher than in 1880–1884, and in 1905–1909 it came within 7 per cent of the average of 1870–1874. If the comparison is carried back to the first half of the '80's, when the English-speaking mine workers were given more days per man than ever since the defeat of the strike of 1875 up to 1900, it appears that in 1905–1909, during the height of Southern and Eastern European immigration, the average mine worker was given 15.5 per cent more work than at the time when the Slav and Italian employees in the anthracite mines were a negligible quantity. This means that the

[1] See Appendix, Table XXVIII.

[2] Computed from the *Report of the United States Geological Survey: The Production of Coal*, 1910, pp. 189–190.

recent immigrant labor supply has been smaller in proportion to the demand for labor in coal mines than the supply of mine workers from Northern and Western Europe thirty years ago.

As stated above, the reports of the Immigration Commission for every district concur in that the native labor supply was inadequate for the operation of the mines from the very beginning, that the supply of immigrants from the British Isles and Germany soon also proved insufficient, and that the mine operators from remoter districts were bidding in the Eastern labor market for immigrants of every nationality willing to work in the Western mines. If it is true that the demand for labor exceeded the available supply, it necessarily follows that wages must have risen. That such has been the fact is not denied by the Immigration Commission. It seeks, however, to qualify it in accordance with its preconceived ideas about the immigrant. We are told that in Pennsylvania "*the companies were not compelled* as a result of agitation or protest *to increase wages* . . . in order to hold the native and former workmen, since they were able to fill their places . . . with recent immigrants who were content with the wages . . . which prevailed in the bituminous regions. *It is true that wages have risen* in the industry, but as a rule only to meet the competition of other industries which use unskilled labor."[1]

Thus "the companies were not compelled . . . to increase wages," because the recent immigrants "were content" with the prevailing wages, and yet somehow "wages have risen." It might be inferred that the companies voluntarily increased wages though the recent immigrants did not ask for it, were it not for the concluding statement that the raise was made "to meet the competition of other industries which use unskilled labor." Apparently then in those "other industries" wages were also raised, and the recent immigrants, though "content" with lower

[1] *Reports of the Immigration Commission*, vol. 8, p. 424.

wages in coal mines, were equally content to quit the mines and accept higher wages in other industries. The most important of those industries in Pennsylvania is the iron and steel industry, in which most of the unskilled laborers are also recent immigrants. So it would seem that in order to hold these new employees the iron and steel companies were compelled to increase wages, and the coal companies in order to hold their own recent immigrants had to follow suit.

An index of the increase in the earnings of the Pennsylvania coal miners since the beginning of the "new immigration" is furnished by the average wages per ton in the anthracite coal mines at the XI. and XIII. Censuses, which increased from 83 cents in 1889 to $1.14 in 1909, *i. e.*, 37.3 per cent. At the same time the progress in the use of mechanical power raised the average output per wage-earner.[1]

In the unionized bituminous coal mines of the Pittsburgh district the scale is agreed upon at joint conferences held biennially since 1898 between the operators and the United Mine Workers. This is the period of the great influx of Southern and Eastern Europeans into the coal mines of the Pittsburgh district. Table 127 shows substantial increases in the scale for undercutting by machine and day-occupations, in which English-speaking mine workers are employed, as well as for loading which is the work of Southern and Eastern Europeans, and for pick mining, at which men of all races are employed. In other words, the Southern and Eastern Europeans have had the same measure of success in bargaining for wages as the English-speaking employees.

While wages have increased, the hours of labor have been reduced from ten to eight. Moreover, "many kinds of work, such as entry cutting, room turning, removing clay, etc., for which formerly nothing was paid, now have a regular scale. This 'dead work,' in a mine employing

[1] *XIII. Census*, vol. xi., *Mines and Quarries*, pp. 188, 189.

one hundred and fifty men, would add about $1.50 per week to the wages of each of them. It means an addition of about ten per cent to a miner's pay."[1]

TABLE 127.

UNION SCALE OF WAGES IN BITUMINOUS COAL MINES, 1898–1908.[2]

Occupation	1898–1900	1906–1908	Increase per cent
	Per ton	Per ton	
Pick mining	$0.66	$0.90	36.4
Air Machines.			
Undercutting in rooms	.125	.1708	36.6
Loading in rooms	.36	.456	26.7
Electric Machines.			
Undercutting	.08	.11	37.5
Loading	.36	.47	30.6
Inside Day Work.			
Track layers, bottom cagers, drivers, trip riders, water and machine haulers, and timbermen	Per day 1.90	Per day 2.56	40.0
Pipemen for compressed air plants	1.84	2.50	30.4
All other inside labor	1.75	2.36	34.9
Trappers (boys)	.75	1.13	50.7

The advances in the scale of wages paid to various classes of employees in non-unionized mines of Pennsylvania[3] are shown in Table 128, condensed from the report of the Immigration Commission.

Wages for all grades of employment have increased since 1895. The rate of increase for common laborers, who are practically all Southern and Eastern Europeans, is higher than for machine bosses, who are Americans or English-speaking foreigners.

The report of the Immigration Commission contains statistics of average daily earnings for 79,575 mine workers classified by race and nativity. As there is no classification of each racial group by occupation, the elaborate averages

[1] Leiserson, *loc. cit.*, p. 319. [2] *Ibid.*, p. 320.

[3] That the mines are non-unionized appears from the fact that they are running on a ten-hour basis.

TABLE 128.

WAGE SCALE OF EMPLOYEES IN THE COAL MINES OF ONE STEEL COMPANY IN PENNSYLVANIA, 1895–1908.[1]

Occupations	Daily wages		Increase per cent
	1895	1908	
Machine boss	$2.50	$3.20	28.0
Boss driver	1.53	2.65	66.7
Team driver	1.50	2.50	66.7
Tipple foreman	1.42	2.50	76.1
Single driver	1.31	2.40	83.2
Sheer (mule)	1.71	2.40	40.4
Motorman	1.75	2.40	38.2
Trip rider	1.55	2.25	45.2
Blacksmith	1.62	2.20	35.8
Stable man	1.25	2.10	68.0
Carpenter	1.25	2.00	60.0
Coupler	1.21	1.95	61.2
Tipple engineer	1.20	1.80	50.0
Tipple man	1.07	1.55	44.9
Switchman	1.25	1.45	16.0
Laborer	1.03	1.45	40.8
Oiler (dilly road)	1.06	1.35	27.4
Patcher	1.00	1.20	20.0
Trapper (boy)	.70	.90	28.6

and per 1000 ratios computed from "80 or more males reporting," are of no value for comparative purposes. The fact that the Mexican earns $2.44 per day, whereas the American of native parentage earns only $2.31,[2] does not mean that the Mexican has a higher standard of living and therefore "insists" upon a higher wage, whereas the American, with his lower standard of living, is "content" to accept a lower wage. The higher average of the Mexican is simply the result of a different distribution of the Mexicans by locality and grade of work. A selection of race groups graded according to percentage earning each specified amount per day is presented in Table 129. It clearly

[1] *Reports of the Immigration Commission*, vol. 8, Table 322.

[2] *Ibid.*, vol. 6, p. 50.

shows that the immigrants from Southern and Eastern Europe are often earning more than native Americans of native stock and English-speaking immigrants.

TABLE 129.

PER CENT OF ADULT BITUMINOUS COAL MINE WORKERS OF SELECTED RACES EARNING EACH SPECIFIED AMOUNT PER DAY, BY LOCALITY.[1]

Earning $2.00 per day and over.			Earning $3.00 per day and over.		
Rank	Locality and race	Per cent	Rank	Locality and race	Per cent
	Middle West:			Middle West:	
1	Russian	95.0	1	Croatian	69.9
2	Croatian	94.3	2	German	46.3
3	South Italian	90.8	3	South Italian	45.0
4	Scotch	89.1	4	English	41.7
5	White of native father.	87.2	5	Russian	37.9
6	Welsh	86.2	6	Scotch	36.9
7	North Italian	84.3	7	Irish	31.3
8	Irish	83.7	8	Welsh	27.4
	Pennsylvania:		9	Slovak	26.2
			10	White of native father.	25.1
1	Slovenian	76.5		Pennsylvania:	
2	Lithuanian	76.4			
3	Russian	73.3	1	Lithuanian	13.5
4	White of native father.	70.1	2	White of native father.	7.7
	South:			South:	
1	Slovak	82.9	1	Slovak	19.4
2	Polish	73.1	2	White of native father.	12.9
3	Magyar	67.9		Southwest:	
4	White of native father.	65.8			
	Southwest:		1	Lithuanian	56.8
			2	South Italian	38.3
1	Slovenian	97.2	3	German	31.6
2	White of native father.	96.1	4	White of native father.	18.9

Comparable data on the earnings of employees engaged in the same class of work are available only for West Virginia. The average earnings of pick-miners for one month were as follows: American, white, $78.18; Magyar

[1] *Reports of the Immigration Commission*, vol. 6, Tables 34–35, pp. 54–56.

and Slovak, $76.68; South Italian, $69.11.[1] There is no substantial difference between the Magyar and Slovaks, on the one hand, and the white Americans, on the other; their wages averaged about $3.00 a day. The earnings of the Italians were lower, but this may have been due to the fact that some of them did not work every day in the month.[2]

The conclusion of the Commission with regard to the Virginia and West Virginia coal fields is that "although it is not clear that the employment of the immigrant has reduced wages . . . *it is obvious* that if immigrant labor had not been available either a much higher wage would have been paid, more labor-saving devices used, or less development would have been possible."[3] In other words, wages have not been reduced, but had there been no immigrants on hand, either wages would have been higher, or they would not have been higher. The conclusion is indisputable.

The Immigration Commission holds the recent immigrants responsible for the evils of the company houses and the company stores. It is the usual method of reasoning: the company house and the company store exist only because the recent immigrants "consent" to accept them.[4] This is a consistent application of the theory of "freedom of contract": wages are low, because wage-earners "consent" to accept low wages; hours of labor are long, because laborers "consent" to work long hours; factories are unsanitary, because operatives "consent" to work in unsanitary factories. Every problem involved in the relation between labor and capital finds an easy solution in this philosophy.

The fact is that the real estate and the mercantile end of a mining company's business are often no less important, as sources of income, than the mine. There are mining companies whose sales of coal do not cover their operating

[1] *Reports of the Immigration Commission*, vol. 6, p. 202. [2] *Ibid.*
[3] *Ibid.*, p. 223. [4] *Ibid.*, pp. 659, 666.

expenses, but the renting of houses to employees and the profits of the commissary store yield enough to pay dividends on the entire investment. This system is much older than immigration from Southern and Eastern Europe.

An item in the Pottsville *Miners' Journal* for January, 1850, states that there were 42,000 houses rented by the operators in the anthracite coal fields. From the earliest records of mining, operators have erected abodes for their employees, and the practice has been continued until very recent times among all the companies.[1]

Company houses are as usual in the South, where the white miners are mostly of old American stock, as in those fields where recent immigrants predominate.

The company store has also had a long history.

The Pottsville *Miners' Journal* states that in 1848 . . . men worked for $3.50 a week and took that out in orders. . . . In 1850, the laborer got from 60 cents to 65 cents a day and the miner from 80 cents to 90 cents. These were low wages but they were actually lower than the amounts specified, for the men were not paid in money. They had to take their earnings out in goods which made a difference of from 15 to 20 per cent against the wage-earner.[2]

Many and persistent attempts have been made to do away with this evil, all of which so far have come short of their object. It was an issue of the Bates strike of 1849. The Workingmen's Benevolent Association of 1868–75 attempted to remove it. It was one of the planks in the platform of the Knights of Labor who flourished in the Middle and Southern coal fields in 1886–88. And the labor organization which now flourishes in the anthracite coal fields has undertaken to correct this evil. What the employees could not do by labor unions their representatives have tried to do by legislative enactment. In June, 1881, a law was passed to enforce payment in lawful money of the United States or "any order or other paper whatsoever, redeemable for its face value in lawful money of the United States." This law was declared unconstitutional. . . . In June, 1891, another act was passed, making it unlawful for "any mining or manufacturing corporation of the commonwealth, or the officers or stockholders of any such corporation, to engage in or carry on any store known as company store." . . . Another attempt was made at the recommendation of an investigating committee in 1897 to abolish this evil. All these

[1] Peter Roberts: *The Anthracite Coal Industry*, p. 130.

[2] *Ibid.*, p. 109.

legislative acts have come short of their objects. The company store still flourishes. . . . Their number is not as large as they once were; they are gradually dying out, but the institution dies hard.[1]

In West Virginia "every mining company has a company store, and the operatives are compelled to deal in the company store, because they are paid only once a month, but may between pay-days obtain trading scrip which is good only at the company stores."[2] Nearly one half (46 per cent) of all mine workers in West Virginia are native white Americans, and only 30 per cent are immigrants from Southern and Eastern Europe.[3] It is clear that the recent immigrant is no more responsible for the company store than the native American miner.

It is a fair conclusion from all available facts that the terms of employment in the coal mines at present are in no respect less favorable to the mine worker, and that the wages are higher, than in the past, when the bulk of the mine workers were native Americans or immigrants from Northern and Western Europe.

The ability of the wage-earner to influence the terms of employment in large-scale industry finds full expression only in collective bargaining. The history of labor unions in the bituminous coal-mining industry, according to the Immigration Commission's version, has been a constant struggle on the part of the English-speaking mine workers to organize the Southern and Eastern Europeans and to hold them in line.

In the Pennsylvania bituminous mining area the entire period from 1870 to 1894 was marked by a series of labor dissensions and strikes, each of which left the labor organizations in a weaker condition than did its predecessor, for the reason that the older employees, who were the leaders in the movement for higher wages and better working conditions, finding themselves unable to control the conditions imposed by the increasing employment of recent immigrants, and finally realizing that it

---

[1] Peter Roberts : *The Anthracite Coal Industry*, pp. 129–130.

[2] *Reports of the Immigration Commission*, vol. 7, p. 201.

[3] *Ibid.*, p. 161.

was impossible to control the incoming supply of immigrant labor, abandoned the Pennsylvania mines and sought similar employment in other bituminous localities where the pressure of competition of recent immigrants was not so strong. . . . Practically, the same situation with the same results was experienced in the mines of West Virginia. Recent immigrants did not enter the mines of that State in large numbers . . . until after the year 1890. The competition was soon felt, however, and the significance of their presence revealed by the strikes which occurred in the Fairmont, Elk Garden, and other fields in the years 1894 and 1895. Natives and older immigrant employees left the mines, as they had done in Pennsylvania, thus creating vacancies which were filled by the employment of additional numbers of recent immigrants, who reduced the strength of the labor organizations. The rapid expansion of the mining operations after 1894 also brought into the mining fields a constantly growing number of Southern and Eastern Europeans, who completely inundated the older employees and unconsciously, but effectually, demoralized the labor unions and put a stop to any efforts toward organization. . . . [In the Middle West] during the past ten years . . . although the labor unions have largely maintained their strength, conditions have changed and the preservation of the standards of the organization has been a matter of the greatest difficulty. Mining operations have undergone a great expansion, and recourse has been had to races of recent immigration in greater and greater numbers. These newcomers have entered the labor organizations principally because they have considered it a necessary step preliminary to securing work in the mines, and not because they have had any sympathy or interest in the labor-union program. They have also manifested comparatively little activity in its behalf.[1]

The preceding summary abounds in errors of fact which produce a distorted view of the history of trade-unionism in the bituminous coal-mining industry. The cardinal fact of that history is that so long as the English-speaking mine workers were in the majority, their organizations were ephemeral and their strikes mostly unsuccessful; it is only since the Southern and Eastern Europeans have become an important factor in the coal mines that the miners' organization has gained strength. The growth of the United Mine Workers of America appears from Table 130 next following. Whereas in 1890 scarcely 15 per cent of all mine workers in the United States were affiliated with

[1] *Reports of the Immigration Commission*, vol. 1, p. 535.

labor unions, in 1904 the proportion of organized mine workers exceeded one half of the total number employed.[1] Since 1898 terms of employment in the bituminous coal mines are periodically agreed upon between conferees of the conventions of organized mine operators and organized mine workers, holding sessions after the fashion of two houses of an industrial parliament.

TABLE 130.

MEMBERSHIP OF THE UNITED MINE WORKERS OF AMERICA, 1890–1904.[2]

Year	Number	Year	Number
1890	20,912	1898	32,902
1891	17,044	1899	61,887
1892	19,376	1900	115,521
1893	14,244	1901	198,024
1894	17,628	1902	175,367
1895	10,871	1903	247,240
1896	9,617	1904	260,075
1897	9,731		

The Industrial Commission says in a survey of the history of the miners' unions up to the end of the past century:

Labor organization among the coal miners has passed through extraordinary vicissitudes. The Welsh, Scotch, English, and Irish miners were well organized and maintained high wages, but in 1875, not owing to the presence of immigrants, but as a result of a strike against a falling market, their organization was entirely broken and their wages greatly reduced. Not until 1897, in the bituminous field, and 1900, in the anthracite field, was a reorganization effected, this time not of the original British stock alone, but also of the mixed nationalities from Southern and Eastern Europe. . . . While there have been serious problems in the organization of mixed nationalities, an equally serious problem which has confronted the organization of these immigrants has been the competition of the unorganized Americans of native stock. This was fully shown in the experience of the miners prior to 1897, when their organizations in Northern Illinois were defeated by the native Americans in Southern Illinois. In the first mining district of Illinois the per cent of Americans is only eleven, and in the seventh, in the Southern part of the State, it is eighty. Yet, it was these American miners in the thick and more easily mined veins of the Southern section

[1] Frank Julian Warne: *The Coal Mine Workers*, pp. 120, 206, 212, 218.

[2] *Ibid.*, pp. 117, 120, 212, 218.

whose competition reduced wages so low that they were actually earning less than in the Northern districts. The success of the strike in 1897 consisted mainly in the fact that the Southern American-born miners were brought into the Union and placed on a basis of equal competition with the foreign-born miners. A similar condition at the present time confronts the mining organization of the four great States of the bituminous field in the competition of West Virginia, where the native whites of native parents number 57½ per cent and the colored miners number 21 per cent of the total number of miners, compared with 20 to 48 per cent native whites of both native and foreign parentage in the other States. Prices and wages in West Virginia are 30 to 70 per cent below those under similar conditions in the other States. . . . The organization of 150,000 bituminous mine workers, over one half of whom are foreign-born of diverse races, is menaced more by the unorganized Americans of native stock than by their own internal divisions.[1]

In another part of the same report the history of the contests in Illinois is given in greater detail:

The jeopardy and defeat of the unions has been owing as often to the competition of unorganized Americans of native stock in new fields, as in the competition of the foreign-born. This is fully demonstrated by the experience of the miners prior to 1897, when they were defeated by the competition of Southern Illinois, and, since 1897, when they were jeopardized by the competition of West Virginia. Beginning with 1886 . . . the local organization of miners known as the Federation of Miners and Mine Laborers acquired such strength that it was able to summon the operators of Pennsylvania, Ohio, and Illinois to annual conferences for the purposes of agreements regarding the scale of wages in these competitive States. . . . During the entire period of these interstate conferences, from 1886 to 1893, it has been impossible for the unions to organize Southern Illinois. The miners in that section were predominatingly Americans. They were farm laborers who had turned to the mines as a source of ready cash. . . . Their rates per ton for mining coal were twenty-eight to thirty-eight cents, as compared with sixty-two to seventy cents in the Northern fields. . . . In order to protect the miners in the Northern, thin-veined districts, and permit their coal to come into the market at living wages, the union has forced the miners in the Southern, thick-veined districts to increase their earnings from the lowest in the State to the highest in the State. This is one of the necessities of the system of differentials in arranging scales of prices for different sections of the same competitive field, and it was exactly the evil of the former unorganized condition that the American

[1] *Reports of the Industrial Commission*, vol. xv., pp. xxxv.–xxxvi.

miners in the Southern field had reduced their compensation so low notwithstanding the greater productivity of the mines, that they were earning less than the meager wages of the foreign-born miners in the Northern fields. . . . *The present high wages of the Southern field are not, therefore, owing to a higher standard of living or superior capacity for organization of Americans as compared with foreigners, but are owing to the initiative and interference of foreigners, who, in self-protection, forced the Americans to a higher position than the one they were willing to accept.*[1]

The Immigration Commission quotes the opinion of "the older employees"—"that in general the immigration of Southern and Eastern Europeans has been very disastrous to the labor unions in the coal-mining industry. In some districts the unions have been entirely disrupted, and old operatives assert that this was directly due to the coming of the later immigrants."[2] The illustrations cited by the Commission in support of this claim prove the very opposite of it. In the strike of 1884 in the Connelsville coke region the Slav, Magyar, and Italian workmen joined the American and Irish strikers. The strike was defeated, but "the percentage of recent immigrants was relatively small"; no reason is given why the defeat should be attributed to that small number rather than to the weakness of the English-speaking majority. In 1890 the strike was again defeated, although "in this case also the immigrants joined the strike." In 1894 the men struck again. "The Americans, English, and Irish were leaders of the strike and the immigrants very generally joined the organization which had been effected only two weeks previously." The strike originally extended to seventy-seven out of eighty-five plants; after six weeks of striking ninety-two per cent of all ovens were idle. By that time, however, many of the strikers "were enduring severe hardships." Still the majority held out for two months longer, and a minority stayed out in all for five months. The strike was defeated. That was the end of the organization in that field.[3]

[1] *Reports of the Industrial Commission*, vol. xv., pp. 407–409.

[2] *Reports of the Immigration Commission*, vol. 6, p. 332.

[3] *Ibid.*, pp. 332–334.

It is sought to fasten the responsibility for the defeat of these strikes upon the Slav, Magyar, and Italian strikers; "the American and Irish leaders" are said to have "found difficulty in restraining them from violence during the strikes." In general, it is remarked that "in strikes the recent immigrant members . . . are often inclined to resort to violence and other methods that bring the union and its cause into disrepute."[1]

In view of the recent developments in the McNamara case these protestations of "the American and Irish leaders" may be accepted *cum grano salis*. "The undesirable alien" is a convenient scapegoat to appease public opinion, which is not burdened with memories of the long ago. The terrorism of the Molly Maguires has a literature. Rioting is chronicled as an incident of almost every strike of importance in the coal mines for the last sixty years. The first great strike of which there is any record occurred in the spring of 1849 under the leadership of the Bates union.

"The strike was accompanied by violence. Miners, armed with cudgels, formed themselves into bands and marched down the Black Valley to collieries which were working, and by intimidation compelled the men to join their ranks."

In the strike of 1868 an effort was made by the strikers to draw into the contest all mine workers of the anthracite region.

> They marched to the Mahanoy Valley and stopped the collieries there, then they advanced to the Schuylkill Valley and did the same there. Thus most of the Southern and Middle collieries were closed. They resolved then to continue their march to the Wyoming Valley and persuade the miners there to join their ranks. The employees of the Wilkes-Barre District joined them. Along the line of march they compelled all classes of workmen to throw down their tools and fall into line. The mechanics of Wilkes-Barre were forced to quit work and join the strikers; the same was done with the force working on the Wilkes-Barre jail at the time. The sheriff of Luzerne County addressed them and asked them to disperse, but to no purpose.

---

[1] *Reports of the Immigration Commission*, vol. 6, pp. 332–333.

On January 10, 1871, the Workingmen's Benevolent Association declared a general strike in all anthracite collieries in sympathy with the miners of the Northern field. Practically all collieries were shut down and remained so until May, when "a few shafts were started by the Delaware, Lackawanna & Western Company. Riots ensued. The military power of the State was called out and in a conflicit between it and the strikers, two of the miners were shot and several wounded. . . . Labor was utterly defeated in the contest."

In 1877 the great railroad strike tied up the anthracite coal mines. The miners of the Delaware, Lackawanna & Western and of the Delaware & Hudson collieries joined in the strike. "Labor riots were the order of the day."[1]

This is the record of the anthracite region only. The battle of the Homestead strikers with the Pinkertons in 1892, the troubles in the metalliferous mines of Colorado and Idaho, the recent strike of the firemen on the Southern railways, and many other episodes in which none but English-speaking workmen were involved, conclusively prove that violence in strikes is not a racial characteristic of "the recent immigrants from Southern and Eastern Europe."

Since the United Mine Workers has won the support of these immigrants, who now form the backbone of that organization, very little is heard of strike riots. For the past fourteen years, as stated, terms of employment in the bituminous mines are peaceably agreed upon between representatives of organized mine operators and organized mine workers.

The United Mine Workers has so far failed in its efforts to gain a foothold in West Virginia and in the Southern fields. But its defeat is not attributable to recent immigrants. "Until 1897 the immigrant labor employed was not in excess of 10 per cent of the total operating forces."[2] Consequently, the defeat of the strikes of 1894

[1] Roberts, *loc. cit.*, pp. 172–181.

[2] *Reports of the Immigration Commission*, vol. 7, pp. 146–147.

and 1895 could not have been brought on by recent immigrants. The next strike took place in 1902. "A majority of the mines were closed for a considerable period." The operators imported strike-breakers—Americans, as well as immigrants—and the strike ultimately failed.[1]

Since that time West Virginia has been a non-union field. But it had been a non-union field also previous to the strike of 1902, when 57.8 per cent of all mine workers were native white of native parentage and 73.4 per cent belonged to the English-speaking races. Yet shortly before the strike of 1902, prices and wages in West Virginia were "30 to 70 per cent below those under similar conditions in the other States."[2]

On the other hand, in Alabama only 13 per cent of all mine workers are foreign-born, and only 10 per cent from Southern and Eastern Europe, while 26 per cent are native white of native parentage and 31 per cent English-speaking white, the other 59 per cent being negroes. Yet "a very small proportion of natives . . . are identified with organized labor . . . for the reason that in only one small district of the Southern field is organized labor recognized."[3] A series of questions naturally arises: Why is organized labor not recognized in the Southern field? Why have the natives not organized? Why have they not won recognition for organized labor? There seems to be no chosen people endowed with special trade-union qualifications: there are well-organized mines with a predominantly non-English-speaking force and unorganized mines manned chiefly by Anglo-Saxons.

The inability of the immigrants to understand the English language may have been an obstacle to organization among them in the early days when they were few. At present, however, when every European language is spoken in every mining field, there is no difficulty in finding a

[1] *Reports of the Immigration Commission*, vol. 7, pp. 150–151.

[2] *Reports of the Industrial Commission*, vol. xv., pp. 407–408.

[3] *Reports of the Immigration Commission*, vol. 7, pp. 142, 196.

sufficient number of English-speaking persons of each nationality who can represent their countrymen in union matters.[1]

There are no available statistics of the distribution of union membership by nationality. It can be estimated, however, for the State of Illinois. In 1904, 51,167 out of 54,685 mine workers in that State, *i. e.*, 93 per cent were affiliated with the United Mine Workers of America.[2] According to the census of 1900, 78 per cent of the total number of mine workers in Illinois were of "English-speaking" parentage.[3] Assuming that every one of the latter class was a member of the organization 15 per cent of the remaining 22 per cent, *i.e.*, 75 per cent of all persons of Slav and Italian parentage, must likewise have been affiliated with the organization. In fact, the percentage of organized Slavs and Italians must have been higher, since their proportion among the coal miners of Illinois had increased from 1900 to 1904. Moreover, it is reasonable to assume that some of the English-speaking mine workers did not belong to the union, which would further add to the estimated percentage of organized Slavs and Italians. On the other hand, in Kentucky 99.5 per cent of all mine workers were of English-speaking parentage, and in Tennessee 99 per cent.[4] But the proportion of union men among them was 21 per cent in Kentucky and 24 per cent in Tennessee.[5]

The most significant test of the strength of the organization is its recognition by the Steel Trust:

> The Slav in the mines is paid from 50 to 90 per cent more per hour than his countrymen working in the mills and factories of Pittsburg, at jobs requiring the same amount of skill and strength. In many cases the same company is compelled to pay these different rates for the same class of labor. The great steel mills and glass factories

[1] The proportion of English-speaking persons among the Southern and Eastern European coal miners enumerated by the Immigration Commission varied for different nationalities from 30 to 75 per cent.—*Reports of the Immigration Commission*, vol. 6, p. 196, Table 122.

[2] Warne, *loc. cit.*, p. 117.

[3] See Appendix, Table XXVII.

[4] *Ibid.*

[5] Warne, *ibid.*

of the district are all non-union. The companies which own them also own many of the coal mines of Allegheny and Washington counties. These are all union mines, and the United States Steel Corporation, Jones & Laughlin, the Pittsburgh Glass Company, as mine owners, sign agreements with the unions which provide for an eight-hour day and a scale of wages almost double what they pay for the same labor in the manufacturing plants. Prof. John R. Commons has summed up, for the *Pittsburgh Survey*, a comparison of the men in the mills with those in the mines, in the following words:

"Taking everything into account—wages, hours, leisure, cost of living, conditions of work—I should say that the common laborer employed by the steel companies in their mines is 50 to 90 per cent better off than the same grade of labor employed at their mills and furnaces; that the semi-skilled labor employed at piece rates is 40 to 50 per cent better off; but among the highest paid labor, the steel roller and the mine worker are about the same."[1]

It should be borne in mind that the highest-paid positions, both in the mines and in the mills, are controlled exclusively by native Americans or by the old immigrant races, whereas the unskilled positions are practically all held by Southern and Eastern Europeans. In the semi-skilled positions, the English-speaking and the non-English-speaking workmen meet on common ground. It thus appears that the activity of the union has secured the best terms for the Southern and Eastern Europeans, and a very substantial improvement for all employees where the Southern and Eastern Europeans are a factor in the labor situations, whereas in the highest grades controlled by the English-speaking races, the organized mine-workers have gained no better terms than those which the steel companies were willing to offer to the unorganized steel workers.

It is worthy of note that the Immigration Commission, while dwelling upon the failure of the United Mine Workers to extend its control to the bituminous fields of Pennsylvania outside of the Pittsburgh district, has passed in silence the signal success of the same organization in the anthracite coal fields, where the same nationalities are employed as in the bituminous mines of Pennsylvania.

[1] Leiserson, *loc. cit.*, pp. 318–319.

The history of organization in the anthracite coal field begins as early as 1848. In that year the "Bates Union," so-called, was organized. It existed only two years. There was no organization in the anthracite coal fields until 1868, when the Workingmen's Benevolent Association was founded. It succeeded in organizing for a while 85 per cent of all mine workers. But in 1871, after an unsuccessful strike, it lost the Northern field, which remained unorganized for twenty-six years. In the Middle and Southern fields it led a moribund existence until 1875. For nine years there was again no organization. From 1884 to 1888 there were first two organizations which in 1887 consolidated into one under the auspices of the Knights of Labor, which was at that time in the heyday of its triumphs. But a disastrous strike which lasted from November, 1887, to March, 1888, put an end to the organization of the anthracite coal miners.

In 1897 the United Mine Workers undertook the organization of the anthracite mines. Its growth was slow until 1900, when it engaged in its first great strike which was won after all collieries had been practically tied up for six weeks.[1] The strike of 1900 was followed by the great struggle of 1902 which was ended by the award of President Roosevelt's Anthracite Coal Strike Commission.

This brief survey shows that all organizations of the English-speaking workers were short-lived and seldom survived one unsuccessful strike. It is only since the advent of the Southern and Eastern Europeans that the union has taken a firm hold of the industry.

Dr. Roberts, reviewing the history of unionism in the anthracite coal industry, says:

> John Graham Brooks, when he studied the Lattimer riots of 1897, found on the Hazleton Mountain over a dozen nationalities. He expressed the conviction that it was a hopeless task to attempt to form them into a labor organization. Paul de Rousiers, in his essay on *Les Tentatives de Monopolisation de l'Anthracite*, expressed a similar

---

[1] Roberts, *loc. cit.*, p. 184.

opinion. He compared the present personnel of anthracite employees, "largely composed of Polanders, Hungarians, and Lithuanians, who are turbulent and incapable of being advantageously formed into an association," with the Americans, Germans, and English of 1868, who so successfully organized the Workingmen's Benevolent Association, and believed they could not be successfully organized into a labor organization. Both eminent men have proved to be false prophets. The stanchest members of the union are the Slavs, and the organizers of the United Mine Workers of America have successfully overcome racial differences, national antipathies and industrial prejudices, and formed into one body the fifteen or sixteen nationalities now constituting the anthracite mining communities.[1]

The opinions of those "false prophets" were still reiterated after the strikes of 1900 and 1902 by labor men, who "had learned nothing and forgotten nothing," and were embodied by the Immigration Commission in its report.

These foreigners, [says Dr. Roberts elsewhere] have proved capable of forming labor organizations which are more compact and united than any which ever existed among the various English-speaking nationalities, who first constituted these communities. It is conceded by men intimate with the situation throughout the coal fields during the last strike, that its universality was more due to the Slav than to any other nationality. There would have been in all probability a break in the ranks in Schuylkill County had it not been for the firm and uncompromising stand of the Slavs in favor of the strike. They have been trained to obedience, and when they organize they move with a unanimity that is very seldom seen among nations who pride themselves on personal liberty and free discussion.[2]

These lines were written by Dr. Roberts previous to the strike of 1902. The significance of the latter was that the other side to the controversy was a trust which was (and is) in complete control of the whole anthracite coal industry. The outcome of the contest has been the creation of a democratic organization of all mine workers to which the trust cannot deny recognition, with a machinery for fixing wages and other terms of employment, as well as for the settlement of disputes.

After twenty years of immigration from Southern and

[1] Roberts, *loc. cit.*, pp. 196–197. [2] *Ibid.*, pp. 171–172.

Eastern Europe, the coal miners are more strongly organized than they had ever been before the English-speaking mine workers relinquished the lower grades of work to the recent immigrants; the hours of labor have been reduced, wages have risen, and the majority of the older employees have advanced on the scale of occupations.

On the other hand, a "small part [of the 'pioneer employees and their descendants'] consisting of the inert, unambitious, thriftless element, have remained on the lower level of the scale of occupations where they are in open competition with the majority of the races of recent immigration in comparison with whom they are generally considered less efficient."[1] It is said in their behalf that their anxiety to be "removed from contact and *competition* with the immigrant" has "forced" them "into day or shift work at a lower rate of pay than in digging coal."[2] In order to escape the ruinous competition of the recent immigrant, the English-speaking miner, it would seem, is willing to accept lower wages than the immigrant. It may be questioned whether this small residue of English-speaking mine workers who are "considered less efficient" than the Southern and Eastern Europeans could have succeeded better in competition with native or English-speaking miners, had there been no immigration from Southern and Eastern Europe. Probably the reference to "competition with the immigrant" is merely a pleonasm, the idea being that the English-speaking miner is willing to make a financial sacrifice in order to be "removed from *contact* with the immigrant." The objection to the recent immigrant is accordingly inspired by pure and simple race prejudice. This is, however, beside the question, so long as it is maintained that immigration should be treated "upon economic or business considerations."[3]

[1] *Reports of the Immigration Commission*, vol. 1, pp. 536–537.

[2] *Ibid.*, vol. 6, pp. 666–667; vol. 7, p. 222.

[3] Recommendations of the Immigration Commission.

CHAPTER XXII

WORK ACCIDENTS

THE greatest of all the dangers of the new immigration, which have been discovered by the investigation of the Immigration Commission, is that their employment in mines and manufactures jeopardizes the lives of American wage-earners. The Commission has devoted to the subject a special chapter in its report on bituminous coal mines.[1] Its conclusions are summarized by Professors Jenks and Lauck as follows[2]:

The lack of industrial training and experience of the recent immigrant before coming to the United States, together with his illiteracy and inability to speak English, has had the effect of ***exposing the original employees to unsafe and unsanitary working conditions***, or has

[1] *Reports of the Immigration Commission*, vol. 6, chapter viii., pp. 209–241; also, pp. 491–492, 543, 651–652; vol. 7, pp. 68–69.

[2] The Commission is, of course, not responsible officially for the statement of those authors. But the book is very largely a verbatim transcript of the most essential portions of the Commission's voluminous report. On the subject of accidents, the report of the Commission says in Volume 6:

"The responsibility for accidents rests in most cases with the men injured . . . they know little or nothing of rock formations, of fire damp, of the properties of coal dust, and of the handling of explosives —matters about which every coal miner should be thoroughly informed. To determine whether a piece of slate or roof is or is not likely to fall often requires a considerable degree of experience, and the majority of the Slavs, Magyars, and Italians have not this experience. Another element of danger is contributed by the fact that few of the recent immigrants speak or understand English, while almost none are able to read or write the language. It is probable that the instructions of the mine bosses and inspectors are, because of this fact, frequently

led to the imposition of conditions of employment which the native American or older immigrant employees have considered unsatisfactory and in some cases unbearable. *When the older employees have found dangerous and unhealthy conditions prevailing in the mines and manufacturing establishments and have protested, the recent immigrant employees,* usually through ignorance of mining or other working methods, *have manifested a willingness to accept the alleged unsatisfactory conditions.* In a large number of cases, the lack of training and experience of the Southern and Eastern European affects only his own safety. On the other hand, his *ignorant acquiescence in dangerous and unsanitary working conditions may make the continuance of such conditions possible and become a menace to a part or to the whole of an operating force of an industrial establishment.* In mining, the presence of an untrained employee may constitute an element of danger to the entire body of workmen. There seems to be a direct causal relation between the extensive employment of recent immigrants in American mines and the extraordinary increase within recent years in the number of mining accidents. *It is an undisputed fact that the greatest number of accidents in bituminous coal mines arise from two causes: (1) the recklessness, and (2) the ignorance and inexperience, of employees.* When the lack of training of the recent immigrant abroad is considered in connection with the fact that he becomes a workman in the mines immediately upon his arrival in this country, and when it is recalled that a large proportion of the new arrivals are not only illiterate and unable to read any precautionary notices posted in the mines, but also unable to speak English and consequently without ability to comprehend instructions intelligently, the inference is plain that *the employment of recent immi-*

---

misunderstood. An inspector, for example, tells an immigrant miner, in English of course, that his roof needs propping. The miner seems to understand, but does not, and a fall results. In some mines printed signs are used to indicate the presence of gas or other peril. These are quite unintelligible to most of the foreigners, because, through lack of training, they are unable to recognize the presence of danger, and further, because of their keenness for earning money, the immigrants are often willing to work in places where more experienced or more intelligent men would refuse to work. For the same reasons they will frequently be satisfied with and accept mine equipment too defective for safety. . . . The ignorance and inexperience of the workmen of the races of recent immigration employed in mines are responsible in a large measure for the high death rate reported. Owing to the large number of factors affecting the situation, no hard and fast conclusion can be drawn, but the inference from the data available clearly warrants the assertion that the employment of immigrant mine workers has a direct bearing upon mining casualties." (pp. 232–233, 241.)

grants has caused a deterioration in working conditions. No complete statistics have been compiled as to the connection between accidents and races employed, but the figures available clearly indicate the conclusion that there has been a direct relation between the employment of untrained foreigners and the prevalence of mining casualties.[1]

The two causes from which, according to this explanation, the greatest number of accidents arise, are but the familiar defenses in an employer's liability case under the common law: (1) negligence of the injured employee or of a fellow-servant, (2) assumption of risk by the injured employee.

The Immigration Commission rests its conclusions on the opinions of State mining officials and experts of the Federal Government, seemingly supported by an array of statistical figures. An examination of these authorities, however, will show that they have merely accepted the mine operator's point of view without turning their attention to the technical and the economic side of coal mining in the United States.

Miss Eastman, in her study of work accidents for the *Pittsburgh Survey*, has carefully scrutinized the sources of the accepted explanation of the causes of work accidents. In vivid conversational style she thus characterizes the typical attitude "of those best informed upon the subject"[2]:

"So you have come to Pittsburgh to study accidents, have you?" says the superintendent, or the claim agent, or the general manager, as the case may be. "Well, I 've been in this business fifteen years and I can tell you one thing right now,—*95 per cent of our accidents are due to the carelessness of the man who gets hurt.* Why, you simply would n't believe the things they 'll do. For instance, I remember a man,"—and he goes on to relate the most telling incident he knows to prove his assertion. This is the almost invariable reaction of the Pittsburgh employer and his representatives to a query about industrial accidents. And the statements of such men are the chief source of effective public opinion on the subject in Pittsburgh.[3]

---

[1] Jenks and Lauck, *loc. cit.*, pp. 189–190.

[2] Phrase used by the Immigration Commission (*Reports*, vol. 6, p. 216).

[3] Crystal Eastman: *Work-Accidents and the Law*, p. 84.

The returns of the mine inspectors on the causes of accidents are based upon the results of the coroners' inquests. Miss Eastman questions the reliability of the evidence secured at the inquests:

> Foremen and fire bosses are required at once to inspect a room where an accident has occurred, and, if death results, one of them is always summoned to the inquest. He almost invariably testifies, "I found plenty of posts in the room." Since it is his business by law to see that there are plenty of posts in the room, and since the inquest is very casual, unimpressive, he could hardly be expected to testify otherwise. Private conversation with miners sometimes brings other information to light. . . . An old Scotch miner of sixty, said . . . that he "had often seen the foreman and boss hurry to a room where an accident had happened and fill it with posts, so that when the inspector arrived there would be plenty of posts on hand."[1] The coroners' records were, as a rule, meager, sometimes illegible, and almost never clear and satisfactory in detail. The testimony, moreover, has a tendency to lean to one side. The witnesses are employees of the company, including almost always the superior of the man killed. It is to his interest to clear himself of all implications; second, to clear his employer. *The easiest and safest way* of accomplishing these ends *is to blame the dead man.*[2]

Thus, when we read in the reports of the Pennsylvania Department of Mines for 1907 that "a careful examination of the reports shows that 332 accidents, or 41.19 per cent, were due to the carelessness of the victim,"[3] this statement means no more than that the reports which reached the department "blamed the dead man" in two cases out of every five. Of course, 41.19 per cent is still short of a majority, but it is turned into a majority of 62.29 per cent by omitting "the 273 fatalities of the Naomi and Darr mines, which were caused by the carelessness of other persons."[4] These undefined "other persons" include "officials in direct charge of the mines." The propriety of omitting two great mine disasters, which resulted in the

[1] Crystal Eastman: *Work-Accidents and the Law*, p. 39.

[2] *Ibid.*, p. 85.

[3] *Reports of the Immigration Commission*, vol. 6, p. 216.

[4] *Ibid.*, p. 216. (Quoted from the report of the Pennsylvania Bureau of Mines.)

loss of 273 lives through the carelessness of "other persons," is open to question.[1] Yet that statement of the Pennsylvania report is the only direct statistical evidence in support of the Commission's conclusion "that the responsibility for a *majority* of the accidents in coal mines rests with the men injured. This being the case"—continues the Commission—"it is evident that an inquiry as to the responsibility of a given race for accidents may perhaps best be answered by showing the extent to which its numbers are sufferers from accidents."[2]

Disinterested mining experts, however, do not accept the apologetic theory of the mine operators as an "undisputed fact."

At the summer meeting of the Mining Institute of America, held in 1910, shortly after the Cherry Mine holocaust, the causes of mine fires were discussed in a paper, from which the following is quoted:

> In looking over the accounts of some of the mine fires which have startled the general public more than others, I was forcibly struck with three of them (Avondale, Hill Farm, and Cherry), especially in the general aspect at least of the *similarity of their cause* and effect, and of the cycle of years between each. The Avondale Mine was *a single-shaft opening. The structural material used in the shaft lining, partitions, derrick, and breaker, was composed of wood.* The fire originated at the bottom of the shaft, caused by the carelessness of the furnace man in lighting the furnace fire, thereby setting fire to the wooden partition, etc. This fire occurred in the month of September, 1869, and in it 109 lives were lost. As you remember, *no adequate means were at hand with which to extinguish the fire.* . . . The Cherry Mine disaster . . . originated at the No. 2 seam landing of the escapement shaft and was

---

[1] Dr. John Randolph Haynes, Special Commissioner on Mining Accidents of the State of California, in a paper read at the last annual meeting of the American Association for Labor Legislation, at Washington, D. C., questioned the independence of State mining inspectors: "They do not wish to lose their positions, which they are very likely to do if they annoy the owners of coal mines, who very commonly own the railroads which carry the coal, and enjoy intimate relations with banks and other corporations that exercise quiet but effective power in State politics."—"A Federal Mining Commission," *American Labor Legislation Review*, vol. ii, No. 1, p. 145.

[2] *Ibid.*, p. 233.

caused by the ignition of hay from the flame of a crude, improvised, unprotected illuminating contrivance. The flame from the hay was communicated to the *overabundance of wood supporting material at the landing,* and adding thereto the *inadequate means available to successfully deal with a fire of such magnitude,* with the ill-judged actions of the inexperienced men at the bottom, the trap was complete and the men caught therein, so we have now to record the greatest and most disastrous mine fire in the history of the coal-mining industry of this country, so far as the loss of life is concerned. Two hundred and sixty-eight lives were lost in the Cherry Mine disaster.

It has always appeared to me that *the causes of mine fires were so apparent* to the thoughtful and intelligent mining men that their occurrence and their ill effects were unnecessary. . . . The prevention of mine fires lies in the *removal of the causes, which are well known,* and the knowledge of means and methods to be employed for their elimination, being within the range and scope of the ability of the ordinary mine official, the wonder is that they do happen. *To secure freedom from mine fires* I believe lies almost entirely within the intelligently directed *administrative powers of the mine management,* and in my opinion *if the mine officials are careful,* alert, and capable, immunity from them can be secured. . . .

Every coal mine should consist of two separate openings and one of them should be used exclusively for an escapement. . . . The escapement shaft, if over one hundred feet in depth, should be equipped with safe and efficient hoisting apparatus. The structure at the hoisting shaft should be built of steel, and the engine and power house should be built of concrete, brick, or masonry; the shaft linings to be of concrete, and *the shaft bottoms, if needing supports for the roof, should be of steel I beams, concrete, or brickwork;* doors between main shaft and escapement shaft should be so located as to be easily accessible to the workmen from all parts of the mine by *convenient traveling ways,* other than those which lead directly to the bottom of the hoisting shaft; mule stables, if not entirely prohibited in the mines, should be built of incombustible material and *illuminated with protected incandescent electric lights;* all oil, electric, and gasoline pump houses should be kept free from combustible material, and be built of concrete, brickwork, or masonry. When the main workings of a mine have advanced five thousand feet in length and the remaining extent of the property and the other conditions warrant it, an auxiliary escapement opening should be provided and *equipped with efficient and necessary machinery; a water system under sufficient pressure* . . . should be installed at all important mines, . . . and all parts and connections kept in first-class condition and ready for use at all times; all electric cables or wires, etc., should be well supported and insulated, and not allowed to come in contact with combustible material. . . . ***A telephone system*** should be provided at important mines so that communication can be had between persons outside, and all important stations inside of them; ***refuge chambers***, efficiently constructed and equipped and conveniently located, should be provided in all large and dangerous mines.

Mines should be provided with a ***powerful reversible fan***, and it should be placed on a separate shaft, ***cased in steel***, and fitted with ***relief doors***.[1]

These details have been quoted in order to show that effective prevention of accidents in mines presupposes a carefully planned equipment involving considerable expense. A separate roadway for miners means additional tunneling work. Two separate openings for every coal mine cost twice as much as one. Refuge chambers require additional excavation and construction work. Concrete or brick is more expensive than wood, which is generally used as structural material in coal mines. A powerful reversible fan placed on a separate shaft cased in steel is another item of expense; so is a water system under sufficient pressure, a telephone system, etc. All this is well known to mine superintendents, "but they are pressed for dividends by the presidents and their companies; the presidents are not heartless, but they are pressed for dividends by their directors who . . . are interested in the mines only as a matter of profit."[2]

The dilemma of the mine superintendent was set forth in a paper on "Mine Accident Prevention," which was recently read before the Alabama Coal Operators' Association by Mr. J. J. Rutledge, a geologist and mining engineer of many years' experience, who has made his way from the bottom up, beginning as assistant mine foreman and advancing to the positions of mine manager and superintendent. He has visited many of the important coal mines in this country, and has been brought into close personal contact with mine foremen and superintendents. He is of the opinion that "*the person who is the greatest factor in the pre-*

[1] "Mine Fires," by Thomas K. Adams. *Mines and Minerals*, December, 1910.

[2] Haynes, *loc. cit.*, p. 145.

vention of mine accidents is the mine foreman or manager. . . . He should never *cancel any requisition for supplies that are absolutely required.* Perhaps *the greatest abuse of this sort is the cancellation of supplies which are required to make ventilation more effective.*" But it is not unusual that the foreman or manager "is handicapped or *hindered in his work by the failure to receive proper supplies or equipment from his superiors.*" That he might "be encouraged to demand the same and . . . *be insured against possible loss of employment by reason of his making such a demand* . . . the law should back him up in making such demands."[1] It is an undisputed fact that poor and defective methods of ventilation largely increase the danger of gas explosion: "An adequate air supply is not only required as a safeguard against the accumulation of dangerous gases, but is prerequisite to the maintenance of the health of miners and animals employed underground."[2]

But the mine manager who is not "insured against possible loss of employment" will take his chances and cancel requisitions for "supplies that are absolutely required." These conditions naturally breed a spirit of carelessness among mine officials, which is, according to expert opinion, "first among the causes of the high fatality rate in American mines." Such was the conclusion reached by three European government experts, among them the Belgian Inspector-General of Mines, who made an examination of American mines upon the invitation of the United States Government. By way of illustration, one of these experts related the following incident:

While passing through a mine in West Virginia with a party carrying both naked and safety lamps, he lifted his lamp toward the roof to test for gas and was surprised to find it present in very dangerous quantities. Turning to the mine superintendent, he remarked, " You should not

---

[1] J. J. Rutledge: " Mine Accident Prevention." *Mines and Minerals*, December, 1910.

[2] F. L. Hoffman: "Fatal Accidents in Coal Mines." *Bulletin of the United States Bureau of Labor*, No. 90, p. 471.

allow naked lamps to be used in this mine." "Oh," replied the superintendent, easily, "we are installing a ventilating system that in a few months will rid the mine entirely of gas and render the use of safety lamps unnecessary." "Before that time arrives," protested the European expert, "your mine will be blown up." And this is precisely what happened. The naked lamps were not excluded, the mine was blown up a few weeks later, and hundreds of miners lost their lives. . . . No European mining superintendent would dream of taking such chances as he foolishly took at the cost of so many lives; and, if he were so inclined, the government inspector would not permit him to do so.[1]

Mine explosions and mine fires impress the imagination by the appalling destruction of lives in a single accident. A great many more lives, however, are sacrificed under ordinary circumstances in every-day accidents, which find their way only into the statistical reports of State mine inspectors, being too common to be noticed by the newspapers.

Every advance in mining engineering within recent years has had the effect of increasing the risks of the miner in the United States. One of the original dangers in underground coal mines is from falls of roof, which are the result, at least in part, of insufficient timbering. This risk has been considerably increased by the use of high explosives.[2] With the installation of improved mining machinery, exposure to unguarded machines has been added to other perils of mining.[3] Electrocution threatens the miner as a result of the application of electricity to mining. The chief inspector of coal mines for Pennsylvania gave warning of this danger in his report for 1901:

Electricity in various forms has been the cause of many of the deaths in soft coal mines, either from the men coming in contact with the electric trolley wire, or with the electric wire that carries the power to the electric cutting machines. In my opinion, *separate travelling ways should be provided for the workman*, when the haulage is done by electricity.[4]

---

[1] Haynes, *loc. cit.*, p. 143.
[2] Eastman, *loc. cit.*, pp. 38–39.
[3] Hoffman, *loc. cit.*, pp. 476–477.
[4] *Ibid.*, pp. 478–479.

When this recommendation was adopted in one Colorado mine ten years later, the *Engineering and Mining Journal* found the fact of sufficient interest as news to print the following letter from a correspondent:

> This mine has introduced *a decided novelty in the form of a separate roadway for the miners to enter and leave the workings*, thus doing away with the necessity of their travelling along the haulage-ways, and providing an additional avenue of escape in time of danger.[1]

The displacement of the mule by the cable car or electric motor has been the source of a new danger to the life of the miner. Many miners are killed by the running trains of coal. This is, of course, clearly the result of their own negligence: why do they travel in the haulage-way? The fact is, however, that the man-entry and track are dark from beginning to end and low, so that one would have to travel in a stooping position all the way. The track is covered with loose slate and big chunks of coal. Therefore the miners prefer the haulage entry, where there are occasional lights, a smooth path to walk, and a higher roof.[2] Most of these risks are humanly preventable,[3] and their continuance is due to economic conditions beyond the control of the mine worker, even with a perfect command of English.

The economic cause of the high rate of fatalities in American coal mines was squarely stated by Dr. J. A. Holmes, Director of the Bureau of Mines, in an address delivered at the annual meeting of the National Civic Federation in New York, November 23, 1909:

> There can be no permanent industry without reasonable profits. It is unjust and irrational that in this great and essential branch of industry *reasonable profits or even the payment of operating expenses* should be *dependent upon methods involving unnecessary sacrifice of human life*. . . . Ruinous competition exists not only between the operators in the same fields, but between the operators of one field as against those in another field or in another state where different mining laws and regulations are in force. This competition is . . . forcing

---

[1] *The Engineering and Mining Journal*, January 14, 1911, p. 135.

[2] Eastman, *loc. cit.*, pp. 38–39.

[3] *Ibid.*, p. 46.

even the larger operator to ***mine coal under conditions which he cannot approve***, but from which he finds no escape. . . . Each must live (or succumb) by underbidding the other, which he can do only through following the wasteful and unsafe mining methods which prevail in this country to-day in spite of the desire of every operator, to improve them. The American mine owner is as humane as the mine owner of any other country, and he would like to follow every practice and use every appliance for safety to be found in Great Britain, or France, or Belgium, or Germany, or elsewhere, but he pays his miners higher wages and, at the same time, receives for his coal at the mine half the price received for similar coal by the operator in those countries. . . . The ruinous competitive system upon which coal mining in the United States is based at the present time should be changed and the price paid for coal at the mines should be such as will permit and secure safe and efficient mining—mining unaccompanied by either this large loss of life or waste of resources, mining which can have due regard not only to the safety, but also to the health and comfort of the men who toil underground.[1]

Thus in the opinion of the head of the bureau created for the purpose of safeguarding the lives of the mine workers, "unnecessary sacrifice of human life" is conditioned by competition among mine operators.

According to the inspector-general of mines of Belgium (quoted above), "similar dangerous conditions once existed in France and Belgium, now the safest coal-mining countries in the world," but they were removed by stringent legislation and by an effective enforcement of the law.[2] In Europe wooden shafts are not permitted, the maximum amount of explosives to be used in one blast is limited by law, all machinery must be properly guarded, etc. Dr. Holmes believes that the adoption of similar regulations in the United States would prevent three fourths of the present

[1] Joseph A. Holmes: "Coal Mine Accidents and their Prevention," *Thirty-Fifth Annual Report of the Chief Inspector of Mines of the State of Ohio*, 1909, pp. 126–128.

[2] Haynes, *loc. cit.*, pp. 148, 150–151. Clarence Hall and Walter O. Snelling: "Coal Mine Accidents: their Causes and Prevention." *Bulletin of the United States Geological Survey*, No. 333, p. 6. Eastman, *loc. cit.*, p. 46. Hoffman, *loc. cit.*, pp. 476–477.

loss of life,[1] which implies that "the greatest number of accidents in bituminous coal mines" (contrary to the view accepted by the Immigration Commission), do not arise from "the recklessness, ignorance, and inexperience of employees."

This opinion is derived from the statistics of accidents in the United States and foreign countries. The comparative rates of fatal accidents in American and foreign coal mines are shown graphically in Diagram XXV., reproduced from

DIAGRAM XXV.

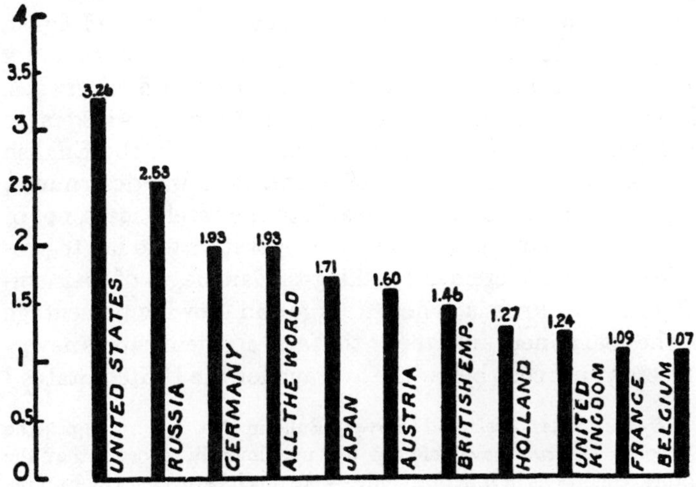

XXV. Fatal accident rates in coal mines per 1000 workmen employed in the United States and foreign countries.

the recent study of the Minnesota Bureau of Labor on the subject of industrial accidents.[2] The rate of fatal accidents in the United States is thrice as high as in France and Belgium, which shows that two thirds of the fatal accidents in the American mines could be prevented. Considering,

[1] Haynes, *loc. cit.*, p. 140.

[2] *Twelfth Biennial Report of the Bureau of Labor, Industries and Commerce of the State of Minnesota*,, 1909–10, p. 203.

however, that the natural conditions in American mines are more favorable for the safe extraction of coal than in any other country in the world,[1] Dr. Holmes's estimate that three fourths of all mining accidents are due to absence of proper precautions is quite conservative.

The difference between the accident rate in the United States and those in Austria and Russia deserves special attention, a large percentage of American mine workers being Austrian and Russian immigrants. The American fatality rate is twice as high as the Austrian. Of course, the popular explanation is, that the Austrians and Russians employed in American mines do not understand the English language, whereas in their home countries they work under the direction of foremen who speak their own languages. In so far as the failure of foreign-born mine workers to understand warnings and instructions given in the English language may affect the rate of accidents in American mines, the difference is clearly chargeable to the carelessness, not of the mine workers, but of the mine operators who fail to provide competent foremen speaking the languages of their employees. In Prussia, where a large and growing percentage of the coal miners are Poles,[2] the fatal accident rate is nevertheless 37 per cent below the average for the United States.[3]

[1] *United States Geological Survey*, Bulletin No. 333, p. 13. The European experts above referred to "unanimously reported that the natural conditions in American mines were much better than in Europe. They found, for example, that up to the present time Americans were not operating in the very deep levels of four thousand feet and lower, not uncommon in Europe, where the task of supplying fresh air and getting rid of dangerous gases is very difficult. In America, also, only thick seams more easily ventilated are, as yet, generally worked. . . . Of late years, with the gradual exhaustion of higher levels, of the thicker seams, and of the supplies of supporting timbers, conditions have come to resemble more nearly those found in Europe, and it is for this reason that the percentage of fatalities has so rapidly increased in the past decade."—Haynes, *loc. cit.*, pp. 141–142.

[2] *See* Chapter VIII., p. 182. The average for 1900–1904 in Prussia was 2.06 per 1000 employees.

[3] *United States Geological Survey*, Bulletin No. 333, p. 8.

This comparison may be pursued further. If it is true that the rate of fatalities in the United States is increased by the employment of immigrants from Southern and Eastern Europe, it may be expected that the rate will be higher in those States where the percentage of Southern and Eastern Europeans is higher among the coal miners. The comparative numbers of lives lost per thousand employees and per one million tons of coal mined in the principal mining States during the twenty-year period 1889–1908 are shown on Diagram XXVI, the distance from left to right representing the percentage of persons of Slavic and Italian parentage among the miners in 1900.[1] These States produced, in 1908, 86.6 per cent of the total output of bituminous coal in the United States.[2]

We find the highest rate of fatal accidents per one million tons mined, in Oklahoma, with 14 per cent of Southern and Eastern European mine workers; next follow Tennessee and Alabama, with 1 per cent and 2 per cent of Southern and Eastern Europeans respectively. On the other hand, in Pennsylvania with 36 per cent, and Illinois with 22 per cent, the rate of accidents is much lower, and approximately the same as in Ohio with 9 per cent, and Indiana with 5.5 per cent. The course of the other curve is the same: West Virginia, Alabama, and Tennessee, with small percentages of Southern and Eastern European mine workers, have higher fatality rates per one thousand employees than Pennsylvania and Illinois with much larger percentages of Southern and Eastern Europeans.

[1] For rates of fatal accidents *cf.* Hoffman, *loc cit.*, p. 452; the percentages of miners of Southern and Eastern European parentage were computed from *XII. Census Report on Occupations*, Table 41. The figures are given in the Appendix, Table XXVII. The census classification of breadwinners by occupation, nativity, and state makes no distinction between coal miners and metalliferous miners. This comparison accordingly comprises only such States in which there are no metalliferous mines, or the number of metalliferous miners is negligible, compared with the number of coal miners.

[2] *Statistical Abstract of the United States*, 1910, Table 120, pp. 208–209.

DIAGRAM XXVI.

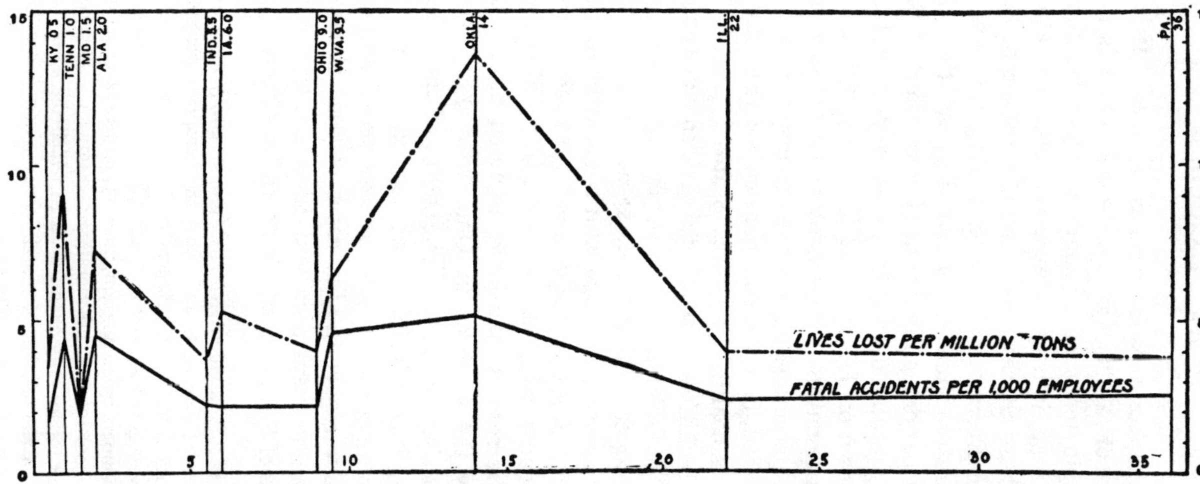

XXVI. Fatal accident rates in coal mines, 1889-1908, and percentage of miners of Slavic and Italian parentage in 1900, in the principal states.

These comparisons are not invalidated by the increase of the proportion of Southern and Eastern Europeans among the coal miners since 1900. The investigation of the Immigration Commission in 1900 found 64.3 per cent of Southern and Eastern Europeans among the coal miners of Pennsylvania, while the official statistics for West Virginia in 1908 showed 28.9 per cent of the same races[1]; and yet the average fatal accident rate per one thousand employees or per one million tons in West Virginia was much higher than in Pennsylvania.

The Immigration Commission lays great stress on the fact that the percentage of fatalities among the foreign-speaking miners in those two States is relatively higher than among the English-speaking employees. This difference, however, proves nothing without a further classification of both language groups by occupation. The distribution of the English-speaking and non-English-speaking mine workers on the scale of occupations is not uniform, and there is a wide range of variation in the degree of risk incident to each occupation. The influence of the first factor will be clear from the following. Machine runners and car loaders work side by side in the mine. The machine runner is the man who runs the mining machinery—necessarily a skilled miner; the car loader is a common laborer. And yet we find that in 1899–1908 the proportion of native white among machine runners who lost their lives in West Virginia was 80.8 per cent, while the proportion of Southern and Eastern Europeans among car loaders killed was 48.4 per cent; on the other hand, the proportion of Southern and Eastern Europeans among machine runners killed was only 6.4 per cent, while the proportion of native white among car loaders killed was 24.3 per cent.[2] It would be absurd to infer from these figures that the Southern and Eastern Europeans were more experienced and more careful

[1] *Reports of the Immigration Commission*, vol. 6, p. 226, Table 140; p. 228, Table 143.

[2] Hoffman, *loc cit.*, p. 640.

than the native white, when the truth is that there are few Southern and Eastern Europeans among the machine runners and few native white among the car loaders. Inasmuch, however, as there are several loaders to one machine runner, more loaders are killed than machine runners. The effect of these arithmetical aberrations upon the general average is to swell the ratio of Southern and Eastern Europeans to the total of fatal accidents.

The effect of the nature of the risk upon fatal accidents by race and nativity is shown in Table 131.

TABLE 131.

NUMBER AND PER CENT DISTRIBUTION OF FATAL ACCIDENTS IN COAL MINES OF WEST VIRGINIA BY PRINCIPAL CAUSES AND NATIVITY OF PERSONS KILLED, 1899–1908, AND PER CENT DISTRIBUTION OF EMPLOYEES BY NATIVITY, 1900.[1]

Race or nativity	Per cent of employees	Falling coal, slate, etc.		Explosions		Other causes[2]	
		Number	Per cent	Number	Per cent	Number	Per cent
Native white	46.3	392	41.2	246	30.0	194	55.9
Negro	21.8	207	21.8	130	15.8	84	24.2
Northern and Western Europe	3.0	68	7.1	59	7.1	8	2.3
Eastern and Southern Europe	28.9	285	29.9	387	47.1	61	17.6
Total	100.0	952	100.0	822	100.0	347	100.0

If the "relative number of fatalities among the employees of a given race or group of races" can "serve as a valuable indication of the extent to which the high death-rate in the mines is to be attributed to the employment of men by

[1] *Bulletin of the Bureau of Labor*, No. 90, Table XX., p. 646. *Reports of the Immigration Commission*, vol. 6, p. 228, Table 143.

[2] Cars (inside and outside), motors and machinery, electrocution and falling into shafts.

that race or group,"[1] then the following conclusions logically follow from the preceding table:

1. While the recent immigrants contribute no more than their proportionate share of fatalities from falling coal, slate, etc., the high death-rate from explosions is attributable to them. On the other hand native Americans contribute less than their quota of accidents from these causes.

2. The older immigrants from Northern and Western Europe contribute twice their share of fatalities from falls of roofs and explosions, which indicates that the employment of older immigrants is a menace to the safety of the men inside the mines.

3. The native white contribute more than their quota of fatalities from cars, motors, machinery, and contact with electric wires, whereas the Southern and Eastern Europeans contribute considerably less than their quota, which indicates that the high death-rate from those causes is attributable to the employment of men of native American stock.

4. The replacement of native Americans by Southern and Eastern European immigrants who apparently show greater aptitude for handling complicated modern machinery than native Americans, would tend to reduce the fatality rate from cars, motors, machinery, and electric shocks. On the other hand the displaced American mechanics could be employed to advantage as common laborers in the mines, which would tend to reduce the fatal accident rate from falling roofs and explosions.

The palpable absurdity of these conclusions proves that the premises from which they are deduced are untenable. The low percentage of Southern and Eastern Europeans among the sufferers from accidents due to machinery, motors, etc., merely indicates that they do not come in contact with these death-dealing agencies as often as Americans. Similarly, the lower ratio of native white among the sufferers from falling roofs and explosions is

[1] *Reports of the Immigration Commission*, vol. 6, p. 233.

attributable to the fact that a large proportion among them are employed in supervisory positions, where they are not exposed to the ordinary risks incident to working underground.

It is sought to deduce a causal connection between the increase of the fatal accident rate and the employment of recent immigrants from their ignorance of mining conditions which exposes them to greater danger. If this be so, it is an argument, not against immigration, but against the development of the coal mining industry. It is evident that if the mining industry is to grow apace with the development of the country, new men must continually be engaged. No one is born with mining experience, even in the United States, and there is no other place where mining experience can be gained except in a mine. The danger resulting from allowing inexperienced men, whether native or foreign-born, to work in a coal mine merely emphasizes the need of providing by law for the employment of a sufficient proportion of experienced miners to supervise the work of new employees.[1] So dangerous, however, are the working conditions in American mines that, according to Mr. Hoffman, "mine experience, even of considerable length, is not necessarily a protective factor."[2] His opinion rests upon a classification of accidents by occupation and length of experience. It appears that in every occupation the majority of those who were killed in West Virginia in 1899–

[1] Says Mr. John Laing, chief of the West Virginia Department of Mines, in a letter to the Immigration Commission: "In our large mines where in the past labor was turned loose to shoot coal, load coal, and care for themselves, we now have an officer known as 'assistant mine foreman' employed to every thirty-five men, who works in the mine and whose specific duty is to see that all coal is properly mined, that all places are timbered, that a system of ventilation is properly brought forward, etc., before a miner be permitted to do blasting of any kind."—*Reports of the Immigration Commission*, vol. 6, p. 238.

[2] "It is significant," says Mr. Hoffman, "that there should have been 43 deaths of men who had been at work from 10–14 years, 13 deaths of men with 15–19 years of mine experience and 11 deaths of men with 20 or more years' experience."—*Loc. cit.*, p. 485.

1908 had an experience of not less than one year, and in some occupations one of more than five years, *e. g.*, fire bosses 100 per cent; track layers 60.8 per cent; machine runners 59.5 per cent, etc. Among the miners, the most numerous and exposed class, 39.7 per cent had an experience of over five years.[1]

The preceding classification deals with length of experience, without regard to race or nationality. It might be argued that the Southern and Eastern Europeans are handicapped by ignorance of the English language even after years of employment in the mines and possibly swell the numbers of victims with long experience. This supposition is dismissed by the West Virginia statistics in which the accidents are classified by nativity and length of experience, as shown in Table 132:

TABLE 132.

NUMBER AND PER CENT OF TOTAL ACCIDENTS TO COAL MINERS, CLASSIFIED BY NATIVITY AND LENGTH OF EXPERIENCE IN WEST VIRGINIA, 1899–1908.[2]

Length of experience	Number			Per cent		
	English-speaking white	Southern and Eastern European	Negro	English-speaking white	Southern and Eastern Europeans	Negro
Under 1 year..........	124	150	66	18.1	24.4	22.8
1–5 years.............	221	306	115	32.2	49.6	39.8
Over 5 years..........	341	160	108	49.7	26.0	37.4
Total............	686	616	289	100.0	100.0	100.0

This table shows that experience of the mine workers counts for very little in fatal accidents: one half of all English-speaking mine workers had had an experience of

[1] Hoffman, *loc. cit.*, Table XVII., p. 643.

[2] *Ibid.*, Table XIX., p. 645.

more than five years when they lost their lives. Of the Southern and Eastern Europeans killed, one fourth had worked more than five years in the mines and three fourths more than one year. The smaller percentage of Southern and Eastern Europeans who lost their lives after an experience of more than five years cannot be taken as proof that inexperience was the cause of death in all other cases: it must be borne in mind that most of the Southern and Eastern European miners in West Virginia are recent immigrants, who for this arithmetical reason alone must contribute a larger number to the death roll of persons with brief experience. If it is sought to explain the prevalence of more recent immigrants among the victims of accidents by their negligence, due to inexperience, it must follow as a corollary that the higher percentage of miners of long experience among the English-speaking victims proves them to be twice as careless or as ignorant as the Southern and Eastern Europeans. This assumption does not agree, however, with the fact that the percentage of recent employees among the victims of accidents is approximately the same for every language or race group. It is clear that the knowledge of the English language gives the new mine worker scarcely greater immunity from accident than that which the law of chance allows to the non-English-speaking miner. The cause of accidents in coal mines is not philological, but technological.

Withal, it is an undeniable fact that the fatal accident rate has increased in the bituminous coal mines of the United States within the last twenty years, simultaneously with the increasing numbers of Slavs and Italians employed in the mines. This coincidence is accepted as sufficient proof that the increasing employment of Southern and Eastern Europeans in coal mines has been the cause of the increase in the fatal accident rate. This explanation is contradicted, however, by the statistics of accidents in the anthracite coal mines of Pennsylvania, for which there are data going as far back as 1870. In 1909, 60 per cent

Diagram XXVII.

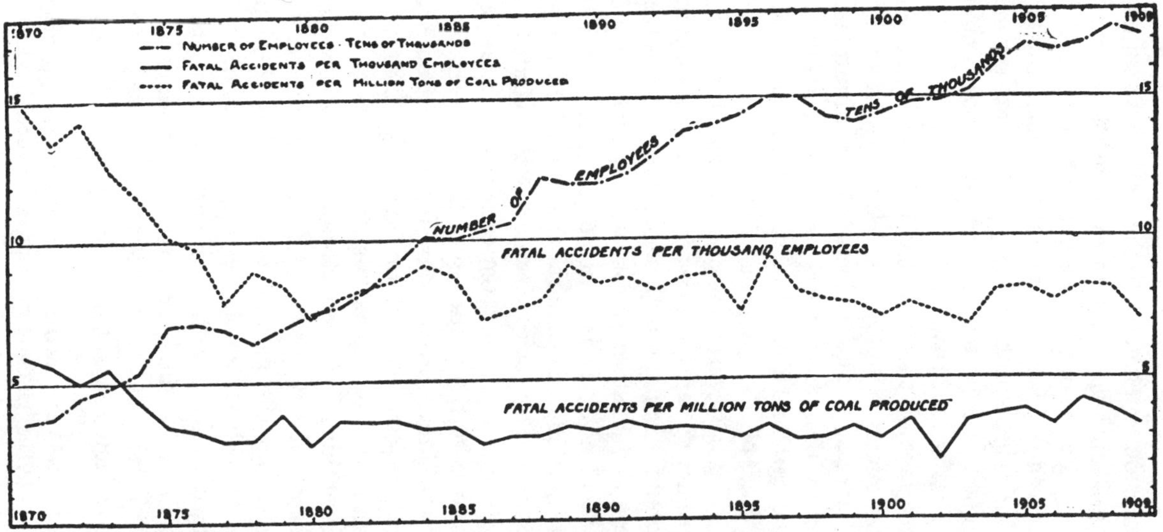

XXVII. Fatal accident rates in anthracite coal mines, 1870-1909.

of the inside employees in the anthracite mines were of the non-English-speaking races.[1] As shown on Diagram XXVII,[2] the greatest relative numbers of fatal accidents were recorded back in 1870–1874, when the employees were all English-speaking. The lowest rate per one million tons mined is reported for the year 1903, and the next lowest for the year 1909.

In the face of this fact, the increase in the number of recent immigrant employees cannot stand as an explanation of the increase of the accident rate in bituminous mines. The European mining experts, mentioned before, lay stress upon the "gradual exhaustion of higher levels, of the thicker seams, and of the supplies of supporting timbers, . . . and it is for this reason (they hold) that the percentage of fatalities has so rapidly increased in the past decade."[3]

No doubt "contributory negligence" on the part of the Southern and Eastern European may figure as a factor in many accidents. It is claimed, *e. g.*, by American and English-speaking miners, that the lives of the mine workers are endangered by the carelessness of the recent immigrants whose "desire . . . for large earnings . . . leads them to neglect to take the proper measures . . . relative to timbering and other precautions, for the reason that these measures require the loss of time from their productive work and the consequent decrease in earnings."[4] This claim is nothing but the outworn common-law defence of "negligence of fellow-servant," in an employer's liability action. From the modern point of view the employer's duty to furnish his employees a safe place of work is not discharged by leaving the necessary timbering to be done by volunteers for the common good without extra compensation. It is his duty to hire special men for that work and to keep the mine safe at his own expense. Be it as it may,

[1] *Report of the Department of Mines of Pennsylvania, 1909*, Part I. pp. 25–26. [2] The figures will be found in the Appendix, Table XXVIII.

[3] Haynes, *loc. cit.*, p. 142.

[4] *Reports of the Immigration Commission*, vol. 6, p. 652.

it is well to remember, however, that in those days when there were no "ignorant foreigners" to whom the responsibility for mine accidents could be shifted, it was the "recklessness" of the English-speaking miners[1] that was to blame. As far back as 1875, a Pennsylvania mine inspector said in his report: "I am sorry to have to report that a majority of the accidents that occur in the coal mines are the result of recklessness of the workmen themselves."[2] This comment was as general in the early reports of the Pennsylvania state mine inspectors, according to Dr. Roberts, as in the recent reports quoted by the Immigration Commission. It is evident that an American farmer boy who for the first time goes down into a mine is as incapable of a proper appreciation of the dangers of mining as a recent Slav immigrant. But even an experienced miner faced every day of his life with the "one universal characteristic" of American mining conditions—"the criminal disregard of the considerations of safety"[3]—at length comes to feel that "a man may as well pass in his checks that way as any other."[4] If he is to continue as a miner, he must develop a frame of mind akin to that of a soldier in war-time. While carelessness on the part of the miners may be a contributory cause in many accidents, the "carelessness" itself is, as Dr. Roberts put it—a "psychological effect of accidents."[5]

In the iron and steel mills there is the same disposition as in coal mining to shift the responsibility for accidents to the ignorance of the "Hunkie." Speaking of the "personal factor" in industrial accidents, Miss Eastman subordinates it to "the pressure and speed at which the plant is run,—an expression of the employer's direct financial interest in the output."

One of the older and wiser mill superintendents in the Pittsburgh District told me [says she], that the one greatest cause of danger in

---

[1] *Reports of the Immigration Commission*, p. 232.

[2] Roberts, *loc. cit.*, p. 154. [3] Haynes, *loc. cit.*, p. 148.

[4] Words of a miner quoted from the report of a Pennsylvania mine inspector, Roberts, *loc. cit.*, p. 154. [5] *Ibid.*

the steel mills is the tremendous rush of the work. "In the mills in England," he said, "they begin to work about 6, stop at 8:30 for forty-five minutes for the men to get breakfast; stop again at 1 for an hour for the men to get dinner, and stop again at 5:30 for half an hour. At these periods everything stops. The machinery is quiet. This is the reason why the English mills do not produce as much steel in the same length of time as the American mills. Here the machinery never stops. Another shift is always ready and waiting to step into the place of the shift that is leaving. Not a moment is lost. If a mill stops three minutes for repairs, or for any other cause, a detailed report of this must be made by the man in charge. If this happens two or three times under one man, the matter will be taken up with a question as to his efficiency. Under this kind of a drive, how can anybody be careful?"

When we read then, of a man who went up to make repairs without stopping the crane, or of a man who tried to throw a belt without slowing down the shaft, we must not lay the resulting accident unquestioningly to his own personal, ill-considered haste. Perhaps he was but a part of a great machine going too fast for safety. Every man in the process must keep the pace of the whole. He can no more go his own gait than a spoke in a wheel can go its own gait.[1]

But the Southern and Eastern European is charged with more than ignorant carelessness or passive acquiescence in dangerous conditions,—the very existence of such conditions "has been due to . . . his tractability or subserviency":

> When the older employees have found unsafe and insanitary working conditions prevailing in the mines and industrial establishments, *and have protested*, the recent immigrant employees, usually through ignorance of mining or other working methods, have manifested a willingness to accept the alleged unsatisfactory condition.[2]

As an illustration of such ineffective "protests," the commission cites a case where an American miner was discharged for refusing to work in a chamber which was in need of timbering, and was replaced by a foreigner.[3] Similar examples could, doubtless, be multiplied at will, considering the general disregard for safety in coal mines. Such indi-

[1] Eastman, *loc. cit.*, pp. 64, 85, 94.

[2] *Reports of the Immigration Commission*, vol. 1, p. 501.

[3] *Ibid.*, vol. 6, p. 241.

vidual objections, however, scarcely amount to a "protest." If the English-speaking miners had shown a disposition to "protest" against dangerous working conditions, it certainly must have found some expression in their strikes. We learn that during the twenty-year period from 1881 to 1900, there occurred 2515 strikes in the coal and coke industry, involving 14,575 establishments. Of the latter number there were *nine (9) in which strikes were declared against dangerous working conditions.*[1] These figures conclusively prove that the American miners made no concerted protest against dangerous working conditions even in the early '80's, when the Southern and Eastern Europeans employed in the mines were but a handful.

To what extent, if at all, individual objections of the "older employees" would have been effective in advancing the introduction of better working conditions, in the absence of Southern and Eastern European immigrant employees, can be judged by a comparison with another extra-hazardous industry, viz., steam railroads, in which the proportion of non-English-speaking employees is very small.[2]

[1] *Sixteenth Annual Report of the Commissioner of Labor*, pp. 352–353, 480–481.—The objects for which these strikes were ordered were as follows:

	Number of establishments	Succeeded
For better ventilation	4	3
The same and for repair of machinery	1	1
For change of machinery	1	—
Against use of electrical mining machines without jacketed motors	1	—
For company to have roadway in mine sprinkled	1	—
For enforcement of mining laws concerning the placing of timbers	1	1
Total	9	5

[2] According to the census of 1900, the ratio of non-English-speaking workmen employed on the railroads was only 7.5 per cent.—*Reports of the Immigration Commission*, vol. 1, pp. 821–829.

There is a marked distinction in this respect between different classes of railroad employees. The trainmen are as a rule, English-speaking, the Slavs, Hungarians, and Italians being employed mainly on construction work. In Diagram XXVIII. are plotted the accident rates per 1000 employees in bituminous and anthracite coal mines and on railroads, for the twenty-year period from 1889 to 1908.[1] The accident rate for all railway employees is not much lower than the rate for coal miners. But the fatal accident rate among trainmen is a great deal higher and has been steadily increasing since 1894.

The number of accidents resulting in personal injuries to railroad employees is still greater. In 1891–1909 it varied from one in every thirty-three, to one in every seventeen employees. The ratio of injured trainmen varied during the same period from one in every twelve, to one in eight. It stood at the last figure in 1906–1908 and declined to one in nine during the year 1909.[2] This means that in nine years' service every trainman has a probability of one hundred per cent to sustain personal injuries.

The ratio of native Americans to all railroad employees killed in work accidents, according to available information, was 72 per cent in the Pittsburgh district,[3] and 62.8 per cent in Illinois; the proportion of those who suffered personal injuries in Illinois was 66.6 per cent.[4] The trainmen who run the greatest risk of death, or personal injury, are all English-speaking and cannot be replaced by non-English-speaking immigrants. Strike statistics show that the employees in all industries combined under the head of "transportation" struck for 212 different causes

[1] The figures on which this diagram is based are given in the Appendix, Table XXIX.

[2] *Statistical Abstract of the United States*, 1910, Table 181, p. 284.

[3] Eastman, *loc. cit.*, p. 14, Table 3; number of native Americans—89, out of a total of 123 killed in accidents.

[4] *Fifteenth Biennial Report of the Bureau of Labor Statistics of Illinois*, pp. 161, 251.

DIAGRAM XXVIII.

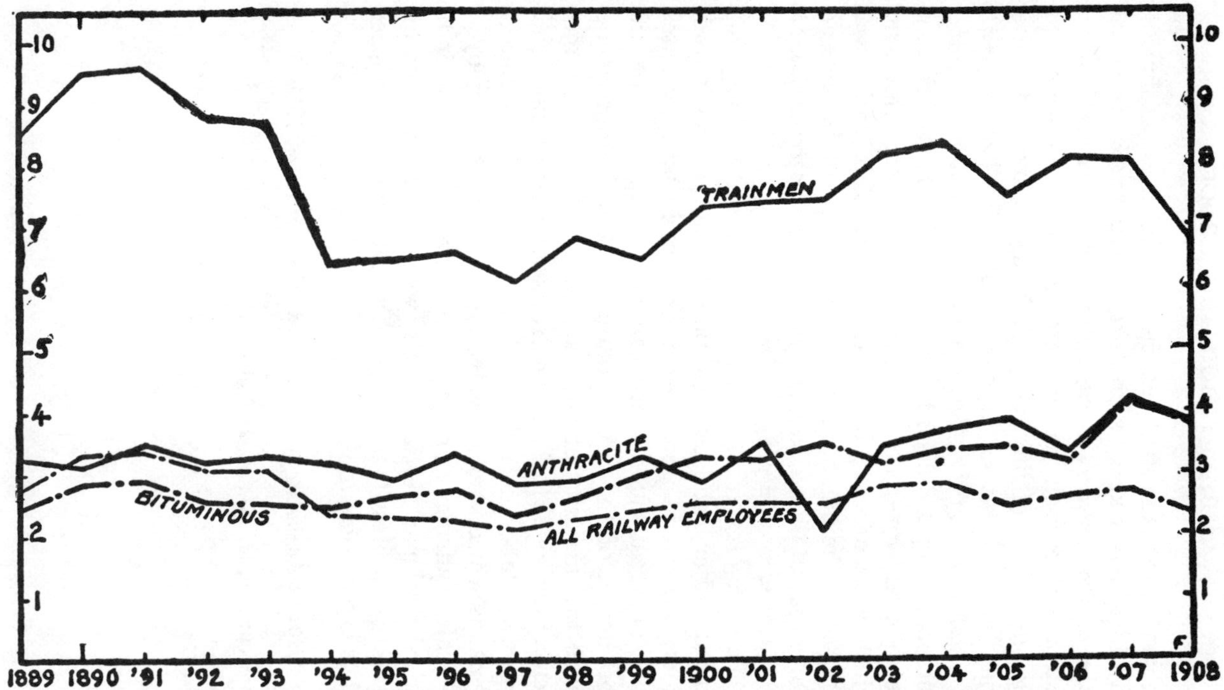

XXVIII. Fatal accident rates per 1000 employees on railroads and in coal mines, 1889-1908.

in 3436 establishments, but the number of establishments in which *strikes were declared against unsafe machinery and other dangers incident to employment was only seven.*[1]

This comparison may be extended to all classes of employment, loss of life and limb being an incident rather than an accident of modern industry. The *Sixteenth Annual Report of the United States Commissioner of Labor* enumerates 1422 different causes of strikes for the twenty-year period 1891–1900. The total number of establishments which were affected by strikes during that period was 117,509. The number among them where *strikes were declared against unsafe machinery and other dangers incident to employment was only eighty-three.*[2]

These figures testify that "acquiescence in dangerous and unsanitary working conditions" is the general attitude of organized and unorganized workers in labor disputes. This apparent indifference cannot be explained by the obstruction of the Southern and Eastern Europeans because the majority of the wage-earners as late as 1900 were of native birth.[3] It may reasonably be assumed that organized labor does not feel strong enough to enforce demands which would involve large outlays by employers for safe equipment and other improvements. The individual workman realizes that it would be quixotic on his part to "protest" singly against evils which organized labor is powerless to remedy.

[1] *Sixteenth Annual Report of the Commissioner of Labor*, Table X. pp. 510–513. [2] *Ibid.*, Table XI, pp. 519–541.

[3] Hourwich, *loc. cit.*, p. 327, Table VIII.

PART IV

CONCLUSION

CHAPTER XXIII

PROBABLE EFFECTS OF RESTRICTION—A FORECAST

IT was recognized by the Immigration Commission that the industrial expansion of the preceding twenty years would have been impossible without "the new immigration." But the Commission held "a slow expansion of industry" preferable to "immigration of laborers of low standards."[1] The Commission accordingly recommended that "a sufficient number be debarred to produce a marked effect upon the present supply of unskilled labor."[2]

What is "a sufficient number"? A learned advocate of restriction, Prof. Fairchild, referring to the period from December, 1907, to August, 1908, when emigration exceeded immigration by 124,124, finds that "this figure is almost *infinitesimal* compared to the total mass of the American working people or *to the amount of unemployment at a normal time.*" The net result of the emigration movement of those nine months was tantamount to a prohibition of immigration, yet it had "a very trifling palliative effect." [3]

The slowing down of the pace of industrial development must necessarily curtail the opportunities for advancement of the wage-earners who are already here.[4]

[1] *Reports of the Immigration Commission,* vol. 1, p. 45. [2] *Ibid.*, p. 47.

[3] Henry Pratt Fairchild: "Immigration and Crises," *The American Economic Review*, December, 1911, p. 758.

[4] The skilled crafts whose organizations were urging the adoption of the recommendation of the Commission for the exclusion of unskilled immigrants were apparently willing to swallow the recommendation in favor of legislation that would facilitate the importation of skilled labor under contract. (*Reports of the Immigration Commission,* vol, 1, p. 47.)

On the other hand, the unemployed could gain nothing from a slow growth of industry. In times of rapid industrial expansion the demand for labor is more active than in times of industrial stagnation. Inasmuch as unemployment is not due to an absolute oversupply of labor, but results from seasonal and cyclical variations in the general demand for labor, as well as from variations in the demands of individual employers, it is clear that these causes could not be removed by reducing the supply of labor. If the industries of the United States can furnish steady employment all year round to eighty per cent of all wage-earners and in times of maximum activity to ninety-five per cent,[2] but must have the full one hundred per cent ready on call, there being no agency for dovetailing the demands of scattered individual employers, these ratios will not be affected by the scale of national production.

If instead of letting the number of factory workers grow to seven million by 1909, the law had kept it at 5,600,000, as it had been in 1904, *i.e.*, twenty per cent below the 1909 figure, the industrial reserve of twenty per cent would not have been wiped out, but would have only been smaller in proportion. Yet the 1,120,000 irregularly employed in 1904 exerted the same economic pressure on the 4,480,000 who were employed all year around, as the 1,400,000 on the 5,600,000 in 1909. The problem of the five per cent irreducible minimum of unemployed was no less serious when they were only 280,000 in 5,600,000, than when they grew to be 350,000 in 7,000,000. The mere exclusion of unskilled immigrants, and even of all immigrants, will not provide employment for all masons and carpenters in the winter, or for the full winter force of a Wisconsin logging camp in the summer. Nor will the restriction of immigration revolutionize the world of fashion, so as to permit of the filling of orders for ladies' garments out of

[1] All figures in this example are merely estimates based upon the statistics of the XII. and the XIII. Census. They are used only for purposes of illustration.

season. In order to provide regular employment for the industrial reserve, all industries would have to be run upon a common time schedule, like railway trains are run on connecting lines. No plan of such a reorganization of industry has as yet been proposed that would be acceptable to all advocates of immigration restriction, let alone the proprietors of half a million independent mining, manufacturing, and mercantile establishments. It is hardly reasonable to expect a systematic adjustment of business activity on such a gigantic scale to grow up spontaneously from a purely negative measure shutting out immigration.

As a theoretical proposition, it seems quite plausible that the exclusion of "a sufficient number" of immigrants "to produce a marked effect upon the supply of unskilled labor" must force employers to pay scarcity rate of wages. It is needless, however, to indulge in abstract speculation on the possible effects of a reduced supply of unskilled immigrant labor, when such a condition actually exists in the United States throughout the agricultural sections. Few immigrants seek employment on the farms. At the census of 1900 the total number of Southern and Eastern European male farm laborers in the United States was only 37,401.[1] The number of all foreign-born male farm laborers had actually decreased from 1890 to 1900.[2] Moreover, there is a constant stream of native labor from the farms to the cities, which has led to an actual decrease of the rural population in many agricultural counties. Farmers generally complain of scarcity of farm labor during the agricultural season. Nevertheless, the wages of farm laborers are lower than the wages of unskilled laborers in mines and mills, where the proportion of recent immigrants is rapidly increasing. Scarcity of labor has not forced the farmer to pay scarcity wages, but has merely retarded the growth of farming. In many places the area under cultivation has actually decreased. On the other hand, the problem how

[1] *Reports of the Immigration Commission*, vol. I, Table A, pp. 821–829.
[2] *Occupations, XII. Census*, Table XXXIV, p. cviii.

to increase production with the same supply of labor has been solved by labor-saving machinery. The shutting-out of unskilled immigrants would have similar effects in manufacturing and mining. The labor that would thus be displaced would form one substitute for immigration.

The coal mines of Alabama and other Southern States which have failed to attract immigrants utilize the labor of farmers and their sons. The 2,300,000 tenant-farmers in particular offer great possibilities as an industrial reserve available during the winter months when the demand for labor in the coal mines is most active. The farm being their main source of subsistence, they are able and willing to offer their labor during the idle winter months more cheaply than freshly-landed immigrants. The efforts of trade-union organizers among this class of English-speaking workers have met with scant success. With the farmer who works in a mine during the winter months, the dominating interest is his farm, whereas his interest in his employment is but transitory. He may not return to the mine the next winter; he accordingly expects no benefit from an eventual gain in wages, whereas a protracted strike may deprive him of his earnings which are needed immediately to pay interest on a mortgage or to buy a machine. He is therefore reluctant to enter into a labor contest. The substitution of the cheap labor of the American farmer for the labor of the Slav or Italian immigrant would tend to weaken the unions and to keep down wages.

The discontinuance of fresh supplies of immigrant labor for the cotton mills of New England would give a new impetus to the development of the cotton industry in the South, where there is an abundant supply of child labor. The shortage of immigrant labor could also be made up for in part by the available reserve of cheap female labor.

The employment of all these substitutes for regular wage-earners certainly has its limitations. Summer is the most active season in many manufacturing industries.

Other industries are localized and cannot spread out to agricultural districts. But there is in the United States, as in all industrial countries, a steady flow of labor from rural to urban districts. In the absence of immigration of unskilled laborers the depopulation of the rural districts would be accelerated. A stimulated movement of labor from the farm to the factory must act as a drawback on the growth of farming, and the prices of foodstuffs would rise in consequence, which would tend to offset the advantages to the wage-earners from a possible rise of wages.

Still, should all the substitutes for immigrant labor prove inadequate for the needs of the employers, it does not necessarily follow that scarcity prices would rule in the American labor market. It must be borne in mind that capital is international.

Billions of American capital are already invested in Mexican and other foreign undertakings. At present this is but a minor item compared with the profits of American industries annually reinvested at home. If, however, a scarcity of labor were created in the United States, more American capital would seek investment abroad. Instead of investing their profits in new mines and mills in the United States, American capitalists would export their money to build up new enterprises in countries with cheap labor.

The increased investment of American capital in the industrial development of foreign countries with cheap labor must eventually react upon labor conditions in the United States. Certain of the most important American industries depend in part upon the export trade. At present the great smelting works of New Jersey import ore from Mexico and employ Slav immigrants to smelt and refine it into lead and copper, a great deal of which is then exported to Europe. Should the immigration of Slav laborers be barred the lead and copper producers could accommodate themselves to the situation by erecting plants in Mexico and exporting the refined lead and copper directly to London. Such a plan would not be a new departure in the world of industry. American, English, French, Belgian, and German manufacturers in the past found it more profitable to establish factories in Russia than to export their products to that country. A scarcity of labor in the United States would induce many American manufacturers to extend that policy.

Such an emigration of American capital would materially affect the export trade of the United States and eventually throw out of employment a number of American wage-earners dependent upon that trade.

It is evident that while restriction of immigration can limit the supply of labor, it is powerless to prevent a corresponding limitation of the demand for labor.

The Immigration Commission believed that "a slow expansion of industry," in the absence of "the immigration of laborers of low standards," would raise "the American standard of wages." Yet the Commission did not explain how a mere Platonic desire to maintain a high standard of living could of itself raise the rates of wages, unless the relation of demand and supply in the labor market were favorable to the wage-earner. The recent crisis has furnished a practical illustration bearing upon this point. When the operations of the steel mills were reduced, a great many men were laid off. The companies, however, offered their skilled men positions as laborers.[1] Neither their high American standard of living, nor their high standard of wages, nor their efficiency enabled them to insist upon higher wages than those which had been paid to unskilled laborers before the crisis. "A slow expansion of industry" is synonymous with an inactive demand for labor, and it is an elementary maxim of Political Economy that an inactive demand for labor is unfavorable to increases in wages.

[1] "The few unskilled places that were open were filled by Americans who were normally skilled workmen, but who at the time of the depression were compelled to take any kind of work they could get."—*Reports of the Immigration Commission*, vol. 8, pp. 39, 40.

"Skilled American employees . . . were glad to turn to unskilled occupations at twelve to fifteen cents an hour."—*Ibid.*, p. 597.

CHAPTER XXIV

THE LESSONS OF THE WAR

THE World War offered an opportunity to test the effects of restriction of immigration under the most favorable conditions. During the war immigration was reduced to a very low level. Departing aliens at times outnumbered both the newcomers and returning immigrants. Though the outbreak of the war was followed by a year of industrial depression in this country, the United States soon became the chief producer of war supplies for the Allied nations. Beginning with the spring of 1916 the supply of labor in the United States fell short of the demand in the labor market. The entrance of the United States into the war withdrew more than two million workers from industry. The government assumed the function of regulating wages in the leading industries, with the co-operation of the officers of the American Federation of Labor. Prominent men of avowed labor sympathies were placed at the head of the War Labor Board. If the economic condition of the American wage earner can be improved by suspension of immigration, here was the opportunity to observe its beneficial effects.

Indeed, the final report of the Commission on Industrial Relations, prepared by Mr. Basil M. Manly, Director of Research and Investigation, contains the following statement: "The great diminution of immigration as a result of the European war, has already begun to show its salutary effects."[1] The report does not specify the particulars in which these "salutary effects" had manifested themselves by August 9, 1915, which is its official date. It baldly asserts that the "evidence presented to the Commission" warrants

[1] *Industrial Relations: Final Report and Testimony*, vol. i, p. 144

the conclusion "that the enormous influx of immigrants during the past twenty-five years has been the *largest single factor* in preventing the wage scale from rising as rapidly as food prices." [1] The evidence was not published by the Commission; reference is only made in the Director's letter of submittal to reports presented to the Commission by Professor Lauck and Mr. Sydenstricker. The data contained in these reports were perused by them in a book published in 1917.[2] This is what they actually have to say on the subject:

> The recent advances in wage rates which have been occasioned by the unusual demand for labor at a time of restricted immigration constitute, of course, a certain advantage in economic status to wage earners in many instances. . . . How far these increases in rates, aside from the increases in earnings made possible by steady employment during a period of great industrial activity, have kept pace with increases in prices of necessaries and of the ordinary comforts used by wage-earning families, is impossible of statement until accurate statistics are obtained and published.[3]

A vast amount of statistical data on every aspect of the economic situation has since been published. A brief summary of the available evidence will be sufficient to disprove the optimistic assurance of the Industrial Commission.

At the annual meetings of the American Economic and the American Statistical Association held at Atlantic City in December, 1920, two series of index numbers of physical production were presented, one by Dr. Walter W. Stewart, the other by Dr. Edmund E. Day. Though their indices differ for particular years, yet both show a growth of production during the war period much in excess of the rate of the preceding quadrennial period.

A comparative summary of the principal items of both series for the years 1910, 1914, and 1918 is presented in Table 133 next following, where the index numbers are con-

[1] *Industrial Relations: Final Report and Testimony*, vol. i, p. 144.

[2] W. Jett Lauck and Edgar Sydenstricker: *Condition of Labor in American Industries*, p. xi.

[3] *Ibid.*, pp. 70–71.

verted to the base of 1914 as 100. The comparative growth of manufactures, mining, agriculture, and population, during the war and the preceding period beginning with 1899, is shown graphically in Diagram XXIX, reproduced from Doctor Day's Chart A.

TABLE 133

INDICES OF MANUFACTURES, MINING, AND TRANSPORTATION, 1910, 1914, 1918[1]

Year	Manufactures		Mining		Transportation
	Day's	Stewart's	Day's	Stewart's	
1910....	97	98	100	94	96
1914....	100	100	100	100	100
1918....	125	144	138	132	139

This unparalleled growth of industry was marked by extraordinary profits. The following analysis is quoted from a survey presented to the United States Railroad Labor Board by Prof. W. Jett Lauck, on behalf of a number of labor unions. His evidence is taken from the financial reports of 205 large corporations, with an aggregate capital stock of over $5,000,000,000. Their annual net income increased from an average of 8.7 per cent for the pre-war period 1912–1914, to an average of 23.9 per cent for the war period 1916–1918.

After all expenses of operation and maintenance had been paid (says Professor Lauck), after all charges for replacement of capital had been set aside—in fact, after every conceivable or imaginary expense had been met—these great groups of corporations, controlling the various products essential to our life, made profits which were sufficient to replace the entire value of the capital stock within a period of slightly over four years. This is proved by their own published reports.

[1] "An Index Number of Production," by Walter W. Stewart. *American Economic Review*, March, 1921, p. 68. "The Measurement of Variations in the National Real Income," by Edmund E. Day. *Quarterly of the American Statistical Association*, March, 1921, p. 555.

DIAGRAM XXIX.

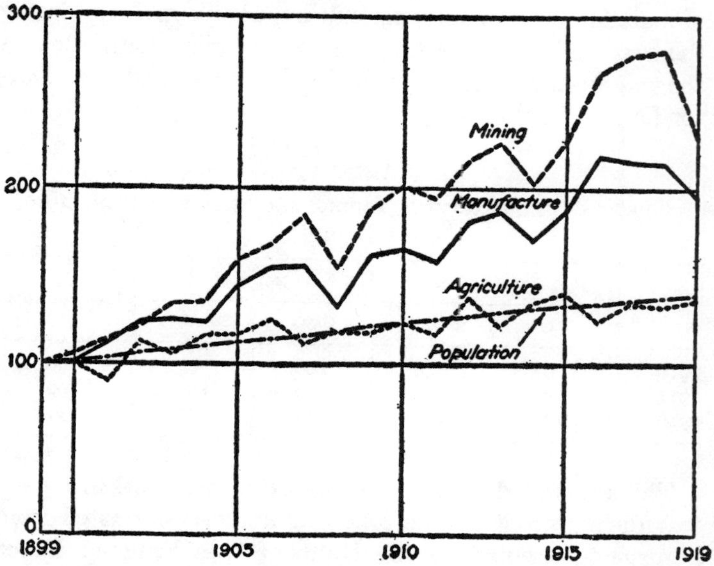

XXIX. Indices of Physical Production for Agriculture, Mining and Manufacture, 1899–1919.

Those corporations were not at all exceptional. The extraordinary profits of industry during the war appear in a document submitted to the Senate by the Treasury Department, entitled "Corporate Earnings and Government Revenue." This document shows the incomes of approximately 20,000 corporations. Altogether they earned in 1917 an average return on capital stock of 33.5 per cent, after all taxes had been deducted.

Over one-fourth of these corporations, 5,724 in number, showed net profits of over 50 per cent on capital stock. And over one-tenth of them (2,030) showed net profits of over 100 per cent. In other words, there were over 5,000 corporations which, in 1917, earned over one-half the value of their capital stock and over 2,000 that earned the entire value in a single year.[1]

[1] W. Jett Lauck: *The Relation Between Wages and the Increased Cost of Living*, pp. 7, 9–12.

The preceding analysis was made by a representative of organized labor. The same conclusions, however, are reached by Professor Friday, who, in his study of the relations between profits, wages, and prices, endeavors to take a judicial attitude, although inclining at times toward the capital side. The net income of all corporations, as reported to the Bureau of Internal Revenue, amounted in 1914 approximately to $3,700,000,000; in 1916 it more than doubled, reaching well nigh $8,600,000,000. When the United States entered the war, the corporations were made to yield to the government in excess profit taxes about $2,000,000,000, and yet their profits for the year 1917 remained at the level of the previous year. Of course the net earnings of the various classes of corporations widely varied. The earnings of mining and manufacturing corporations in 1917 were nearly 330 per cent of those of 1913, the largest pre-war year. A classification of manufacturing, mining, and mercantile corporations according to the percentage ratio of their net income to invested capital shows that more than one-half of the total net income was earned by concerns which made 30 per cent or over. The profits of railroads and other public utility corporations, being regulated by the public authorities, did not rise to such heights, yet in 1916 they were 53 per cent above the 1913 level, and in 1917 they still remained 30 per cent above the pre-war level. "The popular impression," sums up Professor Friday, "that the war has brought a large increase in profits is fully borne out by the facts. The growth has been large, even after the payment of income and excess profits taxes." [1]

A glance at Diagram XXIX will show how far the growth of population lagged behind the industrial expansion of the war years. This was directly due to the decrease of immigration. The annual net immigration or emigration of breadwinners from July 1, 1914, to June 30, 1919, is shown in Table 134.

[1] David Friday: *Profits, Wages, and Prices*, pp. 14, 15, 18, 36, 38, 39.

TABLE 134.

NET IMMIGRATION OR EMIGRATION OF BREADWINNERS, 1915–1919.[1]

Year ended June 30th	Net immigration (+) or emigration (−)
1915	− 29,709
1916	+ 52,111
1917	+134,263
1918	− 3,007
1919	− 15,519
Total	+138,149

The excess of all alien arrivals over all departing aliens, including dependents ("persons without occupation, mostly women and children," in official terminology) aggregated during the same period 431,884. Thus, the additions to the population through immigration during the war period represented mostly dependents of immigrants who had previously settled in the United States. The addition of 138,149 immigrant breadwinners was by far insufficient to make up for the mortality among earlier immigrants.[2]

The effects of the cessation of immigration upon the state of the labor market are reflected in the statistics compiled by the New York State Industrial Commission. From the month of March, 1916, to the end of the year 1918, the supply of labor registered at the public employment offices varied from 97.1 per cent to 47.1 per cent of the demand for labor.[3]

Such was the relation of supply and demand at the gateway of the United States. That this condition was not exceptional, is evidenced by the suspension of the contract-labor law in 1917, 1918, 1919, and 1920, in order to enable

[1] See Appendix, Table XXXI.

[2] During the ten years from July 1, 1910, to June 30, 1920, the excess of arriving over departing aliens aggregated 3,123,000 persons (see Appendix, Table XXX.). The increase of the foreign-born population from the XIII. to the XIV. Census (1910–1920) was only 358,000 (see Table 7 on p. 88). The decrease of the number of foreign-born by death thus amounted to 2,765,000.

[3] See Appendix, Table XXXII.

mine operators and other employers in the Southwest to import Mexican laborers under contract.[1] During those four years 50,800 Mexican contract laborers were imported under departmental regulations which were tantamount to peonage.[2] This measure is justified, in a report of a committee appointed by Ex-Secretary of Labor Wilson, by "the fact that immigration from Europe had practically ceased." It is explained that "a dire and imperative need was met in making the exceptions and permitting Mexican labor to enter this country on easy terms to meet the abnormal demand for common labor." It should be remembered that Mr. Wilson was made the first Secretary of Labor as the spokesman for organized labor, having been a vice-president of the American Federation of Labor and a district president of the United Mine Workers. Obviously such a striking departure from the policy of organized labor must have been necessitated by a genuine scarcity of labor.[3]

The effects of the war upon the state of the labor market during the war are well summarized in the following excerpt from a recent book on war-time strikes:

> In times of emergency and consequent abnormal labor demand, there arises a competition for men which disturbs to a marked degree the wage relationships of normal times. For normal times, as our economic system is constituted, have always meant times of labor surplus. . . . When, however, the demand for men far exceeds the supply, employers compete among one another and are willing in many cases to pay wages even higher than union rates. In open-shop industries men were offered these increased rates irrespective of their union membership. . . . A further consequence of the abnormal war conditions was an unprecedented mobility of labor. Every method, including patriotic appeals in the press and on public platforms, was used to bring home to the workers of other localities the need of men in places where war

[1] *Monthly Labor Review*, November, 1920, p. 223.

[2] See note in the Appendix.

[3] Still, the same Secretary Wilson, in a press statement under date of January 10, 1918, said that there was "an ample supply of labor both for the army and for industry." (The *Evening Telegram*, New York, January 13, 1918.) Apparently, however, such official pronouncements must be taken with a grain of salt.

material was being produced. Influenced both by the patriotic motive and the desire for better wages, men and women left their homes and traveled to distant cities. This movement of the workers was accelerated by the action of employers who, not content with elaborate newspaper advertisements offering high rates of wages, even went as far as to send labor scouts all over the country. Both of these practices had to be curtailed by the government when toward the end of the war the competition for men became fiercer than ever and the U. S. Employment Service was organized in an effort to control the situation. . . . Workers not only left their homes but they changed from one industry to another with a freedom never before known. General wage levels were a matter of common knowledge. And the worker knew not only the pay of men in his own industry but also that of workers in many other trades.[1]

According to scholastic theory, "with employers competing more eagerly to get workmen, with the better employers ready to pay appreciably higher wages than before, with resident laborers not subject to fresh competition from abroad, the time is ripe for a real increase of wages." [2] Did this ideal combination of economic factors during the late war actually produce the "salutary effects" anticipated by the Commission on Industrial Relations?

Applying the standard chosen by the Commission, *viz.*, the rise of the wage scale apace with food prices, we find that the purchasing power of union wages considerably declined during the war, as shown in Table 135.

A painstaking study of the movement of real wages gauged by retail prices of food has been made by Professor Douglas

[1] Alexander M. Bing, *War-time Strikes*, pp. 196–197. According to a special study of mobility of labor made by the United States Bureau of Labor Statistics for the decade 1910–1919, "each year, on the average, the number of persons who quit, who were laid off or were discharged, as well as the number who had to be hired, was much larger than the total number of workers on the force at any one time." During the period from the entrance of the United States into the war, to the armistice (*i.e.*, from May, 1917, to October, 1918), the monthly mobility rates were far above the average. "Mobility of Labor in American Industry," by Paul F. Brissenden and Emil Frankel: *Monthly Labor Review*, June, 1920, pp. 41–43.

[2] "Hourwich's Immigration and Labor," by Robert F. Foerster: *The Quarterly Journal of Economics*, August, 1913, p. 668.

TABLE 135.

PURCHASING POWER OF UNION WAGE RATES, MEASURED BY RETAIL PRICES OF FOOD, 1913–1918.[1]

Year	Per hour	Per week
1913	100	100
1914	100	99
1915	101	101
1916	94	93
1917	78	77
1918	79	77

and Miss Lamberson. They have arrived at the following conclusions concerning the effects of the war upon the condition of the American wage worker:

All the evidence seems to indicate that at the termination of the great war the return in commodities which the American workman received for an equal length of time worked (one hour) was from 7 to 17 per cent less than it was before the sharp, upward movement of prices in 1916. The purchasing power of the established week's work, moreover, was from 10 to 20 per cent less than in 1915. American labor, as a whole, therefore, cannot legitimately be charged with having profiteered during the war. Rather, like Alice in Wonderland, it was compelled to run faster in order to stay in the same place.[2]

The material for these conclusions was taken from the wage statistics of ten leading industries. The authors, therefore, caution the reader against generalization from their results without certain reservations, of which the following are the most important:

[1] *Monthly Labor Review*, March, 1919, p. 120. The United States Bureau of Labor Statistics has expressed the view that union rates of wages are merely minimum rates and that in practice union workers earn more than that minimum. Other students, however, take the opposite view. "The union rates of pay are the so-called minimum rates. As a matter of experience, however, these minimum rates are usually the prevailing rates." Hugh S. Hanna and W. Jett Lauck: *Wages and War*, p. 2. This view is concurred in by Mr. Bing, an employer of labor, of large business experience, who served the government during the war. Bing, *loc. cit.*, p. 196.

[2] "The Movement of Real Wages," by Paul H. Douglas and Frances Lamberson: *The American Economic Review*, September, 1921, pp. 425–426.

The industries covered do not include such war-time industries as munitions plants. Some of the occupations within these industries enjoyed increases in wages more than sufficient to compensate for the increase in the cost of living. On the other hand, neither are the railroad workers and the coal miners included, and their wages notoriously lagged behind the increase in prices. Farm laborers also lost during the war period.[1]

Still, in recent studies of the United States Bureau of Labor Statistics, and in the compilations of the National Industrial Conference Board, retail prices of food alone have been considered unsatisfactory as a measure of the cost of living, inasmuch as they do not reflect the changes in other items of the family budget, notably rent.[2] The adequacy of other standards, however, has likewise been questioned.[3] Professor Litman, in his study of prices during the war, comes to the following conclusions:

As to any definite conclusions regarding increased cost of living and the effect of this increase upon the status of the workingman and his family, one may subscribe without reservation to the statements of

[1] "The Movement of Real Wages," by Paul H. Douglas and Frances Lamberson: *The American Economic Review*, September, 1921, pp. 421–422.

[2] According to the United States Bureau of Labor Statistics, the average cost of housing for thirty-two cities showed practically no change from 1913 to the end of 1917; in December, 1918, it increased 9.2 per cent from the 1913 average. The increase in rents came as the aftermath of the war. *Monthly Labor Review*, July, 1921, p. 112.

[3] "At the present time, index numbers of the cost of living, like all other index numbers, are still in the experimental stage of development. They cannot yet be considered instruments of precision like thermometers or micrometer calipers. And no one is at this time justified in sitting with an eye peeled on the index number of the cost of living and measuring its movement in one direction or another, and believing that whatever the index registers is above question or criticism. For retail price quotations of standardized goods and services are not easy to collect, and when one index number is compared with another, small but not unimportant discrepancies frequently appear. . . . They are due to differences in the manner of collecting price quotations, in the instructions to enumerators, in the training and judgment of the enumerators, and in the kinds of goods and services that are included in the survey by each agency."—Leo Wolman: "The Cost of Living and Wage Cuts," *The New Republic*, July 27, 1921.

the United States Commissioner of Labor Statistics, that after all these years of investigation and statistical toil in the cost-of-living field, we don't know clearly the difference between the higher cost of living and the cost of higher living.[1]

Yet, after a careful examination of all available data, Professor Litman cautiously concludes that "it does not seem that wages rose as rapidly as the prices of commodities.[2]

This view is concurred in by those who speak for organized labor. The following is from Prof. Lauck's statement before the United States Railroad Labor Board, quoted on a previous page:

An examination of the experience of every industry shows, practically without exception, that wage increases have lagged behind price increases, and usually very far behind. . . . They [the workers] have merely struggled as best they could and in the only way they could to keep their old standards of living. In this struggle they have met with only very partial success. For the great body of wage earners, wagcs have not kept step with prices. As a result, labor as a class is now worse off than it was before the war. Almost without exception a day's wage buys less than it did in 1912 to 1914. In other words, in the distribution of the income of the country, labor is receiving a smaller proportion than it did before the war, while capital—in the form of profits, interest, and rent—is receiving a very much larger proportion.[3]

On the other hand, the same statistical material leads Professor Friday to the opposite conclusion, *viz.*, "that the real wages of labor have risen, and are higher to-day than they were in 1914."[4] But at the end of the same chapter, he qualifies this general statement as follows:

There are so many different kinds of labor, so many different kinds of wage payment, and so many different rates of pay, that the task of obtaining a general view of the course of wages is considered by experts to be one of the most difficult and complicated scientific undertakings

[1] Simon Litman: *Prices and Price Control in Great Britain and the United States During the World War*, p. 201.

[2] *Ibid.*, p. 197.

[3] *Loc. cit.*, p. 5.

[4] Friday: *Profits, Wages, and Prices*, p. 107.

in the whole field of economics. . . . Consequently all general statements regarding wages, of which many are always appearing in print and on the platform, should be accepted with extreme caution.[1]

His own computation of the increase in wage rates and employment of from ten to twelve million workers shows that the yearly earnings per employee increased from 1913 to 1917 slightly over 30 per cent,[2] whereas it appears from other sources that the cost of living during the same period increased 42 per cent.[3]

The most conclusive corroboration of the decline in real wages is furnished by the investigations of the Bureau of Child Hygiene of New York City, which show a decided increase of the proportion of malnourished school children during the World War. The figures are presented in Table 136.

TABLE 136.

PROPORTION OF MALNOURISHED SCHOOL CHILDREN IN THE BOROUGH OF MANHATTAN, NEW YORK CITY.[4]

Year	Per cent
1914	5
1915	6
1916	12
1917	21

This condition was not peculiar to New York City only. Dr. Thomas D. Wood, in an address delivered before the National Council of Education, February 28, 1918, estimated "that between 15 and 25 per cent of our school children are undernourished." [5]

Was this lagging of wages behind the advancing cost of living due to the failure of the wage workers to "insist" upon a higher rate of wages—to put it in the language of the eco-

[1] Friday: *Profits, Wages, and Prices*, pp. 110–111.
[2] *Ibid.*, p. 122.
[3] *Monthly Labor Bulletin*, February, 1921, p. 61.
[4] "What Is Malnutrition?" by Lydia Roberts. *Children's Bureau, Publication No. 59*, p. 7.
[5] *Ibid.*, pp. 7, 19.

nomic experts of the Immigration Commission? The statistics of strikes during the world war prove that labor did not submissively acquiesce in the terms offered to it by employers.

In the period from 1881 to 1905 there occurred on an average 1,532 strikes a year. During the three years 1916–1918 the number of strikes averaged more than twice as many, *viz.*, 3,697. The annual average number of strikers during the decade, preceding the predominance of the "new immigration" was 267,000, and in the first decade of its ascendancy 344,000.[1] During the years 1916–1918, the annual average number of strikers rose to 1,310,000,[2] *i.e.*, 391 per cent above the average of 1886–1895, whereas the number of persons engaged in manufacturing and mechanical pursuits, trade, and transportation, increased from the X. to the XIII. Census (1880–1910) only 208 per cent.[3] Nor were those strikes unorganized outbursts of inarticulate discontent. The percentage of strikes in which the workers were members of unions rose from 82 in 1915 to 90 in 1917, and remained at 83 in 1918.[4]

Moreover, strikes were not the only means by which labor was able to assert its claims:

> During the war the principle of collective bargaining was of necessity, albeit in many cases rather grudgingly, recognized by all employers engaged on direct government work or in the production of essentials. The Quartermaster Corps, the Ordnance Office, the Emergency Fleet Corporation of the Shipping Board, the National War Labor Board, the Fuel Administration, and many other government agencies, sought to secure greater and more continuous production by means of collective agreements covering wages.[5]

[1] See Table 104, on p. 345.

[2] Alexander M. Bing: *War-time Strikes*, pp. 292–293.

[3] *XIII. Census Reports*, vol. iv, p. 41.

[4] Bing, *loc. cit.*, p. 297.

[5] Royal Meeker, Commissioner of Labor Statistics: "Employees Representation in Management of Industry," *Monthly Labor Review*, February, 1920, p. 2.

Neither could the presence of the "un-Americanized" foreign worker serve as an explanation for the decline of real wages. It has been brought out, on the basis of the calculations of the Bureau of Applied Economics, that whereas the real wages of common laborers in the iron and steel industry—of whom 64 per cent are foreign born—have gone up, those of locomotive firemen—of whom 84 per cent are native-born Americans—have declined to a point 31 per cent below "the minimum budget under American standards." [1]

Among the potent factors in the decline of real wages must be noted the movement of labor from agriculture to urban industries in response to the attraction of higher wages. In consequence, agricultural production during the war barely kept pace with the growth of population,[2] while the demand for breadstuffs was increased by exports abroad, as indicated in Table 137. The great interests which control

TABLE 137.

WHEAT PRODUCED, EXPORTED, AND RETAINED FOR CONSUMPTION, FISCAL YEARS 1911–1918.[3]

Millions of bushels	Years ended June 30		Increase (+) or decrease (−) Per cent
	1911–1914	1915–1918	
Produced [1]	2,750	3,190	+ 16
Exported, domestic [2]	435	915	+110
Domestic, retained for consumption	2,315	2,275	− 2
Per cent exported	16	29	...

[1] The production is of the calendar year preceding the fiscal year.
[2] Including wheat flour reduced to wheat.

the agricultural produce market were thereby enabled to raise the prices of food. What the wage earner gained in

[1] Editorial in *The New Republic*, February 25, 1920, p. 373.—*XIII. Census Reports*, vol. iv, Table VI: Laborers in blast furnaces and steel rolling mills, iron foundries, and other iron and steel factories; locomotive firemen (computed).

[2] See Diagram XXIX.

[3] *Statistical Abstract of the United States*, 1918, p. 559. For statistics of exports of other breadstuffs, see Appendix, Table XXXIII.

money wages, he was forced to surrender in the higher prices of necessities of life. This fact is established by Prof. Wesley C. Mitchell's study of prices during the war, from which Table 138 is compiled.

TABLE 138.

INDEX NUMBERS OF THE YEARLY PRODUCTION AND PRICES OF VEGETABLE PRODUCTS, 1913–1918.[1]

Years	Production	Prices
1913	100	100
1914	106	95
1915	112	98
1916	100	111
1917	107	173
1918	106	191

The next question to be considered is, What were the substitutes for immigrant labor during the war years? The movement of workers from agriculture to urban industries has already been referred to. It struck the public eye in the migration of Negroes from the agricultural South to the industrial East and Middle West. The volume of that migration is officially estimated at from 400,000 to 500,000. "Shortage of labor in Northern industries" is given as "the direct cause of the increased Negro migration during the war period." "The agricultural regions of the Southern states began to suffer for want of the Negro worker." [2]

[1] "History of Prices During the War," by Wesley C. Mitchell: *W. I. B. Price Bulletin No. 1*, p. 45.—"In vegetable husbandry the harvest depends partly upon the acreage sown, which the farmer can control, but quite as much upon the weather. Thus the annual supply of vegetable products increased in the dull year 1914 and increased largely again in 1915. Nineteen sixteen was a bad year, and all the efforts to encourage agriculture in 1917 and 1918 did not bring the harvests close to the 1915 record." (*Ibid.*, p. 46.)

[2] "The Negro at Work During the World War": *Department of Labor Division of Negro Economics*, George E. Haynes, Director. Second Study on Negro Labor, p. 10. See also: Emmett J. Scott: *Negro Migration During the War*, pp. 3, 14.—According to a preliminary statement issued by the Bureau of the Census, the Negro population of Kentucky, Tennessee, Alabama, Mississippi, and Louisiana decreased from 1910 to 1920 by 142,598. On the other hand, of the total numerical increase in the Negro population of the United States during that de-

Another substitute for immigrant labor was found in the employment of women. The statistics on the subject are scattered in government publications. An illustration is furnished by the Annual Report of the Director-General of Railroads for 1919, from which we learn that in October, 1918, the number of women employed on the railroads had increased, from the entrance of the United States into the war, by about 70,000, which represented an addition of 225 per cent.[1]

The increased employment of children in industry during the war emergency was still another substitute for immigrant labor. The subject is dealt with in a report of the Children's Bureau, from which the following is condensed:

> By the latter part of 1915 the effect of foreign orders for war goods was beginning to make itself felt in the increased employment of children. Beginning with the autumn of 1915 an unprecedented rise began in the number of children entering gainful employment, and heavy increases were practically everywhere recorded for 1916 and 1917, even before the United States entered the war. After the entrance of the United States into the war the number of children taking out employment certificates continued to rise. The forces at work pushing children into industry included *the growing cost of the necessities of life* combined, in many cases, with the absence on military duty of members of the family who had previously contributed to its support. High wages offered by employers hard pressed for help proved a powerful magnet, drawing into business and industry many children under sixteen who in normal times would have remained in school. In several cities the increase in 1918 was so striking as to arrest attention even in that year of generally large increases. In Washington, D. C., there was an increase of more than 163 per cent in 1917–18 (July 1st to June 30th) over 1916–17. In Louisville, Kentucky, there was an increase in 1918 of 52 per cent, following an increase in 1917 of 174 per cent, so that the

---

cade, 69 per cent took place in the North, although its Negro population in 1920 was only 14 per cent of the total for the United States. In several of the Northern states the rates were extraordinarily large, *e.g.*, in Pennsylvania, 46.7 per cent; in Ohio, 67.1 per cent; in Michigan, 251 per cent; in Illinois, 67.1 per cent.

[1] *Monthly Labor Review*, March, 1920, p. 156

number of children receiving employment certificates was in 1918 over four times as great as in 1916. In Philadelphia an increase of 82 per cent in 1917 was followed by a still further increase of 15 per cent in 1918. It should be kept in mind that the figures here given relate only to children legally certificated, and give no indication of the numbers going to work without complying with the law. Reports from labor commissioners and factory inspectors indicated the difficulty experienced during the war years in adequately administering child-labor laws. Parents and children, tempted by the high wages offered the children *at a time when the excessive cost of living presented a serious problem*, would connive at evasions of the law in order to have the children work in factories and munitions plants. In Philadelphia violations of the child-labor law were four times as great in 1917 as in 1916. In inspections made by the Children's Bureau of sixty-three shipyards where steel ships were being built, approximately 60 per cent of the children found at work who claimed to be sixteen and were without certificates were actually only fourteen or fifteen years of age. The reply of the Assistant Secretary of the Industrial Commission of Wisconsin to an inquiry sent out in 1918 by the Children's Bureau in regard to this subject pointed out the fact that "The general effect of the war upon the enforcement of the child-labor law has been to increase the difficulty of enforcing the law. The scarcity of adult labor has made the employer more ready to take minors into his employ. Many employers now employ children who have never done so before to any extent." [1]

What is the lesson that can be drawn from the experience gained in the late war? Amidst the present industrial crisis one must not lose sight of the fact that this is but one of the cyclical disturbances of the capitalistic system which will be followed by resumption of "business as usual." There will be profits which will seek investment in new fields. Prior to the war most of that surplus was applied to the expansion of American industry, which created a demand for immigrant labor. If restriction of immigration is to become the permanent policy of the United States, our recent war experience does not warrant the assumption that the resulting scarcity of labor will inure to the benefit of the American wage worker.

[1] "Trend of Child Labor in the United States, 1913–1920," by Nettie McGill. *Monthly Labor Review*, April, 1921, pp. 6–10.

It seems likely that the restriction of immigration of labor from Europe will lead to emigration of American capital to Europe.

That this is not mere speculation, appears from an official report of the Commercial Secretary of the British Embassy in Berlin, who states that arrangements have been in progress between American capitalists and German corporations, looking toward the investment of American capital in German industry. The electrical and textile industries and shipping are mentioned.[1]

The decline of real wages during the late war is merely a repetition of the story of the Civil War; the cause of it has been stated in a previous chapter.[2] The bargaining power of the wage earner does not extend to the market in which he appears as a consumer. Advances in wages come as a result of the slow process of collective bargaining, involving the use of the cumbersome machinery of arbitration, with occasional resort to industrial warfare, whereas the prices of commodities consumed by the wage earner are controlled by monopolistic combinations, which promptly add every ad-

[1] *General Report on the Industrial and Economic Situation in Germany in December, 1920*, p. 6. Presented to Parliament by Command of His Majesty. London, 1921.—In a press dispatch cabled from Paris under date of September 11, 1921, it was reported that an agreement was signed between representatives of a big American syndicate and the Archduke Frederick of Austria and his family, by which the syndicate took over the whole of the Archduke's estates in the dismembered Austrian Empire. These estates include the rich steel works and mines at Teschen, vast forest lands stretching across many miles of several new Central European republics, farms, factories, etc. The value of the property is conservatively estimated at $200,000,000. In the syndicate which is taking the control of this property are mentioned names prominent in American financial circles. The negotiations began in the summer of 1919. An arrangement was made in October, 1919, whereby the Archduke was to transfer his various properties and interests to a corporation which was then organized in Switzerland. The deal involves litigation in the courts of the new republics, and ex-premier Viviani of France is reported to have been retained as counsel to represent the claims of the Austrian Archduke before the League of Nations.

[2] See p. 306.

vance in wages to the market price of the finished product.[1] Thus the raise of wages of one group of workers is in effect charged up to the working class as a whole.

The leak is in the control of prices. The government, during the war, assumed the authority to regulate prices, but it delegated this authority to representatives of the interests which were to be regulated.[2] The profiteering which resulted from the methods of price control adopted by the various war agencies, was exposed in a report submitted by the Federal Trade Commission to the Senate in the summer of 1918. The profits assured to the big interests were "enormous . . . far beyond anything that was necessary to keep men in industry and to stimulate their initiative and enterprise." [3] What is wanted in order to secure to the worker a real advance in wages, is regulation of profits in the interest of the consumers, of whom the wage earners constitute the most numerous single group.

Restriction of the supply of labor does not touch the problem of price control. Immigration laws can prevent the American capitalist from employing foreign labor in the United States. But with the present rates of exchange he may find it as profitable to employ the same labor in Europe in the manufacture of goods for the world market. The reduction of the supply of labor will be met by a reduction of the demand for labor. Restriction of immigration will merely speed the advance of financial imperialism.

[1] "Wage earners, as soon as they could make their economic demands felt, thereupon received wage increases so that they might in a measure cope with the advance in the cost of living. This meant increased labor costs to the producers and middlemen, and they instantly advanced prices again. Almost without exception, these price advances were out of all proportion to the increase in labor costs. This necessitated further wage increases to labor, and we find the vicious circle established, with the profiteers invariably in command of the situation."—"Profiteers," by W. Jett Lauck: *The Socialist Review*, July, 1920, p. 52.

[2] "Most of the important positions in the Food Administration were entrusted to successful organizers and administrators of private business enterprises."—Litman: *loc. cit.*, p. 211.

[3] Friday: *loc. cit.*, p. 155.

Appendix

IN ANSWER TO CRITICS[1]

THE first edition of this book was attacked by two authors of books on immigration. This record of the critics calls for an examination of their objections.

Prof. Fairchild goes at it with the habits acquired in marking examination papers. It could not escape his trained eye that the name of Prof. Willcox was misspelled (with one "l" instead of two). The error is repentantly admitted, and has been corrected in the present edition. He is less fortunate, however, in other attempts of a similar kind. Thus he finds fault with the remark in the footnote on p. 60 that the conclusion of the Immigration Commission that "'the employment of the wife, or keeping boarders or lodgers, is less frequent among the native-born of foreign father' . . . is derived from the reports in just four families, whose heads are native-born of foreign father." He has taken the pains to look up the reference, and announces to have found that there were 26 such families instead of 4. Examination of Table 44, on p. 310 of the volume quoted shows, however, in the column headed "number of wives having employment or keeping boarders or lodgers," *exactly* 4 such wives. As there is, presumably, one wife to each family, this is equivalent to four families. The critic has evidently been misled by the figure 26, which is shown in another column headed "number of selected families," for the "total native-born of selected families."

This desire to pick flaws reaches a climax on p. 762 of Prof. Fairchild's review. In Table 8 the author has copied from the *Reports of the Immigration Commission*, the sta-

[1] Henry Pratt Fairchild, in *The National Municipal Review*, vol. ii, (1913).—Robert F. Foerster, in *The Quarterly Journal of Economics*, August, 1913.

tistics of the movement of third-class passengers between the United States and European ports during the calendar years 1899–1909. The number of west-bound passengers is reported to have fallen from 1,378,000 in 1907, to 420,000 in 1908, which shows a decline of *958,000*; the net immigration, *i.e.*, the excess of east-bound over west-bound passengers for the year 1908, is *237,000*. These figures are commented upon by the author as follows:

> During the industrial crisis of 1908, immigration dropped at once *nearly a million*, compared with the high-water mark of the previous year. . . . The result was a net loss of *nearly a quarter of a million* through emigration (p. 92).

Prof. Fairchild has not troubled himself to look at Table 8, instead of which he has made a computation of his own from some other source—he does not take the reader into his secret—and has obtained the figures 859,642 and 41,198, respectively, instead of those commented upon by the author. On this ground the author is charged with "intent to mislead." The American academic world prides itself upon its "catholicity": there are two sides to every question, etc. But, when met by heterodox opinion, the priest of the Temple of Wisdom loses his scholarly poise and falls into the ways of the *vulgus profanum*.

Concerning the merits of the criticisms, it must be noted that both reviewers reject the statistical method of treatment of the subject of immigration. Prof. Fairchild exhorts against "the besetting sin of the professional statistician, the assumption that nothing is true which cannot be proved by statistics" (p. 763). He is seconded by Dr. Foerster, who believes that "we must go heavily armed with hypotheses. . . . For to-day [he says] guarded deductive reasoning is indispensable, and often by appropriate tests is found valid" (pp. 670, 671).

It will be remembered that a Commission was appointed by Congress to investigate the immigration question, and that after nearly three years of study the Commission brought out a report recommending restriction of immigration, in support of which it presented many volumes of statistical material. This evidence is ruled out by the learned economists, who prefer to go back to deductive reasoning and hypotheses. Is it because they realize that the truth of the conclusions of the Commission "cannot be proved by statistics"? Still, since other university professors who directed its investigations tried to prove the case for restriction of immigration by statistical evidence, it was incumbent upon the negative side to show that their statistics had failed to establish the truth of their contentions.

Let us consider, however, whether deductive reasoning would do better than the inductive method. The prerequisite for the application of the deductive method is the existence of axioms and postulates based upon common observation of facts. In pure mathematics these facts are few and simple, and are within the daily experience of every person. Economic science, on the contrary, deals with a great number of complex phenomena which are not within the knowledge of everybody. The so-called deductive Political Economy is in reality also based upon observed facts, but the field of observation is confined to the narrow environment of the scholar. A pertinent illustration is the theory of wages to which both reviewers swear allegiance, *viz.*, that the demand for labor at periods of shortage of labor "must of necessity have raised the wages of laborers already in the country, if the foreign sources of supply had been cut off." [1] The experience of labor in the late war, as well as in the Civil War, has discredited this theory. Mere facts, however, have no place in the speculative theory of the reviewers.

> What importance can it have—says Dr. Foerster—to ask whether wages in an immigrant occupation are higher or lower now than they once were? Legislators must ask, how does unrestricted immigration affect wages (p. 658).

[1] Fairchild, *loc. cit.*, p. 760.—See also Foerster, *loc. cit.*, p. 668.

Obviously he thinks that that question can be answered by intuition, without a comparative study of the actual rates of wages. Economists have not agreed, however, upon the premises from which the legislators could readily deduce an answer satisfactory to Dr. Foerster. Prof. Commons, who made a study of immigration for President McKinley's Industrial Commission, reached the conclusion that immigrants come in response to demand for labor, which is dependent upon industrial expansion, and that when the expansion of industry is strong, "there is no overcrowding of the labor market" and "the new labor as well as the existing labor may secure advances in wages" (see pp. 114, 302). In order to answer Dr. Foerster's hypothetical question, the legislators must therefore first ascertain the following facts:

(1) Is American industry expanding fast enough to create a demand for immigrant labor or, on the contrary, is there an overcrowding of the labor market?

(2) Has immigrant labor, as well as native labor, actually secured advances in wages, or has immigration retarded the advance of wages?

Answers to these questions imply that very "historical comparison" which is spurned by Dr. Foerster (p. 657). He claims that the Immigration Commission attempted to study the movement of wages in connection with immigration, and indulges in the following speculation:

> If wages declined as immigrants entered a field and underbid the workers, that would presumably prove that immigration lowers wages" (p. 658).

This hypothesis merely proves that Dr. Foerster speaks of the reports of the Immigration Commission without having familiarized himself with them. The Commission never attempted a historical study of wages, nor has it proved Dr. Foerster's hypothesis. The burden of proof is obviously on the restrictionist, who contends that contemporary immigration is responsible for low wages. The author's task has been purely negative, to show the lack of evidence to support the contentions of the restrictionists. How was he to go about it? We are taught by Dr. Foerster that "wherever wages change we must note what else characteristically changes" (p. 670). In conformity with this rule, the author compared the wages of immigrant and native railway men for a number of years. Census statistics of wages in manufactures were compared by states in parallel columns with percentages of foreign-born. If wages declined as immigrants entered a field, states with a large percentage of immigrants would show lower average earnings than those with a smaller percentage of immigrants. Likewise, the movement of wages of railway employees for a period of years would show a greater advance in those occupations in which native Americans predominate than in those in which immigrants are employed. This is, however, not the case.

Both reviewers find fault with the author for making comparisons of money wages "without reference to the relative cost of living." That the author is fully aware of this factor the reader can see from the following sentence, appearing on p. 294: "A rise or a fall in money wages is no indication of an increase or decrease of the resources of the wage-earners, unless coupled with comparative statistics of the cost of living." But when the movement of wages is compared by occupations for a number of years, the change in the cost of living affects all workers alike and may, therefore, be eliminated. The defects of our statistics of the cost of living do not permit of a thoroughgoing comparison of real wages over different sections of the country. But, relying upon Dr. Nearing's conclusion in his *Wages in the United States*, "that average wages are rather constant for a given industry from state to state," we may properly infer that the cost of living must likewise vary but little from state to state. From such data as are available, it does not appear that immigration has had a depressing effect upon real wages. In the woolen mills, "since the immigrants from southern and Eastern Europe and Asiatic Turkey have begun to enter the unskilled occupations in large numbers, the percentage of increase in the wages of unskilled operatives has been greater than the percentage of increase in the rates of skilled workers, who are practically all of the English-speaking races" (p. 390). Mr. Fitch, in his study of the steel workers for the Pittsburgh Survey, has brought out the fact that the wages of the unskilled immigrants have kept pace with the cost of living, whereas the wages of the skilled native workers have been reduced (see pp. 404–409). Comparisons of the standard of living of the workers at different periods beginning with 1800 show a decided improvement of the condition of labor, going parallel with immigration (see pp. 295–297). This was, of course, due to the industrial progress of the country, in which the workers had a share. Prof. Fairchild thinks that, with the wonderful development of industry in the United States, the share of the workers should have been larger if it had not been for the influx of immigrants. But this is begging the question.

He cites the example of Germany, where the expansion of industry improved the condition of labor, and asks why it has not had the same effect in the United States, the inference being that in the United States the advancement of labor was retarded by immigration. He overlooks, however, the fact that the period of German industrial expansion was also a period of immigration of Polish and Italian workers to Germany. Thus improvement of the condition of labor came along with immigration.

But, cleverly interjects Dr. Foerster, if statistics "really prove that heavy immigration does not hurt the terms of employment of labor, then they also prove that such immigration betters the terms of employment" (p. 662). He assumes that because a certain proposition is true, the converse proposition, too, must be true. Perhaps, however, one must not expect from an economic scholar a familiarity with Euclid's rules of deductive reasoning.

From an economic point of view immigration is merely a movement of labor to the market where there is a demand for it, precisely as the movement from the country to the city. Immigration to the United States supplied the unskilled labor which was wanted by the rapidly expanding American industries. The expansion of industry created a lively demand for skilled workers, as well as many positions of a supervisory character—these positions were filled by native workers and older immigrants. To this extent immigration indirectly did better their terms of employment. This tendency has been recognized by the experts of the Immigration Commission (see p. 163).

On the other hand, reduction of the supply of labor, instead of raising wages, may react upon the demand for labor. A demonstration was furnished by the "non-essential" industries during the late war. The supply of foreign labor was cut off, shortage of labor necessitated the suspension of building activities, with the result that whereas from 1897 to 1917 relative full-time weekly earnings in the building trades had grown faster than the average for ten leading industries, in 1918 they fell behind the average.[1] The after-effect of the suspension of building operations has been the present housing crisis, which has raised the cost of shelter 58 per cent since the armistice.[2] This is tantamount to a reduction of the real wages of the working class, as a whole, for the benefit of the landlord class.

Deductive reasoning proves as fallacious in relation to the problem of unemployment. Prof. Fairchild rules out all the evidence disproving the hypothesis that immigration is responsible for unemployment. It is wrong to assume, he thinks, that the effects of immigration upon the labor market must manifest themselves immediately; they may be cumulative, and will tell a few years later, during a period of industrial depression. Indeed, inasmuch as over five million immigrants were admitted to the United States within the

[1] Douglas and Lamberson, *loc. cit.*, Table IV.

[2] *Changes in Cost of Living and Prices*. Bureau of Applied Economics. Bulletin No. 6, Addendum, September 25, 1920. (Estimate of the National Industrial Conference Board.)

past ten years, and there are to-day over five million unemployed in this country, is it not self-evident that had those five million aliens been kept out, there would be a job for everybody in this country to-day? Yet on the other hand, Australia, with a total population of five millions to a continent as large as the United States, and without immigration, has also known unemployment on a scale as large in proportion as the state of New York. Prof. Fairchild dismisses this argument "without opinion," to use a legal phrase. The fallacy of his interpretation of cyclical unemployment lies in the ready assumption that unemployment is the result of an excessive supply of labor, whereas, to quote Mr. Beveridge, "it depends upon the nature of the demand for labor, not upon the volume of the whole supply" (see Chapter VI). The advocates of restriction of immigration overlook the fact that parallel with the immigration of labor to the United States prior to the war there was going on an immigration of European capital to the United States. It was estimated that the total amount of European capital invested in permanent securities and loans in the United States was approximately $6,500,000,000.[1] This was equal to about 14 per cent of the total capital invested in American industries (exclusive of agriculture).[2] The foreign-born non-agricultural population constituted about the same percentage of the total non-agricultural population of the United States.[3] In other words, European capital came together

[1] George Paish, *The Trade Balance of the United States*, pp. 174, 175. (Senate Document 579, Sixty-first Congress, 2d Session.)

[2] The wealth invested in mines and quarries, factory land and improvements, manufacturing machinery, products of mining and manufacturing in stock, steam railroads, canals and shipping, telegraphs, telephones, street railways, central electric light and power stations, private waterworks, and other business property, was estimated for 1904 at $46,900,000,000.—*Wealth, Debt, and Taxation* (Bureau of Census), pp. 12, 17, 22, 27.

[3] The proportion of foreign-born among the farmers in the United States was 13.2 per cent in 1900 (*Occupations at the XII. Census*, Table XXXVI., p. cxiii.), *i.e.*, approximately the same as among the population at large.

with European labor to assist in the development of American industry.

The Immigration Commission contended that there was, nevertheless, an oversupply of unskilled labor due to immigration. The guiding idea of its report is the belief that native Americans and older immigrant workers had been displaced by recent immigrants. In support of this theory the Commission quoted census statistics for the decade 1890–1900. On closer examination, however, the figures of the censuses of 1890 and 1900 proved quite the opposite of what the Commission intended to prove. Yet Prof. Fairchild would not give up a hypothesis merely for want of facts to support it. The decade 1890–1900, he objects, is inconclusive, because it was a period of light immigration, but if the author had consulted the figures of the XIII. Census, which followed a decade of heavy immigration, they would tell another story. Regardless of the general rule that the burden of proof is not on the negative, but on the affirmative —in the present case, upon that side which affirms the theory of "racial displacement"—it is characteristic of Prof. Fairchild's easy methods of reasoning that at the time he made this guess the occupation statistics of the XIII. Census had not yet been published, so he manifestly did not know what they would show.

The present writer was not satisfied, however, to rest his conclusions on the period relied upon by the Immigration Commission, but, anticipating such hypothetical objections as those of Prof. Fairchild, he perused the report of the Massachusetts state census of 1905, which showed "no material change in the make-up of the industrial forces during the first five years of the present century" (see p. 176). The years 1900–1905 were marked by heavy immigration; the total for the five-year period, 3,841,646, exceeded the total for the previous decade;[1] the net immigration for the five calendar years 1900–1904, preceding the Massachusetts state census, was nearly equal to the net immigration for the

[1] *Reports of the Immigration Commission*, vol. i, pp. 56, 57.

next five years, 1905–1909, preceding the XIII. Census of the United States (see Table 8, on p. 90); Massachusetts is one of the states with a large immigrant population. In the absence of any data to the contrary, the results of the Massachusetts census could properly be accepted as an indication that the data for 1890–1900 still held good in 1910.

The XIII. Census report on occupations was subsequently published in an uncompleted form, with a new classification which rendered its figures non-comparable with those of the preceding censuses.

Another of the popular myths related to the subject of labor supply is the alleged "stimulation" of immigration. The author has quoted the statement of the Immigration Commission that "owing to the rigidity of the law and the fact that special provision is made for its enforcement, there are probably at the present time relatively few actual contract laborers admitted." This does not satisfy Prof. Fairchild. He insinuates that the author has deliberately omitted other qualifying statements of the Commission. He quotes a sentence to the effect that "a very large number . . . come in response to indirect assurance that employment awaits them" (which, as a matter of fact, he could have found on p. 94 of this book, reproduced in almost identical language from another page of the same volume). He further quotes the opinion of the Commission that "it is certain that European immigrants, and particularly those from southern and eastern Europe, are, under a literal construction of the law, for the most part contract laborers" (p. 761). He is not disturbed by the glaring contradiction between this conclusion and the other that "owing to the rigidity of the law" and its effective enforcement there are "few actual contract laborers admitted." He fails to perceive the distinction between a statement of facts and a conclusion, and is apparently unfamiliar with the time-honored rule of evidence that one may accept the testimony of witnesses concerning facts, without accepting their conclusions from those facts.

Closely connected with the subject of unemployment is

the effect of machinery upon the demand for labor. Here again deductive reasoning has failed our learned economists. Prof. Fairchild denies "the assumption (*sic!*) that labor-saving machinery supplants skilled labor to a much greater extent than unskilled labor" (p. 763). He is seconded by Dr. Foerster, who has picked out a number of exceptions, of which only one need be mentioned here: "The old cobbler was not superior to the worker in the modern shoe industry" (p. 665). He should brush up on his Taussig, where he will find the following:

> The cobbler of former days put together a shoe by himself; in a modern factory the shoe goes through some eighty different processes. . . . The machines now used . . . have extended the principle of the automatic repetition of identical movements to tasks long thought too intricate to be amenable to such methods. . . . The skillful workman and the adaptable tool retain a large place in industry; but the range of their work tends to become more and more restricted.[1]

This proposition has become a truism. The author has quoted a statement of Professors Jenks and Lauck which incidentally refers to the fact that "the invention of mechanical methods and processes" has resulted in the employment of "unskilled industrial workers as a substitute for the

[1] *Principles of Economics*, by F. W. Taussig, vol. i, pp. 35–36.—That the theory originated by Prof. Fairchild and Dr. Foerster had been unknown to their predecessors in the field of economics, appears from the following references: "The effect of improvements in machinery," according to an early writer, consists "in substituting one description of human labor for another—the less skilled for the more skilled." —Andrew Ure: *The Philosophy of Manufactures*, p. 321 (Third edition, London, 1861). "A factor that has had a real tendency to lower the actual average earnings of the wage-earner in many of the industries is the displacement of the skilled operative by machinery, which permits the substitution of a comparatively unskilled machine hand. This tendency is noticeable in many lines of industry."—*Twelfth Census, Manufactures*, vol. i, p. 123. President McKinley's Industrial Commission, discussing the effects of immigration upon wages, remarked that "machinery . . . by displacing the skilled mechanic, makes room for the unskilled immigrant."—*Report of the Industrial Commission*, vol. xv, p. xxiii.

skilled operatives formerly required" (see p. 290). That in some cases the machine has substituted a new kind of skill for the old one, may be conceded. But the error is in the deductive reasoning from insufficient facts, which are generalized out of all proportion to their real place in modern industry. If Dr. Foerster had taken note of the statistics compiled by Mr. Fitch in his study of the steel workers (reproduced in Table 121 of this book) he would realize that the skilled workers constitute only about one-sixth of the force of a modern steel plant, whereas more than three-fifths are unskilled laborers. Owing to his misconception of the effects of machinery he fails to see that the introduction of new labor-saving machinery as a substitute for immigration would displace the skilled labor of the native American workers and reduce them to the condition of unskilled laborers (see Chapter XXIII).

The contempt of both reviewers for facts is reflected in their judgments on every economic and social problem. Discrimination between recent immigrants from southern and eastern Europe and older immigrants from northern and western Europe, runs through the whole report of the Immigration Commission, yet Dr. Foerster wonders, are there really "persons who ask for restriction on the ground that former immigrants were 'more desirable' than the present ones"? (p. 658). He ridicules the idea that "a reduction in the day's work, all other things being equal, provides more days of work for every employee." Yet it is a fact that the American Federation of Labor has repeatedly urged the shortening of the work day on this very ground.[1]

Prof. Fairchild, speaking of child labor, says:

> The only reasonable basis of comparison is the total number of children of the given ages in each nativity group in the country. If the author had made this comparison . . . it would have appeared that *nearly three times as large a percentage of all children of foreign parents,*

[1] See Report on Unemployment, by John Koren, in "Waste in Industry," by The Committee on Elimination of Waste in Industry of the Federated Engineering Societies (1921), p. 296.

of the given ages, are employed in the specified occupations as children of native parents (p. 762).

As a matter of fact, the author did make such a comparison in Table 94, on p. 320, with the result that the percentage of children of foreign parents employed in manufactures was found to be exactly the same as that of children of native parents, and not "three times as large," as Prof. Fairchild imagines.

Dr. Foerster interprets the employment of children in large numbers in the Southern mills as the effect of immigration. The Southern manufacturers are compelled to employ children in order to meet the competition of the cheap immigrant labor of the North. Reference to Table 114 shows, however, that the average yearly earnings of adult males in the cotton mills of South Carolina were at the census of manufactures of 1905 about equal to the earnings of children in the cotton mills of Massachusetts ($244 and $233, respectively), and that the earnings of adult males in Pennsylvania were more than double the earnings of adult males in North and South Carolina. It was a case of the native Southerner underbidding the immigrant. The absence of adequate laws against child labor in the South is thus obviously due to the demand for *labor*, not for *cheap* labor—adult male labor is cheap enough in the South. In the North, too, child labor was employed in the early days of the cotton manufacturing industry; later, however, with the growth of immigration, the cotton mills secured a supply of adult labor which made it practicable to dispense with child labor (see Chapter XIV).

In reference to pauperism, Dr. Fairchild boldly asserts that it would be difficult to find "statistics which would not go to show that *the amount of pauperism among the foreign-born was vastly out of proportion to their total numbers in the population*" (p. 762). It does not matter that Tables 106–109 do present such statistics, drawn from official sources, and that the Immigration Commission, though unfriendly to immigration, after an investigation which covered the activities of associated charities in forty-three cities, came to the conclusion that "the recent immigrants, even in cities in times of relative industrial inactivity, did not seek charitable assistance in any considerable numbers" (p. 354).

A brief chapter has been devoted by the author to the refutation of Gen. Walker's theory that immigration has displaced millions of unborn Americans. To Prof. Fairchild's mind, however, the reiteration of Gen. Walker's hypothesis by other prominent writers (none of whom has contributed a single new fact in support of it) somehow vests it with added authority. *Magister dixit.* He is not disturbed by his own admission, in his book published a short time before, that "the proposition . . . is absolutely incapable of mathematical proof." [1]

To prove that the world-wide "volitional limitation of the family" has no relation to immigration to the United States, figures were quoted, in the first edition of this book, from Mr. Newsholme's *The Declining Birth Rate*, showing the number of children born to an average family of the British aristocracy to have declined within half a century from 7 to 3.[2] The decline of the birth-rate among the upper classes of England led Prof. Karl Pearson to the following conclusions:

> The mentally better stock in the nation is not reproducing itself at the same rate as of old. . . . For the last forty years the intellectual classes of the nation, enervated by wealth or by love of pleasure, or following an erroneous standard of life, have ceased to give in due proportion the men wanted to carry on the ever-growing work of the Empire.[3]

Still, if facts do not count with Prof. Fairchild against a preconceived idea backed up by authorities, the authority of Prof. Willcox, ranged on the opposite side of the question,

[1] Henry Pratt Fairchild: ***Immigration***, pp. 341–342.

[2] These statistics have since been superseded by a nation-wide investigation, the results of which are quoted in the present edition.

[3] Quoted in the first edition, p. 226, from ***The Declining Birth Rate***, by Arthur Newsholme, pp. 42–43.

ought to have appealed to him. That he has not a word to say about Prof. Willcox's arguments, although he has noticed the wrong spelling of Prof. Willcox's name, is ground for suspicion that he did not read the chapter on Race Suicide, and based his peremptory judgment on the brief summary on p. 18.

Verily, there are none so blind as those who would not see.

Note to page 499.

IMPORTATION OF MEXICAN CONTRACT-LABORERS.

Under the departmental regulations, Mexican contract laborers are admitted on the express condition that they will remain at work with the employer by whom they were imported. If a contract laborer deserts his employer and attempts to seek work elsewhere, he is to be deported from the United States. There is a possibility that a contract laborer who has deserted his employer might successfully conceal his identity and find other employment. To guard against such an emergency the employer is ***required*** to withhold a part of the wages of the contract laborer, pending the fulfillment of his contract, and to deposit the same with a postal savings bank in the name of the laborer. In case the latter deserts, he forfeits the amount deposited for his benefit. To be sure, the regulations require the employer to pay his contract laborers the prevailing rate of wages.[1] But this is merely ***nudum jus***, which could not be enforced in practice. Suppose the employer pays his imported laborer under the prevailing rate, what remedy has the latter to enforce his claim? He dare not leave his job and seek employment on better terms, for fear of deportation. For the same reason he dare not strike for higher wages. He must accept the wages stipulated in his contract (made in Mexico) although they may be below the prevailing rate paid for the same work in the same locality. "That wages paid and conditions provided" for the imported Mexican laborers were "perhaps in many cases not ideal," is admitted in a report of an investigating committee appointed by Secretary Wilson. It is learned from the same report that 10,691 imported contract laborers, *i.e.*, 21 per cent of the total number, deserted.[2]

[1] "The New Mexican Immigration," by J. B. Gwin: *The Survey*, August 3, 1918, p. 491.

[2] *Monthly Labor Review*, November, 1920, p. 223.

STATISTICAL TABLES

TABLE I.—ANNUAL AVERAGE IMMIGRATION DISTRIBUTED BY OCCUPATIONS (IN THOUSANDS), 1861–1910.[1]

Occupation	1861–1870	1871–1880	1881–1890	1891–1900	1901–1910
Professional	1	2	3	2	10
Skilled	30	33	54	44	132
Agricultural pursuits, total	22	26	37	25	159
Common laborers	53	60	133	103	227
Servants	9	11	25	33	92
All other occupations	10	11	13	12	33
Total	125	143	265	219	653

TABLE II.—FLUCTUATIONS OF EMPLOYMENT OF MALE WAGE-EARNERS IN THE MONTH OF MAY, 1899.[2]

Greatest number laid off [3]

Industry	Number
Glucose	1,267
Fur hats	1,650
Jewelry	1,924
Steam fittings and heating apparatus	1,680
Total	6,521

[1] *Monthly Summary of Commerce and Finance*, June, 1903, pp. 4408–4411. *Reports of the Immigration Commission. Abstract of the Statistical Review of Immigration to the United States, 1820–1910*, Tables 11–12. *Annual Reports of the Commissioner-General of Immigration*, 1899, Table VII., p. 19; 1900, Table VII., p. 21; 1901, Table IX., p. 26; 1902, Table IX., p. 29; 1903, Table IX., p. 33; 1904, Table IX., p. 30; 1905, Table VIII., p. 29; 1906, Table VIII., p. 31; 1907, Table VIII., p. 31; 1908, Table VIII., p. 35; 1909, Table X., p. 46; 1910, Table X., p. 45.

[2] Compiled from *U. S. XII. Census Report on Manufactures*, Pt. I, Table 2, pp. 20 *et seq.*

[3] Difference between the greatest number employed at any time during the year and the number employed in May (*i.e.*, the least number).

TABLE II.—(Continued).

Greatest number of temporary help wanted.[1]

Industry	Number
Awnings, tents, and sails	1,312
Bags, paper	338
Baskets and rattan and willow ware	1,889
Belting and hose, leather	63
Blacksmithing and wheelwrighting	3,045
Boxes, wooden packing	2,771
Brass castings and brass finishings	721
Bread and other bakery products	2,661
Bicycle and tricycle repairing	3,696
Carpets, rag	290
Carriages and wagons	14,187
Cars, general shop construction and repairs by street railroad companies	576
Cheese, butter, and condensed milk, factory product	5,789
Clothing, men's, custom work and repairing	16,861
Cork, cutting	123
Corsets	84
Dyeing and cleaning	771
Dyestuffs and extracts	178
Electroplating	483
Furniture, cabinetmaking, repairing and upholstering	2,384
Gas, machines and meters	193
Gloves and mittens	561
Grease and tallow	142
Grindstones	487
Hosiery and knit goods	1,723
Lamps and reflectors	439
Lock and gun smithing	100
Lumber, planing mill products, including sash, doors, and blinds	13,399
Lumber and timber products	93,238
Monuments and tombstones	4,403
Painting, house, sign, etc.	48,838
Paperhanging	5,637
Paper and wood pulp	4,002
Photographic materials	55
Pipes, tobacco	138
Plumbers' supplies	834
Refrigerators	383

[1] Difference between the number employed in May (*i.e.*, the greatest number) and the least number employed at any time during the year.

TABLE II.—(Concluded).

Industry	Number
Safes and vaults	137
Ship and boat building, wooden	5,346
Slaughtering, wholesale, not including packing	743
Tin and terne plate	1,594
Tobacco, chewing, smoking, and snuff	3,983
Tobacco, cigars, and cigarettes	6,348
Washing machines and clothes wringers	212
Window shades	247
Zinc, smelting and refining	590
Total	252,017

TABLE III.—MAXIMUM AND MINIMUM NUMBER OF WAGE-EARNERS EMPLOYED IN MANUFACTURES DURING ANY ONE MONTH, NUMBER AND PER CENT UNEMPLOYED, 1899, AND PER CENT FOREIGN-BORN ENGAGED IN MANUFACTURING AND MECHANICAL PURSUITS, 1900, BY SEX AND BY STATES.[1]

Rank according to per cent		State[2]	Number employed (00's omitted)				Unemployed		Per cent foreign-born
Foreign-born	Unemployed		Maximum month		Minimum month		Number (00's omitted)	Per cent of greatest number employed	
		I.—MALES							
1	5	North Carolina	May	47,9	August	42,5	5,4	11.3	1.0
2	30	South Carolina	November	32,8	July	26,0	6,8	20.5	1.7
3	19	Georgia	March	70,2	July	59,9	10,3	14.6	2.8
4	14	Virginia	May	60,0	January	52,0	8,0	13.3	3.9
5	1	Tennessee	May	44,4	August	41,0	3,4	7.7	4.5
6	42	Mississippi	October	28,4	July	19,6	8,8	31.0	4.6
7	25	Alabama	October	49,2	July	40,3	8,9	18.1	5.5
8	33	Arkansas	November	28,5	July	22,1	6,4	22.5	6.4
9	35	Oklahoma	May	2,2	July	1,7	5	22.7	9.0
10	17	West Virginia	May	31,9	July	27,4	4,5	14.1	10.3
11	22	Kentucky	May	56,9	January	48,0	8,9	15.6	11.5
12	47	Louisiana	November	54,3	July	28,3	26,0	47.9	12.4
13	43	District of Columbia	September	16,7	February	11,1	5,6	33.5	13.0
14	13	Indiana	May	144,5	December	125,3	19,2	13.3	14.7
15	48	Indian Territory	November	2,4	June	1,1	1,3	54.2	15.2
16	36	Florida	March	36,0	July	27,8	8,2	22.8	16.0
17	20	Delaware	September	19,2	February	16,3	2.9	15.1	17.7
18	24	Maryland	September	80,2	January	66,6	13,6	16.8	18.4

[1] Compiled from *XII. Census Report on Manufactures*, Vol. I, Table 3, pp. 62–63; *Occupations at the XII. Census*, p. 164, Table 34.

[2] States where the number of males or females, respectively, employed during the maximum month was less than 1000, are not included.

TABLE III.—(Continued).

Rank according to per cent: Foreign born	Rank according to per cent: Unemployed	State	Number employed (00's omitted): Maximum month		Number employed (00's omitted): Minimum month		Unemployed: Number (00's omitted)	Unemployed: Per cent of greatest number employed	Per cent foreign-born
19	44	Texas	October	56,5	June	37,6	18,9	33.5	18.9
20	23	Kansas	May	33,3	January	27,8	5,5	16.4	19.4
21	27	Missouri	May	115,2	January	93,1	22,1	19.2	20.6
22	10	Ohio	May	304,6	January	266,5	38,1	12.5	24.1
23	38	Maine	September	60,6	January	45,5	15,1	24.9	24.2
24	39	Iowa	September	54,9	January	40,0	14,9	27.2	26.5
25	40	Oregon	June	16,9	January	12,3	4,6	27.2	28.8
26	21	Vermont	May	26,9	January	22,8	4,1	15.2	29.6
27	2	New Mexico	May	2,6	February	2,4	2	7.7	30.0
28	26	Nebraska	September	22,6	February	18,4	4,2	18.6	30.7
29	45	Idaho	May	1,7	January	1,1	6	35.3	31.9
30	7	Pennsylvania	May	596,7	January	531,5	65,5	11.0	33.2
31	31	California	September	80,4	January	63,2	16,9	21.0	34.4
32	41	Washington	May	38,0	January	27,0	11,0	29.0	34.9
33	3	New Hampshire	May	49,0	January	45,0	4,0	8.2	37.8
34	18	Arizona	May	3,5	November	3,0	5	14.2	37.5
35	16	Colorado	October	24,3	February	21,0	3,3	13.6	38.4
36	12	New Jersey	May	191,6	January	166,4	25,2	13.2	38.5
37	11	Wyoming	August	2,3	February	2,0	3	13.0	40.9
38	6	Connecticut	May	135,2	January	121,2	14,0	10.4	41.6
39	15	Illinois	May	345,7	January	299,2	46,5	13.5	44.8
40	28	Michigan	May	151,2	January	121,6	29,6	19.6	44.8
41	32	Wisconsin	May	134,0	January	104,1	29,9	22.3	44.8
42	8	New York	May	639,9	January	564,5	75,4	11.8	44.9
43	4	Massachusetts	October	355,2	January	322,8	32,4	9.1	46.3
44	37	Utah	September	6,2	February	4,7	1,5	24.2	46.6
45	9	Rhode Island	September	66,9	January	59,0	7,9	11.8	47.0
46	29	Montana	May	10,6	February	8,5	2,1	19.8	51.8
47	46	North Dakota	September	2,7	February	1,6	1,1	40.7	53.5
48	34	Minnesota	May	74,2	January	57,5	16,7	22.5	53.8
		UNITED STATES	May	4333,9	January	3800,9	533,0	12.3	32.7
		II.—FEMALES							
1	5	North Carolina	May	16,7	July	14,7	2,0	12.0	0.2
2	3	South Carolina	March	10,1	September	9,3	8	7.9	0.5
3	11	Georgia	April	11,6	July	10,0	1,6	13.8	0.7
4	34	Mississippi	October	2,1	July	1,4	7	33.3	0.8
5	24	Alabama	May	4,3	July	3,3	1,0	23.3	1.0
6	14	Virginia	October	13,2	July	11,1	2,1	15.9	1.4
7	8	Tennessee	May	6,2	February	5,4	8	12.9	1.6
8	30	West Virginia	October	4,0	July	2,8	1,2	30.0	3.6
9	23	Kentucky	April	10,0	August	7,8	2,2	22.0	4.1
10	31	Indiana	September	22,8	July	15,9	6,9	30.3	5.4

TABLE III.—(Concluded).

Rank according to per cent: Foreign born	Rank according to per cent: Unemployed	State	Number employed (00's omitted): Maximum month		Number employed (00's omitted): Minimum month		Unemployed: Number (00's omitted)	Unemployed: Per cent of greatest number employed	Per cent. foreign-born
11	19	Louisiana	March / December	6,0	July	4,8	1,2	20.0	5.6
12	36	District of Columbia	April	2,2	August	1,3	9	40.9	5.9
13	28	Kansas	October	3,7	February	2,7	1,0	27.0	6.5
14	37	Delaware	September	5,8	July	2,4	3,4	58.6	6.6
15	16	Missouri	September	25,7	July	20,6	5,1	19.8	8.4
16	29	Iowa	September	9,5	January	6,8	2,7	28.4	9.6
17	27	Maryland	September	36,0	February	26,3	9,7	26.9	9.7
18	9	Ohio	October	56,9	January	49,4	7,5	13.2	10.0
19	25	Texas	May	3,4	August	2,5	9	26.5	10.4
20	33	Oregon	September	2,2	August	1,5	7	31.8	12.4
21	6	Pennsylvania	April	131,6	July	115,8	15,8	12.0	13.0
22	12	Vermont	April	4,8	July	4,1	7	14.6	14.6
23	32	Colorado	October	2,3	January	1,6	7	30.4	14.8
24	26	Nebraska	October	3,0	January	2,2	8	26.7	15.8
25	38	California	August	27,6	August	11,4	16,2	58.7	17.0
26	21	Washington	May	1,4	August	1,1	3	21.4	19.1
27	15	Wisconsin	October	17,4	January	14,6	2,8	16.1	19.9
28	35	Florida	March	2,0	July	1,3	7	35.0	20.3
29	18	Michigan	October	25,6	July	20,5	5,1	19.9	22.7
30	10	New Jersey	October	55,1	July	47,7	7,4	13.4	25.2
31	20	Illinois	April	64,1	July	51,6	12,5	19.5	26.1
32	22	Minnesota	May	10,5	July	8,2	2,3	21.9	27.0
33	4	Connecticut	October	44,3	January	40,7	3,6	8.1	27.9
34	13	New York	October	244,4	July	208,0	36,4	14.9	29.6
35	17	Maine	October	21,1	February	16,9	4,2	19.9	32.8
36	2	Rhode Island	December	30,8	August	28,4	2,4	7.8	39.5
37	7	Massachusetts	April	149,5	August	130,6	18,9	12.6	40.6
38	1	New Hampshire	December	22,5	August	21,1	1,4	6.2	46.2
		UNITED STATES	October	1089,8	July	949,3	140.5	12.9	21.4

TABLE IV.—PERCENTAGE RATIOS OF UNEMPLOYED AND OF FOREIGN

Rank according to per cent: Unemployed	Rank according to per cent: Foreign white	Occupation	Unemployed at any time during the year	Foreign White
		Males		
1	1	Telegraph and telephone operators.	9.6	6.3
2	34	Confectioners.	11.2	35.9
3	47	Bakers.	11.3	56.4
4	32	Butchers.	11.5	35.2
5	49	Brewers and maltsters.	12.1	71.9
6	27	Bartenders.	12.5	31.1
7	7	Porters and helpers (in stores).	12.6	19.8
8	37	Cotton mill operatives.	13.1	38.3
9	14	Street railway employees.	13.3	24.2
10	19	Machinists.	13.4	27.7
11	18	Blacksmiths.	13.7	27.7
12	5	Printers, lithographers, and pressmen.	15.0	15.9
13	10	Steam railroad employees.	15.8	20.08
14	30	Paper and pulp mill operatives.	16.9	33.0
15	11	Servants and waiters.	17.0	21.5
16	22	Steam boiler makers.	18.4	29.6
17	46	Bleachery and dye works operatives.	19.3	53.0
18	9	Draymen, hackmen, teamsters, etc.	19.3	20.4
19	39	Woolen mill operatives.	19.5	43.1
20	36	Brass workers.	19.6	37.3
21	3	Messenger, errand, and office boys.	19.7	10.8
22	21	Upholsterers.	20.9	28.1
23	48	Cabinet makers.	20.9	56.5
24	6	Plumber and gas and steam fitters.	22.0	19.1
25	24	Tool and cutlery makers.	22.0	30.2
26	2	Oil well and oil works employees.	22.8	10.5
27	38	Textile workers (not specified).	23.8	41.8
28	26	Wood workers (not specified).	24.6	30.8
29	43	Leather curriers and tanners.	24.8	47.7
30	31	Gold and silver workers.	25.3	34.5

WHITE BREADWINNERS IN THE PRINCIPAL OCCUPATIONS, 1900.[1]

Rank according to per cent: Unemployed	Rank according to per cent: Foreign white	Occupation	Unemployed at any time during the year	Foreign White
31	44	Wire workers.	25.3	49.8
32	15	Tinplate and tinware makers.	25.9	24.9
33	50	Tailors.	27.0	75.8
34	29	Tobacco and cigar factory operatives.	27.2	32.6
35	35	Iron and steel workers.	28.1	35.9
36	42	Silk mill operatives.	29.3	47.1
37	28	Boatmen and sailors.	33.3	31.8
38	25	Coopers.	34.3	30.8
39	8	Sawing and planing mill employees.	35.1	20.1
40	41	Marble and stone cutters.	39.5	44.6
41	45	Hat and cap makers.	41.0	50.4
42	16	Carpenters and joiners.	41.4	25.4
43	13	Painters, glaziers, and varnishers.	42.4	23.5
44	40	Miners and quarrymen.	44.3	43.7
45	20	Laborers (not specified).	44.3	28.1
46	4	Paper hangers.	44.5	13.5
47	23	Brick and tile makers.	48.4	30.0
48	33	Masons (brick and stone).	55.5	35.3
49	17	Plasterers.	56.1	25.8
50	12	Glass workers.	59.9	22.7
		Females		
1	1	Telegraph and telephone operators.	10.7	6.2
2	14	Servants and waitresses.	14.8	25.9
3	18	Cotton mill operatives.	14.9	38.2
4	3	Printers, lithographers, and presswomen.	16.5	7.3
5	5	Bookbinders.	16.7	11.0
6	8	Dressmakers.	19.8	16.5
7	10	Hosiery and knitting mill operatives.	20.0	17.9
8	7	Box makers (paper).	20.4	14.5
9	16	Woolen mill operatives.	21.1	32.1
10	9	Shirt, collar, and cuff makers.	22.1	16.6
11	15	Textile workers (not specified).	22.1	30.7
12	11	Seamstresses.	24.2	18.5

[1] *XII. Census. Occupations*, pp. ccxxvii. *et seq.*, Tables LXXXVIII. and LXXXIX.; pp. cxiv.–cxvi., Table XXXVII.

TABLE IV.—(Concluded).

Rank according to per cent: Unemployed	Rank according to per cent: Foreign white	Occupation	Unemployed at any time during the year	Foreign White
13	12	Silk mill operatives.	25.8	23.0
14	4	Milliners.	26.3	10.9
15	17	Tailors.	26.4	38.2
16	13	Tobacco and cigar factory operatives.	27.2	25.2
17	6	Boot and shoe makers and repairers.	42.5	14.1
18	2	Laborers (not specified).	44.1	6.8

TABLE V.—BITUMINOUS COAL MINES: GREATEST AND LEAST NUMBER EMPLOYED, PER CENT UNEMPLOYED AT ANY TIME DURING THE YEAR 1902, AND PER CENT FOREIGN WHITE MINERS IN 1900, IN THE PRINCIPAL STATES.[1]

Rank according to per cent		State[2]	Number employed		Per cent unemployed	Per cent foreign white miners
Foreign-born	Unemployed		Greatest	Least		
1	3	Texas	2,035	1,881	7.6	62.7
2	11	Wyoming	4,920	3,481	29.2	59.2
3	2	Pennsylvania	93,620	87,355	6.7	58.7
4	5	Illinois	39,557	32,809	17.1	48.5
5	10	Iowa	10,719	7,749	27.7	39.7
6	9	Kansas	8,120	6,179	23.9	33.6
7	4	Ohio	27,770	24,241	12.7	27.0
8	8	Indian Territory	5,109	4,054	20.7	26.9
9	1	Maryland	4,881	4,706	3.6	22.3
10	7	Indiana	11,614	9,408	19.0	21.3
11	12	West Virginia	26,197	16,564	36.7	14.3
12	6	Arkansas	2,826	2,304	18.5	13.6

[1] Compiled from *Census Report on Mines and Quarries*, 1902, pp. 710–715, Table 60; *Occupations at the XII. Census*, Table 41.

[2] All States with less than 1,000 employees have been omitted; likewise New Mexico, Colorado, Missouri, and Washington, there being a large number of metalliferous miners in those States who are not segregated from coal miners in the census statistics of occupations.

TABLE VI.—LABORERS, MALE: PER CENT FOREIGN WHITE AND PER CENT UNEMPLOYED, BY STATES, 1900.[1]

Rank according to per cent		State	Foreign White	Unemployed
Foreign White	Unem-ployed			
1	22	North Carolina	0.1	42.1
2	5	Georgia	0.4	37.4
3	12	South Carolina	0.4	39.8
4	13	Alabama	0.6	40.6
5	36	Tennessee	0.6	45.5
6	20	Virginia	0.7	41.6
7	11	Mississippi	0.9	39.7
8	50	Indian Territory	1.5	65.0
9	33	Arkansas	1.6	45.0
10	6	Florida	1.7	38.0
11	42	Kentucky	3.3	49.0
12	49	Oklahoma	3.3	56.5
13	8	District of Columbia	4.1	38.6
14	30	West Virginia	5.5	44.2
15	26	Louisiana	5.7	43.5
16	40	Kansas	8.8	47.1
17	4	New Mexico	8.9	37.0
18	48	Indiana	9.8	52.1
19	28	Maryland	12.7	44.0
20	44	Missouri	13.3	49.4
21	23	Oregon	14.4	42.4
22	35	Texas	16.8	45.3
23	9	Delaware	17.5	39.3
24	38	Idaho	19.6	45.9
25	47	Iowa	20.9	51.2
26	41	Nevada	22.8	48.0
27	43	Ohio	24.3	49.3
28	18	Nebraska	26.2	41.5
29	2	Vermont	26.4	35.1
30	14	Colorado	27.4	40.8
31	3	Wyoming	28.6	35.5
32	24	Washington	29.9	43.0
33	34	Maine	30.2	45.0
34	46	Utah	30.2	49.6
35	37	South Dakota	31.3	45.7
36	29	California	32.9	44.0
37	15	Pennsylvania	33.4	40.8
38	17	Arizona	40.8	41.2
39	31	Montana	41.0	44.6
40	32	Michigan	41.1	44.8
41	1	New Hampshire	43.3	33.6
42	45	Illinois	44.1	49.4

[1] Computed from *Occupations at the XII. Census*, Table 41.

TABLE VI.—(Concluded).

Rank according to per cent: Foreign White	Rank according to per cent: Unemployed	State	Foreign White	Unemployed
43	16	Wisconsin	48.0	41.0
44	27	New York	50.2	43.7
45	25	North Dakota	52.1	43.4
46	19	New Jersey	52.9	41.5
47	39	Minnesota	53.5	46.6
48	7	Connecticut	60.8	38.1
49	21	Massachusetts	65.8	41.8
50	10	Rhode Island	65.6	39.4
		United States	28.1	44.3

TABLE VII.—COTTON MILL OPERATIVES, MALE: PER CENT FOREIGN WHITE AND PER CENT UNEMPLOYED, BY STATES, 1900.[1]

Rank according to per cent: Foreign White	Rank according to per cent: Unemployed	State	Foreign White	Unemployed
1	13	North Carolina	0.2	14.8
2	7	South Carolina	0.2	11.4
3	20	Alabama	0.3	17.6
4	9	Mississippi	0.3	11.5
5	19	Georgia	0.4	17.1
6	15	Virginia	0.9	15.4
7	1	Maryland	1.2	7.5
8	22	Tennessee	1.8	29.6
9	10	Kentucky	3.1	13.0
10	14	Texas	5.3	15.2
11	23	Louisiana	7.2	34.0
12	3	Indiana	9.1	9.4
13	4	Delaware	17.8	11.1
14	16	Pennsylvania	19.6	16.1
15	8	Colorado	23.9	11.4
16	12	New York	30.7	14.3
17	17	New Jersey	36.8	16.4
18	21	Vermont	48.2	21.7
19	5	Connecticut	60.5	11.1
20	11	Rhode Island	63.4	13.1
21	18	Maine	65.9	16.5
22	6	Massachusetts	72.3	11.1
23	2	New Hampshire	74.5	9.1
		United States	38.4	13.0

[1] Computed from *Occupations at the XII. Census*, Table 41.

TABLE VIII.—PERSONS EMPLOYED IN ALL INDUSTRIES OF MASSACHUSETTS, 1888–1908.[1]

Year	Greatest number	Least number	Excess of greatest over least number	Year	Greatest number	Least number	Excess of greatest over least number
1888	221,307	169,610	51,697	1899	420,701	312,054	108,647
1889	293,321	224,887	68,434	1900	440,363	322,200	118,163
1890	322,288	251,107	71,181	1901	456,137	339,405	116,732
1891	335,919	260,419	75,500	1902	483,392	373,385	110,007
1892	352,939	271,399	81,540	1903	500,348	377,563	122,785
1893	345,388	222,370	123,018	1904	493,354	363,245	130,109
1894	310,167	206,423	103,744	1905	534,712	411,869	122,843
1895	351,915	258,776	93,139	1906	565,472	448,830	116,642
1896	358,529	241,363	117,166	1907	607,151	453,349	153,802
1897	377,399	272,204	105,195	1908	570,712	383,588	187,124
1898	386,383	271,847	114,536				

TABLE IX.—IMMIGRANT BREADWINNERS DESTINED FOR MASSACHUSETTS, 1897–1908.[2]

Year	Number	Year	Number	Year	Number
1897	17,147	1901	30,174	1905	56,349
1898	15,983	1902	39,747	1906	55,737
1899	21,724	1903	49,941	1907	64,764
1900	29,369	1904	43,998	1908	31,335

[1] *Massachusetts Statistics of Manufactures*, 1889, pp. 61, 68, 202; 1890, pp. 91, 257, 315; 1891, pp. 91, 127, 135; 1892, pp. 33, 47, 399; 1893, pp. 41, 53, 311; 1894, pp. 51, 89, 204; 1896, pp. 28, 70, 168; 1897, pp. 30, 70, 175; 1898, pp. 29, 31, 33, 35, 73, 169; 1901, pp. 70, 80, 82, 87; 1903, pp. 30, 32, 39, 42.—*Annual Reports of the Bureau of Labor*, XXXVII., pp. 285, 288, 316; XXXVIII., pp. 322, 353, 355, 367, 403; XXXIX., pp. 2, 36; XL., p. 2.

[2] *Report of the Commissioner-General of Immigration*, 1897, Table IX; 1898, p. 26; 1899–1901, Table VII; 1902–1908, Table IX.

TABLE X.—INCREASE OR DECREASE (—) OF THE NUMBER OF BREAD-WINNERS, CLASSIFIED BY SEX, NATIVITY, AND OCCUPATION, IN THE UNITED STATES, 1890–1900 (THOUSANDS).[1]

Occupations	Aggregate	Native white: Native parents	Native white: Foreign parents	Foreign white	Colored
All occupations, exclusive of farmers:					
Both sexes	5,304	2,538	1,580	504	682
Males	4,081	2,014	1,232	425	410
Females	1,223	524	348	79	272
A. Professional service:					
Both sexes	312	164	105	28	15
Males	199	101	65	24	9
Females	113	63	40	4	6
B. Business and clerical pursuits:[2]					
Both sexes	1,423	587	495	135	206
Males	1,070	415	376	101	178
Females	353	172	119	34	28
C. All other occupations:					
Both sexes	3,569	1,787	980	341	461
Males	2,812	1,498	791	300	223
Females	757	289	189	41	238
I. Occupations showing a general decrease in the demand for labor:					
Both sexes	—21	—5	—3	—11	—2
Males, total	—20	—4	—3	—11	—2
Brick and tile makers, etc.	—10	—1	—1	—7	—1
Dairymen	—8	—2	—1	—4	—1

[1] *Occupations at the XII. Census*, Table 34, p. cviii., and Table 2, pp. 10 *et seq. Compendium of the XI. Census*, 1890, Part III, Population, Table 78, pp. 452 *et seq.*

[2] Agents, bankers, and brokers, officials of banks and companies, manufacturers and officials, etc., boarding- and lodging-house keepers, bookkeepers and accountants, clerks and copyists, stenographers and typewriters, commercial travelers, salesmen and saleswomen, hotel keepers, merchants and dealers (wholesale), restaurant keepers, saloon keepers, livery-stable keepers, and undertakers.

TABLE X.—(Continued).

Occupations	Aggregate	Native white: Native parents	Native white: Foreign parents	Foreign white	Colored
All others in this group[3]	—2	—1	—1	......	......
Females: total	—1	—1	......	......	......
Dairywomen	—1	—1	......	......	......
II. Occupations in which native white have been displaced by immigrants or their children:					
Both sexes	7	—59	37	29	......
Males, total	—22	—72	34	15	1
Boatmen, canalmen, pilots, and sailors	3	—3	2	4	......
Boot and shoemakers and repairers	—11	—12	4	—2	—1
Carpenters and joiners	—18	—25	16	—8	—1
Masons (brick and stone)	—1	—6	5	—4	4
Tailors	38	—1	4	35	......
Woodworkers (not otherwise specified)	—10	—7	1	—4	......
All others in this group[4]	—23	—18	2	—6	—1
Females, total	29	13	3	14	—1
Cotton mill operatives	28	25	—1	4	......
Seamstresses	—1	—9	3	5	......
Tailoresses	3	—1	—1	5	......
Other textile mill operatives	—3	—2	2	—2	—1
All others in this group[5]	—2	......	......	2	......

[3] Includes boxmakers (paper), broom and brush makers.

[4] Includes distillers and rectifiers, harness and saddle makers and repairers, hat and cap makers, leather curriers and tanners, marble and stone cutters, millers, and plasterers.

[5] Includes bleachery and dye works operatives, hucksters and peddlers.

TABLE X.—(Concluded).

Occupations	Aggregate	Native white: Native parents	Native white: Foreign parents	Foreign parents	Colored
III. Occupations in which immigrants have been displaced by native white:					
Both sexes	879	678	288	—82	—5
Males, total	810	661	241	—40	—52
Agricultural laborers	685	588	184	—10	—77[6]
All others in agricultural pursuits[7]	13	16	7	—14	4
Blacksmiths	16	9	10	—2	—1
Clerks and copyists	55	24	32	—2	1
Hostlers	11	5	3	—1	4
Saw and planing-mill employees	24	14	3	—9	16
All others in this[8] group	6	5	2	—2	1
Females, total	69	17	47	—42	47
Servants and waitresses	69	16	47	—41	47
Paper- and pulp-makers	......	1	......	—1	......
IV. Occupations showing a general increase in the demand for labor:					
Both sexes	2,704	1,173	658	405	468
Males	2,044	913	519	336	276
Females	660	260	139	69	192

[6] Negroes only. There are no comparative data for other colored agricultural laborers at the XI. Census.

[7] Includes gardeners, florists, nurserymen, etc., lumbermen, wood choppers, etc., stock raisers, herders, and drovers.

[8] Includes brewers and maltsters, potters, telegraph and telephone linemen, trunk and leather-case makers, etc.

TABLE XI.—NUMBER AND INCREASE OR DECREASE, OF FOREIGN-BORN WHITE MALE BREADWINNERS, CLASSIFIED BY NATIONALITY AND OCCUPATION (THOUSANDS), 1890–1900.[1]

Occupations.	German			Irish			English and Welsh.			Scotch.			Bohemian.			Hungarian.			Italian		
	1890	1900	Increase (+) or Decrease (−)	1890	1900	Increase (+) or Decrease (−)	1890	1900	Increase (+) or Decrease (−)	1890	1900	Increase (+) or Decrease (−)	1890	1900	Increase (+) or Decrease (−)	1890	1900	Increase (+) or Decrease (−)	1890	1900	Imcrease (+) or Decrease (−)
Farmers, planters, and overseers	282.7	263.7	−19.0	93.4	67.0	−26.4	72.2	57.7	−14.5	16.1	16.5	+ .4	14.4	18.1	+ 3.7	.8	1.4	+ .6	2.2	4.4	+ 2.2
Manufacturers and officials, etc.	10.7	18.0	+ 7.3	2.9	7.9	+ 5.0	4.6	9.6	+ 5.0	1.0	3.3	+ 2.3	.3	.5	+ .2	.2	.6	+ .4	.2	1.1	+ .9
Merchants and dealers (except wholesale)	69.6	66.5	− 3.1	25.2	20.6	− 4.6	16.6	15.2	− 1.4	3.9	4.4	+.5	1.2	2.1	+ .9	1.3	2.9	+ 1.6	7.0	16.0	+ 9.0
Agents and salesmen	19.9	30.5	+10.6	10.2	14.9	+ 4.7	10.3	14.2	+ 3.9	2.7	4.6	+ 1.9	.4	1.0	+ .6	.4	1.4	+ 1.0	.5	2.0	+ 1.5
Professional service	27.9	30.0	+ 2.1	14.4	13.9	+ .5	17.2	19.7	+ 2 5	3.7	5.8	+ 2.1	.6	1.0	+ .4	.4	1.0	+ .6	2.3	3.8	+ 1.5
Bookkeepers, accountants, clerks, and copyists	26.7	23.0	− 3.7	15.4	15.4	.0	16.2	16.1	− .1	4.7	5.3	+ .6	.6	.7	+ .1	.5	.9	+ .4	.8	1.6	+ .8
Building trades	95.6	83.6	−12.0	46.7	41.9	− 4.8	40.4	32.8	− 7.6	12.3	12.5	+ .2	2.7	3.7	+ 1.0	.5	1.4	+ .9	3.3	10.2	+ 6.9
Blacksmiths and machinists	36.2	39.7	+ 3.5	21.7	21.2	− .5	21.1	20.5	− .6	6.7	7.8	+ 1.1	1.0	1.8	+ .8	.3	.9	+ .6	.4	1.6	+ 1.2
Steam railroad employees.	20.4	18.8	− 1.6	36.5	31.2	− 5.3	9.1	8.3	− .8	2.3	2.7	+ .4	.7	.8	+ .1	1.3	1.6	+ .3	10.3	17.3	+ 7.0
Miners and quarrymen	19.2	19.0	− .2	27.9	22.9	− 5.0	56.7	44.9	−11.8	11.8	9.7	− 2.1	.9	1.6	+ .7	7.3	26.5	+19.2	9.7	25.5	+15.8
Saw- and planing-mill employees	10.2	7.1	− 3.1	2.3	1.7	− .6	1.6	.9	− .7	.4	.4	.0	1.3	.7	− .6	.1	.1	.0	.2	.5	+ .3
Tailors	36.3	28.3	− 8.0	5.8	3.8	− 2.0	3.8	2.3	− 1.5	1.1	1.0	− .1	3.3	4.9	+ 1.6	1.8	3.7	+ 1.9	2.3	7.8	+ 5.5
Textile mill operatives	15.5	12.0	− 3.5	19.6	14.6	− 5.0	23.8	19.6	− 4.2	4.7	3.6	− 1.1	.2	.4	+ .2	.3	1.0	+ .7	1.2	3.9	+ 2.7
Laborers (not specified)[2]	154.9	129.6	−25.3	202.4	158.9	−43.5	36.4	28.3	− 8.1	7.8	7.3	− .5	8.2	10.0	+ 1.8	11.8	19.8	+ 8.0	39.0	91.8	+52.8
Agricultural laborers and all others in this class	97.0	84.6	−12.4	35.9	30.4	− 5.5	26.7	21.6	− 5.1	6.5	7.2	+ .7	3.6	4.8	+ 1.2	.7	1.4	+ .7	6.5	12.2	+ 5.7
All others	414.9	421.6	+ 6.7	245.4	247.9	+ 2.5	130.7	127.3	− 3.4	32.5	37.8	+ 5.3	11.9	19.3	+ 7.4	8.8	23.8	+15.0	28.2	76.7	+48.5
Total	1,337.7	1,276.0	−61.7	804.7	711.2	−90.5	487.4	439.0	48.4	118.2	129.9	11.7	51.3	71.4	20.1	36.5	88.4	+51.9	114.1	276.4	+162.3

[1] *XI. Census*, Part II., Table 109, p. 484. *Reports of the Immigration Commission*, vol. 1, pp. 821–829, Table A.

[2] Laborers in 1890 include in some agricultural districts agricultural laborers.

TABLE XII.—FOREIGN-BORN ENGAGED IN GAINFUL OCCUPATIONS IN GERMANY, 1900.[1]

Occupations	Thousands	
	Males	Females
Agriculture	59	21
Trade	37	10
Transportation	13	..
Manufactures	245	32
Common labor	26	10
Professional pursuits	18	10
Living on income from property	18	16
Servants	1	23
Total	417	122

TABLE XIII.—FOREIGN-BORN IN GERMANY, BY COUNTRY OF BIRTH (THOUSANDS), 1880–1900.[2]

Year	Total	Austria-Hungary	Russia	Italy	All other countries
1880	419	150	57	8	204
1890	518	206	53	13	246
1900	823	362	89	62	310
Increase 1880–1900	404	212	32	54	106

[1] Ergänzungsheft zu den Viertelsjahrsheften zur Statistik des Deutschen Reichs, 1905. Heft I. Die Deutschen im Auslande und die Ausländer im Deutschen Reich, p. 40.

[2] *Ibid.*

TABLE XIV.—FOREIGN-BORN POPULATION FROM THE SCANDINAVIAN COUNTRIES AND FROM SOUTHERN AND EASTERN EUROPE, BY STATES, 1880, 1890, 1900, AND 1910.[1]

States	From the Scandinavian Countries				From Southern and Eastern Europe			
	1880	1890	1900	1910	1880	1890	1900	1910
Minnesota....	107,768	215,215	236,670	243,899	7,577	21,988	30,544	76,833
Iowa........	46,046	72,873	72,611	66,586	2,777	3,562	6,709	34,593
The Dakotas..	17,869	65,588	76,051	100,654	6,978	18,787	33,735	65,559
Nebraska......	16,685	46,341	40,107	39,592	7.006	12,984	16,283	47,177
Montana.....	644	6,411	9.741	15,513	191	2,533	6,655	23,644
Idaho........	1,185	3,506	5,621	9,775	100	776	1,280	7,074
Wyoming.....	511	2,382	2,989	4,078	78	1,320	2,282	9,607
Utah........	12,755	16,863	18,285	17,826	237	789	1,519	10,482
Washington..	1,524	21,413	26,254	68,228	424	4,949	7,657	44,784
Oregon.......	1,942	7,333	9,007	20,153	991	4,005	4,129	22,503
Total......	206,929	457,925	497,336	586,304	26,359	71,693	110,793	342,256
All other.....	233,333	475,324	566,973	664,196	152,339	626,677	1,603,071	4,466,244
Total, U. S...	440,262	933,249	1,064,309	1,250,500	178,698	698,370	1,713,864	4,808,500

TABLE XV.—EMIGRATION FROM THE UNITED KINGDOM, BY DESTINATION OF EMIGRANTS, 1840–1909.[2]

Year	North American Colonies	United States	British South Africa	Australia and New Zealand	Other Countries	Total
1840	32,293	40,642	......	15,850	1,958	90,743
1841	38,164	45,017	......	32,625	2,786	118,592
1842	54,123	63,852	......	8,534	1,835	128,344
1843	23,518	28,335	......	3,478	1,881	57,212
1844	22,924	43,660	......	2,229	1,873	70,686
1845	31,803	58,538	......	830	2,330	93,501
1846	43,439	82,239	......	2,347	1,826	129,851
1847	109,680	142,154	......	4,949	1,487	258,270
1848	31,065	188,233	......	23,904	4,887	248,089
1849	41,367	219,450	......	32,191	6,490	299,498

[1] Compiled from the *United States Census of 1880*, vol. i., pp. 492–495; *XIII. Census. Population*, vol. i., Table 33, pp. 834–838.

[2] Compiled from *Statistical Abstracts of the United Kingdom of Great Britain*. Reprint of the *Statistical Abstracts for the United Kingdom for 1840–1854*, p. 84; 14, p. 122; 29, p. 161; 42, p. 239; and 57, p. 363.

TABLE XV.—(Continued).

Year	North American Colonies	United States	British South Africa	Australia and New Zealand	Other Countries	Total
1850	32,961	223,078	......	16,037	8,773	280,849
1851	42,605	267,357	......	21,532	4,472	335,966
1852	32,873	244,261	......	87,881	3,749	368,764
1853	34,522	230,885	......	61,401	3,129	329,937
1854	43,761	193,065	......	83,237	3,366	323,429
1855	17,966	103,414	......	52,309	3,118	176,807
1856	16,378	111,837	......	44,584	3,755	176,554
1857	21,001	126,905	......	61,248	3,721	212,875
1858	9,704	59,716	......	39,295	5,257	113,972
1859	6,689	70,303	......	31,013	12,427	120,432
1860	9,786	87,500	......	24,302	6,881	128,469
1861	12,707	49,764	......	23,738	7,561	91,770
1862	15,522	58,706	......	41,843	5,143	121,214
1863	18,083	146,813	......	53,054	5,808	223,758
1864	12,721	147,042	......	40,942	8,195	208,900
1865	17,211	147,258	......	37,283	8,049	209,801
1866	13,255	161,000	......	24,097	6,530	204,882
1867	12,160	126,051	......	14,023	4,748	156,982
1868	12,332	108,490	......	12,332	5,033	138,187
1869	20,921	146,737	......	14,457	4,185	186,300
1870	27,168	153,466	......	16,526	5,351	202,511
1871	24,954	150,788	......	11,695	5,314	192,751
1872	24,382	161,782	......	15,248	9,082	210,494
1873	29,045	166,730	......	25,137	7,433	228,345
1874	20,728	113,774	......	52,581	10,189	197,272
1875	12,306	81,193	......	34,750	12,426	140,675
1876	9,335	54,554	......	32,196	13,384	109,469
1877	7,720	45,481	......	30,138	11,856	195,195
1878	10,652	54,694	......	36,479	11,077	112,902
1879	17,952	91,806	......	40,959	13,557	164,274
1880	20,902	166,570	......	24,184	15,886	227,542
1881	23,912	176,104	......	22,682	20,304	243,002
1882	40,441	181,903	......	37,289	19,733	279,366
1883	44,185	191,573	......	71,264	13,096	320,118
1884	31,134	155,280	......	44,255	11,510	242,179
1885	19,838	137,687	......	39,395	10,724	207,644
1886	24,745	152,710	......	43,076	12,369	232,900
1887	32,025	201,526	......	34,183	13,753	281,487
1888	34,853	195,986	......	31,127	17,962	279,928
1889	28,269	168,771	......	28,294	28,461	253,795

TABLE XV.—(Concluded).

Year	North American Colonies	United States	British South Africa	Australia and New Zealand	Other Countries	Total
1890	22,520	152,413	......	21,179	22,004	218,116
1891	21,578	156,395	......	19,547	20,987	218,507
1892	23,264	150,039	......	15,950	20,799	210,042
1893	24,732	148,949	......	11,203	23,930	208,814
1894	17,459	104,001	......	10,917	23,653	156,030
1895	16,622	126,502	20,234	10,567	11,256	185,181
1896	15,267	98,921	24,594	10,354	12,789	161,925
1897	15,571	85,324	21,109	12,061	12,395	146,460
1898	17,640	80,494	19,756	10,693	12,061	140,644
1899	16,410	92,482	14,432	11,467	11,571	146,362
1900	18,433	102,797	20,815	14,922	11,848	168,815
1901	15,757	104,195	23,143	15,350	13,270	171,715
1902	26,293	108,498	43,206	14,345	13,320	205,662
1903	59,652	123,663	50,206	12,375	14,054	259,950
1904	69,681	146,446	26,818	13,910	14,581	271,435
1905	82,437	122,370	26,307	15,139	15,824	262,077
1906	114,859	144,817	22,804	19,331	23,326	325,137
1907	151,216	170,264	20,925	24,767	28,508	395,680
1908	81,321	96,869	19,568	33,569	31,872	263,199
1909	85,887	109,700	22,017	37,620	33,537	288,761

TABLE XVI.—CONGESTION IN DUBLIN: CLASSIFICATION OF TENEMENTS OF FOUR ROOMS OR LESS, BY NUMBER OF ROOMS AND BY NUMBER OF PERSONS PER TENEMENT, 1901.[1]

Persons per tenement	Number of tenements of ——			
	1 room	2 rooms	3 rooms	4 rooms
1	3,278	702	172	101
2	5,544	2,234	779	597
3	4,392	2,231	900	772
4	3,384	2,240	952	816
5	2,302	2,022	825	818
6	1,477	1,575	765	680
7	797	1,205	620	562
8	362	773	433	422
9	145	367	238	320
10	47	175	163	201
11	13	62	74	98
12 or more	6	34	50	97
Total	21,747	13,620	5,971	5,484

[1] *Census of Ireland, 1901. General Report*, p. 173, Table 50.

TABLE XVI.—(Continued).

Summary

	Number of tenements
Total	59,263
With 4 rooms or less	46,822
Number of persons per room:	
Not more than one	10,351
Not more than two	15,039
Not more than three	9,996
More than three	11,436

TABLE XVII.—"REPRESENTATIVE" HOUSEHOLD EXPENDITURES FOR FOOD IN THE IRON DISTRICT OF THE SOUTH, FOR THE PERIOD OF ONE WEEK IN 1909.[1]

Household number	Nationality	Income	Persons per household		Nutrition units per household	Expenditure for food	
			Adults	Children		For the week	Per man per day
2	South Italian	$10.50	2	3	21.7	$6.48	$0.30
3		9.00	2	1	14.7	6.11	0.41
4		22.00	3	2	28.7	8.16	0.28
6		10.50	2	5	28.7	10.35	0.36
7		16.00	3	2	24.5	9.10	0.37
9	American White	19.00	3	1	23.8	7.65	0.32
10		25.00	2	3	21.7	7.88	0.36
11		18.00	2	3	21.7	7.80	0.36
12		12.00	2	—	12.6	3.65	0.29
13		23.00	2	1	15.6	9.63	0.62

TABLE XVIII.—EARNINGS AND EXPENSES IN MASSACHUSETTS, 1800, 1830, and 1860.[2]

	1800	1830	1860
Expenses of a family of four	$429	$431	$587
Earnings:			
Master carpenter	325	455	520
Journeyman carpenter	260	390	455
Master mason	500	500	625
Journeyman mason	375	438	500
Master painter	325	455	520
Journeyman painter	260	......	455
Laborer	......	226	325

[1] *Reports of the Immigration Commission*, vol. 9, pp. 215–221.

[2] *Third Annual Report of the Massachusetts Bureau of Statistics of Labor* (1871–1872), pp. 514–517.

TABLE XIX.—AVERAGE INCOME AND EXPENDITURES OF WAGE-EARNERS IN SPECIFIED OCCUPATIONS, IN NEW JERSEY, 1885.[1]

Occupations	Number of families	Average number in family	Average number at work	Earnings of head of family	Income of family	Expenditures of family	Surplus (+) or deficit (−) Of family[2]	Of head of family[3]
Glass-blowers.	48	4.9	1.3	$941	$1,070	$737	+$333	+$204
Other glass-workers....	34	4.8	1.6	693	813	654	+ 159	+ 58
Blacksmiths...	11	5.9	1.6	712	747	674	+ 73	+ 19
Iron-workers..	15	4.8	1.5	493	573	538	+ 35	− 45
Shoemakers...	32	5.1	1.4	542	583	565	+ 18	− 23
Carpenters....	12	5.5	1.5	545	678	661	+ 17	− 16
Machinists....	24	4.9	1.5	558	629	619	+ 10	− 61
Flax-mill workers....	28	4.9	1.7	374	482	501	−19	− 127
Silk-mill workers....	34	4.2	1.5	322	368	459	−91	− 137

TABLE XX.—AVERAGE INCOME AND EXPENDITURES OF UNSKILLED LABORERS IN NEW JERSEY, CLASSIFIED BY NATIVITY AND SOURCE OF INCOME, 1885.[4]

Item	Breadwinners in the family: Father alone			Father and children		
	Native	English	Irish	Native	English	Irish
Number of families	20	1	9	12	3	6
Earnings of:						
Father............	$381	$519	$246	$368	$494	$249
Children..........	....	....	....	222	175	246
Total.......	$381	$519	$246	$590	$669	$495
Expenditures.........	361	567	272	578	634	531

[1] *Eighth Annual Report of the New Jersey Bureau of Statistics of Labor and Ind.* (1885), p. 147.

[2] Income of family less expenditures of family.

[3] Earnings of head of family less expenditures of family.

[4] *Eighth Annual Report of the Bureau of Statistics of New Jersey*, 1885, pp. 30–34.

TABLE XX.—(Concluded).

Item	Breadwinners in the family					
	Father alone			Father and children		
	Native	English	Irish	Native	English	Irish
Number of families	20	1	9	12	3	6
Surplus (+) or deficit (−).........	+$20	−$48	−$26	+$12	+$35	−$36
Earnings of father over expenses Surplus (+) or deficit (−)	+20	−48	−26	−210	−140	−282

TABLE XXI.—AVERAGE WAGES AND AVERAGE EXPENSES OF WORKING FAMILIES WITH DEFICITS, IN OHIO, 1885.[1]

Occupation	Number reporting	Persons in family	Rooms to family	Persons to one room	Wages earned by family	Average expenses of family	Deficit	Per cent of workers from S. & E. Europe, 1890
Stonecutters ..	4	5.0	4.5	1.1	$505	$507	$2	3.5
Macninists....	27	4.2	5.3	0.8	556	571	15	2.4
Cabinet-makers.....	6	4.5	4.3	1.05	481	537	56	3.5[2]
Iron workers..	21	5.7	5.7	1.0	679	745	66	5.3
Wood carvers..	5	5.6	3.4	1.6	659	772	113	2.1[3]
Cigar makers...	20	4.8	3.2	1.5	394	508	114	4.5
Miners	57	5.8	4.1	1.4	303	422	119	2.9

[1] *Eleventh Annual Report of the Ohio Bureau of Labor Statistics* (1885), Table 27, p. 117. *IX Census, Population* Part II., p. 596.

[2] Cabinet makers and upholsterers.

[3] Woodworkers other than cabinetmakers, carpenters, and joiners.

TABLE XXII.—ORGANIZED WORKERS AND MALE WHITE BREADWINNERS, ENGAGED IN NON-AGRICULTURAL PURSUITS, IN ILLINOIS AND NEW JERSEY, CLASSIFIED BY NATIVITY.[1]

	Illinois, 1886		New Jersey, 1887	
Nativity	Breadwinners	Organized	Breadwinners	Organized
Number:				
Native	423,290	25,985	243,093	24,463
Foreign-born	308,595	57,163	137,385	26,704
Total	731,885	83,148	380,478	51,167
Per Cent:				
Native	57.8	31.3	63.9	47.8
Foreign-born	42.2	68.7	36.1	52.2
Total	100.0	100.0	100.0	100.0

TABLE XXIII.—MALE LABOR UNION MEMBERSHIP AND IMMIGRATION, NEW YORK STATE, 1897–1910.

Year	Labor union membership[2]	Immigrant breadwinners destined for New York[3]	Year	Labor union membership	Immigrant breadwinners destined for New York
1897	162,690	55,871	1904	378,859	193,430
1898	163,562	53,310	1905	370,971	241,689
1899	200,932	70,740	1906	386,869	269,477
1900	233,553	99,104	1907	422,561	297,300
1901	261,523	106,817	1908	361,761	173,022
1902	313,592	154,872	1909	360,319	145,036
1903	380,845	198,620	1910	453,801	207,021

[1] *Fourth Biennial Report of the Bureau of Labor Statistics of Illinois*, 1886, pp. 224–226; *Population at XI. Census*, Part II, pp. 552–553; *ibid.*, Table 116, p. 586; *Tenth Annual Report of the Bureau of Statistics of Labor and Industries of New Jersey*, p. 15.

[2] *Annual Report of the Bureau of Labor Statistics of New York State*, 1910, vol. II., Table 34, p. xlix.

[3] *Reports of the Commissioner-General of Immigration*, 1897, p. 38; 1898, p. 26; 1899, p. 17; 1900, p. 20; 1901, p. 17; 1902, p. 29; 1903, p. 33; 1904, p. 30; 1905, p. 34; 1906, p. 37; 1907, p. 35; 1908, p. 39; 1909, p. 57; 1910, p. 55.

TABLE XXIV.—URBAN POPULATION, MEMBERSHIP OF LABOR UNIONS AND PERCENTAGE OF ORGANIZED INDUSTRIAL WAGE-EARNERS IN NEW YORK AND KANSAS, 1900–1909.[1]

Year	Urban population both sexes.[2]		Union membership of both sexes			
			Number		Percentage of industrial wage-earners[3]	
	New York	Kansas	New York	Kansas	New York	Kansas
1900	5,293,111	330,903	245,381	6,341	18.3	5.7
1901	5,486,849	347,191	276,141	8,649	20.6	7.8
1902	5,675,587	363,479	329,101	7,715	24.6	7.0
1903	5,864,225	379,767	395,598	9,657	29.6	8.7
1904	6,052,963	395,953	391,676	12,074	29.3	10.9
1905	6,241,701	412,241	383,226	12,454	28.6	11.2
1906	6,430,439	428,529	398,494	12,187	29.8	11.0
1907	6,619,177	444,817	436,792	13,058	32.6	11.8
1908	6,807,915	461,005	372,459	23,995	27.8	21.6
1909	6,996,653	477,293	372,729	21,385	27.9	19.3

TABLE XXV.—DAILY WAGES IN STEEL COMPANY NO. 1, 1880–1908.[4]

Occupation[5]	1880	1885	1890	1895	1900	1903	1908
I. Bessemer Department:							
Laborer.........	$1.23	$1.00	$1.10	$1.10	$1.10	1.30	$1.45
Water tender....	....	....	....	1.05	....	2.10	2.20
Fireman.........	1.38	.89	....	1.00	....	1.70	1.90
Carpenter.......	....	....	....	1.22	1.35	1.75	1.90
Metal breaker...	2.20	1.32	1.55	1.33	....	1.55	1.65
Skull cracker....	....	....	1.60	1.18	1.38	1.55	1.64
Ashman.........	1.45	.95	....	1.00	....	1.50	1.55

[1] *Annual Report of the New York Bureau of Labor*, 1909, p. xxxviii, Table 7; *Annual Reports of the Kansas Bureau of Labor*, 1900–1909.

[2] Census figures for 1900, estimates for subsequent years.

[3] The number of industrial wage-earners at the XII. Census (1900) in New York was 1,337,000, and in Kansas, 110,000. The method of classification and computation is explained in an article by the writer in the *Journal of Political Economy*, 1911, March and April: "Social-Economic Classes of the Population of the United States."

[4] *Report of the Immigration Commission*, vol. 8, pp. 448, 449.

[5] Only such occupations have been selected for which comparable data are available.

TABLE XXV.—(Concluded).

Occupation	1880	1885	1890	1895	1900	1903	1908
Pump man......	....	1.08	....	....	....	1.30	1.40
Ganister mixer..	1.45	....	....	1.00	....	1.30	1.35
Dumper........	....	....	1.10	1.00	....	1.30	1.35
Clean-up.......	....	.68	.75	1.00	....	1.30	1.35
II. Blast Furnaces:							
Laborer.........	1.10	1.04	1.00	1.00	1.20	1.30	1.38
Engineer........	3.00	1.65	1.60	1.60	2.20	2.50	2.65
Water tender....	....	....	1.35	1.30	1.65	2.10	2.25
Blacksmith	1.84	....	1.26	1.45	1.60	2.00	2.10
Helper........	....	....	1.10	1.15	1.25	1.30	1.38
Gasman.........	1.55	....	1.17	1.35	1.30	1.84	2.05
Carpenter	1.55	....	1.50	1.45	1.60	1.80	1.90
Fireman.........	1.27	1.00	1.17	1.30	1.50	1.75	1.85
Hot-stove tender	....	....	1.26	1.45	1.60	1.70	1.80
Boiler blowers...	....	....	1.10	1.00	1.20	1.55	1.60
Scale men.......	....	....	1.15	1.35	1.50	1.50	1.60
Coke fillers......	1.55	....	1.25	1.00	....	1.50	1.60
Cinder man.....	1.55	1.15	1.20	1.26	1.40	1.45	1.55
Fillers..........	1.50	1.15	1.25	1.35	1.44	1.40	1.50
Pushers.........	....	....	1.00	1.20	1.32	1.35	1.45
Greasers........	....	....	1.00	1.20	1.32	1.30	1.38
III. Mechanical Department:							
Brick mason:							
Minimum.....	1.85	1.57	1.95	1.80	1.80	2.25	2.47
Maximum.....	2.45	3.42	2.50	3.00	3.65	3.24	3.60
Pattern maker: .							
Minimum.....	1.55	1.54	....	....	....	1.48	1.55
Maximum.....	2.50	2.43	....	....	....	3.00	3.25
Blacksmith:							
Minimum.....	1.65	....	1.35	1.62	2.10	1.43	1.57
Maximum.....	2.70	....	2.20	2.58	2.70	2.92	3.25
Boiler maker:							
Minimum.....	1.60	1.62	1.75	1.65	1.60	1.48	1.62
Maximum.....	2.75	2.25	2.50	2.47	2.85	2.67	2.95
Roofer:							
Minimum.....	1.50	1.31	1.60	1.54	1.55	1.30	1.45
Maximum.....	2.00	2.50	2.70	2.50	2.75	2.40	2.65
Carpenter:							
Minimum.....	1.60	1.60	....	2.00	1.55	1.29	1.41
Maximum.....	2.50	1.80	....	2.20	2.40	2.37	2.60
Painter:							
Minimum.....	1.20	....	....	....	....	1.98	2.17
Maximum.....	2.10	....	....	....	....	2.25	2.47
Mason (helper):							
Minimum.....	1.10	.70	....	1.15	1.15	1.10	1.20
Maximum.....	1.30	1.48	....	1.35	1.40	1.35	1.48

TABLE XXVI.—PER CENT OF MACHINE-MINED BITUMINOUS COAL AND PER CENT RATIO OF FOREIGN-BORN FROM SOUTHERN AND EASTERN EUROPE FOR EACH OF THE PRINCIPAL COAL-PRODUCING STATES, 1900 and 1910.[1]

State	Mined by machinery		Ratio of Southern and Eastern Europeans to total population[2]		Per cent of miners of S. and E. European parentage
	1910	1900	1910	1900	1900
Ohio........	84.44	46.53	5.5	1.5	9.0
Kentucky...	64.03	43.91	0.3	0.1	0.5
Indiana.....	48.87	27.36	1.8	0.5	5.5
Pennsylvania	45.51	33.65	10.9	4.9	36.0
West Virginia	45.37	15.09	1.2	0.6	9.5
Illinois......	38.63	19.73	7.9	3.0	22.0

TABLE XXVII.—PER CENT OF MINERS OF SOUTHERN AND EASTERN EUROPEAN PARENTAGE,[3] LIVES LOST PER MILLION TONS, AND PER 1,000 EMPLOYEES, IN BITUMINOUS COAL MINES.[4]

State	Per cent of miners of S. and E. European parentage, 1900	Fatal accidents per 1,000 employees, 1889–1908	Lives lost per million tons, 1866–1908
Pennsylvania....	36.0[5]	2.71	3.83
Illinois..........	22.0	2.33	3.94
Oklahoma........	14.0	5.07	13.57
West Virginia....	9.5	4.64	6.36
Ohio............	9.0	2.14	3.95
Iowa............	6.0	2.15	5.22
Indiana..........	5.5	2.32	3.73
Alabama........	2.0	4.55	7.27
Maryland.......	1.5	1.77	1.96
Tennessee.......	1.0	4.38	9.04
Kentucky.......	0.5	1.60	3.34

[1] *U. S. Geological Survey, Production of Coal*, 1910, p. 51. These six States produced 90 per cent of the total output of machine-mined coal in the United States for 1900–1909, and 80 per cent of the total output of bituminous coal for 1910.

[2] Advance information issued to the press by the Director of the Census.

[3] Computed from *XII. Census Report on Occupations*, Table 41.

[4] *Bureau of Labor Bulletin No. 90*, Table XXIX, pp. 452, 671.

[5] Includes both bituminous and anthracite mines.

TABLE XXVIII.—NUMBER OF EMPLOYEES AND FATAL ACCIDENT RATES IN THE ANTHRACITE MINES OF PENNSYLVANIA, 1870–1909.[1]

Years	Employees (thousands)	Fatal accidents per 1,000 employees	Fatal accidents per 1,000,000 tons produced	Years	Employees (thousands)	Fatal accidents per 1,000 employees	Fatal accidents per 1,000,000 tons produced
1870	36	5.93	14.89	1890	120	3.15	8.40
1871	37	5.60	13.52	1891	123	3.47	8.61
1872	45	4.98	14.32	1892	130	3.21	8.16
1873	48	5.48	12.57	1893	138	3.30	8.63
1874	53	4.33	11.59	1894	140	3.19	8.75
1875	70	3.40	10.17	1895	144	2.93	7.39
1876	70	3.24	9.73	1896	150	3.34	9.32
1877	67	2.90	7.85	1897	150	2.83	8.04
1878	64	2.92	8.95	1898	142	2.89	7.78
1879	69	3.81	8.44	1899	141	3.28	7.62
1880	73	2.75	7.22	1900	144	2.86	7.16
1881	76	3.59	7.98	1901	148	3.47	7.65
1882	82	3.54	8.30	1902	148	2.03	7.26
1883	91	3.53	8.56	1903	152	3.41	6.89
1884	101	3.28	9.10	1904	161	3.69	8.08
1885	100	3.31	8.68	1905	168	3.83	8.19
1886	103	2.71	7.16	1906	166	3.35	7.72
1887	107	2.97	7.50	1907	169	4.20	8.23
1888	122	2.98	7.81	1908	175	3.88	8.12
1889	120	3.32	9.09	1909	171	3.31	7.07

[1] *Report of the Pennsylvania Department of Mines*, 1909, Part I, Table L., p. 57.

TABLE XXIX.—NUMBER OF FATAL ACCIDENTS AND RATIO PER 1000 EMPLOYEES ON RAILROADS AND IN COAL MINES, 1889–1908.[1]

Years	Number				Ratio per 1000 employees			
	Railroad trainmen	All railroad employees	Anthracite mines	Bituminous mines, U.S. and Canada	Railroad trainmen	All railroad employees	Anthracite mines	Bituminous mines, U.S. and Canada
1889	1,179	1,972	397	681	8.55	2.80	3.31	2.45
1890	1,459	2,451	378	852	9.53	3.27	3.15	2.84
1891	1,533	2,660	428	952	9.61	3.39	3.47	2.92
1892	1,503	2,554	418	880	8.85	3.11	3.21	2.57
1893	1,567	2,727	456	969	8.70	3.13	3.30	2.53
1894	1,029	1,823	446	956	6.41	2.33	3.19	2.44
1895	1,017	1,811	421	1,053	6.45	2.31	2.93	2.62
1896	1,073	1,861	502	1,123	6.59	2.25	3.34	2.74
1897	976	1,693	423	947	6.08	2.06	2.83	2.32
1898	1,141	1,958	411	1,049	6.67	2.24	2.89	2.59
1899	1,155	2,210	461	1,249	6.45	2.38	3.28	2.97
1900	1,396	2,550	411	1,501	7.30	2.51	2.86	3.25
1901	1,537	2,675	513	1,579	7.35	2.50	3.47	3.21
1902	1,670	2,969	300	1,837	7.40	2.49	2.03	3.47
1903	2,061	3,606	518	1,815	8.13	2.75	3.41	3.16
1904	2,115	3,632	595	2,018	8.33	2.80	3.69	3.33
1905	1,993	3,361	644	2,178	7.51	2.43	3.83	3.40
1906	2,302	3,929	557	2,093	8.08	2.58	3.35	3.19
1907	2,542	4,534	708	2,838	8.00	2.71	4.19	4.15
1908	1,845	3,405	678	2,723	6.67	2.37	3.89	3.82

[1] Figures for 1891–1908 from *U. S. Statistical Abstract*, 1910, Tables 180 and 181, p. 284, also Table 168, p. 265; *U. S. Bureau of Labor Bulletin 90*, Table xxiv., pp. 655–659; *Bulletin 32*, p. 8.

TABLE XXX.—ARRIVAL AND DEPARTURE OF ALIENS (THOUSANDS), 1908–1920.[1]

Fiscal year ended June 30.	All Aliens			Immigrants	Emigrants	Excess of immigration over emigration
	Admitted	Departed	Net Increase			
1908........	925	715	210	783	395	388
1909........	944	400	544	752	223	529
1910........	1,198	380	818	1,042	202	840
1911........	1,030	518	512	879	295	584
1912........	1,017	615	402	838	333	505
1913........	1,427	612	815	1,198	308	890
1914........	1,403	634	709	1,218	303	915
1915........	434	384	50	327	204	123
1916........	367	241	126	299	130	169
1917........	362	146	216	295	66	229
1918........	212	193	19	111	95	16
1919........	237	216	21	141	124	17
1920........	622	428	194	430	288	142
Total...	10,179	5,483	4,695	8,312	2,970	5,342

[1] *Annual Report of the Commissioner-General of Immigration*, 1920, Table XVI A, p. 191.

TABLE XXXI.—IMMIGRATION AND EMIGRATION OF BREADWINNERS,[1] FISCAL YEARS 1915–1919.[2]

Year Ended June 30	Admitted		Departed	
	Immigrant aliens	Non-immigrant aliens	Emigrant aliens	Non-emigrant aliens
1915.........	209,760	72,361	175,609	136,221
1916.........	194,060	45,671	112,376	75,244
1917.........	190,985	46,758	50,353	53,127
1918.........	65,655	81,788	69,483	80,967
1919.........	82,818	73,388	101,293	70,432

TABLE XXXII—COMPARISON OF PERSONS SEEKING WORK AND WORKERS CALLED FOR BY EMPLOYERS AT PUBLIC EMPLOYMENT OFFICES IN THE STATE OF NEW YORK: NUMBER OF WORKERS REGISTERED FOR EACH ONE HUNDRED PLACES OPEN, 1916–18.[3]

MONTH	1916	1917	1918
January..................	136.2	88.1	91.0
February.................	121.6	84.4	84.3
March....................	97.1	78.8	68.2
April....................	73.5	81.7	61.0
May......................	73.4	83.7	53.8
June.....................	78.5	79.4	50.5
July.....................	67.1	75.9	60.7
August...................	75.9	73.9	53.7
September................	74.3	75.6	52.7
October..................	72.1	80.7	47.1
November.................	74.8	91.3	59.3
December.................	77.2	85.8	71.7

1 All aliens, exclusive of "persons without occupation, mostly women and children."

2 *Annual Reports of the Commissioner General of Immigration*, 1915–1919, Table VI.: occupations of aliens admitted and departed.

3 Compiled from *The Labor Market Bulletin*, published monthly by the Bureau of Statistics and Information of the New York State Industrial Commission. Beginning with July, 1918, the reports on which the above table is based comprise the operations of the Employment Bureaus of the New York State Industrial Commission and of the U. S. Employment Service in New York State. Previous to that date, the reports related only to the Employment Bureaus of the New York State Industrial Commission.

TABLE XXXIII.—EXPORTS OF PRINCIPAL BREADSTUFFS, OTHER THAN WHEAT, FROM THE UNITED STATES, 1910–1918.[1]

Article	July 1st to June 30th		Increase
	1910–1914	1914–1918	
	Thousands	Thousands	Per cent
Barley, bushels	35,166	106,895	204
Rye, bushels	4,054	52,327	1,191
Rye, flour, barrels	24	1,140	4,650
Corn meal, barrels	1,668	3,417	105
Oatmeal, pounds	106,061	580,607	447
Rice, pounds	85,397	574,879	573

[1] *Statistical Abstract of United States*, 1918, pp. 477–478 (computed).

INDEX

C

H

J

T

U

W

Z

THE END